We Shook Up the World

We Shook Up the World

THE SPIRITUAL REBELLION OF MUHAMMAD ALI AND GEORGE HARRISON

Tracy Daugherty

UNIVERSITY OF OKLAHOMA PRESS : NORMAN

Publication of this book is made possible through the generosity of Edith Kinney Gaylord.

Library of Congress Cataloging-in-Publication Data

Names: Daugherty, Tracy, author.
Title: We shook up the world : the spiritual rebellion of Muhammad Ali and George
    Harrison / Tracy Daugherty.
Description: Norman : University of Oklahoma Press, [2024] | Includes bibliographical
    references and index. | Summary: "A dual biography of George Harrison and
    Muhammad Ali, two complex icons of the 1960s, culminating in 1974, when both men
    reemerged in their respective professions. These men displayed that tenacity of the
    rebellious spirit of a vanishing era that challenged the cultural and political hegemony
    of the West and American military dominance"—Provided by publisher.
Identifiers: LCCN 2023034951 | ISBN 978-0-8061-9371-7 (hardcover)
Subjects: LCSH: Ali, Muhammad, 1942–2016—Religion. | Ali, Muhammad, 1942–2016—
    Political and social views. | Harrison, George, 1943–2001—Religion. | Harrison, George,
    1943–2001—Political and social views. | African American boxers—Biography. |
    Rock musicians—Great Britain—Biography | Muslims—United States—Biography. |
    Hindus—Great Britain—Biography. | Social change—Religious aspects. | Civilization,
    Modern—20th century.
Classification: LCC GV1132.A44 D38 2024 | DDC 781.66092 [B]—dc23/eng/20231024
LC record available at https://lccn.loc.gov/2023034951

The paper in this book meets the guidelines for permanence and durability of the Committee on Production Guidelines for Book Longevity of the Council on Library Resources, Inc. ∞

1 2 3 4 5 6 7 8 9 10

For David Turkel and Jon Lewis
For Colleen Mohyde
For Kent Calder

A man does not attain freedom from the results of action by abstaining from actions, and he does not approach perfection simply by renunciation. . . . For the mere maintenance of the world, you should act. . . . Whatever the greatest man does, thus do the rest; whatever standard he sets, the world follows that.

Bhagavad Gita

A man is worked on by what he works on. He may carve out his circumstances, but his circumstances will carve him out as well.

Frederick Douglass

The rubble had been cleared away, but strange grasses and wild herbs had sprung up where the war-demolished houses had been.

Muriel Spark

Contents

Acknowledgments

George Harrison once said he liked stories of "the rock and roll years when you see what happened [historically] . . . and you remember that Eddie Cochran was singing this tune [at the time] . . . I like nostalgia in that respect." Such has been my approach in *We Shook up the World*: a careful layering of perspectives.

The biographies of Harrison and Muhammad Ali as presented in this book are enfolded within a larger framework of cultural history. As such, they are not intended to lay bare the men's psychologies or to expose previously unknown secrets. Rather, this book offers a collective portrait of an era, using two prominent men as guides to the heart of the material. In this approach, the already-existing public record, journalism's famous "rough draft of history," assumes primary interest. Instead of uncovering the gossip we didn't know, the point of this exercise has been to take what we *thought* we knew and connect it to other pages of the public record to forge new perceptions, fresh insights. The point is to see the past anew.

I gratefully acknowledge my indebtedness to investigative reporters, interviewers, and biographers who came before me (evident extensively in the notes). In particular, I want to cite Hunter Davies (*The Beatles*, 1968), Philip Norman (*Shout!* 1981), Bob Spitz (*The Beatles*, 2005), and Mark Lewisohn (volume one of his ongoing project, *Tune In*, 2013). As valuable as these books are in advancing our understanding of George Harrison in his cultural context, they tell an incomplete story, presenting him as one-fourth of a group.

Two serious biographies of Harrison have appeared, *George Harrison* by Alan Clayson, published in 1996, before Harrison's death, and *George Harrison: Behind the Locked Door* by Graeme Thomson (2013). Both books extend the myth that Lennon and McCartney could have managed without the contributions of Harrison and Starr. A cursory study of the Beatles' musical catalog reveals the error of this view. Additionally, neither biography offers sufficient depth in the matter of Harrison's religious faith and its links to his experiments with Indian music.

Walter Everett and Tim Riley have both contributed excellent studies of the Beatles' musicianship and importance to their period, in the *Beatles as Musicians* (Everett) and *What Goes On: The Beatles, Their Music, and Their Time* (Everett and Riley). Ian Macdonald's *Revolution in the Head: The Beatles' Records and the Sixties* also adds significantly to our knowledge in this regard.

In 1991, sportswriter Thomas Hauser published a monumental oral history of Muhammad Ali, *Ali: His Life and Times*. Jonathan Eig's *Ali* (2017) is the first full-scale Ali biography. These are excellent books, focused on Ali in his athletic context. Books exploring the boxer's wider cultural impact have tended to be for the academic market. Michael Oriard's "Muhammad Ali: The Hero in the Age of Mass Media" (1995) was an early seed for this book.

I am also indebted to Manning Marable's *Malcolm X: A Life of Reinvention* (2011), Randy Roberts and Johnny Smith's *Blood Brothers: The Fatal Friendship of Muhammad Ali and Malcolm X* (2016), and Les Payne and Tamara Payne's *The Dead are Arising: The Life of Malcolm X* (2020).

Thanks to Hannah and Arlo Mullin, to Debra, Charlie, and Joey Vetter, and to Ted Leeson and Betty Campbell.

Long ago, Ehud Havazelet encouraged me to write this book. Bob and Mary Jo Nye were sweetly supportive. At the University of Oklahoma Press, Kent Calder and Joe Schiller provided invaluable aid and patient, exacting advice. Chris Dodge was a keen and insightful copy editor. Marjorie Sandor made everything possible. She fights the good fight and brings all the music.

Prologue

"You Don't Ever Want to Die"

It is a global story. In reliving it, we will travel far in distance and in time, beginning with early February 1974. George Harrison had flown to India for the first time in six years to stay with his friend and mentor, the sitar player Ravi Shankar, to visit Varanasi, also known as Benares, and to return to the holy city of Vrindavan on the banks of the Ganges, said by some to be Krishna's birthplace. The Beatles had disbanded, Harrison's marriage was ending, and he was grieving for his mother, recently dead from cancer. His commitments to India's sacred texts and prayerful chanting had profoundly changed his relationship to Western music and the music industry. Despite impressive commercial success as a solo artist in the immediate post-Beatles years, he was already suffering attacks from mainstream rock-and-roll journalists over his droning compositions and didactic song lyrics.

He was thirty-one years old. He had spent a decade as one of the world's most famous men. Now he hoped to revitalize his faith, energy, and musical inspirations on the trip to India. At the heart of his renewal was the visit to Varanasi, the center of the earth in Hindu cosmology. He wanted a reminder, a vivid means of placing human life in perspective—in the context of death. Years earlier, at the beginning of his relationship with Pattie Boyd, who had now left their marriage for Harrison's buddy, Eric Clapton, Harrison had gone to Varanasi to watch the sacred burning of corpses. Ashes washed in the Ganges were thought to be blessed. "It was an astonishing sight to see bodies burning on the banks as we stepped out of [a] boat," Boyd recalled years later in her memoir. "I was unable to look away, although I wanted to." In a separate reminiscence she wrote that "bears and monkeys on chains in the streets beside beggars and mutilated children" appeared wherever they went in Mumbai, Jodhpur, or Jaipur. Shankar introduced the couple to his spiritual guru, Tat Wale Baba, said by his devotees to have ceased aging when he was thirty-five. Tat Baba explained the laws of karma, of action and reaction, to Harrison. In Varanasi, Harrison observed the sadhus, mendicants who'd renounced the material world, chanting and soliciting food in the streets. Shankar took the couple to Kumbh Mela, a Hindu festival held, among other locations, at the confluence of the Ganges, Yamuna, and Saraswati Rivers. Kumbh Mela is celebrated roughly in twelve-year cycles determined by the astrological positions of the sun, moon, and Jupiter. It is one of the largest peaceful gatherings in the world. "Kumbh," a term first recorded in the Rig Veda, is Sanskrit for "pitcher." In Vedic texts, it is associated with the nectar of immortality. "Mela" means "to meet." The festival is a union near the waters of eternal life. Pilgrims feed monks, feed the poor, and bathe themselves in the rivers, chanting rhythmic prayers, to cleanse their sins. "We found ourselves in a crowd of about three thousand, most of whom had come on foot [from across India]," Boyd recalled. "I remember sitting with Ravi at the festival and seeing a man with a bamboo stick sitting nearby. He kept putting his tongue into the stick, so I asked Ravi what he was doing. He explained that a snake was inside the stick and he was getting a little bit of venom to get high."

Late in the day, Harrison bought a *bhang ki thanddai*, a yogurt-and-almond drink laced with hashish (legal in Varanasi), associated with Shiva's sacraments. After a few sips, he viewed the rising full moon and the pink dust shimmering in the air as from a great distance in time—as if from another life.

But it was the body-burning that made the most indelible impression. The setting sun, as darkly orange as flaming coal, slanted through clouds of roiling smoke as men in groups of three, silent and black as underworld couriers, carried corpses wrapped in white linen to the riverbank. In firelight flickering among the ghats, the stone steps descending into the river's west side, the linens glowed like alabaster lamps, ruffled by rounded lumps—heads stiff with rigor mortis—or pierced, among the folds, by bruised arms and legs dumbly animated by the carriers' motions. The carriers entered the water and placed the bodies into wooden boats rocking on lulling waves. The boatmen shifted their bamboo oars; the instruments creaked in stirrups made of twine. Incense and smoky body oils choked the thickening air. The river, its surface agitated, dull as weathered tin, waited.

Once more, now, in early February 1974, Harrison was startled and moved by the rising flames, the smoke, the bodies' juices and odors, the incense and flowers accompanying the dead to the banks of the river, the swarms of ashes in the purple evening sky. Earlier he had walked through the center of Varanasi, past unhurried cows, pigs, and goats, the carcasses of puppies crushed by tractors and tuk-tuks, erratic auto-rickshaws, and the street markets buzzing like wasps, offering cashmere and silk, hand-rolled cigarettes, and illegally recorded music on cheap cassettes (including the Beatles). He had wound his way toward the ghats, near the spot where it was said the Buddha delivered his first sermon, to stand among sadhus shrunken inside thin, peach-tinted robes, among women wrapped in saris selling lemon-colored parrots. He stood among girls beating laundry on the gritty, wet steps, men soaping the sides of apparently indifferent water buffalo. He stood among the many open-air cremations—the loud crackling, the light like circles of fireflies—among the dying and the dead, savoring the Ganges's promise of salvation.

It was an irony or a paradox: this most pure spot was also among the filthiest patches on Earth. Human life, reduced to its essence: divinity and dust.

In this place, the closest place to heaven that he knew, his perspective always widened. Before he'd made this trip, friends back in England had been urging him to take his music on the road, to capitalize on the recent successes of his albums. He had soured on touring long ago, after the Beatles' tumultuous experiences in 1966 when they endured death threats, especially in the American South, following John Lennon's remark that the band was more popular than Jesus. The Beatle saga had been a nightmare, Harrison always said. But that was the narrow view. Here in Varanasi, he could almost imagine traveling again, sharing with audiences the pleasures of Indian ragas, evoking the profound truths he was witnessing now by the Ganges. He could imagine the joy of *bringing* this experience to people, journeying with fellow players who saw what he did in music: a devotional practice, a way of putting God into sound.

Meanwhile, in the Pennsylvania woods, just off Route 61, thirty-two-year-old Muhammad Ali, training to regain his heavyweight boxing title in a fight with George Foreman, was also obsessed with mortality. Like George Harrison, he had spent the past ten years as a worldwide celebrity, earning both extravagant praise and critical barbs.

Early one morning in July 1974, he left his rural training camp in a white Cadillac, on his way to a nearby boys' camp. The boys' camp had been established to rehabilitate juvenile troublemakers using tactics of tough love, putting them to work chopping trees and clearing brush. Ali had agreed to stage a boxing exhibition to entertain the boys. He loved doing that sort of thing, and it was good PR in this pastoral, largely white artists' community where he'd chosen to erect his compound. "I love the feel [here]," he told his friends. "There's lots of energy." But some of the locals remained leery of him. They had not forgotten or forgiven his views on race, on Vietnam. So he staged goodwill demonstrations throughout Schuykill County and kept his camp open to visitors.

On this warm July morning he had eaten an early breakfast fixed for him by Lana Shabazz, a member of his staff. Then he'd hopped into his Caddy. On his way to the boys' camp, he was accompanied by Dave Kindred, a sportswriter from the *Louisville Courier-Journal,* Ali's hometown paper, and an old pal of Kindred's. Kindred reported the story later. Ali wheeled his car erratically down steep logging roads, deeply rutted, topping eighty-five miles per hour, talking up a storm. Kindred and his buddy glanced at each other; they feared for their lives. "Muhammad, are you afraid of dying?" Kindred asked him.

"You don't ever want to die," Ali said.

"Glad to hear that."

"But the man who built this road is dead now. The man who built that farm-house over there is dead. There are guys I fought, Sonny Liston, Zora Folley, Eddie Machen, Alejandro Lavorante, dead. Liston rottin' in his grave, nobody cares."

Liston, Ali's first major opponent, had died in 1970 under a fog of rumors— spread by Elvis Presley among others—that the Las Vegas mob, for whom Liston allegedly dealt drugs, had murdered him, injecting him with heroin.

"We ain't nothin,'" Ali continued in the car. "We're nobody. We don't own nothin' on this earth. We just borrow things. When you die, another man comes along, and your daughter calls him Daddy." He took a right turn onto a narrow, twisting deer path. "Death is the tax the soul has to pay for having a name and a form."

In camp, sometimes in the evenings after a day-long workout, he'd gather his entourage around the ring along with a smattering of visitors. "I want to say something right now," he'd announce. "This might make you all think. Life is not really long. Let's say the average person is thirty years old. If you're thirty years old you're not but about seven years old. Add up all the seven, eight, nine hours you slept for thirty years. Out of thirty years add up all the nights when you went to bed and this morning don't remember a thing. You've been unconscious for about eight years if you're thirty years old. How much traveling have you done in thirty years? From home to another country to another city to school to church. You've probably spent two years of your life just going back and forth to where you're going. So there's eight years of sleeping and two years of traveling." He challenged his listeners to contemplate time spent sitting in school, in movie theaters, in sports stadiums. "So life is real short . . . add up your traveling, add up all your sleeping, add up all your school, add up all your entertainment, you've probably spent half your life doing nothing." The best thing a person could do, he'd insist, was prepare "to meet God." "[God] wants to know how do we treat each other, how do we help each other."

After a decade of unprecedented fame, of magnificent achievements starting to fade, perhaps it was natural for George Harrison and Muhammad Ali to consider finality. Already, in 1974, it was apparent that none of the ex-Beatles would ever escape the weight of their years as lovable mop-tops, no matter how accomplished they became as individuals. It was clear that, after a lengthy layoff from the ring, the result of his conflict with the US government over the war in Southeast Asia, Ali would never again be the athlete he was, even if he did manage to make an astonishing comeback.

In general, the 1970s was a period of "dishonor and dysfunction," a time of "deepening shame," in the words of writer Richard Hoffer—particularly in America. *The Late Great Planet Earth* by Hal Lindsey, predicting an immediate apocalypse, became the decade's biggest international best seller. Inflation, the Arab oil embargo, the energy crisis, Kent State, the scandals of Watergate and My Lai, the humiliation of the unfolding end games in Vietnam, Cambodia, and Laos. The sixties mantra of revolution had devolved into Andy Warhol's repeated Mao paintings, begun in 1972, the leader's round face flattened, deliberately superficial—the commercial packaging of protest. *New West* magazine called the Pet Rock the "perfect Seventies symbol": it "just sat there doing nothing."

Harrison and Ali had been honored—and they'd been burdened—by their symbolic status as cultural representatives. In the 1960s Ali became one of the most charismatic people on the planet. His stance against the war enshrined him as an icon of the decade's revolutionary spirit, loved by some, hated by others. Harrison used his celebrity in the sixties to forge paths between Eastern philosophy and Western religion, mixing Eastern and Western music, a cultural revolution no less momentous than the period's political upheavals. He broke musical boundaries by combining rockabilly rhythms, country, blues, and Indian classical music. Ali altered boxing by jabbing and dancing in the ring, keeping his hands down, countervailing traditional wisdom. Theirs were rebellions of *style*, spreading, influencing bigger social spheres.

These men had been uniquely positioned to lead in a violently disruptive time. But now the press noted Ali's receding youth and the Beatles' breakup as signs of the period's erosion.

Yet it was in 1974, following Harrison's trip to India and Ali's training regimen in Pennsylvania, that both men embarked on highly visible ventures—large-scale gestures capping all they had accomplished and hoped to achieve in the previous decade.

Historians have often cited 1974 as a useful end point for what we loosely call the 1960s. Richard Nixon's resignation of the presidency and the retreat of US military forces from Vietnam together provide a solid demarcation between the cultural sixties and their aftermath. The public receptions given to Harrison's and Ali's activities in 1974 offer remarkable insights into how America began to process its immediate past and tried to shape a future.

Ironies lined the lives of George Harrison and Muhammad Ali, suggesting how unlikely each life story was, how easily the stories might never have happened, how quickly the whole could have unraveled.

Harrison lived the freewheeling life of a rock star, openly admitting he'd engaged in serial sexual affairs and drug experimentation, yet above all else his fans revered him in the late sixties for his heartfelt expressions of the period's spiritual yearning.

"How can people consider Ali a historic figure from the 1960s?" Mark Kram, a *Sports Illustrated* writer, once asked a fellow reporter. "He wasn't for civil rights; he was for separation of the races. He wasn't for women's rights; he treated them like second-class call girls. He was never really against the war; he was told not to go by [his spiritual leader] Elijah Muhammad because it would be a PR disaster for the Muslims. These were the hot issues of the sixties, and he was on the wrong side of history in all of them. Yet people today somehow think Ali belongs right next to Martin Luther King."

In part, this book explores the puzzles of why people considered Muhammad Ali an important cultural figure and how George Harrison encouraged spirituality from the raging center ring of sex, drugs, and rock and roll. Ironies are never simple. Nor were these men. Nor were the times.

Harrison's path crossed Ali's on only a few occasions, yet their names are linked in history. In tracing their parallel careers and insisting on crucial ties between them, I am countering an intuitive view that, of the Beatles, John Lennon most warranted comparisons with Ali. Both men were confident, aggressive, and brash; both came to be associated publicly with the antiwar movement. In contrast, Harrison was less outspoken and wary of his celebrity.

Yet the similarities between Lennon and Ali did not extend far below the surface. It was Harrison who shared with the fighter a profound and genuine spiritual awareness. His struggle to maintain his spirituality in the glare of a celebrity culture more outlandish than the world had ever known lent a special gravity to his career matched closely by Ali's. No other popular figures traveled their paths, quite, or achieved what they did as a result of their choices. Risking their livelihoods, they rejected the Christianity and many of the Western values held by a majority of their audiences. They embraced religious practices considered exotic and strange by many of their devoted followers. Most importantly, their achievements were significantly altered and defined by the choices they made; their parallel movements placed them at the center of the postcolonial world's dramatic shifts. Because of the borders they crossed—spiritual, cultural, and geographic—and because new technologies elevated their fame to stratospheric levels, George Harrison and Muhammad Ali, more than any of their pop cultural peers, came to embody the world that made them. In turn, they helped fashion that world.

In retrospect, Harrison's involvement with Eastern cultures, his efforts on behalf of Bangladesh, and Ali's contact with Africa and contradictory stances on pan-African movements reframe our understanding of what occurred worldwide in the 1960s and 1970s. Thus, the details of these men's stories become markers in a much broader tale, a tale at the heart of this book: the shattering of the postcolonial world and the rise and fall of the American century. Harrison and Ali became lead characters in this narrative: their stories came to us through fresh lines of communication dreamed into existence, it seemed, for the sole purpose of enchanting us with *these* particular figures. Ali and the Beatles were new, as were our ways of knowing them. As were the visions they revealed to us, intentionally or not.

For Americans of the Baby Boom generation, Harrison and his mates shrank global distances. When Harrison turned to Indian aesthetics for his sustenance, he, in particular, educated international audiences about the tremors they were feeling. Many of Ali's fights occurred in locations exotic to most Americans. Zaire (the once and future Congo), Malaysia, the Philippines, the Bahamas. These venues were settled on through complex and often shady negotiations involving international banking laws and personal and corporate hustles. But they also materialized because dictators leading these fledgling countries wanted to prove to their former masters that they had arrived on the world scene. They believed the quickest way to do this was to host the world's most famous man—to surround him with spectacle. Even more satisfying for them: in the 1960s, when he first became Muhammad Ali, the world's most famous man had resisted the world's greatest superpower and won his battle with its government. Receiving him in splendor was much more gratifying, more symbolically potent, than receiving a US president.

It is impossible to speak of Muhammad Ali's late career without considering its postcolonial nature (just as his early fights cannot be severed from America's civil rights struggles). As Ali noted on the eve of his bout with George Foreman in Zaire in 1974, many nations go to war to attract attention. It was so much cheaper to invite him to fight.

In 1974 Harrison mounted his US tour—the first ex-Beatle to tour the States since the band's end—just when Ali had staged his championship comeback against Foreman. As a result, Western nations had a chance to reevaluate the recent past through two of their most powerful social symbols.

The spectacle of a touring Beatle—he would never really be an *ex*—and a jabbing Ali, defying time's sucker punch, gave observers a moment to ponder their present and consider how they got there and to ask what they wanted from the future.

If it seems odd to suggest that entertainment provided as much opportunity for historical reassessment as politics or the day's unfolding tragedies, we will see, during the course of this story, how central popular culture had become to grasping and spreading information and how thoroughly bound pop culture was to current events.

Not only was the Beatles' sound evocative of the 1960s, it was also a product of the period's technology and social rhythms. Not only were Ali's fights distilled versions of America's racial tensions, they were also, in some cases, virtual life-and-death struggles. As Joyce Carol Oates observed in her book *On Boxing*, the sweet science is not a metaphor for life. It *is* life.

This book is mostly about the 1960s, but 1974, a pivotal year in the careers of George Harrison and Muhammad Ali, becomes the culminating peak here because it was a moment when both men's values were tested. That year their achievements and, in many ways those of the masses, were placed in stark perspective. But the importance of 1974 cannot be grasped without understanding what preceded it and what occurred in its aftermath.

PART ONE

The Shaken World

CHAPTER 1

The Quiet One and the Marvelous Mouth

The world trembled in the 1960s. Ancient national alignments frayed as many of the geopolitical arrangements made after World War II unraveled in uprisings and demands for independence, roiling the global economy and undermining cultural foundations planet-wide. The lives of George Harrison and Muhammad Ali would be resoundingly altered by such events; these men absorbed the rhythms of change and helped spread them by means of the fresh technologies fueling their fame (and much of the world's turbulence). The 1960s, culturally defined here as running from the late 1950s to the mid-1970s, began, broadly speaking, with glimmers of political hope, represented most forcefully in the West by the youthful face of John F. Kennedy. By the period's end, old colonial outposts, particularly in the East, lay in shambles, their detritus flowing straight into the West's gluttonous bloodstream, sometimes a poison, sometimes a glorious high. The world's power of self-destruction was awesome to behold. "It is not an overstatement to say that the destiny of the entire human race depends on what is going on in America today," Eldridge Cleaver had written in *Soul on Ice*. "This is a staggering reality to the rest of the world; they must feel like passengers in a supersonic jet liner who are forced to watch helplessly while a passel of drunks, hypes, freaks, and madmen fight for the controls and the pilot's seat."

In 1970 John Lennon sang "The dream is over," referring to the end of the Beatles and indirectly to the rebellious spirit of the 1960s. But that spirit wasn't quite exhausted. In 1974 Lennon's former bandmate George Harrison returned to America, where the Beatles' fame had always been greatest. In what turned out to be in many ways a career-culminating spectacle, he showcased the values he believed lay at the heart of the sixties. At the same time, Muhammad Ali, whose rise to fame had coincided with that of the Beatles, and who would always be linked to them, made a bold attempt to reclaim the glory he had gained in the preceding decade. He claimed to share that glory with those who lived the "dream."

The importance of Harrison's and Ali's high visibility in 1974 began ten years earlier when the young guitar player and the budding boxer stood on the cusp of worldwide fame. In February 1964, the Beatles were about to make their first personal appearance in the United States, where, among hundreds of other teenage girls in the Broadway theater hosting Ed Sullivan's weekly show, Richard Nixon's daughters Julie and Tricia would scream in ecstasy at their music. On February 18, in Miami Beach, the Beatles met Muhammad Ali, then known as Cassius Clay, on the eve of his fight with the heavyweight champion Sonny Liston—the fight that would make his career.

The young men had gathered for a photo shoot in the 5th Street Gym. Most of the journalists assigned to cover the event thought it was a waste of time. They figured that before long nobody would remember the Beatles or Cassius Clay. Less than three months had passed since John Kennedy had been shot to death in Dallas. Images from the August 1963 March on Washington were still prevalent in the press. News of church bombings and civil rights workers vanishing in Mississippi would soon compete for media space with confusing dispatches from Southeast Asia. There would be no room for pop frippery such as long-haired boy bands and loud-mouthed, has-been boxers (the nation's sportswriters assured their readers that Liston could not possibly lose to Clay).

At the time, both boxing and rock and roll were on the ropes. In 1959 California governor Edmund Brown campaigned to ban professional boxing because of its dangers and the sacks of dirty money supporting it. In Washington, D.C., Senator Estes Kefauver had opened a congressional investigation into organized crime's grip on the fight world. Sonny Liston was called to testify at the hearings. When asked directly if he was owned by the mob, he said, "You know your boss, but you don't know who he's with. You know he pays you, that's all."

After winning a gold medal at the 1960 Olympics in Rome, Cassius Clay said he would save the sport of boxing. And he would.

In the world of popular music, the electric guitar, first developed in the 1930s, had risen in prominence, unsettling veteran US record executives. The instrument fit the modern Age of Technology (electric guitars were even featured on the covers of science fiction comic books, played by robots on other planets). As a new instrument, it had no tradition behind it, so young players were free to invent its uses and sounds. Older producers distrusted this free-form approach; they preferred formulaic music with proven commercial appeal, played on more venerable instruments, like piano and clarinet. Industry bosses did not see how an act like the Beatles, lacking a single identifiable lead singer, could be viable. Increasingly, popular music belonged to laconic crooners: Pat Boone, Bobby Darin, and a well-groomed Elvis tamed by his stint in the army.

Swifter than anyone could have imagined, the Beatles' raw, exuberant sound, anchored by airtight harmonies, would blow this old world off its axis.

In the 5th Street Gym on that warm February day in 1964, none of the news people saw how thoroughly the Beatles and Cassius Clay would absorb the world's positive and negative energies. In the beginning, their representative status was largely symbolic, driven by self-mythologizing, well-funded PR campaigns, reporters in search of good copy, and young people fingering extra cash in their pockets. But there were solid intersections between the singers and the boxer and the social movements of their time: reasons why they became avatars of their moment in history.

To begin with, television was crucial to what they accomplished. From his very first days in the ring, at the age of twelve, Cassius Clay appeared on TV. He won his first fight as an amateur, a three-round bout on November 12, 1954 on a program called *Tomorrow's Champions*, broadcast locally on WAVE-TV in Louisville, Kentucky, sponsored by a local cop named Joe Martin. Martin taught boys to box in the basement of the Columbia Auditorium downtown, and he'd taken on Clay when Clay came running into the basement one day, crying, yelling that his bike had been stolen. He hoped to give the thief a good "whuppin'." The boy never got his bike back, but a month later he got his face on TV. He decided he liked it. Weighing in at a slender eighty-nine pounds, he won a split decision over a fellow named Ronnie O'Keefe. He earned three dollars. "Those boys really went at it," Martin said. As a beginner, Clay "looked no better or worse" than the other boys Martin taught, but "he had more determination than most boys, and he had the speed to get him someplace." He'd cry if he didn't perform as well as he thought he should: "He was a kid willing to make the sacrifices necessary to achieve something worthwhile." And the camera loved him. He became the biggest star in his school (where he was also one of the poorest pupils). "At twelve years old I wanted to be a celebrity," he said later. "I wanted to be world famous . . . [so] I could rebel and be different from all the rest of them and show everyone behind me that you don't have to Uncle Tom, you don't have to kiss you-know-what to make it . . . I wanted to be free. I wanted to say what I wanna say . . . Go where I wanna go. Do what I wanna do."

Very publicly, he took on his school's biggest bully—a fearsome street-brawler—and pounded him until the kid was exhausted. After that, Cassius Clay was an even bigger local star, the "baddest dude" anyone knew.

The boxing and the television turns sanctioned his ambitions, his brashness. They made him the equal of the white boys who stepped into the ring with him. Already, at twelve, he was poised to become a new kind of athlete. Just six years later, the Summer Games in Rome would be the first Olympic contests commercially broadcast, and Cassius Clay's image would dominate the screen. It wasn't just his beauty, his grace, his experience with cameras. To his fellow athletes, his boasts could be annoying—"This guy is such a jerk. He's never going to amount to anything," thought the American shot-putter, Dallas Long—but on television he came across as centered and charming.

Something else: his personal ambitions surged just as the context for athletics was changing. His desire to rebel fit the moment in the Eternal City that summer, when Clay stepped onto the Roman stage. "Television, money, and drugs were bursting onto the scene, altering everything they touched," said David Maraniss. "Old-boy notions of pristine amateurism, created by and for upper-class sportsmen, were crumbling . . . and could never be taken seriously again. Rome brought the first . . . doping scandal, the first runner paid for wearing a certain brand of track shoes. New nations and constituencies were being heard from, with increasing pressure to provide equal rights for Blacks and women as they emerged from generations of discrimination and condescension."

The terms of the sixties were being set, and the cameras were rolling. They tended to linger on the thin, bronze face of Cassius Marcellus Clay, smiling irresistibly like the boy he was, enjoying the limelight, eating up a world he already knew was his.

In the background: delegations from newly independent nations such as Ethiopia, poisoned twenty-five years earlier by Mussolini's warplanes; protests by South African civil rights activists, urging the International Olympic Committee to expel the apartheid delegation following the recent Sharpeville massacre; the personal drama of Milkha Singh, the "Flying Sikh," who'd watched Pakistani Muslims murder his parents during the partitioning of Pakistan and India—his countrymen saw his track victories as national redemption.

The Games that summer coincided with "increasing tension in divided Berlin and violence in the rebellious Congo," Maraniss wrote. And through it all, Cassius

Clay, "Uncle Sam's unofficial goodwill ambassador" (so named by the American press corps), beamed. It didn't matter that the world's journalists scoffed at his unorthodox fighting style. He never got inside, they complained, never put the full force of his body behind his punches. He dropped his gloves. Clay dismissed their talk. "I know how far I can go back, when it's time to duck or tie my man up," he explained. "I learn there is a science to making your opponent wear down. I learn to put my head within hitting range, force my opponent to throw blows, then lean back and away, keeping my eyes wide open so I can see everything, then sidestep . . . jab him again, then again. . . . It takes a lot out of a fighter to throw punches that land in the thin air. When his best punches hit nothing but space, it saps him."

The proof was in the ring. After he won his medal, "He slept with it, he went to the cafeteria with it," said gold medal sprinter Wilma Rudolph. "He never took it off." A foreign journalist said to him, "With the intolerance in your country, you must have a lot of problems." "Oh, yeah, we've got some problems," Clay answered. "But get this straight—it's still the best country in the world." To a Soviet interviewer, he said, "We got qualified men working on [the race] problem. We got the biggest and the prettiest cars. We get all the food we can eat . . . as far as places I can't eat goes, I got lots of places I can eat. . . . Russian, there's good and bad in every country, and if there weren't good and bad, we wouldn't be talking about Judgment Day."

A rebel, yes, but completely unpredictable—that was part of his charm. Returning to the States, he convened an impromptu airport press conference, reciting one of his earliest poems: "To make America the greatest is my goal / So I beat the Russian and I beat the Pole / And for the USA won the medal of Gold / The Greeks said you're better than the Cassius of Old."

Without missing a beat he turned pro, signing with a group of white Louisville businessmen who'd agreed to sponsor his career. His winning appearances on television grew even more frequent.

In England the Beatles were busy conquering British TV—a slower process than Clay's march in the States. They made their screen debut on October 17, 1962, on Granada Television, a Manchester station. Ringo Starr had only been a member of the band for two months, replacing drummer Pete Best. They had not had time to rehearse; the show was taped between live concert appearances at the Cavern Club in Liverpool. "They were very scruffy characters, but they had a beat in their music which I liked," said the show's producer, Johnnie Hamp, who'd learned of the group through their manager, Brian Epstein. They played their debut single, "Love Me Do" and a cover of Richard Barrett's "Some Other Guy."

George Harrison, nineteen, had been seeing a Liverpool girl, Iris Caldwell, since he was twelve. "We'd walk down Lilly Lane which was like a lovers' lane and kiss and cuddle," Caldwell recalled. She said that "every single time" the Beatles appeared on TV, "George would phone up my mum and say, 'What was that like?' And she'd say, 'Oh, it was all right, but none of you have got any personality. If you don't smile, you're not going to get anywhere.' So the next time he said, 'I smiled this time, was it all right?' She said, 'It was better, but you still need to smile more.'"

The group spent many grueling months touring Britain, generating mixed press notices and word of mouth. One newspaper compared their concerts to Hitler's Nuremburg rallies. But their persistence paid off. It eventually led to the band's most important televised gig on November 4, 1963, on the occasion of the Queen's Royal Variety Performance in London's Prince of Wales Theatre. Since 1912, the annual charity show, once known as the Royal Command Performance, had been Britain's most extravagant show biz night. The Beatles' Liverpool fans, abandoned in the dingy old Cavern, feared the band had sold out, accepting the invitation. Paul McCartney dismissed the idea. The Beatles would never change, he said: "We don't all speak like [the] BBC." To prove the point, John Lennon ("fantastically nervous, but I wanted to say something to rebel a bit") announced from the stage, "For our last number, I'd like to ask your help." Nervously, he licked his lips. "The people in the cheaper seats, clap your hands." Titters echoed in the hall. "And the rest of you, if you'd just rattle your jewelry." He ducked his head as if awaiting a blow. He grinned like a naughty little boy. The audience roared. Relieved, Lennon rolled into a grating, gritty "Twist and Shout," compelling Princess Margaret to nearly leap from her seat.

"It's one of the best shows I've seen," the Queen Mother pronounced afterward. "The Beatles are most intriguing." The concert was an astonishing class breakthrough, carried off on sheer energy and charm.

"YEAH! YEAH! YEAH! You have to be a real sour square not to love the nutty, noisy, happy, handsome Beatles," read a headline in the following day's *Daily Mirror*. The *Express* ran five front-page stories on the band over the next seven days.

The performance earned the Beatles their first important notice in America. In an article titled "The New Madness," *Time* magazine said the group was the "very spirit of good clean fun." NBC and CBS television had just expanded their evening news broadcasts from fifteen minutes to thirty. As a result, they needed lighter fare as filler. One night, correspondent Edwin Newman on NBC's

Huntley-Brinkley Report mentioned the Beatles in a story, concluding, "One reason for [their] popularity is that it's almost impossible to hear them [over fans' incessant screaming]." Five days later, the day JFK was murdered, CBS aired the first profile of the Beatles in the United States, calling them "the authentic voice of the proletariat." The clip was a teaser on a morning show, previewing a four-minute segment to be played that night on the evening news. The Beatles got bumped after the president's assassination.

In addition to television, the Beatles made a staggering number of live appearances on BBC Radio. Their radio performances—and their arrival in the United States in early 1964—coincided precisely with the popularity of transistor radio among teenagers internationally. Before transistors replaced vacuum tubes, radio sets were bulky living room furniture. In October 1954, Texas Instruments, an outfit geared to produce heavy equipment for the petroleum industry, combined with a television antenna company to create an exciting new technology. Three years later, the Tokyo Telecommunications Engineering Company, rebranding itself as Sony, introduced a five-transistor radio, a version of which would go on to sell over seven million units by the mid-1960s. The boom in portable radio really occurred in 1963 when sales in the United States rose from 5.5 million to nearly 10 million. In 1964, after the Beatles' appearance on *The Ed Sullivan Show*, transistor radios became far and away the nation's most popular Christmas stocking stuffer.

This revolution in listening technology erupted just when radio needed it. Since the mid-1950s, television sets had largely replaced vacuum tube radios in America's homes. Milton Berle and other radio personalities had made the move to TV. Programming was drying up. Then along came a world you could fit in your hand. Teenagers were no longer trapped with their parents; they could transport their entertainment—outside, to their rooms, to school. Using earplugs, they could hide under bed covers at night, listening without their parents knowing. Programming adapted to this portable new medium with fast-paced Top Forty countdowns featuring crazy contests and fast-talking deejays spinning rock and roll platters. The Beatles' short tunes, with their irresistible hooks, suited the format.

Capitol Records, a subsidiary of Britain's EMI, had to be ordered by the company to release the Beatles' records. Dave Dexter, Capitol's A&R man, hated rock and roll—he found it "juvenile and maddeningly repetitive." He preferred to work with easy-listening artists, the likes of Nat King Cole and Peggy Lee, but Beatlemania had become too phenomenal to ignore. In late October 1963, Ed Sullivan, America's premiere variety show host, just happened to arrive in

Heathrow Airport when the group returned from a Swedish concert tour. A thousand screaming fans greeted them. Sullivan presumed the Royal Family had arrived, but someone told him, "It's the Beatles." "Who the hell are the Beatles?" he asked. *The next Elvis Presley*, he grasped, surveying the scene. Within weeks, after a series of transatlantic negotiations, he made a deal with Brian Epstein to book the group for three appearances on his show at the incredibly cheap price of $10,000. Epstein didn't care. American exposure was all he wanted.

"On the plane over . . . we knew," Lennon said in 1970, recalling the Beatles' first North American visit. "We would wipe them out if we could just get a grip on you [Americans]. We were new. When we got here you were all walking around in fucking Bermuda shorts with Boston crewcuts and stuff on your teeth." Similarly, Paul McCartney "always knew exactly where he was going, even though people often used to tell him [the Beatles] would never make it," said Iris Caldwell.

Harrison, always humbler than his mates, wasn't sure of the Beatles' future. (Unlike the others, he had actually been to America, to visit his sister, who had moved with her husband to Illinois.) On the plane to New York, he said, "America's got everything so why should they want us?"

Historians have noted that Cassius Clay and the Beatles brought exuberant energy to public life again following the gloomy aftermath of the JFK assassination. Some observers suggested their lucky timing accounted for their astounding popularity. "We needed a fling after the wake," said rock critic Lester Bangs. Simplistic but not inaccurate. The Beatles in particular would always be associated with the forever-young face of John F. Kennedy.

The day JFK was shot, the band released its second album in Britain, *With the Beatles* (a bastardized version of which would become their first US LP a few months later, retitled *Meet the Beatles*). It featured George Harrison's first complete composition—a song strikingly different from Lennon-McCartney numbers, not upbeat and happy but rather a dark, brooding tune—written while he had a nasty cold—called "Don't Bother Me." Its melody was based around a five-note blues scale propelled by a crisp rhythm and blues lick. It was "an early indicator that Harrison wasn't driven to please the audience," music critic Simon Leng would write much later. If most Beatle music offered a snappy antidote to grief and worries about the nuclear arms race, there were those who found Harrison's disturbing sound a more accurate reflection of the moment. In early

1964, "'Don't Bother Me' felt like the spookiest song on earth" Greil Marcus would write decades later.

From the first, Harrison wrote idiosyncratically "because he never thought he was any *good*, really," his son Dhani has said. Like his bandmates, he couldn't read music, was self-taught, and had become a stage star before developing as a musician. The Beatles' hectic touring schedule and the fact that they couldn't hear themselves perform impeded their technical growth. This tormented Harrison. He valued his craft. He always strove to improve—unlike Lennon, who once professed satisfaction with basic competency: "Whatever media you put [me] in, [I] can produce something worthwhile," Lennon said. "I'm not technically very good, but I can make it fucking howl and move."

"My father once said to me, 'I play the notes you never hear,'" Dhani said. He had a clear view of his limits. "He focused on touch and control. . . . He knew he was good at smaller things, not hitting any off notes, not making strings buzz, not playing anything that would jar you. 'Everyone else has played all the other bullshit,' he would say. 'I just play what's left.'" In essence, this meant changing the terms of musical tension and release. Most early rock and roll was based on three-chord progressions: Harrison strayed beyond that, using sharps and flats to delay or alter the path to a phrase's resolution. He called these "naughty chords." Frequently he'd balance his melodies on the upbeats rather than follow the standard practice of emphasizing the downbeat. More intricately, he really *did* play the "notes you never hear," incorporating microtones between the major and minor chords in standard Western music—a staple of Black soul singers whose records he had memorized and of the North Indian classical music he would turn to as early as 1965.

"He looked very hard for the notes that were most suggestive of the whole," Dhani said. Music writer Jayson Greene remarks that this self-effacing approach meant his "lead guitar was never a 'lead' in the traditional sense" but rather "just one voice in an imaginary choir."

In the United States, the Kennedy assassination benefited the Beatles in at least one measurable way. On December 10, Walter Cronkite resurrected the four-minute CBS News profile of the group that had originally been scheduled for November 22. He was desperate "to lift the spirits of the devastated American public with a cheerful segment," asserts Randy Lewis, a television critic. The timing of the piece, featuring the band performing "She Loves You," increased the

Beatles' impact far beyond anything the first air date would have accomplished. "The film clip triggered an astonishing chain reaction," Lewis says. Following suit, NBC's *Jack Paar Show* played a tape of a Beatles performance on January 3. Though Paar mocked the group—"I understand science is working on a cure for this"—his viewership that night jumped from seventeen million to thirty million. Anticipation grew for the band's American arrival. "The Beatles are coming," *Life* magazine announced on January 31. Capitol Records scurried to prepare an ad campaign, urging its sales reps to wear Beatle wigs and spread them among retailers: "Get these Beatle wigs around properly, and you'll find you're helping to start the Beatle Hair-Do Craze that should be sweeping the country soon," read a promotional memo. Capitol had released "I Want to Hold Your Hand" as a US single on December 26; the record needed no help climbing the charts. Derision in the press, as in a Donald Freeman piece in the *Chicago Tribune*—"If they ever submitted to a barber who loves music—snip! snip! snip!—that would be the end of the act"—only heightened the excitement.

And by then American teenagers had learned from watching film clips of their British counterparts how to respond to the Beatles: you screamed your bloody head off.

On February 7, 1964 at 1:20 p.m., the Beatles landed at the recently renamed John F. Kennedy Airport in New York. Four thousand teenagers, two hundred reporters, and one hundred police officers met them. Few members of the press took them seriously as musicians, but most were impressed by their instincts as entertainers. They were quick, witty, and charming. "What do you think of Beethoven?" one reporter asked the group. "Great," said Ringo. "Especially his poems."

The Ed Sullivan Show received 50,000 applications for 728 tickets for the Sunday, February 9, performance. On February 8, the *New York Times* announced, "Mr. Harrison, who is known as the quiet Beatle, awoke yesterday with a sore throat. He was treated by Dr. Jules Gordon [the house doctor at the Plaza Hotel], used a vaporizer and rejoined his colleagues at the studio late in the afternoon. 'I should be perfect for tomorrow,' he said." In fact, he became known as the "quiet Beatle" by virtue of this piece, and he was quiet because his throat hurt. The situation was far more serious than the press realized. He was suffering from strep, and throat problems would dog him at key moments throughout his career.

The following night, after heavy medication, Harrison managed to take the stage. Sullivan announced, in his usual robotic cadence, "Yesterday and today our theater's been jammed with newspapermen and hundreds of photographers from all over the nation, and these veterans agreed with me that the city has never witnessed the excitement stirred by these youngsters from Liverpool." The group performed "All My Loving," "Till There Was You," "She Loves You," "I Saw Her Standing There," and "I Want to Hold Your Hand." Seventy-three million viewers tuned in—40 percent of the US population—at that time the largest audience in history for an entertainment program.

Later a legend arose that crime came to a halt nationwide while the Beatles were on TV. The *Washington Post* wrote that "there wasn't a single hubcap stolen in America" during the Sullivan show—the paper's cheeky way of suggesting the Beatles' audience consisted of juvenile delinquents. *Newsweek* reported it as a fact.

At that time, only one other celebrity in the country had the power to generate publicity on a scale equal to the Beatles, and that was Cassius Clay. He was a "publicist's dream," said sports announcer John Condon. Whereas many fighters, unaccustomed to public speaking, were leery of microphones, Clay always asked reporters, "What do you want me to do?" "He wore a bow tie all the time in those days. Everything was brand new to him, and he was full of life," Condon recalled. He'd board New York subways, telling people, "I'm Cassius Clay. I'm going to be heavyweight champion of the world."

"I didn't know what to make of him. . . . I thought it was an act . . . and in a way it was," Condon said. "He was putting everybody on, because if you sat down and talked to him alone, he was a different person. He would become serious in a man-to-man conversation. But when he was on, so to speak, he just ate everybody up and had everybody falling in love with him."

His trainer, Angelo Dundee, said, "Muhammad was never as talkative as people thought. In private . . . a lot of the time he was real thoughtful and quiet. . . . [But he] was the most available superstar of our era, and I pride myself on that. I used to point the newspaper guys out to him and say, 'Those are your people. Open up to them. Work with them. They can help.' . . . He knew how to promote himself. God, he could do that."

In 1961, shortly after winning the gold medal in Rome, he met a freelance photographer named Flip Schulke. "Man, how about shooting me for *Life?*" Clay asked him. "I'd love to, but I'd never get it past the editors," Schulke answered. The Olympics were over. There was no story here. Clay asked him what kind of photography he specialized in. "Underwater," Schulke said. Right away, Clay responded, "I never told nobody this, but me and Angelo have a secret. Do you know why I'm the fastest heavyweight in the world? I'm the only heavyweight that trains underwater. You know why fighters wear heavy shoes when they run? They wear those shoes because, when you take them off and put the other shoes on, you feel real light and you run real fast. Well, I get in the water up to my neck and I punch in the water, and then when I get out of the water, I'm lightning fast because there's no resistance . . . Tomorrow morning, you can see me do it. I do it every morning . . . and no one's ever seen it before. I'll let you photograph it for *Life* magazine as an exclusive."

On September 8, 1961, *Life* ran a gorgeous five-page spread of Cassius Clay's muscled arms streaking through crystalline water, surrounded by bubbles as if he were floating in champagne. The truth was he couldn't swim. He'd never done anything like this before. He'd conned Schulke into creating a work of art with him.

Just as 1963 was the year of British Beatlemania, it was Clay's year to be everywhere in the US media. Long-form magazine journalism was taking off; for filling pages, Clay was unbeatable. Few writers took him seriously as a long-term boxing prospect—just as they dismissed the Beatles as musicians—but his entertainment value was beyond question. "It may not seem like much that a fighter should size up the fight business as show business, but damned few before Cassius Clay ever did," Tom Wolfe wrote of him in *Esquire*. Columbia Records signed him to do an album of monologues and poems. "I'm going to be like Elvis Presley," he bragged. In March, the Bitter End, a Greenwich Village coffee shop in which Bob Dylan had attracted attention two years earlier, invited Clay to recite his poems one evening. "I'm a beatnik," he said. Later that month, *Time* featured him on its cover. "Cassius Clay is Hercules," said the magazine. Its writers lacked the boxer's poetic immediacy: "The mysteries of the universe are his Tinker Toys. He rattles the thunder and looses the lightning."

The William Morris Agency wanted to sign him as an entertainer, planning lucrative film and TV deals. Clay considered it. "Maybe if we make enough personal appearances, we don't have to fight so much and get banged around," he told his Louisville sponsors. "We should make it while we're hot."

The second half of the year turned dark in America. In June, Mississippi civil rights activist Medgar Evers was shot to death in his driveway. Federal troops forced Governor George Wallace to admit Black students to the University of Alabama. In September, eighteen days after the March on Washington, four white segregationists blew up an African American church in Birmingham, killing four girls. Then came Dallas.

"If the world was all sports, there would be no guns and no wars," Clay lamented publicly, not yet a polarizing figure.

In late November, Jack Paar was still over a month away from grasping the rising Beatle spectacle, but he sensed the need to lighten the national mood. A week after the assassination, Paar aired a show on which Clay had appeared. It was a brilliant performance all around, light-hearted and charming. The pianist Liberace was Paar's other guest that night. Clay strolled onto the stage, shook Liberace's hand, crumpled as if overpowered, and then grinned to signal it was a joke. The Liston fight was then two months off. "Sonny Liston rather take off his sport coat, soak it in gasoline, and run through Hell before he fight me," Clay announced, winning the audience. "If it wasn't for me, the whole [fight game] would be dead. Fighters don't come on shows like yours." True enough. He performed with Liberace. "You recite something and I'll make up the music," Liberace said, assuming his seat at a grand piano. Clay stood in his sleek dark suit near Liberace's candelabra: "This is the legend of Cassius Clay / The most beautiful fighter in the world today. . ."

Harold Conrad, the publicist for the Clay-Liston bout, saw the PR value in bringing the Beatles together with one of the boxers in Miami Beach. He knew their paths were about to cross, and he was determined to take advantage of it. Since December 1960, Clay had been living in the city, training with Angelo Dundee in the 5th Street Gym. The gym was owned by Angelo's brother, Chris.

Dundee was the perfect fit for Clay because he saw that a direct approach would not work. "You didn't have to push [him]. It was like jet propulsion. Just touch him and he took off," Dundee said. "The important thing was, always make him feel like he was the guy. He used to say, 'Angelo doesn't train me.' And I didn't; he was right. I directed him, and made him feel that he was the innovator. He'd come out of the ring after a sparring session, and I'd say, 'You threw a great left hook, the way you turned your shoulder with it, your body with it, your toe with it, fantastic.' The next time he sparred, he'd throw it that way."

The Cuban fighters in the gym called him *Niño con boca grande*—"Boy with the big mouth."

Dundee understood Miami's complex racial geography. He'd found Clay a room in the Mary Elizabeth Hotel in Overtown, a Black neighborhood where visiting entertainers stayed. Ella Fitzgerald, Nat King Cole, and Sammy Davis Jr. couldn't rent rooms in the nice hotels they worked, so they retreated to Overtown after their nightly shows. The hotel lobbies were full of pimps and prostitutes. Clay would have nothing to do with them. "The hardest part of the training is the loneliness," he told a local journalist. "I can't go out in the street and mix with the folks out there 'cause they wouldn't be out there if they was up to any good. . . . Here I am surrounded by showgirls, whiskey and nobody watching me. All this temptation and me trying to train to be a boxer. It's something to think about."

So far in his life, he'd succumbed to temptation only once, while attending a Golden Gloves tournament in Chicago when he was sixteen. A cabbie had taken him and a buddy to Forty-Seventh and Calumet Avenue, guaranteeing they'd find prostitutes. Clay wound up in a graffiti-covered room that night with a woman who offered him a "trip around the world." "She grabbed me with both her hands, pulling me to her," he recalled. "'Just push,'" she said. Afterward, she asked him, "'Did you reach your climax? . . . Didn't you get a ticklish feeling?' . . . I said, 'No.' There was nothing else to say. She pushed me off. . . . I couldn't look at her."

Since coming to Miami, he'd devoted his hours to boxing.

On March 1, 1961, purely as a formality, Cassius Clay registered for the army with the Selective Service System. On the form, he listed his previous work experience as "Winning the World Light heavy Weight Olympic Boxing Champion at Rome."

Eventually he moved into a small white house in an all-Black Miami neighborhood at Northwest Fifteenth Court. The neighbor children banged in and out of his screen door day and night, always welcome. He loved children. In the evenings, he'd set up a movie screen on his front lawn and play scary movies for the kids. *Invasion of the Body Snatchers* was one of his favorites. He also replayed his fight films.

In the mornings at dawn, in his sweats, he'd run along Biscayne Boulevard. Dundee received more than one early morning phone call from the cops. They'd detained the young man. They wanted to know if he really was a boxer in training or a hoodlum running from a crime in a neighborhood he shouldn't have been near. Miami's demographics were changing, with a large influx of anti-Castro Cubans. Whites were even more nervous than usual.

Clay was scheduled to fight Sonny Liston in Miami Beach for the heavyweight title on February 25, 1964. Then the Beatles hit town. They'd made their Sullivan appearance. They landed in Florida on February 13. Sullivan had booked them for a second show, a special to be broadcast from downtown Miami on February 16. Then they'd stay in South Florida eight more days, relaxing before returning to Europe.

Nearly ten thousand teenagers surrounded them at the airport before a limo whisked them to the Deauville Hotel on Collins Avenue. Sergeant Buddy Dresner of the Miami Beach Police Department had been assigned to oversee their security. He'd supervised John Kennedy's guard detail in the city just days before the president was slain in Dallas. He arranged for a decoy limo to arrive first at the hotel to distract waiting fans and then he sped the Beatles in a second car to the rear of the building. The hotel was overrun, scotching plans, the following morning, for a *Life* magazine photo shoot in the pool. Myron Cohen, a comedian scheduled to appear with the band on the Sullivan show, called an old friend of his, Jerri Pollak, a nightclub singer, and asked if they could escape to her house. "Tell the boys to come over," she said. She prepared cold cuts for them. The magazine photographer asked them to jump in the backyard swimming pool (*keep your hair dry!* he warned). He directed them to burst into song for him. *Life* published the iconic photograph several days later.

On Sunday, February 16, Harold Conrad took Sonny Liston to watch the Beatles perform on *The Ed Sullivan Show*. "Are these motherfuckers what all the people are screaming about?" Liston said. "My dog plays better drums than that kid with the big nose." He refused to meet them, despite their insistence that, if they had to make an appearance with one of the fighters, they'd rather meet Liston than that "loudmouth who's going to lose," Lennon said.

"It was all part of being a Beatle, really; just getting lugged around and thrust into rooms full of press men taking pictures and asking questions," Harrison said wearily years later.

After the fact, conflicting stories emerged about how the February 18 Beatles-Clay meeting was actually arranged. Photographer Harry Benson, working for *Life*, was tasked with recording the event. Originally he'd been scheduled to fly to Africa, to cover the revolt of the Ugandan army, under Idi Amin, against British colonialists. Then he got assigned to the Beatles. He was sorely disappointed until he met the band. They were all young men, like Ali (who was twenty-two). He fell in love with them.

He claimed that he tricked the Beatles into believing he was taking them to meet Sonny Liston. When they discovered the truth, at the entrance to the 5th Street Gym, they were furious. Certainly the gym, on the corner of Fifth and Washington on Miami Beach's southern tip, about two blocks from the ocean, was no great shakes. It sat on the second floor of a squat building above what was originally Howie's Bar and Liquor Store, the Thrifty Market, and a drugstore selling newspapers from New York. Chris Dundee, a wiry Groucho

Marx lookalike, had opened the gym in 1950, just as South Beach went into steep decline (all the new money moved north to establish condos and extravagant hotels—the Fontainebleau and the Eden Roc). He'd come to Florida in the late 1930s, from Philly and New York, where he'd learned to promote fights under the aegis of mobster Frankie Carbo. Carbo still controlled much of the boxing world (he'd had a piece of Sonny Liston). Dundee, the "capo di tutti capi," the big boss, dealt with the mob whenever he had to, but he tried hard to keep his fighters clean. His brother Angelo, tall, thoughtful, and quiet' only paid attention to the ring.

The Beatles were used to rat-eaten places: they'd played their share of joints worse than this. Fifteen creaky, linoleum-covered steps led to the gym. "I'm on my way to hell," Willie Pastrano, the light heavyweight champ in '63, used to moan as he shuffled up the stairs toward Emmett "Sully" Sullivan, the gnome-like guardian of the inner sanctum. Sully charged visitors twenty-five cents to watch the workouts—fifty cents if Cassius Clay was training that day.

"Fifty cents, bub," he'd wheeze.

"But I'm the press."

"Yeah! Yeah! Press my pants, you mud toitle." "No Dead Beats," said a weathered sign above his head. "No Girls Allowed."

The space had once been a Chinese restaurant. Fighters claimed it still smelled like chicken soup, along with the taint of sweat, rubbing alcohol, and forgotten socks. The ring was surrounded by a warped wooden bench, a fly-specked mirror at the back, dented lockers, a blackboard listing sparring sessions, fight posters hiding holes in the walls, and pale pink concrete trim. Chris Dundee didn't really have an office—his pants pockets were his place of business. He was always producing wads of bills wrapped in rubber bands to pay off sports writers, gossip columnists, anyone who could do his fighters any good or get them out of trouble. He negotiated contracts at the nearby Puerto Saqua, over steaming platters of Cuban steak, black beans, and rice.

When the Beatles walked into the gym, the old, cigar-chomping men who regularly gathered to grouse about Cassius Clay's atrocious style (hands down, no body shots—look at how he leans away from punches, someone's gonna clip him one day!) stared at them with open disdain. Reporters milled about, wondering how long this would take. Clay had not yet arrived.

Robert Lipsyte, a young *New York Times* reporter had been assigned to cover Clay. "[Because] I was unworthy," he said. "The real reporter, the [regular] boxing reporter, didn't think it was worth his time to go down there. It was going to be a one round knockout [when Clay got into the ring with Liston]." "So [the paper] send[s] me down and my instructions are as soon as I get to Miami Beach: rent a car, drive back and forth between the arena where the fights are going to be held and the nearest hospital so that I don't waste any deadline time following Cassius Clay into intensive care. So I do this, and I drive to the 5th Street Gym and as I'm going up the stairs there are these four little guys. Who knew? I wasn't a teenage girl . . . I didn't know who they were!"

They'd come from the beach. They all wore white cabana shirts. Lipsyte introduced himself. Lennon said, "I'm Ringo." Starr said, "Hi, I'm George." They could turn on the charm when they wanted, but they could also be brusque. After all, they were rough-and-ready Liverpudlians. They weren't used to waiting. "Where the fuck's Clay?" Starr said. Finally, Lennon spun on his heels: "Let's get the fuck out of here," he said.

Like the boys and girls of middle-class America who composed their most fervent fan base, the four Liverpool lads were children of the World War II generation. Liverpool was a port city in northern England, gray and industrial, dense with thick Victorian buildings and massive stone structures modeled on the Greek Parthenon. In the seventeenth century, its shipping lanes made it the "Gateway to the British Empire," its tall-masted boats sailing to the malarial swamps of West Africa, trading cotton with Arab and African slave-runners for human cargo. "The first known slave ship to sail from Liverpool was *Liverpool Merchant,* which left port on 3 October 1699 and transported 220 Africans to Barbados," according to literature from the International Slavery Museum in Liverpool. "By 1750 Liverpool was sending more ships to Africa than the other main slaving ports of Bristol and London put together. . . . The estimate is that on Liverpool ships alone, there were more than 1.5 million enslaved Africans—that's a low estimate," museum director Richard Benjamin told an American delegation in 2008. Liverpool became England's most successful broker of human flesh because "it had dry docks, it had infrastructure to build the ships, the people to command the ships and to make the goods that were sold—it had everything," Benjamin explained.

Because of this legacy and the influx of poor Irish families, economic refugees, over several decades, Liverpool had become one of the most diverse cities in England by the time the Beatles were born there. It had developed a degree of racial and class tolerance unknown in other parts of the country. "There was an honesty that we had, a very simple, naïve honesty, and I think that had a lot to do with where we came from," Harrison said. "The people [in Liverpool] . . . say you have to have humor to live in a place like that. . . . That kept us going."

During the Beatles' childhoods, sectors of the city remained bombed-out from the war—whole neighborhoods "just *gone*," people said, particularly around Penny Lane, close to the docks. After Britain declared war on Germany in 1939, an air blitz pounded Liverpool from August 1940 to May 1941. Four thousand citizens were killed, and over 120,000 houses were damaged or destroyed. Mass burials occurred all over the city, leaving common graves every few blocks. The Bishop of Liverpool said that God would know who all these people were.

George Harrison and Richard Starkey (who later adopted the stage name Ringo Starr) hailed from poor families; John Lennon and Paul McCartney were lower middle class, but all four experienced early tragedies (Lennon and McCartney both lost their mothers when they were young, while Lennon and Starkey came from broken homes.) Nevertheless, British boys of the Beatles' generation would not face the need for military inscription—they would be blessed with more leisure time than their fathers had been and given more opportunity to develop their interests. For the Beatles, from a very young age, this meant an intense devotion to music.

Their raw sound, based largely on American rock and roll, most of which they heard from the 45s sailors brought back to the port of Liverpool, was forged literally in the war rubble of their city and in the postwar squalor of Germany, in the Hamburg nightclubs where they honed their act each night before all but one had reached the age of twenty.

If, as Wordsworth said, poetry is emotion recollected in tranquility, the Beatles' sound was the lingering memory of war transfigured by the leisure bought with postwar prosperity. Such was the movement of the mid-twentieth century, and from their beginnings, the Beatles had captured this lightning in a bottle.

Harrison, the youngest of the group, was born on February 25, 1943, to a homemaker and a war vet, a former seaman. Harry Harrison struggled to make a living. He worked off and on as a bus driver. For years the family lived without hot water and relied on an outhouse rather than indoor plumbing. "Cold? It was cold in those times," Harrison said. "We only had one fire. . . . And in the winter there used to be ice on the windows and in fact you would have to put a hot water bottle in the bed and keep moving it around for an hour before getting into the bed." He grew up, along with his older brothers Peter and Harry and his sister Louise, breathing chemically tainted air from nearby steel factories and the sweet-and-sour blood odors of slaughterhouses at the end of the cobbled lanes by his house.

Yet for all the hardships, the home life was loving and stable. He adored his father, but it was Harrison's mother Louise who centered his world. Whenever the kitchen fire went out or food was scarce, she shrugged and said, "Lord willing, we'll be all right. It could always be worse." In 1958, when his friend John Lennon's mother was killed by a drunk driver, Harrison followed Louise wherever she went. He was "terrified that I was going to die next," she said. "He'd watch me . . . all the time."

Through her, he learned to puzzle through life's inequities rather than just shout about them. His surroundings gave him a keen awareness of cruelty, injustice, and hypocrisy; his mother taught him to analyze these circumstances and take firm stands against them.

His mother baptized him in Our Lady of Good Help Church, but at an early age he dismissed her Catholicism. He saw all too clearly how pubs outnumbered churches on the city streets and how quickly the parishioners headed for the pubs after Mass. "[Priests smelling of tobacco] used to come round to all the houses in the neighborhood collecting money. . . . They built a large church out of all the donations. . . . I felt then that there was some hypocrisy going on, even though I was only about eleven years old." He liked the stained glass windows and the incense. The Stations of the Cross, the idea of "Christ dragging his cross down the street with everybody spitting at him," intrigued him because he could easily imagine a unique soul raising the ire of those who refused to understand him. Everything else church-related seemed like "bullshit."

Far more exciting to him, in a spiritual sense, was the polished meteorite set in cement by the Wavertree Baths. It had landed in a farmer's field outside Liverpool. Harrison would crawl on it as a boy, put his arms around it, trying to grasp the depths of space it had traveled to get there.

He started classes at the Liverpool Institute in 1954 (Charles Dickens had once lectured there). It was a long bus ride from his house, and the distance meant he could rarely stay late for extracurricular activities. He developed a sense of social isolation, a resentment of his classmates' cliquishness, a hatred of gossip. A few years later, when he was old enough to attend Dovetale Grammar School, "the darkness [really] began," he said. "I realized [life] was raining and cloudy with old streets and backward teachers and all of that, and that is where my frustrations seemed to start. You would punch people just to get it out of your system."

He recognized the sadism and love of power motivating many of his teachers. He stuck up for classmates who were bullied. More than anything, authority *disappointed* him. "I had already made my mind up when I was about twelve that I was not going into the army at any cost and then at school from about thirteen years old to sixteen or seventeen they had these cadet guys," he said. "I could never figure it out . . . every Monday afternoon, or Wednesday, you would look out and see these boys and they would all be there marching up and down with the geography teacher or the maths teacher, all dressed as soldiers, going 'hup, two, three, four' . . . I would think, 'WHAT?'"

Now and then his schooling was interrupted by lengthy hospital stays. Kidney trouble. Tonsillitis. "I had a really sore throat [once], and . . . the infection spread and gave me nephritis, an inflammation of the kidneys," he said. It was during this convalescence, bored, that he decided to learn guitar. He loved Hoagy Carmichael; he loved the country singers his dad played on the windup gramophone he'd bought as a merchant seaman—Hank Williams, Jimmie Rodgers—and he'd just discovered Elvis. His mother gave him three pounds, and he bought a "cheapo horrible little guitar . . . it had a concave neck, so the most you could get out of it was a couple of chords. All the frets buzzed and the strings hit the frets."

A friend of his father's showed him some basic chords and played a few tunes for him. In the afternoons, he'd take his guitar and practice down by the Picton Clock Tower in Wavertree, near the first house his family lived in. The tower, built in 1884, was surrounded by iron street lamps trimmed with carved stone dolphins. Concrete plaques on its base offered meditative poems on mortality and time—aphorisms the likes of which the mature Harrison would often use as song lyrics: "Time wasted is existence; used is life." Harrison practiced until his fingers bled.

From the tower he could hike to a series of tunnels leading up a small hill—a favorite haunt of Liverpool kids. Years later, when he bought Friar Park, a former Catholic school in Henley-on-Thames, a place he occupied from 1970 until he died, he cleared tunnels and caves on the grounds, and he erected a clock tower in the garden, re-creating his childhood.

Once Harrison had learned enough chords to impress John Lennon and Paul McCartney, overriding their worries that he was too young to join their band, he asked his brother Pete, "Would you pack in work and have a go at [music] if you were me?" His father had found him a job as an apprentice electrician in a local shop. Pete said, "You might as well—you never know. . . . And if it doesn't work out you're not going to lose anything." "[So] I packed in my job, and joined the band full time and from then, nine-to-five never came back into my thinking," Harrison later recalled.

Bruno Koschmider, a former circus clown, now a music promoter from Hamburg, had been trolling England looking for groups he could hire cheaply to work his club, the Kaiserkeller. The Beatles, building their repertoire in local dives, came to Koschmider's attention through Allan Williams, a self-made impresario in Liverpool. Hamburg "was known to be a dodgy place . . . the famous stripper-land . . . with gangsters, where sailors were murdered," McCartney said. But none of the boys hesitated when Koschmider made them an offer. "I wanted to get out [of Liverpool]. I wanted to get the hell out. I knew there was a world out there and I wanted it," Lennon said later. "I think about Liverpool. The people I went to school with. Lads full of talent and hope . . . And even then, when we were all just startin' out, they decided to go to work, to go to a job, to work in some bloody office, and I would see them, and they'd be old eighteen months later. Old. Just hunched up, like, walkin' like their fathers. . . They were young, like us, and then—then they were old. And some of them were pissed at us [later], because they thought they could've become Beatles too. And maybe they were right. But they didn't. They decided to die early."

With his mother's full support, seventeen-year-old George Harrison followed his older mates to Hamburg, the "naughtiest city in the world" (though Louise certainly didn't know that at the time). Since he was underage he had to be smuggled into Germany using a false visa.

Upon arriving in the city on August 17, 1960, Harrison learned vivid new lessons about victory and defeat in war: the losers' home was a pile of rubble no less horrifying than the winners'. The Allies had relentlessly bombed Hamburg's shipyards, U-boat pens, and oil refineries. In 1943 Allied fighter planes had ignited one of the largest firestorms of the war, killing over thirty-five thousand civilians. For all that, the place looked no worse than vast stretches of Liverpool. The Reeperbahn, the red-light district where the Beatles would be living and playing, was—for all its seediness—hopping.

"[In the Reeperbahn], we were put in this pigsty, like a toilet it was, in a cinema, a rundown sort of fleapit," Lennon recalled. "*We were living in a toilet.*"

In the club, they would play all night, every night, honing their performance chops. "All these gangsters would come in—the local Mafia," Lennon said. "They'd send a crate of champagne on stage, imitation German champagne, and we had to drink it or they'd kill us. They'd say, 'Drink, and then do 'What'd I Say.' We'd have to do this show, whatever time of night. If they came in at five in the morning and we'd been playing seven hours, they'd give us a crate of champagne and we were supposed to carry on. My voice began to hurt with the pain of singing. But we learnt from the Germans that you could stay awake by eating slimming pills, so we did that."

At the Beatles' shows, gangs of British servicemen piled into the bar, shouting nationalistic slogans, insulting the German waiters, trying to stiff them on the bills. The soldiers picked fights "over nothing," Lennon said. "The waiters would get their flick-knives out, or their truncheons, and that would be it. I've never seen such killers." The shows often ended with the band weeping, from police tear gas lobbed into the club to break up brawls.

And then, of course, "We all got our [sexual] education in Hamburg," McCartney said. "They were all barmaids. It wasn't your average sweet virgin that you were mixing with."

"I certainly didn't have a stripper in Hamburg," Harrison recalled. "There were young girls in the clubs and we knew a few, but for me it wasn't some big orgy." On the Beatles' second trip to the city, in 1961, he had his "first shag." It was nothing like his experiences with Iris Caldwell back home. He brought a girl to bed one night "with Paul and John and Pete Best all watching," he said. "We were in bunkbeds. They couldn't really see anything because I was under the covers. But after I'd finished they all applauded and cheered. At least they kept quiet while I was doing it."

"The rest of us were a little more experienced," McCartney said. "George was a late starter."

It was the memory of Iris that held him back. In Liverpool the goal was to bond with the person you were with. But in Hamburg the point seemed to be to impress your mates: sex as competition, an initiation rite intended to bind you to the lads. Once admitted into the club, Harrison would never resolve this paradox.

There was something else he never got over. In one of the Beatles' early trips to Germany, the authorities deported him once they discovered he was underage. Always afterward, he would remember the feeling of guilt that he had jeopardized the band's future right when they were taking off. He was a lost little boy the day he boarded a train for home hauling a "crappy suitcase and things in boxes, paper bags with my clothes in, and a guitar." "I had too many things to carry and was standing in the corridor of the train with my belongings around me, and lots of soldiers on the train, drinking," he said. "I had visions of our band staying on there with me stuck in Liverpool, and that would be it."

But back home the Beatles reconvened in the Cavern Club and stayed together, returning to Hamburg a year later, their music stiffened by hard experience—dues paid, as the blues kings sang. They'd learned their tones, syncopation, and structures from the tensions in American music, fault lines embedded in the generational experiences of Black families. George Harrison's fingers bled while playing the rhythms of America's racial legacy. He'd come by these rhythms naturally, as a child of Liverpool's rich history.

✡

Cassius Clay was an early, ardent Elvis fan and a fan of rock and roll generally. His father, Cash, always claimed that if it weren't for racist white music producers he would have been a great singer. Young Cassius hoped to follow suit after seeing Elvis on *The Ed Sullivan Show*.

Later he realized that Presley's musical roots lay in Black traditions: gospel, work songs, blues. This insight shook him just as he was old enough to study his father's painted murals. Cash made his living as a sign painter: "Deliveries and Female Disorders," "Joyce's Barber Shop," "Three Rooms of Furniture." For twenty-five bucks a pop, and an occasional chicken dinner, he also crafted scenes from the Bible in Louisville churches. Jesus was always a white man in these paintings, yet the Gospels said everyone was made in God's image. The Lord's blue-eyed son sure as hell didn't look like him or his father, Clay thought.

Despite what the Bible said, in this fancy horse-breeding town, the people who looked like him were condemned to be servants, like his mama cleaning houses.

Born on January 17, 1942, and raised in Louisville's segregated West End, Clay had plenty of time, as a kid, to ponder Black and white. Like George Harrison, he was surrounded by hypocrisy, but his mother, Odessa, worked hard to keep the family stable. They'd named him Cassius Marcellus Clay. He loved it. It was like a little poem. The name had a powerful local history. His great-grandfather had been a slave owned by Kentucky senator Henry Clay. Though Clay trafficked in human bondage, he aspired to abolish slavery, a system he called "the darkest spot in the map of our country."

Unusually restless as a baby, young Cassius would bang his head against the back of his chair, like a boxer taking punches, when he couldn't get to sleep. "He could beat on anything and get rhythm," Odessa said. He was as light-skinned as his mother. Like a young chick, he seemed to imprint on her (later he called her "Bird" because of her chirping laughter). When he began to motor round the house, he'd run from room to room on tiptoe. The family told Odessa he was imitating the way she moved in high heels. From an early age, he referred to himself as pretty. He once went to school wearing lipstick. He seemed to equate his mother's gentleness with her skin color. Once he asked her if she was really a Negro.

Generally he was wary of his father, darker in color; later in life, his wariness extended to other men with very dark skin. In prefight trash talk, he was always harsher on his Black opponents than on white fighters, often engaging in racial slurs, most notably against Joe Frazier in the 1970s. His trainer was a white man. His first sponsors were wealthy white businessmen. After his retirement, when he fell into financial trouble, he asked a friend to find him a white lawyer because he believed Black lawyers would try to "screw" him. All of this contradicted the separatist rhetoric he heard from the Nation of Islam.

His father could be fabulously entertaining, singing Nat King Cole around the house, dressing up, mimicking regional accents, pretending to be a foreigner in impromptu comedy skits performed for the neighbors. But Cash could be scary when he lowered his voice and talked about how the white man had cheated him of lucrative opportunities, how the Black man should follow Marcus Garvey and establish a separate nation. And when he was drinking—gin, his preference—he became terrifying.

In the summer of 1957, the Louisville Police Department responded to a domestic disturbance call at the Clay residence on Grand Avenue. Officer Charles Kalbfleisch discovered young Cassius bleeding from his thigh. Shaking, Odessa told Kalbfleisch that Cash, drunk, had cut her son with a knife when the boy tried to protect her from him. In the end, no charges were filed. "They'll kill each other," Kalbfleisch said, meaning Black families, "and when you go to court two or three months later, they've forgotten."

Joe Martin, Clay's boxing coach, remembered seeing the boy in the gym three days after the incident. "I knew the kid was scared to death of his old man." Yet ultimately young Cassius would not reject the traits he inherited from his father—the acceptance of violence under certain circumstances, the bragging, the desire to be the center of attention, the disdain for white authority. In time he would also develop his father's cavalier attitude toward women.

In his parents, "you saw the two component parts of [Clay] walking the earth in separate forms," said journalist Jack Olsen. "The bombastic fast-talking father, the complete egoist, and that lovely, sweet, warm, wonderful mom. . . . [Clay] had not integrated the maternal and paternal sides of his personality. You could see Cassius Senior come out in those pugnacious bellicose statements, and five minutes later you'd see his mother come out in some lovely sweet gesture or lyrical line. It was like a noninsane schizophrenia."

As a boy Clay remained staunchly protective of his mother—and of his younger brother Rudy (named after Rudolph Valentino). Cassius seized on Rudy as if he were a prize teddy bear and enlisted him to aid his athletic training. "He used to ask me to throw rocks at him," Rudy said. "I thought he was crazy, but he'd stand back and dodge every one of them. No matter how many I threw, I could never hit him."

With the money from Cash's paintings and Odessa's house-cleaning jobs, the Clay family lived a lower-middle-class life, but as southern Blacks they endured the Jim Crow rules of the time and place. Young Clay knew there were parts of town to avoid. He knew to act subservient around white officials. He knew when he saw his mother walking home exhausted after cleaning other people's houses that the world was made for white people. He lay in bed at night crying, asking his mother why colored people had to suffer.

He learned that masking was essential, like feinting and dodging in the ring; the habit, ingrained early, extended beyond safety needs to cover a host of awkward situations. For instance, in his teenage years feminine beauty stunned him into near-silence. He'd force himself to preen and brag in front of girls. "He was like a live chick walking through Colonel Sanders," said Areatha Swint, a high school friend. "He drew [girls] like a magnet." But his shyness held him back. He fainted once outside Swint's apartment after kissing her at her door.

His masking also hid his family's economic realities. Often in the afternoon, after school, he'd run for miles alongside city buses. He told his friends he needed to do this because he was training to be an athlete. The truth was that he couldn't afford bus fare. He was too ashamed to admit it.

Like George Harrison, he rejected his mother's god. He saw sadists running the schools. He longed for escape. If any of his teachers had encouraged his musical talents, he might have opted for a life of rock and roll. Instead he wound up gravitating toward the boxing ring. Black Americans had always distinguished themselves in sports. Clay studied the history—he learned how southern plantation owners had arranged barn fights among their slaves for gambling and entertainment purposes; how heavyweight champion Jack Johnson had outraged white American society in the early twentieth century, dating white women; how Joe Louis, the Brown Bomber, had carried the nation's hopes against the German Max Schmeling during Hitler's rise to power. Clay understood how symbolically important a fighter could become.

In his risky pursuit, he was fortunate to have the support of his mother, just as George Harrison had Louise's blessing. And just as Harrison's sense of injustice grew once he discovered Hamburg's ruins, so too did Cassius Clay develop a larger vision. It happened for him when he read about Emmet Till's murder: a Black boy beaten to death because he'd dared to address a white woman. Till's killers were never brought to justice. Clay understood that the same conditions permitting "Whites" and "Colored" signs to be posted above separate water fountains in downtown Louisville permitted white men to get away with bludgeoning boys who looked just like he did. He would hone his skills in the ring. He would fight—and fight back.

"We're [getting] the fuck out of here," Lennon said. He headed for the gymnasium stairs, past a row of busted seats salvaged from an abandoned movie theater.

"But [then] some state troopers just pushed us . . . into this dressing room," said Robert Lipsyte. "I guess Clay's people wanted a photo op too." Someone locked the door. "[The Beatles were] screaming and banging on the door . . . and cursing and they were very angry at having been abducted. Then suddenly the door bursts open and the five of us in unison, we just gasp. I mean, it was the first time. We had no idea how big he was. He filled the doorway. He was just wearing boxing shorts. He glowed." Clay was six foot three, 218 pounds. "He was carrying a big staff like a prophet," Lipsyte recalled. "And there was this wonderful hushed moment when the five of us just looked at this gorgeous creature from another planet."

"Hello there, Beatles. We oughta do some road shows together. We'll get rich," Clay said.

Then he led them to the ring, and together they climbed through the sagging ropes. Clay balanced his gloved fist against Harrison's shaggy head, knocking him against the others. They play-wobbled, ready to drop like dominoes. The older journalists in the gym barely masked their impatience. But Lipsyte noticed how compatible the men were—larger than life. "As if they hadn't just met each other, they went through what seemed like a total choreographed routine." Clay called them the greatest. He said they "shook up the world." (In reality, he didn't know much about them; later he asked Lipsyte, "Who *were* those faggots?")

But when the cameras clicked they bonded. They were sealed together inside the bubble of greatness, even if others weren't yet willing to acknowledge it. They stood apart, and they knew it. Their play had a natural spontaneity, a graceful rhythm.

Clay called McCartney the prettiest adding "but not as pretty as me."

He picked up Ringo, the smallest of the Beatles, and held him like a doll. Then: "Squirm, you worms!" Clay shouted. The Beatles dropped to his feet. He pounded his bare chest. Harrison folded his hands in prayer. His Beatle bob brushed the dried blood of young boxers who'd sacrificed their bodies in the ring—celebrity, the only immortality they could imagine.

In the short time they spent together, Clay and the Beatles relished their awareness that they were special, that this ridiculous photo stunt was the prelude to much larger things. Lennon, just one step ahead of Clay in losing his private life to the world, said, "The bigger you get, the more unreality you have to face. The more real you get, the more unreal *they* get." Clay said, "You're not as dumb as you look." "No, but you are," Lennon shot back. Clay paused. Then he saw Lennon's grin. He laughed, and the silliness resumed.

The American press had followed the lead of the *New York Times* in dubbing George Harrison the "quiet Beatle" because he had been so subdued in his illness. Clay was known as the "Louisville Lip," the "Marvelous Mouth," or "Gaseous Cassius" because of his bragging and his poetry. Despite the differences implied by these tags, the men were more alike than not, as the years ahead would prove.

For one thing, as children they had both been prone to spiritual questioning. At night, unable to sleep, closing his eyes, Harrison experienced a feeling of rapidly withdrawing from his body, from Earth, and traveling some vague distance before finding himself back in bed. Many years later, as a devotee of transcendental meditation, he would experience similar sensations, his head filling with light when he shut his eyes, accompanied by the warmth of being absorbed into some vaster entity.

Clay was a firm believer in prophecies. From a very young age, he boasted, "I am a man of destiny." (As a young fighter, he predicted with uncanny accuracy—and no small amount of showmanship—the round in which he would knock out his opponent.) "I don't know what it was, but I always felt I was born to do something for my people," he said. "Eight years old, ten years old; I'd walk out of my house at two in the morning and look at the sky for an angel or a revelation or God telling me what to do."

He wanted to believe in literal magic and learned as many tricks as he could, so as to summon the power of enchantment. As one of his schoolteachers explained, "If you can't stand the world you live in and you can't change it, you've got to believe in magic, in predictions."

Neither Harrison nor Clay could change the rough surroundings of their childhoods. So they developed a mystical bent: an interiority in which they felt connected to larger energies, a self-denying discipline (for physical training, music, prayer).

The mystical aspects of their personalities, combined with their celebrity, would soon make George Harrison and Muhammad Ali lightning rods for the world's unpredictable currents.

When they descended from the ring, the Beatles went "off to their history and [Clay] off to his," said Robert Lipsyte. "[They] were in perfect sync at that moment. You could see it was not that they were fostering any kind of political revolution. It was this kind of breezy disrespect for everything that had gone before them."

CHAPTER 2

Elijah and Malcolm

"He's the fifth Beatle," Jimmy Cannon said of Cassius Clay. "Except that's not right," Cannon reconsidered. "The Beatles have no hokum to them." Cannon was an old-school sportswriter for the *New York Journal-American*. He was one of the most consistent critics of Clay's unorthodox fighting style. "In a way, Clay is a freak," he wrote. "He is a bantamweight who weighs more than two hundred pounds." Cannon also despised the young man's braggadocio—he was as noisy as a scruffy rock and roller.

Still, in the lead-up to the February 1964 championship bout with Sonny Liston, Clay's clowning, his poetry, and his relentless self-promotion seemed harmless. No one gave him a shot at the title, but some writers suggested this young upstart couldn't tarnish the heavyweight crown any more than the current champ. "Sonny Liston was a mean fucker," said Harold Conrad, the fight's PR man. "This was a guy who got arrested a hundred times, went to prison for armed robbery, got out, went back again for beating up a cop, and wound up being managed by organized crime. When Sonny gave you the evil eye—I don't care who you were—you [shrank]."

Jimmy Cannon notwithstanding, younger journalists saw Clay's youth, good looks, and humor as the perfect foils for that "mean fucker." They saw his bragging as an exquisite performance—learned, Clay said, from the TV wrestler Gorgeous George. George deliberately egged audiences to boo him, to yell for his defeat in the ring. He stoked the crowd's passions, knowing he'd fill more seats that way. Clay got it. Adding a dash of Little Richard to his wrestler routine, he worked hard to promote his fight with Liston.

Liston got it too. "A boxing match is like a cowboy movie," he told *Sports Illustrated*. "There's got to be good guys, and there's got to be bad guys. That's what the people pay for."

Clay was a prankster. Fans wanted to see him punished. But they also hated Sonny Liston. Under these circumstances, Clay was the natural good guy. But tickets weren't selling. The Convention Hall at Miami Beach had a capacity of 16,448, which would have guaranteed $1.2 million at the gate. Fewer than half the tickets had sold days before the fight. Promoter Bill MacDonald, a former bus driver turned millionaire, worried he'd been overly ambitious in scaling the arena or that volatile weather was scaring fans away (a massive rainstorm drenched the city hours before the bout). Other explanations included the reasonable assumption that few people wanted to pay a large sum to see a match destined to last a few seconds: the writers all said Liston's first punch would end matters quickly.

More on the mark, MacDonald thought, was the feeling that Clay's loud mouth had "got[ten] out of hand." Worse, rumors had begun to circulate about his affiliation with a strange cult, something called the Nation of Islam or the Black Muslims. Apparently this group touted militancy and scorn for the civil rights movement.

Observers were starting to think maybe there *wasn't* a good guy in this fight. To MacDonald's chagrin, Jim Murray wrote in the *Los Angeles Times*, "[This will be] the most popular fight since Hitler-Stalin—180 million Americans rooting for a double knockout."

Charles "Sonny" Liston, the grandson of a slave, was not born into this world as much as dropped into its dirt in a cypress-board shack in Sand Slough, St. Francis County, Arkansas. When he testified before the US Senate in 1960, he said he was born in 1933. In 1953, registering for a Golden Gloves tournament, he listed his birthdate as 1932. During his career, he'd offer half a dozen other dates. The truth was he didn't know. No one in his family bothered to remember. He said his father, a tenant farmer, had sired twenty-five children—mules for his plow, a cotton-picking crew. Liston never knew most of their names.

By 1960 he was already a "mean fucker." He had learned to box in the Missouri State Penitentiary while serving a stint for armed robbery. Upon his release, he was guided by organized crime to wreck the ranks of professional boxing. He was a lucrative prize. In a stunningly short time, Liston defeated the class of the heavyweight division. He emerged as the prime contender for Floyd Patterson's crown. Patterson enjoyed wide esteem among white audiences—he was soft-spoken, polite, the stereotyped Negro who knew his place. At first, he ducked Liston because of Liston's ties to the Mafia. In the 1960 Kefauver hearings, Lt. Joseph Kuda of the St. Louis Police Department testified that John Vitale, head of the St. Louis crime family, owned 12 percent of Sonny Liston; Frank "Blinky" Palermo, a Philly hood, owned another 12; and Frankie Carbo held a whopping 52 percent share. Carbo had long been associated with the Genovese crime family and with Murder Inc. He had ties to the outfit operating Madison Square Garden. Through those connections, he controlled much of what happened in the boxing world, "manipulat[ing] odds by causing fixed results in fights," according to a 1946 FBI report. Patterson claimed it wouldn't do to let Liston sully boxing's image. Liston scoffed: Patterson was just a coward, he said.

Patterson knew that Liston had legitimately earned a shot at the title—*in* the ring. "I knew if I'd want to sleep comfortably I'd have to take [him] on . . . [and] maybe if Liston wins, he'll live up to the title. He may make people look up to him."

The fight was scheduled for Chicago's Comiskey Park on September 25, 1962. This bout offered obvious good and bad: it was "Saint v. Sinner," said the British writer Sam Leitch.

The saint crumbled at two minutes and six seconds of the first round. Three left hooks, a right, and a final left put him down. Cassius Clay attended the fight, wearing a dark suit with a black bow tie. He stood and gaped at the dazed former champ.

In his dressing room afterward, Liston told an interviewer, "If the public will give me a chance to prove it, I will be a worthy champion."

It was not to be. Within days, journalist Dan Parker wrote, "The leopard cannot change its spots, and this Big Cat, Liston, certainly didn't impress anyone as a penitent sinner, eager to atone for his errors during his training period. He is probably the most anti-social fighter in history." Another writer, Reg Gutteridge, didn't bother to hide his racism: Liston was a "muscular mass of menace," he said, and the fight was "as one-sided as a lynching."

Somehow, before flying home to Philadelphia, Liston got word that the city was planning a ticker-tape parade in his honor. He had received a congratulatory telegram from the mayor. Proud, and determined to make people prouder of him yet, he worked on a speech during the flight. Journalist Jack McKinney traveled on the plane with him. "I want to reach my people," Liston told him. "I want to reach them and tell them, 'You don't have to worry about me disgracing you.' . . .

I want to go to colored churches and colored neighborhoods. I know it was in the papers that the better class of colored people were hoping I'd lose, even praying I'd lose, because they were afraid I wouldn't know how to act. . . . I want to go to a lot of places, like orphan homes and reform schools. I'll be able to say, 'Kid, I know it's tough for you, and it might even get tougher. But don't give up on the world. Good things can happen if you let them.'"

McKinney recalled that, after landing, Liston waited patiently for the plane's door to open. He carefully straightened his tie and hat. He stepped out and . . . a few journalists were there. And airport workers.

"I watched Sonny. His eyes swept the whole scene," McKinney said. "He was extremely intelligent, and he understood immediately what it meant. His Adam's Apple moved slightly. You could feel the deflation, see the look of hurt in his eyes. . . . He had been deliberately snubbed. Philadelphia wanted nothing to do with him. It was going to be a whole new world. What happened . . . that day was a turning point in his life. He was still the bad guy. He was the personification of evil. And that's the way it was going to remain. He was devastated."

"Some day they'll write a blues song just for fighters," Liston once said. "It'll be for a slow guitar, soft trumpet and a bell."

"[Liston] is a man unafraid because he's never had the imagination to be afraid of anything," Tom Tannas, a veteran boxing manager observed following the Patterson fight.

But Cassius Clay scared Sonny Liston.

For the next year and a half, after winning the heavyweight title, Liston, angry, determined to be meaner than ever—the world be damned—scheduled only one fight, a rematch with Floyd Patterson in Las Vegas. The fight ended in another first-round KO, Patterson sprawled across the canvas.

But instead of praising Liston's abilities, journalists attacked him as "insufferable . . . bullying and cocky." "The world of sport now realizes it has gotten Charles (Sonny) Liston to keep," Jim Murray wrote in the *LA Times*. "It's like finding a live bat on a string under your Christmas tree."

"Colored people say they don't want their children to look up to me," Liston said. "Well, they ain't teaching their children to look up to Martin Luther King, either." The hell with them. He spent his time trying to avoid the Louisville Lip, who'd mounted a harassment campaign, hoping to force the champ to give him a shot at the title.

"He's got one of them bulldog kind of minds," Clay said. "The big thing for me was observing how Liston acted outside of the ring . . . to try to get a good picture of how his mind worked. And that's when I first got the idea that if I would handle the thing right, I could use psychology on him . . . work on his nerves so bad that I would have him beat before he ever got in the ring with me."

By now, in Philadelphia, Liston had amassed a petty arrest record, enough to force him and his wife Geraldine to move again, this time to Denver. Late one night, Clay pulled up outside of Liston's Colorado house in an old passenger bus he'd bought, painted red and white like the stolen bicycle that inadvertently led him to boxing. "Come on out of there! I'm going to whup you right now! Come on out of there and protect your home! If you don't come out of that door, I'm gonna break it down!" he yelled from the curb. Liston opened the door, groggy, wearing a long silk robe. "What do you want, you Black motherfucker?" he said. But Clay had him: Liston was paralyzed, knowing a street fight in the middle of the night would put him away, given his rap sheet.

Neighbors called the police, and the cops sent the Lip on his way.

But suspicions grew in Liston's mind: this boy was dangerous. Not as a physical challenge but as lunacy unleashed. Equally worrying were stories about the Nation of Islam. Clay wore dark suits and bow ties. Liston's associates told him this was the uniform of the Muslims. Were those assholes behind him? Liston didn't know much about the group, but he understood they had a paramilitary unit—to be feared as much as the mob. The stories made him even madder. Was the world going to squeeze his balls from two directions?

Cassius Clay had, in fact, been introduced to the Nation of Islam as early as the age of sixteen. In 1958, on a vacation to Atlanta with his brother Rudy, he spoke to members of the Nation outside Muhammad's Temple Number 15. Later he referred to that moment as being "fished off a street corner." (We know of his contact with Atlanta because the FBI had organized wiretaps to monitor the Muslims' activities there.)

After his second trip to Chicago for a Golden Gloves tournament in 1959—a year after his encounter with the prostitute—he returned to Louisville carrying a 45 record he'd picked up, a calypso song titled "A White Man's Heaven Is a Black Man's Hell," performed by Minister Louis X, later known as Louis Farrakhan. Clay loved the tune's gentle rhythm. He high-stepped all over Louisville's West End singing the lyrics: "Why are we called Negroes? / Why are we deaf, dumb, and blind?" His aunt, Mary, believed the song "brainwashed" him. "They musta fed him something before he came back," she said.

In December 1961 he was roller-skating with friends at the Broadway Roller Rink in Louisville, a segregated amusement center. Upon leaving, he noticed a crowd across the street listening to a Black man in a Mohair suit and bow tie. The man was praising the Honorable Elijah Muhammad, the leader of the Nation of Islam. He offered Clay a newspaper. "My brother, do you want to buy a *Muhammad Speaks* . . . so that you can read about your own kind, read the real truth of your history, your true religion, your true name before you were given the White Man's name in slavery?"

Clay didn't bother to read the articles, but a cartoon on page 32 intrigued him. Signed "Eugene XXX"—the pen name of Eugene Majied—the comic depicted a slave, dressed as a Muslim, being punished by his overseer for reciting an Arabic prayer. Years later he would remember it: "I liked that cartoon, it did something to me."

The Nation of Islam had natural appeal for a southern Black man whose father had scorned whites and lauded the separatist goals of Marcus Garvey. The Muslims' professed discipline—the strict diets, the regular observances—also spoke to the dedicated, self-sacrificing young athlete.

It didn't take long after his move to Miami and the 5th Street Gym for the Nation to find him again. One day, he spied a street corner preacher "fishing for the dead," the "deaf, dumb, and blind—brainwashed of all self-respect and knowledge . . . by the white slave master." The man's name was Sam Saxon. He was a poolroom hustler, a janitor, a food salesman at various Miami racetracks, and a devout Black Muslim. He called himself Captain Sam, and he offered the young fighter a copy of *Muhammad Speaks*.

This time Clay read what was in it—the prophecies of Elijah Muhammad: Allah had spiritually tested the Black man, allowing white Christians to enslave him, Muhammad said, but the day was coming when war would ravage the world and Blacks would conquer the Earth.

Saxon took Clay to meetings at a local mosque. The principal minister, a man named Ishmael Sabakhan, became Clay's teacher. One day, another preacher, a man called Brother John, delivered a sermon, asking, "Why are we called Negroes?" (Clay memorized this speech word for word.) "It's the white man's way of taking away our identity. If you see a Chinaman coming, you know he's from China. If you see a Cuban coming, you know he's from Cuba. If you see a Canadian coming, you know he's from Canada. What country is called Negro?" American Blacks had been handed slave names, he said, names erasing their ancestry.

Saxon, Sabakhan, and Brother John introduced Clay to the words of Malcolm X—the Nation's most charismatic speaker. Malcolm mocked the civil rights movement, the lunch counter protests. "Anybody can sit," he said. "An old woman can sit. A coward can sit. . . . It takes a man to stand." He warned white listeners, "You might see these Negroes who believe in nonviolence and mistake us for one of them and put your hands on us thinking that we're going to turn the other cheek—and we'll put you to death just like that."

In 1962 Clay and his brother traveled to Detroit specifically to hear Elijah Muhammad and Malcolm X speak at Olympia Stadium. Before the rally began, Clay ran into Malcolm at a nearby luncheonette. Malcolm was slender and tall, with a ginger beard and thin black glasses. Clay walked up to him. He told the minister—as he told everyone—that he was going to be the next heavyweight champion of the world. This meant nothing to Malcolm. Elijah Muhammad had condemned boxing and sports in general as forms of white oppression.

But Malcolm's speech that day galvanized Clay. "How could a Black man talk about the government and white people and act so bold and not be shot at?" he said later. "How could he say these things? Only God must be protecting him. He was fearless. That really attracted me."

Two years later, on the eve of Clay's fight with Sonny Liston, Miami reporters spotted Malcolm X lurking around the 5th Street Gym. They noticed Clay dressing like Malcolm. The fighter's dietary habits were strange, even stricter than most boxers' regimens. Was it true he didn't eat pork? "Poke give me a headache," Clay admitted one afternoon to broadcaster Myron Cope. "Doctors told me poke 90 percent live cell parasites. Poke 90 percent maggots."

Stories about his religious beliefs, his odd affiliations, snuck into the press. Bill MacDonald, the fight promoter, panicked. His "good guy" was tanking. Advance ticket sales were depressed. When reporters asked Clay directly about his interest in the Muslims, he answered defensively that Muslims didn't drink or indulge in drugs. They didn't cheat on their spouses. Was he member of the Nation of Islam? "No, I'm not, not now," he said. "But the way you keep pressing me I just might be. They're the cleanest people next to God."

The Nation of Islam was a peculiar, homegrown product of US history, neuroses, and stubborn realities. It sprang into being as a result of the country's internal colonial tendencies.

The Nation began in Detroit in the 1930s—Detroit, future home of Motown, the sound of Black struggles, joy, and independence, the Motor City rhythms quickening the Beatles' pulse. Along with Chicago, Detroit was an epicenter of the southern Black diaspora, the "blues people" seeking release from bondage.

Detroit—the industrial "other side of the Cotton Curtain." Home of the Brown Bomber, beboppers, Smokey Robinson, and the Honorable Elijah Muhammad.

In Georgia, where Elijah Muhammad came from, he was known as Elijah Poole, a railway worker, the son of sharecroppers and itinerant preachers. As a child he witnessed the senseless lynching of a Black man. He married, had two kids, and moved to Detroit in 1923, at the age of twenty-six. He thought "life might be better" in Detroit. But "even there the first year I saw my people shot down right in the street without any justice whatsoever," he said. He drank and barely scraped by, growing more and more asthmatic, breathing cinders in the foundries he worked in.

Then in 1930 he met a man who claimed to be God. This man remains hard to pin down—certainly, the FBI files concerning "God" are a mess. Smugly, a field agent reported, in 1943, "Allah has proved to be very much of a human being since he has an arrest record in the Identification Division of the FBI." But the FBI could get no closer to identifying "God" than to concede it had fifty-eight different aliases for him, didn't know if he was Black or white, born in New Zealand or Pakistan or Portland, Oregon, and had no idea where he'd ended up, how or why or even if he'd died.

Elijah Muhammad's account of this person was unequivocal: "I asked Him, 'Who are you, and what is your real name?' He said, 'I am the one that the world has been expecting for the past 2,000 years.' I said to Him again, 'What is your name?' He said, 'My name is Mahdi; I am God, I came to guide you into the right path that you may be successful and see the hereafter.' He described the destruction of the world with bombs, poison gas, and finally with fire that would consume and destroy everything of the present world."

Meanwhile, the FBI was trying to determine if God had once bootlegged white lightning and trafficked morphine in Los Angeles. What the bureau knew (or thought it knew) from Elijah Muhammad was this: in 1930, in Paradise Valley, the "Bottoms" of Detroit, people were starving and dying, addicted and unemployed. There Elijah Poole met a man named Wallace Farad or Wallie D. Ford or W. H. Fard or Wallie Ford. According to a November 9, 1943, FBI report forwarded directly to J. Edgar Hoover, "Mahdi" told Poole that "Negroes were Moslems as were all of the dark races and that by registering with the nation of Islam the colored people would be given their correct names from Mecca and their slave names would be taken from them." An additional report explained that Farad had "many [fanatical] beliefs . . . including a belief that Japan has had for many years a monster airplane, known to the Moslems as a 'mother airplane.' The 'mother airplane' is said to carry 1,000 small airplanes, each of which carries bombs, which will be used against the white man. Each bomb is said to be such size to penetrate the earth's surface for a distance of one mile, and to destroy an area of fifty square miles when it explodes . . . All members . . . have a belief in ALLAH, also [known as] Mr. W. D. FARAD, and contend that this individual will return to help them liberate themselves from the yoke of the white man's rule."

The best that can be assembled from these puzzle pieces is that Elijah Poole met a man from *somewhere* who had absorbed a mix of Black nationalist ideas from Marcus Garvey and Timothy Drew. Drew was a New Jersey rail man who rebranded himself Noble Drew Ali and founded the Moorish Science Temple of America in Newark in 1913, preaching an odd combination of race pride and semi-Islamic ritual. (From the beginning, in America, Black Muslims were not unknown—many were shipped as slaves from Africa.)

Farad carried copies of the Bible and the Koran. He claimed that Blacks were members of a lost Asiatic tribe, descended from the Old Testament's Moabites. Allah was their true God. He said he'd come from Mecca; his father was a Black man named Alphonso, and his mother was a Russian Jew called Baby Gee.

Farad prowled the Bottoms day and night, refining his teachings, seeking converts to his cause. Allah, the Original Man, of whom he was an incarnation, he said, was born of a spinning atom seventy-six trillion years ago. His descendants, the Black people, belonged to a tribe called Shabazz.

White people were a race of devils created by a rogue Black man, an evil, big-headed scientist named Yakub. Over time, said Farad, white skin and blood were diluted through a series of eugenics experiments on the Greek island of Patmos—including the sacrifice of Black babies. White people lived savagely in the caves of Europe for two thousand years, mating with animals, eventually dominating the earth and enslaving Black people. Allah was testing the Black man, but salvation would come in the twentieth century, when the Mother Plane, a human-built planet carrying bombs, would attack Earth and finish off the white race.

In America, he said, the institution of slavery had brainwashed Black people, keeping from them true knowledge of their origins and destiny. Farad had come to wake them up.

His message resonated powerfully with Elijah Poole, alcoholic, desperately poor, nearly disabled because of his damaged lungs. Poole was among the first to swear allegiance to Farad's Allah Temple of Islam, sobering up, refusing to eat pork, praying every day. He helped Farad organize the Fruit of Islam, a group of men trained in the martial arts, assigned to maintain order in outdoor meetings. Anyone who disrupted a rally or questioned Farad's teachings got a beating.

In 1932 Farad offered his followers more specifics about the end of the world. The Mother Ship was "made like the universe," a series of wheels within wheels, he said. American "tricknology" could not understand its composition or dynamics. Years ago, it had been manufactured in secret by "our Asiatic brothers" in Japan.

At one point, one of Farad's disciples, impassioned by his stridency—a man named Robert Harris—knifed a fellow Muslim in the chest, killing him, offering him as a human sacrifice to the Temple of Allah. Naturally, this interested the Detroit police. They investigated Farad and confiscated a stack of his writings, including his promise to the children of his congregation that they would earn a trip to Mecca if they "cut off the head of four [white] 'devils.'"

On this incendiary evidence, the police arrested him, committed him to the psychopathic ward of Detroit's Receiving Hospital, and offered him a ticket out of town if he'd renounce his teachings. He did so and, escorted by two detectives to the Chicago train station, vanished on December 7, 1932.

Meanwhile, the police harassed his former parishioners, arresting them at their jobs, erasing their names from welfare rolls. Many of them drifted away from the temple. But not Elijah Poole. He mounted large protest campaigns outside the courthouse. Encouraged by this show of support, Farad returned to Detroit, recast his group as the Nation of Islam, gave each member an Arabic name, and continued to preach on the down-low.

He renamed Elijah Poole "Elijah Muhammad."

By May the cops had caught him again. Interrogators forced him to label his teachings "a racket." He promised he'd leave town for good. To Elijah Muhammad, he reiterated he was the universal God. In late May 1933 he announced to his followers, "Don't worry, I am with you. I will be with you in the near future to lead you out of this hell." He hugged Muhammad and said, "Tell them, Elijah, I love them." He drove away in a black Ford sedan.

That is one story. Over the years, Elijah Muhammad's explanations of what actually happened to Farad were maddeningly contradictory. No one knows where he went. Rumors circulated that Muhammad may have done him in, in a power grab. The FBI lost track of "God"—and later stoked the confusion. Under its COINTELPRO program, attempting to destabilize the Nation of Islam, it disseminated false information about the man and fell prey to its own tangled lies.

Elijah Muhammad swore that Farad had personally ordained him to "give life to the dead." Several of Farad's confused followers refused to accept Muhammad as Mahdi's replacement. Many more spread rumors of foul play, casting deep suspicion on the self-proclaimed "Messenger." Police harassment of the splintered group did not let up. Finally, in 1935, dismissing Detroit's Muslims as "hypocrites," fearing for his life, Elijah Muhammad took his family and left the city, eventually establishing a temple in a former animal hospital on Chicago's South Side.

To Farad's founding doctrines he added more vigorous assertions of racial pride, proposing a separate Black nation in the South. He said Black people needed no favors from white America. He encouraged his flock to become economically self-sufficient, supporting Black schools, groceries, and cafés. He promoted healthy diets and family discipline. He designed formal dress uniforms for the Fruit of Islam, dark blue coats and pants, resembling the outfits of railway porters. He militarized their ranks, stepping up hand-to-hand combat training and teaching the group to march in formation. He founded a newspaper, *Muhammad Speaks*, insisting that every member of the Nation sell a certain number of copies each month. All proceeds went to the temple.

His ascension to power in Chicago was not entirely smooth. "All members [of the Nation] were told not to register for the draft as they 'were already registered in Mecca.' They were also told that they could not fight in the 'white man's war,' but that they should remain to help the Japanese and all dark races in their fight for supremacy," an FBI field agent reported to J. Edgar Hoover. For this Muhammad was arrested, charged with draft evasion and sedition, found guilty, and imprisoned from 1943 to 1946.

While incarcerated, he was given a number of psychological tests. The "patient" was "diagnosed" as possessing a "marked persecutory trend both against himself and his race," convinced he was being "pursued and slandered by his enemies." He was a "paranoid type," suffering from "dementia praecox," and his claim to have communicated with God "in visual and auditory form" suggested schizophrenia.

He was, however, aggressively well-organized both individually and as the leader of his group. Once out of jail, he continued to expand the Nation of Islam, as its one true prophet. He instilled in his followers a powerful sense of dignity. By the time Cassius Clay heard of the Nation of Islam, it had established temples in almost every American city. Its members owned restaurants, apartment houses, and farms.

Elijah Muhammad was never a charismatic man. He was diminutive and pale, with a soft, squeaky voice. He often lost his breath. How did he manage to attract such a large following, and impress such powerful personalities as Malcolm X and Cassius Clay?

In *The Fire Next Time* (1963), James Baldwin offered a clue. Muhammad's "peculiar authority" came from his face, whose "central quality . . . is pain," Baldwin wrote. "Pain so old and deep and Black that it becomes personal and particular only when he smiles."

His pain, a reservoir of his people's collective anguish, convinced Cassius Clay that every word he spoke was the absolute truth.

Clay's aunt, Mary, once remarked, "Why, you have to be almost totally illiterate to be sold that Muslim bill of goods! I'll just plain old give you the facts. *You have to be illiterate!*" But the strange, elaborate narrative pulsed with archetypal power absorbed from ancient myths, biblical poetry, and Black folklore. Yakub was a classic trickster figure, familiar from Yoruba origin stories passed through generations of families descended from slaves; the Mother Ship was a modern incarnation of the prophecy of Ezekiel: "And I looked, and, behold, a whirlwind came out of the north, a great cloud, and a fire . . . [then] the appearance of . . . wheels and their work was like unto the color of a beryl"; a vanished god promising to return was a staple of most of the world's religions.

And what held the whole together, made it a viable vision, was the social pathology *making it necessary.* "Without the failings of Western society," said historian Louis E. Lomax, "the Black Muslims could not have come into being."

Malcolm Little was on his way to becoming Sonny Liston, except he couldn't box.

In March 1946, he was sent inside for eight to ten years at the Charlestown State Prison in Massachusetts for a series of armed robberies in Boston. He wasn't physically imposing like Liston, but his fierce intelligence, intense gaze, and impatience with bullshit made his fellow inmates fear him. He'd earned the nickname Detroit Red because of his slightly reddish hair and his origins as a petty thief in Detroit. Most of the other prisoners called him Satan.

Elijah Muhammad was soon calling him X. Impressed with Malcolm's intelligence, sincerity, and charisma, Muhammad asked him to train as a Nation of Islam minister.

The FBI kept watch on Malcolm from the moment he was paroled on August 7, 1952. Their surveillance of him would not cease until he died in 1965.

For a year, while studying to be a minister, Malcolm labored as a dockworker. Eventually Muhammad appointed him assistant minister at the temple in

Detroit. Soon Malcolm went to Boston. He recruited fresh members—he was gifted at bringing people into the fold—and established a new temple in Roxbury. After that he was dispatched to Philadelphia to serve as acting minister in place of a disgraced leader. In Philadelphia Malcolm developed the jazz-like, hypnotically rhythmic cadences that drew thousands to his voice and would captivate Cassius Clay. In one typical sermon, he expressed incredulity that white people considered Blacks "subversive." "Here is a man [the white man] who has raped your mother and hung your father on a tree, is he subversive? Here is a man who has robbed you of all knowledge of your nation and your religion and is he subversive?"

Behind such assertions, Malcolm's emphasis was notably different than Elijah Muhammad's—an early hint of the nascent rift between them. The rift would one day prove fatal to Malcolm. In most of *his* sermons, Muhammad stressed self-knowledge, patience, the long-term promise of salvation. Malcolm called for action.

Their split was openly apparent as early as 1955. From April 8 to April 24, 1955, at the invitation of India's prime minister Jawaharlal Nehru, representatives from twenty-nine Asian and African countries met in Bandung, Indonesia. There, as a collective, the leaders condemned decades-old colonial models putting the West in charge of Eastern nations. They denounced worldwide racism and Western exploitation of the planet's resources and labor. They rejected Cold War tactics and realignment resulting from postwar conflicts.

Though little noticed by most US citizens since it didn't get much mass media coverage, the Bandung Conference signaled an early shot across the bow in what became a cascading series of independence struggles challenging world order. The conference galvanized Malcolm; the lessons he took from it would one day emerge from Muhammad Ali's mouth and enter the West's cultural bloodstream.

Speaking in Detroit at the King Solomon Baptist Church on November 10, 1963, Malcolm said: "In Bandung . . . was the first unity meeting in centuries of Black people. And once you study what happened at the Bandung Conference . . . it actually serves as a model for the same procedure you and I can use to get our problems solved. At Bandung all the nations came together from Africa and Asia. . . . Despite their religious differences, they came together . . . despite their economic and political differences, they came together."

What Malcolm saw, before almost anyone else, was that the Bandung "unity meeting" offered a blueprint for world revolution.

Elijah Muhammad ignored it.

In 1957 Malcolm came to large-scale public attention beyond the borders of Black communities. By then his growing visibility had become a source of conflict with Muhammad's family. They perceived Malcolm as too popular, too powerful, a threat to their leader.

Muhammad had put him in charge of Harlem's Temple Number 7. The building sat among rat-filled tenements, soiled streets, and stinking, trash-filled alleys. Yet Malcolm had found his place. Harlem was home to many ex-Garveyites, politically savvy brothers and sisters. The Ahmadiyah Movement, a quasi-Islamic sect founded in India, recruited a number of devotees in Harlem's back rooms. Its late leader, Mirza Ghulum Ahmad, had once—like W. D. Farad—called himself the Mahdi, the Muslim Messiah signaling the end times. These groups competed, yet their agendas overlapped; Malcolm's message reached sympathetic ears. He recruited Louis Walcott, Louis X, whose calypso record would so enchant the impressionable Cassius Clay.

On April 26, 1957, police officers broke up a physical confrontation between a Black couple at 125th and Lenox Avenue. Johnson X Hinton, a member of Malcolm's temple, witnessed cops beating the man. Police ordered Hinton to leave the scene. He refused, snapping, "You're not in Alabama—this is New York." Patrolman Mike Dolan clipped him with a nightstick.

Later that day, Malcolm marched with about fifty members of the Fruit of Islam to the 28th Precinct station house, demanding Hinton be released from jail and admitted to Harlem Hospital. As hours passed, the throng outside the station grew to over two thousand. Nervously, the police assured Malcolm the prisoner would be given proper care. Once Malcolm was satisfied, he waved his arm. The gathering dispersed without incident. One witness said it was "eerie, because these people just faded into the night. It was the most orderly movement of four thousand to five thousand people I've ever seen in my life—they just simply disappeared—right before our eyes." *The New York Times* took notice. So did the FBI. So did the New York cops. "No one man should have that much power," said the precinct's chief inspector.

Elijah Muhammad agreed. He had established a public policy: the Nation of Islam was to practice political disengagement. It could not afford a severe white backlash (it had already stirred enough trouble). Yet in September 1960, when Fidel Castro, Cuba's new leader, came to New York to attend the UN's General Assembly, Malcolm extended him a hand in solidarity with the world's "dark" revolutionaries. He offered the Cuban delegation rooms in Harlem's Hotel

Theresa, blocks from Mosque Number 7. He put the Fruit of Islam on twenty-four-hour alert to "assist Castro in the event of any anti-Castro demonstrations."

The prophet was not happy.

A month later, Malcolm greeted Ghanaian president Kwame Nkrumah in Harlem. On a stage erected beside the Hotel Theresa, Nkrumah said the "strongest link between the people of North America and the people of Africa" were American Negroes. Malcolm nodded assent.

The prophet was displeased a year later when Malcolm initially resisted his order to cooperate with members of the Ku Klux Klan in Atlanta. Muhammad insisted that the Klan and the Nation of Islam shared many goals, including separatism. He wanted to forge a nonviolence pact with the militant organization. At the meeting, a Klan leader asked Malcolm if he'd join a plot to murder Martin Luther King, Jr. Astonished, Malcolm refused. He couldn't believe his mentor had put him in a position to even discuss such a grotesquerie.

No bones about it: commercial sports were a form of indenture for the Black man, Elijah Muhammad said. No Negro in America ever emerged from the maw of organized athletics with his soul or his freedom intact. Worst of all was the sanctioned brutality of boxing. Just ignore it.

Yet, "I am interested in him as a human being," Malcolm X said of Cassius Clay. "Not many people know the quality of the mind he's got in there. He fools them. One forgets that though a clown never imitates a wise man, the wise man can imitate the clown. He is sensitive, very humble, yet shrewd—with as much untapped mental energy as he has physical power."

"Malcolm X and [Clay] were very like close brothers. It was almost as if they were in love with each other," said Ferdie Pacheco, Clay's ring doctor.

Weeks before the Clay-Liston fight, with ticket sales in the toilet, Bill Mac-Donald did not want Malcolm around. Sonny Liston had done his part to secure his "bad guy" image: to one reporter he remarked of his opponent, "He's a fag, I'm a man."

Half-heartedly, defensively, Clay "swore" to the *Miami Herald* "by all that's holy . . . I'm not a Black Muslim any more than you are." "I'm not mad at the white people. If they like me, I like them." No one believed him; he admitted he enjoyed hearing the Muslims preach. "I feel free since I learned the truth about myself and my people," he said.

It was hard for many fans, Black *and* white, to consider him a "good guy" when he denounced Martin Luther King Jr.'s integration efforts: "I believe it's human nature to be with your own kind. I know what restroom to use, where to eat, and what to say. I don't want people who don't want me. I don't like people who cause trouble. I'm not going out there to rile up a lot of people." The civil rights protests were not like boxing matches, he said: "There's no referee in the street."

Journalists simply didn't know what to make of his socioreligious beliefs. Most dismissed him as hopelessly confused or full of crap. Writing in *Ebony*, Alex Poinsett was one of the first reporters to see him as Malcolm did. "[When] Cassius Clay declares, 'I am the greatest,' he is not just thinking about boxing. Lingering behind those words is the bitter sarcasm of Dick Gregory, the shrill defiance of Miles Davis, the utter contempt of Malcolm X," Poinsett wrote. "Cassius Marcellus Clay is a blast furnace of race pride. His is a race pride that would never mask itself with skin lighteners and processed hair."

When Malcolm arrived in Miami in mid-January, at Cassius Clay's invitation, it became impossible for the press to gloss over the boxer's connections to the Nation of Islam or to "the violently anti-white New York chief of the Muslims."

The FBI had tapped Malcolm's New York phone. One night agents overheard Clay tell him he would pick him up, along with his wife Betty and their children, at the Miami airport. Immediately the FBI's Miami field office was notified to tail Clay's 1963 Chrysler with the Florida license plate 1E-1621, to "determine" the "subject's" motives. Clay checked Malcolm and his family into the Hampton House Motel on Northwest Twenty-Seventh Avenue. For the next few weeks, between training sessions, he drove to the motel every day to play with Malcolm's daughters. "Our children were crazy about him," Malcolm said. Betty was relieved to see her husband relax in the fighter's presence: he was rarely free of apprehensions, sorrow, and enormous tension. Malcolm "loved [Clay] like a younger brother," Betty said. He took pictures and dozens of reels of home movies. He advised his young protégé that his success in the future would depend on how well he understood the motives and true natures of people scrambling for his attention.

Malcolm was wary of reporters, but he did not keep a low profile in Miami. Ever since his youth, when he'd moved to Boston to frequent nightclubs, working as a shoeshine boy at the Roseland Ballroom, he'd been fascinated with Black celebrity, the power of determined folks to overcome race obstacles and achieve stupendous success. He never forgot his encounters with Lionel Hampton, Count Basie, and Duke Ellington.

In Miami he loved meeting the show biz kings glued to Cassius Clay, basking in the massive publicity the kid could generate. He especially liked Clay's friend, the glamorous young singer Sam Cooke, who, even more than Elvis, represented to Clay the pinnacle of fame.

Malcolm was aware that his presence in the city was "tricky" for Clay. But the young man had shrewdly grasped the situation. He was resolving how to sidestep it. "He should be a diplomat," Malcolm observed.

Advance ticket sales for the fight were not improving. It didn't help that the army was said to be readying Clay's draft papers. The rumors were premature. In any case, Liston had said the army wouldn't want this kid after he was "done with him."

As a PR move, Bill MacDonald and Harold Conrad arranged for Clay to stage a sparring exhibition at the Miami Beach Auditorium to raise money for children with cerebral palsy. MacDonald hoped the event would remind the public that Clay was just a "nice, sweet kid." But a few days later, Clay told reporters, "In Cleveland [recently], the Negroes tried to integrate and you could see what happened. The white people hit the Negroes and the Negroes hit the white people. Bam-bam, bam-bam!" He said Negroes were not treated like "Americans." Once more, the press compared his rhetoric to the speeches of Malcolm X.

His ring-play with the Beatles prompted scorn from Jimmy Cannon and other old-timers. Sportswriters were also busy noting how many mob bosses had descended on the beaches, hoping to see Liston shut the *boca grande*: Sam Giancana, Felix Aldersino, Paul Ricco, those who'd worked with Old Man Kennedy to get his son Jack elected president, and with Attorney General Bobby Kennedy to try to bump off Castro.

When a Black reporter for the *Atlanta Daily World* wrote that "Clay, through his association with Malcolm X, [Elijah] Muhammad, and other Black Muslims, has revealed himself as a white-hating racist at the time when intergroup progress is being made throughout the South," MacDonald concluded that he had a bigger problem than sluggish ticket sales. He might be courting a race riot—with an increased possibility of violence, given all the gangsters in town.

He warned Clay that he would cancel the fight if the young boxer didn't denounce the Muslims right away. He'd lose his chance at a world championship.

Encouraged by Malcolm, Clay didn't hesitate. "My religion is more important to me than the fight," he announced.

Historians Randy Roberts and Johnny Smith write in their book *Blood Brothers* that when Conrad learned of MacDonald's plans, he insisted that MacDonald *couldn't* cancel the fight. "The hell I can't . . . you're a Northerner," MacDonald had responded. "You don't understand . . . Miami is the Deep South and is just as segregated as any town in Mississippi. How can I promote a fight down here with a guy who thinks we're white devils?"

Conrad sought a compromise: if Malcolm left town, could the fight go on? Reluctantly, MacDonald agreed.

Malcolm's presence was tricky everywhere, not only in Miami. It wasn't just the FBI or the likelihood that anyone who came in contact with him would be wiretapped and followed. It wasn't just the death threats from white racists. In February 1964 it was—more than anything else—the fact that he'd fallen into disfavor with his surrogate father, his mentor, his leader, Elijah Muhammad.

Their falling out had long been inevitable, given their political views, but in the lead-up to the Clay-Liston fight, specific events precipitated the break.

In deliberate defiance of Muhammad's order to "cool it," Malcolm gave the speech at Detroit's King Solomon Baptist Church, described above in conjunction with the Bandung Conference. He asserted, "Revolution is bloody, revolution is hostile, revolution knows no compromise. . . . The Black revolution is sweeping Asia, is sweeping Africa, is rearing its head in Latin America. The Cuban Revolution—that's a revolution. They overturned the system . . . [T]he white man is screaming . . . How do you think he'll react to you [the American Black man] when you learn what a real revolution is?"

He said nothing about the Nation of Islam.

A few days after this speech, back in New York, he met with Cassius Clay, who'd come to town to film *The Jack Paar Show*. The Selective Service had just informed Clay that he had to take a physical to determine his eligibility for the armed services. "I've just spent four hours with God today," Clay told reporters after visiting Malcolm in Mosque Number 7. "He's going to fix it so I don't have to serve in the army." Malcolm dismissed any thought of Black men fighting white men's wars, and he would not stay silent about politics. After the KKK bombed Birmingham's 16th Street Baptist Church, killing four Black girls, Malcolm said that, as the father of daughters, he'd be damned if he'd turn the other cheek.

After the killing of Medgar Evers on June 11, 1963, Martin Luther King Jr. called for more strenuous efforts to end prejudice and enable integration across the fifty states. Malcolm responded, "Whenever sheep try to integrate with the wolf, then there is a step forward for the wolf." He called the August 1963 March on Washington a "circus" led by "Toms": "The Negroes spent a lot of money, had a good time, and enjoyed a real carnival atmosphere. Now that the show is over, the Black masses are still without land, without jobs, and without homes. . . . Their Christian churches are still being bombed, their innocent little girls murdered. So what did the March on Washington accomplish?" He castigated President Kennedy for co-opting Black anger and turning it into a party—and he would not have been shocked to learn that Kennedy's brother, Bobby, the attorney general, was in the process of approving FBI wiretaps of Martin Luther King, Jr.'s Atlanta office and home. Malcolm concluded: "While King was having a dream, the rest of us Negroes are having a nightmare."

In the midst of this public turmoil, Malcolm struggled with personal doubts about Allah's Messenger. For years he had heard rumors about Elijah Muhammad's infidelities, children born out of wedlock. He had always ignored the gossip. But beginning in 1962, the FBI, based on testimony from paid informants, leaked stories to the press about Muhammad's mistresses—at least seven of them, former secretaries for the Nation of Islam. This prompted many members to quit. Malcolm listened more carefully. He confronted the leader directly at Muhammad's palatial Chicago compound (paid for by years of tithing and sales of *Muhammad Speaks*). Sitting with Malcolm by the swimming pool, Muhammad quietly explained that his duty as a prophet was at stake. "I'm David [from the Bible]," he said. "When you read about how David took another man's wife, I'm that David. You read books about Noah, who got drunk—that's me. You read about Lot, who went and laid up with his own daughters. I have to fulfill all of those things."

"I believed he was divine, divinely taught and divinely guided," Malcolm admitted later. "[But then] he found himself confronted with a moral question which he could not face up to as a man. And his failure to face up to that as a man made me begin to doubt him, not only as someone divine—divinely guided—but it made me doubt him as a man. And in the face of that, I began to analyze everything else he taught."

Malcom's biggest sin: he had outgrown his teacher, emotionally and intellectually.

Elijah Muhammad's priorities were decidedly worldly now (even if his spiritual beliefs remained sincere): he was determined to protect his privileges, his luxuries. The Black man's salvation was a long way off, but in the meantime Elijah was doing just fine, and revolution would not assist his comfort. Such rabble-rousing had to stop—especially from his most stubborn capable minister, a man with the talent and ambition to usurp the prophet, should he wish. In the summer of 1963, he ordered Malcolm, "Be careful about mentioning Kennedy in your talks . . . use USA or the American government [instead]." White Americans loved their handsome young president. Insulting him would create a wave of resentment the Nation of Islam could not afford.

In late November, when word came from Dallas of JFK's assassination, Malcolm remarked to an associate, "That devil is dead."

The Nation's official position was otherwise: "The death of President KENNEDY today was very tragic." The Messenger warned his followers, "You are to show no jubilation about the matter. No matter how you feel, don't talk to your friends or on your jobs about the assassination. . . . The Christians have deep feelings about what has happened and if you say the wrong thing, you can find yourselves in serious trouble. You might even be killed."

Just over a week later, at the Manhattan Center after a speech, Malcolm quipped in a hasty Q&A that Kennedy's killing was an instance of "the chickens coming home to roost." He added, "Being an old farm boy myself, chickens coming home to roost never did make me sad; they always made me glad."

He said Kennedy's killing was a sign of Western civilization's decline, tied to "the rise of the dark world." "Our present generation is witnessing the end of colonialism, Europeanism, Westernism, [and] white supremacy."

Three days later, on December 4, Elijah Muhammad announced that Malcolm X had been suspended from the Nation of Islam for ninety days, ordered to relinquish his ministerial duties, and remain silent. He told the press on behalf of the Nation, "We with the world are very shocked at the assassination of President Kennedy."

Muhammad had seized on Malcolm's faux pas to exercise power over his hard-charging protégé, to initiate events that would eventually lead to his expulsion from the Nation of Islam and worse. Each man felt sorely betrayed by the other.

Repeatedly, Malcolm insisted that a much more significant killing than Kennedy's had occurred two years prior to Dallas, unbeknown to most Americans. In the Congo, Patrice Lumumba, the first democratically elected leader of that nation (once a colonial outpost of Belgium) had been executed with the tacit approval, if not the direct help, of the CIA, seeking US Cold War advantage and control of the Congo's resources.

Malcolm told Cassius Clay he believed that Dallas was just a warning shot in a worldwide revolution. From 1960 to 1963, twenty-four African countries had fought for and earned their independence from Western powers. Unless Black Americans tied their demands to the struggles of their international brothers they would achieve nothing, Malcolm said—they would just be "trying to crawl back to the plantation."

He had evolved a global vision. He first glimpsed this wider perspective by studying the Bandung Conference in 1955, and then he reinforced his outlook by traveling in 1959 to the Middle East. There he had discovered that his Muslim brothers in Egypt, Saudi Arabia, and the Sudan mourned America's "racial trouble" as much as their own. He fully confirmed his views by listening to Lumumba.

On June 30, 1960, the day Belgium granted the Congo its independence, Lumumba declared in a tense ceremony in front of the Belgian king, "We are proud of [our] struggle, of tears, of fire, and of blood but our wounds are too fresh and too painful still for us to drive them from our memory. . . . We have known ironies, insults, blows that we endured morning, noon, and evening, because we are Negroes. We have seen our lands seized in the name of allegedly legal laws which in fact recognized only that might is right. We have seen that the law was not the same for a white and for a Black, accommodating for the first, cruel and inhuman for the other."

He was talking about the Congo, but he could just as easily have been reciting the history of Mississippi.

Following Lumumba's assassination in 1961 (on JFK's Inauguration Day), Malcolm addressed a rally at the Audubon Ballroom: "Lumumba [is] the greatest man who ever walked the African continent. He didn't fear anybody. He had those people so scared they had to kill him. They couldn't buy him, they couldn't frighten him, they couldn't reach him. Why, he told the king of Belgium, 'Man, you may let us free . . . but we can never forget these scars.' The greatest speech—you should take that speech and tack it up over your door. This is what Lumumba said: 'You aren't giving us anything. Why, can you take back these scars that you put on our bodies? Can you give us back the limbs that you cut off while you were here?' No, you should never forget what that man did to you. And you bear the scars of the same kind of colonization and oppression not on your body, but in your brain, in your heart, in your soul, right now."

This was an international vision far beyond Elijah Muhammad's capacity to imagine. Muhammad knew—as did the US government and the governments in Africa and Europe—that Malcolm had the potential to become a leader on as grand a scale as Gandhi or Martin Luther King Jr.

He was not preaching pacifism. Nor was he saying much about Islam. And he had the ear of the man who would soon become the most famous figure on the planet.

On January 2, 1964, a few weeks before Malcolm went to Miami, he had an awkward phone conversation with Elijah Muhammad (recorded, of course, by the FBI). After this talk, he understood that his relationship with the man had dangerously frayed. "I've been hearing about Malcolm this and Malcolm that, and even Malcolm being called a leader," Muhammad said coldly. "You made an error."

Malcolm apologized, "Messenger, I'd rather be dead than say anything against you."

"[Then] why are you checking into my personal affairs? . . . How can you take this poison and pour it all over my people?" He warned Malcolm that he would be watching him ("to see if you become stronger, strong enough to resist this poison"). Then he slammed down the phone.

A few days later, Malcolm learned that the Nation's headquarters had quarantined him. Black Muslims were forbidden to approach him. He heard that, in one midwestern mosque, a minister had told his flock, "If you knew what the Minister did, you'd go out and kill him yourself." Such open talk would not have spread without approval from the top. And Malcolm knew it was serious. He had seen men with whom Muhammad was displeased beaten nearly to death by the Fruit of Islam.

Eugene XXX, the cartoonist whose work in *Muhammad Speaks* had so intrigued the teenage Cassius Clay, would soon publish in the paper an image of Malcolm's severed head bouncing toward a mountain of skulls.

This was Malcolm's situation when Clay invited him to Miami with his family. Clay certainly knew there was friction between his friend and Elijah Muhammad, but Malcolm underplayed its grimness, insisting everything would be fine again once the prophet lifted the ninety-day suspension. Clay served as a shield for Malcolm—or so Malcolm hoped. The fighter's publicity value was enormous, and even though Muhammad still condemned commercial sports and privately expressed his belief that Clay would soon be forgotten after losing to Sonny Liston, he ordered the editors of *Muhammad Speaks* to include a few stories on Clay. They would increase the paper's circulation. Malcolm believed if he could complete the full conversion of the boxer to Islam, and deliver him in person to the Messenger, he would regain favor. There would not be a bigger story in the world than Cassius Clay declaring himself a Muslim.

In the meantime, Malcolm made home movies of his daughters romping with Clay—happy domestic scenes intended to soften the minister's public image.

His strategy for reinstatement in the Nation came to this: Cassius Clay had to beat Sonny Liston. Almost no one in the world believed this was possible. But the world, whether it knew it or not, *needed* Clay to win, Malcolm thought. Even as the mob flocked to Miami, even as the Beatles came to town, even as the odds in Vegas in favor of the Ugly Bear (Clay's nickname for Liston) reached seven to one, US military planes were bombing the liberated areas of the Congo to secure power for the dictator Joseph Mobutu, who had conspired to murder Lumumba.

Malcolm and his international brothers had work to do.

At the obligatory weigh-in, on the day of the fight, Clay exploded at Liston, "Hey, sucker, you a chump. Are you scared? Somebody's gonna die at ringside tonight." He ran around the room like a "skittish colt," said one reporter, further convincing Liston he was unbalanced. Dr. Alexander Robbins, the attending physician at the weigh-in, recorded Clay's heart rate as 120. Normally it was 72. "Clay is nervous and scared and he's burning a lot of energy," the doctor concluded. Pressed later by Jimmy Cannon, Robbins elaborated, "He is hysterical. He has a fear of death . . . a fear of getting killed. He acted like a maniac. He's definitely out of control."

Malcolm X believed otherwise. Days earlier, at Clay's tiny house at Northwest Fifteenth Court, with the kitchen air full of the smells of black beans and collard greens, with the laughter of children on the front lawn, he had convinced the young boxer his fight with Sonny Liston was an explicit example of Crescent versus Cross. Allah had foreordained his victory, part of a divine plan to spread Islam across the globe. "This fight is the truth," he said. "It's a modern Crusades—a Christian and a Muslim facing each other with television to beam it off Telstar. . . . Do you think Allah has brought about all this intending for you to leave the ring as anything but the champion?" He shook his head. "To be a Muslim is to know no fear," Malcolm said.

His world depended on it.

A thunderstorm right before the fight guaranteed that the undersold arena would not fill at the last minute. Attendance—compared to what it could have been—was dismal. The hall was only half full, eighty-three hundred fans paying a total of $400,000 (MacDonald needed to recoup at least twice that much to break even). Yet the Cassius Clay–Sonny Liston championship bout revolutionized sports viewership and added a whole new dimension to the notion of celebrity.

The final take worldwide topped $5 million, most of it going to Theater Network Television, Inc. (TNT). The company had purchased the live television rights. Partnering with major motion picture theater chains, RKO, Loew's, Warner, and Balaban and Katz, as well as sports arenas and concert halls, TNT beamed the fight live to 271 venues with a seating capacity of approximately 1.1 million people. Additionally, the WABC radio network paid $115,000 for the live radio broadcast rights, reaching brand-new markets in Asia, Africa, and South America.

Eurovision broadcast the Clay-Liston fight to 165 million people in Ireland, Spain, Sweden, Finland, Yugoslavia, Norway, and Czechoslovakia.

NASA had a policy prohibiting its satellites from being used for commercial purposes, but TNT paid the space agency an enormous undisclosed sum to make an exception in this case. Technically, the arrangement worked this way: TNT filmed the fight live and then, via kinescope, transmitted the broadcast onto videotape. The network then piped the tape to NASA's Earth station in Andover, Maine. At that point, NASA maneuvered its intercontinental relay satellite into position to receive the signal from Andover and bounced the signal to a station in Brittany, England, to be captured by Eurovision and fed to transmitters across the continent.

The Mother Ship could not have more efficiently conquered the globe.

It was not boxing, per se, that mobilized this state-of-the-art technology. With the general public, boxing had been on life-support for years because of its morally dubious status. Following the recent deaths of boxers Davey Moore and Benny "The Kid" Paret after fights, and after the Kefauver hearings' exposure of boxing's link to the underworld, almost all of the weekly fight programs on America's television networks, including ABC's once enormously popular *Fight of the Week,* had vanished. Major advertisers, such as the Gillette Safety Razor Company, did not want their brands associated with ugliness.

Then came Cassius Clay. If his antics and questions about his beliefs were enough to scare away traditionalists who would normally fill arenas, his appeal to the young and rebellious, and to regions of the world being reached for the first time by communications equipment, was incalculable. These once-ignored countries were beginning to feel their potential, as was Cassius Clay. His controversies were also their dilemmas. He embodied their desires. He was forging a fresh identity just as it was becoming possible to disseminate images instantly worldwide. It was a perfect rush of energy, fashioning a whole new kind of cultural hero.

Nelson Mandela, imprisoned in South Africa in 1962 for resisting apartheid, said he listened to Cassius Clay's rise on the radio and drew invaluable inspiration from it.

On the night of February 25, 1964, the Miami Beach Convention Hall—graced above its doors with the words "Dedicated to Peace, Achievement and Progress"—hosted a diverse crowd reflecting culture's changing personality. Not only were sports figures such as Yogi Berra and Sugar Ray Robinson present. Politicians, actors, TV stars (Ed Sullivan), mobsters, and writers such as Norman Mailer and George Plimpton turned up, drawn by the young fighter's glow, a major reversal from boxing's near-extinguishment just two years earlier.

Malcolm X was there. He had left Miami, at Harold Conrad's urging, so Conrad could talk Bill MacDonald into proceeding with the fight. But Malcolm snuck back to town for the bout. Sitting right behind him, in row seven, was Sam Cooke. A former gospel singer with the Soul Stirrers, Cooke had achieved astonishing crossover success with smooth R&B songs like "You Send Me," "Cupid," "Chain Gang," and "Twistin' the Night Away." (Cooke landed thirty Top Forty hits on the US charts between 1957 and early 1964.) Perhaps even more impressively, he had become one of the few Black artists in the music industry to control his career, purchasing his master tapes from RCA, founding his own record company, and establishing a publishing and management corporation. He and Cassius Clay recognized in each other the same boundless energy, improvisational intelligence, and effortless charisma. Like the Beatles, Clay had always wanted to be bigger than Elvis. Sam Cooke had beaten him to it. Cooke was now being managed by Allen Klein, who would one day manage the Beatles.

Malcolm and Sam: two extremes on the spectrum of Black celebrity. Clay was torn between them. He yearned for Malcolm's wisdom and honored the discipline he developed. He envied Sam Cooke's show biz savoir faire, his ease with the many women he attracted. Clay was still shy with women, and he believed the old fighters' maxim that too much sex sapped a warrior's strength. Cooke's buddy, the record producer Bumps Blackwell, said Sam "would [always] walk past a good girl to get to a whore." Clay, working hard to resist temptation during training ("OOOO. Sometimes it's so hard to be righteous!"), admired the singer's daring: risking *dangerous* sex must be as exciting, he thought, as climbing into a ring with an unpredictable opponent.

Clay wanted to be Malcolm. He wanted to be Sam. The holy man and the singing star: was it possible to have it all?

Just before the announcer stepped into the ring, Malcolm X slipped into Clay's dressing room to say a silent prayer with the fighter, facing east toward Mecca. The dressing room was unsettled. Drew "Bundini" Brown, a long-time figure in the boxing world had joined Clay's entourage as an advisor and inspirational guru, on the recommendation of Sugar Ray Robinson. Wispy, gnome-like, Bundini flitted about, weeping with joy, assuring Clay that "Shorty" was with him. Shorty was Bundini's name for God. Bundini wasn't having much effect. Clay's mood was dark. He trusted no one. "Watch out," Captain Sam had been telling him. "The white power structure is out to get you." "Dundee [is] Mafia," said the other Muslims. "You can't trust him, you can't trust Pacheco, and the other white guys around you."

"The whole thing was ridiculous, but he was worried," Ferdie Pacheco said. Three or four times, Clay told his brother Rudy to empty his water bottle, refresh it, and tape it shut again. "Finally, I said, 'Who's gonna poison you, Angelo or me? . . . If I was gonna poison you I would've done it with some shot.' And with Angelo . . . the Muslims kept telling him Angelo was Italian, with ties to Frankie Carbo, the same people who were around Liston. You can build paranoia in a fighter faster than you can in anybody. Just with a hint. The fact was that everyone in boxing had had relations with Frankie Carbo in the forties and fifties. If you knew boxing, you knew at least that much. But the Muslims were just guys from Chicago who knew nothing about boxing. They didn't even think sports were any good, until [Clay] furnished them with a good living. So the water bottle got emptied again and again."

Finally satisfied, Clay emerged into the spotlight in the center of the arena, surrounded by Muslim brothers. The crowd booed. He glanced down at Sam Cooke, who had moved to seat seven in row seven, double good luck. Clay smiled at the singer's calm. He bounced on his feet. He danced.

Liston, "somber and menacing . . . aptly named the most frightening man on the planet," according to Steve Ellis, TNT's announcer, entered the ring, towels draped on his shoulders and chest, swelling his size. He'd pulled the hood of his robe up, making it look like an executioner's outfit.

He wouldn't look at the Muslims.

Portable typewriters clacked around the ring. "It's even money Clay won't last [through] the National Anthem," one writer remarked. Liston had predicted a knockout in three—then cut it to two after Clay's performance at the weigh-in.

The ring announcer, Frank Freeman, approached the microphone. "This bout is under the auspices of the Veterans of Foreign Wars, Post Number 3559," he said. In fact, the VFW had nothing to do with the fight (and would, of course, want nothing to do with Cassius Clay in the years ahead after he changed his name to Muhammad Ali). In 1964 the Florida Statutes forbade prizefighting "for reward" to be staged in the state unless the bout was sanctioned by a civic organization. Chris Dundee, owner of the 5th Street Gym, had entered into an agreement with Bill MacDonald to donate $500 to the VFW for the use of their name: a false appearance to circumvent the statutes. Based on this fiction, the Miami Boxing Commission licensed what was, in essence, an illegal fight.

Referee Barney Felix called the fighters to the middle of the ring to give them instructions. Liston glowered at Clay. Later Clay admitted he was frightened: "He hit hard; and he was fixing to kill me . . . But I was there; I didn't have no choice but to go out and fight." The crowd's reaction was different: an audible gasp filled the arena when the men met face-to-face. Even wearing the bulked-up towels, Liston looked small next to Clay. At just over 210 pounds, Clay was more massive through the chest and shoulders. He was two inches taller. And about ten years younger. "He was the most perfect physical specimen I had ever seen, from an artistic and an anatomical standpoint, even healthwise," said Pacheco. "You just couldn't improve on the guy. If someone came from another planet and said, 'Give us your best specimen,' you'd give them [Clay]." And Liston hadn't trained properly. In Miami, he'd spent as much time drinking as sparring, and his overconfident manager had gone out, on at least two occasions, to Twenty-Third and Collins to find his fighter some hookers.

In round one, Liston immediately threw a left, then another. He missed both times, expending precious energy. "The punches you miss are the ones that wear you out. You miss enough and it begins to wear at your head and your body," Angelo Dundee said. Clay was the first to score, a crisp left jab. He kept his hands at his sides, dangerously, as Liston pressed him, swinging. Clay danced mostly to the left, pulling his head back, slipping punches. Liston whiffed by inches—sometimes by less than an inch: blows that would have floored his opponent if they'd landed. But his failure to connect was no fluke. Again and again, Clay anticipated everything Liston had, ducking trouble by fractions.

Liston lumbered forward. Clay hit him with jabs. Instinctually, the crowd seemed to know when two and a half minutes had passed: Clay had survived longer than Floyd Patterson did in the ring with Liston. A surge of excited energy lifted the room. Then Clay unleashed a three-punch combination to the top of Liston's head. It shook the older man. The bell rang, but for eight more seconds, the fighters kept at it until Felix pulled them apart.

"I remember I came to my corner thinking, 'He was supposed to kill me. Well, I'm still alive,'" Clay said later. More than that: the younger man had completely dominated the opening minutes. Liston was so angry and confused he wouldn't sit. "It was obvious he went back to the corner thinking, 'Now what the fuck do I do?'" Ferdie Pacheco said. "Sonny had nothing to hit, he was hitting open air." Clay had trained to go hard the first two rounds, cover up in the third, take it easy through the fifth while Liston tired, then come back strong. The strategy was working. Also, the first round had taught him: "Liston's eyes tip you when he is about to throw a heavy punch. Some kind of way, they just flicker." He could see the man loading up.

From his stool Clay glared at the ringside writers and photographers, who'd thought he'd be finished by now. He stretched his mouth and gave a silent, gloating scream.

Round two opened with a hard, right-hand body shot from Liston. Clay recovered quickly, floated away, and kept Liston off him, extending his left arm into the older man's face. The fight had developed into a slugfest, which no one had expected—but the renowned puncher was missing as wildly as a beginner, while the silly, prancing kid was doing real damage to the champ's cheeks and chin. Briefly Liston trapped him on the ropes, but Clay glided away again, jabbing. His clockwise canter was hypnotic but just when Liston thought he'd grasped the motion, just when he cocked his arm to catch him, Clay wagged in the opposite direction or jerked back abruptly. He was like a weather vane spinning, leaving the champ huffing like a horse.

Clay noticed a puffy pink mouse beginning to swell just beneath Liston's left eye. He flicked a series of left jabs at the angry, padded flesh, slowing Liston's approach. "The old champ was as clumsy as a guy groping for a light switch in the dark with a hangover," said the *LA Times*'s Jim Murray.

Early in the third round, Clay's concentrated hammering of Liston's welt opened it up. "Cassius went after Liston . . . [he] had incredibly swift hands and a manner of punching where he twisted his fist at the moment of impact, which had the effect of a pretty sharp knife," said Mort Sharnik, a *Sports Illustrated* writer. "He hit Liston with a one-two combination; a jab followed by a straight right. And it was like the armor plate on a battleship being pierced . . . Liston's skin had seemed so thick, I didn't think it could possibly burst like that. And I said to myself, 'My God; Cassius Clay is winning this fight.'"

"I saw the blood, and I knew that eye was my target from then on," Clay said.

"Liston is in desperate trouble!" Steve Ellis screamed. "[His] face is bleeding and he can't stop the punches coming into him!" "[Liston is] clubbing savagely, trying to fend off this young challenger, but those fists tonight haven't made much impression. . . . Clay seems contemptuous of the punches."

"Come on, you bum!" Clay shouted at the champ. Liston bled from his nose.

"Sensation [is] piling upon sensation," Ellis gushed. "The honors are all with Cassius Clay."

By round four, Liston was tentative, slow, pulling his punches, afraid they wouldn't land anyway. Clay kept poking the eye. "That left hand is drawn toward Liston's face," Ellis said. "Clay is making every critic in the place look silly."

Liston had aged "twenty years in four rounds," Harold Conrad saw.

But back in his corner, Clay was blinking in pain. "He's got something in his eyes!" Ellis noticed. Clay screamed that he couldn't see. His face stung. Angelo Dundee touched a pinkie to the corner of Clay's eye and dabbed his own face. A burning sensation—like thousands of needles. He sponged water under Clay's eyes, but it didn't help.

Clay believed Liston's "trainers [were] dirty," juicing Liston's gloves with some nasty substance to blind him—maybe at Liston's insistence. Dundee believed lineament smeared on Liston's shoulders got into his eyes. Or maybe the coagulant Liston's corner men used on the cut, wintergreen or ferric chloride, had affected Clay.

In any case, a series of crucial decisions were made on the spot. As Clay screamed, "I can't see! Cut 'em off! I can't see! Cut off the gloves!" Dundee stood firm. "This is the big one, Daddy!" he shouted. "Cut the bullshit! We're not quitting now! You gotta go out there and run!"

"He was ready to quit," said Ferdie Pacheco. "And it had nothing to do with lack of courage, because this was a kid who'd been fighting since he was twelve years old. And . . . he'd been poked and banged and busted and clobbered many times . . . but this was something beyond what he'd experienced, and I was there. I could see it. His eyes were aflame. And Angelo was spectacular." He didn't back down. Clay took a breath. In that instant he decided to follow this man he'd been warned not to trust.

The Muslims at ringside, standing just below the fighter's stool, were shouting, "This white man is trying to blind Clay! It's a conspiracy!" Chris Dundee told his brother the Muslims thought he was working for Liston: "They're looking to do a number on you." Angelo picked up the sponge he'd used on Clay's eyes. He swabbed it across his face to show them it was nothing but water.

The referee had noticed the uproar and started to approach Clay's corner. Angelo stood in his way until the bell rang. Then he told his fighter, "Run!"

"Clay isn't putting up much of a defense [now]," Ellis said, calling the fifth round action. "Liston will be merciless. . . . Liston is hurting him."

"Take a stiff tree branch in your hand and hit it against the floor and you'll feel your hand go *boinggg*," Clay said later. "Well, getting tagged is the same kind of jar on your whole body, and you need at least ten or twenty seconds to make that go away. . . . You're numb and you don't know where you're at. There's no *pain*, just that jarring feeling."

Liston jarred him again and again in the round's early minutes. Clay back-pedaled, missing the grace he'd shown before. "I was just trying to keep alive, hoping the tears would wash out my eyes," he said. "I could open them enough to get a good glimpse of Liston, and then it hurt so bad I blinked them closed again."

By the middle of the round, Steve Ellis noticed with astonishment—was it possible?—"[Clay] is playing around! Clay is playacting with him!" His eyes were beginning to clear. He stuck his left fist in front of Liston's face and held it there as if shooing a pesky child. "He's pawing him away!" Ellis said, almost laughing with amazement. And then: "This is what's significant: Liston [has been] hitting him at will and he's still standing. He's taunting him [now], making a fool of the champion."

"Cassius can't see, and still Liston couldn't do anything with him," said Ferdie Pacheco. "What can I say? Beethoven wrote some of his greatest symphonies when he was deaf. Why couldn't Cassius Clay fight when he was blind?"

Clay's ability to take a punch—a strength none of the sportswriters thought he possessed—had saved him. "Liston has got a scowl on his face now. His lips are twisted," Ellis said. When the bell rang, Ellis declared the match "the most . . . sensational heavyweight fight since before the war."

Liston seemed to know he had lost his best chance to win the battle. His bullying hadn't worked, his dirty trick hadn't worked (if it was a dirty trick) . He came out flat-footed in the sixth, out of gas. Clay blasted him with a solid right, followed by a swift left jab. He brushed away the man's listless arms. Liston retreated. "It's all Clay," Ellis announced. "His corner is jubilant. Liston is now looking completely at sea. He doesn't know what's going on."

He went to his stool shaking his head. Clay danced.

Liston spat out his mouthpiece. "That's it," he told his corner.

He looked like "an instant middle-aged man," Mort Sharnik said. "He looked like a middle-aged truck driver who had driven into an abutment. He was swollen all over: his eyes, his face, his body."

Tears mingled with blood on his cheeks.

Later, recovering in the hospital, Liston would say, "That wasn't the guy I was supposed to fight. That guy could hit."

Clay didn't have a mark on his face.

As it became apparent Liston wasn't rising for round seven, Ellis shouted, "Something has happened in Liston's corner!" Clay raised his arms and danced to the center of the ring. "But why is he retiring? What has happened?"

Then Ellis had to yell above the crowd, "Police are lining the ring to stop people from getting in!"

Cassius Clay was the new heavyweight champion of the world.

He stood on the ropes, taunting the writers who'd given him no chance. The writers edged close, fearfully eyeing the Muslims.

"I folded my arms and tried to appear the coolest man in the place," Malcolm X wrote later, "because a television camera can show you looking like a fool yelling at a prizefight."

Liston's corner men were now taping his left shoulder. Dr. Alexander Robbins, the commission's official medic, announced that Liston had torn a tendon. "It was all bullshit," one of Liston's trainers said afterward. "We cooked that shoulder thing up on the spot." In fact, hospital tests that night confirmed an injury, perhaps from before the fight or because of a wild swing in the ring—in any case, it was not by any means the worst physical setback Liston had ever endured.

Clay had fought blind. Liston quit because his shoulder hurt. That was the tale of the fight.

As newspapermen and television reporters gathered around the new champion, Clay shouted, "I'm the greatest thing that ever lived! I talk to God every day! With God with me can't nobody be against me! And I upset Sonny Liston and I'm just twenty-two years old! I *must* be the greatest!" He raised his fists once more. "I shook up the world! I'm pretty! I'm a *baaad* man! You must *listen* to me!"

He spotted Sam Cooke in the crowd. "Let this man up here! Sam Cooke!"

The reporters wanted to know about his eyes. "My face is still burning," he said. "The man's trainers are dirty." What did he think about Liston's shoulder? "An excuse. His injury is a cut eye." He demanded again that the men move aside for his friend. The reporters kept jabbering about Liston. Cooke squeezed into the ring. The new champ turned to the cameras. "Sam Cooke!" he shouted. "This is the world's greatest rock and roll singer!"

✿

Sonny Liston wept as he left his dressing room and walked to his car outside the arena. His arm hung in a sling, and the left side of his face was bandaged.

Politely, he stopped to answer a reporter's question, his voice just a whisper: "I tried to throw a left hook. It missed. I felt something snap. I just couldn't throw a punch. Not the jab anyway. My arm was killing me."

Losing, he said, made him feel the way he felt when the president was shot. Later he would tell Harold Conrad, "Don't [people] know what that title meant to me . . . You know what it means to me to hear a kid say, 'Hello, Champ?'"

Back at the Fontainebleau Hotel, where many of the reporters gathered post-fight, Beau Jack, one of the hotel's shoeshine men, a former lightweight, now barely getting by, said aloud what many of the writers were thinking: "Sonny's better off dead."

Martin Luther King, Jr. called Cassius Clay to congratulate him on winning the championship. Clay told the civil rights leader he appreciated his work (though he'd said just the opposite in public); he was King's brother, backing him "one hundred percent." He told King to take care of himself and to "watch out for them whities."

The FBI recorded the call.

✿

"Well . . . don't you think it's time for this young man to stop spouting off and get serious?" Malcolm X asked the football player Jim Brown. They were among the small, quiet group accompanying Clay to Malcolm's room at the Hampton House Hotel after the fight. Clay's sponsors from Louisville, convinced, like everyone else, that he was going to lose, had not planned a victory party and now scrambled to arrange a huge celebration with champagne, celebrities, and the press at the Fontainebleau. Clay refused. He retreated from the hul-labaloo and the entreating women outside his dressing room door, went out for ice cream, then retired with his two role models, Malcolm and Sam, and a handful of others, to the Hampton House. Malcolm, Jim Brown, and Clay talked about the future of race relations in America. Brown was aware that night for the first time that a terrible schism had occurred between Malcolm and Elijah Muhammad. He feared correctly that Clay would soon be forced to decide where his loyalties lay.

Clay fell asleep on Malcolm's bed and then, early in the morning, returned to his house at Northwest Fifteenth Court, where neighbors and their children had gathered on his lawn to congratulate him. "Sam Cooke had three beautiful young ladies come over . . . And these three ladies grabbed [the champ] and they said we're gonna go out and celebrate," said a member of Clay's entourage. "But he would not go out and celebrate. At exactly quarter to one he told the three girls, 'I'm sorry, ladies, you are gonna have to leave. I'm gonna go to bed.' Now can you imagine that? . . . A young beautiful guy like that?"

At the following morning's press conference Clay was unusually subdued. Perhaps he was already aware that the wound between Malcolm and the Messenger could not be healed. "I'm through talking," he told the gathered reporters. "All I have to do is be a nice, clean gentleman." He said he planned to retire from boxing as soon as he made enough money. Boxing was not his priority, and he certainly didn't want to hurt anyone or be hurt. "I feel sorry for Liston. He's all beat up," he said. He wanted to be the people's champion, "roam the streets, talk to the poor folk and the drunks and the bums. I just want to make people happy."

He bristled when someone asked wasn't it true he was a "card-carrying member of the Black Muslims?"

"Card-carrying? What does that mean?" Sounded like McCarthyism, he said. "I believe in Allah and in peace. I don't try to move into white neighborhoods. I don't want to marry a white woman. . . . I'm not a Christian anymore. I know where I'm going and I know the truth and I don't have to be what you want me to be. I'm free to be what I want."

The next day, at a second press conference, he gave white reporters a brief history lesson: "Black Muslims is a press word. It's not a legitimate name. The real name is Islam. That means peace. Islam is a religion and there are 750 million people all over the world who believe in it, and I'm one of them." He denied that the Muslims were a hate group. They were not communists. It was simply a fact that, even though he was the heavyweight champion of the world, he could not enter certain neighborhoods in America, and that was not right. Still, he did not want to go where he was not welcome. Muslims were not troublemakers: "Followers of Allah are the sweetest people in the world."

He added, "I'm a good boy. I never have done anything wrong. I have never been in jail. I have never been in court. I don't join integration marches. I don't pay any attention to all these white women who wink at me." He concluded the briefing by quoting a line from one of Malcolm's speeches: "A rooster crows only when it sees the light. Put him in the dark and he'll never crow. I have seen the light and I'm crowing."

Predictably, the white press reacted with scorn. "Most of the writers, particularly the older ones, felt more comfortable with the mob figures around Liston than with the Muslims around Clay," said Robert Lipsyte.

"The fight racket, since its rotten beginnings, has been the red-light district of sports," Jimmy Cannon wrote. "But this is the first time it has been turned into an instrument of hate. It has maimed the bodies of numerous men and ruined their minds but now, as one of Elijah Muhammad's missionaries, Clay is using it as a weapon of wickedness in an attack on the spirit." Cassius Clay's devotion to the Nation of Islam, he said, was a "more pernicious hate symbol than [Max] Schmeling and Nazism."

The World Boxing Association decided that Clay's conversion to Islam represented "conduct detrimental to the best interests of boxing," "setting a very poor example for America's youth," and recommended suspension.

A dizzying series of developments unfolded over the next few days. Clay announced that, from then on, he was "Cassius X"—he had rejected his slave name. His parents were dismayed. Cash said the Muslims had stolen his boys (Rudy had joined the Nation too). Cassius had always loved his name; now he was demeaning the family. Cash said the Muslims had threatened his life to try to keep him from disparaging the Nation. Odessa said the Muslims hated *her* because her skin was too light.

Elijah Muhammad gave a speech at the Chicago Coliseum, claiming he and Allah had secured victory for the young fighter. Though he still opposed "sport and play," he welcomed Cassius X into the fold in order to protect him. Privately, monitored by the FBI, he complained to associates that Malcolm was "nursing" the fighter "like a baby." Muhammad was determined to drive a wedge between them. After all, Cassius X possessed the power of publicity. Jonathan Eig has determined that Elijah Muhammad's name appeared in the *New York Times* on 31 occasions in 1964, Malcolm was mentioned in 100 articles, and 203 pieces were devoted to Cassius Clay—second only, in the world of Black celebrity, to

Martin Luther King Jr., who won the Nobel Peace Prize that year. Comedian Dick Gregory put it this way: "When you saw King, you saw sound bites. Most folks never heard, 'I have a dream.' They heard little tidbits of it." But Cassius Clay? "This motherfucker would be in your fucking face for as many rounds as the fight last. King never got that kind of time. You watch him beat a white boy down to the ground and there ain't a goddamn thing you can do about it. Then he'd go and talk, *praising Allah!* This had never happened before. Never, ever happened before in the history of the planet."

On March 2, newspapers reported—based on leaks from the FBI, determined to fracture the Nation—that Cassius Clay stood "solidly in Malcolm's corner." Malcom was attempting to "establish a cult of his own," the papers said. He intended to "participate more actively with other Negro groups in every phase of the current Negro revolution."

Two days later, in New York, Clay toured the United Nations with Malcolm, visiting Asian and African delegates. He said he was eager to see Mecca and hoped to travel with Malcolm: "I'm the champion of the whole world and I want to meet the people I'm champion of."

"It was 'obvious,' journalist Murray Robinson concluded, that Malcolm had 'set out to make the heavyweight champion an international political figure.'"

Additionally, Malcolm was beginning to see the United Nations as a more fruitful organization than the Nation of Islam in tying America's civil rights struggles to the larger issue of international human rights.

During his extended stay in New York, Clay met Sam Cooke in the Columbia Records studios to record a duet with him, a rocking version of "The Gang's All Here." His bid to be bigger than Elvis was headed for failure. Said one music business insider, "Malcolm X has cost him a fortune in endorsements, TV shots, and disc sales."

In the meantime, press reports had begun to appear questioning the legitimacy of the Liston fight. The *New York Journal-American* said that, twenty-four hours before the match, Liston's managers paid Clay's lawyers $50,000 as part of a contract giving them control over Clay's next opponent—the assumption being that Sonny Liston would get a rematch. This raised suspicions that the fight had been fixed (if Liston won, why would his managers care about Clay's next opponent?). Suspicions grew when high-profile figures complained about the unsatisfying conclusion—the champ just *quitting?* Ed Sullivan said, "I saw the Liston-Clay fight. This was a stinker of all time. I swear the Beatles could have beaten the two of them. No kidding."

Dr. Robbins, the fight medic, addressed the skeptics, pointing out that Liston's shoulder *was* severely injured, and his face had required six stitches and plastic surgery. "There is no doubt in my mind that the fight should have been stopped," he said.

More embarrassing news: reporters got wind of the fact that in January, about a month before the fight, Clay had been called to the US Armed Forces Induction Center at Coral Gables, south of Miami, to take a mental aptitude test to assess his fitness for military service. He failed miserably. Doctors assigned him an IQ of 78—a result so dismal that some reporters wondered if he'd faked it. The army classified him 1-Y, fit for induction only in case of a national emergency. Sheepishly, he said, "I said I was the greatest, not the smartest."

One writer asked: if he passed the test in the future, would he register as a conscientious objector? "I don't like that name. It sounds ugly," he said. "I just want to do what's right. I don't want to go to jail, and I don't want to get into trouble."

On March 5, Elijah Muhammad phoned him with good news: Muhammad was granting him a new identity. From henceforth, he said, you will be known as Muhammad Ali. The Messenger rarely bestowed such an honor on a member of the Nation, usually only after many years of loyal service. (Malcolm had never been so recognized.) But Clay's achievement was extraordinary, bringing glory to Allah, the Messenger said. Clay was flattered; still, he wasn't sure—he *did* love "Cassius Marcellus."

But the next day, Muhammad boxed him into a corner. He delivered a public radio address. "This Clay name has no divine meaning," he announced. "Muhammad Ali is what I will give to him as long as he believes in Allah and follows me." *Muhammad* meant "worthy of praise, *Ali* meant "lofty."

Malcolm heard the announcement on his car radio. "That's a political move!" he shouted, slamming the wheel. "He did it to prevent him from coming with me!"

On March 8, Malcolm told the press he intended to leave the Nation of Islam. He said he was still loyal to the Messenger and hoped to advance Muhammad's vision on his own, with greater freedom of movement.

Muhammad professed to be shocked at Malcolm's decision, concealing from the press how much he had pushed his former protégé from the ranks: "I am stunned. I never dreamed this man would deviate from the Nation of Islam." Behind the scenes, he was sending emissaries from Chicago to visit Ali at the Hotel Theresa, cajoling, possibly threatening him to secure his loyalty to Muhammad. They promised him a wife, one of the Messenger's granddaughters.

Malcolm had an office in the Hotel Theresa. It was across the street from Lewis Michaux's African National Memorial Bookstore, a gathering spot for Black intellectuals and a treasure trove of volumes on Pan-Africanism and the history of American slavery. Malcolm had drafted the beginnings of many of his speeches in Michaux's store. Often, as he moved back and forth between it and the hotel, he ran into Ali, even as Ali kept his distance. Malcolm had been blunt with him and Rudy. He told them Elijah Muhammad was a false prophet who had slept with women outside of marriage. Rudy considered this blasphemy. He got so angry one day, he wrestled Malcolm to the floor. Ali pulled them apart. He didn't know what to believe. Before, Malcolm had *praised* the Messenger—now this? Muhammad had become a generous, protective father to Ali (light-skinned, like his mother, with all the *good* qualities).

Finally, one night Muhammad called Ali at the hotel and ordered him to "stop seeing Malcolm starting today."

The writer Alex Haley had been working with Malcolm since 1963 on material that would be published, after Malcolm's death, as *The Autobiography of Malcolm X*. One day Haley sat with Ali at the Hotel Theresa to conduct a *Playboy* interview. He asked Ali about his relationship with Malcolm. "I don't want to talk about him no more," Ali mumbled. Pressed, he said, "You don't just buck Mr. Muhammad and get away with it."

He stopped accepting Malcolm's calls—Malcolm knew he was being wiretapped—but the men could not avoid seeing each other inside the hotel, and they didn't try. One day a reporter from the *New York Post* saw Ali pop into Malcolm's office for a "swift low-voiced chat." Malcolm told another reporter, "We are brothers and we have much in common," but he would not elaborate on the status of their friendship.

Malcolm felt a vise tightening on him. He heard a credible rumor that a former associate of his at Harlem's Mosque Number 7 had ordered a bomb to be planted in his Oldsmobile. He purchased a semi-automatic rifle to protect his family at home in Queens (in a house provided for him by the Nation of Islam—how long would *that* arrangement last?).

And in fact, within days, he got a call from an assistant to Elijah Muhammad's son, Herbert, informing him that an eviction notice had been drafted. Herbert was going to become Muhammad Ali's fight manager, and Ali would no longer be traveling with Malcolm to Africa.

This saddened but did not surprise him. Nor was he surprised when Ali announced to the press, "I am religious. I am not going to do anything that is not right. I don't know much about what Malcolm X is doing, but I do know that Muhammad is the wisest." Malcolm understood Ali had no choice but to save himself. After all, he was the one who'd advised the young man, "Nobody leaves the Muslims without trouble."

Ali landed in Ghana in mid-May 1964, following the disorienting shock of modern travel, the erased gradations between East and West, the miracle of air travel. Bodies hurtled from snow and cold to blazing sun in the time it takes to nap and dream.

President Kwame Nkrumah had instructed Ghana's radio stations and newspapers to hail Ali as a visiting hero, a "source of inspiration to the youth of the world." Ali could undercut the "superiority complex of the white man" and "assist positively to bring about [Nkrumah's] cherished aims of projecting the African personality," freed from colonialism.

Ali would not have traveled here without Malcolm's prodding; Malcolm's desire to transform him into an international political figure had succeeded.

Gazing from an open-air wooden bus, intoxicated by the smells of almonds, cloves, bananas, and cardamom, Ali was amazed to see buildings, beaches, hospitals, and schools rather than straw huts, lions, and alligators.

He shouted to the people in the streets, "Who's the king?"

"You are!" the crowds—especially children—responded.

The scene was repeated in Nigeria and Egypt. Outside of the United States, his name *meant* something. He felt the strength of the land, the ancestors—the timelessness of Africa—filling his senses.

Prior to the Liston fight he had confessed to Mort Sharnik that he wasn't sure he could live up to his public image. "I'm like Columbus," he said. "I think the world is round, but I'm a little scared because now I'm reaching the point where I'll find out if it's really round and I can sail around it or is it flat and will I fall off . . . I think I'm going to do what I say. But I won't know for sure until I get there."

In Africa, as the champ, he was finding sure footing in the world.

"I'll remember that trip for as long as I live because that was where I saw Cassius Clay became Muhammad Ali," said his friend Osman Karriem.

Sounding like Malcolm—rather than the Uncle Sam booster he was in 1960, returning from Rome—he said that in America his brothers and sisters were "getting killed . . . bombed in churches . . . [because] the so-called master doesn't want his slave to be his equal."

Malcolm had arrived in Accra a week before Ali—and learned that the boxer was the most popular Muslim-American in the world. People asked Malcolm what he was like. Malcolm was thrilled for his brother and wistful not to be traveling with him.

But he had his own goals—foremost, the hajj, the pilgrimage to Mecca. Wearing traditional Muslim attire, bearded, robed, carrying a cane, he witnessed in Mecca a coming-together "of all races, colors, from all over the world." A "*brotherhood!*" he exclaimed, astonished. Thereafter, though he still shunned most white Americans, he said he no longer believed all white people were devils.

He delivered a lecture in the Great Hall of the University of Ghana in which he called the United States a "colonial power" on a par with Portugal, France, and Britain. "Only a concerted attack by the Black, the yellow, the red and the brown races which outnumber the white race would end segregation in the US and the world," he said.

He met with Kwame Nkrumah, seeking support for a UN resolution Malcolm was planning that would charge the United States with human rights violations. Nkrumah, dependent on US aid, would not agree. In fact, he feared merely *meeting* Malcolm would jeopardize financial and military assistance from the West. He surmised, quite rightly, that Malcolm's every movement in Africa was being monitored by the US State Department. Nkrumah agreed to the meeting only after W. E. B. Du Bois's widow, Shirley, an expat living in Ghana, urged him to do so.

Again and again, in Senegal, Morocco, and Algiers, Malcolm's Middle Eastern brothers disappointed him, sympathizing with the plight of the American Negro yet refusing to support the UN initiative, unwilling to risk losing America's money.

But Malcolm, adopting an orthodox Sunni Muslim name, El-Hajj Malik El-Shabazz, felt surer of his own identity and aims than ever before. The Muslim Students' Society of Nigeria bestowed upon him the honorific *Omowale*: "The son who has returned."

On May 17, a sweltering Sunday morning, back in Accra, he finished packing his bags, preparing for his return flight to New York. He met some companions, including the poet Maya Angelou, in front of the Ambassador Hotel. Just then, Muhammad Ali walked by along with the Messenger's son Herbert and a few other men. "The next moment froze," Angelou recalled. Malcolm knew Ali couldn't openly acknowledge him in front of Herbert, but he couldn't contain his delight at seeing his old friend. "Brother Muhammad! Brother Muhammad!"

he called. Ali hesitated. "Brother, I still love you, and you are still the greatest," Malcolm said.

Softly, glancing away, Ali answered, "You left the Honorable Elijah Muhammad. That was the wrong thing to do, Brother Malcolm." He turned and walked away.

Malcolm stood still. Ali, clearly fearful, blustered a loud performance for Herbert's benefit: "Man, did you get a look at him? . . . Man, he's gone. He's gone so far out he's out completely. Doesn't that just go to show, Herbert, that Elijah is the most powerful? Nobody listens to that Malcolm anymore."

Before leaving the continent, Malcolm paused to wire Ali: "Because a billion of our people in Africa, Arabia, and Asia love you blindly, you must now be aware of your tremendous responsibilities to them." He warned Ali not to let his enemies—by which he meant the Nation of Islam—exploit his reputation.

But now, standing, sweating lightly in the shadow of the Ambassador Hotel, watching his brother walk away, Malcolm said, "I've lost a lot. A lot. Almost too much."

CHAPTER 3

Ravi and Prabhupada

In George Harrison's autobiography he recalls meeting, in the early 1970s, the pilot of the Electra plane the Beatles rented for their US tour, six months after their meeting with Cassius Clay. The pilot confessed to Harrison that the plane's wings were "full of bullet holes." "Crazy guys" had been "at the end of the runway" shooting at them ("trying to pot us off," the pilot said). Harrison attributed this to jealous boyfriends, but maybe it was something more, something political.

Harrison hated flying, a paralyzing fear he shared with Muhammad Ali. He was the worrier on tour. McCartney and Starr fed on the hectic pace, the waves of adulation ("I loved it. I loved the decoy cars and all the intricate ways of getting us to the gigs. It was just so much fun," Starr said). Lennon quickly grew bored with the daily routine—the plane, the cars, the strange new bed every night. It was Harrison's role to point out that only nine months had passed since John F. Kennedy had been killed by a gunman in the streets of an American city, so why, right before their kickoff concert in San Francisco on August 19, were they considering riding in a convertible during a ticker-tape parade? No way, he said.

On August 21, 1964, in Seattle, their limousine got crushed just minutes after police had whisked them out of it. The Edgewater Inn Hotel erected a 350-foot-long plywood fence topped with barbed wire around the parking lot to keep boisterous fans wearing Beatle wigs away. Harbor Patrol boats skimmed the shoreline to prevent waterborne assaults on the boys. In store windows: displays of Beatle dolls for sale, Beatle lunch boxes. At the afternoon press conference, a journalist asked how long the band thought its popularity could last. "Till death do us part," Harrison said, not smiling.

Las Vegas, Los Angeles, Denver, Chicago ("There had been riots in the Black ghettoes, and . . . the cops [were] tense," Harrison recalled), Philadelphia, Milwaukee, Jacksonville . . .

Bomb threats. British flags burned and torn in the streets.

In Dallas, on September 18—after the Beatles had done twenty-four shows in twenty-four days and were on the brink of collapse—their plane landed at Love Field, and their motorcade followed the same route JFK had taken his last day alive, through Dealey Plaza, past the grassy knoll and the underpass (the Beatles all ducked in the back seat of the car).

Jesse Curry, the Dallas police chief who had taken heat from J. Edgar Hoover for screwing things up in the assassination aftermath, oversaw the Beatles' security. Just months earlier, he'd been hospitalized for stress. Friends said he was drinking. Days before the Beatles' arrival, he'd admitted to a colleague, "I wake up every now and then at two and three in the morning thinking about Kennedy, Oswald, and Ruby and can't get back to sleep. I suppose it will haunt me to my dying day."

If the president hadn't been killed on his watch, Curry would have been remembered instead for organizing the most peaceful school desegregation process in the South.

He arranged for twenty-nine patrolmen to escort the Beatles safely to the Cabana Hotel. It would be another week before the Warren Report went public, before Gerald Ford and his fellow authors tried to sell the story that Lee Harvey Oswald was the lone assassin, but already in Dallas rumors suggested that the night before Kennedy's murder key figures in an assassination plot met in the Bon Vivant Lounge at the Cabana—Jack Ruby, his mob pals (angry at the president's brother for his vendetta against organized crime), maybe Lee Oswald or a man posing as his double. The Beatles had landed in Conspiracy Central.

They knew it too. At the obligatory press conference, they tried to stay breezy but allowed they were "more scared here" that they'd been at other stops. Harrison fidgeted behind the others, impatient with what he'd come to see as a silly and pointless ritual. He was already fed up with playacting Beatle George.

Two hundred police officers were assigned to the Dallas Memorial Auditorium that night. Even so, a number of Dallas parents seemed as nervous as the Beatles and refused to let their kids attend the concert, fearing public violence. The band rushed through thirty minutes of tunes, and then, just after 11:00 p.m., ran to their Electra parked on the runway at Love Field. If shots were fired, they missed. The plane's owner, Reed Pigman, president of American Flyers Airlines, from whom Brian Epstein had chartered transportation, had hatched a plan with Epstein to give the boys a needed day off before their final concert in New York. From Dallas, they'd take the Electra to a private landing strip, built in wartime in Walnut Ridge, Arkansas—two hours north of Sonny Liston's birthplace, to the degree that Sonny Liston's birthplace could ever be located—and from there Pigman himself would fly them in a twin-engine seven-seater to his ranch in Alton, Missouri, for twenty-four hours of home cooking and horseback riding.

Harrison described the trip: "Pigman met us in a little plane with one wing on top and with one or maybe two engines . . . [He] had a little map on his knee, with a light, as we were flying along and he was saying, 'Oh, I don't know where we are,' and it's pitch black and there are mountains all around and he's rubbing the windscreen trying to get the mist off. Finally he found where we were and we landed in a field with tin cans on fire to guide us in."

Two years later, Pigman, flying that same plane, was transporting close to a hundred army recruits to a training camp in Georgia, prior to deployment in Vietnam. He suffered a heart attack at the wheel and crashed in Oklahoma, killing nearly everyone aboard.

The Beatles endured this madness because they were now the kings of the record industry. It was a crooked and clueless business. In 1963, when Allen Klein met Sam Cooke, the 45 rpm single, introduced by RCA, was only fourteen years old. It had become the vehicle, insanely lucrative, for rock and roll, but it didn't start out that way. In the beginning, the major labels, RCA, Columbia, and Capitol, didn't invest in either singles or rock and roll music, leaving the door open for small independents—Sun, Chess, Atlantic, and the Black-owned Vee Jay, which first brought the Beatles to the US market. The independents introduced Elvis, Ray Charles, Carl Perkins, Chuck Berry, Roy Orbison, and Little Richard. In October 1955 RCA had recognized its mistake ("It smells but it sells," RCA executives said of rock and roll) and paid $35,000 to buy Elvis's contract from Sun Records.

Ever since, it had become standard practice for the labels to keep their artists in debt, so they'd pump out product hoping to catch up. Financially, it was a form of modern slavery. "The artists never had any money," Klein learned. "They were always paid with an advance, which they would spend, and then the session costs came off their money. So they were always in the hole. And they were frequently represented by someone who didn't want someone else to come in and show them what they hadn't been doing right." The same mob that controlled much of the fight world took its share of record profits. Morris Levy, owner of Roulette Records, had ties to the Genovese crime family and to boxing king Frankie Carbo.

John Lennon knew he was a slave. "You exist in this kind of vacuum. . . . It's work, sleep, eat and work again. We work mad hours, really," he said.

"We used to play clubs. . . . And it was fun . . . but then we got famous and it spoiled all that, because we just go round and round the world [now] singing the same 10 dopey tunes," Harrison complained.

Pattie Boyd, a fashion model whom Harrison had met during the filming of the Beatles' first movie *A Hard Day's Night* said Harrison never understood the band's fame. His guitar playing was "okay as far as he was concerned, but why was he suddenly world-famous? He always wanted to find out, why him? He never grasped it." He thought the Beatles were "typical of a hundred [other] groups."

"We were lucky," he'd say. "We got away with it first."

Onstage every night the band heard the crowd's presence like the roar of the sea rushing to engulf them. Starr's drums weren't miked; the guitars were run through 60-watt Vox amplifiers, producing faint vibrations more than sounds. Unable to hear his bandmates, Starr watched McCartney's wagging ass to determine what song they were playing and where they were.

"The music was dead," Lennon said. Back in Hamburg, in the early days, "what we generated was fantastic . . . and there was nobody to touch us in Britain. But as soon as we made it, the edges got knocked off. Brian Epstein put us in suits and all that, and we made it very, very big. We sold out. . . . We had to reduce an hour or two hours' play . . . to the same twenty minutes every night. . . . The Beatles' music died then. . . . We killed ourselves then to make it—and that was the end of it. George and I are more inclined [than Ringo or Paul] to say that."

During shows, fans pelted the stages with lipstick tubes, hairbrushes, rolls of toilet paper inscribed with love notes, binoculars, jelly beans, and every so often a truly dangerous object such as a steel railroad spike.

Even on their earliest concert dates, the band was pressured to comment on the escalating war in Vietnam. On August 2, 1964, as the Beatles' first US tour was getting underway, the USS *Maddox*, patrolling in the Gulf of Tonkin, was said to be fired upon by North Vietnamese torpedo boats. Later, members of Congress questioned the veracity of these reports, but in any case the Johnson administration used the Gulf incident to increase the US military presence in Southeast Asia.

As forcefully as the press pushed the group for opinions on the war, Epstein pressured them to avoid addressing controversial topics. Lennon and Harrison chafed against being muzzled.

For Harrison, the tour's highlight was meeting Bob Dylan in New York, in the Delmonico Hotel, on August 28. He sat quietly on the bed talking to Dylan, with whom he felt an immediate, respectful bond. They laughed about the fact that Dylan had misinterpreted the lyrics to "I Want to Hold Your Hand," hearing "I can't hide" as "I get high."

At the end of the summer, Harrison felt grateful to be getting out of the United States alive. Each day had seemed like a week.

"Because we were famous, we were supposed to have people, epileptics and whatever, in our dressing room all the time. We were supposed to be good for them," Lennon said. "When we would open up, every night, instead of seeing kids there, we would see a row full of cripples along the front. . . . It seemed that we were just surrounded by cripples and blind people all the time, and when we would go through corridors they would all be touching us. It was horrifying."

"All these poor unfortunate people," Harrison said. "They gave their money, and they gave their screams. But the Beatles . . . gave their nervous systems. They used us as an excuse to go mad, the world did, and then blamed it on us."

The Beatles' US tour redefined in scale, intensity, and logistics the traveling theatrical revue. One promoter said, "The Beatles and Elvis are in show business. After that, any comparison is just a joke. No one . . . has had the crowds the Beatles had."

This was true, in part, because of timing. Entertainment, particularly sports and rock and roll, were both distractions from what was happening internationally. While countries in much of the world, following two major wars, struggled to define themselves in a new global order, the United States, triumphant, became the dominant world power, spreading its influence as much through its vibrant popular culture as through military and economic means.

Meanwhile, divided by competing independence movements, many fledgling nations were convulsed by chaos resulting from colonialism, official incompetence, corruption, power contests, and poor leadership. They were cauldrons of deep unrest. Their internal strife gave the world's emerging superpowers—the

United States, the Soviet Union, and China—opportunities to test their Cold War agendas, seeking advantage, exploiting the resources of smaller nations.

Most obviously these deadly maneuvers played out in the Middle East, Korea, and Vietnam. Yet following the Holocaust in Europe, two of the centuries' worst genocides decimated Rwanda, adjacent to the Congo, and the area now split among Pakistan, Kashmir, and Bangladesh. These genocides were the direct result of the twentieth century's great shifts: the reckless partitioning of lands with little regard for historical, ethnic, cultural, and religious affinities, and the rush to independence of untried nations, unleashing inevitable power struggles and economic hardships.

The United States may have been dominant after World War II, but by the 1960s it was dangerously close to unraveling from within. The era was marked by unprecedented economic prosperity—hence, the massive youthful crowds paying to hear the Beatles. And with more free time and greater resources, social groups and political activists could organize, solidify their bases, and contest some of America's historical contradictions.

In particular, the nation's vexed history in race relations, civil rights, and economic inequality came under intense scrutiny in political circles, academia, popular culture, and finally on city streets. Muhammad Ali would bring these issues to boxing. Late in the decade, the growing unpopularity of the war in Vietnam would cause a generational rift and add to the country's uncertain self-image: was the United States a model society for the rest of the world or just another cruel empire in the old colonial mold?

For members of the comfortable US middle class, information about the planet's fault lines came largely through TV, movies, records, magazines, and sports. This was the culmination of a long-standing trend in the West. Mike Marqusee, a political historian, once noted, "Modern, secular spectator sports . . . first emerged from the womb of parochial ritual and folk pastime in mid-eighteenth century England. Their midwives were rapid urbanization, the spread of market relations and the growth of an ambitious elite with both time and money to squander."

Because of the mass media—the shorthand narratives of television and magazines—pop culture icons became tied to broad social movements, and the news media covered them obsessively. It was only natural, then, that the Beatles and Muhammad Ali crashed into public consciousness immediately after the assassination of John F. Kennedy.

Today we use the word "globalization" to refer to the interdependence of national economies, work forces, and trade relationships. What is less understood is that these mutual dependencies resulted from a cracked world. World War II was the earthquake. Major aftershocks erupted in the 1950s and 1960s. We have been living with constant tremors ever since.

Writers have long attempted to define, explain, or mythologize the 1960s, the period symbolized by the Beatles and Ali. As a summary of the era, many of these observers refer to East meeting West, but it is perhaps more accurate to say that East *flooded* West, materially and spiritually.

Prior to mid-century, Western nations colonized the East. But with the outbreak of African and Asian independence movements, and the redrawing of maps after World War II, what had once been exploitive relationships became cases of codependency.

This tilt was accompanied in the West and especially in the United States by an unprecedented monetary boom. For all its positive effects, such as the growth of a well-off middle class, the boom forced massive shocks on the system. By the 1960s, US culture was like an old dirt-and-gravel wagon road overrun by elegant cars: exciting but barely manageable. The resulting chaos nearly shattered the nation's infrastructure.

As history's largest group of consumers, the middle class fueled a market for a popular culture through which these global changes were represented, symbolized, documented, debated, and rightly or wrongly understood. The nature of art, sport, performance, and celebrity changed dramatically during this period and could not be considered apart from political and social change.

George Harrison was already seeking escape from it all. He asked Pattie Boyd to marry him the day they met. They flirted and joked together. But what really drew him to her was her personal history. Until he met Ravi Shankar, and later the teachers from India to whom he would devote his most serious attention, Boyd was his guide to the world beyond the one he knew, and to worlds beyond that.

Her mother had been born in India and raised in England. Her grandparents were old colonials in the Far East and in Africa. Her father, a handsome RAF man, had been badly injured in Malta in the early 1940s when a bomber he was flying collided with another plane on a runway. He survived the explosion, but his face and right hand were terribly burned. He never fully recovered from his emotional and physical devastation; his self-isolation would ruin his marriage and force his daughter to develop an early independent streak.

When Boyd was four, the family moved to one of her grandfather's compounds in Kenya, a half hour from Nairobi. She grew up among lions and giraffes. They lurked in the bushes all around her, among nasturtiums and peach trees and Kikuyu servants who taught her horseback riding and navigation by the night sky. In 1952 the Mau Mau uprising, aimed at the overthrow of British rule and the eviction of white settlers, threatened her family and their servants (the Kikuyu were threatened with death if they did not stop working for white people). A year later, Boyd found herself back in England in a "fairy world" of Christmas lights.

Harrison was fascinated by her tales of foreign rituals, beliefs, meals, and the complexities of tribal cultures—when the couple found privacy and time enough to talk. They were accompanied on their first date by the dapper Brian Epstein, who not only managed the Beatles but also chaperoned them, as a father might, through the world of high society. "I didn't resent his presence," Boyd said. He "seemed to know everything about wine, food, and London restaurants. And perhaps if George and I, two very young, very shy people, had been on our own in such a grown-up restaurant, it would have been too intense. As it was, we had a lovely evening and sat side by side on a banquette listening to Brian, hardly daring to touch each other's hand."

Their courtship—and later their marriage—was never free of the mania. Boyd wondered what she'd gotten into. Harrison didn't have time to wonder. He just did what Epstein told him, especially when it came to signing contracts. Epstein's deal with the Beatles gave him 25 percent of their total income. Dick James, a music publisher and a friend of Epstein's, controlled the Beatles' songwriting interests through what McCartney much later described as a "slave contract," giving James 50 percent of all royalties and Epstein another commission on top of that. "As an 18- or 19-year-old kid, I thought, 'Great, somebody's gonna publish my songs!'" Harrison reflected years later. "But [James] never said, 'And incidentally, when you sign this document here, you're assigning me ownership of the songs.'"

At the time, between touring, recording, running from fans and the press, and trying to get to know Boyd, he didn't consider not trusting these men who assured him they had his best interests at heart.

At the end of 1964 he packed his guitar and tried to get away from the madness, but the press dogged him and Boyd from London to Amsterdam to Vancouver to Honolulu. He refused to play the old tabloid game, posing for the press. As the couple fled to an even more remote Pacific island, he turned toward the photographers and writers and called from the airplane doorway, "Why don't you just leave us alone?"

✩

"You see what you're doing to my husband, don't you?" Betty Shabazz said to Muhammad Ali in the lobby of the Hotel Theresa in mid-February 1965.

"I haven't done anything. I'm not doing anything to him," Ali protested.

A few days earlier, at 2:45 a.m., a Molotov cocktail had smashed through the living room window of the house where Betty and Malcolm X were sleeping with their children—the house Malcolm had refused to leave. He grabbed his four daughters. Choking on smoke, he and Betty stumbled into the yard, Malcolm clutching a .25 caliber pistol he'd managed to snatch from his bedside. It stunned him that the Nation of Islam was willing to murder his family ("I have no compassion or mercy or forgiveness for anyone who attacks sleeping babies," he said.) He wasn't shocked to be the primary target.

Later the Nation told the press he'd burned his own house for publicity.

Wherever he traveled he was followed by the Fruit of Islam—even to places where the only people who could have known his itinerary were FBI agents. Clearly informants had infiltrated the Nation.

"Just tell [Malcolm] he's as good as dead," an anonymous caller warned Betty one day.

"I'm probably a dead man already," Malcolm confided to Mike Wallace of CBS News. Wallace was good for carefully timed publicity, which Malcolm hoped would keep him safe, but he was hardly a sympathetic contact. In 1959 he had hosted a TV documentary titled *The Hate That Hate Produced*, sealing for white America the image of Malcolm as a devil.

The FBI, granted extended permission by Bobby Kennedy to tap Malcom's phones after his return from Africa, overheard him say one night, of Elijah Muhammad, "Any man who will go to bed with his brother's daughter, and then turn around and make five other women pregnant and then accuse all these women of committing adultery, is a ruthless man."

Listening in on Muhammad, federal agents heard him say it was time to make an example of "that no good long-legged Malcolm." Facing such hypocrites, "you . . . cut their heads off," he said.

"Malcolm will soon die" and "Malcolm should have been killed by now!" other highly placed Nation officials had said. "[He is] worthy of death," said Louis X, his former protégé.

Malcolm knew all this—the FBI was concertedly leaking stories to the press to stoke divisions in the group. He'd seen the cartoon in *Muhammad Speaks*, Eugene XXX's drawing of his severed head. And he knew that among the people condemning him was Muhammad Ali.

"Malcolm X and anybody else who attacks or talks about attacking Elijah Muhammad will die," Ali told reporters. "I don't even think about him. He's nothing but a fellow who was [a] dope addict, a prisoner, a jailbird who had no education, couldn't read or write, who heard about the Honorable Elijah Muhammad, who took him off the streets, cleaned him up and educated him."

Ali was boxing outside the ring now, masking, head-faking, disguising his punches. He didn't fool everyone. "He'd be talking with you about something, and one of the Muslims would come into the room and the conversation would change completely," sports columnist Jerry Izenberg observed. Ali was performing desperately, erratically, trying to save his life.

Malcolm knew this too. "He's just a boy," he told friends. "He doesn't know what he's doing. He's being used."

A few weeks before Malcolm's house was torched, Leon Ameer, Ali's press secretary, was nearly beaten to death by the Fruit of Islam. Soon thereafter Ameer was found dead in his Boston hotel room. The Nation suspected Ameer of warning Malcolm about a specific death threat. Ameer had also been saying that Ali was privately upset with the Nation. The champ didn't like how Nation officials constantly required "numerous donations," Ameer said.

He told a reporter that Ali's life would be in danger if he didn't watch out.

Malcolm spent the last few months of his life pledging to "support fully and without compromise any action by any group that is designed to get immediate meaningful results" in the area of race relations: conciliatory words aimed at Martin Luther King Jr. He urged civil rights groups to unite. He met with John Lewis of the Student Nonviolent Coordinating Committee and with Mississippi organizer Fannie Lou Hamer. On August 26, 1964—two days before the Beatles met Bob Dylan in New York—he bumped into King in the visitors' gallery of the US Senate, their one and only meeting. The Senate had just passed the Civil Rights Act, legislation both men supported (though Malcolm cautioned reporters, "You can't legislate goodwill."). "Well, Malcolm, good to see you," King said. "Good to see you," Malcolm replied. The two leaders shook hands and then parted.

(At the time, FBI reports characterized the saintly MLK as a "'tom cat' with obsessive degenerative sexual urges" and the despised Malcolm as an individual "who neither smokes nor drinks and is of high moral character.")

Sam Cooke's "A Change Is Gonna Come" had been released as the B side of the single "Shake" shortly after Cooke was brutally murdered in Los Angeles after taking a hooker to a seedy motel in December that year. Now it was climbing the R&B charts and "A change is gonna come" would be chanted in early March by some of the protesters in Selma as they were beaten on the Edmund Pettis Bridge. Meanwhile, Malcolm had created the Muslim Mosque, Inc., and the Organization of Afro-American Unity to promote his appeals for justice.

He taught his disciples to broaden their vision, just as he had widened Cassius Clay's horizons. "[This is the] era in which we witnessed the emerging of Africa," he reminded them. "The spirit of Bandung created a working unity that made it possible for the Asians, who were oppressed, and the Africans, who were oppressed . . . to work together toward gaining independence." That remained the model. Consequently, Black Americans needed to keep their eyes on the US government's continuing evils in the Congo, he said. (On November 24, 1964, white hostages were killed in Stanleyville during a rescue attempt staged against Congolese rebels by Belgian and American soldiers; Malcolm described this disaster as another example of "chickens coming home to roost.") In supporting the Mau Maus in Kenya, rising against the British, he said: "When you put a fire under a pot, you learn what's in it."

Further distancing himself from the Messenger, he said, "I believe in one God, and I believe that one God had one religion. . . . God taught all the prophets the same religion . . . Moses, Jesus, Muhammad, or some of the others. . . . They all had one doctrine and that doctrine was designed to give clarification of humanity."

In January and February 1965, Malcolm was most passionate about expanding the Black struggle in America beyond a civil rights plea to a human rights initiative. He intended to do this by using the UN Charter, the UN's Declaration of Human Rights, and its Convention on the Prevention and Punishment of the Crime of Genocide. "As long as you call it civil rights your only allies can be the people in the next community, many of whom are responsible for your grievance. But when you call it human rights it becomes international. And then you can take your troubles to the World Court. You can take them before the world. And anybody anywhere on this earth can become your ally," Malcolm declared on February 16.

He continued to be disappointed by his comrades in Africa, who released a statement under the auspices of the Organization of Afro-American Unity expressing concern over "manifestations of racial bigotry and racial oppression against Negro citizens of the United States of America" but did not endorse his UN plan, fearing a loss of US aid.

Malcolm knew the UN Charter backwards and forwards (Article 55: "the United Nations shall promote . . . universal respect for, and observance of, human rights and fundamental freedoms for all without distinction as to race, sex, language or religion"); he knew that, in 1945, Secretary of State John Foster Dulles had fought against the charter precisely because he thought it would create difficulties for "the Negro problem in the South."

Malcolm knew that the genocide convention, drafted in response to Hitler's atrocities, forbade "deliberately inflicting on [a] group conditions of life calculated to bring about its physical destruction in whole or in part," and he believed this to be the history of America.

He drafted a document to submit to the UN entitled "Outline for Petition to the United Nations Charging Genocide Against 22 Million Black Americans." It declared, "We have appealed to the conscience of America, but her conscience slumbers."

The case was prepared. The US State Department took it seriously enough to consider Malcolm's plan a threat to national security. The CIA was requested to take "covert action against Malcolm X"; the Justice Department considered prosecuting him under the Logan Act, which made it a crime for US citizens to discuss with foreign powers activities detrimental to the US government.

Meanwhile, the FBI continued to monitor his phones. Along with the New York Police Department's Bureau of Special Services, it infiltrated his inner circle and his security team.

Elijah Muhammad was only one of his problems.

"Nobody listens to that Malcom anymore," Muhammad Ali had said. How wrong he was.

"Wa-Alaikum-Salaam," Malcolm said to the crowd. It was February 21, 1965, at the Audubon Ballroom, an old theater on West 165th Street in Manhattan that was as creaky as Miami's 5th Street Gym. As Malcolm stood behind the plywood lectern onstage, near an old white grand piano and a set of drums, he gazed out at folks, including his wife and three of his four little girls, seated on folding chairs or on rickety seats arranged in sloppy rows across the scuffed wooden floor. The ceiling was low, the lighting dim and flickering. That morning he had awakened in New York's Hilton Hotel (where he had slept alone to protect his family). The phone rang. An anonymous caller said in a low, threatening voice, "Wake up, brother," then clicked off.

Backstage at the Audubon, minutes before he stepped out to speak, he told his associates, "I don't feel right about this meeting. I feel that I should not be here. Something is wrong, brothers." Still, he had asked his security detail not to frisk people entering the hall. He didn't want his followers subjected to humiliating suspicions. Gene Roberts, a member of his security team, and also an undercover cop assigned to spy on Malcolm, had warned his superiors that the man was in serious need of protection. Yet no officers were assigned to the ballroom that day. "They had the mentality of wanting an assassination," Gerry Fulcher, an NYPD official, admitted later.

Strangely, twenty cops were posted two hundred yards away, across the street from the Audubon, at the Columbia-Presbyterian Medical Center, as if anticipating a scene there.

"Brothers and sisters . . ." Malcolm began. A man wearing a black overcoat stood and tossed a homemade smoke bomb into the middle of the crowd. He shouted, "Get your hand out of my pocket!" and immediately two other men stood. They began to wrestle. The spectacle drew Malcolm's bodyguards, including Gene Roberts, away from the stage, leaving him alone behind the rostrum. "Now, now, brothers, break it up. Be cool, be calm," Malcolm urged. "Hold it! Hold it! Hold it! Hold it!"

Just then a man stepped forward, not fifteen feet from Malcolm, and pulled a sawed-off shotgun from under his coat.

Malcolm's daughter, Ilyasah Shabazz, who was two at the time, says, "I was there that day . . . I have no memory of it." Her sister Qubilah, who was four, recalls: "Noise and screaming and confusion and Daddy not coming home."

Their blankness accurately conveys the trauma and terror of everyone present. (A witness heard one of the children cry, "Are they going to kill everyone?") The girls were shielded from the horror by their mother, who fell on them on the floor while shots were fired and chairs went flying. "They're killing my husband!" she screamed.

Futilely, Gene Roberts tried to give Malcolm mouth-to-mouth resuscitation. Someone tore Malcolm's shirt open. His chest was a lake of blood. His body was placed on a stretcher and rushed across the street to the Columbia-Presbyterian Medical Center and the idle cops. Their presence near the shooting did not insure an orderly or pristine investigation of the crime scene, any more than the LA police had effectively scoured the Hacienda Motel after Sam Cooke's murder.

Malcom X was pronounced dead at 3:30 p.m.

One of the conspirators, Talmadge Hayer, known as Talmadge X at Mosque Number 25 in Newark (the press identified him as "Thomas Hagan"), was caught at the scene. He confessed his involvement in the plot—he knew what he had to do, he said, when he saw the drawing of Malcolm's head in *Muhammad Speaks*. Along with four other members of the Newark mosque—none of whom were ever questioned by police—he acquired a twelve-gauge shotgun, a Luger, and a .45 automatic for the job.

Eventually two other men, both members of the New York mosque, Norman 3X Butler and Thomas 15X Johnson, were sentenced to twenty years in prison along with Talmadge Hayer for Malcolm's murder. "Butler and Johnson didn't have nothing to do with this crime," Hayer told the court. Still, with their petty arrest records and involvement with the mosque, they were easy foils for the New York cops, who wanted to clear the case as quickly as possible. (On November 18, 2021, both men would be officially exonerated.)

For decades, it was an open secret among Newark Muslims that a member of the mosque there, William Bradley—Willie X—had fired the fatal shots with the shotgun. New York authorities failed to reopen the case even when Hayer finally filed an affidavit naming his co-conspirators. Bradley lived out his life, peacefully, in Newark.

More troubling, as Manning Marable, historian and biographer, pointed out: the "convergence of interests between law enforcement, national security institutions, and the Nation of Islam undoubtedly made Malcolm's murder easier to carry out." It remains hard to say what the FBI and the police authorized based on the reports of their informants tucked inside the Nation and in Malcolm's camp.

Perhaps more to the point, shortly after the killing, a journal called *Spark*, a "Socialist Weekly of the African Revolution," accused the American ruling class of assassinating Malcolm X because he, along with nine African states, was about to charge the United States with genocide at the United Nations.

Standing among overturned chairs in the Audubon Ballroom while women and children wailed and Malcolm bled out onstage, an old man shook his head. "There ain't no goddam hope for our people in this lousy country," he said to no one in particular. "You got to fight them lousy whites and fight the stupid niggahs too. There ain't no goddam hope!"

✪

The day Malcolm died, a fire broke out in Muhammad Ali's apartment on the South Side of Chicago, where he was living now, near Elijah Muhammad. The incident occurred around 10:00 p.m. while Ali attended a service at the mosque during which a minister coldly announced Malcolm's murder.

Officials ruled the apartment fire an accident, but Ali would always believe "somebody started it on purpose." Malcolm's supporters? Or Elijah Muhammad's emissaries, warning him he would be next if he ever considered straying from the fold?

Two days later, early in the morning, Mosque Number 7 in New York went up in flames.

The Chicago Police Department assigned an escort detail to Ali, fearing Malcolm loyalists might try to harm him. After all, he was now Elijah Muhammad's most visible supporter. "I'm with God," he told reporters. "If I'm gonna die for truth, I'm ready to die. I ain't afraid. I ain't afraid of nothing." Of Malcolm, he said, "Malcolm X was my friend and he was a friend of everybody as long as he was a member of Islam. Now I don't want to talk about him no more."

At a Nation rally on February 26, celebrating the "Savior" Wallie Farad, Elijah Muhammad insisted, "Malcolm was a hypocrite who got what he was preaching. Just weeks ago he came to this city to blast away with his hate and his mudslinging. He didn't stop here, either, but he went around the country trying to slander me." Onstage, Muhammad Ali sat next to the prophet, applauding, shouting, "Amen!" and "Yes, sir!" Meanwhile, police officers were responding to bomb threats outside the rally.

On the day of Malcolm's funeral in New York—February 27—Ali performed a boxing exhibition in Chicago at the Nation of Islam's Unity Bazaar. He was training for a scheduled rematch with Sonny Liston. He clowned for children who'd gathered near the ring. Among those watching him that day were Chicago plainclothesmen and FBI field agents.

Inside the Faith Temple Church of God in Christ on Amsterdam Avenue in New York, Betty Shabazz, pregnant with twins, leaned over her husband's coffin and kissed its glass covering. The actor Ossie Davis delivered a eulogy. Malcolm was not a "fanatic, a racist," he said. Those who called him a violent demagogue never really knew him. "Did you ever talk to Brother Malcolm? Did you ever touch him, or have him smile at you? Did you ever really listen to him?"

Afterward, at the Ferncliff Cemetery in Hartsdale, in the bitter cold, a group of Muslim brothers insisted on taking the grave diggers' shovels and doing the job themselves. Respectfully, the workers backed away. Said one of Malcolm's mourners, "No white man is going to bury Malcolm."

Publicly, Muhammad Ali remained true to his promise: he refused to speak of his old friend. Clearly, though, he became familiar with *The Autobiography of Malcolm X*, the book Alex Haley published after Malcolm's death. Haley had conducted a series of interviews with the minister. From these discussions, he constructed a classic conversion narrative, using a literary approximation of Malcolm's voice: the lost soul on the road to perdition who hears the words of his savior; the years in the wilderness doing the work of the Lord; the disillusionment upon discovering he has followed a false prophet; the rebirth and a promise of true salvation. Haley's accounts of Malcolm's difficult childhood and his brutal encounters with racism humanized him for a white audience.

Ali was not a great reader—he may have been dyslexic—but he came to know the book, and for the rest of his life he echoed Malcolm's words and ideas. In 2004, he said, "Turning my back on Malcolm was one of the mistakes that I regret most in my life."

Numerous reporters saw an older Ali grow teary looking at photos of Malcolm. "I wish I'd been able to tell Malcolm I was sorry, that he was right about so many things. But he was killed before I got the chance. . . . Malcolm and I were so close and had been through so much. But there were so many things for me to consider . . . I felt that [Elijah Muhammad] had set me free! I was proud of my name and dedicated to the Nation of Islam as Elijah presented it. At that point in my journey, I just wasn't ready to question his teaching . . . I thought [Malcolm] had gone too far." Eventually he saw Malcolm "as a visionary, ahead of us all." "Malcolm was the first to discover the truth," he wrote in his autobiography.

In 1965 he couldn't have said any of these things. Herbert Muhammad watched him intently. Ali was the Nation's most valuable commodity. Herbert said, "[My father] informed me that [with] his name being Muhammad Ali, all the Muslims around the world would rally around him, and they'll see him as the Statue of Liberty, and that when they come they'll want to get his pictures and autograph and that would be a good way for him to let the world know that he's a Muslim from the Nation of Islam." It would be just like "when the people come out to

[see] the Beatles," Herbert said. It was Herbert's task to insure that Ali remained loyal. "My father put that job on me and asked me to show him the way."

Herbert, pudgy, quiet, somewhat aimless apart from his father's directions, was thirteen years older than Ali. Once, as a boy, he set up a speed bag in his father's garage and practiced punching. Elijah Muhammad caught him at it and scolded him, "I don't want you around the ring, boxing for any little fat white man with a big cigar. Don't be around any sport world. Sport is the ruin of our people. Turns them into children who're used and then left broken. Stay out of it." But by 1965 Elijah believed that, through Muhammad Ali, sport would be manna for Islam.

When Ali first met Herbert Muhammad in Chicago, soon after the Liston fight, Herbert was conducting various odd jobs for the Nation and editing *Muhammad Speaks*. He spent most of his time in his photography studio. In the past, he had taken portraits of Kwame Nkrumah, Gamal Abdel Nasser, and many Black statesmen. In the mid-sixties he mostly snapped photos of nude women and made short soft-core films. He talked women into posing for him in exchange for lavish gifts. The FBI became interested in him not just because he was a member of the Nation of Islam but also because he had a history of domestic violence.

About a week before he met Ali, he convinced Sonji Roi to let him photograph her. Roi answered phones in the *Muhammad Speaks* offices. She had also worked as a part-time fashion model and cocktail waitress. Sam Cooke knew her from his days roaming Chicago clubs. A couple of times the police had picked her up for solicitation. She was twenty-seven years old, and she looked like a Motown singer. She was slender and graceful, with dark eyes and a strong, firm chin, giving her an air of friendly confidence.

"I delivered her picture to [Ali] . . . about two days after I met [him]," Herbert said. She had never seen the boxer, but "she signed an autograph" on an 11 x 14 portrait, "from one champ to another."

In chaperoning Ali—and separating him from Malcolm—Herbert and Elijah Muhammad, no strangers to helping themselves to whatever they wanted, did not hesitate to offer women to Ali as part of the Nation's package. Publicly, Muslim women were treated with respect. Privately, at least in the Messenger's family, they were chattel. Ali got the message.

Herbert told Roi he could introduce her to the heavyweight champ. "I wasn't impressed. I didn't know anything about boxing," she later recalled. "I didn't know who he was talking about, but I said okay. You're always meeting someone. Later, Herbert starting bringing all sorts of women to Ali . . . Ali liked pretty women. They both did. But I went and met him." They met at a place called the Roberts Motel. "We liked each other and that was how it started."

Ali was so smitten with Roi that he asked her to marry him the night of their arranged rendezvous. "I didn't know if he was serious or not," she said. "I didn't know anything about him. But I was alone in the world. I didn't have a mother to go home and ask. I had to make the decision myself. After we spent some time together, I felt needed by him. He was strong, but he didn't know a lot of things. He needed a friend, and . . . I said to myself, there's nothing else I'm doing with my life. I can do this. I can be a good wife to this man."

"Man, you don't marry this girl," Herbert raged at Ali when he heard the news. He'd just wanted to show the champ a good time. A fun night out. "She works at a cocktail place wearing one of those little bunny things on her behind. You don't marry no girl like this."

But Ali did marry her—in a car, he said, where he declared before God and two Muslim brothers that he fully accepted this woman as his wife. No, no, Herbert said: "Legally you still ain't married in the United States. If they find out you got this girl and you're running around to various places on the highway, you're gonna be in trouble." So on August 14, 1964—just over a month after they'd met—Ali and Roi were formally married in a private ceremony.

"She agreed to do everything that I wanted her to do," Ali said. No smoking, no drinking, no tiny skirts. No pork.

"I told him, 'I'll wear the long clothes, I'll follow the diet, I won't wear makeup. It doesn't make sense, but I'll do all that if it's what you want me to do. He was a good husband," Roi said, looking back in later years. "He's precious; he's sweet; he's gentle. His only interest was making other people happy . . . He used to sing to me. Ben E. King, 'Stand By Me'; that was his favorite. And Sam Cooke. . . . The best times we had together were when everybody else was gone and he could be himself, and it wasn't necessary for him to be the Muslim. . . . I just wanted for us to be happy, and we would have been if people had left us alone."

But the Nation "wanted to control his entire life," she said. "When nobody was around, he'd want one thing from me; and then in public it was another. I couldn't understand his two faces."

Elijah Muhammad insisted they move into an apartment in Chicago to be near him (this was the apartment that burned the night Malcolm died). When Roi suggested they buy a house of their own, Ali explained that a house did not make sense because the Mother Ship was coming in three years to take them away. If that was true, she said, why did Elijah Muhammad live in a mansion? "Woman," Ali replied. "You're too wise. Don't be asking them questions."

Reporters wanted to interview the champ's new wife, but the Nation would not grant them permission. The leaders feared Ali was too distracted by Roi. It was time for him to train seriously for his rematch with Sonny Liston. He had gained thirty pounds. He seemed to be losing interest in boxing just as the Nation was counting on his riches.

Public doubt about the first fight had increased. Liston's refusal to rise from his stool "tarnished the victory," said Ferdie Pacheco—made it seem somehow illegitimate. "All you knew for sure . . . was that this kid had survived."

For his part, Angelo Dundee worried that Ali no longer feared Sonny Liston: an arrogant mistake.

In his final months, Malcolm X seemed to move knowingly toward his martyrdom. At the beginning of 1965 George Harrison felt equally confident that his movements were being guided. He sensed glimmers of a destiny awaiting him. It seemed that he had been heading there all along.

It started with a "chance meeting" in February in the Bahamas, four days after Malcolm's assassination. The Beatles had arrived in Nassau to film exteriors for their second movie, *Help!*

At the time, the Bahamas was still officially a colony of Great Britain, though a year before it had begun an experiment in self-government. The Beatles were surrounded by Black faces, descendants of slaves from Ghana and the Congo imported to the islands by American Loyalists who'd fled there, mostly from Georgia and South Carolina, in exile after the American Revolution. Britain abolished slavery in 1807, but the former American colonists continued to infuse the Bahamas with indentured servants to pick and pack their cotton.

By 1965, another former British colony was on the move in the West. Swami Vishnu Devananda, from Rishikesh, India, had relocated to the Bahamas to promote hatha yoga to Westerners, not as a religious practice but as a health benefit. For him, spreading information about the exercises was both an act of beneficence and a bold capitalistic venture: the very ideal of Western existence.

He had written a book, *The Illustrated Book of Yoga*. One day, wearing orange robes and spotting the Beatles riding bicycles under palm trees (they were awaiting instructions from Richard Lester, their frenetic film director), he approached Harrison and handed him a copy of his guide to ancient techniques—the asanas,

"lubricating routines for joints, muscles," he said. He explained that these practices had been largely lost in modern India but that "all this knowledge [had]
returned to [him] from past lives."

It happened to be Harrison's twenty-second birthday. Harrison tucked the
book into his bag without glancing at it. But he held onto it. "[Vishnu Devananda]
told me years later that whilst meditating he had a strong feeling that he should
make contact [with me]," Harrison wrote in his autobiography.

Like John Lennon, whose title song for the movie was a cry from the heart,
Harrison was floundering. The "whole Beatle thing was just beyond comprehen-
sion" at that point, Lennon would remember. "I was eating and drinking like a
pig, and I was as fat as a pig, dissatisfied with myself, and subconsciously I was
crying for help."

"The Beatles were [already] doomed," Harrison said. "Your own space . . . it's
so important. That's why we were doomed because we didn't have any. It's like
monkeys in a zoo. They die."

The only way he could stand to sit around the movie set was to smoke loads
of pot—first cultivated, someone had told him, in the Himalayas.

Vishnu Devananda would leave the Bahamas and eventually establish the
Sivinanada Yoga Vedanta Centre Corporation near Montreal, North America's
largest yoga organization. George Harrison would leave the Bahamas with *The
Illustrated Book of Yoga* in his suitcase and fly back to London, where, a few
days after his encounter with Vishnu Devananda, he would pick up a sitar. The
silly plot of *Help!*, a spoof of James Bond movies, included dark-skinned bad
guys representing a mysterious Indian cult ("See what you've done with your
filthy Eastern ways!" Lennon shouts in one scene). The film's music composer,
Ken Thorne, had hired an ensemble of Indian musicians to add color to the
soundtrack, using sitar, tabla, flute, ghunghroo bells, tanpura, and dilruba on a
Beatle medley titled "Another Hard Day's Night."

One day, in the Twickenham Film Studios, preparing to shoot a restaurant
scene, Harrison noticed one of the musicians' sitars on the floor. He cradled
it in his lap, plucked a few strings, and was enchanted by the sound. Nothing pleased him more than doodling on an instrument, seeking new pitches,
ranges, rhythms. He asked the sitar player, a man named Motihaar, to explain
the instrument: its provenance (medieval Asia), its resonance (up to twenty-
one strings over raised, curved frets called *pard*ā, and a group of sympathetic
strings—*tarb*—stretched across a calabash gourd). Harrison was more and
more intrigued. He only had time to finger a few shapes before the director

called him to his mark; the Beatles' schedule did not permit him to think of the sitar again for several months, but the impression it made, so soon after his brief meeting with Vishnu Devananda, convinced him later that his life had been converging toward this moment even before he was born. There were just too many conjunctions tilting him toward India. When he was little, his mother listened to a "Sounds of India" program on the family's crystal radio ("When I first consciously heard Indian music, it was as if I already knew it," he said). Mona Best, mother of the Beatles' first drummer, Pete, was of mixed Anglo-Indian blood. A Hindu idol, waving multiple golden arms, adorned her front hall in the house where the teenaged Beatles used to practice. She ran a basement coffeehouse, the Casbah, where the Beatles played, decorating it with East Asian fabrics. In Hamburg, the Beatles became the house band at the Indra Club, named for the Hindu god of the skies. The club was distinguished, above its entrance, by a flashing neon elephant. A standard tune in the band's repertoire at the club was its cover of "The Sheik of Araby," a comic Eastern parody sung by Harrison. Back in Liverpool, the boys played another coffeehouse, the Jacaranda on the edge of Chinatown, where they heard Lord Woodbine's Caribbean stylings and Indian rhythms. When Harrison met Pattie Boyd, she told him of her mother's Eastern origins.

Looking back, Ravi Shankar, the sitar maestro who would soon meet Harrison and become the single most important influence on his life, said, "It does seem like he already had some Indian background in him. Otherwise, it's hard to explain how, from Liverpool, with his background, and then becoming so famous, what reason did he have to get so attracted to a particular type of life and philosophy, even religion? . . . George had something which we call in our language *tyagi*, which means the feeling of unattachment. He had everything— all the wealth, all the fame, whatever he wanted. But he was not attached to it. It didn't seem to matter much to him, because he was searching for something much higher, much deeper. . . . It seems very strange really. Unless you believe in reincarnation."

Within a month or so of picking up the sitar, Harrison became even less attached to the everyday world, thanks to his dentist. One warm spring night, Harrison, Boyd, Lennon, and Lennon's wife (Cynthia) were having dinner with John Riley, a tooth-pulling swinger, and his girlfriend. (Riley wanted to be the Beatles' disco pal as well as their doctor.) Coolly, he announced that he'd spiked their coffee with lysergic acid diethylamide 25. At the time LSD was not illegal. Initially produced by Sandoz Pharmaceuticals as a potential cure for migraines, it had become a source of curiosity to the US military in its search for mind-control drugs, and then it escaped the researchers' labs to become a mental plaything among members of the developing counterculture.

"I'm sure [Riley] thought [LSD] was an aphrodisiac," Harrison said. "I remember his girlfriend had enormous breasts and I think he thought there was going to be a big gang-bang and that he was going to get to shag everybody. I really think that was his motive."

Angry and frightened, the Beatle couples left in Harrison's Cooper Mini, "going about ten miles an hour," Lennon said. "It was as if we suddenly [had] found ourselves in the middle of a horror film," Cynthia recalled. They went to a club in Leicester Square. "We all thought there was a fire in the lift. It was just a little red light, and we were all screaming, all hot and hysterical," Lennon said.

Once he'd settled at a table, Harrison "suddenly . . . felt the most incredible feeling." He would recall, "[It was] something like a very concentrated version of the best feeling I'd ever had in my whole life. It was fantastic. I felt in love, not with anything or anybody in particular, but with everything. Everything was perfect, in a perfect light, and I had an overwhelming desire to go round the club telling everybody how much I loved them." Well-being washed through him in waves, even after he'd left the club. "There was a God, and I could see him in every blade of grass . . . every blade of grass was just throbbing and pulsating. . . . It was like gaining hundreds of years of experience in twelve hours."

All at once, he said, he understood that "everything in the physical world is governed by duality: everything is heaven and hell. Life is heaven and it is hell; that's the nature of it. And so [what] acid does is shoot you into space, where everything is so much greater. The hell is more hell, if that's what you want to experience, or the heaven is more heaven."

Something else: "I had this lingering thought that just stayed with me after that, and that thought was, 'Yogis of the Himalayas.' I don't know why . . . suddenly the thought was in the back of my consciousness. It was like somebody was whispering to me, 'Yogis of the Himalayas.'"

"[Muhammad Ali] once asked [me] why he couldn't have visitations from God," Mort Sharnik said. "[He] was saying that Moses spoke to God and the prophets spoke to God, and why couldn't he speak to God? And I had the feeling he sensed he was a special vessel, that he might be ordained for special things."

That was one of his two faces.

The other, tougher one had hardened in the cyclone of speeded-up time that had seen him defeat Sonny Liston, pledge his faith to Allah, turn from Malcolm, get married on the fly, and attract scorn from the press. Old friends shunned him—or were kept from him—as the Fruit of Islam tightened its circle around him. "Since [Malcolm's] assassination, Ali has not been part of my life," Betty Shabazz admitted. "I . . . believe there were people who saw Muhammad Ali only as a bread ticket, and were not concerned for his person, soul, or future. They cared about what Ali could do for them, rather than strengthening his character and beliefs as Malcolm sought to do. And that's a shame, because Ali was important . . . a great number of young people once felt that they were the greatest because of him, and it's very evident now that a lot of our young people do not feel that they are the greatest."

In the past, Ali had courted hatred in fun, playing the big mouth everyone wanted to shut so tickets would sell. Now the hatred—and fear of his attachment to the Muslims—was real, unprovoked, and ugly. In responding to it, he followed the cue of none other than Sonny Liston.

The world be damned.

"There was a whole new atmosphere around Ali . . . [when he] was getting ready for the rematch with Liston. It was a chilly atmosphere, and . . . [he] began to take on [a] dual personality," Jerry Izenberg said. "He'd be talking to you about something, and then one of the Muslims would come. . . . My feeling was, he wanted to please them. I think he was afraid of losing them. . . . When he found the Muslims, he'd found an extraordinarily strong reason to be Black. He was no longer somebody who could be cast aside because of his color. And I think he was afraid that if he didn't become SuperMuslim at that stage of his life, somehow that would mean he was failing them."

His aunt Mary wasn't fooled. "Cassius is about the cleanest thing in the whole confounded Muslim organization," she said. "If they haven't once been hustlers, well, they're hustling now! If they haven't been robbers, they're robbing now! . . . You know I'm not lying. . . . Cassius falls for all that business about not drinking and no smoking, but he don't know they drink behind the doors, and cuss, and whip their mamas . . . and they'd kill you just as quick as they'd kill me, and don't you forget it!"

Ali's zealousness provoked a growing crisis with Sonji Roi. "Why can't women wear short dresses?" she'd demand. "Why do you call white people 'devils' when you have so many white friends?" One night he picked up a wet towel and harshly rubbed the makeup off her face. Later he admitted her direct challenges shook the certainty he was trying to develop: "Every difference was a threat."

Publicly he smiled. "My wife and I will be together forever," he said.

The one person he treated with respect was Sonny Liston. No taunting. No antics. The rematch with Liston was originally scheduled for the Boston Garden on November 16, 1964. On September 14, Ali and Liston held a joint press conference at the Logan Airport Motel. Ali was confident but subdued. When Liston said he would stalk "Clay" in the ring—"There ain't but one way to catch a coon. You got to trick him and trap him"—Ali did not respond.

A reporter asked about Allah. Angrily, Ali snapped, "Why you ask about my faith? You ask Goldwater about *his* faith?"

"I'm not fighting no Ali Millamed," Liston grumbled. "I met him as Cassius Clay and I'm gonna leave him as Cassius Clay."

Did Ali feel insulted by that?

"No, sir," he answered the newsman. "He don't understand." Politely, quietly, he turned to Liston and said, "Please, call me Muhammad Ali."

A week before the fight, Ali suffered an incarcerated inguinal hernia the size of an egg in his right bowel. It required immediate surgery, and the rematch was rescheduled for May 25, 1965. "That damned fool," Liston said, hearing the news. "That damned fool."

In the interim, following Malcolm's assassination, the fire in Ali's apartment, the burning of the New York mosque, and continuing questions about the legality of the promotional contract—Boston Garden got nervous. Sponsors backed out of the fight. Finally, after scouring the country, promoters convinced St. Dominic's Arena, a small youth center and junior hockey rink in Lewiston, Maine, to host the bout.

The delay harmed Liston. In Denver, he had trained seriously, quit drinking. He had slimmed down. He had busted open the face of one of his sparring partners. "Blood is like champagne to a fighter," said one of his trainers, approvingly. "It gives his ego bubbly sensations." But after the postponement, when Liston moved his training to Plymouth, Massachusetts, in a fancy facility overlooking Cape Cod, he lost his focus. His diligence slipped. Starting over was just too hard, especially for a man who was thirty. Or thirty-seven. Or forty.

Writing in *Sports Illustrated*, Gilbert Rogin described an "almost tragic expression of hurt and irremediable loss" etched into Liston's face. He quoted one of Liston's training partners: "You can see it in his eyes. They don't look so scary anymore. They look sad and confused." His cheek muscles sagged.

Bill Cayton, a veteran fight manager, remarked, "I believe that sometime between [the] two fights [with Ali] Sonny Liston went on drugs. I've always believed that. The people handling him at that time, some of them at least, were heavily involved in the drug traffic, which back then meant heroin. And of course, in those days they didn't have drug tests for fighters, so if someone was on heroin you wouldn't know. But Liston deteriorated so much between the first and second fights."

Muhammad Ali had been training in Miami Beach. He had grown half an inch since the first fight. He was slender and muscled, fully recovered from his hernia operation. "I'm so beautiful I should be chiseled in gold," he said.

He was sparring as much with his wife as much as with partners in the ring. One evening Roi wore a short orange knit dress to a party. In front of the guests, Ali tugged at the hem, trying to pull it over her knees. He had bought the dress for her, but he didn't want her wearing it in front of other men. She cried. He followed her into a bathroom and pawed at the dress until it tore. "I slapped her," he said years later, painfully remembering that night. "It's the only time I did something like that. . . . I was young, twenty-two years old, and she was doing things against my religion, but that's no excuse. A man should never hit a woman."

She left him and flew to Chicago. After eighty-five dollars in phone bills, days of abject apologies from Ali, she returned to give him another chance. But they continued to spat.

On April 1, Ali gathered his entourage and a handful of reporters, loaded them onto the red bus he'd bought when he was stalking Sonny Liston, and pointed it north toward Lewiston, Maine. He was still afraid to fly.

Ali joked with his friends about driving through Selma: "Don't worry, when we shout at girls it's gonna be colored girls so nobody get hung."

A week before the fight Ali had perfected the role of the "bad guy." "I didn't like the way Ali handled himself," said Jerry Izenberg. "I remember being in a dressing room with him. . . . He was on the rubbing table. Luis Sarria [one of his trainers] was giving him a massage . . . and a reporter asked, 'You've heard the stories about Malcolm's people making an attempt on your life,' something like that. And Ali looked up and said, 'What people? Malcolm ain't got no people.' . . . I got mad, because in my mind Malcolm stood for certain things. And I thought, 'You son of a bitch. One minute, Malcolm is great, and then all of a sudden he's nobody because somebody tells you he's nobody.' I was really pissed about it."

In Maine Ali trained by letting his sparring partners bash him as he stood against the ropes, preparing for the pain he might experience. He ran laps each morning past a Smith & Wesson gun factory. To local reporters he joked, "Maine is the land of the bear. How am I going to recognize the ugly one?"

His wife flew into town. She spent her days at a Holiday Inn on the turnpike reading James Bond novels. She knew Ali didn't like her talking to the press, but she *did* manage to tell an interviewer, "I can't wait for this fight, and all the worrying, to end. Then I'm going to steal my man and run away with him and hide somewhere."

At night, when Ali returned to the inn from his workout gym, people crowded round him demanding autographs. He said, "They act like the Beatles are in town." He signed pictures of Elijah Muhammad.

Sonny Liston spent the night before the fight staring silently at a television screen. A movie called *Zulu:* white soldiers wielding repeating rifles, wiping out the Zulu nation. His tiny motel room overlooked the town's cemetery.

He was a nine-to-one favorite.

The textile town of Lewiston, Maine, with about forty thousand inhabitants, was the smallest town in forty-two years to host a heavyweight championship fight. (In 1923, tiny Shelby, Montana, had been the site of Jack Dempsey's title defense against Tommy Gibbons. Shelby wanted to pay Jack Dempsey in sheep.)

Lewiston's citizens were unprepared for the army of bow tie–wearing strongmen patrolling its streets (entering town past a sign that said, "Moose Area Next Eighteen Miles"). Rumors circulated that Malcolm X's loyalists were going to kill Muhammad Ali, perhaps in the ring. The FBI sent five agents to Ali's hotel one day to say the bureau believed the stories. Agents posted a twelve-person, twenty-four hour guard around him. Photographer Howard Bingham recalled, "We'd run at sunup, the two of us [Ali and me], and the cops would start out running with us but couldn't keep up. One of them would hand me a gun, then they'd wave us on."

When a journalist asked Ali how much his armed protection was costing American taxpayers, Ali replied testily, "The Negro has the fear put in him by your people. But you people run the country and you should go out on the highway and stop anybody coming after me."

"They're coming to get *him,* not me, right?" Sonny Liston asked members of his camp. Ali was fast: a stray bullet could miss him and hit Liston instead. Liston had also heard that the Fruit was planning to murder *him* if he didn't throw the fight. And the mob had cast him aside. The chatter rattled him. "He just didn't seem like Sonny," said his wife. The day of the contest he barely said a word to anyone. Diarrhea seized his bowels.

Ticket prices were relatively low—ranging from twenty-five to one hundred dollars—but still too high for most locals. With 2,434 seats sold, St. Dominic's Arena was less than half full the night of the bout. Yet once again, thanks to closed-circuit television, the event was seen around the world as it was beamed to 258 locations. The worldwide audience was estimated at eighty million people, with an expected return of at least $1.5 million. "At the same moment Clay and Liston are bouncing punches off each other's noggins, Early Bird will be bouncing the picture story of the brawl into TV-equipped homes abroad. This, perhaps, is not quite the scientific triumph and the lofty purpose the United States had in mind when it embarked on its billion-dollar satellite program," the *Boston Globe* ventured.

To protect its investment, Sportsvision, the closed-circuit TV company airing the fight, took out a $1 million life insurance policy on Muhammad Ali.

As the arena doors opened, nearly three hundred police officers circled the ring: one lawman for every eight paying customers. "All those police in the hall just for me?" Ali joked. "I'm a great, great person!" The cops body-searched every Black man who entered and picked through purses, coats, and cases, on the alert for "poison gas bombs." The event was incredibly "ugly," Jerry Izenberg said. Not even the ringside presence of Jackie Gleason, Frank Sinatra, and Elizabeth Taylor could break the gloomy anxiety.

Robert Goulet mangled the national anthem, turning "dawn's early light" into "dawn's early night," and "gave proof through the night" to "gave proof through the fight." The next day, sportscaster Bud Collins, referring to the singer, said, "Clay hit the wrong guy."

Goulet's goofs almost seemed deliberate, in keeping with Ali's roiling of the nation's mood. Said one fan, "Are you *sure* that was the national anthem?"

Whatever was about to happen in the ring, the veteran journalist Jimmy Breslin figured the opening bell would signal a new era. Liston was the mob's last heavyweight fighter, he wrote. Ali belonged to a new breed of gangster. "They come out of Chicago and they murder and extort, and it is anybody's guess what their leader Elijah Muhammad . . . will do to get at money this simple kid will collect for defending the championship." He added, "We're all in the wrong business. We ought to go out and open a religion."

The writers sitting next to Breslin as the fighters were introduced glanced skittishly at the shadows in the room. "We're in the front row," one realized. "We're sitting ducks for some guy with ideas."

Former heavyweight champion Jersey Joe Walcott refereed the match. He motioned the boxers together for instructions. Ali (booed by the crowd) snarled at Liston. "Did you notice the way Liston was sweating under those hot lights?" Howard Cosell remarked, viewing a film of the fight later for ABC's *Wide World of Sports*. Liston, wearing only a single towel this time, draped thinly around sagging shoulders, gazed into Ali's eyes with a look of profound melancholy. Somehow, whatever passed for his spirit had already moved far beyond this moment.

In his corner, Ali bowed his head in prayer. Then the bell, and the slow blues began.

The round's first few seconds repeated the men's initial match, Ali moving to his left, Liston following with off-the-mark jabs. The crowd yelled with each Liston swing as if their noise might do some damage; Liston's fists certainly weren't up to the challenge. Ali landed a straight right lead, but he seemed in no hurry to do much of anything. He moved with extreme confidence, almost daring Liston to squeeze him against the ropes. When Liston pressed forward, he came with his head up and his balance off, resting on a poorly planted left foot.

Several of the arena's customers were still standing in long concession lines when the fight was called at one minute and forty-four seconds into the round. They didn't see a thing. Neither did most of the people watching. "The Phantom Punch," reporters called it later: a short right hand over Liston's missed jab, straight into his temple, lifting his left foot off the ground, toppling him. He fell like a teddy bear in a sideshow shooting gallery. Former champ Joe Louis, observing ringside, said Ali's punch had nothing behind it—it was like "throwing Corn Flakes at a battleship," but it was enough to send Liston to the canvas, apparently stunned. Even Ali didn't believe what he was seeing. "Get up and fight, sucker!" he yelled. This wasn't good. Folks doubted his first victory; he needed a decisive win to silence the skeptics.

Walcott, startled, failed to hustle Ali to a neutral corner. Ali loomed over Liston then he finally stepped away. He danced jubilantly. There was never an official count. Liston, arms splayed, rolled over, tried to stand, and fell again. Finally, after seventeen seconds, he got to his feet. Walcott signaled for the fighters to resume the action. "Liston still has reflexes. Look at him duck," Cosell observed, reviewing the fight film later. But Nat Fleischer, the publisher of *Ring* magazine, yelled, "It's over! He's out!" He had been counting. The timekeeper, Francis McDonough, also said they were done. Puzzled, Walcott walked over to Fleischer while the fighters flailed away. Then Walcott waved his arms. Finished. Ali had successfully defended his heavyweight title.

Boos showered the ring. "Fix!" people screamed. "Fake! Fake!" Ali danced some more, but in his corner he told his brother Rudy, "He laid down." "No," Rudy said, "you hit him." "Did I hit him?" Ali protested, but Rudy insisted, "Nah man, you hit him."

The whole mess was as "ugly as a Maine lobster," *Sports Illustrated* would declare.

Immediately afterward, in the ring, in a post-fight interview with Steve Ellis, Ali couldn't identify whether a "left hook or a right cross" had floored Liston: "I was moving too fast." He was more comfortable attributing the victory to "Almighty Allah and his Messenger." "I've been living a righteous life and you see what happens. All this talk of people coming with bombs and machine guns scared him but it didn't scare me."

Journalist Paul Gallender later claimed, with no solid evidence, that the Fruit of Islam had kidnapped Geraldine before the fight to force Liston to take a dive. In fact, Geraldine burst into Liston's dressing room immediately after the bout. "You could have got up!" she yelled.

Quietly Liston implored one of his aides, "Tell her. Tell her. I got hit."

"It was a perfect shot," said José Torres, former light heavyweight champion. "It happens once in a million years. Liston . . . moved into it. I don't think he even saw it. It wasn't a fake. You'd have to be a fighter to know it."

Former heavyweight champ James Braddock said, "I have a feeling this guy [Ali] is a lot better than any of us gave him credit for."

But doubts persisted, linked to rumors that John Vitale was telling people beforehand that the fight would end in round one. Former FBI agent William Roemer said, "We learned that there very definitely had been a fix in that fight," but there was never any conclusive proof, even after an extensive investigation.

Liston's remarks were contradictory—from "I was groggy" to "it was the way the fight had to go" to perhaps the most plausible explanation: "I was down but not hurt, but I looked up and saw Ali standing over me. Now there is no way to get up from the canvas that you are not exposed to a great shot. Ali is waiting to hit me, the ref can't control him. I have to put one knee and one glove on the canvas to get up. You know Ali is a nut. You can tell what a normal man is going to do, but you can't tell what a nut is going to do, and Ali is a nut."

Geraldine got the clearest last word: "I think Sonny gave that second fight away," she said. "[But] I didn't see the money if he was paid to lose."

After that, Liston began his long limp into the shadows. James Baldwin offered this quiet valedictory of him, "He is inarticulate in the way we all are when more has happened to us than we know how to express, and inarticulate in a particularly Negro way—he has a long tale to tell which no one wants to hear."

Ali was as frustrated as anyone. He knew he *still* hadn't convinced nonbelievers he was the world's greatest fighter. He assured Steve Ellis, "You have never seen the real Muhammad Ali. I haven't even had time to warm up."

Most of the public agreed with Francis McDonough, the fight's much maligned timekeeper: "That lousy bum Clay. If Clay had gone to a neutral corner like he was supposed to, this whole thing wouldn't have happened. The bum shouldn't be allowed to fight anymore."

Among Blacks as well as whites now, Muhammad Ali was one of the most hated men in America, and it was only going to get worse.

Jerry Izenberg remembered a celebration in the courtyard of the Holiday Inn following the fight: Ali was laughing and carrying on with his entourage, with the Muslims. Sonji Roi appeared on a second-floor balcony. She called to her husband, "Come upstairs."

"It was obvious there was great feeling between them," Izenberg said. "And the guys were saying, 'No, man, don't go, stay down here.'" Ali started to walk up, but five or six Muslims stood at the bottom of the stairs blocking his way—not in an overtly threatening manner but enough to get their message across. Ali called to his wife, "Go to bed." Izenberg wanted to shout at the Muslims, "Why don't you leave this guy alone and leave her alone and see if they can get together and work out their lives?"

Herbert Muhammad had introduced them and now he schemed to push them apart. An FBI informant reported to his superiors that Herbert treated Ali "in a manner such as a 'pimp' would treat a prostitute . . . attempting to downgrade [him] as much as he can in order to keep him completely under control."

Herbert Muhammad told Ali that Sonji had tried to sleep with him, even after she'd married Ali. Biographer Jonathan Eig insists it was the other way around. Ali's brother, Rudy, told friends Herbert couldn't persuade Sonji to do what he wanted, so he decided to get rid of her.

The couple's existing disagreements were easy enough to exploit. "How [can] I stand by seeing you act like a tiger in the ring, and out of it your knees trembling before some religious superstition, like a man who believes in ghosts?" she challenged him. "I ask . . . you to question it. Just ask yourself the questions, and in the quiet dead of night, answer. Don't even whisper your answer out loud. Just to yourself. You world heavyweight champion muthafucker."

"You traded heaven for hell, baby," Ali warned her.

On June 23, 1965, less than a month after the fight in Lewiston, Ali, with the encouragement of Herbert Muhammad, filed a complaint in Dade County, Florida, Circuit Court seeking an annulment of his marriage, on the grounds that Roi had fraudulently promised to follow the tenets of Islam. Publicly, she said she still loved her husband and hoped to save their union. To friends, she said, "They've stolen my man's mind." Malcolm X, Sonji Roi, maybe even Sonny Liston, had all been sacrificed so Ali could serve the Messenger in the way the Messenger intended.

A final divorce decree was granted on January 10, 1966. The Nation forbade Ali from talking with Roi—even changing his phone number more than once to keep her from reaching him.

"I just about went crazy, sitting in my room, smelling her perfume, looking at the walls," he admitted. "But it was something that had to happen."

"He went through hell," Rudy concurred. "Not to be able to hold her, make love to her. It hurt him real bad. She's the only woman he ever really loved. His true love, his only one."

"I know what it's like to be loved, because he really loved me," Roi said. "Someone else made the decision—I'm sure of that—and it hurt me. I wanted to fight it. I loved the man. But I looked around and I didn't see a friendly face in the crowd. I wasn't going to take on all the Muslims. If I had, I'd probably have wound up dead."

"I know what it's like to be dead," Peter Fonda assured George Harrison.

Harrison had just dropped acid for the second time. The Beatles were back in the United States for another nerve-wracking series of concert dates (following a European tour, rehearsals, and the premiere of *Help!*). They arrived in the States in mid-August 1965, just as violence was winding down in LA's Watts neighborhood. Thousands of National Guardsmen had finally quelled looting following a clash between white police officers and Black citizens. As the Beatles' plane landed, they studied newspaper images of a city resembling "an all-out war zone in some far-off foreign country," in the estimation of one Los Angeles police sergeant. The band was scheduled to play the Hollywood Bowl in two weeks. Harrison feared getting hit onstage by more than just jelly beans.

This time around, pressure from the press to speak out on politics was worse than before. Urban riots, explicit sex in the movies, and America's first televised war immersed the news media in irresistible dramas. It became a competitive game to try to mire the Beatles in controversy—especially since the US military had just announced a refinement of its role in Vietnam. US troops were no longer advisory; they were free to take the offensive in the field. All pretense had fallen: the United States was now conducting an aggressive—if inefficient—war in Southeast Asia.

Brian Epstein worked harder than ever to tailor the band for tabloids rather than the editorial pages. God forbid the Beatles earn press coverage as hostile as Muhammad Ali's. (In *their* country, they were hailed as heroes, honored by their queen!)

After performing a total of eleven shows in eight days in New York City, Toronto, Atlanta, Houston, Chicago, suburban Minneapolis (Bloomington, Minnesota), and Portland, Oregon, the Beatles retreated, for a brief respite, to a house Epstein had rented for them in Beverly Hills, just off Mulholland Drive. The house was owned by actress Zsa Zsa Gabor.

Harrison was miserable, missing his girlfriend, phoning her every day. The bandmates slept until two each afternoon and then dragged themselves to the backyard pool like casualties recuperating at a sanitarium. All was not well in the band. "John and I had decided that Paul and Ringo had to have acid because we couldn't relate to them anymore," Harrison said. "Not just on the one level—we couldn't relate to them on any level, because acid had changed us so much. It was such a mammoth experience that it was unexplainable. It was something that had to be experienced, because you could spend the rest of your life trying to explain what it made you feel and think. It was all too important to John and me."

While in New York, Harrison had obtained a foil packet of acid-laced sugar cubes. He carried it through the tour, saving the treat for LA.

Starr was game. "I'd take anything," he said, ever the team player. "It was a fabulous day. The night wasn't so great, because it felt like it was never going to wear off. Twelve hours later and it was, 'Give us a break now, Lord.'"

McCartney refused to participate. He'd been frightened by stories he'd heard—how the drug might alter your mind permanently and you'd "never get back home" (a prospect Lennon embraced). McCartney didn't appreciate the peer pressure ("We were all slightly cruel," Lennon admitted). Harrison didn't like what he perceived to be McCartney's moralistic judgment. For him, this wasn't just a high. It was about seeing God. Arguably, he never again trusted Paul.

That August, in Los Angeles, the coincidences mounted, tugging Harrison further toward a future he felt may have already been his past. The events came within days of one another, offering unexpected insights and results.

Word got out among fans that the Beatles had holed up in Beverly Hills. A dozen police officers and private security men from the Burns Agency were dispatched to protect the house, surrounded now by growing crowds. The Beatles could not go out. Visitors came to them.

On the afternoon of August 24, David Crosby and Roger McGuinn of the Byrds, along with Peter Fonda (four years before of his era-defining role as the American road hippie in *Easy Rider*) stopped by. From afar, the Byrds and the Beatles had formed a mutual admiration society. "There were girls at the gates, police guards," McGuinn recalled of their arrival at the house. "We went in and David, John Lennon, George Harrison and I took LSD to help get to know each other better." They all affirmed that acid aided them in "discover[ing] the truth about spiritual things." They retreated to a large bathroom in the house, sat around a giant shower stall, and passed around a guitar. They took turns playing their favorite songs. "John and I agreed 'Be-Bop-A-Lula' was our favorite 50s rock record," McGuinn said.

"I had a concept of what had happened the first time I took LSD, but the concept is nowhere near as big as the reality when it actually happens," Harrison said. "So as it kicked in again, I thought, 'Jesus, I remember!'" He was trying to play the guitar, a fragment of Bach. He went outside to the swimming pool, feeling euphoric, but then he felt a "bad vibe." Somehow, a reporter had sneaked past security—one of the journalists determined to get the Beatles on record saying something shocking. While the Beatles' road managers Mal Evans and Neil Aspinall worked to eject the man before he witnessed the Beatles tripping, Harrison's experience of the drug worsened. He began to think he was dying. Suddenly Peter Fonda appeared beside him, trying to help: "I told him that there was nothing to be afraid of and all that he needed to do was relax. I said that I knew what it was like to be dead because, when I was ten years old, I'd accidentally shot myself in the stomach and my heart stopped beating three times while I was on the operating table because I had lost so much blood."

John Lennon overheard him talking to Harrison and became irate. "For Christ's sake, shut up!" he yelled. "We don't care, we don't want to know!"

Fonda remembered, "[Lennon] looked at me and said, 'You're making me feel like I've never been born. Who put all that shit in your head?'"

Later this incident formed the basis of Lennon's song, "She Said She Said."

It was a "morbid and bizarre" afternoon, McGuinn recalled—but before the day was done the elements came together for George Harrison. One of the Byrds' producers, Jim Dickson of World Pacific Records in Los Angeles, also produced Ravi Shankar's American releases. He had introduced Crosby and McGuinn to Shankar's music and told them of Shankar's influence on John Coltrane. In his vocalizations, Crosby tried to imitate Coltrane's improvisational approach to melody, while McGuinn studied Shankar's modal inventions. He played a guitar raga for Harrison and Lennon as they sat by the pool—Harrison considerably calmer now—and Harrison was gripped. The music sounded both completely familiar and like nothing he had ever heard. He was glad to learn about Ravi Shankar—the world's best sitar player, McGuinn assured him.

The sitar. LSD. Awareness of God and death. *The Yogis of the Himalayas.*

"What do you think about God?" McGuinn asked him.

"We don't know about that," Harrison demurred—trained by Epstein to avoid saying anything *heavy,* even in an intimate situation (reporters might be lurking about). Harrison spoke as a Beatle, using the royal "we," rather than as an individual—like Muhammad Ali treading carefully under the gaze of the Nation of Islam.

That summer, the summer of 1965, the Beatles had become bigger than Elvis, as they had dreamed. On August 15 they had been the first rock and roll band to play a sports stadium, Shea, home of baseball's New York Mets—"an orange and blue ass pit of a venue," a journalist called it. A rickety stage was erected on second base, a fair distance from the crowd, at that time the largest audience in pop music history, at nearly fifty-six thousand people, caged behind chain link fencing circling the stadium's seats. Despite the fence and two thousand security personnel, several fans managed to take the field and nearly reach the stage.

Right before the show, the Beatles had been taken by limo from the Warwick Hotel to a helipad on the East River. From there, over the blue, glittering skyline, a chopper ferried them to the World's Fair Building in Queens. "[The helicopter pilot] started zooming round the stadium, saying, 'Look at that, isn't it great?' And we were hanging on by the skin of our teeth, thinking, 'Let's get out of here!'" Harrison recalled. The sight of the crowd packed into the venue below, like colored pills in a box, terrified him. The pilot switched on a radio so they could hear the deejay over Shea's PA system announcing, "You hear that up there? Listen . . . *it's the Beatles!* They're *here!*" With a tsunami roar, thousands of flashbulbs exploded. Geoffrey Ellis, one of Brian Epstein's assistants, sitting in the cockpit, later recalled, "All those kids . . . kept looking up to the heavens as though God was descending to the earth."

Two days before the Beatles boarded that chopper, a sixty-nine-year-old pharmacist-turned-mendicant walked aboard a large black cargo ship in Calcutta, bound for Boston. He carried only a small suitcase with a tiny typewriter and a tape recorder, an umbrella, a supply of dry cereal, and a stack of his own painstaking translations of ancient Sanskrit manuscripts. He knew no one in the States. He had about a days' worth of currency (in US terms). He believed his destiny was to bring consciousness of Lord Krishna to the ill and suffering West.

Part of his destiny was to meet George Harrison, and it would be impossible to tell which man benefited the most from the encounter.

Harrison would know him as Swami Prabhupada (in Sanskrit, "he who has taken shelter at the lotus feet of the Lord"). His given name was Abhay Charan De. He was born to a cloth merchant on a street named Harrison Road in Calcutta in 1896. His father was a follower of the Gaudiya Vaishnavism tradition within Hinduism—that is, the worship of Krishna as a personal god.

One of the major Hindu deities, Krishna is first mentioned in Vedic texts from the first millennium BCE, and in the Bhagavad Gita, the Bhagavata Purana, and the Mahabharata. He is depicted in many guises, most popularly as a blue-skinned child-god, playing the flute and cavorting with *gopis,* adoring goat-herding girls. (Harrison came to relish this image of the free-spirited musician-god.) Krishna is filled with compassion, tenderness, and love.

Prabhupada grew up chanting "Hare Krishna" and studying ancient texts declaring the material world an illusion. An eternal soul, the atman, lives inside every individual, the texts said, waiting to be freed from the painful cycle of death, rebirth, and suffering.

As a student at Calcutta's Scottish Church College in the 1920s he supported *svaraj,* the push for independence from British rule. He believed Mohandas Gandhi when Gandhi insisted that British schools instilled a slave mentality in Indian students. Nevertheless, Prabhupada completed his studies and went to work for a chemical industrialist. His father arranged a marriage for him with another member of the merchant class. But he had also become a disciple of an elderly sadhu, Bhaktisiddhaānta Sarasvati Thākura. Sarasvati noted Prabhupada's writing skills and said his calling was to translate the Vedas for Western readers, provide commentaries on them, and disseminate the sacred words to the English-speaking world.

Decades passed before Prabhupada felt he had fulfilled his duties as son, husband, and father, clearing his path to pursue his destiny. World War II and the partitioning of India and Pakistan in 1947, causing intense Hindu-Muslim fighting, interrupted his plans but also strengthened his resolve. "They fought, and so many died," he said. "And after death there was no distinction who was Hindu or who was Muslim—the municipal men gathered the bodies together in piles, to throw them somewhere."

He left his family and his business, maintaining his wife and children in a Calcutta apartment. He moved to the holy city of Vrindavan, legendarily God's birthplace, eighty miles south of New Delhi. Destitute, dependent on donations to fund his translation of the Bhagavad Gita, he nearly lost faith—especially, once, after suffering heat stroke and becoming severely disoriented in the streets. On another occasion he was gored by a bull. He lay for hours on the roadside. "But those difficulties were *assets*," he concluded. "It was all Krishna's mercy."

In 1965, when he was about to turn sixty-nine, he met a sympathetic businessman with contacts in the West who was willing to help him obtain the documents he'd need to travel to the United States. On August 13, he boarded the steam-powered cargo carrier *Jaladuta*. His highest aim in the physical world was to die in Vrindavan, on the banks of the Yamuna River; now he might never see it again. At Krishna's mercy, he was heading for an unknown, possibly hostile land to do the impossible.

The ship's captain later reported that he had never seen the Atlantic as calm as it was during that voyage. Prabhupada credited Krishna. Still, he suffered terrible seasickness and two mild heart attacks along the way. In a fever-dream, he saw himself in a small wooden boat rowed by his god. "Do not fear," Krishna said.

Prabhupada landed at Boston's Commonwealth Pier at 5:30 a.m., September 17. By that time, George Harrison was back in London, following the Beatles' last US concert date, where he wasted no time finding a copy of Ravi Shankar's album *Portrait of Genius*, a selection of ragas highlighting sitar and tabla.

Sitting aboard ship as it idled at the pier, Prabhupada grabbed a sheet of paper and wrote, "My dear lord Krishna, You are so kind upon this useless soul, but I do not know why You have brought me here. Now You can do whatever You like with me. But I guess You have some business here, otherwise why would You bring me to this terrible place?" He signed the page, "The most unfortunate, insignificant beggar."

For several weeks, he lived a peripatetic existence among contacts provided by his Indian patron. One of them, a Sanskrit scholar living in an apartment overlooking the Hudson River in New York, gave Prabhupada a small room to stay in. Through this man, Prabhupada met Ravi Shankar, briefly, nine months before George Harrison would meet him in London. The scholar was well acquainted with Shankar and his brother Uday.

Prabhupada enjoyed spending days wandering the streets of Manhattan alone, even on bitter winter mornings, carrying his umbrella and wearing a wool cap he'd borrowed that was trimmed with flapping fur muffs. With his heavy, drooping eyelids and thick red lips slightly parted, he seemed always on the verge of asking a question. People who saw him in his saffron-colored robes and pointed white shoes said "he looked like the genie that popped out of Aladdin's lamp."

The Paradox, a macrobiotic restaurant at 64 East Seventh Street on the Lower East Side (where occasionally a young conceptual artist named Yoko Ono waited tables and served salads), gave Prabhupada his first small American audience. News spread among the restaurant's regulars, devotees of healthy diets and alternative living philosophies: a swami had arrived in New York and was staying with a Sanskrit scholar uptown. People went to hear him speak. They bought copies of his translated texts.

One day someone robbed his small room. He lost his typewriter and his tape recorder, the essential tools of his writing. One of the Paradox regulars invited Prabhupada to stay with him in an apartment in the Bowery. The loft there quickly became a pilgrimage site for young dropouts and street people in the East Village, drawn to Prabhupada's simple message: God is sound; let sound fill you. He cooked elaborate vegetarian dishes for his guests—*prasādam*, ritualistic food offerings. These were the only meals many of the kids got each week. Others were attracted to the joyous *kirtanas*—the group chanting sessions led by Prabhupada—or to the moody *bhajanas* he'd sing, accompanied by hand cymbals: sacred North Indian folk melodies. A number of his devotees had come to New York because they wanted to be rock musicians. Others had come on vague spiritual searches. They were willing to try anything. LSD. Chanting. Dal.

Pine-scented incense filled the air.

Well over one hundred blocks north, in Harlem, the Nation of Islam was trying to reopen the mosque following its spasmodic destruction after Malcolm died. The believers there had temporarily lost their center. Here on the Lower East Side, a new and different sort of center was rapidly forming, composed mostly of white, middle-class dropouts. Around St. Mark's Place, head shops, bookstores, poster galleries, and record stores opened. It was Manhattan's precursor to San Francisco's Haight-Ashbury. In the middle of it all: a hip swami. "I am an old man," he'd tell his followers. "I may go away at any moment." They didn't believe him. A miracle had brought him to them. Miracles would keep him here.

Michael Grant, a young musician and LSD lover who came to the loft mainly for the food, saw the growing crowds around Prabhupada and decided to help him find a bigger place. Through the classified ads in the *Village Voice*, he located an abandoned storefront on Second Avenue. For $196 a month, Prabhupada could live there. He'd have room enough to invite devotees for *prasādam, kirtana,* teachings. They'd each pitch in on the rent.

The store's old, hand-painted sign remained out front: "Matchless Gifts."

Prabhupada hung a calendar image of the blue-skinned flautist on a wall, the room's centerpiece.

From this humble space, overlooking two funeral homes, a gravestone cutter, an import-export business, and a Mobil filling station, Prabhupada would begin to fulfill his destiny. Before leaving Vrindavan, he had written three books, in addition to the translations he'd completed of ancient texts. In the next twelve years, he would produce over sixty volumes of teachings in English. Before departing Vrindavan, he had initiated one disciple. In the next dozen years, he would personally welcome more than four thousand men and women into the fold—including a shell-shocked Beatle.

In early October 1965, overwhelmed by Ravi Shankar's *Portrait of Genius*, George Harrison popped out to a little shop on Oxford Street called India Craft. It was one of many such stores opening in London as immigration to Great Britain from Pakistan and India steadily increased. "[The shop] stocked little carvings and incense," Harrison said. And he bought a "crummy-quality" sitar there. He brought it back to Kinfauns, the house he'd bought in Esher, and played it for Pattie Boyd. She saw how much he needed to escape (and grasp) the mania. "He knew that he would have ended up in a menial job and lived a very ordinary life in Liverpool had not the fates intervened," Boyd said. "George was . . . desperate to know what was in him that made it turn out so different. He really wanted to find out what kind of divine spirit had made this happen."

How else—but for divine intervention—to explain the insanity? *Help!* had trafficked in racist stereotypes (he was embarrassed by it now), and the Indian musicians never received credit for their contributions. They should have been furious. Yet one of them, Pandit Shiv Dayal Batish, wanted Harrison to know he felt it a great honor to have met the Beatles: "Working with [you] . . . not only earned us fame and popularity in the West, it also brought us respect within our own Indian community." The mania twisted everything into unpredictable ironies.

Harrison brought the sitar to Abbey Road studios, but he didn't know what to do with it. The Beatles were about to begin recording new songs for what would become their first mature album, *Rubber Soul*. The songs reflected recent influences: Dylan, acid, ragas, pot.

Harrison's contributions showcased a growing lyrical and musical complexity. He had always said he wanted to take his time writing and not do corny stuff. His words were blunt, as always, with few attempts at poetry, but they were getting more incisive. And the songs' structures more aptly conveyed their content. "Think for Yourself," a sharp invective against an obtuse lover, embodies impatience using a grating fuzz-box on the bass line and abrupt chord changes from A minor and D minor to B, circling back to C and G. The song affirms Harrison's disinterest in ingratiating himself to listeners. It is energized by his fascination with fresh sounds (the fuzz-box) and, on some level, by his anger at the American press. Though aimed at an intimate, the song suggests weariness at being told what to think.

"If I Needed Someone," written for Boyd, was Harrison's first classical Indian song, in the sense that it was founded on a drone, a tonic A continuing even when the chorus line switches to G major. The guitar faintly mimics a high-register tambura, while underneath, like an ache of desire, a harmonium provides a persistent moan. Harrison invoked Roger McGuinn's chiming guitar riff from "The Bells of Rhymney," a debt he happily acknowledged when he sent McGuinn a copy of the song.

In addition to recent influences, the Beatles' new music reflected a changing dynamic in the group. Until now, Harrison had taken a backseat to the hit-making writing partnership of Lennon-McCartney. This was evident in the studio, in the attitude later expressed by sound engineer Geoff Emerick. Of a particular recording session, Emerick noted, "This was, after all, a Harrison song and therefore not something anyone was prepared to spend a whole lot of time on."

But the shared LSD experience had brought Harrison and Lennon closer, leaving McCartney out of the mix. Like McCartney, Lennon still treated Harrison as a pesky little brother, but he talked to him more intimately now, respected his search for something more meaningful than Beatlemania. An unspoken tug-of-war began between Harrison and McCartney for John Lennon's affection and respect (boastful and headstrong Lennon had always been the de facto band leader). At the moment, through explorations of expanding consciousness and Indian music, Harrison was winning the battle.

Lennon's "In My Life," a retrospective view of love and loss, and "Nowhere Man," a confession of aimlessness, sounded more like Harrison meditations than McCartney's love ballads or narrative snapshots.

Though critics have usually linked "Norwegian Wood" to Dylan's acoustic influence, it is arguably *Lennon's* first Indian song, even without sitar. It features an E major drone underneath the D-chord melody, and a descending line similar to the raga shapes McGuinn had demonstrated for Lennon and Harrison beside the swimming pool in California.

"We were at the point where we'd recorded the 'Norwegian Wood' backing track . . . and it needed something," Harrison remembered. "I picked the sitar up—it was just lying around. I hadn't really figured out what to do with it. It was quite spontaneous. I found the notes that played the lick. It fitted and it worked." (He did think that "[the] sound was bad.")

At one point he broke a string. The sitar wasn't made for Western tuning, and the sympathetic strings weren't happy. George Martin had once been hired to produce the soundtrack of a Peter Sellers movie; in doing so, he had worked with Indian musicians from an organization called the Asian Music Circle. He suggested giving them a call to see if they had some spare strings—thus opening another fortuitous connection for George Harrison.

The Asian Music Circle had been founded in 1946 by an Indian émigré, Ayana Deva Angadi, and his English-born wife, the heiress Patricia Fell-Clarke. Angadi's father had sent him to England in the 1920s to study for the civil service exams so he could work for the British Raj. He rebelled and committed to fighting British imperialism from his perch in London. In 1943 he married Fell-Clarke, also in rebellion from her upbringing. She pursued the arts, particularly portrait painting. Together they founded the Music Circle with the aid of acquaintances they had made in the world of arts, most notably the American violinist Yehudi Menuhin. Menuhin served on their board, raised funds, and established classes and concert series featuring internationally known Hindustani musicians, including Ravi Shankar.

When the Angadis got the call from Abbey Road, they rushed over in person to deliver the goods. Harrison invited them to stay, to watch the rest of the "Norwegian Wood" session. He plucked the new string. The recording console went haywire, meter needles leaping into the red. This was the first of many occasions, over the next few years, when the Beatles' musical experiments would require more sophisticated equipment.

Entranced by Harrison's face while he concentrated on the music, Patricia Angadi sat quietly in a corner, sketching him sitting next to Lennon. McCartney looked on.

One day McCartney tried to win Lennon back by taking him to the Indica Gallery. The Indica was a bookshop and art gallery run by pals of McCartney's girlfriend, Jane Asher. McCartney said, "[I've been trying to] cram everything in, all the things I've missed. People are saying things and painting things and writing things and composing things that are great, and I must know what people are doing." Through the Indica and other cultural centers he had been introduced to the poetry of the Beats, to the free jazz of Albert Ayler, to the electronic music of Karlheinz Stockhausen. He knew Lennon would share his enthusiasm for the avant-garde.

On a bookshelf at the gallery, Lennon picked up a copy of *The Psychedelic Experience: A Manual Based on the Tibetan Book of the Dead* by Harvard researchers Timothy Leary and Richard Alpert (later known as Baba Ram Dass). The authors used an eighth-century Buddhist text as a guide to the hallucinogenic experience. "Do not cling to your old self," they wrote. They described a process of "ego-death" as LSD's effects took hold, and the ego's reintegration as the drug wore off. They predicted that, in the next few years, mass populations would experience mystical revelations through LSD, revolutionizing the world's religions.

Lennon read the whole book while sitting in the gallery. McCartney had been right to bring him here. But the book only strengthened his bond with Harrison. He couldn't wait to tell his younger bandmate he'd found an intellectual framework for what they'd experienced together.

"Tomorrow Never Knows," the creative result of Lennon's reading, was truly a band effort, but essentially it was a product of Harrison's obsession with Indian music filtered through Lennon's sensibility. Built entirely on a C drone and driven by a relentless tabla-like beat, a snare-crack followed by skipping snaps on a loose tom-tom, the song fulfills Lennon's desire to "sound like the Dalai Lama chanting from a mountaintop, miles away," an effect Geoff Emerick achieved by running Lennon's voice through a Leslie speaker—the device, with revolving bass and treble, giving Hammond organs their wavery, distant sound. (Lennon thought it would be just as effective to hang him by the ankles from a rope attached to the ceiling and whirl him around a circle of microphones.) A set of tape loops, edited together randomly in a perpetual cycle, distorted so McCartney's laughter sounded like seagulls, added a dreamy background to the lyrics, which urged listeners to "lay down all thoughts [and] surrender to the void"—the primary aim of meditation.

Underneath it all, Harrison added a droning tambura.

Later, in a book called *Revolution in the Head*, Ian Macdonald wrote of the song: "The Indian drone, as brought into First World culture by this track, challenges not only seven centuries of Western music, but the operating premise of Western civilization itself. When Lennon's voice rises out of the seething dazzle of churning loops, the first words it utters, 'Turn off your mind,' are a mystic negation of all progressive intellectual enterprise. The message: it is not the contents of one's mind which matter; rather, what counts is the quality of the containing mind itself—and the emptier, the better. This proposition . . . was radically subversive in 1966."

Harrison and Boyd became regulars on Fitzalan Road, at the Asian Music Circle. They befriended the Angadis and many of the musicians who worked with them. Harrison began to take sitar lessons—his first official music study. Boyd took up the dilruba, a bowed instrument. One day, Shiv Dayal Batish, a member of the Music Circle who had played on the *Help!* soundtrack, got a call from "Mr. Harrison" requiring a dilruba. When the instrument arrived from Calcutta, Harrison sent a limo to pick up Batish. Upon reaching Kinfauns, Batish was impressed by Harrison's cultural sensitivity: he "came forward with folded hands observing the Indian style of Namaste."

Harrison's house filled him with "awe and wonder." "Peace was prevalent" in the main sitting room, he said, "thoroughly carpeted with a variety of Oriental carpets. To me it looked as if the whole room was partitioned into segments, perhaps, with a view to make it possible and convenient for the occupant groups to be able to sit separately without losing the visual angle."

Boyd was a marvelous student, he said, smart and steady and accurate. The perfect complement to her musician partner.

When Harrison asked her to marry him, he sought Brian Epstein's permission. (What would it do to the Beatles' image if the quiet one got hitched?) Once again, she paused to examine the path she was considering. Certainly, she saw, it was an "unreal life." "[The bandmates] hadn't had a chance to grow up in the way most people do . . . so cocooned. . . . They never knew whom they could trust. In many respects they were still children. They had few real friends apart from each other. . . . They knew little about life and, with Brian looking after their every need, they had no reason to learn." But she had embarked on an exhilarating exploration with Harrison—cultural, musical, spiritual, intimate.

They arranged a quiet ceremony in a register office in Surrey on January 21, 1966. Then they had to endure a press conference organized by Epstein. "It was so terrifying that I have almost blanked it from my memory," Boyd said later. She told the newsmen she wanted three children "but not immediately" ("there was plenty of time").

At Kinfauns, a passion grew in Harrison for gardening—the bungalow had been built next to the spacious grounds of a former vegetable garden at the Claremont Girls School. The school had once belonged to Lord Robert Clive, "founder of Britain's Indian empire," Boyd said. The couple became vegetarian after reading about the cruel treatment of calves in the making of veal. They doted over a beloved Persian cat named Korky. They tried hard to develop a normal rhythm together, but nothing would ever be normal. Occasionally Beatles fans broke into the house. Girls hid under the bed. Items of Boyd's clothing disappeared. Maurice Milbourne, the gardener Harrison had hired to teach him what to do, found the vegetable beds trampled each morning.

On the streets of London, Boyd was followed and kicked by miniskirted girls who said they hated her for stealing their favorite Beatle. She received threatening letters.

She found some solace in getting to know the other Beatle wives, Cynthia Lennon, a quiet blonde, somewhat reserved, and Maureen Starkey, a former hairdresser who'd first met Ringo (her "Ritchie") at a Beatle show in the Cavern Club in Liverpool when she was seventeen years old. She was "jolly and friendly," Boyd said, dark and sleek—and at heart, still a simple Beatle fan.

Boyd would later write, "We'd be in the same room but [George] wasn't really with me: he was in his head. Most of the time I didn't mind. I'd think, Oh, good, he's writing a new song—he was always happiest when he was being creative."

She was highly social, whereas Harrison, traumatized from touring, rarely wanted to leave the house or meet new people. He had a small appetite; he didn't eat out much. Brian Epstein had introduced him to fine wines. He drank more alcohol than Boyd was used to. It relaxed him around strangers, he said.

Apart from the other Beatles, he was closest, during this period, to the Angadis. Patricia Angadi liked to paint the couple—they were the most beautiful people she had ever seen. One day in June 1966, she invited them for dinner. "Guess who's coming?" she said. She was referring to Ravi Shankar.

"Something clicked from the very beginning with George," Shankar would later write. Harrison, for his part, later recalled, "[Ravi] was very friendly and easy to communicate with." He seemed bigger than he was because of all his energy. "By this time the Beatles had met so many people—prime ministers, celebrities, royalty—but I got to the point where I thought, 'I'd like to meet somebody who could really impress me.' And that was when I met Ravi. He was the first person who impressed me in a way that was beyond just being a famous celebrity. . . . I mean . . . Elvis impressed me when I was a kid, and impressed me when I met him because of the buzz of meeting Elvis—but you couldn't later on go round to him and say, 'Elvis, what's happening in the universe?'"

Shankar, then in his mid-forties, had achieved an impressive level of international fame. He had been performing around the world since he was a child, first as a member of an Indian ballet troupe with his older brother Uday, and then as a sitar master, trained for years by a renowned teacher, Baba Allauddin Khan. His father had abandoned his mother for a British woman in London; in earliest youth, Shankar was shuttled back and forth between East and West, educated in both Eastern and Western traditions and knowledgeable in a variety of musical styles. This had led to his popular collaborations with Yehudi Menuhin and John Coltrane. Finally, in spirit, he had returned to his homeland's sacred musical traditions, to the concept of *Nada Brahma*, Sanskrit for "Sound is God." It was this, more than the fame or the experience of performing, that attracted George Harrison to him, not just as a musician but also as a seeker of truth. "Ravi was my link into the Vedic world," Harrison said. "Ravi plugged me into the whole of reality."

"From the moment we met, George was asking questions, and I felt he was genuinely interested in Indian music and religion," Shankar said. "He appeared to be a sweet, straightforward young man." Shankar had heard of the Beatles—barely. He hadn't listened to their music. It amused him that rock stars were interested in the sitar. The Beatles weren't the first to use the instrument on record. The Yardbirds and the Kinks had experimented with Indian sounds. But "Norwegian Wood" was the first rock song to feature the sitar so prominently. Harrison wouldn't discuss it with Shankar. He was embarrassed by his playing on the record.

A short time later, when Shankar *did* hear the song, he told Harrison, "My goodness, what is this sort of thing you are playing there, George? If you don't mind me saying so, it's the sort of frightful *twangy* thing you hear on Radio Bombay advertising soap powders." Surrounded by sycophants who assured him everything he did was fantastic, Harrison was grateful for Shankar's bluntness. The ability to be acutely honest with each other became another bond between the men.

At the Angadi dinner, Harrison came right out and asked Shankar if he would give him sitar lessons. "I told him that to play sitar is like learning Western classical music on the violin or the cello. It is not merely a matter of learning how to hold the instrument and play a few strokes and chords, after which (with sufficient talent) you can prosper on your own, as is common with the guitar in Western pop music," Shankar insisted. "I said, 'I have given many years of my life to sitar, and by God's grace I have become very well known—but still I know in my heart of hearts that I have a long way to go. There's no end to it. It is not only the technical mastery . . . you have to learn the whole complex system of music properly and get deeply into it.'"

Harrison said he understood the seriousness of the undertaking. He would try his best to devote time and energy to it. Unfortunately, the Beatles were preparing to tour again—forever and always on the road—first to Germany, Japan, and the Philippines, then back to the States.

Shankar agreed to drop by Kinfauns within a few days.

One afternoon "Ravi came to my house for an hour or two, and he showed me how to get started," Harrison said. "One thing he said was, 'Do you read music?' I said 'No,' and my heart sank—I thought, 'I probably don't even deserve to waste his time.' But he said, 'Good—it will only confuse you anyway.'" The discipline of the ragas was based on an oral tradition. "The moment we started, the feelings I got were of his patience, compassion, and humility," Harrison said. "He wasn't grudging at all, and he wasn't flash about it, either." Shankar taught him the proper use of the pick (the *Misra*), downstrokes (*da*), upstrokes (*ra*), up-and-down motions (*diri diri*), and sets of exercises on the scales, *da ra diri diri*. He demonstrated *Krintan*, the technique of hitting a note above the one you intend to finish on, linking the sounds. He taught Harrison to bend the strings (*Meend*)—"murder on your fingers," Harrison said. At one point, the telephone rang. Harrison stood to answer it, stepping casually over the sitar. Shankar whacked his leg. You must show the instrument proper respect, he said.

He was beginning to glimpse the hectic life of a Beatle. He sensed Harrison's dread of being hurled into the mania again. How could a person under so much pressure ever slow down enough to develop the necessary discipline to become even just adequate on the sitar? Still, Shankar maintained his commitment to the young man. He made Harrison promise to come to India once the Beatles' tour was over.

In time, the cynics' view of the Harrison-Shankar relationship—and there were many cynics in both men's orbits—posed Shankar as an opportunist, exploiting Harrison for money (Shankar was often on shaky ground, financially; he went bankrupt three times). The cynics said that Harrison, insecure in the Beatles, used Shankar to forge a new musical identity. On some level, these dynamics may well have been in play, but to reduce a lifelong friendship as deep as the one shared by these men to a mere transactional exchange is to ignore the men's complexities as well as the complex nature of friendship.

"I felt strongly that there was a beautiful soul in him, and recognized one quality which I always have valued enormously and which is considered the principal one in our culture—humility," Shankar said.

Muhammad Ali had long ago decided he couldn't afford to be humble. "Where do you think I would be next week if I didn't know how to shout and holler and make the public sit up and take notice?" he said. "I would be poor for one thing, and I would probably be down in Louisville, Kentucky, my hometown, washing windows or running an elevator and saying, 'Yes, suh' and 'No, suh' and knowing my place."

If anything had humbled him, it was his poor showing on the military's IQ tests. Those embarrassing scores were once again under public scrutiny. Since the Liston fight in Lewiston, he had survived a turbulent few months. The divorce from Sonji. Doubts about the "Phantom Punch." An altercation with his father one night, when the old man showed up drunk, waving a knife, screaming about those thieving Muslims ruining his family's name. Neighbors had to restrain Ali to keep him from hurting his father.

And then there was the Floyd Patterson fight in Las Vegas, six months after Lewiston (on the second anniversary of the Kennedy assassination). In his second heavyweight title defense, Ali taunted Patterson while pummeling him in the ring, "Come on, black man, fight for America." In the buildup to the bout, Patterson had questioned Ali's ability to be a role model and refused to call him by his Muslim name. Ali dubbed his opponent the "white man's Black man." Round after round he rocked Patterson with straight right hands, shouting, "What's my name? What's my name?" Under siege since announcing his allegiance to

Allah, and since Malcolm's murder, Ali was exhibiting a cruelty he'd not shown before. (Ali won the bout by TKO in the twelfth round.)

On Thursday, February 17, 1966, Local Draft Board 47 in Louisville was rumored to be preparing an announcement of his eligibility for military service. Until this week, his low IQ score had disqualified him. But with the war heating up in Vietnam, with the army in need of more recruits, standards had been changed—nakedly dropped—so more young men would be available to the draft.

At around this time, the Nation of Islam announced it was forming an organization, Main Bout, Inc., to manage the promotional rights to Ali's fights. The sports world recoiled; the Muslims, the Negroes, were trying to control boxing.

Suddenly Ali's draft status was under review (an FBI memo later revealed that J. Edgar Hoover had personally ordered agents to see what could be done about him).

Since splitting with Sonji (marriage would have given him another exemption from the draft), he had abandoned the Chicago apartment and spent most of his time in Miami, in what he called "Spooktown," in the house at Northwest Fifteenth Court. That's where he was early in the afternoon on February 17 when word came from Louisville: 1-A.

On the front lawn, with children playing all around him, he told a growing circle of newsmen,

> For two years the Army told everybody I was a nut[,] and I was ashamed. And now they decide I am a wise man. They embarrassed my parents. . . . Even my ex-wife was ashamed. Yeah, it bothered me a bit. Now, without ever testing me to see if I am wiser or worser than before, they decide I can go in the Army. . . . I can't understand how they do this to me. Why be anxious to take me—a man who pays the salary of at least 200,000 men a year? . . . me, who in two fights pays for six new jet planes? I'm fighting for the government every day. I'm laying my life on the line for the government every day. Nine out of ten soldiers would not want to be in my place in the ring. It's too dangerous.

For the rest of the afternoon, pacing his front porch, playing with neighbor kids, he sang softly, "How many roads must a man walk down / Before you call him a man?"

That night, his "Why me?" plea played on the *CBS Evening News with Walter Cronkite*. It appeared right after a segment featuring Dan Rather in Vietnam. Rather crouched in spiky bushes, wearing battle fatigues. He asked a frontline

American soldier what message he had for President Lyndon Johnson. "I'd just like to let him know that I'm behind him," the soldier said.

Ali earned no sympathy from an already hostile press. The "Black Benedict Arnold," one reporter called him. "Not since A. Hitler was stirring up a mess of trouble some 30 years ago has there been anyone to compare with our boy Cassius Clay when it comes to making enemies and having a bad influence on a lot of people," wrote another.

The next day, Sam Saxon reminded Ali that the Nation of Islam forbade Black men from fighting white men's wars. "You got nothing against those Viet Cong," he said. That's right, Ali agreed.

Later that day, on the phone, Ali told a writer from the *Chicago Daily News*, "I am a member of the Muslims and we don't go to no wars unless they are declared by Allah himself. I don't have no personal quarrel with those Viet Congs."

Next to his fighting motto, "Float like a butterfly / Sting like a bee" (coined by Bundini Brown), the "Viet Cong" statement was the one by which he would be most remembered.

A Michigan newspaper said that exempting Ali from the draft because he was a Muslim "makes as much sense as exempting members of the Ku Klux Klan."

Editorialists across the country noted Ali's contradictory responses to the draft notice: was he upset because war was against his religion or because he felt he was being singled out or because he wanted to keep earning money? And by the way, those Viet Cong with whom he had no quarrel? They were killing thousands of American boys each year.

In Miami, his buddies warned him that if he went in the army, some cracker sergeant from rural Georgia was liable to drop a grenade down his pants and blow his balls off.

✧

As reported in the *Chicago Daily News*, Ali said, "Those Vietcongs are not attacking me. All I know is that they are considered Asiatic Black people and I don't have no fight with Black people." For these words, the Illinois State Athletic Commission demanded that Ali come before them and apologize. If he did not apologize, the commission would not sanction his upcoming match, booked for Chicago, with Ernie Terrell.

The proceeding, held in downtown Chicago on February 25, 1966, looked exactly like what it was: a tribunal, a bank of hostile white officials sitting in judgment at a dais above a solitary Black man. Policemen lined the room.

Ali wore a dark suit, white shirt, and bow tie. He said, "First of all, I'm not here to make a showdown plea or apologize as the press has projected I will. My apology is only to apologize for what embarrassment and pressure may have been put on you, not me. I should have told these things to the government—the draft board—not the reporters. I didn't mean to insult anyone or the people with children, sons, in Vietnam."

Flabbergasted, chairman Joe Triner said, "Then you are not apologizing for the unpatriotic statement you made?"

"I'm not apologizing for anything like that because I don't have to."

At bottom, whatever lay behind Ali's refusal of the draft—vanity, fear and cowardice, conscience, confusion, or a combination of these—his appearance before the Illinois State Athletic Commission revealed the man's essence: he was a proud Black person insisting on his dignity in the face of massive white resistance.

Triner and Chicago mayor Richard Daley kept addressing him as "Mr. Clay."

"My name is Muhammad Ali," Muhammad Ali said in a measured, low voice.

Americans were setting fires around the world. In Watts and in Pleiku, Vietnam. Ali felt the heat. The Beatles, about to embark on a world tour, would feel it too.

Before leaving England, the band members spoke to journalist Maureen Cleave of London's *Evening Standard*. "[America's] a lousy country to be in where anyone who is Black is made to seem a dirty nigger," said McCartney, the nice one, the cute one. "There they [are] in America, all getting house-trained for adulthood with their indisputable principle of life: short hair equals men, long hair equals women. Well, we got rid of that little convention for them."

If anyone had remembered his words later, McCartney might have become the most hated Beatle in America. But by summertime, when the US press quoted Cleave's articles (courtesy of Epstein's PR man, hoping to pump up ticket sales for the tour), one of Lennon's statements had overshadowed his bandmate's. "Christianity will go," he'd said. "It will vanish and shrink. I needn't argue about that. I'm right and I will be proved right. We're more popular than Jesus now; I don't know which will go first—rock and roll or Christianity. Jesus was all right, but his disciples were thick and ordinary. It's them twisting it that ruins it for me."

By August, when the Beatles reached Memphis, Tennessee, their images would be melting in gas-fueled flames. Hooded Ku Klux Klansmen, defending Western Christianity, would toss hundreds of Beatle records, Beatle dolls, and Beatle wigs into soaring bonfires.

✿

"We were the generation who didn't suffer from the war and we didn't want to have to keep being told about Hitler," Harrison said. "We were more bright-eyed and hopeful for the future, breaking out of the Victorian mold of attitudes and poverty and hardship. . . . And then we bumped right into Vietnam."

Before boarding a flight to Munich on June 23, 1966, John Lennon told a British journalist, "Epstein [has] always tried to waffle on at us about Vietnam, so . . . George and I said [to him], 'Listen, when they ask next time, we're going to say we don't like the war and we think [America] should get out.'"

Hearing this, Epstein worried about trouble on tour—with good cause. Shortly after the band landed in Germany, Harrison received an anonymous letter stating, for no apparent reason, "You won't live beyond the next month."

Pattie Boyd remembered getting miserable phone calls and plaintive letters from Harrison, telling her how lonely he was. But then he'd plunge into hedonism. There were rules at home with the people you loved. On the road, it was always and forever Hamburg, where sex began.

In Japan, Harrison thought he'd traveled back in time to World War II. Policemen wearing gas masks and flashing rifles herded the crowds at the Beatles' concert venue. Lennon spoke out against the Vietnam War for the first time: "We think about [the war] every day, and we don't agree with it and we think it's wrong . . . That's all we can do . . . and say that we don't like it." Asked what he wanted in life, Lennon said, "Peace."

The band stopped next on Vietnam's doorstep: Ferdinand Marcos's Philippines. Formerly a Spanish, an American, and a Japanese colony, the entire country lived in lockdown. Marcos, an authoritarian kleptocrat, welcomed an opportunity to greet the Beatles, to prove he was a progressive fellow. Nine years later, his power more brutal than ever, he would host the "Thrilla in Manila," the third bout between Muhammad Ali and Joe Frazier.

The moment the Beatles deplaned in Manila, armed guards separated them from their bags (and their pot), and from Epstein and the rest of their crew, and shoved them into a car and took them to a boat in the Manila Harbor. It was that "hot/Catholic/gun/Spanish Inquisition attitude," Starr said. On the boat, they were surrounded by wealthy Filipinos, solicitous prostitutes, and security men. It was never entirely clear who their hosts were—government officials, concert promoters, or, as they came to suspect, a rival gang of entertainment moguls who wanted to be seen partying with the Beatles. After several angry phone calls, Epstein got the boys off the boat and into a hotel at four in the morning.

"[Before long] we were woken up by bangs on the door . . . and there was a lot of panic going on outside," Harrison said. "Somebody came into the room and said, 'Come on! You're supposed to be at the palace.' We said, 'What are you talking about?' . . . 'You're supposed to be at the palace! Turn on the television.' We did, and there it was, live from the palace. There was a huge line of people either side of the long marble corridor, with kids in their best clothing, and the TV commentator saying, 'And they're still not here yet' . . . We sat there in amazement. We couldn't believe it, and we just had to watch ourselves not arriving at the presidential palace."

Epstein had overlooked, ignored, or forgotten an official invitation—not a request—to deliver the band to a public gala sponsored by First Lady Imelda Marcos. She complained bitterly that these arrogant foreign musicians had snubbed her. Dozens of death threats arrived at the British embassy.

That afternoon, the band performed two concerts at the Rizal football stadium, designed to accommodate thirty thousand people. Well over two hundred thousand jammed the field—unscrupulous promoters had made a killing overselling it.

Surviving the shows, the Beatles then nearly failed to escape the country. The following morning, hotel staff refused to assist them, police declined to provide security escorts to the airport, the airport resembled an armed military camp, and no one helped the crew carry bags, equipment, and amplifiers. Suddenly the boys were surrounded by the same thugs who'd met them when they landed, the men who'd herded them onto the boat, now kicking, shoving, and shouting at them, "This is what happens when you insult the first lady."

"Mania was going on with people trying to grab us, and other people trying to hit us," Harrison recalled.

On the tarmac, Inland Revenue presented Epstein with a tax bill on the concert earnings, not part of the contract: a way of extorting the band's money. Mal Evans was badly beaten. Even after the Beatles had boarded their plane, there were long delays on the runway, snafus (real or not) with passports. Finally the aircraft lifted safely into the air.

Their life had become a "freak show," Lennon declared. A war zone.

"Who fucking needs this?" Harrison said.

Back in Britain, a journalist asked about the Beatles' plans. Harrison answered, "We're going to have a couple of weeks to recuperate before we go and get beaten up by the Americans."

✧

One by one, after Illinois canceled the Ali-Terrell fight, other US venues refused to come near Ali (under pressure from mayors and governors). It was a surprise, then, when the owner of the sixteen-thousand-seat Maple Leaf Gardens in Toronto offered his space. "I'm pleased that someone has finally looked at this as a sports event instead of something else," said Mike Malitz, manager of Ali's closed-circuit television rights through Main Bout, Inc. Malitz was an entertainment lawyer who sometimes worked with Allen Klein.

But Ernie Terrell backed out of the fight, citing irregularities in the contract. Word on the street was that Terrell's mob bosses couldn't fix it so they'd earn money outside the States and thus pressured him to renege on the deal.

In a speech in Chicago, Elijah Muhammad accused the United States of "robbing" Ali, impeding his chance to earn a living: "You want to make a bum of Muhammad Ali, but you won't if he sticks with Elijah." Since Muhammad's son Herbert was now skimming a third of Ali's income, Muhammad's outrage was as much financial as moral.

The journeyman George Chuvalo, a blocky brawler, stepped in to replace Ernie Terrell. The fight was scheduled for the night of March 29, 1966. A week before that, Ali flew to Louisville to address Draft Board 47. The board refused to change his classification but said he could file an appeal with Selective Service within ten days. In the meantime, he was free to leave the country to fight Chuvalo. "This whole thing has been disturbing to me," Ali said to newsmen outside the draft board offices. He wouldn't talk politics. As for the upcoming bout: "It's too bad the fight won't be carried on too many stations because a lot of people want to see me beat. It's always a possibility, too, because I'm human. I may be the greatest, but I'm also human."

He was referring to the fact that Main Bout had invited 280 North American venues to broadcast the closed-circuit feed, but only 32 had accepted. The American Legion and the Veterans of Foreign Wars announced boycotts of any theaters showing the fight. A theater in Cleveland considering the broadcast received a credible bomb threat. California politicians decreed a statewide blackout of the match "in deference to the many families that have loved ones fighting and dying in Vietnam." Though it went unstated, the reason other locations backed away was their refusal to work with a Black-owned promotion company. "Outbursts over [Ali's] draft status" were racist pretexts, a "means of killing two birds with one red, white, and blue stone," *Muhammad Speaks* accused the white power establishment.

On the day Talmadge Hayer, Norman 3X Butler, and Thomas 15X Johnson were found guilty of Malcolm X's murder (they would be sentenced to life in prison), Ali filed his draft appeal.

✧

Chuvalo lasted fifteen rounds. He gave Ali a little trouble in the ring but not nearly as much difficulty as Ali encountered after the fight trying to secure his next contest. Main Bout found no takers. Arenas were skittish. Politicians were happy to grandstand at the Muslims' expense.

Ali pretended not to care. "They want to stop me from fighting. They done run me out of the country . . . I don't want to go . . . [but] it's a world title I got, not a USA title, and it can be defended anywhere in the world," he said. "This is more than money. I'm not disturbed and nervous. Why should I be? In a few hours I could fly to another country, in the East, in Africa, where people love me. Millions all over the world want to see me. Why should I worry about losing a few dollars?"

With the States a closed shop, Main Bout took Ali's next three fights to Europe—just as the Beatles were preparing for their most controversial tour.

Training in London, Ali told a tabloid writer one day, "The American press keeps me in shape because if they do this to me now, when I'm world champion, I know how devilish they're going to be if I lose."

In Europe, the closed-circuit television market was better than in the States. Ali's victorious outing against the Brit Henry Cooper, less than two months after the Chuvalo bout, was the first athletic event beamed from Europe on Intelsat 1, an Early Bird satellite. Ali predicted his next two fights, one in England, the other in Germany, would be witnessed around the world as well as in outer space. "Don't laugh," he said. "I know [the aliens] are out there and I know who they are. Some people think it's swamp fire, but it's flying saucers. They saw my fight in Toronto and they were at Lewiston, Maine."

He said, "Boxing is nothing, just satisfying some bloodthirsty people. I'm no longer Cassius Clay, a Negro from Kentucky. I belong to the world, the Black world. I'll always have a home in Pakistan, in Algeria, in Ethiopia."

✧

In the days before the Beatles' 1966 US tour kicked off, Brian Epstein became aware of how much trouble Lennon's comments on Christianity had caused. *Datebook,* a teen magazine in the States, had picked up Maureen Cleave's articles and run a headline: "JOHN LENNON SAYS: 'BEATLES MORE POPULAR THAN JESUS!'" Massachusetts radio station WAQY banned Beatle records and sponsored a community bonfire for Fab Four novelty items ("to show them they cannot get away with this sort of thing"). KZEE in Weatherford, Texas, "damned" Beatle music "eternally." In Reno, Nevada, KCBN broadcast anti-Beatles editorials. A KKK Grand Dragon in South Carolina nailed Beatle albums to a wooden cross and set it on fire.

Lennon was unrepentant. "What I said stands," he told Epstein. He wasn't going to lie about what he felt. "We have been Beatles as best we ever will be— those four jolly lads," he said. "But we're not those people anymore."

Drolly, Harrison asked, "Why can't we bring all this out in the open? Why is there all this stuff about blasphemy? If Christianity is as good as they say it is, it should stand up to a bit of discussion."

Epstein considered canceling the tour. He issued a formal statement to the American press: "What [Lennon] meant was that he was astonished that in the last fifty years the Church of England, and therefore Christ, had suffered a decline in interest. He did not mean to boast about the Beatles' fame." This satisfied no one.

Again he urged Lennon to make a public apology. Lennon refused. "I didn't want to talk because I thought they'd kill me," he said. '[T]hey take things so seriously [in America]. I mean, they shoot you and then they realize that it wasn't that important."

On August 11, on the twenty-seventh floor of Chicago's Astor Towers, TV and newspapermen were preparing for the usual Beatles press conference. Epstein called the four together for a last-minute meeting in his suite. He poured them all drinks. Then he turned to Lennon. "Look, you do realize the implications of this, don't you? You can't go out there with a few one-liners. It's not a joke, and it's not just you getting yourself off the hook. Either we have to get positive press out of this or the tour is going to be called off. We're not talking, John, about you rescuing your own reputation. We're talking about you saving the group's tour." He paused. "I fear the Beatles might be assassinated during the tour."

Carefully, Lennon set his drink on the glass tabletop in front of him. Then he burst into tears. "I didn't mean to cause all this," he said, shaking. He said he'd do "anything."

How had he created "another little piece of hate in the world?"

In the event, with his mates fidgeting nervously beside him, he bowed his head before the microphones. To the gathered press he muttered, "If I'd have said, 'Television is more popular than Jesus,' I might have got away with it." In the back of the room Epstein cringed. The stubborn fool was going to make things worse. "I'm not anti-God, anti-Christ, or anti-religion. I was not knocking it. I was not saying we are greater or better. I think it's a bit silly. If they don't like us, why don't they just not buy the records?"

This wasn't working.

"I just said what I said and it was wrong. Or it was taken wrong. And now it's all this."

"But are you prepared to apologize?" someone asked.

"I wasn't saying what they're saying I was saying." Now he didn't look abject. He looked like he wanted to hit somebody. "I'm sorry I said it—really. I never meant it to be a lousy anti-religious thing. I apologize if that will make you happy. I still don't know quite what I've done. I've tried to tell you what I did do, but if you want me to apologize, if that will make you happy, then—okay, I'm sorry."

"Okay, can you just actually say to the camera how sorry you are?"

Christ! The Beatles gave one another knowing, bitter smiles. Nothing would ever be enough.

In Chicago (reeking of the stockyards), Detroit, Cleveland, Washington, and Philadelphia, the Beatles went through the motions, and so did the fans—rote screaming, shouting, and fainting. In Cleveland's Municipal Stadium, three thousand people dropped from the stands onto the field, rushing the stage. "Run for your lives!" security personnel called to the band. The boys dropped their instruments and headed for a trailer behind home plate.

Five days later, as their plane descended into Memphis, Lennon looked glumly out the window. He said, "So this is where all the Christians come from." Nothing broke the gloom until Harrison said, "Send John out first. He's the one they want."

But on the ground it was no joke. A robed Klansman told a television reporter: "We're known as a terror organization, and we have ways and means to stop [the Beatles]."

The place resembled a Third World country controlled by an army of white men waving guns. Police loaded the bandmates into an armored car and told them to lie down, fearing snipers. Protesters lined the route to the hotel, shaking fists and hateful signs. As the car pulled under the hotel awning, a small, blond-haired boy, eleven or twelve, banged on the back window, startling McCartney. "I will never forget . . . [he] barely came up to the window, [but he] was screaming at me through the plate glass with such vehemence."

When they took the stage that night they huddled closer together than usual. Epstein scanned the rafters for gunmen. The Beatles began a smiling performance.

During Harrison's "If I Needed Someone," a shot echoed. *Was* it a shot? "My heart stopped," McCartney said. He and Harrison edged automatically toward Lennon, to see if he was okay. Someone had thrown a cherry bomb onto the stage. As if war had been declared, the Beatles spontaneously kicked into the most spirited performance they'd given in years, raging back at the crowd with the fury of their 4/4 drive, their punch, their bite, and their unbreakable harmony. It was a bit of the old Hamburg. But then a string of firecrackers went off, and they just rushed through the rest of the set, ready to abandon the sweltering arena as quickly as possible.

In the days ahead, they were nearly electrocuted twice onstage, first at Cincinnati's Crosley Field, where a downpour overwhelmed the canvas covering, exposing wires. In St. Louis, McCartney said, the stage resembled a "mud hut in the middle of somewhere." They canceled the Cincinnati gig, despite hostile screams of "We want the Beatles!" rising over rain bursts, because McCartney was so afraid of the sloppy wiring that he vomited in the wings.

Though it will not appear in history books, August 23, 1966, was perhaps as emblematic of the era as any day in 1960s America. At two o'clock on that afternoon, in Louisville, Kentucky, Muhammad Ali, carrying a copy of the Koran and a copy of Elijah Muhammad's *Message to the Blackman in America*, entered the US Post Office, Court House, and Custom House to try to convince a sixty-six-year-old white judge that he was a sincere conscientious objector who should not be shipped to Vietnam.

At that same moment, in Manhattan, at the New York Hilton on Sixth Avenue, Secretary of Defense Robert McNamara was addressing a convention of the Veterans of Foreign Wars, defending the government's new draft policies.

On the street outside, members of a group called Youth Against War and Fascism marched and chanted, carrying signs: "Bring the GIs Home Now." "Big Firms Get Rich, GIs Get Killed."

Also on the streets, surrounding the Warwick Hotel, on Fifty-Fourth, across Sixth Avenue and around the corner from the Hilton, a crowd five times the size of the antiwar protesters waited to catch a glimpse of the Beatles. The Beatles were inside telling the press that the United States should get out of Vietnam.

"War is wrong and it's obvious it's wrong. And that's all that needs to be said about it," Harrison spoke into a taped-together microphone. Roughly half the journalists applauded.

In Louisville, Muhammad Ali told Judge Lawrence Grauman,

It's true that I was raised as a Baptist and while being raised as a Baptist I never understood the teachings of the Christian preacher and I never understood why Heaven was in the sky and I never understood why Hell was under the ground and I never understood why the so-called Negroes had to turn their cheeks and have to take all the punishment while everyone else defends themselves and fought back. [But when] I went to the mosque . . . the Minister . . . was preaching on the subject of why we are called Negroes. . . . He said the Russians have names such as Mr. Krushchev and Africans have names such as Lumumba. We call ourselves Mr. Tree, Mr. Bird, Mr. Clay . . . and he said these were names of our slave master, and by me being an intelligent man and the Lord blessing me with five senses, I have to accept it.

In Louisville Ali said: "I'll die right now in this courtroom, because I know this is the truth I'm talking."

In New York Robert McNamara said to the Veterans of Foreign Wars: "I do not believe that the qualifying standard for military service should now be lowered" (in fact, this was precisely the policy he had just approved). "What I do believe is that through the application of advanced educational and medical techniques we can salvage tens of thousands of these men, each year, first for productive military careers and later for productive roles in society."

On Sixth Avenue, protesters chanted, "McNamara, Secretary of Aggression!" Around the corner, fans shouted for the Beatles.

In Washington, Representative Paul Fino, Republican from New York, had this advice for Judge Grauman as he considered Muhammad Ali's request to be exempted from military service: "I . . . hope very much that Cassius Clay will fight his next championship in a rice paddy."

Just another summer day in the good ol' USA.

The Beatles' dynamic, already fraying before the tour, most evident in the Harrison-McCartney struggle, suffered further on the road. For all their musical chemistry, McCartney and Harrison were poles apart in personality and ambition. The playwright and musical composer Lionel Bart, observing the Beatles in action, said, "It was clear from the start that show business ran deep in Paul's veins and he was committed to a lifetime on the stage." The tour had ground him down, as it had the others, but he took the difficulties in stride as part of the life he had chosen.

Not so Harrison. "We've had four years of doing what everybody else wants us to do," he told California radio station KRLA. "Everything the Beatles have done so far has been rubbish."

When asked at a press conference what directions he might take in the future—was he going to try other new instruments now that he'd learned to play the sitar?—he bristled: "I haven't learned to play the sitar. I mean, Ravi Shankar hasn't *learned* to play it and he's been playing it thirty-five years."

"Ooh!" McCartney teased him.

Ren Grevatt, a reporter from *Melody Maker* who'd accompanied the Beatles from city to city, wrote, "I've noticed that George Harrison is getting deeper and deeper every day and will probably end up being a bald recluse monk. He's trying to figure out life, but don't let this sound mocking—he is very serious."

"Can I please go home to my mummy now, please can I?" Starr whispered in the band's small dressing room at Dodger Stadium, following their performance. Outside, for over two hours, police had been swinging batons to move crowds off the field. Fans had damaged the Beatles' getaway car, knocking it out of commission. The boys were in limbo until another van could be found.

They were wearier than they had ever been—wearier than they'd thought it possible for young men to be. By this point, bruised and stiff from so many cramped accommodations, even McCartney agreed he needed an indefinite break from the madness. "We didn't make a formal announcement that we were going to stop touring," Starr said. But as they landed in San Francisco, in fog and rain, the four of them knew their show in Candlestick Park on August 29 would be their last. At least for a while. They would not return next year to the United States.

On the way to the concert, their bus driver nearly got lost in residential neighborhoods, trying to outrun chasing fans. Once safely inside their dressing room, changed into their crisp Edwardian suits, the band had to endure another informal press conference. *Did Lennon consciously borrow from baroque composers?* "I don't know what baroque is," Lennon snapped. "I wouldn't know a Handel from a Gretel."

On the field, the national anthem blared through the stadium's PA system. Someone unfurled a banner over a railing: "Lennon Saves."

Right before taking the stage, McCartney asked one of the crew members to tape the show on a small cassette recorder for him—a personal keepsake of the Beatles' final public performance. Each of the Beatles carried a small camera with him to capture the moment—they were stunned witnesses too of this wild phenomenon. As it was possibly coming to an end, they wanted souvenirs.

Bay breezes lashed them as they ran from the dugout to the stage. The crowd's screams were "like clouds bursting," Joan Baez would later recall. The Beatles plugged in and began a thirty-three minute set with an uninspired version of Chuck Berry's "Rock and Roll Music." The amps kept popping as if they might explode. Later Lennon described the performance as a "puppet show."

Summer was over. So were the Beatles as a live act. They would never again play together in America. Though their finest work still lay ahead of them in the studio, they were in essence finished as a performing unit, driven from the stage by the insanity—well-meaning and malicious—welling up from the center of Western culture. (Over thirty years later, Harrison's second wife, Olivia, swore he was still suffering post-traumatic stress from those days.)

After Muhammad Ali's September 1966 bout in Germany, he would fight in Houston two months later, winning a third-round TKO against thirty-three-year-old veteran Cleveland Williams, his fifth title defense of the year. Less than two months later, on February 6, 1967, he would defend his title again, in the same venue, the Houston Astrodome, against Terrell. He then would stage one more fight, defeating Zora Folley in Madison Square Garden on March 22, 1967, before vanishing from the ring for over three and a half years, driven away by uniquely American psychoses—and the power of the US government.

Main Bout, Inc., folded, bowing to the reality that a Black-owned organization would not be allowed to assume too much authority in the States.

Within a few years, the US public had projected onto Muhammad Ali and the Beatles a skein of hopes, fears, and lusts. Together, the boxer and the singers had arrived as saviors, buoyant, laughing, offering unfettered joy in the murk of a national tragedy. They surprised and delighted audiences by revealing nuances and depths no one expected. More than mere entertainers, more than fads, they turned out to be artists in their fields, influencing other fields. They backed up their boasts, fulfilled their promises. They pleased some, angered others, by challenging traditions and mores (in music, sports, fashion, sex, religion, and class)—all titillating and fun, until it wasn't anymore. That national tragedy they appeared to extinguish, the JFK assassination, would not disperse. The violence of it, the madness of it, deepened throughout the middle of the decade, a festering wound. (Think of Sonny Liston's face in 1964.) Up above, satellites spread the madness across the globe. The Beatles and Ali had promised delight; instead they had delivered controversies. Ali and the Beatles were the most visible faces on the planet, and they had to own the mess. They represented what we had *made* them represent (despite warning us they didn't have to be what we wanted them to be). Now we needed scapegoats.

Thus, in their prime, the Beatles and Muhammad Ali saw their careers blocked. At play was what Malcolm X described as Western malignancy: intolerance in its many horrid forms, intolerance fueled by grievance and the desire for instant gratification. At the end of 1966 the Beatles and Ali might have been on their way to becoming ghosts. In the case of Ali, he might have lived up to what F. Scott Fitzgerald wrote in the notes to his last, unfinished novel: "There are no second acts in American lives. There are no second chances." But Ali would prove Fitzgerald wrong.

As for the Fab Four, their future together was not guaranteed after their tour ended in San Francisco. Flying back to England after the concert in Candlestick Park, George Harrison settled into his seat and closed his eyes. "Right—that's it," he said. "I'm not a Beatle anymore."

PART TWO

The Inner Light

CHAPTER 4

Within You

Philip Goldberg, author of *American Veda*, a useful history of Eastern spirituality in the West, wrote—hyperbolically but not entirely falsely—that when the Beatles went to India it "may have been the most momentous spiritual retreat since Jesus spent those forty days in the wilderness." "Our understanding and practice of spirituality would never be the same," he said. "[The] tectonic plates of Western culture shifted."

But it was really George Harrison who went to India. The other Beatles followed him there. Lennon went on a genuine search for meaning; as was his pattern, he quickly grew bored and embittered with the experience. Starr went to be with his buddies—he was a band member in the truest sense of the word. McCartney went to see what he could see but also to keep tabs on the Harrison-Lennon connection. Was he about to lose his partner to foreign influences?

No one was more pleased than McCartney when, near the end of the 1960s, Lennon disavowed gurus. Pointedly, during band rehearsals in the recording studio, McCartney laughed about Lennon's approach to the Maharishi and said, "It just wasn't you." He had finally wrested his partner back from his younger rival. When Lennon wrote "Across the Universe," a meditative song (featuring the chant, "Jai Guru Deva, Om"—"Glory to the teacher of God"), McCartney wrote "Let It Be," a prayerful tune praising "Mother Mary"—his own mother, he was quick to say, but the Christian undertones were clear. As the music made plain, a religious war (more broadly, a cultural war) had erupted in the Beatles—a fight for the soul of John Lennon. Ultimately, McCartney and Harrison both lost their grip on the man. Yoko Ono and drug addiction would take him away from them.

In the meantime, as Lennon pursued "ego-death" on LSD, McCartney asserted his ego, his leadership, his musicianship, and kept the Beatles afloat commercially, writing hits such as "Lady Madonna" and "Hey Jude," moving the group past the darkness of the '66 tour, the death threats, and the unsettling controversies. More than anything, the release of the album *Sergeant Pepper's Lonely Hearts Club Band* in the summer of 1967 reasserted the Beatles' place at the top of the pop world. Critics and musical historians agreed with the listening public that *Pepper* was a peak—in its vision, its musicality, its technical innovations, and its ambition. It established rock music, and the long-playing album, as an art form to be taken seriously. It was a personal triumph for Paul McCartney, who had shepherded the project to completion and written most of the LP's songs.

Notably, George Harrison was almost absent from the album. Mentally and spiritually he had remained in India. His major contribution to *Pepper* (offered after the band had rejected one of his earlier songs) sounded like nothing else on it: "Within You Without You," a classical Indian raga based around a snippet of a Ravi Shankar melody featuring Harrison on tambura and sitar—and none of the other Beatles. McCartney wasn't even in the country when the recording was completed.

It was McCartney's commercial instinct, his love of show business, of the British music hall (the spirit behind *Pepper*) that kept the Beatles selling records between 1967 and 1970. But it was Harrison's spiritual turn toward India that kept them culturally relevant, themselves gurus to a large portion of the generation born in the late 1940s and 1950s, a generation increasingly distressed by the materialistic, colonial legacies of the West. In 1967 and 1968, psychedelia (the Beatles in their *Pepper* suits) joined the sound of the sitar and the smell of incense as manifestations of spiritual pursuit. The Beatles, wearing shoulder-length hair and flowing beards—Savile Row sadhus—appeared to be modern-day prophets. Goldberg writes: "In the late 1960s . . . a constellation of forces came together—mass communication and ease of travel; social unrest; war and nuclear anxiety; psychedelic drugs; and alienated . . . youngsters with the time and money to explore new ways of being. The Beatles' journey to the banks of the Ganges blew the gates between East and West wide open. In a flash, more Americans learned about Indian spirituality than in all the previous centuries."

Of course, the West's brushes with the Vedas long preceded George Harrison, paving the path he would take. In the modern era, in the nineteenth century,

British colonialists translated Vedic scriptures. (The East India Company hired Sanskrit scholars to better understand the marketplace it was exploiting.) The translations, shipped across the Atlantic, changed the lives of Ralph Waldo Emerson, Henry David Thoreau, and Walt Whitman—early American countercultural figures.

A segment of the American psyche had long been eager for the arrival, on US shores, of actual gurus from the East, when they began to appear in the late nineteenth and early twentieth centuries. "Despite more than fifty years of interest in Indian thought, few New Englanders had met a Hindu," wrote an excited Bostonian, after hearing Swami Vivekananda address a conference called the World Parliament of Religions in Chicago in 1893. Vivekananda made a powerful impression. He was "a handsome monk in [an] orange robe," gushed Harriet Monroe, the editor of *Poetry* magazine. He began addressing the audience: "Sisters and Brothers of America"—after which there was applause reportedly lasting for at least two minutes. "I am proud to belong to a religion that has taught the world both tolerance and universal acceptance," he went on to say. "We accept all religions to be true." And then he quoted what Goldberg calls "a traditional hymn": "As the different streams, having their sources in different places, all mingle their water in the sea, so, O Lord, the different paths . . . crooked or straight, all lead to Thee."

Eventually one of Vivekananda's followers, Swami Prabhavananda, would form the Vedanta Society of Southern California, attracting Hollywood notables such as Aldous Huxley, Christopher Isherwood, and Gerald Heard. The society further spread Vivekananda's teachings among Westerners. "The struggle to become . . . divine, to reach God, and see God . . . constitutes the religion of the Hindus," Vivekananda said. William James, a founder of American psychology and author of *The Varieties of Religious Experience*, studied with Vivekananda, befriended him, and considered Vedanta "the paragon of all monastic systems."

After Vivekananda, Paramahansa Yogananda has had the profoundest effect on the West—to date, his *Autobiography of a Yogi* has sold over four million copies in English. He first came to the United States in 1920 to speak at a conference organized by the Unitarian Association. At the conference he told audiences in packed venues that religion was less about dogmas and beliefs than "God-consciousness, or the realization of God both within and without." In that sense, he said, there is only one religion for there is only one God: "In reality, God and man are one, and the separation is only apparent." Through yoga and meditation, we free the "spiritual self" from "physical and mental distractions" by redistributing the "life electricity" within us, discharging it in the "form of light" within our minds.

George Eastman (founder of the Kodak Company), Leopold Stokowski (conductor of the Philadelphia Orchestra), botanist-horticulturist Luther Burbank, and Margaret Woodrow Wilson (President Wilson's eldest child) numbered among Yogananda's disciples.

Eventually Yogananda settled in Los Angeles, opening the Self-Realization Fellowship, selling his *Autobiography* through mail order, and training Sri Daya Mata to take his place when he died. He appreciated the marriage between "spiritual India" and "efficient America," he said. He passed away of a coronary occlusion in 1952—but was resurrected in 1967, at George Harrison's behest, on the cover of *Sergeant Pepper*.

In September 1966, shaken from the American tour, Harrison had traveled to India with his wife—ostensibly to take further sitar lessons with Ravi Shankar. "I do not believe that sitar and the world of music was anything more than a pretext for a much deeper spiritual connection between Ravi Shankar and the Beatle," said Vivek Bharat Ram, a friend and student of Shankar's. "It was a unique relationship that can only be explained by Samskara [the Hindu concept of lives linked from one birth/death cycle to another]. I am convinced that [they] were connected in a previous life for them to so quickly establish rapport and familiarity. . . . These two had no blood ties, no cultural or community affiliations and were vastly different personalities. So there can be no simple, rational explanation to define the relationship. We were all aware of its special nature."

"It was quite amazing to see the two constantly holding hands and hugging each other. They were very physically demonstrative about the affection they had for each other," said Vivek's brother, Arun.

"My heart melted with love for [George, when he arrived in Bombay (now Mumbai)]," Shankar later remembered. "[His] quest was beautiful, although at the same time it was more like a child's; he wasn't fully matured. . . . Nevertheless his interest in and curiosity for our traditions, mostly in the fields of religion, philosophy and music, was quite genuine." In teaching Harrison, Shankar could become the engaged, present father that he, Shankar, never had. (As a very young man, Shankar did have a son, Shubho, with whom he was not particularly close and whom he rarely saw.)

And though Harrison cherished his parents, he found in Shankar a figure to demolish the hypocrisies he'd witnessed in childhood. "[In India,] Ravi and his brother gave me a lot of books by some wise men," he said.

One of the books which was by Swami Vivekananda said *if there is a God, you must SEE him. And . . . if there is a soul, you must PERCEIVE it. Otherwise, it is better NOT to believe. It's better to be an outspoken atheist than a hypocrite. . . .* I had been brought up . . . well, they had tried to raise me a Catholic. They had told you just believe what they're telling you and not have the direct experience. This for me; going to India and having somebody saying, "no, you can't believe ANYTHING until you have direct perception of it" . . . *I thought, WOW, fantastic, at last. . . somebody who makes some sense.*

"Ravi used to say that George was far more Indian than foreign," recalled Shankar's widow, Sukanya. "And we were all surprised at how comfortable he used to be with Indian food and sitting cross-legged on the floor. One almost forgot he was a foreigner. And he was really a devoted Hindu."

Shankar had advised Harrison to travel incognito to avoid the press. He grew a mustache and cut his hair short. He and Pattie Boyd registered at the Taj Mahal Hotel in Bombay under the names Mr. and Mrs. Sam Wells. The ruse worked at first. He was able to visit the holy sanctorum inside the Venkateswara Temple in Tirupati, a pilgrimage site off-limits to non-Hindus. Temple officials did not recognize him; they merely tried to prevent him from entering because he was a foreigner. Coolly, he replied, "But I am a Hindu and an Indian." "What is your name?" asked one of the guards. "Krishna." He said this with such conviction that no one questioned him.

The sitar lessons, administered by Shankar or by one of his advanced students, Shambhu Das, were painstaking and slow. Back in England, Harrison had quickly grasped the fundamentals of the instrument, as well as the broad structural concepts of Indian classical music, but he and Shankar both understood it would take him years to absorb the sitar's nuances, to develop improvisational techniques. There was another challenge too. "My hips were killing me from sitting on the floor, and so Ravi brought a yoga teacher to start showing me the physical exercises," Harrison said.

And then his cover got blown. Somehow, the press discovered that a "hero of popland" was in their midst. Hordes of fans, girls in saris, swirled beneath his hotel balcony. "What do they want?" he cried to his wife. "I am not God!"

Reporters tried to wrangle interviews with him. He pleaded for privacy. "I'm not pretending," he said. "I am not here for just a joke. I have specially taken away the time from the Beatles to learn sitar from Ravi Shankar. I cannot learn if I go about signing autographs . . . I am not a Beatle all the time just as you are not a journalist all the time."

Finally Shankar convinced him to hold a press conference in his hotel room to mollify the reporters. This dynamic would be repeated on Harrison's 1974 US tour—Harrison increasingly hostile to the press, Shankar playing go-between.

The *Times of India* found Harrison sitting cross-legged in his room, dressed in white pajamas and a fawn-colored silk kurta. Throughout the interview, he insisted he should not be the focus of so much attention—why were so many young Indians unaware of the splendid cultural traditions they had inherited? "All the great philosophers of the West have looked to the East," he said. "The ancient Indians and the Chinese were far more advanced than their counterparts in the West." And further: "I believe much more in the religions of India than in anything I ever learned from Christianity."

He seemed ashamed of his role in popularizing the sitar in rock music. "[I don't want it to be a] bandwagon gimmick, with everybody leaping aboard it just to be 'in' . . . I really want to learn the music properly and take it seriously."

The press conference did not succeed in keeping reporters off his back, so Shankar made hasty arrangements to get "Mr. and Mrs. Sam Wells" out of the city. In the next few days, they visited the Ellora Caves in Maharashtra, a complex of monasteries and temples—Hindu, Buddhist, and Jain—carved into towering basalt cliffs, dating to 600–1000 BCE. The god and goddess of destruction and creation—Shiva and Parvati—cavorted vividly across the walls, often assuming explicitly erotic poses. "Making love, fighting with demons"—Boyd was amazed. This was not religion as she knew it.

Shankar spirited them away to Dal Lake in Srinagar, to a fleet of five houseboats there. They stayed for a week, Shankar sharing his quarters with his long-time lover, a younger woman named Kamala Chakravarty (he was unhappily married, in an arrangement made when he was young). The setting was placid and remote, the water clear, traffic nonexistent. "To suddenly find yourself in a place where it feels like 5000 BC is wonderful," Harrison recalled. "It was the first feeling I'd had of being liberated from being a Beatle. . . . I'd wake up in the morning and a little Kashmiri fellow, Mr. Butt"—the owner of the houseboats—"would bring us tea and biscuits and I could hear Ravi in the next room, practicing."

"They were polite, down to earth, and behaved so well with all of us," said Ghulam Rasool Dar, at the time a nineteen-year-old boatman on the lake. "They would sit for hours plucking the strings of their sitars. During sunrise and sunset, they wanted to enjoy the more peaceful settings—and what better place than the middle of Dal Lake? I would row the boat every morning and evening, sometimes for an hour and sometimes for two, and they would be busy with their sitars. All they wanted from me was that I row the boat gently so they were not disturbed."

One night, Mr. Butt invited his guests to dinner at his house. He was Muslim; the women of his household, who had prepared the food along with a castrati cook ("fixed" so he could work in the kitchen), were not allowed to mingle with the men. Separately, Boyd and Kamala met the women for tea. The language barriers and rigid social customs did not detract from the amazement of the occasion: Hindus, Muslims, and Westerners sharing an ancient ritual.

In a quiet display of reverse colonialism, Harrison apprenticed himself to his Indian companions.

Finally Shankar wanted to show his new friends his birthplace—Benares, on the banks of the holy River Ganga. There Harrison and Boyd witnessed bodies burning on the ghats, gray ashes dispersing into the river's muddy currents; up above, on the streets of the city, the cedar-scented market stalls bursting with red and yellow spice mounds, damp smells of fish, the laughter and movements of the living; and weaving among the stalls and among the ghats, nameless sadhus looking like vagrants.

There was chanting, the crackling of flames, a hint of hashish in the air.

Shankar had taught Harrison a Sanskrit phrase, *Vasudhaiva kutumbakam*, from the *Upanishads*—"The world is one family," Hinduism's highest moral value, Shankar said.

Yogananda in his *Autobiography of a Yogi* wrote: "Krishna . . . is always shown in Hindu art . . . [playing an] enrapturing song that recalls to their true home the human souls wandering in *maya*-delusion." This became George Harrison's major aim in making music. Back in London, he listened to Paul McCartney describe his idea for the next Beatle album: "Let's develop alter egos . . . [and] actually take on the personas of [a music hall] band." Harrison stared at his mate as if he was crazy.

If Lyndon Johnson hadn't signed the Immigration Act of 1965, the history of Hinduism in the West would have looked much different than it does today.

Initially, Prabhupada had intended to remain in America for only two months, until his visa ran out. The Immigration Act lifted restrictions on Asian immigration and allowed him a longer stay—time enough to turn the old Second Avenue storefront, Matchless Gifts, into a small Indian temple. A signboard out front stated: "Classes on *Bhagavad-gita*, Monday, Wednesday, and Friday, 7 p.m.; Chant *Hare Krishna Hare Krishna Krishna Krishna Hare Hare Hare Rama Hare Rama Rama Rama Hare Hare* . . . and your life will be sublime!"

Inside, the fragrance of incense, of dark brown chickpea stew, eggplant and tomato curry, red peppers, creamed spinach with milk curd, yellow rice, and golden potatoes. In the front of the room, seated before a wall poster of a smiling blue-skinned god, a frail old man in saffron robes intoned, so softly his scraggly young listeners strained to hear, "There are eighty-four species of life. That means eight million and four hundred thousand forms of different varieties of life. The purpose of human life is to get out of these species. . . . All of us are suffering the pangs of *janma-mrityu-jara-vyadhi*—birth, death, old age, and disease. An intelligent man can stop this process. . . . And the whole thing begins with chanting and hearing."

Patiently, Prabhupada explained, "Krishna's name is not different from Krishna Himself. Therefore, as soon as my tongue touches the holy name of Krishna, I am immediately associating with [Him]."

Since so many of Prabhupada's young followers were aspiring musicians, his insistence on sound as the essence of God caused the greatest excitement in the weekly meetings. People flocked to hear him clapping his finger cymbals or tapping the *mrdanga*, the deep, hypnotic drum. Irving Halpern, an East Village flute-maker, said, "Whenever a new musician [stopped by] . . . [Prabhupada] would extend his arms. . . . I mean, there was this gesture that every musician knows. You just know when someone else wants you to play with them . . . and this very basic kind of musician communication was there with him."

Jazz players in local clubs began improvising melodies around the Hare Krishna chant—they'd heard it on the street, passing by the storefront, or walking past the Swami's devotees. At one point, Prabhupada paid to make a limited-edition recording of the chant. His followers passed copies of the record around the Village. They even sent one of the 45s to London, to the Beatles, not believing it would reach them—but why not?

Druggies composed a significant portion of the Swami's cortege. The neighborhood was swarming with addicts. Stuck there, on trashy streets smelling of urine and shit, Prabhupada had no choice but to appeal to the suffering souls he saw. The risk was that they would never develop the committed discipline to follow God for life. But Prabhupada's mission was to spread the word—Krishna would handle the rest.

He asked his adherents to print flyers: "STAY HIGH FOREVER! No More Coming Down. Practice Krishna Consciousness . . . TRANSCENDENTAL SOUND VIBRATION."

One night, several members of Timothy Leary's Millbank Colony—an LSD retreat in upstate New York—drove to the city to hear the Swami's message. He told them drugs were part of *maya*, a curtain drawn over pure consciousness, preventing self-realization. "But have *you* ever taken LSD?" one young man asked.

"No. I have never taken any of these things, not even cigarettes or tea."

"If you haven't taken it, then how can you say what it is?"

He said a drug-high was like a trip on a rocket ship. You reach a peak and then you come back down; your spacecraft cannot travel forever.

The Millbank crowd did not return.

Similarly, the Swami's rants against promiscuous sex chased away potential recruits such as Ed Sanders of the Fugs, a rock group whose songs "Slum Goddess of the Lower East Side" and "Group Grope" were Village favorites.

Inevitably, the Vietnam War made its way to Matchless Gifts. One night, someone asked the Swami, "If God is so kind, why is He allowing so many of our American boys to be killed in Vietnam?"

"You are daily killing so many animals, so God is saying, 'Send your *sons* to the slaughterhouse,'" Prabhupada replied. "If we want peace, we have to worship God."

This was not the call to action the hard-core war protesters wanted to hear, but, as with sex and drugs, Prabhupada refused to tailor his message to please Americans.

A disciple of Vivekananda had warned him that chanting and wearing robes was not the way to reach Westerners. The disciple advised Prabhupada to buy business suits and to groom himself like an American. The remarkable aspect of Prabhupada's mission was precisely this: unlike previous gurus' attempts to generalize Hinduism for Westerners, trimming its religious trappings and presenting it as a set of exercises anyone could practice (e.g. meditation and yoga), Prabhupada made clear he *was* promoting a religion requiring daily devotion, a specifically Indian religion, whose God was Krishna. He was not selling anything. He was saving souls.

This did not mean he lacked business sense. He set about incorporating his "society," legalizing it as a nonprofit organization, to protect and promote it financially. He called it the International Society for Krishna Consciousness (ISKCON). Three of its seven stated purposes: "To systematically propagate spiritual knowledge to society at large . . . propagate consciousness of Krishna, as it is revealed in the *Bhagavad Gita* . . . [and] bring the members closer together for the purpose of teaching a simpler and more natural way of life."

The society had been mentioned in the *Village Voice* and elsewhere, and ISKCON leaflets were circulating around the Village and mailed to residents, drawing the attention of Allen Ginsberg, who lived nearby on East Tenth Street. The Beat poet, looking very much like a young Walt Whitman, came one night to the storefront, lugging a harmonium. He joined the *kirtana*. Prabhupada quoted the Bhagavad Gita to him—*Whatever a great man does, others will follow*—and asked Ginsberg to continue chanting wherever he traveled. "The main thing . . . was an aroma of sweetness he had, a personal, selfless sweetness like total devotion," Ginsberg recalled. "And that was what always conquered me, whatever intellectual questions or doubts I had."

In the early fall, with the weather sufficiently warm, the Swami moved his *kirtanas* to Tompkins Square Park, tucked among brownstone tenements between Seventh and Tenth. On Sundays, the park was full of Puerto Rican families, children and dogs, and young couples, as well as hippies, drug dealers, and heroin addicts. Prabhupada, wearing a canary-colored robe and cradling a drum, walked the eight blocks from the storefront, leading a core of his followers, then found a patch of grass and began chanting.

"Hey Buddha! Hey, you forgot to change your pajamas!" Puerto Rican teens taunted him. People stared down from the brownstone windows. "Hippies!" "Hey, A-rabs!" "What are they, Communists?" Prabhupada's followers were stunned that such a gentle figure could provoke so much hostility. He didn't seem to notice, smiling blissfully, eyes closed.

Word got around about the spectacle in the park. Eventually the *New York Times* took notice: "Swami's Flock Chants in Park to Find Ecstasy," read a headline on October 10, 1966. The article under the headline included Allen Ginsberg's endorsement. Improbably, the old man *had* started a movement in America, exactly as he'd set out to do.

In late 1966, Prabhupada sent Michael Grant, now renamed Mukunda Goswami, to San Francisco, to explore the possibility of opening a Krishna temple there. The Haight-Ashbury neighborhood sounded like fertile ground.

Mukunda arrived in the Haight in December. The US government had made LSD illegal just two months before, but the drug was everywhere on the streets. The neighborhood was distinguished by once-posh Victorian houses gone to seed following the 1906 earthquake, the Depression, and the Second World War. Rents were cheap; groups of teenage runaways from all over the country crashed together in the empty old homes, pooling their resources to cover monthly costs and purchase drugs. Allen Ginsberg, aware that the Haight was swiftly becoming a countercultural mecca, came from New York to extol the wonders of hallucinogens: "How can we change America?" he declared in public gatherings. "Everybody . . . try the chemical LSD at least once—every man, woman and child over fourteen in good health. Then I prophesize we will have seen some ray of glory or vastness beyond our social selves, beyond our government, beyond America even, that will unite us into a peaceful community." He proposed "drugs, orgies, music and primitive magic as worship ritual." For him, Prabhupada's chanting was just another element in the ongoing party.

Eventually Mukunda found a cheap house to rent on Frederick Street in the Haight. He and a handful of friends—including his new wife, Janaki Dasi; Sam Speerstra, an old college buddy from Oregon (whom Prabhupada christened Shyamasundar Das Adhikari); and Speerstra's wife, Melanie Nagel (Malati Dasi)—begged for money on the streets. They sold spices and oils to head shops and planned ways to establish Krishna as a presence in the neighborhood. Speerstra had once lived in the Haight and knew Grateful Dead manager Rock Scully and Sam Andrew, a guitarist with Janis Joplin and Big Brother and the Holding Company. He suggested staging a rock concert featuring prolonged Krishna chanting—he could confer with Scully and Andrew. Maybe Ginsberg could help them. He liked the Swami. Mukunda loved the idea. Perhaps even Prabhupada might attend. "Thousands of people would hear him!" Janaki Dasi exclaimed.

Chet Helms, manager of the Avalon Ballroom was up for it: he liked a good party. The bands agreed to play for $250 apiece.

Planning began for the Mantra-Rock Dance, for after the first of the year. Meanwhile, Nagel offered "Love Feasts" at the Krishna house for hungry people on the streets, *prasādam*, free dishes of peppers, peas, potatoes, and curries. Word got out about the group. They chanted in small parks, under trees. The *Oracle*, the neighborhood's alternative newspaper, wrote them up. Mukunda came across an interview with George Harrison in an old issue of the *Oracle*. Harrison said a person could use meditation mantras to get to the essence of music. Mukunda addressed a letter to him, arguing the opposite: music carried a soul into the heart of the mantra. He did not expect the letter, like the 45 record the initiates had sent to London, to reach its destination.

Joan Didion appeared in the Haight to write about the hippies. She interviewed Mukunda; thus, a tiny bit of Krishna consciousness snuck into the *Saturday Evening Post*.

Just two days before Prabhupada arrived in San Francisco for the Mantra-Rock Dance, the Human Be-In ("A Gathering of the Tribes") took place in Golden Gate Park on January 14, 1967—a vast celebration of hippiedom and a protest against the banning of LSD. Gary Snyder, Timothy Leary, and Baba Ram Dass spoke. Ginsberg chanted mantras, further embedding Hinduism into the Western counterculture.

By mid-afternoon on January 16, over fifty people had gathered at United Airlines Gate 22 at the San Francisco airport to greet the Swami with chanting. Allen Ginsberg showed up with a bouquet of flowers. "We were quite an assorted lot . . . even for San Francisco," said Roger Segal, one of the young greeters. "Mukunda was wearing a Merlin the Magician robe with paisley squares all around, Sam was wearing a Moroccan sheep robe with a hood—he even smelled like a sheep—and I was wearing a sort of blue homemade Japanese samurai robe with small white dots. Long strings of beads were everywhere. Buckskins, boots, army fatigues . . . the whole phantasmagoria of San Francisco at its height."

The tiny old man appeared in the jetway, shuffling in his saffron robes. He opened his arms to Ginsberg's flowers. At baggage claim he danced to the chanting.

He had never flown before. "The houses looked like match boxes," he said to Mukunda. "Just imagine how Krishna sees things!"

His energy amazed his young companions. At the house on Frederick Street, he graciously spoke to amused reporters from the *San Francisco Chronicle*, preparing another feature on the Haight.

The thought of the old man presiding over a rock extravaganza puzzled many of his followers. "Swami says even Ravi Shankar is *maya*!" remarked one concerned believer on the eve of the concert.

The night of the show, Timothy Leary was ushered to a special seat inside the auditorium, as was Owsley Stanley III, the Bay Area's one-man LSD industry (and John Lennon's personal acid source). The Hell's Angels arrived in a pot-cloud.

A light show began: red, yellow, and blue amoebas writhing across the low ceiling and the cramped hall's dirty walls. Backstage, Janis Joplin, weaving, gripping a bottle of Jim Beam, humming Eric Burdon's version of "House of the Rising Sun," confronted Mukunda. "Hey, you're one of the Krishnas, right? Why do you feel you have to chant that mantra?"

"Because it makes you feel good," he said.

She sneered.

Prabhupada arrived at the ballroom, driven in a 1949 Cadillac Fleetwood by one of his New York followers. Devotees inside the hall blew conch shells as he walked down the center aisle from the entrance to the stage. The light show gave way to slides, images of Krishna playing his flute and cavorting with his consorts. The audience cheered, standing. Prabhupada spotted Allen Ginsberg in the wings. "You can speak something about the mantra," he said.

Ginsberg took the stage, playing his harmonium. "I'd like you to sing aloud with me," he said to the crowd. "It's meditation that's musical. It'll take you to another dimension."

He paused. Slides of Krishna dancing with the Gopis flashed behind him on the wall.

"Sometimes you can have a bad acid trip, and I want you to know that if you ever do, you can stabilize yourself on re-entry by chanting this mantra. . . . Now, I want to introduce you to [the] Swami . . . who brought this mantra to the place where it was probably most needed, to New York's Lower East side—to the dispossessed, to the homeless, the lost, the anarchists, the seekers."

The audience roared.

"He left India, where life is peaceful, where he could have remained happily chanting in a holy village where people never heard of war and violence, where life is slow and meaningful. But instead, he's here with us tonight, his first time in this city, his first time in America, and he's come to share with us something precious, something to treasure, something serene."

Prabhupada ambled to the microphone. He spoke slowly. "This chant . . . will lead us to the spiritual world," he said. "You may begin tonight or any time. The mantra is not only for Indians. . . . Krishna is *everyone's* father . . . God is for all human beings, beasts, aquatics, insects, trees, plants—all varieties. That is God."

As Ginsberg led the chant, the audience joined in. "People didn't know what they were chanting for," remembered Janaki Dasi. "But to see that many people chanting—even though most of them were intoxicated—made Swami very happy."

On the wall, grinning Krishna played his flute.

Prabhupada raised his hands and began to twirl and dance. The crowd followed his movements. Behind him, the Grateful Dead plugged in their instruments; tentatively, Big Brother pounded on their untuned strings.

Roger Segal said, "The ballroom appeared as if it was a human field of wheat blowing in the wind. It produced a calm feeling in contrast to the [usual] Avalon Ballroom atmosphere of gyrating energies. The chanting of Hare Krishna continued for over an hour, and finally everyone was jumping and yelling, even crying and shouting."

Remarkably, the world's most ancient religion, based on humanity's oldest Eastern texts, was expanding through Western Black music channeled through modern electronics. Its message would soon explode, once the Swami met the Beatle.

"Om Vishnupāda Paramhamsa. . . . All glories to the assembled devotees!" Prabhupada muttered into the mike. As Ginsberg introduced the rock stars one by one, the Swami slipped away, back to the house on Frederick Street. "This is no place for a *brahmacāri*," he thought. As thrilling as the night had been—praise Krishna—he felt in every cell of his withered limbs what he truly was: an old man in exile, far from where he wanted his physical body to die, caught in a strange, confusing land.

Muhammad Ali's exile from boxing began when he declared himself a minister of the Nation of Islam and a conscientious objector to war on religious grounds.

Lawrence Grauman, the judge who had heard his case in court, was not likely to be sympathetic to him. For one thing, Grauman couldn't understand how a man who practiced gladiatorial violence could disavow it in other contexts ("Because I never lose my head in the ring," Ali explained. "There is a difference in intent"). And for another thing, Judge Grauman was extremely race-conscious. Everywhere he traveled in public, he'd point out dark faces. "Look!" he'd say. "There's another one." "A Black person, someone from India, whatever they were, every time he saw one, he made a comment," his son later recalled.

But on November 25, 1966, in a sixteen-page letter sent to the Appeal Board for the Western District of Kentucky Selective Service System, Judge Grauman declared he was "impressed by [Ali's] statements." The young fighter had been forthright and convincing (he had kept his head and charmed the old man); Grauman concluded Ali was "sincere on religious grounds [against] participation in war."

Unfortunately for Ali, Grauman's role in the matter was merely advisory. The US Justice Department had the final say, and it was clear from the way the Department cherry-picked Grauman's comments in its response to him that it had made its decision in advance. (Grauman had noted, in passing, that "human conviction" might not sit very deep in Ali. He was immature. He might grow "disenchanted with the Muslims and voluntarily join . . . the United States Marines." The Justice Department (DOJ) seized on this statement as a reason to dismiss everything Ali said.)

"Neither the fact that he has 'no personal quarrel' with the Viet Cong nor his related objection to the Black Muslims getting involved in the Vietnam war [matters]," the DOJ concluded. "[His] objection must be a general scruple against 'participation in war in any form' not merely an objection to participation in a particular war . . . [T]he registrant's conscientious-objector claim is not sustained."

Time was running out for Ali to continue boxing. He managed to squeeze in two more fights: one in the Houston Astrodome against Ernie Terrell (a dominant performance in which Ali repeated the punishment he'd given Floyd Patterson, demanding "What's my name?" each time he pounded his opponent—unwisely, Terrell had insisted on calling him "Clay") and another in Madison Square Garden against Zora Folley. That Ali could fight at all on US soil had solely to do with money: the Astrodome was a new venue, looking for revenue, respect, and publicity; the Garden, on New York's Eighth Avenue, was about to shut down before moving to a new location above Penn Station on Thirty-Third Street.

Reporters and public officials scorned Ali for treating Terrell so cruelly in the ring. "It was a kind of lynching," Jimmy Cannon wrote. "This, the Black Muslims claim, is one of their ministers. What kind of clergyman is he?" Said Congressman Robert Michel of Illinois, "While thousands of our finest young men are fighting and dying in the jungles of Vietnam, this healthy specimen is profiteering from a series of shabby bouts. Apparently, Cassius will fight anyone but the Viet Cong."

At this stage, Howard Cosell of ABC-TV was about the only American sports-caster granting Ali respect, calling him by his Muslim name, speaking to him seriously about his fights and his predicament with the government. "Look at what was happening then," Cosell said later. "The birth of the drug culture, the birth of the pill, riots in the streets, an ugly unwanted war, assassinations. . . . That time period was incredible, and Ali understood it; he was at the heart of it; he helped shape it all. And the powers he fought!"

Ali told Cosell he couldn't make white folks happy unless he was beaten. "If I put [Terrell] away in one round, it's bad. If I put him away in three rounds, it's bad. If I talk to him, it's bad. If I whip him clean, it's bad. I'm just wrong if I do it, wrong if I don't."

A week before the Folley match, on March 15, 1967, Ali heard from John Condon, a PR man at the Garden, that the Louisville draft board had just announced Ali's induction day: April 11. "If what you say is true, this is gonna be my last fight," he said.

The night before the bout, he asked former champ Sugar Ray Robinson to meet him at his suite in the Loews Midtown Hotel. He needed to talk, he said. Robinson found him agitated regarding the impending induction. Ali explained he couldn't go into the army because Elijah Muhammad wouldn't let him. Robinson said he advised Ali, "I don't care what Muhammad told you, but I do care about you. If you don't go in the army, you'll go to jail. When that happens, they'll take your title away. When you come out of jail, you won't be able to fight. Do you realize you're forfeiting your entire career?"

"But I'm afraid, Ray. I'm real afraid."

"Afraid of what? Afraid of the Muslims if you don't do what they told you?"

Ali wouldn't answer. He had tears in his eyes.

"I never thought of myself as great when I refused to go into the army," he said. "All I did was stand up for what I believed. There were people who thought the war in Vietnam was right. And those people, if they went to war, acted just as brave as I did. There were people who tried to put me in jail. Some of them were hypocrites, but others did what they thought was proper and I can't condemn them for following their conscience. . . . I wasn't trying to be a leader. I just wanted to be free."

Above all, he did not believe in asking for America's mercy. He did not believe mercy was in America's power to give, nor did it reside in America's DNA: "We [Black people] weren't brought here to be citizens in white America. The intention was for us to work for them—and like it." So it made no sense to plead for equal treatment. "When you put your whole trust and your whole future in another people, then you're putting yourself in a position to be disappointed and deceived. You cannot disappoint me. You cannot deceive me if I'm not looking for anything from you."

On his lawyer's advice, he moved to an apartment in Houston, switching his draft board from Louisville. Generally, said the lawyer, Houston courts were more generous with draft appeals than courts in other cities.

Ali was scheduled for induction on April 28. Meanwhile, he flew back to Louisville to see his family. An open housing battle had erupted in the city. Black leaders had asked the city's Board of Aldermen to levy fines against sellers or landlords who discriminated on the basis of race, religion, or national origin. Ali still did not believe Black people should *want* to live in white neighborhoods, but he was sympathetic to families who had been unfairly evicted from their homes. He lent his public support to the battle—along with another visitor to the city, Martin Luther King Jr.

On March 29, 1967, at a Louisville hotel, the men had their first and only face-to-face meeting. The FBI monitored their private conversation in King's room and said they mostly told jokes. Later, in the lobby, in front of the press, they stood together as "Black brothers," Ali claimed.

"This was a renewal of our friendship," said King. "We are victims of the same system of oppression. Although our religious beliefs differ, we are brothers."

Ali said, "The same dog that bit him bit me."

More significantly, King had finally announced his opposition to the war in Vietnam. Seven months after the Beatles had declared an official stand against the conflict, and in the midst of Ali's draft troubles, King had at last defied those supporters of his who feared he would harm the civil rights cause if he linked it to antiwar sentiment. He had come around to Malcolm's view that civil rights in the United States needed to be joined to an international struggle for human rights. "Rather than have the American Dream slain in the jungles and swamps of Vietnam, we pledge ourselves to do everything in our power to end that war," King said. (Immediately, J. Edgar Hoover said King had become "an instrument in the hands of subversive forces seeking to undermine our nation.")

King openly acknowledged that Muhammad Ali's courage and outspokenness had served as models for him.

In turn, Ali drew strength from the minister's presence. Despite the confusion, doubt, and fear plaguing him, he was growing solidly into his conviction. In Louisville he told the open housing advocates that their cause was *his* cause. Their common enemy was the United States. "Why should they ask me, [a] so-called Negro, to put on a uniform and go ten thousand miles from home and drop bombs and bullets on brown people in Vietnam while so-called Negro people in Louisville are treated like dogs and denied simple human rights?" He went on to say, "If I thought the war was going to bring freedom and equality to twenty-two million of my people, they wouldn't have to draft me. I'd join tomorrow. But I either have to obey the laws of the land or the laws of Allah. . . . So I'll go to jail. We've been in jail for four hundred years."

He sang "A White Man's Heaven Is a Black Man's Hell." He said he would not help the United States enslave other peoples.

Ali wrote a new poem: "Tell little children whatever they believe, / Stand up like Muhammad Ali." He said to the press, "Tell all the fans and all the people that their idol, the living legend—they may be looking at him for the last time. It will be sad from here on out. Watching two heavyweights slugging and butting each other. There'll be no more poems, no more Ali shuffle. You can take this game to the graveyard. Look and look close and remember me."

Within nine months, Louisville passed the open housing law.

By April 1967, ten thousand young men a month were drafted in America. Thirteen thousand American soldiers had been killed in Vietnam, a disproportionate number of them Black (22.4 percent, though they accounted for only 11 percent of all American servicemen).

Just after 8:00 a.m. on April 28, a cool, misty morning in Houston, a taxi pulled up in front of the Armed Forces Examining and Entrance Station in the federal building at 701 San Jacinto Street. Muhammad Ali emerged, smiling tightly, wearing a dark blue suit. He was one of thirty-five men called for induction in Houston that day, most of them bound for Fort Polk in Louisiana.

"Gee Gee, do the right thing," his mother had told him the night before on the phone from Kentucky. "Gee Gee" was her nickname for him, based on the first sounds he'd uttered as a baby. "If I were you, I would go ahead and take the step. If I were you, I would join the army. Do you understand me, son?"

"Mama, I love you," he said. "Whatever I do, Mama, remember I love you."

She cried.

A few demonstrators walked in slow circles around San Jacinto Street, waving signs: "We Love Ali," "Ali, Stay Home," "Draft Beer—Not Ali," "I Want to Be a Mau Mau." One young man burned a piece of paper, claiming it was a draft card. An elderly white woman approached the boxer. She said she'd attended all his fights. When he thanked her, she hissed that she couldn't wait to see him get his ass kicked.

On the building's third floor, Ali joined other young men in a waiting area of Houston's Draft Board Number 61. Most of them gripped duffel bags or suitcases. "You all look very dejected," he said to the boys. They laughed and grinned. They asked him about his fights. He told a few jokes. Someone asked him if he was afraid to go to Vietnam. He crouched, pretending to hold a rifle. He peered wildly. "The Viet Cong don't scare me," he said. "If they don't get me, two guys from Georgia would. I'd have to watch for the Viet Cong and the guys behind me, too."

One of the draftees said he wished Ali could come with him wherever he was going: "It would lighten our trip."

Another draftee whispered to a newsman, "I kind of feel sorry for the old guy"—Ali was five or six years older than the others—"He can't get away from this mess."

The draftees were given a series of physical examinations. Ali shuffled in his underwear. His mental aptitude was tested no further.

At lunchtime, the boys were offered food boxes: a ham sandwich, an apple, an orange, and a slice of cake. Ali threw the ham away.

Meanwhile, Raymond X, a minister in Houston's Mosque Number 45, paced the waiting area alongside reporters. He pointed to a slumped draftee: "See that black man over there? He's got two babies, his back's half broken, and Uncle Sam wants him. Give me liberty or give me death! Where's the Negroes working in this building? Only one here and he's pushing the Red Cross coffee pot."

Finally, the induction officer lined the candidates against a wall in room 1B. He announced, "You are about to be inducted into the Armed Forces of the United States in the Army, the Navy, the Air Force or the Marine Corps. . . . You will take one step forward as your name and service are called, and such step will constitute your induction into the Armed Forces indicated."

One by one, Lieutenant Steven S. Dunkley read the names. Jason Adams, army. Luis Cerrato, army. The crooked line shortened.

Then: "Cassius Marcellus Clay." Ali did not move. "Cassius Clay—Army." Nothing. "Cassius Clay, will you please step forward and be inducted into the Armed Forces of the United States?" Ali stood still. "Refusal is a criminal act," the officer informed him. "You could go to jail for five years. There could be a $10,000 fine. Do you want a second chance?"

"Thank you, sir, but I don't need it."

"Please give us in writing your reason for refusal."

Ali then stepped forward and wrote, "I refuse to be inducted into the armed forces of the United States because I claim to be exempt as a minister of the religion of Islam."

A military spokesman walked into the waiting room. He announced to reporters, "Ladies and gentlemen: Cassius Clay has just refused to be inducted into the United States Armed Forces. Notification of his refusal is being made to the United States Attorney."

Ali entered. He moved with calm dignity, illuminated, it seemed, by a light from within. He passed around copies of a four-page statement prepared by his lawyers: In it he said, "I strongly object to the fact that so many newspapers have given the American public and the world the impression that I have only two alternatives in taking this stand—either I go to jail or go to the army. There is another alternative, and that alternative is justice."

By the end of the day, Edwin Dooley, chairman of the New York State Athletic Commission, announced that the commission had "unanimously decided to suspend Clay's boxing license indefinitely and to withdraw recognition of him as World Heavyweight Champion," saying "[Ali's] refusal to enter the service is regarded by the commission to be detrimental to the best interests of boxing."

Right away, other state athletic commissions followed suit. So did the World Boxing Association.

It was bad enough that the "best interests of boxing" had never been imperiled by illicit gambling, mob activity, domestic abuse, or any religious faith other than Islam. What galled was the illegality of the actions taken by boxing's purist guardians. Without having been charged with a crime—the case was still pending and would certainly be appealed, if necessary—without being given due process under the US Constitution's Fourteenth Amendment, Ali was stripped of his ability to earn a living, to protect his property and his liberty.

That day, precisely as Ali and his fellow draftees were sitting in Houston's federal building waiting to be called into the armed forces, General William Westmoreland, preparing the country for a widening war effort, addressed a joint session of the US Congress. "Backed at home by resolve, confidence, patience, determination and continued support, we will prevail in Vietnam over the Communist aggressor," he said. His speech earned nineteen standing ovations from the nation's representatives. Afterward, Congressman L. Mendel Rivers said, "'My country, right or wrong,' could never be truer. It's too late to question whether it's right or wrong."

That night Ali called his mother: "Mama, I'm all right," he said. "I did what I had to do. I sure am looking forward to coming home to eat some of your cooking."

Shirley Povich asserted in the *Washington Post*: "It is too bad he went wrong. He had the makings of a national hero." Jimmy Cannon wrote in the *New York World Journal Tribune*: "[Clay] is the assassin who killed the great heavyweight championship of the world." And Bud Collins, in the *Boston Globe*, said America better figure out its war business pronto because, love him or hate him, Ali had set an example for thousands of kids who were now going to claim they had no quarrel with the Viet Cong.

Ali was arrested on charges of sedition, fingerprinted, and photographed. He posted a $5,000 bond for bail. On May 8, a federal grand jury in Houston (seating one Black member in a group of twenty-one) indicted him after minimal deliberation. A trial lay ahead.

Outside the courthouse, a Black woman yelled at Ali that he was a fool. "Your attorneys want to take all your money and then they'll leave you," she said. "What are you doing this for, anyway?"

"For religion," he said.

"Are you serious?" she said.

"Yes, I'm serious. I'm ready to die for it."

Indirectly, through Arthur Krim, an entertainment lawyer and presidential advisor, Lyndon Johnson offered Ali a deal: in exchange for entering the army and traveling to military bases around the world, giving boxing exhibitions for soldiers, he would not be forced to wear a uniform or see combat. He might even be able to continue fighting professionally while serving.

Ali refused the offer.

In *Sports Illustrated*, the basketball star Bill Russell wrote: "[Ali] has something I have never been able to attain and something very few people I know possess. He has an absolute and sincere faith. . . . I'm not worried about Muhammad Ali. He is better equipped than anyone I know to withstand the trials in store for him. What I'm worried about is the rest of us."

Less than two weeks later, an all-white jury in Houston, six men, six women, found Ali guilty of draft evasion. As Ali sat quietly in the courtroom beside his lawyers, sketching on a yellow legal pad an airplane crashing into a mountain, the judge mandated the maximum sentence of five years in prison and a $10,000 fine. Ali was granted freedom while his lawyers appealed the sentence, but within weeks the judge confiscated his passport. Banned from boxing in the United States, he was now unable to pursue his living anywhere in the world. And meanwhile Congress extended the draft.

In Guyana, huge crowds picketed the US embassy, protesting the US government's treatment of Ali. Ali's Egyptian supporters jammed the streets of Cairo. Ghanaian newspapers ran fierce editorials denouncing America's racist persecution of the boxer. A Pakistani protester fasted outside the US consulate.

Britain experienced its very first antiwar demonstrations; prominent among the signs at the rallies, "LBJ, Don't Send Muhammad Ali to War."

Even at home, support for Ali came from surprising corners. Floyd Patterson, who detested Ali's connection to the Nation of Islam, spoke up for him. "What bothers me is Clay is being made to pay too stiff a penalty for doing what is right," he said. He caught the gist of the government's punitive message: "The prizefighter in America is not supposed to shoot off his mouth about politics, particularly if his views oppose the government's and might influence many among the working class that follow boxing."

The seasoned reporters gathered in a back room of the Lion's Head Bar in Greenwich Village one mild afternoon in late June 1967 understood that what happened in the shaken world could be shaped by the manner in which it was reported.

Comprising "left-wing writers, alcoholics, and other bohemians," according to one of its members, the group met to discuss how it could counter the government's persecution of Muhammad Ali. It was an "injustice on a historical scale," according to another member, Jack Newfield, a writer for the *Village Voice*. His friends Jimmy Breslin, Pete Hamill, George Plimpton, and Norman Mailer agreed. "Without so much as a hearing, Ali was dispossessed of what is his," Plimpton sputtered into his beer. Heads nodded. "Forget the war. We're *all* against it. It's just wrong to punish Ali for having the courage to take a stand."

"We need a national voice," said one of the others. Someone to speak on Ali's behalf—a media figure trusted by ordinary Americans. "How about Cosell?" someone else said.

As reported by Dave Kindred, Plimpton paid a visit soon afterward to the sportscaster's office in New York. Cosell had a huge public megaphone as an announcer on *ABC's Wide World of Sports*, and he had a friendly rapport with Ali—often, on the air, they did a sort of Laurel and Hardy routine, ribbing each other, always good-naturedly. "My sympathies are obviously with Muhammad," Cosell informed Plimpton that day. "But the time, at this stage in the country's popular feeling, is not correct for such an act on my part."

But "voices should be raised," Plimpton persisted.

Cosell gestured out the window. "Georgie-boy, I'd be *shot*, sitting right here in this armchair, by some crazed redneck . . . over there in that building if I deigned to say over the airwaves that Muhammad Ali should be completely absolved and allowed to return to the ring." He shook his head. "I have consistently referred to him as Muhammad Ali, not Cassius Clay, and that is contribution to his cause greater than any made by any other journalist. In the end, this is a matter for adjudication by the courts, not by journalists . . . you and your little committee are embarked on a quixotic journey against giants."

So even the media had its limits, though those limits were constantly shattered.

Just five days after Ali's conviction in Houston, the Beatles—by now also staunchly antiwar—set a new technological precedent, performing live before the largest global audience ever, on the BBC television show *Our World*. Using a new Early Bird satellite, the BBC linked thirty-one TV networks for the first time around the world, reaching an estimated audience of between four hundred million and seven hundred million people. The show featured artists from nineteen nations, including Maria Callas and Pablo Picasso. The Beatles were the headliners.

Four days before the broadcast, Eastern bloc countries led by the Soviet Union canceled their participation in the event to protest the West's support of Israel in the Middle East's recent Six-Day War.

For the program the Beatles wore flamboyant psychedelic costumes—orange paisley jackets, silk, suede, and fur. They were surrounded by confetti, colorful balloons, and "flower-waving crowds of Beautiful People," according to a BBC executive. They performed a new Lennon composition, "All You Need Is Love," featuring a distinctive electric guitar solo by Harrison and a pastiche of classical Western melodies—"Greensleeves," "La Marseillaise"—fading in and out of the background, suggesting the passing of the old beneath the lovely tide of the new. Love and peace would conquer all, in spite of the Soviet Union and in spite of Vietnam: the hypnotic chant "Love is all you need," like an Indian mantra, was insistent, clear, and irresistible. And it was far more effective or at least far-reaching than anything a gruff sportscaster like Howard Cosell might utter about a world awash in injustice.

Culturally speaking, you didn't need a weatherman to know which way the wind was blowing.

While the Beatles sang about love, Ali was preparing to get married again. And again Herbert Muhammad played an outsized role in the arrangements. After his trial in Houston, Ali had returned to Chicago. One afternoon he dropped by the Shabazz Restaurant on Seventy-First Street, a Nation of Islam establishment, for soup and bean pie. Herbert had told him the seventeen-year-old girl behind the counter might make a good wife: she was a "Princess of Islam."

"What's that mean?" Ali asked.

"It means she's never been tampered with. She's a virgin. She doesn't know anything about anything. . . . She's raised and grown and trained to be a wife and a mother."

She shared a last name with George Harrison's wife. Her name was Belinda Boyd. She had been born into the Nation. Her parents were members of the Messenger's inner circle. By the time she was eight, she was babysitting Elijah Muhammad's grandchildren. All her life, her education had consisted of religious indoctrination. She could not have been more different from Sonji Roi.

Ali walked up to her at the restaurant counter. She was tall and slim, demure, wearing a floor-length dress and prim head covering. "Do you know who I am?" he asked her. They had, in fact, met before. Both recalled the meeting. In 1960, when she was a ten-year-old fourth grader, Ali had visited her class as the new Olympic champion. Children clamored for his autograph, but she scorned him. "You're proud of this name?" she said.

"I certainly am. My mama gave me this. These are Roman names. You know what the Romans did? They ruled the world."

"Clay? Is that like dirt and mud? You don't know who you are." She told him it was a slave name. She ripped up his autograph. *Ten years old*, rebuffing the Olympic champ! So strong! So self-assured! She wore her hair in a long thin braid down her back. Ali called her "The Indian." He never forgot her.

As for her, she thought, "If I had to be a man, this is what I would look like." She acted unimpressed.

Seven years later in the Shabazz Restaurant, she feigned indifference once more. "You gonna butt the line?" she snapped at Ali. Abashed, he stepped back and waited his turn.

For the rest of that summer he showed up nearly every day at the restaurant. He'd ask the "Indian" how she was doing. "I wasn't interested in having no boyfriend," she said. "I wasn't interested in getting married at all." But she did tell him he'd done the right thing in refusing the draft. Hearing this from a pretty young woman after all the crap he'd taken made him feel better than he'd felt in months. And she began to admire his potential as a Muslim. "I wanted to mold him so he could be like my father," she admitted.

One rainy evening, as she was waiting for a bus, Ali pulled up in a silver Eldorado. He offered to drive her home. She said no, a single girl shouldn't ride alone with a man. She boarded the bus and Ali followed it for several blocks until she reached her stop. She was still three miles from home. Again she refused a ride. While she walked, he turned on his emergency flashers and drove slowly beside her, chatting with her through his open window.

Eventually he met her family, charming them all. Her mother was impressed by his generosity and his genuine love of children.

Belinda said,

I think [I] was a challenge [to him], because he'd become quite a guy with the women, and people said to him, "It doesn't matter what you do, you'll never get to Belinda." He'd tell them, "Man, you're crazy! All women want me." But still they'd say, "No, Belinda is different. She's strict, she's strong, she's moral." And I think it drove him crazy. If he'd asked me to marry him, I probably would have said no, but it didn't happen that way. He just kept coming around to the house a lot. My parents liked him. And finally, he didn't ask me, he told me. He just said, "You're gonna be my wife." I said, "Right," and that was it.

They were married on August 18, 1967, in a small ceremony at Ali's place on South Jeffery Boulevard. Herbert Muhammad served as best man.

Ali loved showing her off to his friends in the Nation. "[S]he don't say nothing. There can't be but one big mouth in the family," he'd say.

"I liked it that way," Belinda later recalled. She played her role perfectly. Quiet and retiring in public, completely in charge at home. And they were content together. "He was my first love . . . [and] in the beginning he was beautiful. On the outside, he was always sure of himself, but inside, I could tell there was a little insecurity. Not about his boxing; he was very secure at that. But in other ways, I think he was unsure of himself, and spent a lot of his time searching for who he was."

It didn't take her long to see that Herbert and the Nation drained most of his income—or that his generosity and desire to please people frittered away much of what remained (not to mention the fact that he'd fallen behind in his alimony payments to Sonji). It struck her that—given his exile from boxing—she had "married a man with no job."

It had been a turbulent summer in the United States. Chicago, where Ali settled with his wife, was one of the few major cities unscathed by race riots in 1967. There were sixteen dead and 353 injured in Newark where Malcolm's ghost haunted the mosque; 1,189 injured in Detroit among two thousand damaged buildings after police raided an all-Black nightclub celebrating a pair of soldiers returning from Vietnam; and racial violence too in Minneapolis, Milwaukee, Buffalo, and Birmingham, Alabama.

On July 23, in the burned-out center of Newark, at a Black Power conference, organizers floated a number of proposals designed to give attendees a morsel of optimism in the midst of so much failure, hostility, oppression. *Should birth control programs be resisted because they target the extermination of Negroes?* The audience shouted tepid approval. *Should May 19, Malcolm X's birthday, be declared a national holiday?* A more enthusiastic, moderate response. *Should the bigots who stripped Muhammad Ali of his title be condemned?* A mighty roar followed.

"The Beatles are here, the Beatles are in town!"

It was August 7, 1967. Harrison's presence in the Haight caused a scuffle.

He and Pattie Boyd had flown to California to visit her sister Jenny. They attended a series of concerts by Ravi Shankar. After leaving LA, they decided to explore the San Francisco hippie scene. "I went there expecting it to be a brilliant place, with groovy gypsy people making works of art and paintings and carvings in little workshops," Harrison said. "But it was full of horrible spotty drop-out kids on drugs, and it turned me off the whole scene. I could only describe it as being like the Bowery, a lot of bums . . . many of them young kids."

"Everybody looked stoned—even mothers and babies—and they were so close behind us they were treading on the backs of our heels," Boyd later recalled. "It got to the point where we couldn't stop for fear of being trampled."

"It certainly showed me what was really happening in the drug culture," Harrison said. "It wasn't what I'd thought—spiritual awakenings and being artistic—it was like alcoholism, like any addiction. . . . That was the turning-point for me—that's when I went right off the whole drug cult and stopped taking the dreaded lysergic acid. I had some in a little bottle (it was liquid). I put it under a microscope, and it looked like bits of old rope. I thought that I couldn't put that into my brain any more. . . . 'This is not it.' And that's when I really went for the meditation."

Months earlier, Paul McCartney had finally succumbed to peer pressure and tried LSD. Immediately he'd told the press how it changed his life, made him "a better, more honest, more tolerant member of society."

"Paul needs an audience," George Martin said, shrugging, when informed that McCartney had gone public about the group's drug use. Harrison felt McCartney's comments breached the band's trust. "I thought Paul should have been quiet about it," he said. For a year and a half McCartney had resisted the experience. "And then one day he's on the television talking all about it."

Lennon fumed: viewed through the lens of the men's creative competition, this was classic Paul, cautiously testing a thing before taking full credit for its invention. Harrison didn't care quite as much: he was simply moving on.

On the flight back from San Francisco, still shaken from his experience in the Haight, he was sitting behind the pilots when "the plane went into a stall—we hadn't got very high before we went into a steep turn and the plane made a lurch and dropped. The whole dashboard lit up saying 'UNSAFE' right across it. I thought, 'Well, that's it.'" Several weeks back—around the time McCartney announced his acid use—Harrison had received a 45 record in the mail: a Hare Krishna chant made by a group of Americans. The recording thrilled him. He'd shared it with Lennon, and the two of them had chanted together until their jaws hurt.

Now, as the jet lurched above the hills of California—eventually righting itself—he closed his eyes and whispered, "*Hare Krishna Hare Krishna Krishna Krishna. . .*"

Ali and his wife prayed together every morning, noon, and night in their small brick house on the South Side of Chicago. The house had once belonged to Herbert Muhammad, but his father made him give it to Ali, so Ali could live near the Messenger.

Belinda worried whenever her husband left the neighborhood without bodyguards. He had made a lot of enemies, stirred plenty of talk ("People who'd never thought about the war—Black and white—began to think it through because of Ali. The ripples were enormous," said Julian Bond). People approached Ali on the streets to chat, to commiserate, to ask for autographs. They handed him leaflets ("What kind of America is it whose response to the poverty and oppression in Vietnam is napalm . . . whose response to the poverty and oppression in Mississippi is silence?") He didn't worry about his safety. He walked with Allah, he said. He moved among his people.

Back home, he loved nothing more than watching old westerns on TV with Belinda. "You better get out of town, Belinda," he'd drawl. She'd rise from the couch, stare him down, put her hands on her hips, and say, "Naw, cuz I'm about to draw!" They'd laugh and laugh. She said his sexual appetite was insatiable—though unmindful of *her* pleasure. She enjoyed his body anyway. What could she expect of a man whose father, to her horror, bragged in front of Ali's mother, "I'm a whore-runner." Cash liked "stallions," he said—women with big legs and big boobs, "but I ain't leaving my wife for that crap. . . . My wife knows what I'm doing."

"I was happy," Belinda said, even though, in their first few months together, they'd had to dip into her college savings. "The government had taken away his title, and we thought boxing was gone forever. We didn't have much money, but we said, 'It don't matter; we're gonna make it.'"

The Beatles finally met Sonny Liston, but Sonny was made of wax and stood next to a waxy George. Madame Tussauds lent its effigy of the boxer to Peter Blake, the designer of the *Sergeant Pepper* album cover, along with wax figures of the Beatles in their mop-top phase. They appear on the cover collage of photos and cardboard cutouts of dozens of other celebrities and historical figures, jammed into a tableau suggesting a funeral for the old Beatles attended by their new incarnation, Sergeant Pepper's Lonely Hearts Club Band (four mustachioed men in psychedelic-colored regalia, "part German marching band, part military band," in Lennon's words). Together the images raised questions about the enduring and transient qualities of celebrity.

"To help us get into the character of Sergeant Pepper's band, we started to think about who our heroes might be," McCartney said. "'Well then, who would this band like? . . . Who would my character admire?' We wrote a list. They could be as diverse as we wanted: Marlon Brando, James Dean, Albert Einstein."

Starr said he didn't care who appeared on the cover: he'd go along with whatever the others suggested. Lennon wanted Hitler and Gandhi, humanity's extremes. Obviously, Hitler would never get past the record executives—surprisingly, Gandhi got nixed as well. "At that time, EMI [the Beatles' British label] was very much a colonial record company," McCartney explained. "It still is—they sell records in India and China—so they were/are very aware of Indian sensibilities . . . 'You can't have Gandhi . . . It might be taken the wrong way. He's rather sacred in India, you know.'"

McCartney listed artists, writers, and movie stars: Magritte, Aldous Huxley, Groucho Marx. Initially, Mae West refused to lend her likeness: "No, I won't be in it. What would I be doing in a lonely hearts club?" It took individual, pleading letters from each of the Beatles, professing undying love for her, to change her mind.

Harrison named eight holy men, including Babaji and Yogananda.

In the final, iconic cover, Sergeant Pepper's Band stands holding its orchestral instruments behind a big bass drum. In front of the drum, "Beatles" is spelled out in red flowers, surrounded by pot plants and yellow flowers in what appears to be the shape of a guitar. Next to mop-top George at the left, Sonny Liston stands draped in a white boxer's robe, arms loosely folded. Ali was either not asked for permission to use his image or did not give it. In any case, by the summer of '67 he was a notorious draft-dodger—undoubtedly, EMI would have axed him.

Madame Tussauds let Peter Blake keep the Liston figure. "They were going to melt old Sonny down," he said. Liston was a has-been. For years, Blake kept the effigy in his studio. "Underneath his robe he's . . . rather fragile," he said, "so he doesn't go anywhere anymore."

In a couple of years, a college disc jockey in the United States would start a rumor that Paul McCartney had died mysteriously and been replaced by a double. Beatles albums were said to contain clues to his death, and the *Sergeant Pepper* cover was said to be rife with markers. On the back of the album cover, the four bandmates are pictured together, three facing forward and McCartney turned away.

In retrospect, the most important image on the cover—signaling change within the group, leading to the Beatles' eventual demise—was the instrument George Harrison cradled in his hand. Lennon grips a French horn (*mine's the biggest!*), Starr a trumpet, McCartney an oboe. Harrison holds a flute—the holy and seductive symbol of Krishna.

"I'd just got back from India, and my heart was still out there. After what had happened in 1966 . . . I was losing interest in being 'fab,'" Harrison said. "It was difficult for me to come back into the sessions. In a way, it felt like going backwards. Everybody else thought that *Sergeant Pepper* was a revolutionary record . . . [but] I had gone through so many trips of my own and I was growing out of that kind of thing."

In the "Summer of Love," when *Sergeant Pepper* was released, Ravi Shankar, long known and respected in the West, became a full-fledged star based on his association with Harrison and his appearance at the Monterey Pop Festival, the world's first large-scale rock revue. He performed with the tabla maestro Alla Rakha and awed the crowd with a frenzied afternoon raga—after lecturing the audience to respect the music's complexities, and expressing impatience with what he considered bad etiquette: smoking, drinking, and talking during musical performance.

Also that summer John Coltrane died—Coltrane, who had been Shankar's student, who had come to combine the influence of Islamic, Arabic, and Indian improvisation in his jazz, connecting them to the spoken blues riffs of Malcolm X's calls to action.

But Shankar and Coltrane would not establish the world's new musical terms. Nor would Yehudi Menuhin, the first Jew to perform in postwar Germany, a musical ambassador for peace, whose collaborations with Shankar, dating back to the 1950s, initiated modern East-West fusions. It was George Harrison—whom "nobody was really expecting . . . much of," in the words of sound engineer Geoff Emerick—with a remarkable song, "Within You Without You." "Personally," said Emerick, "I thought it was just tedious." Later, he would change his mind. He would have been impressed right away had he fully understood the swirl of forces animating the composition.

The classical music of northern India, the music that freed Harrison's deepest talents as well as his spirituality, is the oldest musical system in the world. In 1500 BCE the Aryans arrived in India from Central Asia bringing the Vedas, orally transmitted scriptures, the third volume of which, the Samveda, was chanted using three notes, later expanded into seven, linked by the yogis to the human body's seven chakras, or energy points. During meditation, the chants were said to redistribute energy, or light, throughout the chakras, leading the meditator to God, the source of pure consciousness.

Hazrat Inayat Khan, the Sufi master whom Muhammad Ali would one day embrace, wrote "In the Vedas of the Hindus we read: Nada Brahma—sound, being the Creator. . . . When we come to the Bible, we find: 'First was the word, and the word was God.' And when we come to the Qur'an we read that the word was pronounced, and all creation was manifest. . . . The origin of the whole [of] creation is sound." This became George Harrison's central truth.

By the seventh century, the structure of the raga had evolved from the oral Vedic tradition, "raga" in Sanskrit meaning, loosely, "color"—or, as historian Peter Lavezzoli writes, "the feelings or moods evoked by a special combination of notes."

Different ragas are played at different times of day, prompting various moods. "Technically . . . a raga lies somewhere between a scale and a melody," Lavezzoli explains. It begins with a meditative *alap*, a sort of instrumental prayer or invocation with an improvisatory feel, not strictly related to melody or metrics but hinting at the structure of sounds to come. The *alap* is usually followed by a moderately paced, rhythmic *jor*, during which the tabla, the drum, establishes a time signature, *tala* (seven beats, sixteen beats, and so on). Finally, the whole builds toward the *jhala*, a swift, climactic ending. In between, spaces open and close among the notes allowing for improvisation and call-and-response dynamics among the instruments. In addition to his attempts to technically master the sitar, Harrison concentrated on learning the raga structure as well as its spiritual sources.

"[My sitar training] really did help me as far as writing strange melodies, and also rhythmically it was the best assistance I could ever have had," he said. His immediate affinity for the music was striking, but he was not entirely unprepared. By the nineteenth century, the activities of the East India Company had to some degree culturally cross-pollinated East and West. In the 1880s, Verdi's opera *Otello* included "Oriental" folk themes, the likes of which continued with Rimski-Korsakoff's *Scheherazade* (1888) and Tchaikovsky's *Nutcracker* (1892). On a more accessible level, the British Music Hall (so beloved of Paul McCartney) based many of its comic skits around the rumored exotic activities of people at the far eastern reaches of the British Empire. The skits were always accompanied by "Oriental" folk melodies. Across the pond, in the United States, this form of entertainment became the minstrel show with its unfunny "coon songs."

In 1920s Britain, another refinement of Eastern influence surfaced in the craze for Hawaiian music, and Harrison embraced ukuleles and slide guitar with extraordinary passion. As a child listening to the radio, he had heard, in addition to his mother's Radio India program, his father's favorite, Hoagy Carmichael, who wrote a series of "Oriental tunes." In the 1980s Harrison would cover Carmichael's songs, and their influence was apparent in the soundtrack he would write for the movie *Shanghai Surprise*.

From Eastern traditions, Carmichael learned to push his lyrics beyond the standard Tin Pan Alley love story. "Hong Kong Blues," for instance, is a woeful tale of opium addiction. Similarly, in keeping with musical explorations of the spirit, Harrison's mature writing almost always focused on questions of identity and human purpose. His love songs might as easily be addressed to God as to a woman. The bent notes of the blues prepared him for the sitar's arcing strings. The joy-in-suffering/suffering-in-joy nature of the soul music he had always loved intended so much more than entertainment.

In sum, by the time he met Ravi Shankar and other Eastern teachers, Harrison was ready to hear what he heard.

In the 1950s, Shankar had been crucial in resurrecting Indian classical music—it had fallen into disfavor in India, partially as a result of its microtonal complexity but even more because of its appropriation by colonials for parody. In India it was associated with silly popular movies—and with "[a] prostitute's quarters, and with the bazaar, where its most accomplished practitioners were reportedly found," according to musician Amit Chauduri. More than anyone, in the '50s, Shankar and Ali Akbar Khan reconnected this musical tradition with the Vedas and brought it to sophisticated audiences around the globe. Their collaborations with Menuhin and Menuhin's goal of using sound to promote peace emphasized the music's core in Vasudhaiva Kutumbakam—a unitary worldwide family.

But there was a down side, for Shankar, in bringing his music to the West. Even before he met George Harrison, musical purists in India criticized him for bastardizing the nation's ancient traditions. This criticism intensified after "Norwegian Wood" sparked the sitar craze in rock music and the music attached itself to hippies. "[George] really wanted to learn. I never thought our meeting would cause such an explosion," Shankar said, perplexed and stung by the attacks on him.

"It became like a fashion, everybody was into playing sitars. . . . Then later, as all fashions disappear, Ravi had to start all over again and rebuild his audience," Harrison admitted, upset by his role in the mess.

In the mid-1960s, sitars in rock—never more than frills or flourishes in the background, usually out of tune—were simply an extension of the nineteenth-century appropriation of Eastern exoticism, perpetuating stereotypes, reducing Indian sounds to a suggestion of Oriental mystery.

Harrison had *found* himself in Indian music ("To me it is the only really great music now, and it makes Western three-or-four-beat type stuff seem somehow dead."). He intended to repair the damage he'd done to it. Between 1966 and 1968 he wrote three pioneering songs, having nothing to do with the Beatles or acid rock, honoring the world's oldest musical tradition, bringing it *whole* (if condensed into pop format) into the modern Western world.

"Love You To," a meditation on mortality from the Beatles' *Revolver* album, begins with an unmeasured *alap* on sitar, followed by a four-beat *tala* on tabla, introducing the tambura. After two verses, the sitar improvises for several beats before the song modulates between metrical units of sevens, fives, and threes. It ends on a *drut* (a fast tempo) and fades.

Harrison recruited Anil Bhagwat of the Asian Music Circle to play tabla. "The session came out of the blue," Bhagwat said.

A chap called Angadi called me and asked if I was free that evening to work with George. I didn't know who he meant—he didn't say it was Harrison. It was only when a Rolls-Royce came to pick me up that I realized I'd be playing on a Beatles session. When I arrived at Abbey Road there were girls everywhere with Thermos flasks, cakes, sandwiches, waiting for The Beatles to come out. George told me what he wanted and I tuned the tabla with him. He suggested I play something in the Ravi Shankar style, 16 beats, though he agreed that I should improvise. Indian music is all improvisation. . . . It was one of the most exciting times of my life.

Over the years, musical scholars have speculated that Harrison plays sitar only during the free-form *alap* and that an unnamed player from the Asian Music Circle must have stepped in after that. They argue that the playing is too sophisticated for Harrison to have grasped in such a short time. Others suggest that the picking style (very much like a Western guitarist) and the slightly out-of-tune instrument suggest that it *is* Harrison playing throughout the song. Either way, Peter Lavezzoli writes, "'Love You To' remains the most accomplished performance on sitar by any rock musician."

Typically, Emerick approached recording this Harrison song with "boredom," but he quickly grew fascinated by the challenge of miking Indian instruments. By the end of the session, he grudgingly admitted the results were striking. Harrison, he said, had matured incredibly as a musician and as a writer.

Of "Love You To," musicologist David R. Reck has written, "One cannot emphasize enough how absolutely unprecedented this piece is in the history both of popular music and of European orientalism. For the first time an Asian music was not parodied using familiar Western stereotypes and misconceptions, but rather transferred in toto into its new environment, with sympathy and rare understanding."

With his next offering, for the *Sergeant Pepper* sessions, Harrison was ready to make another leap forward. Working again with musicians from the Asian Music Circle—and none of the other Beatles ("George barely even noticed that the others had departed [the studio]; he may have even welcomed them leaving him to work on his own," Emerick said)—Harrison premiered "Within You Without You," a song in the mode of Hindu devotionals called *bhajans*, about the illusory nature of the material world and the need to discover the eternal soul. The lyrics acknowledged bhakti, divine love, with the power to "save the world," and *bhramam*, the infinity residing in every individual ("life flows on within you and without you").

The words came not only from the ancient texts he'd been reading but also from a philosophical conversation he'd had with Klaus Voorman, an old Hamburg buddy living now in England. "Klaus had a harmonium in his house, which I hadn't played before," Harrison remembered. "I was doodling on it, playing to amuse myself, when 'Within You' started to come. The tune came first . . . The words are always a bit of a hangup for me. I'm not very poetic. My lyrics are poor, really. But . . . it's great if someone else likes it."

When he first played the tune for Geoff Emerick and George Martin, Martin found it "dreary." Like Emerick, he would soon change his mind.

Harrison gathered the musicians he wanted from the Asian Music Circle. "They [had] jobs like bus driving during the day and only play[ed] in the evening, so some of them just weren't good enough, but we still had to use them," he recalled. "They were much better than any Western musician could do, because it at least is their natural style, but it made things very difficult. We spent hours just rehearsing and rehearsing."

Peter Blake hung around the Abbey Road studio with some friends, soaking up the atmosphere, seeking inspiration for the still-developing album cover. He later remembered, "They had a carpet on the floor and there was incense burning. George was very sweet—he's always been very kind and sweet—and he got up and welcomed us in and offered us tea. We just sat and watched for a couple of hours. It was a fascinating, historical time." Emerick agreed: "It was very calm and peaceful in the studio that evening. Harrison was gracious and welcoming when Peter Blake arrived; for perhaps the first time during the 'Pepper' sessions, I could see that George was completely relaxed."

From Shankar, Harrison had learned to teach songs orally using Indian notation. "Indian music is written . . . very simply like our tonic sol-fa," he said. "Instead of Do, Re, Mi, and so on, they sing Sa, Re, Ga, Ma, Pa, Dha, Ni, Sa. . . . You indicate how high or low, or how long each one is, by putting little marks under each note. The first notes of 'Within You' to go with the words *We were talking* would go Ga, Ma, Pa, Ni." In the studio, Harrison sang these notes to the players. Then he asked, "Okay, should we try it from the beginning?"

Like "Love You To," "Within You Without You" begins with a short *alap*, played on the dilruba. In the middle of the five-minute song, the tabla switches from sixteen to ten beats while a *jawab-sawal*, a call and response, begins first between the dilruba and Harrison's sitar, and then between the sitar

and a Western string orchestra: life's dual nature—physical and spiritual—
in action.

Then the tabla dives into a deep 4/4 groove to bring the song back to its verse.

"The results were nothing short of magical," Emerick conceded. "None of us
really appreciated how difficult the sitar was to play." George Martin, conducting the orchestra, struggled to blend the Western instruments with Eastern
microtones. "Thankfully he had the help of George Harrison, who acted as a
bridge between the Indian tonalities and rhythms, which he understood quite
well, and the Western sensibilities of George Martin and the classical musicians," Emerick said (classical strings would be overdubbed). "I was never more
impressed with both Georges than I was on that very special, almost spiritual
night," Emerick said. He also noted, "From then on, many of George Martin's
orchestrations began exhibiting that same kind of Indian feel, with string sections
doing slight pitch-bending. It put a stamp on his arrangements and gave them
a unique sound."

"Finally, with the lights down low and candles and incense burning, George
tackled the lead vocal, and he did a great job," Emerick asserted. "Mind you, he
does sound quite sleepy on it . . . he'd been up all night working on the track!"

As the song fades, the listener hears an audience laughing, a sound effect
Harrison insisted on adding. "Well, after all that long Indian stuff you want
some light relief. It's a release after five minutes of sad music," he explained.
"You were supposed to hear the audience anyway, as they listen to Sgt. Pepper's
show. That was the style of the album."

"I think he just wanted to relieve the tedium a bit," George Martin remarked
of the laughter. "George was slightly embarrassed and defensive about his work.
I was always conscious of that."

It didn't help that he rarely felt fully supported by his bandmates, his producer,
or his sound engineer. But when it finally came together the way Harrison heard it
in his head, "Within You Without You," impressed them all in spite of themselves.
"He is clear on that song. You can hear his mind is clear and his music is clear,"
Lennon said in 1980. "It's his innate talent that . . . brought that song together.
George is responsible for Indian music getting over here [in the West]. That song
is a good example."

Sergeant Pepper was released in the later spring of 1967, and it was atop the
Billboard 200 list in the United States from July 1 into October. "A hallucinatory cabaret revue . . . [*Pepper*] quickly became one of the canonical icons
of [the] 1960s," music scholar David R. Reck wrote, "joining such works as

J. R. R. Tolkien's *The Lord of the Rings*, Hesse's *Siddharta*, the *I Ching*, and the *Tibetan Book of the Dead*."

Harrison would write one last Indian song, "The Inner Light," while still a member of the Beatles. "Within You Without You" prompted Juan Mascaró, a Sanskrit scholar at Cambridge University, to write him a letter: "A few days ago two friends from abroad gave me the recording of your song 'Within You Without You.' I am very happy. It is a moving song and may it move the souls of millions; and there is more to come, as you are only beginning on the great journey."

Mascaró sent Harrison a copy of his translation of the Tao Te Ching, a book of verses attributed to Lao Tzu (Laozi). Harrison built "The Inner Light" around one of the verses, using the words from the translation almost verbatim: "Without going out of your door / You can know all things on earth. / Without looking out of your window / You can know the ways of heaven. / The farther one travels, / The less one knows."

The song did not feature sitar, tabla, or tambura. It was driven instead by a sarod, a harmonium, and Harrison's plaintive voice. With its simple instrumentation and its chord changes, it more closely resembled South Indian temple hymns than North Indian classical music.

None of the other Beatles appeared on the track. Harrison recorded it in India, while working on the soundtrack to a forgettable film called *Wonderwall*. He cared little about the movie, but, when the director said he could write whatever he wanted, he seized the opportunity to create a mini-anthology of Indian sounds and songs. While staying in Bombay, he recorded "The Inner Light" with a small group of Indian musicians: Aashish Khan (sarod), Hanuman Jadev (shehnai), Hariprasad Chaurasia (flute), Mahapurush Misra (pakhawaj), and Rijram Desad (harmonium).

Lennon and McCartney were so impressed with the song that they decided to place it on the B side of the Beatles' new single, "Lady Madonna"—the first time a Harrison composition had ever appeared on a 45. By the time it was released in England and the States, the Beatles had followed George Harrison to Maharishi Mahesh Yogi's ashram in Rishikesh, India.

CHAPTER 5

Sour Milk Sea

On June 18, 1967, in the *Washington Post*, a review appeared of *Sergeant Pepper's Lonely Hearts Club Band*, saying:

> With "Sgt. Pepper's Lonely Hearts Club Band" Her Majesty's knights in psychedelic armor come to rescue the form, creating the first pop tone poem. In their latest album the Beatles have managed to create a musical infinity through a miraculous metamorphosis of Eastern and Western musical ideas, some centuries old, others from our own era and more than a few from the future. When combined with John Lennon's perceptive lyrics (and honed wit), the Sgt. Pepper metamorphosis becomes a wildly contemporary continuum—structured pop music with a beginning, middle and end linked by riotous sounds, words, colors, images and musical tension. It is a bit fantastic, and certainly unprecedented.

The review was written by confessed "music freak" Carl Bernstein. Five years later, Bernstein, along with Bob Woodward, would expose the Watergate scandal for the *Post*, beginning the end of Richard Nixon's presidency.

On the day the review appeared, Nixon was preparing an article on US foreign policy for *Foreign Affairs* magazine. Entitled "Asia after Viet Nam," the article began, "The war in Viet Nam has for so long dominated our field of vision that it has distorted our picture of Asia. A small country on the rim of the continent has filled the screen of our minds; but it does not fill the map. Sometimes dramatically, but more often quietly, the rest of Asia has been undergoing a profound, an exciting and on balance an extraordinarily promising transformation."

Nixon was speaking here of the decade since the Bandung Conference that so excited Malcolm X, the struggle of former colonial outposts to achieve independence. But his concerns were far different than Malcolm's, less focused on Asia's future than on America's ability to profit from the region's changes. He was not at all eager to see the East's independence movements as models for US minority populations.

During his presidency, Nixon's response to Asia's "promising transformation" would help propel genocide in Bangladesh, Ravi Shankar's family's home. Millions of people would perish.

In 1967, at the ninth annual Grammy Awards, Shankar's collaboration with Yehudi Menuhin *West Meets East*, a series of violin and sitar duets exposing previously hidden cultural connections, won the Chamber Music Performance category, while *Sergeant Pepper*, featuring George Harrison's extended *bhajan*, won Album of the Year.

In this atmosphere of change, Muhammad Ali's public image too saw a remarkable evolution. "The power structure seems to want to starve me out," he said. "The punishment, five years in jail, ten-thousand-dollar fine, ain't enough. They want to stop me from working, not only in this country but out of it . . . and that's in this twentieth century. You read about these things in dictatorship countries, where a man don't go along with this or that and he is completely not allowed to work or to earn a decent living."

Next to boxing, his greatest skill was talking, Belinda said. Why not do it for money? She wrote letters to colleges and universities around the country to see if any were interested in inviting him to lecture. Sitting with him on their blue velvet couch in front of their small marble fireplace, she helped him write notes for speeches, memorize and practice talking points. He studied Elijah Muhammad's *Message to the Blackman in America*, tape recorded himself reading passages aloud, and played the recordings until he'd memorized the phrases. "Putting the lectures together was hard work. . . . I wrote them . . . on note cards, studied them every day, and practiced giving speeches in front of a mirror with Belinda listening. . . . I did that for about three months until I was ready." He added, "Talking is a whole lot easier than fighting."

Temple University in Philadelphia offered him $1,000, and Cheyney University, a historically Black college in Cheyney, Pennsylvania, ponied up $500. After that, he signed with Richard Fulton, Inc., a nationwide speaker's bureau. The company prepared fifty thousand promotional flyers. Soon Ali was in great demand.

He took Belinda to a parking lot near their house to teach her to drive the Eldorado. She earned her license, and they hit the road together—in the era of *Easy Rider* and Ken Kesey's Magic Bus, they made their own colorful trip across America, spending much of what he earned on the lecture circuit on motel rooms, gas, and car repairs. They'd drive most of the night, rise at dawn, and drive some more—Sam Cooke and Lloyd Price crooning from the eight-track tape player.

"I was as close to him as his jugular vein," Belinda said. "He didn't want to go anywhere without me. We were a team. Going out to conquer the world. We did it together. There wasn't no sitting back."

Of the two, she had the sense of direction. If she fell asleep while he drove, inevitably she'd wake to find they were lost.

At first, the speeches didn't connect. He would harangue audiences, speaking too long, upsetting people with his negative views of integration and intermarriage ("No intelligent white man or white woman in his or her white right mind wants Black boys and Black girls comin' round their homes to marry their white sons and daughters"). Students booed him when he expressed support for the staunch southern segregationist George Wallace.

"Go home, draft-dodger," someone shouted at one of his early appearances.

Another student offered to take his place in Vietnam for $1,000. "No, brother, your life is worth more than $1,000," Ali responded.

One night, upset with the hecklers, he told Belinda, "I ain't doing this."

"Yes, you are," she said. "This is our livelihood."

With her help he devised a response. The next time someone yelled in the middle of a speech, he paused. "Ladies and gentlemen . . . A long time ago when I was a little boy I used to take a rock and throw it at this donkey. I kept throwing rocks and my mama said to me, 'Cassius, you stop throwing rocks at that donkey because you are going to kill that donkey and one day that donkey is going to come back and haunt you.'" He paused again. Then he said, "Ladies and gentlemen, I do believe that ass is here tonight."

It worked. He charmed people. He got smoother, tighter. He moved away from race—at least directly—concentrating on his antiwar stance. "Whatever the punishment, whatever the persecution is for standing up for my beliefs, even it means facing machine-gun fire . . . I'll face it," he'd say. Or, "Damn the money. Damn the heavyweight championship. I will die before I sell out my people for the white man's money." This message proved to be enormously popular, especially on majority white campuses where Beatles posters hung in many of the dorm rooms.

"The speeches were important, not just for Ali but for everyone who heard them," Robert Lipsyte said. "He was leading people into areas of thought and information that might not otherwise have been accessible to them. And a lot of young people wouldn't have thought this stuff through if it hadn't been a celebrity lightning rod telling it to them."

"If you want to see a man at his best, take a look at Ali in his prime," Jim Brown agreed. "[He] was a true warrior. It was unbelievable, the courage he had. . . . He was a champion who fought for his people. He was above sports; he was part of history. The man used his athletic ability as a platform to project himself right up there with world leaders, taking chances that absolutely no one else took."

By a circuitous route, he had become what Malcolm X had hoped he would become.

One afternoon, deep in Alabama somewhere, on the way to a small college, Ali stopped the car at a filling station. "It was like 'Deliverance,' little boys on the porch with banjos and shit," Belinda recalled. "Then some rednecks come out with little beards, hair all over them. Like Neanderthals. I'm thinking this is a real hick town and we can get lynched down here and no one will ever know."

Ali filled his tank and then went around back to the bathroom. One of the bearded men approached Belinda's window. "How the hell are you?" he said.

"I'm just fine, brother."

"Let me tell you something. That boy with you?"

She waited.

"Is he Cassius Clay?"

"Yes, that's Muhammad Ali."

He stepped back from the Caddy. "Jesus Christ, Jesus Motherfucking H. Christ," he screamed. "Jesus H. Christ. I got Muhammad Allah here!"

Folks appeared from out of the woods—or so it seemed to Belinda. They asked Ali to sign whatever they could find, magazines, even toilet paper. Someone came with homemade cookies. Another woman appeared with fried chicken wrapped in a shoebox. Under the swaying, mossy oaks they all had a grand old time.

An FBI memorandum, dated July 25, 1967, reads: "Cassius Clay, alias Muhammad Ali, is an admitted active member of the Nation of Islam (NOI), which is a highly secretive organization whose membership is made up entirely of selected Negroes who advocate and believe in the ultimate destruction of the white race and complete control of the civilized world by the Negro cult . . . [It is] an ideology completely foreign to the basic American ideals of equality and justice for all, love of God and country."

Sometimes Ali received aid from unexpected quarters. Under the editorship of Harold Thomas Pace Hayes, *Esquire* magazine had developed a reputation, throughout the 1960s, of iconoclastic reporting and provocative imagery in its pages. This trend began in 1963 when Hayes, working with his pugnacious art director, George Lois, decided America needed a Christmas wake-up call after the murder of Medgar Evers, TV footage of white Southern cops turning fire hoses on Black demonstrators, and George Wallace's attempts to prevent Black students from enrolling in the University of Alabama.

On *Esquire*'s December 1963 cover—two months before the Beatles and Cassius Clay posed together in the 5th Street Gym—Hayes and Lois ran a photograph of Sonny Liston, scowling, wearing a big red Santa cap. *Sports Illustrated* said Liston was "the last man on earth America wanted to see coming down its chimney." Advertisers yanked $750,000 worth of ads, but in the long run *Esquire* gained tremendous publicity, and Lois did not check his "aggressively oratorical approach" to presenting in the magazine "what was happening in America."

Now, four years later, to accompany a lengthy profile of Muhammad Ali, Lois had another jazzy idea. He phoned Ali, asked him to come to a photography studio in New York, and showed him a painting by Francesco Botticini depicting the martyrdom of Saint Sebastian. In the painting, the saint, wearing only a loin cloth, stands tied to a tree, shot through the chest, ribs, and belly with arrows. Lois asked Ali to strike the pose.

"Hey, George! This cat's a *Christian*!" Ali said.

Yes, Lois agreed. Sebastian had been persecuted for converting to Christianity just as Ali was being punished for his commitment to Islam. Did Ali think Elijah Muhammad would give the magazine permission to suggest Ali's martyrdom?

The Messenger *had* told the boxer, "The world knows that America has wronged you. Your cause is worldwide, and you can use your fame to help our proselytizing."

After a short deliberation, Muhammad gave Lois the go-ahead.

"We'd practiced on a model beforehand, and when we tried sticking the arrows on the body with glue, they were so heavy that they hung down," Lois recalled. "So we put a bar across the studio's ceiling and hung fishing line to hold up the arrows. It was a pain in the ass, because Ali had to stand very still for a long time till we got all the arrows lined up at the right height. He didn't complain, though. He was one of the few people in public life who was just like his reputation. He was funny. He was relaxed. He wasn't a bullshitter."

Ali wore white shoes and white boxing shorts. He stood against an all-white background, hands held behind his back, head tilted in an attitude of agony, a volley of arrows piercing his chest, one plunged into his right thigh. Fake blood leaked from the wounds. He resembled one of his father's old church murals. The cover was guaranteed to outrage his critics, convinced he was no martyr to America, and to confuse many others: what did it mean for this outspoken Black separatist, an avowed Muslim, to assume the identify of a white Christian saint?

If the confusion *around* Ali was growing, *he* had become less puzzled about his situation. In one of the clearest statements he'd made, he said, "My conscience won't let me go shoot my brother, or some darker people, or some poor hungry people in the mud for big, powerful America." And lest anyone believe he didn't understand what he'd stumbled into, George Lois reported that he became very thoughtful during the photo session. He touched each of the false arrows, ticking off "names of people in this world that were out to get him." Lyndon Johnson, General Westmoreland, Robert McNamara . . .

In the early months of 1968, while the magazine prepared its profile and the final cover design, Martin Luther King Jr. was flying back and forth to and from Memphis to lend his support to Black laborers involved in a sanitation workers' strike. They were protesting poor job conditions in the city. The strike tactics, more and more random, were growing increasingly violent. On J. Edgar Hoover's command, FBI officials offered "cooperative news sources" items of misinformation: "King's famous espousal of nonviolence [has resulted in] vandalism, looting, and riot," they said. They even tried to tie him to the Nation of Islam.

In early April, his flight to Memphis was delayed for over an hour on the Atlanta runway after a bomb threat. King was never sure how serious any particular threat might be—the FBI refused to brief him on the tips it received.

On the evening of April 4, King was standing on a balcony in front of his room at the Lorraine Motel in Memphis, calling down to the parking lot to a saxophone player set to perform that night at a rally King was supposed to lead. "Make sure you play 'Precious Lord, Take My Hand' in the meeting tonight," he said. "Play it real pretty."

But the singing and chanting would be anguished and angry that evening.

In Indianapolis, Robert Kennedy, a recently declared presidential candidate, hearing the news from Memphis, scrapped his planned speech and told a stricken crowd, "Martin Luther King dedicated his life to love and to justice between fellow human beings. He died [from an assassin's bullet] in the cause of that effort."

Kennedy did not mention that, as attorney general, he'd approved FBI wiretaps of King. "In this difficult day, in this difficult time for the United States, it's perhaps well to ask what kind of a nation we are and what direction we want to move in. For those of you who are Black . . . you can be filled with bitterness, and with hatred, and a desire for revenge. We can move in that direction as a country, in greater polarization—Black people amongst Blacks, and whites amongst whites, filled with hatred toward one another. Or we can make an effort, as Martin Luther King did, to understand, and to comprehend, and replace that violence, that stain of bloodshed that has spread across our land."

That very afternoon, copies of *Esquire* had appeared on newsstands across the nation featuring a bleeding Muhammad Ali pierced with arrows. Saint Sebastian, yes, but the pose perhaps also recalled photographs of lynching.

Ali released a statement to the press: "Dr. King was my great Black Brother, and he'll be remembered for thousands of years to come."

In the weeks and months ahead—as Robert Kennedy was assassinated in Los Angeles, on the campaign trail where he'd pursued an antiwar agenda; as the Democratic National Convention in Chicago devolved into street riots; as an aggrieved feminist shot Andy Warhol multiple times; as news of the My Lai massacre (on the heels of the Tet Offensive) undermined the Johnson administration's assertions that the Vietnam War was successful; as an exhausted Johnson declined to run for reelection; as George Wallace's segregationist views earned him over a million votes in the presidential election; and as Richard Nixon secured the White House—the image of Ali as martyr circulated across the United States.

On May 6, the Fifth Circuit Court of Appeals upheld Ali's conviction. Ali's lawyers had argued that Blacks were underrepresented on draft boards around the country—in twenty-three states, no Blacks at all sat on draft boards. The court agreed this was a problem but ruled that "the systematic exclusion of Negroes from draft boards" did not nullify their decisions.

Shortly thereafter, in a Phoenix courtroom, an FBI agent admitted under oath that the US Justice Department had illegally recorded Ali five times in wiretaps of Martin Luther King Jr. The agent said that in one recorded phone call, lasting forty-five minutes, Ali had discussed his religious convictions with King. Presumably, this tape could be invaluable to Ali's case—but, the agent revealed, it had been erased.

Despite the clear violations of Ali's civil rights, the court ruled that the wiretaps had "resulted in no prejudice and had no bearing on the defendant's conviction."

His only recourse now was the US Supreme Court—an unhopeful prospect.

"I'm being tested by Allah," Ali repeated. "If I pass this test, I'll come out stronger than ever."

Talking was easier than boxing, but boxing was what he *did*. It was what he *tasted* in his mouth, even while praying.

He was restless.

On June 19, Belinda gave birth to their first child, Maryum, but even this didn't anchor him. He had always loved children. He doted on "May-May," but diaper-changing and sleepless nights were not his style. As he saw it, Muslim women were trained to do the cooking and the child-raising. That's just the way it was: "Allah made men to look down on women and women to look up to men; it don't matter if the two are standin' up or layin' down," he said. "It's just natural." Since the baby was a girl, his only ambitions for her were to become "a clean, righteous person . . . a good sister, maybe a teacher of Black children."

Now, while Belinda stayed home with the child, he took to the road alone or sometimes with buddies from the Nation.

"If I go to jail [for draft evasion], so be it," he continued to insist. "Somebody's got to do something to knock the fear out of some of these Negroes."

In the popular imagination, the Beatles' escapades in India were limited to the few weeks they spent at a meditation retreat at the ashram of Maharishi Mahesh Yogi in Rishikesh. This was largely true of Lennon, McCartney, and Starr, but Harrison's engagement would last his whole lifetime.

"George is a few inches ahead of [the rest of] us," Lennon admitted when he arrived at the ashram in February 1968. He also observed, "The mystery inside George is immense. It's watching him uncover it all little by little that's so damn interesting."

After only a few days at the retreat, noting his bandmate's intense devotion to prayer and meditation, Lennon remarked, "The way George is going, he will be flying on a magic carpet by the time he is forty."

Lennon went to India hoping the Maharishi would slip him a secret key unlocking an attic in the sky. McCartney went to keep his eye on his writing partner and to size up the Maharishi the way he'd studied Stockhausen, Henry Miller, and Picasso.

Harrison considered himself a Hindu. "I believe in reincarnation. Life and death are . . . only relative to thought. I believe in rebirth. You keep coming back until you have got it straight. The ultimate thing is to manifest divinity, and become one with the Creator," he said.

"Once you take the vows of a monk, [your] past life is forgotten," the Maharishi once said, and what is known of his story, a jigsaw of contradictory information, certainly indicates a cavalier concern for history.

Some sources place his 1917 birth in Panduka village, Raipur district, near an ancient Hindu temple. He was named Mahesh Varma, and his father was said to have been a tax inspector. His passport said he was born in Pounalulla in 1918, four hundred kilometers northwest of Raipur.

Eventually he pursued a physics degree at Allahabad University, where he matriculated as M. C. Srivastava. In 1958, traveling to Burma, he listed his name as Bal Brahmachari ("young, celibate") Mahesh Yogi.

His spiritual life began in his twenties when he met Swami Brahmananda Saraswati, an ascetic who had meditated for decades in a remote forest cave, it was said. Saraswati emerged as a "supreme teacher" at Jyotirmath in Benares, a venerated Hindu site. Maharishi became the Swami's personal secretary. He helped the teacher travel across the country once India achieved its independence.

Maharishi took his vows of celibacy and was initiated as a monk. However, he belonged to the Kayastha caste, consigned for life to managerial tasks. He had no future as a teacher in any religious order, so he left. He admitted later, "[The Swami] never trained me." His spiritual wisdom "just blossomed and blossomed and blossomed." The Swami "must have known" he was special, he said.

On other occasions, he changed his story and said his teacher gave him the secrets of Transcendental Meditation to pass along to ordinary householders in India, regardless of caste or religious background.

The Maharishi moved from Bangalore to Madanapalle to Kerala. His activities are hard to trace. Allegedly, he would arrive in a place, find a spot to spread his deerskin, and erect a handmade sign: "WHO WANTS INSTANT ENLIGHTENMENT?"

Drawing upon his physics background, he told growing audiences, "The truth of Indian philosophy has been supported by the findings of modern science. . . . Electrons and protons are the ultimate reality of matter. All these different forms of matter are nothing but involved energy." Using the "special sounds" of mantras (*man,* "mind," *traya,* "liberation"), individuals could control this "ultimate reality." His unique, up-to-date packaging of ancient yoga, combined with his guarantee that *anyone* could grasp eternal bliss, gave his appearances an exciting aura. One could be spiritual *and* materially successful—there was no need to renounce the world.

This message didn't quite resonate at home. Historian Ajoy Bose observed, "[In] India in the 1950s, still at least three decades away from the consumer boom, a vast majority of people clung to the age-old precept of being pious by rejecting material pleasures. After all, for millions of Indians mired in poverty, it was a convenient way of making a virtue out of a necessity." The Maharishi's pragmatic approach was better suited to the fatted yet spiritually hungry West.

By the time he met the Beatles in August 1967, he had spent nearly a decade traveling in the United States and England, becoming media savvy, assuring middle-class and affluent converts that meditation was easy, like learning to "dance in a hurry—only you do it with your mind."

"Americans are always interested in pills or drops that will give them increased energy," said an early American aide to the guru. "We figured this would have a greater appeal than [a] purely spiritual message."

In India, the Maharishi dispensed mantras for free. In the West, he began to charge fees. Westerners considered nothing valuable unless someone slapped a price tag on it.

LA socialites flocked to grasp this exciting new power. Nancy Cooke de Herrera, a Beverley Hills doyenne, pal of Nancy Reagan and Betsy Bloomingdale, practiced meditation in her three-inch heels. Doris Duke, a tobacco heiress dubbed by the press "the richest girl in the world," sought frequent stress-reduction from the Maharishi following several busted love affairs. Waving a lily at her, he convinced her that tobacco, a "life-destructive plant," brought "bad karma to those who sell it to others." It was her duty to "perform life-constructive acts with [her] money to offset this karma."

She gave the Maharishi $1 million from her charitable trust so he could construct his ashram in Rishikesh overlooking the source of the Ganges, where the Beatles would come to study.

Ravi Shankar never told George Harrison what he really thought of the Maharishi. Shankar was distrustful of "fake gurus" traveling from India selling shortcuts to God. He would mimic the Maharishi's giggle and joke that he, Shankar, "should have put on the robes of a holy man instead of wasting [my] time with the sitar. I would have made far more money with far less effort," he said. But he respected Harrison's search. Harrison's path was his own, and Shankar felt certain he'd learn what he needed to learn.

The trip to Rishikesh was preceded by a pair of dramatic developments in the Beatles' lives. Brian Epstein died of a drug overdose. Sleeping pills and alcohol. He was thirty-two years old. He had been unhappy ever since the Beatles quit touring: he was convinced they no longer needed him. They were changing, maturing; his parental role was diminishing. "I suppose we were so absorbed in our own lives, as children are, that we didn't stop to wonder how Daddy was," Pattie Boyd wrote in her autobiography.

But Epstein's unhappiness ran deeper: he was a closeted gay man whose tastes ran to rough trade. Frequently, his partners beat him, stole his money. He faced constant blackmail threats. His use of alcohol and pills as relaxants finally unbalanced him.

"I had no misconceptions about [the Beatles'] ability to do anything other than play music," Lennon said when he heard the news. "I was scared. I thought, 'We've fuckin' had it!'"

Meanwhile, he had met a strange and amusing figure. At the Indica Gallery one day, John Dunbar, the owner, introduced him to Yoko Ono, a Japanese-born conceptual artist from New York. Dunbar was sponsoring an Ono exhibition entitled *Unfinished Paintings and Objects.* Lennon attended, thinking she might perform some avant-garde sex act as a Happening. Instead, there "was an apple on sale . . . for two hundred quid. I thought it was fantastic," he said. "I got the humor in her work immediately . . . a fresh apple on a stand . . . and it was two hundred quid to watch the apple decompose."

She was small, silent, almost hidden in a mane of long, black hair. She intrigued him. For her part, she saw Lennon as a potential wealthy patron. She contrived to stay in touch with him.

✸

Rishikesh lay over 150 kilometers northeast of New Delhi, where the Lennons and the Harrisons landed at three o'clock one February morning in 1968. McCartney and Starr would come later. The couples were driven in old cars over lumpy dirt roads, across creaking suspension bridges, and past open-country markets hawking bananas, coconut, red mangoes, and jackfruit. Vendors prepared vegetable fritters in sizzling woks set above crackling wood fires. The air was fragrant with the scent of garam masala. The group stopped for lunch at a roadside restaurant near Roorkee: tomato soup, scrambled eggs, potato chips with a side of plain rice, a foretaste of their diet for the next few weeks. In the visitors' book, Harrison wrote "Accha," the Hindi word for "Good."

The ashram, the International Academy of Meditation, consisted of fourteen acres of stone huts and wooden bungalows built on land leased from the Uttar Pradesh Forest Department. It overlooked the Ganges through groves of teak and guava trees, the river gushing from a crook in the gray-white Himalayas into the plains. Peacocks and bright green parrots cried within shifting patches of shadow among scorched banana leaves. Small monkeys frequently dropped from the trees onto the ashram's tables and chairs.

Lepers bathed by the river, down the hill.

The Maharishi made sure the Beatles' bungalows were outfitted with carpets, mirrors, and fabrics to brighten the walls. He had claimed he didn't know how famous the boys were (this was certainly not true). Previous guests at the ashram had complained about the hot, cramped quarters and the food (unattended plates licked clean by dogs roaming the compound, sugar bowls attacked by parrots). It was impossible to "meditate with dysentery," one German visitor groused. The Maharishi wanted to avoid any trouble with the Beatles.

They weren't the only famous folks present: Mia Farrow was there along with her sister Prudence; actress Marisa Berenson came, along with Mike Love of the Beach Boys and Donovan.

The governing coalition of Uttar Pradesh, made up in part of Socialist Party representatives, frowned upon the Maharishi's courtship of wealthy Westerners. The Socialists resented the Maharishi for gobbling up real estate in a valley of landless peasants. "The Beatles and hippies have set up their own colony in

Rishikesh," one parliamentarian announced. At the time, Prime Minister Indira Gandhi was pursuing warmer relations with the Soviet Union at the expense of her partnership with the United States. Her overtures were to have profound consequences for Bangladesh in the early 1970s, but for the moment, in the valley of Rishikesh, they simply turned the locals against the Maharishi and his "stupid" Western students. Newspapers, even some police officers, suspected that the CIA had overrun the ashram. Other valley yogis fumed at the Maharishi's ability to manipulate Western media and generate publicity. To top it off, the elder residents of Rishikesh, accustomed to the genteel men and women of the Raj, could not believe how sloppy and outrageous-looking young Englishmen had become. What had happened to the world?

One result of this hostility was increased police protection around the ashram. Lennon, Harrison, and their wives arrived in a cloud of cops.

That first evening at sunset, as the sky above the river purpled, streaked with pink and gold, Harrison carried a portable tape player into a large meditation hall inside the Maharishi's bungalow. "Is it a new song, George?" asked the Maharishi.

"A new song," Harrison affirmed. He pushed the button: "The Inner Light." "Music is the highest form of education," said the Rig Veda. Harrison hoped the guru would be pleased.

Before the Beatles' arrival, Maharishi had told the press, "Because of the conscious mind expansion brought on by meditation, the Beatles' records will show changes in the future, which I feel will bring out the depths in their talents that even they haven't reached yet."

Initially, Harrison and his wife shared a bungalow—"sparsely furnished, with two skimpy beds," Boyd later remembered—but as meditation practice began in earnest, they disturbed one another, chanting their mantras, so they moved into separate quarters. "John and George were [the] most engrossed in Maharishi's teachings. They would meditate for hours, and George was very focused," Boyd said. "I loved meditating, but I can't sustain that sort of intensity for long. Sometimes I would leave George meditating and make a foray to Mussoorie and Dheradun, Tibetan trading posts." She bought prayer wheels and beads and talked to the vendors. Their lives were difficult; China was stealing their country, driving them out, destroying their culture, they explained. When she returned to the ashram, Harrison was still meditating.

"I had a strange experience when I was in Rishikesh," he said later. "The goal is to really plug into the divine energy. . . . It's hard to actually explain it, but it was just the feeling of consciousness traveling. I don't know where to. It wasn't up, down, left, right—but there was no 'body' there. You don't feel as though you're missing anything, but at the same time the consciousness is complete."

When he wasn't meditating he'd practice the sitar. Paul Saltzman, a twenty-three-year-old Canadian photographer who had come to the ashram sat one evening with Harrison. He was "a decent guy, warmhearted and unpretentious," Saltzman said. They watched a baby monkey drop onto a table in front of them, grab a piece of bread and leap into the trees again. Harrison said quietly, "I'm going to play for a while. Would you like to listen?" They retreated to Harrison's bungalow, the last of the sunlight filtering through his window. He practiced for about twenty minutes, eyes closed. After a long silence, he said, "You can have everything in life. Like we're the Beatles, aren't we? We can have anything that money can buy and all the fame we could dream of, but then what? It isn't love. It isn't health. It isn't peace inside."

His life as Beatle George had intruded again, briefly, with the arrival of McCartney and Starr and the attendant press noise. Starr and his wife were deeply unsure about the experience, didn't like being apart from their kids. Starr had a delicate stomach; he'd brought a suitcase packed with Heinz baked beans to see him through the ordeal. Maureen hated the heat and the flies. The two of them lasted only two weeks at the ashram.

McCartney was happy to be on vacation, away from the vitriol in the newspapers and in magazines critical of the Beatles' latest movie, a television film, *Magical Mystery Tour.* He didn't mind meditating. "It took you back to childhood when you were a baby, some of the secure moments when you've just been fed or you were having your nap. It reminded me of those nice, secure feelings," he said. Otherwise, he kept a guitar in his hand and churned out dozens of songs. Inevitably, he began to speak of the Beatles' next project.

"We're not here to talk music. We're here to meditate," Harrison snapped at him.

"Calm down, man," McCartney said. "Sense of humor needed here, you know."

Harrison felt there was no time to waste. They were surrounded, in these mountains, by yogis and saints. "I believe that I have already extended my life by twenty years," he said. "I believe there are bods [people] up here in the Himalayas who have lived for centuries. There's one somewhere around [here] who was born before Christ—and is still living now."

Harrison was determined to find him. To *be* him.

Lennon couldn't resist playing music with his mate. Eventually the pleasure of joining the fun attracted Harrison too. Each of the three wrote songs in

Rishikesh—altogether over forty tunes, including most of those that would be on the *White Album* and more.

At the ashram, in the Vishvasara Tantra, Harrison found an illustration entitled "Sour Milk Sea" ("Kalladadi Samuda" in Sanskrit)—a depiction of the illusory nature of the material world: "What is here is elsewhere, what is not here is nowhere." He wrote a song around the picture, a violent tempest, praising meditation as a way out of "the shit."

He composed "Long Long Long," a weary soul's whispered seduction of God. He ended the song with a stark G minor chord accompanied by a soft double drum-tap, a "suggestion of death, a new beginning, and an enigmatic question," critic Ian MacDonald would observe.

Sometimes in the evenings, after a day of chanting, Donovan joined Harrison, McCartney, and Lennon playing guitars beneath the guava trees. Listening to the three bandmates sing together, Donovan understood that "what made the music of the Beatles different wasn't their natural high exuberance, their . . . songwriting, or their extraordinary skills at playing. There was something else happening . . . They were using Aeolian [or] antique Gaelic harmonies. When you hear 'Love Me Do,' these are not modern Western harmonies. They're in an antique style, influenced by the drone in Gaelic music. Interestingly, there is a link here with the drone used in Indian music."

Historically, the Roma of Europe had migrated from India. "My belief is that [John and Paul] had discovered this antique Gaelic root in their own country, and when George later heard it coming from the East, it linked with him, too," Donovan said. Listening to Harrison noodle on tunes, he understood that the Beatle's guitar sound came from his desire to marry the strains of the sitar with those of the sarod. "Until 1966, George's . . . tunings were normal," he observed. "What he loved and learned from Indian music he applied to his own very special style of electric guitar playing." Harrison began tuning *down*, in the blues style, to achieve a drone. "Then [in Drop D tuning he] could get very low sounds and very high sounds, and it resembled sitar music," Donovan said. "It resembled drone music, and it reminded [him] of our own antique Gaelic music."

This music was in the air at the time in postcolonial fusions. Traditional Scottish and Irish tunes made a strong comeback in the 1960s, resurrected in part by the British folk movement. Musicians such as Shirley Collins, John Renbourn, Bert Jansch, and Davey Graham and bands such as Pentangle inspired even more influential groups, the likes of the Bothy Band, Planxsty, and the Chieftans. In the United States, in addition to Dylan and Dave Van Ronk, Sandy

Bull combined traditional folk music with Indian ragas and pop songs. Following the French-Algerian War, in 1962, Algerian refugees brought alternative guitar tunings, the sounds of Asia and the Middle East, to the Paris busking scene, of which Graham and Bull were a part. All of these developments—as exciting as rock's revival of the blues—Harrison followed keenly.

Lennon asked Donovan to teach him the finger-picking style he'd borrowed from country, jazz, and flamenco, and Donovan showed him what he knew. Hitting the bass (bottom) string and then strumming—bass-strum, bass-strum—Lennon wrote "Julia," an elegy for his mother, and "Dear Prudence" for Mia Farrow's sister, who was meditating at the ashram days on end without any breaks. Everyone feared for her sanity. "Won't you come out to play?" Lennon sang, sitting at the door of her hut.

McCartney wrote "Blackbird" and "I Will" using Donovan's techniques. "George didn't really want to learn the fingerstyle of Maybelle Carter," Donovan recalled. "He said he really had a Chet Atkins picking style, when he held the flat pick between the thumb and forefinger and then picked the strings with the other fingers. . . . What George was fascinated with [were] these descending chord patterns that I was playing"—A minor to the D minor 9—"and out of it came the most heartrending song . . . 'While My Guitar Gently Weeps.'"

"[One evening], under the tropical stars, we broke out the guitars, and I started to write this song," Donovan said. It was "Hurdy Gurdy Man," about an eternal wandering minstrel listening to humanity's cries across the gulf of the centuries and appearing, when needed, to sing love songs. "George Harrison turned to me and he said, 'I could write a verse for that song, Don. And he did, but I didn't record it. . . [George wrote]: "When truth gets very deep / Beneath a thousand years of sleep, / Time demands a turn around / And once again the truth is found."

"This will do me," Paul McCartney decided one day. He'd been feeling constricted in the ashram, skipping his afternoon meditations, sneaking off to the riverbank to play his guitar in the sun. He'd been worrying about the Beatles' fledgling business, Apple, back in London. Begun as a tax dodge on the advice of accountants after Epstein's death, Apple was, in McCartney's mind, a potential corporate empire funding artists in all media. He was eager to fly home and attend to details.

And he'd long suspected the Maharishi of trying to exploit the Beatles' fame. The Maharishi had been talking about producing a TV special in America on

Transcendental Meditation featuring testimonies from the band. McCartney told him flatly one day that he was not to use their names to further his business affairs. The Maharishi just giggled. While McCartney simmered, Harrison defended the guru. "He's not a modern man," he said. "He just doesn't understand these things."

McCartney's departure left Harrison feeling isolated (Starr had already left) because Lennon's attention was starting to drift badly. He had *not* received the key to the heavens. With help from some members of the Maharishi's staff, he was smuggling whiskey, cigarettes, and pot into the camp. Almost every day, unknown to Cynthia, he received postcards from Yoko Ono: "Look up at the sky and when you see a cloud think of me." He moved into a bungalow of his own, away from his wife—ostensibly to pursue meditation undisturbed but really to answer Ono's mail. "I got so excited about her letters," he said later. "There was nothin' in them that wives or mothers-in-law could've understood, and from India I started thinkin' of her as a woman, and not just an intellectual."

And then Magic Alex appeared at the ashram gate. No one knew how or why he'd been invited. His real name was Alex Mardas. He had entered the Beatles' orbit as an acquaintance of Pattie's sister, Jenny. He loved creating simple electronic gadgets. He enjoyed the power he had to fascinate Lennon with them (on LSD, Lennon could stare at a box of flashing lights for hours). Cynthia Lennon and Pattie Boyd both suspected Mardas had come to bring Lennon home—perhaps at McCartney's urging.

At the ashram, Mardas began a whisper campaign suggesting that the Maharishi had made inappropriate advances to women in the camp. Mia Farrow said she thought the Maharishi had made a pass at her one night while placing flowers around her neck. The local newspapers, intent on smearing the guru, printed lurid headlines: "Wild Orgies at Ashram." One paper even said "Beatle Wife Raped." Dryly, Boyd remarked that she hadn't had the honor, and neither had Cynthia Lennon.

Nevertheless, Mardas exploited these details to plant doubts in Lennon's mind. "He was a wicked man," Boyd said, "a lying minx."

Lennon couldn't tolerate anyone pulling the wool over his eyes. Besides, he had not met God, but he had met Yoko Ono, and he was eager to get back to her. "[George and I] stayed up all night discussing [the accusation], was it true or not true," he said. "And when George started thinking it might be true, I thought, 'Well, it must be true, 'cause if George is doubting it, there must be something in it.'"

Whatever Harrison thought, he was not prepared to leave. He had grown restless, but only because he felt the Maharishi was too protective of him. The guru didn't understand that Harrison had experienced India; he had already walked a path to Hinduism. Meditation was just part of it. He wanted to go to Kumbh Mela, the pilgrimage he and Pattie Boyd had witnessed on an earlier trip. He wanted to the see the monks and sadhus gathered on the banks of the Ganges. The Maharishi resisted his request to leave the ashram, suggesting that he didn't know what he would get himself into. Then he said Harrison could go but only if he rode on the back of an elephant (a good image for the press, publicity for the ashram). No, Harrison said. "Being a Beatle is already seeing life from the back of an elephant. We want to mix with the crowds." The Maharishi, clutching a red carnation, said no.

Harrison's restlessness gave Lennon an opening to work on. Lennon said he believed Magic Alex. Harrison insisted they couldn't confirm the rumors. Can you deny them? Lennon asked. Harrison admitted gurus were in a prime position to take advantage of vulnerable women; he didn't doubt such things happened—but who was he to question anyone's road to God or to judge the faults of teachers who were, after all, only human? That didn't mean the divine couldn't also manifest in them. "All Maharishi ever gave me was good advice and the technique of meditation, which was really wonderful," he said. "I admire him for being able in spite of all the ridicule to just keep going."

But Lennon insisted they were leaving the ashram. Harrison knew the rumors were just an excuse: Lennon wanted to go. Mardas's stories were "total bullshit," but Harrison tried to thread the needle, to be a good Beatle-buddy without hurting the Maharishi. He informed the guru that he wasn't leaving in anger; he wanted to see more of India. He had already told him as much.

Lennon had a very different story of the parting: "As usual, when the dirty work came, I actually had to be leader . . . I said, 'We're leaving.' 'Why?' Hee-hee, all that shit. And I said, 'Well, if you're so cosmic, you'll know why.' He said, 'I don't know why, you must tell me.' And I just kept saying, 'You know why'—and he gave me a look like, 'I'll kill you, you bastard.' He gave me such a look, and I knew then when he looked at me, because I'd called his bluff. And I was a bit rough to him."

Jenny Boyd recalled Maharishi looking small and sad at the gates as they all filed past with their luggage. "Wait," he pleaded with them. "Talk to me."

There were "a lot of flakes" at the ashram, Harrison reflected years later. "The whole place was full of flaky people. Some of them were us."

✿

"We made a mistake," Lennon told the press, hoping to put India behind him as quickly as he had taken it up. He wrote a song, calling the Maharishi a "cunt" (he'd do the same years later, in a fierce invective aimed at Paul McCartney). When Harrison heard the lyrics, he insisted that Lennon tone them down and drop the guru's name. Lennon retitled the song "Sexy Sadie," ostensibly about a hustling seductress.

On the plane home from India, Lennon, drunk on Scotch and Cokes, decided it was time to confess to his wife his numerous infidelities over the years.

"I don't want to hear about it," Cynthia said.

"But you've got to bloody hear it, Cyn. What the fuck do you think I've been doing on the road all those years? There was a bloody slew of girls—"

"In Hamburg, yes, I knew that—"

"An uncountable number, in hotel rooms throughout the bloody world."

This seemed to Cynthia less a spiritual unburdening prompted by meditation than a calculated strategy to drive her away from him. Whether or not this was true, it worked. Soon their marriage was over and Lennon was living with Yoko Ono.

Meanwhile in London, McCartney was setting up Apple, an experiment in "Western Communism," he said: the Beatles as grand arts patrons, giving away money so others could "create beautiful things."

The last thing George Harrison wanted to do was become an Apple executive. He knew "chaos" was "waiting for him in England," said Pattie Boyd, "the new business, finding a new manager, the fans and the press." They flew to Madras to visit Ravi Shankar.

The Beatles were splintering. But they had compiled an astonishing collection of new songs at the ashram. Some segments of the American press were calling them the "great scribes of our era" (*Look* magazine). *Life* dubbed 1968 "The Year of the Guru," thanks to the Beatles. And a *Time* magazine cover story said, "In exchange for . . . teenyboppers, the new Beatles have captivated a different and much more responsible audience. They include college students, professors, and even business executives. Kids sense a quality of defiant honesty in the Beatles and admire their freedom and open-mindedness. They see them as peers who are able to try anything and can be relied on to tell it to them straight."

✺

Harrison, arguably the one most responsible for the "new" Beatles' "defiant honesty," deeply regretted his abrupt departure from Rishikesh. In years to come, numerous female followers of the Maharishi would emerge with credible stories of sexual affairs with him, but this did not dim Harrison's respect for what the man had to teach or his belief that nothing untoward had happened at the ashram in 1968.

For him, the highlight of his experience there was his twenty-fifth birthday, coming just days before the Festival of Shivaratri, a celebration of the wedding of Lord Shiva and his consort Parvati—the union of creation and destruction.

The Maharishi had arranged for a fireworks display and for colorful balloons to hang in the lecture hall. Indian musicians serenaded Harrison, and everyone was given a garland of fresh marigolds to offer him along with their blessings. The Maharishi seated Harrison on a silk cushion beside him. Gently, affectionately, he stroked the young man's hair. He said that ever since he'd seen "George Harrison and his blesséd friends," he had known there was hope for humanity. "Angels were vibrating with the good news; great prophets in different lands and hemispheres were sending the same message, that . . . all creation had been awakened to the certain promise of bliss eternal."

He placed a wreath of orange flowers around the musician's neck. "It's not me, you know," Harrison said, embarrassed.

The guru handed him a snow globe, upside down. "This is the world," he said. "It needs to be corrected."

CHAPTER 6

And in the End

In September 1968, Mukunda Goswami and Shyamasundar Das arrived in London, along with their wives and a devotee named Gurudas. Gurudas had marched with Martin Luther King Jr. in Alabama before joining the Krishna movement. Prabhupada had sent them all on a remarkable journey: these young American ambassadors for an elderly Indian man were dispatched to establish India's ancient religion in the heart of the empire that had long oppressed Asia. They would alter the empire from within. Prabhupada's own teacher, Swami Sarasvati had tried sending disciples in the 1930s to proselytize in Britain only to determine that the *mlecchas*, undisciplined Westerners, did not possess concentration enough to find God.

But Shyamasundar had excited Prabhupada with the possibility that, just as rock groups in San Francisco had started thousands of kids chanting the Lord's name, the Beatles, the biggest rock band in the world, could blow the movement wide open. Clearly, George Harrison was a seeker.

"I am very much eager to open a center in London," Prabhupada wrote Shyamasundar. "As soon as it is possible then I may go there for some time to meet with the Beatles. Any sincere person, never mind whether he is hippy or Beatle, if he is actually searching for something beyond this hackneyed material sense gratification, surely he will find the most comfortable shelter under the lotus feet of Lord Krishna."

Before his disciples left the United States, Prabhupada asked if they had any contacts in Britain. No, they replied. "No matter. Krishna will help," he said.

"When I came to America I knew no one, and Krishna sent all of you to me. Drama will be important in England. It is land of Shakespeare."

The disciples understood that he was telling them not to be discreet but instead to make an effort to stand out. Be outrageous. Get noticed. Though most Indian immigrants to England dressed in suits and ties and formal dresses, the Krishnas were to flaunt their silk robes, face markings, wooden flutes and *mrdangas*. Each of the men shaved their heads soon after arriving in London. "First they ignore you, then they laugh at you, then they debate you, then they accept you," Gurudas reasoned.

Britain required long-term visitors to carry four thousand pounds in cash or traveler's checks. At the airport, security officials checked their funds, asked if they were members of the Scientology cult, and then, satisfied they were harmless, let them through.

The couples boarded together in a three-room apartment in a suburb south of London owned by an Indian widow. They chanted in Trafalgar Square and on Drury Lane in Covent Garden, the center of London's hippie scene. Sure enough, their bald heads and robes drew plenty of attention, including newspaper coverage. They made a little money selling pamphlets, incense, and Prabhupada's books.

Mukunda actually thought it unlikely they'd ever meet a Beatle. But a series of letters written by Prabhupada to his young disciples in the fall of 1968 and in the early months of 1969 reveal how concertedly the Krishnas pursued George Harrison. On December 21, 1968, Prabhupada wrote Shyamasundar, "It is understood . . . that Mr. George Harrison has a little sympathy for our movement and if Krishna is actually satisfied on him surely he will be able to join with us in pushing [Krishna] throughout the world. Somehow or other the Beatles have become the cynosure of the neighboring European countries and America also. He is attracted by [us] and if Mr. George Harrison takes [a] leading part . . . consisting of the Beatles and our Iskcon Boys surely we will change the face of the world so much politically harassed by the maneuvers of the politicians."

In a postscript, he added, "If you have serious engagement with Mr. George Harrison then don't move from London until your business is finished. Have you any copies of Bhagavad-gita? . . . Present one hardbound copy to Mr. George Harrison with my compliments. He will be pleased to read it."

At another point, after receiving disappointing dispatches from London, Prabhupada grew less hopeful. "So far [as] Mr. George Harrison is concerned . . . I think it is not probable to meet him. It doesn't matter, let us grow slowly but surely."

Then one afternoon in a Tube station, Mukunda bought an underground newspaper and noticed an ad announcing the Beatles' new Apple Corps. Apple was seeking work by talented people in all artistic media, possibly offering to fund it.

Mukunda recorded himself and the others singing the Hare Krishna chant. He sent the tape to the address in the ad: 3 Savile Row. Rather quickly, he received a form letter saying the company couldn't help.

Mukunda tried sending a pie to the Apple offices with "Hare Krishna" lettered in the crust. On another occasion, he sent a plastic wind-up walking apple painted with a mantra. Nothing.

Then it occurred to him that Allen Ginsberg might be useful. Ginsberg had been pictured in the paper hanging out with the Beatles. The Krishnas knew the poet from New York and Haight-Ashbury. So Mukunda called Apple. Using the Ginsberg connection, he got an appointment with Peter Asher, Apple's A&R agent.

One chilly day in late December 1968, the Krishnas arrived at Savile Row bearing several vegetarian platters. They were shown into a completely white reception area—white walls, white couch, white drapes. A framed painting of a bright green apple—straight out of Magritte—hung on one of the sheer, pale walls.

Asher, also pale with a shock of vivid red hair cut in the old Beatle style, entered the room, chatting away. "So. I hear Ginsberg's a friend of yours." He took a slice of cake from one of the trays.

"Yeah. He helped us out of some tight spots when we were first getting our movement started in the States," Mukunda said. He explained that they would like to make a professional recording of the Hare Krishna chant to raise funds for a center in England.

"This cake's great. But I don't do record deals. For that you'd have to meet with George."

"How do we do that?" Shyamasundar asked.

"It's not very likely," Asher answered. "Look, I'll mention it to him and see if I can get you an appointment. I guess you guys know he's into Indian stuff, so you might have more of a chance than all the other people who come in here wanting to make an album."

Crestfallen, the Krishnas left feeling the Beatles were out of reach.

But they would get another opportunity. As it turned out, Harrison had met a couple of Hell's Angels in San Francisco. He had invited them to drop by the Beatles' offices if they ever came to London. Two weeks after the Krishnas' meeting with Peter Asher, the Angels made good on the offer. Harrison distributed a memo to the Apple staff: "Hell's Angels will be in London . . . on the way to straighten out Czechoslovakia." (The Soviets had invaded the Central European country, and what the Angels thought they could do about that was anybody's guess.) "There will be twelve in number complete with black leather jackets and motor cycles. . . . They may try to make full use of Apple's facilities. They may look as though they are going to do you in but are very straight and do good things, so don't fear them or up-tight them."

The Angels, among them "Frisco" Pete and "Sweet William" Fritsch along with numerous hangers-on, took complete control of Savile Row, commandeering offices, consuming massive amounts of food and drink at the company's expense. The staff and the other Beatles *were* frightened of them, but one day Jackie Lomax, a singer, one of the artists Apple had signed to produce, watched Harrison send three Angels packing. "These three [guys] just flung open the door and walked straight in," Lomax recalled. "I was looking for the closet, but George walked straight up to the biggest guy in the middle and said, 'What are you doing here? We don't want you here, we're having a meeting.' The guy must have outweighed him by 200 pounds, but he just. . . . walked out the door and George shut it in his face."

Neil Aspinall, in charge of running Apple, asked the bikers to clear out, but they wouldn't budge. "George had invited them, so George was going to have to ask them to go," he said. "[And] I think George did it very well—I can't remember exactly what he said, but it was like, 'Yes/No—Yin/Yang—In/Out—Stay/Go. You know—BUGGER OFF! And they said, 'Well, if you put it that way, George, of course,' and left."

Their brief interlude at Apple had given the Krishnas the opening they needed. When the Angels arrived, they brought with them a couple of people Shyamasundar had known in the Haight: novelist Ken Kesey and the Grateful Dead's manager, Rock Scully, who had been so instrumental in arranging the Mantra-Rock Dance for Prabhupada. Scully invited Shyamasundar to come with him to the Apple offices one morning—maybe they'd get to talk to a Beatle.

Shyamasundar arrived in a drizzle and was turned away by a guard in a sleek black suit. "Just doing my job," the guard apologized. A klatch of girls always waiting to catch a glimpse of the Beatles laughed at the bald-headed boy.

Then a Rolls pulled up to the curb in front of the steps. A small Japanese woman dressed entirely in black stepped out of the back seat. On her way into the building she turned to Shyamasundar. "You must be one of George's," she said. "Come on in."

A small party was in progress in a spacious white lounge. A tiny Christmas tree blinked red lights in a corner next to sofas, coffee tables, armchairs. Fifty or so people stood about the room, drinking. Scully wasn't there. The Japanese woman disappeared. Finally a door opened at one end of the lounge. Apparently a meeting had just adjourned. One by one, Lennon, McCartney, and Starr emerged. They ran for the exit, speaking to no one. Shyamasundar, fidgeting awkwardly by the tree, was readying to leave. Then George Harrison stepped into the room. He glanced warily about, preparing to bolt. When he spotted the shaven head he broke into a smile. Quickly he crossed the room. "Hare Krishna," he said. "Where have you been? I've been waiting to meet you."

Ali informed Belinda he was going to go into nightclubs and tell women, "Stop showing your titties and ass! Put some clothes on!" He would visit prisons, he said, and tell "all them niggers stop smoking, stop drinking, stop taking drugs!"

He continued to travel the college circuit, in spite of various state senators assuring reporters that "Clay" was "encouraged by the Communists" and that his "un-American" talk was subverting young minds.

He ignored his critics. "I'm a baaaad man!" he said.

"The man was immaculate," Belinda said. "He was good. [Life] was beautiful then. That was the Muslim man I married."

Then he made the mistake of saying casually to Howard Cosell in a television interview, "Yeah, I'd go back [in the ring] if the money was right. I have a lot of bills to pay."

The comment drew an immediate response from Elijah Muhammad. The Messenger summoned Ali to his home in Chicago and told him he was suspended from the Nation of Islam. Two days later, *Muhammad Speaks* declared, in a striking, bold headline, "WE TELL THE WORLD WE ARE NOT WITH MUHAMMAD ALI."

Elijah Muhammad wrote, "I want the world to know that Muhammad Ali has stepped down off the spiritual platform of Islam to go and see if he can make money in the sport world. . . . Mr. Muhammad Ali plainly acted the Fool to the whole world. . . . Any man or woman who comes to Allah (God) and then puts his hopes and trust in the enemy of Allah (God) for survival, is underestimating the power of Allah (God) to even help them. . . . Mr. Muhammad Ali desires to do that which the Holy Quran teaches him against." For one year, said the Messenger, Ali "was out of the circle of the brotherhood of the followers of Islam."

He was not allowed to be seen with any Muslims or to take part in any religious activity. His holy name was revoked and he would once again go by his slave designation, Cassius Clay, a name no one respected: "LET THIS BE A LESSON TO THOSE WHO ARE WEAK IN THE FAITH."

Even some members of the Messenger's inner circle—Lana Shabazz, Muhammad's cook, for one—failed to understand why the Messenger had suddenly turned on Ali. Earlier, he had allowed him to fight and even installed his son as Ali's boxing manager.

Now Ali's prospects had dimmed. He was no longer able to bring vast sums of money into the Nation. He was still highly visible, but the press was uniformly negative—a stain on the prophet's reputation.

Ali found himself broke, shunned, and alone, just like Malcolm X in the days before he was assassinated. "It was terrifying," Belinda said.

At loose ends, Ali spent afternoons walking alone underneath Chicago's "L" tracks or hanging out with buddies at an auto garage on the corner of Sixty-Ninth Street and Stony Island Avenue. He'd stop and help people in the neighborhood if he saw he could lend a hand, changing flat tires or carrying groceries. Of his suspension he simply said, "I made a fool of myself when I said that I'd return to boxing to pay my bills. I'm glad [Elijah] awakened me. I'll take my punishment like a man and when my year's suspension is over, I hope he'll accept me back." "Boxing is temporary," Ali noted. "I will be a Muslim until the day I die."

As the party in the Apple lounge grew louder, Harrison sat quietly talking with Shyamasundar. "Do you know these people?" he asked, nodding at a group of Hell's Angels who'd appeared from somewhere in the building. The bald young man said yes, they'd all come from Haight-Ashbury where he was a devotee of Swami Prabhupada along with other "ex-freaks" like him.

Harrison laughed. Apple workers were used to seeing strange-looking people on the premises, but the sight of Beatle George huddled with this robed young American topped the list. Harrison told Shyamasundar he'd heard of Prabhupada. He was convinced that chanting Hare Krishna had saved his life as he was leaving San Francisco once on a sputtering jet.

Shyamasundar explained that Prabhupada espoused a form of Hinduism recognizing Krishna as the sole personal god.

"But what I don't get is why just Krishna?" Harrison said. "I mean, you've got Shiva, Ganesh, Brahma. They're all the same, aren't they? Why don't you chant 'Hare Shiva' or something?" This would remain a sticking point for him. As much as he would come to admire Prabhupada and adore the god Krishna, he was inclined to see Krishna as merely one manifestation among many of the Divine Presence: as he saw it, God infused all things.

Gently, Shyamasundar insisted that Krishna was the "fountainhead . . . uniquely beautiful." God's "impersonal energy" was not as powerful as Krishna's "personal form." "Just like now, which would I prefer, to sit in my pad stoned out on your music, or to be here with you personally sharing some laughs? Your music's great, but I'd rather be here yakking with you in person," he said.

Harrison sketched a map to his house on a cocktail napkin and invited Shyamasundar to drop by on the weekend. The following Sunday, Shyamasundar arrived at Kinfauns driving a red pickup truck the Krishnas had managed to purchase. Harrison played a Bob Dylan album. Shyamasundar talked some more about Prabhupada's teachings: by serving Krishna with devotion, he said, one freed one's soul from further births and secured a permanent spot in the spiritual world. He invited Harrison to come meet the other Krishnas. Harrison agreed; he admitted that after touring the Haight he felt a responsibility to set a good example for young people: "If I don't use this opportunity [to learn about and spread the word of God], then I've wasted my life, haven't I?"

One afternoon in early February 1969, he drove his Porsche to the warehouse on Betterton Street in London where the Krishnas had established a makeshift temple. They served him potato-and-pea *samosas* and sat with him on the floor in front of carved deities of Krishna and his consort Radha on a homemade altar. When Mukunda introduced himself, Harrison said, "Yes, I remember your name. Didn't you write me a letter once? I was intrigued by what you said in it . . . you turned what I was thinking around. You said it was the essence of the mantra we should be seeking, not the essence of music."

But music was something they had in common. Mukunda reached for his *mrdanga*, Harrison pumped a harmonium, and the group happily chanted Hare Krishna. They were all roughly the same age. They were all seekers. They all loved music and laughter. Harrison felt wholly at ease with them. He didn't feel pressured to shave his head or be initiated. They accepted him as a "closet Krishna."

Later, he told Mukunda, "I always felt at home with Krishna. You see, it was already a part of me. I think it's something that's been with me from my previous birth. Your coming to England . . . was just like another piece of a jigsaw puzzle that was coming together to make a complete picture. It had been slowly fitting together. That's why I responded to you all the way I did . . . I felt comfortable with you . . . kind of like we'd known each other before. It was a pretty natural thing."

By the way, he said, he knew of a vacant five-story building over on Baker Street, near the British Museum. He could buy it for them to use as their center. What did they think?

The Krishna movement had found its patron.

Prabhupada wrote Shyamasundar on May 6, 1969, "Mr. George Harrison is sometimes coming forward to help us and sometimes he is not straightforward. But because he is chanting Hare Krishna and he has some faith . . . a little respect for me, I am sure he will come forward to help our movement."

Prabhupada was pleased to learn that Shyamasundar and Mukunda were "tackling very consistently a great personality like George Harrison," he wrote to Shyamasundar later in May. And a month later he wrote, "I am glad that your friendship with Mr. George Harrison is gradually working, so much so that he is now prepared to spend [money]." But in September the Swami warned his devotees, "These monied men and women have to be very cautiously dealt with in spiritual life. We have to sometimes deal with them on account of preaching work; otherwise Lord Caitanya Mahaprabhu [a fifteenth-century Hindu saint] has strictly restricted to mix with them . . . but . . . whatever opportunity is favorable for pushing on Krishna Consciousness we should accept."

The Swami pressed his disciples to secure further contributions from the rock star. The Baker Street building was wonderful. Even better would be several acres in the countryside for a self-sustaining Krishna compound. Harrison considered it and hesitated.

The Swami asked Shyamasundar to convince Harrison to fund the publication of a book he had written explaining Krishna's story: "It will cost nineteen thousand dollars to print five thousand copies, with fifty-four color pages."

"Swami, we must be very careful with George," Shyamasundar replied. "We never ask him for anything [directly]. We just try to give to him, not take anything from him. If he gives, it's something he offers on his own."

"I understand," wrote Prabhupada. "You may inform George that it is my personal request. You will see. Krishna will help you to say it."

Shortly thereafter, on a nasty, rainy night, Shyamasundar dined with Harrison. He was trying to frame his request. He knew his uneasiness showed. Finally, he said, "George, do you remember I was telling you about that book Prabhupada wrote?" Thunder rolled across the sky. Harrison tensed. Were the Krishnas just like everyone else—opportunists always wanting something from him? "Prabhupada asked me to ask you something. He wants you to publish [the book], nineteen thousand dollars—"

Harrison frowned. Thunder clapped again. Then, Shyamasundar said, lightning struck the roof. The houselights blazed. A few of the bulbs exploded. After a stunned silence, a wide-eyed Harrison settled back in his chair. "Well," he said. "There's no arguing with that, is there?"

On his own, Harrison suggested to Mukunda one day, "You've got to record the mantra. It's a great way to tell the world about what you're doing."

"That was our original plan in approaching Apple, but I'm thinking now, you know, we're not professionals."

"You don't have to be! We weren't professionals, either, to begin with."

So one night in late March, the devotees arrived at Abbey Road. Guards escorted them into a large room plastered on all four walls with acoustic tiles. Microphone cords crossed the floor. Mukunda lighted sticks of sandalwood incense and pinned up pictures of Krishna. Harrison insisted that everyone sing; he ushered into the studio thirty or so other people to fill out the choir—janitors, sound engineers, secretaries, anyone he could find in the building. He took his place behind a harmonium. *Hare Krishna Hare Krishna Krishna Krishna . . .*

"Repeat Until Death," he scribbled on a scrap of paper.

"The Hare Krishna Mantra" sold seventy thousand copies the first day it was released by Apple Records in August. Two weeks later, it was number one on the British music charts. On *Top of the Pops*, England's most popular television show, go-go dancers swung their hips to the mantra's pulsing beat, and the recording played over stadium speakers before weekly football matches.

With the power of a Beatle behind them, the devotees had become rock stars. People stopped them on the streets for autographs. Harrison booked them to tour with Joe Cocker, the Moody Blues, Deep Purple. They played the Star Club in Hamburg where the Beatles once rocked the house. In the United States and Europe, performances of the stage musical *Hair* always ended with a spirited version of the mantra, involving the audience.

Prabhupada had a commercial hit on his hands—far greater exposure for Krishna than he had dreamed when he had set sail from India on a cargo ship four years earlier.

Meanwhile, he was planning a trip to England to meet Harrison, maybe by the end of the year. He told Shyamasundar that his visit there would be "the biggest thing in London since the time of the Roman Invasion."

Prabhupada's disciples appeared in Harrison's life at a crucial moment, at a time when "everyone in the world want[ed] to be a Beatle . . . except the Beatles," in the estimation of critic Fred Goodman.

"George came back from Rishikesh and reacted with real horror to what was going on [at Apple]," said Derek Taylor, the Beatles' publicist. He saw it as "John and Paul's madness . . . just [giving] away huge quantities of money."

McCartney had even said as much: "We're in the happy position of not really needing any more money. So for the first time, the bosses aren't in it for profit. If you come and see me and say, 'I've had such-and-such a dream,' I'll say, 'Here's so much money. Go away and do it.' We've already bought all our dreams. So now we want to share that possibility with others."

It sounded great, but none of it was feasible—or true. The Beatles were close to cash-poor. That's why Apple was founded in the first place, as a financial shelter. At the time, Britain imposed on its wealthiest citizens a 95 percent tax rate. McCartney was not going to welcome strangers into his office or his home to hear them pitch their crazy dreams, and neither were the others. Apple simply could not function as a "psychedelic sugar daddy," to use Goodman's term.

But initially Lennon was as enthusiastic as McCartney. "We're just going to do—*everything*!" he crowed. "We'll have electronics, we'll have clothes, we'll have publishing, we'll have music. We're going to be talent spotters." At a press conference, he said to business reps, "We want to set up a system whereby people who just want to make a film about anything don't have to go on their knees in somebody's office. Probably yours."

The Apple office on Savile Row had "the best-stocked bar in town," Pattie Boyd said. "Scotch, VSOP brandy, vodka, wine, champagne, cigarettes, whatever anyone wanted was dispensed liberally to all, from the office juniors to friends, other musicians, and anyone who happened to drop in . . . [and] visitors didn't stop at drinks: they walked out with typewriters, hi-fi speakers, television sets—anything that wasn't screwed down. Security was nonexistent because it had never occurred to anyone that it might be necessary. . . . George said, 'This place has become a haven for dropouts. The trouble is, some of our best friends are dropouts.'"

"The [world's] longest cocktail party" was how Richard DiLello, an Apple staffer, described the company's business model. One day a naked woman walked in off the street dragging her teenage daughter. She asked if someone could find George Harrison right away because the girl wanted to sleep with him.

Each day the staff on Savile Row was overwhelmed by mail: mountains of awful tapes, atrocious manuscripts, terrible eight-millimeter films from dilettantes seeking patronage. Record producing was the one successful endeavor, and its robustness was largely due to Harrison. Though he was skeptical of the Apple enterprise, he did take seriously the idea of helping other artists. More than the other Beatles, he devoted himself to producing new music. After years of being relegated to the role of sideman for Lennon and McCartney, he was accustomed to working hard on other people's projects. He handpicked a few artists he admired: Jackie Lomax, Doris Troy, Ronnie Spector, the Iveys (renamed Badfinger), and Billy Preston, Sam Cooke's old keyboardist. He pursued a diversity of styles: gospel, soul, folk, rhythm and blues, and Wall of Sound. He produced, wrote, arranged, and played on the songs. "George Harrison really was quite a talented producer," said Geoff Emerick. "He knew what he wanted, and he was a very different person when he wasn't on a Beatles session. Perhaps that was because he didn't have to contend with being second-guessed by Paul or John . . . or Yoko." John Barham, an orchestral arranger who often worked with the Beatles, said, looking back: "I sensed that he was honing his skills as a record producer and for the most part enjoying himself. I didn't feel any strain . . . I would say he was happier and more outgoing then."

One significant reason for this was the experience of playing with musicians other than the Beatles. He learned new styles, new techniques—and people appreciated his talents.

It was not like being stuck with the boys, where every day was a scolding. "I'd open my guitar case and go to get my guitar out and [Paul would] say, 'No, no, we're not doing that yet.' It became stifling . . . Paul wanted nobody to play on his songs until he had decided how [they] should go," Harrison said.

He would offer a new tune he had written, only to be shunned. "Sour Milk Sea" would have been one of the strongest songs on the *White Album*. Lennon and McCartney showed little enthusiasm for it. Harrison gave it to Jackie Lomax. "While My Guitar Gently Weeps," a standout, became acceptable to the others only when Harrison brought a new friend of his to Abbey Road to play lead guitar—Eric Clapton, whose skills they all admired.

The album's selections, most written in Rishikesh, were distinctive for their *lack* of Eastern flavor (except for references to the Ganges valley setting: blackbirds, rivers, monkeys). It's as if the band needed a dose of homesickness in order to reassess its Western musical heritage: vaudeville numbers, blues, movie soundtracks, country and western, rock and roll, Tin Pan Alley . . .

Ravi Shankar, aware that, for some time, Harrison had barely touched his guitar, asked him what his roots were. Shankar suggested he return to his foundations for musical nourishment. "I felt more at home in India . . . yet I decided, 'well maybe I should get back to the guitar because I'm not getting any better . . . and I'm not going to be a great sitar player,'" Harrison would write. "I had met a few hundred sitar players who were all sensational, yet Ravi had hopes only for one of them . . . I should have started at least fifteen years earlier."

"While My Guitar Gently Weeps" and "Long Long Long" indicated how firmly the structures, syncopations, and tonalities of Indian music would remain in Harrison's songs even when he did return to his rock and roll roots.

McCartney referred to the *White Album* as the "Tension Album" because the Beatles had nearly ceased to function as a band at this point. After the return from India and Lennon's rejection of the Maharishi, Harrison no longer had major influence in the group. McCartney never let him forget it. He asserted his dominance in the studio. Working through their tensions, the Beatles gave listeners the most vivid echoes of the era. It wasn't exactly "All you need is love."

"Can you take me back where I came from, can you take me back?" Paul sings on a hidden track on the album. The answer was plain: no. After sifting through every imaginable melody, scrap, and ditty, the *White Album* reached a crescendo with a barrage of noise: bombs and singing angels, Gatling guns, car horns, riotous shouts and baby talk, ghost choruses, military fanfares, sexy whispers and agonized screams, and sports fans chanting for blood, followed by an off-key lullaby. The history of Western civilization.

One reason McCartney became so overbearing in the studio was the musical splintering evident among the band's three writers and his desire to impose some unity. Lennon expressed the difference this way: "Paul said, 'Come and see the show.' I said, 'I read the news today, oh boy.'"

But the split was more profound than that. As David R. Reck wrote, Harrison, maturing rapidly, was an almost schizophrenic writer at this point, swinging from hard-driving blues-and-soul based rock (his roots) to classical Indian stylings. His music directly reflected his inner turmoil: "The way I see it is that one half is going where the other half has just been," he said. "I was in the West and I was into rock and roll, getting crazy, staying up all night and doing whatever were supposed to be the wrong things. That's in conflict with all the right things, which is what I learned through India—like getting up early, taking care of yourself and having some sort of spiritual quality to your life. I've always had this conflict." Unable to synthesize his impulses, he nevertheless had a clear idea of what they were and how they related.

By contrast, Lennon's experimental tape loops, feedback, electronic noodling, distorted voices, and backwards guitar riffs tilted toward surrealism—a kaleidoscope of impressions rather than Harrison's direct perception, suggesting a psyche so damaged by trauma (abandonment by his father, the early loss of his mother) that it was unable to stitch together a coherent sense of reality.

Lennon's songs were poetic, Harrison's more elegantly structured. McCartney, the most naturally melodic of the three, worked feverishly to make the Beatles commercially viable, a difficult and often unenviable task.

McCartney also—against his will—had to be the schoolmarm. It isn't clear why or how Lennon and Ono got hooked on heroin; most of his life, Lennon had been dependent on one drug or another—Preludin in Hamburg to keep him up all night or the dreamy escape of LSD. And the Beatles had always been targets for dealers and tempters. Now McCartney became aware that he was in serious danger of losing his partner to apathy and addiction. Lennon gave various reasons for sniffing the drug: he had been busted for possession of hashish, and the trauma of that experience got him started; or it was the pain of Yoko Ono's miscarriage in November 1968; or it was his bandmates' chilly regard for his new lover, "what the Beatles and their pals did to us."

Most likely, he began using after a summer 1968 exhibition of Ono's work at London's Robert Fraser Gallery. Fraser was well known for turning the British art world on to hard drugs, claiming the drugs weren't addictive. In any case, Ono was soon joking that sniffing heroin was the couple's form of exercise.

"This was a fairly big shocker for us because we all thought we were far-out boys, but we kind of understood that we'd never get quite that far out," McCartney said. "John started talking about fixes and monkeys and it was harder terminology which the rest of us weren't into. We were disappointed that he was getting into heroin because we didn't really know how we could help him. We just hoped it wouldn't go too far."

Lennon began missing recording sessions. When he *did* show, Ono was always at his side. He'd bounce from silence and passivity to extreme irritation. Barry Miles, a friend of McCartney's, wrote, "The other Beatles had to walk on eggshells just to avoid one of [Lennon's] explosive rages . . . John was in such an unpredictable state and so obviously in pain."

The Beatles had always protected themselves in Abbey Road as a tight, focused working unit. By bringing Ono to the sessions Lennon was daring his mates to challenge him. While the band practiced, honing song structures, Ono sat next to Lennon talking to him in a low voice. One day she spoke aloud to the group, suggesting a different vocal approach to a song. McCartney paused. Then, barely restraining his rage, he said, "Fuck me. Did somebody speak? Who the fuck was that? Did you say something, George? Your lips didn't move."

Harrison had always been the third voice in the group, behind Lennon and McCartney; now he was demoted to fourth, behind Yoko Ono. It infuriated him. Hurt him.

"He said to me . . . that John sometimes mucked up his head, but the relationship with Yoko and John, and the drugs, that really did fuck up [George's] heart," said Geoff Wonfor, a friend and Apple employee.

Lennon would not admit he had violated the group's work ethic by introducing his lover into the sanctity of the studio, giving his bandmates legitimate reason for discomfort. He would not admit they had cause to be concerned about his drug intake and Ono's powerful influence on him. Instead, he lashed out, blaming their reactions on racism, telling Jann Wenner of *Rolling Stone*,

> You sit through sixty sessions with the most big-headed, uptight people on earth and see what it's fuckin' like. And be insulted just because you love someone. George insulted her right to her face in the Apple office at the beginning, just being straightforward, that game of, "Well, I'm going to be upfront because this is what I've heard and Dylan and a few people said you've got a lousy name in New York and you give off bad vibes." That's what George said to her, and we both sat through it. And I didn't hit him, I don't know why . . . I'll never forgive [Paul and George]. I don't care what fuckin' shit about Hare Krishna and God.

Inevitably, the Beatles' troubles spilled into Harrison's marriage. Frightened, Boyd saw that "some of the lightness [had gone] out of his soul." He had been extremely intense in India and then frustrated, returning to the Beatle grind, when he couldn't maintain complete devotion to meditation. He withdrew inside the house to chant, or he would retreat into his garden. He would fast and refrain from drugs, even sex. And then, after a horrible day at Abbey Road, he would drive home and dive into alcohol or pot. He couldn't find any balance.

He grew short-tempered. He treated the Apple staff roughly. "George could be very easy to be with and down to earth, but he was well aware of who he was," said Chris O'Dell, of Apple. "For us it was like, 'Well, he's George. We'll just have to adjust to his mood, he's not going to adjust to ours.'" His sense of humor, always caustic, became hard to distinguish from genuine anger.

Boyd had never seen him so depressed. His darkness increased. "I don't think I knew half of what was going on [with the Beatles]," she would write. "George would start to say something about Paul, then stop. He appeared unable or unwilling to share his thoughts with me; he wouldn't tell me he felt left out—although I am sure he did. He kept his hurt, frustration, anger, or whatever it was, to himself. We had once been so close, so honest and open with each other. Now a distance had developed between us. At times I couldn't reach him."

Other destabilizing elements undermined the marriage. A group of hard-core fangirls, teenagers mostly, some of them runaways, some from as far away as the United States, had begun congregating on the Apple front steps day and night, waiting to glimpse the Beatles, bringing flowers and gifts. Month after month they stood in the cold and rain, wearing ratty coats. Harrison referred to them as the Apple Scruffs. Unlike the other Beatles, he often stopped and talked with the girls, bringing them tea when the day was particularly cold. He told them he truly could not understand why they were there, but their devotion touched him. For the most part, the Scruffs' relationships with the Beatles were sweet and innocent, but on a couple of occasions the girls crossed lines. One day some of them broke into Paul McCartney's house and stole a pair of his trousers (later he wrote a song about it, "She Came in through the Bathroom Window"). Another Scruff, Carol Bedford from Dallas, Texas, made persistent efforts to snag Harrison's attention. She told him she loved him. He worried about her chronic depression and her willingness to suffer in the cold just to see him. One day he asked her if she had been in Dallas when JFK was shot. He asked her if she knew about Krishna and confessed he believed he was too "impure" to ever be a proper devotee. "At least you try," she told him. "You're very kind," he said. She gave him the number of a therapist she saw in London because she detected that he was depressed too. She asked him how his home life was. "It's crazy," he said. "I love the people I live with. I really do. I just can't live with them." He seemed to mean the Beatles more than his wife. One night he gave her a delicate kiss. It shocked them both.

Their intimacy never went beyond that, and Bedford eventually realized, "I was one of his nightmares. I, who professed to love and care for him, was one of his daily pressures. Therefore, to really care for him, I was forced to stay away from him . . . [to] remove one pressure from his life . . . It became all I could offer."

Meanwhile, Harrison was seeing more and more of Eric Clapton. They were neighbors. Often they stopped by each other's houses to play guitars. Harrison wrote "Here Comes the Sun" in Clapton's garden one afternoon while skipping a bad Beatles session.

Harrison and Boyd were "trying to set me up with different pretty ladies," Clapton recalled. "I wasn't really interested, however, because something else quite unexpected was happening: I was falling in love with Pattie. I think initially I was motivated by a mixture of lust and envy . . . she belonged to a powerful man who seemed to have everything I wanted—amazing cars, an incredible career, and a beautiful wife."

Boyd was aware that he found her attractive. "And I enjoyed the attention he paid me," she would write. Harrison knew this.

So there it was, the road ethos moving in, unpacking its case in the living room: sex as possession, as competition, as a form of male bonding, a perk of rock and roll.

Clapton's envy and his attraction to Harrison's wife initiated a complex psychodrama that would play out for years; it was as much about Harrison and Clapton as about Harrison's marriage to Boyd.

Clapton had been dating one of Boyd's friends, a French model named Charlotte Martin, who had posed for magazine covers with Boyd. He abandoned Martin abruptly to "work out" his feelings for his friend's wife. When he did so, Boyd invited her to stay at Kinfauns to recover from her heartbreak. Martin's idea of recovery was to signal Harrison that she wanted to bed him—perhaps as a blow to Clapton. Perhaps for a similar reason, to compete with Clapton, or to ease his depression, Harrison did not resist Martin's approach.

Boyd knew he had strayed when she smelled sandalwood oil on his skin. He had never worn aftershave or cologne. "I was shocked that George could do such a thing to me," she said. "If I had been a stronger, more confident person I might have guessed that . . . he was just being a boy and would get over it, that it didn't mean he didn't love me, but my ego was too fragile and I couldn't see it as anything other than betrayal."

Feebly, Harrison used Krishna as an excuse to his wife, saying the god "was always surrounded by young maidens." He said he could imagine becoming a figure like that, "a spiritual being with lots of concubines." In truth, he detested his weakness, how easily he fell prey to pettiness, squabbling, and lust. "I hated everything about my ego," he said of that time. "It was a flash of everything false and impermanent which I disliked."

He spent a weekend with his parents, to be quiet, to try to understand how things had gotten so bad with the Beatles, to try to grasp his own behaviors: was he unhappy at home, was his unhappiness affecting the band's dynamics; or was the poisonous atmosphere of the studio ruining his marriage?

Over Thanksgiving holiday in 1968, he went with Boyd to visit Bob Dylan in the United States, an escape from Apple's madness. Since suffering a motorcycle accident (and fame fatigue) in 1966, Dylan had more or less secluded himself in Woodstock, New York. He had not performed in public. "Bob was an odd person," Boyd said. "When we went to see him . . . God, it was absolute agony. He just wouldn't talk. He *would not talk*. He certainly had no social graces whatsoever. I don't know whether it was because he was shy of George or what the story was, but it was agonizingly difficult." Finally, Harrison unpacked the guitars. That broke the ice. He played Dylan a new song he'd written, an erotic lament probably inspired by Charlotte Martin ("I see your eyes are busy kissing mine"). The Beatles would dismiss the song, but Dylan was intrigued by the tune's unusual major seventh chords. He asked Harrison to show him a few tricks with the frets. Harrison wrote a song speaking directly to Dylan, expressing his friendship, trying to break through Dylan's shyness: "Let me into your heart."

Again he experienced the pleasure of playing with someone new and being respected for his musicianship. "He was totally free from the people he thought were holding him back," Boyd said, pleased to see him lighten up.

But then he returned to what he termed the "Beatles' winter of discontent." Once more, Lennon and McCartney refused to give his songs a serious listen. One night, he asked Glyn Johns, a producer at Abbey Road, a favor. Johns later recalled, "[Harrison] asked me if I would stay behind after a session because he wanted to put down a demo on his own with no one else in the room, which made me assume that he was a little insecure about it. I think he had been made to feel that way." Alone with an electric guitar, Harrison ran through an early version of "Something," which would become the Beatles' second-best-selling song after Paul McCartney's "Yesterday."

"I remember listening to that song and thinking, 'Fucking hell, why isn't he playing this to everyone else? What is going on here?' And then him coming in and asking what did I think. That remains my overriding memory of George:

What did I think? I said, 'You've got to be fucking joking. It's incredible, what are you talking about?'"

In this atmosphere, Mukunda and Shyamasundar couldn't have arrived soon enough for George Harrison.

On the studio floor, McCartney said to Lennon, in front of their younger mate, "Our songs have [always] been better than George's." To McCartney, Harrison said, "Look, I'll play whatever you want me to play, or I won't play at all. Whatever it is that'll please you, I'll do it."

It was just the tenth day of the first month of another long year.

Muhammad and Belinda Ali sat in the back seat of a black car gliding quietly through the dark streets of Manhattan at night. Black cloth bags covered their heads. They could see nothing. Their hearing was muffled.

The car stopped. Hands groped them, helping them out, slowly turning them and guiding them up concrete steps into a building. When the bags were removed from their heads they found themselves in a small apartment facing H. Rap Brown. He greeted them warmly. A small, thin man who appeared to be growing out of his Afro rather than the other way around, he pointed out the window. A delicious irony: he was hiding from the cops, but his safe house was right across the street from a police station. He apologized for the secrecy, the bags, all that, but he couldn't be too careful, and they would be safer now if someone questioned them later. It was best for them not to know where they were.

"Something had just blown up and [the cops] said he was behind it," Belinda said later. In fact, Brown was on the FBI's Ten Most Wanted List. A former chairman of the Student Nonviolent Coordinating Committee and briefly minister of justice with the Black Panther Party, Brown was known and feared for his incendiary rhetoric. "Violence is as American as cherry pie," he had said. He called for "Negroes" to "carry on guerilla warfare in all the cities," activities to "make the Vietcong look like Sunday School teachers."

He was thrilled to meet Muhammad Ali. When he had heard that Ali was staying in New York, he spread word on the streets that he would like to talk to the man. "[So] we're sitting there next to this terrorist, this criminal, this revolutionary. Radical!" Belinda said. "Nicest person you ever wanted to meet." She paused. "But he was serious about blowing up shit."

The three of them chatted pleasantly for over an hour, Brown periodically checking the window to make sure the streets were clear. He said he had strongly supported Harry Edwards's Olympic Project for Human Rights and Edwards's calls to boycott the 1968 Games in Mexico City. (Did Ali know that Brown was an athlete? He had gone to Southern University on a football scholarship.) Ali agreed it was a proud moment when Tommie Smith and John Carlos raised their fists on the medal stand. Brown told him that someone had smuggled a flier for the Olympic Project for Human Rights into Nelson Mandela's prison cell in South Africa. Reportedly, Mandela treasured the flier.

When the time came for Ali and Belinda to leave, the bags went back on their heads and Brown's driver dropped them at the Wellington Hotel on Fifty-Fifth Street, where they were staying. Earlier that evening, they'd left Maryum in the room with a friend.

They had come to New York for Ali's unlikely debut on Broadway. A year earlier, he had flown to the city to watch James Earl Jones play Jack Johnson in *The Great White Hope*. The play delighted him; he bragged, "Jack Johnson is the original me." The producers agreed with him. Soon thereafter, Zev Buffman, a veteran of stage musicals, and his financial backers, including Jack Haley Jr., whose father had played the Tin Man in *The Wizard of Oz*, offered Ali a part in a musical called *Buck White*. The play concerned America's legacy of slavery and the rise of Black militancy—not an acting stretch for Ali. For three hundred dollars a week he would play a radical speaker from the Beautiful Allelujah Days (BAD), and he would sing four songs written by poet Oscar Brown Jr., including the show-stopper, "Mighty Whitey": "You've had us in your lock / tight as any cage. / And now you're acting shocked / Cause we are in a rage."

It was his chance to be a singer onstage, like Lloyd Price, Sam Cooke, and the Beatles.

In the play, billed on the marquee as "Cassius Clay," he wore a fake beard and an Afro wig as big as a Japanese maple. He also wore a pelt, leaving his muscled arms gleaming and bare. He attacked the role with gusto, stalking the stage, booming songs, glaring out at the seats. "Was you scared?" he asked visitors at rehearsals.

"Ali was brilliant. I have never seen anyone or anything like it, the way he captured the stage," Buffman said. "I was amazed at his ability to carry a tune—his voice was as attention-grabbling as his charm as a fighter."

The songs were not a problem, but it was difficult for him to memorize spoken lines. "Why can't I just ad lib all the time?" he asked.

"Because then it wouldn't be a play," a fellow actor explained. "It would be something else."

Ali insisted that profanity be removed from the script. "I'd never do a love scene," he said. "Not only with a white woman, any woman. I'm a religious person. Get Billy Graham to play a love scene. Or the Pope. It's the same thing."

Belinda came to rehearsals bringing seventeen-month-old Maryum. Maryum ran among the empty aisles while Belinda drew reporters' stares almost as much as Ali. She was striking and dignified, tall and regal in her black silk pant suits, her hair tied in a bun.

It didn't take long for her to learn that her husband made a distinction between love scenes onstage and offstage. Every afternoon, women flocked around the theater door ogling Ali. He couldn't believe it. He flirted back with them. It was like the groupie scene at a Beatles concert.

The temptation proved too much. Several times Belinda caught him kissing girls in dark theater nooks or in the hallways of the Wellington Hotel. "I thought growing up if I was good and loyal my husband would be good and loyal. I was totally wrong," she said. But she surprised herself by not being too upset at his behavior. She had been raised around Elijah Muhammad, and this sort of hypocrisy was nothing new to her. She had seen that Elijah and Herbert did not necessarily associate sex with love, and she accepted this as a fact about all men.

Ali turned out to be "a sex addict," she lamented. He'd cry and apologize whenever she caught him with a girl. "He would tell me, 'I'm just weak, man. I'm just grateful you're not jumping off leaving me.' I said I'm not going to leave you. I said we got children. I'm not going to let no woman destroy my marriage. . . . And he would say, 'I don't love these people, it was just bam, bam, thank you ma'am. I ain't in love with nobody.'"

She would grab him at the end of rehearsals and drag him back to the hotel. "That would leave the 150 women for the rest of us," said one cast member. "We had carte blanche, something I've never seen at another play. It was a very good situation [for us]."

On the weekends Ali slipped entirely out of his wife's control. Sonji Roi had managed to get in touch with him now that Elijah Muhammad was not watching him so intently. Sonji was living in Philadelphia; frequently now, Ali left Belinda with Maryum in New York to conduct an affair with Sonji. He swore to her she was still his first love.

While in Philadelphia he would stay with members of the mosque there, though the Muslims were not supposed to consort with him. They were a rogue bunch—the FBI called them the "gangster mosque" and monitored their activities involving "narcotics, armed robberies, widespread extortion and loan-sharking." During his visits, Ali was fortunate not to get caught in an FBI sting.

Buck White opened at the George Abbott Theater on December 2, 1969. It closed four days later. Even reviewers who hated the play generally gave Ali high marks. Clive Barnes wrote, "[Ali] emerges as a modest naturally appealing man. He sings with a pleasant slightly impersonal voice, acts without embarrassment, and moves with innate dignity. He does himself proud."

This was a typical response, as were pans of the play in spite of Ali's efforts. The highly choreographed Black Power salutes throughout the performance were simply too artificial to be effective. Young people, for whom the play would naturally have the strongest appeal, could not afford tickets. And picketers outside the theater, protesting Ali's "draft-dodging," frightened away Broadway regulars.

Most of all, "I think the FBI shut it down," said one of the actors. "There were some things that happened that didn't feel right. Even with the [poor] reviews the play should have run for at least a month. The FBI was always around. They didn't want Ali to make money. J. Edgar Hoover wanted to keep him down."

Ed Sullivan agreed.

Ali's most cynical critics, such as Mark Kram of *Sports Illustrated*, used his speaking tours and the brief Broadway stint as proof that he would do anything for money—as if his need to make a living invalidated his antiwar stance.

Then the literary world came to his defense. Once again, George Lois, the art director of *Esquire*, the man behind the Saint Sebastian cover, decided it was time to shake things up. He put a boxing ring on the magazine's November 1969 cover—sans Ali. Instead, standing between the ropes: a dozen prominent male intellectuals, artists, and entertainers beneath the line, "We believe this: Muhammad Ali deserves the right to defend his title."

By the end of the year, Random House had paid Ali $60,000, the first installment on a $200,000 advance for his autobiography, to be cowritten with writer and editor Richard Durham and edited by Toni Morrison. "Writing is as good as fighting," Ali declared happily.

His cause had been helped by the country's mood. The war was increasingly unpopular. Hippies were more acceptable now after the generally peaceful spectacle of Woodstock. Paradoxically, the Nation of Islam's shunning of Ali lent him more credibility in the minds of doubters, apparent proof that he wasn't just marching to Elijah Muhammad's orders. His decisions—like them or not—were his own, and he was willing to suffer the consequences.

His religion was beyond most Americans' grasp, but the public understood that his faith manifested as courage. The slow redemption of Muhammad Ali had begun.

"We haven't got half the money people think we have," John Lennon announced to the press in early January 1969. "It's been pie-in-the-sky from the start. . . . We did it all wrong. . . It's got to be business first, we realize that now. . . . If it carries on like this, all of us will be broke in the next six months."

When Brian Epstein was still living, Paul McCartney tormented him, threatening to enlist someone to run the Beatles' business more efficiently—someone like that creepy American, Allen Klein. In fact, the day Klein heard on his car radio that Epstein had died, he thought, "I got 'em!"—meaning the Beatles. As *the* accountant to the rock world, he knew there was no bigger prize. For years he had heard rumors that Epstein was gullible, harried, naïve, and disintegrating psychologically. When he died, Klein figured he would bide his time and wait for the right moment to strike.

Lennon's announcement that the Beatles were nearly broke was that moment, and Klein used every connection he had in the record business to schedule a meeting with John.

Klein had "all the charm of a broken lavatory seat," said Alistair Taylor, an aide working for Apple. He was "fast-talking, dirty-mouthed . . . sloppily dressed and grossly overweight," another aide complained. Yet these were precisely the qualities that most appealed to Lennon—particularly since McCartney had suggested the Park Avenue lawyers Lee and John Eastman as the band's new managers. The Eastmans were about to become McCartney's new in-laws, the father and brother, respectively, of photographer Linda Eastman, to whom McCartney had become engaged after splitting with Jane Asher.

The Eastmans were the sort of sophisticated men in suits who had screwed Lennon all his life, he said—an assessment George Harrison shared. "Because we were all from Liverpool we favored street people. Lee Eastman was more like a class-conscious type of person," Harrison said.

He wasn't fond of Klein, but he went with Lennon. Lennon convinced Harrison that Klein would make them money right away.

Most of all, Lennon had responded warmly to Klein's stories of an absent dad and a mother dead too young. The men shared similar miserable pasts. Lennon was touched by the "sentimental old Jewish mommy" in Klein: "I believe him when he says he has helped Sam Cooke's old father," he said.

Despite once joking that he was tempted to enlist the brash accountant, McCartney distrusted the man. He had heard stories about Klein, how he would begin by representing artists and then wind up owning them. McCartney knew Klein was under investigation for tax evasion in the United States. He wanted nothing to do with him.

It didn't take Klein long, perusing the Beatles' old contracts, to discover that they had been "fucked around by everybody." This was standard practice in the record industry—and finding it was the easy part. It was also a fairly simple matter for Klein to threaten the record companies into coughing up a little more money. This impressed his clients and earned Klein their trust.

Except for that of Paul McCartney.

Meanwhile, Dick James, Brian Epstein's old friend who had made a fortune buying the publishing rights to the Beatles' songs, got nervous, hearing rumors about the band's squabbling and their management crisis. He decided to sell his share of the Lennon-McCartney catalog to Sir Lew Grade, Britain's biggest entertainment mogul, a man the Beatles hated because he had dismissed them early in the game, then sang their praises once they became a smashing success.

It was bad enough for James to unload the catalog; it was an abomination that Lew Grade was the beneficiary. James wasn't going to announce anything until the deal was complete, killing any chance the Beatles might have had to gain control of their songs.

The Beatles' business troubles amplified their inexorable self-destruction in the studio. McCartney seized the initiative and decided the group should make a documentary film, rehearsing a new set of songs and ending the movie with a concert performance. He arranged to book the band in the cold and drafty Twickenham Film Studios, where much of *A Hard Day's Night* was shot, surrounded by cameras and cameramen all day, every day, filming what turned out to be the group's final split. Lennon's response was to withdraw even further on opioids. Starr showed up as he always had but offered no more energy than was required of him. He was drinking more and more, worrying his wife Maureen, who appeared frequently at the studio to check on her Ritchie. She seemed to be regretting that she had not given meditation more of a chance. She admired Harrison's calm—though she could see he was struggling too. Gamely, he tried to follow McCartney's plan, introducing new material only to have McCartney reject it. "I'm . . . trying to help you, and I always hear myself . . . annoy[ing] you," McCartney told him one day.

"You're not annoying me. You don't annoy me anymore," Harrison responded with great annoyance.

He grew quieter each day, less engaged.

Finally one afternoon a frustrated McCartney said to his mates, "I don't see why any of you, if you're not interested, get yourselves into this. What's it for? It can't be for the money. Why are you here? I'm here because I want to do a show, but I really don't feel an awful lot of support."

Silence.

"You don't say anything," McCartney pleaded with Lennon.

"Hear no evil, speak no evil, see no evil," Harrison said, mocking Lennon's blankness. Another lengthy pause. Harrison said, "Maybe we should get a divorce."

They mustered happiness as a musical unit only when they burst into spontaneous jams of oldies they'd grown up playing together, as if touching again, briefly, distantly, a sweeter, more innocent time. "We used to do it . . ." Harrison said sadly one day, picking at Buddy Holly's "Crying, Waiting, Hoping." "It ended with, ah—"

Hopin' you'll come back . . .

On March 12, 1969, the day Paul McCartney married Linda Eastman, Harrison's woes were compounded when the police raided his house and busted him for marijuana possession.

Happy police overran his place, drinking his tea, watching his television, inspecting his record collection, thrilled to be meeting a Beatle. "This is my house," he kept repeating incredulously. He accused the cops of planting the pot. "I'm a tidy man," he said. "I keep my socks in the sock drawer and [my] stash in the stash box. It's not mine."

Four years later, the police sergeant in charge of the raid would be convicted of "conspiracy to pervert the course of justice" for planting drugs in several of his cases. He was sentenced to four years in prison. Harrison was fined 250 pounds.

Life would take another nasty turn in September when Harrison's mother and father, Louise and Harry, both fell ill. The only good thing about being a Beatle, he had often said, was the opportunity it gave him to take care of his folks. When he first earned money, he had asked his father how much he made, driving a bus. "Ten pounds, two shillings," Harry answered. "A day?" "A week." "Dad, please retire," Harrison had said. "I'll give you three times that to do nothing. It'll put another ten years on your life."

But now he stood face to face with his helplessness. For over eight weeks Louise had been misdiagnosed as suffering from "psychological problems" when in fact she had a brain tumor. Her doctor, who had merely prescribed pills for mild dementia, asked for Harrison's autograph when Harrison arrived to speak with him. Harrison was furious. "[Louise's] skin was covered with goose pimples and she was rambling about people in the room whom we couldn't see," Boyd would later write. Louise didn't recognize her son. "We immediately found another doctor, who sent Louise straight to hospital for X-rays," Boyd recalled. "Four hospitals later, we discovered she had a brain tumor. It was inoperable, but a surgeon drilled a hole in her skull to release some fluid and relieve the pressure." Meanwhile, Harry had been hospitalized for severe ulcers. "It was sad to watch George try to comfort his father when he himself was so low," Boyd wrote. He pretended to each of his parents that the other was going to be fine.

That same month, September 1969 (shortly after the Beatles finished recording *Abbey Road*), Prabhupada arrived in London. Reporters greeted him at the airport. "Do you plan to meet with George Harrison while you're here in England?" they asked.

"Yes, if he would like, I will meet with him. I can meet with anyone who is interested in serving Krishna."

"Are you his guru?"

"I am no one's guru. I am servant, not master."

This answer endeared him to Harrison.

Harrison had talked Lennon into letting Prabhupada stay in a guest room at Lennon's house, a vast Georgian estate called Tittenhurst, outside of London, while the Krishna temple was being readied in the city. Lennon had plenty of space; Tittenhurst was undergoing renovations, and he invited a group of devotees to stay with Prabhupada as long as they would work on the house in exchange for their rooms.

Prabhupada took to Harrison right away. Harrison was a "nice young boy," he said.

"Prabhupada just looked like I thought he would," Harrison said. "I had like a mixed feeling of fear and awe about meeting him . . . [but] I felt that he was just more like a friend. I felt relaxed . . . He was very warm towards me. . . . He wouldn't talk differently to me than to anybody else. . . . Seeing him was always a pleasure."

One afternoon at Tittenhurst, Harrison sat with Prabhupada, Lennon, and Yoko Ono. "What kind of philosophy are you following?" Prabhupada asked them.

"Following?" Lennon said.

"We don't follow anything," Ono replied. "We're just living."

"We've done meditation," Harrison said. "Or I do my meditation, mantra meditation."

Lennon explained that they had received "secret" mantras from the Maharishi, not to be revealed.

"If a mantra has power, why should it be secret?" Prabhupada said. He was no fan of the Maharishi's attempts to sell Indian religion to the West. "It should be distributed. People are suffering."

Harrison had also arrived at this point of view. He had read in Vivekananda, "Anything that is secret and mysterious . . . should at once be rejected. So far as it is true, it ought to be preached in the public streets in broad daylight."

Prabhupada insisted that "Hare Krishna" was the only mantra anyone needed.

"But how would you know?" Lennon challenged him. "Maharishi said exactly the same thing about his mantra, that it is coming down with seemingly as much authority as you."

"If a mantra is coming down in that way then it is potent. The potency is there."

"But Hare Krishna is the best one?" Lennon asked skeptically.

"Yes. You don't require to bother to say anything else. The Hare Krishna mantra is sufficient for one's perfection."

Harrison was troubled by Lennon's cynicism as well as Prabhupada's exclusivity. Like a good harmony singer, he attempted to offer balance: "Surely it's like flowers. Somebody may prefer roses and somebody may like carnations better. Isn't it really a matter for the devotee? One person may find Hare Krishna is more beneficial to his spiritual progress, and yet for somebody else some other mantra may be more beneficial."

Prabhupada appreciated Harrison's effort to calm the waters, but he insisted that Krishna was the Supreme Lord and that those who were "addicted" to Krishna found lasting peace.

His word choice made Harrison wonder if Prabhupada knew—or could sense—Lennon's struggle with heroin. An awkward silence hung in the room until Prabhupada suggested *kirtan*. They chanted together for a few minutes until Harrison excused himself, apologizing, explaining he had to go see his ailing mother.

As Lennon and Ono left, she turned to him and said, "Look how simply he's living." She nodded at Prabhupada's room. "Could you live like that?" Two years later, her question provided the theme of what would become Lennon's best-known song, "Imagine."

The Krishnas' stay at Tittenhurst proved to be "just a hair short of lunatic," Gurudas said. They invited new initiates from London to move in and help with the renovations: "Not the best move." Gurudas described one bald young man climbing atop Lennon's home studio where the Beatles were rehearsing one day. He came crashing through the skylight onto the concrete floor. As he sat up, trying to shake off his daze, Lennon didn't miss a strum. "Must be one of yours," he muttered to Harrison.

Eventually Prabhupada understood they had overstayed their welcome. The temple Harrison had purchased for them in central London was almost ready. Allen Klein was helping him finalize the financing; Prabhupada found himself dealing with one of the most ruthless businessmen on the planet, but it was all for spiritual benefit.

In late December 1969, the Krishnas moved into the temple, erecting a $3,000 altar slab and a blue marble carving of Krishna paid for by Harrison. Prabhupada was proud to report to his devotees that the "Hare Krishna record is [still] selling nicely." For months now he had charted its progress. Back in September, as if he were Klein, or maybe Dick James reassuring his shareholders, he had written, "Yesterday, it sold 5,000 copies, and this week it is on the chronological list as #20. They say next week it will come to be #3, and after that it may come to #1."

The Beatles' wretched business affairs soon reached a nadir. McCartney refused to speak to Allen Klein. The Eastmans advised him to separate himself, legally, from the rest of the band. "Klein and Eastman lurched at each other, collided and fell in a heap," Derek Taylor assessed. "John and Paul each claimed victory for their fighters. George, who saw his peace of mind dependent more and more on remaining neutral, said that in his view both had lost."

ABKCO, Klein's company, began skimming 20 percent of Apple's income before taxes. "They're not four little boys who don't know what they are doing, they're four grown men," Klein said. But that was wrong—they *were* virtually boys, surrounded ever since they could remember by hucksters, sycophants, hangers-on, exploiters, and tempters, given everything they wanted and shielded from what they didn't understand, caught in a bubble of unreality shaped by a level of fame the world had never experienced, cocooned by Brian Epstein until he was gone.

In his absence they were storm-tossed. Everyone wanted a piece of them. Those who had a piece wanted more, and the bandmates no longer had a buffer against the forces of erosion. The dream fed too many people. It was not sustainable without adjustment. They needed someone, just one person, to look after their best interests as individuals and as a unit; someone to see the personal crises they were in—*together*—and to put healing ahead of ego, profit, what the teachers called *Maya*. But no one did.

No one did.

"Everything got too big, too bloody vast for human beings, frail, ill-prepared human beings," said Derek Taylor. "I knew the Beatles were human, I looked at them as leaders and together with everyone else who had grown to love them, I began to build the legend of invincibility." For young people across the world, the Beatles had served as emblems of harmony, friendship, group democracy in action. *All you need is love.* "I looked to the Beatles to show the way and the poor devils were themselves crying out in pain and in vain that they were looking for a Way, a Truth and a Life."

Once ABKCO took charge, and McCartney abandoned ship, Taylor mused, "I guess you could say that Allen Klein straightened out Apple as the Beatles wanted it. The only thing is . . . where is Apple and where are the Beatles?"

Musically, the partnership ended before the contractual obligations did.

Harrison—relieved by his mother's brief remission and his father's recovery—tried to debut over half a dozen songs, three of which would end up as standouts on his first solo album. His bandmates ignored him. Despite his constant bickering with McCartney in the studio, he left the group formally one afternoon after mounting irritation with Lennon. Fed up with Lennon's condescension, coupled with Ono's presence on turf that wasn't hers, he asserted himself. He told Lennon he should have kept his mouth shut about the group's money woes—it was *their* business, not the world's. Lennon was not in his usual drug haze, and he responded flippantly.

Later, Harrison packed up his guitar. "I think I'll be leaving the band now," he said.

"When?" Lennon asked.

"Now. You can replace me. Put an ad in the *New Musical Express* and get a few people in. See you around the clubs."

He walked out. He returned—briefly—a few days later. But the band's days were numbered.

On Thursday, January 30, 1969, at around lunchtime, on a cold, breezy day, the Beatles had performed together for the very last time on the roof of the Apple building on Savile Row. They played (accompanied by keyboardist Billy Preston) for about forty-two minutes for a small crew of staffers, friends, and intimates, including Yoko Ono and Maureen Starkey.

For all its modesty and ill-preparedness, the performance was a fine way to go out. Passersby on the street stopped to listen, as did people poking their heads out of windows in adjacent buildings and climbing onto rooftops: young hipsters browsing boutiques, bankers and accountants, secretaries and mail carriers.

As he played, Harrison looked around the roof, as amazed as ever at where he found himself. Beyond it—as in a Joseph Conrad novel—the open world stretched, obscured in a layer of haze. "I'd like to say thanks on behalf of the group," Lennon said. "I hope we passed the audition."

In April 1970, a BBC reporter addressed a camera, standing in front of a grieving crowd in an afternoon drizzle outside 3 Savile Row: "The event is so momentous that historians may one day view it as a landmark in the decline of the British Empire: the Beatles are breaking up."

"It's always cold, damp, rainy, and cloudy . . . London is Hell," said the elderly man in his saffron robes. "In India the sun always shines."

Prabhupada cleared his throat. He shook his brown, bald head. He gazed out the window of the temple at the grimy streets below. Around him sat his young American disciples. "This England. England today is deteriorated. Not like fifty years ago . . . Hitler ruined their empire, even though he was also ruined." He shook his head again. "The English policy of exploitation was not good . . . Gandhi helped establish Indian people to no longer cooperate with Britishers." He tossed one more thoughtful glance out the window. "Britain is finished," he pronounced. "The British Empire is finished."

PART THREE

The Dream Is Over

CHAPTER 7

"My Friend Came to Me"

It was 111 degrees in Dacca on August 15, 1947, the day the India Independence Bill passed in the UK Parliament, removing the British Empire from its seat of power on the Indian subcontinent. On their way out, the British left a last damning imprint: they split the region into two countries, Muslim-majority Pakistan and Hindu-dominated India. In reality, geographical anomalies made this a three-country split: though politically unified, Pakistan was segmented into two non-contiguous territories, East and West, separated by thousands of miles of north Indian forests.

In the West, home of the central government, Punjabis, Pashtuns, Baluchis, and Sindhis lived together, speaking mostly Urdu; in the East, more densely populated, and economically poorer, Bengalis spoke their own language. A vibrant Hindu minority occupied the area as well. Under the Raj, Punjabis had become the Englishmen's pet military officers, prized as fighters by the British, while the Bengalis—"Bingos"—were considered weak, a non-warrior class. This prejudice remained after the English departure.

West Pakistanis distrusted their Eastern brethren, many of whom referred to their land as Bangla Desh—the Bengali Nation—and they certainly did not welcome Hindus as part of greater Pakistan.

In February 1948, at an East-West assembly in Karachi, eastern representatives proposed Bengali as Pakistan's official language, since, out of sixty-nine million people in the country, forty-four million spoke Bengali. The assembly roundly rejected the proposal. A few months later, Pakistan's governor-general declared flatly, "The state language of Pakistan is going to be Urdu and no other language. Anyone who tries to mislead you is really the enemy of Pakistan." The nascent cultural conflict had erupted into the open.

Four years later, university students in East Pakistan, massing by the thousands, insisting they had traded one colonial master for another, protested Western oppression. Street violence spilled over into Dacca's Provincial Assembly House. Police opened fire on the students, killing four of them.

Years of wearying street clashes followed between enraged students and the military—a force armed largely now by the United States, seeking a noncommunist ally in the region. In 1958 West Pakistan imposed a state of martial law on the East. The order failed to stop the violence.

General Agha Muhammad Yahya Khan seized power in 1969. Drunk on ego and cognac, he was a thoroughgoing authoritarian, but he declared he would hold free elections by the end of 1970, to prove the people's love for him. He controlled the state mechanisms, so he knew he couldn't lose.

Yet on November 13, 1970, a higher power wrested control from him. He had just returned from Washington, D.C., on a mission to secure further US arms from his friend and admirer Richard Nixon (six F-104 fighter planes, seven B-57 bombers, and three hundred armed personnel carriers). Tropical Cyclone Bhola formed rapidly over the Bay of Bengal early on November 8. It traveled northward, intensifying to a peak wind speed of 185 kilometers per hour (115 mph). It was the deadliest cyclone ever recorded. On November 13 it devastated East Pakistan, leaving over half a million people dead, nearly 15 percent of the population, their bodies floating in flooded rice paddies, bobbing among drowned cattle, soon bloated and reeking.

Beyond ordering national flags to be flown at half-mast, Yahya did little in response. Initial relief efforts consisted of one military transport aircraft and a crop-duster hauling crates of medicine and food. Yahya claimed the Indian government would not allow him to fly his military helicopters over its territory from West Pakistan. India denied this.

To blunt growing criticism from the international press, Yahya flew to East Pakistan to personally oversee the aid effort. Journalist Sidney Schanberg said, "There were still bodies floating in inland rivers, mass graves being dug with backhoes, everyone wearing masks because of the smells, throwing lime on it. And he was walking through with polished boots and a walking stick with a gold knob. . . . We asked a couple of questions, and he brushed us off with blah-blah, then went home."

East Pakistan's Bengali nationalist party, the Awami League, charged Yahya with "gross neglect, callous and utter indifference." The party called for his resignation.

Instead, he went smugly ahead with the election—and lost, badly, in East Pakistan. Of 169 contested seats in the eastern assembly, the Awami League took all but two. "*Joi Bangla!*—Victory to Bengal" said hand-painted signs appearing all across Dacca.

The league rightfully asked to be included in forming a new Pakistani government. Yahya refused. He suspended the national assembly. He warned, "It is the duty of the Pakistan armed forces to insure the integrity, solidarity, and security of Pakistan, and in this they have never failed."

US Ambassador Archer Blood alerted the State Department, "I've seen the beginning of the breakup of Pakistan." In the Oval Office, President Richard Nixon, recorded for posterity by his secret taping system, told his national security advisor, Henry Kissinger, "I feel that anything that can be done to maintain Pakistan as a viable country is extremely important."

Kissinger urged inaction. Yahya and his US-supported army would handle matters, he said. (Technically, Pakistan was under a US arms embargo for having violated a war pact with India, but Nixon personally made sure that covert supplies reached the country via Jordan and Iran.)

Nixon prided himself on being an expert on Asia, yet his policies were personal as much as strategic. Yahya was helping him open a back communications channel to China, feeding his fantasy of entering the history books as a visionary diplomat. Meanwhile, India's prime minister, Indira Gandhi, was making friendly overtures to the Soviet Union. For these reasons, Nixon opposed India and supported Pakistan.

But his alliances were also visceral. Yahya was a hard-drinking military man, matching Nixon's gilded self-image. Indira Gandhi was the daughter of Jawaharlal Nehru, the man who had convened the Bandung Conference in the 1950s that so impressed Malcom X. Besides, Gandhi was a woman.

"I don't like the Indians," Nixon said. Visiting Pakistan he said, "Pakistan is a country I would like to do everything for." As author Gary Bass notes, "Nixon found the Pakistanis to be staunchly anticommunist and pro-American. 'The people have less complexes than the Indians,' he said. 'The Pakistanis are completely frank, even when it hurts.'"

He hated the US counterculture's "mystical fascination" with Hinduism. "There is a psychosis in this country about India," he declared. Kissinger agreed with him that the Indians were a "basket case," and that "obsequiousness toward India [was] a prime example of liberal softheadedness." Justice was never the point of foreign policy, Kissinger argued. It was about international stability, even when human rights had to be sacrificed.

Beginning on March 25, 1971, using first the cyclone and then election unrest as excuses to restore law and order, the Pakistani army launched Operation Searchlight, moving savagely though East Pakistan conducting "cleansing" exercises, particularly of the region's Hindu minority population.

Driving M-24 tanks, firing squads entered villages and shantytowns, methodically mowing down citizens, strafing huts and burning them, raping women, lighting children on fire. Intellectuals were targeted. Five hundred students were killed at the University of Dacca in the first two days of the operation. "At least two mass graves on campus. Stench terrible," Archer Blood cabled the State Department.

Awami League leaders were rounded up and shot in their homes.

Archer Blood sent numerous cables documenting atrocities and pleading for US intervention. His anguish was met with "deafening silence," he said. Kenneth Keating, the US ambassador to India, also called for the Nixon administration to "promptly, publicly, and prominently deplore this brutality," as tens of thousands of starving, sick refugees stumbled into northern India, fleeing the terror.

In the Oval Office, Nixon blithely remarked to Kissinger, "The Indians need . . . a mass famine."

"They're such bastards," Kissinger agreed.

Their friend Yahya did not disguise his intentions toward East Pakistan: "Kill three million of them and the rest will eat out of our hands," he said.

Nixon continued to supply him with arms, even though Kissinger admitted, "We are . . . operating . . . at the very edge of legality." In fact, they'd passed that edge long ago. Kissinger joked that Yahya was having great fun massacring Hindus.

In late March, when the death toll in East Pakistan was nearing three hundred thousand, when documentable cases of rape had surpassed forty thousand and over ten million refugees had overwhelmed India, Kissinger reported to his boss, "It looks . . . as if Yahya has gotten control."

"Really?" Nixon said eagerly. "How?"

"The Bengalis aren't very good fighters, I guess."

This conversation took place as Archer Blood was preparing a cable to the administration with the subject line, "Selective Genocide": "Here in Dacca we are mute and horrified witnesses to a reign of terror by the Pak military."

Nixon gave no reply. But he was not sitting idle. Blood expressed his concern that US armaments were being used to support "mass murder." He had personally witnessed American-made C-130 transport planes shuttling soldiers to the East from West Pakistan. He had seen the skies blackened by F-86 Sabres, US jets honed by their use in Korea.

Cable after cable: "Horror stories," "atmosphere of terror," "stunned with grief," "army going after Hindus with vengeance," "Atrocity tales rampant," "Pray for us."

Silence from Washington.

Finally, on April 6, Blood put his career on the line. He sent a cable, signed by twenty-nine other veterans of the US diplomatic corps: "U.S. policy related to recent developments in East Pakistan serves neither our moral interests broadly defined nor our national interests narrowly defined. . . . Our government has evidenced what many will consider moral bankruptcy. . . . Unfortunately the overworked term Genocide is applicable [here]. . . . We, as professional public servants, express our dissent with current policy and fervently hope that our true and lasting interests here can be defined and our policies redirected in order to salvage our nation's position as a moral leader of the free world." Blood would be relieved of his diplomatic duties shortly after this.

The 1970s saw a widening of the world's social fissures, reflected in microcosm in the splitting of the Beatles, particularly John Lennon and George Harrison. These old mates, mirroring global fractures, veered on the issue of political activism versus spiritual enlightenment. Save the world or save your soul? The question stirred young and old as "Jesus Freaks" hit the streets alongside antiwar protesters. The massive social problems of the 1960s, in East and West, remained unresolved. Violence was worsening worldwide. Where did the workable answers lie? And what was pop culture's role, if any, in locating the answers? After all, pop culture had been, for many American consumers, a major information source.

Lennon would soon be living in New York, schmoozing with Abbie Hoffmann, Jerry Rubin, Bobby Seale, and other political activists surveilled by the FBI. For Richard Nixon and J. Edgar Hoover, Lennon with the Black Panthers was as unsettling as Muhammad Ali with the Nation of Islam.

Alternately, George Harrison advocated "conjur[ing] . . . peace" through meditation. "There is no problem if each individual doesn't have any problems. . . .

The problems are created more, sometimes, by people going around trying to fix up the government, or trying to do something."

So everything was illusory: did that make it any less oppressive?

Within the year, Lennon would be singing, "God is a concept by which we measure our pain," while Harrison sang, "My sweet Lord, I really want to see you."

Immersed in Ono, his drug-taking, and their political activity together, Lennon seemed unwilling to look back. The Beatles were finished, and good riddance to them. Harrison, who had been quite ready to escape the band, marshaled a shred of team spirit. On April 25, 1970, he told a New York City radio station, "We all have to sacrifice a little in order to gain something really big. And there is a big gain by recording together—I think musically, and financially, and also spiritually. And also for the rest of the world, you know, I think that Beatle music is such a big sort of scene—I think it's the least we could do is to sacrifice three months of the year, you know, just to do an album or two. I think it's very selfish if the Beatles don't record together."

The Beatles' youngest member was speaking like their wise elder statesman. He said he was hopeful. "The fact that we're all here in these bodies means that we're not perfected. So having accepted we're not perfected, we can allow for each other's inadequacies or failings with a little, you know, with a little compassion. I'm certainly ready to be able to try and work things out."

✣

"Not perfected" was one way to view the world in 1970.

During the Days of Rage in 1968, Prime Minister Georges Pompidou of France had said, "Our civilization is being questioned—not the government, not the institutions, not even France, but the materialistic and soulless modern society." Since then, a gulf had opened between the naïve optimism of the early 1960s and the decade's assassinations—Kennedy, Malcolm, King, Kennedy—leading to Nixon's election and the dawn of the '70s.

For Americans born between 1940 and 1970, the New Deal was the recognizable structure of US government, kept viable by a strong liberal consensus supporting centralized power. Under liberalism, civil rights expanded, along with wider health care, worker protections, immigration reform, arts support, gender equality, and a "war on poverty."

After LBJ signed the Civil Rights Act of 1964 and the Voting Rights Act of 1965, which he predicted would alienate the South, and after Richard Nixon's ascendancy in 1968, the New Deal began to die. The North, America's manufacturing center, the Rust Belt, lost its political clout. The South and the West, often marching proudly under the old Confederate banner or no banner at all, became dominant.

One result of this political shift was the rise of Christian evangelism as a player in US politics. In the United States, the biggest-selling book of 1970—indeed, of the entire decade—was Hal Lindsey's *The Late Great Planet Earth*, a death-loving narrative predicting imminent apocalypse and the Second Coming of Christ. Christ's return would be aided, Lindsey said, by moral US leaders guided by their born-again constituents.

In 1973 the Christian Right would find a fund-raising goldmine in the Supreme Court's *Roe v. Wade* decision, one of the last rulings the court made under the old liberal consensus. (In 1971 the liberal court would also decide Muhammad Ali's status.)

In 1970, when National Guard troops shot to death unarmed students protesting the Vietnam War on the campus of Kent State University in Ohio, no one needed Lindsey's book to imagine imminent apocalypse. "There isn't going to be any revolution," said Country Joe McDonald, whose "Feels Like I'm Fixin' to Die Rag" was one of the era's most popular antiwar anthems. "I know a lot of people wearing Che Guevara stuff . . . [but they're just] a bunch of tripped-out freaks."

As an idea, "revolution" had shrunk to be applied to various groups—Blacks, Chicanos, Asians, women, gays, lesbians—clamoring to be recognized and competing for public money. If unity was the goal, these well-meaning movements were self-defeating. The solution? "You take drugs, you turn up the music very loud, you dance around, you build yourself a fantasy world where everything's beautiful," said Country Joe, proclaiming the spirit of the American 1970s. You say you want a revolution? Well . . .

In the early '70s, Nixon ordered a blistering B-52 bombing campaign against North Vietnam. More than mass destruction, the object was to persuade the Viet Cong that they were dealing with a lunatic and better back off. The bombs were real. People were actually dying. It was hard to tell if Nixon was faking insanity or not.

George Harrison was a refugee from the ugliness of the 1970s. Or he tried to be. After numerous break-ins by Beatle fans, and following his drug bust, Harrison felt that Kinfauns was no longer safe for him. A run-in with a neighbor convinced him to move. Next to his property were the grounds of an old mansion that had been turned into a private school, a lovely park featuring lakes and luscious rhododendrons. Harrison liked to meditate there. One day, ten minutes before closing time, a park guard saw him sitting on the grass and told him to leave. "All I want to do is look at the trees," he said. The man threw him out. "Okay, I'll buy my own park," he said. And he did.

Pattie Boyd came across an ad in the *Sunday Times* placed by an order of nuns, the Salesian Sisters of St. John Bosco. They had been running a school in a vast house built on the site of an old monastery in 1898 by Sir Frank Crisp, a wealthy solicitor and horticulturalist. It was located in Oxfordshire, in Henley-on-Thames, forty miles west of London. The school had closed, and only six nuns and one monk remained on the premises. Upkeep had become physically and financially untenable. The Catholics were selling the place and the accompanying acreage for £125,000. "The house was going to be knocked down," Harrison later wrote. "What a thing, to knock down a house like this. It's hard to credit that they would bring a great iron ball and smash this and bulldoze it, but they would have done." One of the first things that appealed to him when he toured the grounds was an ancient, whimsical sign. Sir Frank had placed it in one of the gardens: "Don't Keep Off the Grass."

Harrison came across a legend etched into a sundial's stone pedestal: "Shadows we are and shadows we depart." It reminded him of the meditations on mortality carved into the Picton Clock Tower near his family's first house. Small boulders surrounding former lakes in the gardens (by then just rubbish heaps) recalled for him the meteorite he had climbed as a boy while contemplating infinity.

He had come home—to Friar Park.

The house, a Victorian Gothic husk (at this point), three stories, featuring turrets and spires and gargoyles carved into the pink façade, consisted of twenty-five bedrooms, a drawing room, a dining room, a ballroom, a library, and a massive kitchen. There was plenty of space for a home recording studio, a meditation room, and a private chapel. From the house's wrought-iron parapets, an observer could gaze over twenty acres of land, twelve of them devoted to formal gardens (gone to seed), a gatehouse, and two lodges. Already Harrison was imagining erecting greenhouses near the gardens where he and Maurice Milbourne, his master gardener, could develop flower species.

Harrison learned that Frank Crisp had been a wildly eccentric man, "a bit like Lewis Carroll or Walt Disney." In his day, Crisp had created a series of lakes on the property, excavated tunnels for grottoes displaying skeletons and distorting mirrors, carved a river through the grounds, surrounded by animal topiaries, and built a replica of the Matterhorn, a hundred feet high, out of millstone grit. He had carved homilies into rocks and walls—"Scan not a friend with a microscopic glass. / You know his faults, now let his foibles pass." He had installed quirky statues around the house: for instance, a grinning priest gripping a frying pan riddled with holes, titled "Two Holy Friars."

Harrison found old specs from the 1920s and '30s detailing the house's former appearance; he was determined to restore it and its gardens to their former glory.

When his sister-in-law Irene arrived to see the house along with his brother Harry, she thought, "'My God! What's he done?' . . . People had dumped cars in the garden and brambles had grown over them. You didn't go for a walk without a machete in your hand to cut your way through. It was a huge, huge project. There was grass growing up through some of the wooden floors. All the beautiful tracery work, a lot of that needed replacing. And the grounds, there was so much that was hidden. But somehow or other he had the foresight to look at it for what it was."

She remembered walking with him one day among the spreading brambles: "There were . . . blue firs [there], and he said at the time, pointing them out, 'Do you realize that when Frank Crisp planted those he knew he was never ever going to see them? He planted those as a stand of trees. They must have gone in as saplings. So he knew that by the time he was an old gentleman he still wasn't going to see this garden looking as he'd planned it.' And he said, 'That's a huge task to take on. To try and look at something and think, I might never see this in my lifetime.' And I think that's how George looked at [Friar Park]. That whatever he did or planned, he might never see it to its fruition, but whatever he did, he did well."

He and Boyd moved into Friar Park on March 12, 1970. They hired an architect to plan renovations, and he and Milbourne began to extricate the gardens from mountains of trash and weeds. He imagined the main house as it once looked and as it would look again—oak doors, sweeping staircases, warm, glowing lamps, marble pillars. "[Sir Frank's] attention to detail was exquisite and just what George understood," Boyd said. Friar Park's combination of gravitas and whimsy, ostentation and delicacy, were manifestations of his personality.

But for now the house was uninhabitable. The couple slept in sleeping bags in one of the lodges while the architect and his crew went to work. "Those first few weeks were so freezing—I don't remember ever being so cold," Boyd would later write. It reminded Harrison of his childhood. "The only two rooms we could warm were the kitchen, a huge room with a lovely big scrubbed-pine table that seated twenty, and the hall, where there was a big fireplace. At night we used to pile up the fire in the hall with logs and sleep in front of it in [our] sleeping bags, wrapped in hats, coats, scarves, gloves, anything we could find." On either side of the fireplace, painted panels depicted the Tree of Life and the Tree of Destiny. A stained-glass window rose from the hall to the second floor.

To Boyd's great discomfort, Harrison contacted Shyamasundar in London and said, "I was hoping some of you could live out here and help me clean [the place] up a bit."

"The idea was that the men would do the gardening and the women would look after us and cook," Boyd remembered. "I wasn't sure of this arrangement but George thought it would be wonderful: we would chant together and there would be good vibes in the house."

Shyamasundar, Mukunda, Gurudas, and their wives came to stay, bringing their kids. Boyd had a hard time distinguishing them from the "lost souls and wannabes" camping on the Apple doorstep. "They may have been spiritual and belonged to a spiritual group, [but] at the end of the day they were just people . . . big fans of the Beatles and George," she wrote. "[And] George was a slightly soft touch for people in the Hare Krishna movement."

"They were just a bunch of moochers as far as I was concerned," said Bobby Whitlock, a keyboard player who had come to England to record with Harrison. Harrison was "an easy touch," he said. "He wanted to do good and well for everyone, especially people that he assumed were of like mind and who would not use and abuse him—but they did, hand over fist, every time he turned around."

Boyd grew particularly irritated in the mornings, waking from a rough night in her sleeping bag to the pungent smells of heavy Indian cooking. "I began to feel that what I considered my home had been taken over," she said. She and Harrison had no time or space for intimacy, despite the vast grounds, now crawling with workers and Krishnas.

Harrison had embarked on what many of his friends considered a folly. Visiting the house, John Lennon said it was so dark that he didn't know how anybody could live in it. But Harrison's sense of peace there was elemental. Friar Park was grandiose and expensive, a massive chunk of the material world. It was also ethereal, with traces of the old monastery still wafting through the smoke of candles and the sandalwood incense he lighted every night. It was frenetic with the activities of workers attempting to restore it, but it was also an unchanging meditation retreat. Harrison was long accustomed to insoluble contradictions. He knew what he was doing. While the 1970s went mad outside his gate—riots in Notting Hill, bombs in Southeast Asia—he was building himself a cathedral.

✺

Lennon and McCartney had busted out of the Beatles, both determined to prove (to the other, more than to anyone else) that they didn't need a band. McCartney went further: he needed no one at all. He played every instrument on his first solo album, overdubbing them one by one. Inside the record sleeve, he included a self-interview stressing how little he missed his former bandmates. Lennon nearly matched him on his own first solo album, requiring only Starr on drums and Klaus Voorman on bass to provide minimal backing behind his primal screams about pain and anger and his intimacy with Yoko Ono. He gave *Rolling Stone* an exclusive interview in which he virtually disavowed every close friendship he'd ever had.

By contrast, Harrison was eager to learn from other musicians. "Solo" was not in his vocabulary. In early May 1970, when word went out that Harrison was planning a project, the buzz throughout the music industry was palpable. Everyone wanted to play with him because of his reputation as a band-oriented player. "He was always laid back, nothing demonstrative," said Peter Frampton, whom Harrison recruited to play acoustic guitar. "Everyone was there because they were great . . . [He'd say,] 'Here's the song, what can you bring to it?' He hired people for their inspiration, and the only thing George ever said was, 'That was a good one" or 'Let's try it again.' No one was left out, it was like we were a band. . . . George was not wrapped up in a me-me-me thing."

His peers admired him. They wanted his album to be a success.

"The sessions felt very comfortable, and George made sure that everybody was happy," Whitlock said. "I recall the wonderful tandoori chicken that was delivered to the studio. In fact, every night was a huge Indian feast. . . There was a constant sweet aroma of burning incense, rose petals were scattered around the floor, and there were large trays of peanut butter cookies. It all created a serene atmosphere. George's sessions were always spectacular in every way."

As a vocalist, Harrison had never been the strongest member of the Beatles, but his voice had a touching, straightforward, plaintive quality, especially on songs of longing—for a girl or for God. As the sessions began for *All Things Must Pass*, he worried about the strength of his throat. Just a year earlier he'd had a tonsillectomy (after which the University College Hospital's switchboards lit up with callers seeking to buy the Beatle's tonsils). He had bounced back from the surgery to deliver a sterling performance while recording his composition "Old Brown Shoe," but he never knew when his throat would fail him.

Phil Spector, nominally the album's coproducer, told Harrison, "I really feel that your voice has got to be heard throughout the album so that the greatness of the songs can . . . come through. We can't cover you up too much (and there really is no need to)."

Nervous, Harrison recruited an army of guitarists, fronted by Eric Clapton, to give him support. "George was a really great guitar player," Bobby Whitlock said. "He just didn't think he was."

"He always bowed to Eric as . . . a technician," Spector said. "But for versatility and ideas, George was far superior. George was more creative, more melodic."

"I've always liked the way George plays guitar—restrained and good," said Bob Dylan, one of the many musicians Harrison partnered with as the Beatles split: Robbie Robertson and the Band, the gospel-steeped Edwin Hawkins Singers, and Delaney and Bonnie, a southern-roots rock group. All of these influences would mark Harrison's career, complimenting his Asian obsession, beginning with *All Things Must Pass.*

It was Delaney Bramlett and Dave Mason who convinced him to attempt slide guitar. Briefly, Harrison had joined Delaney and Bonnie on tour, along with Eric Clapton, at the end of 1969, to escape Abbey Road's poisoned atmosphere. As Graeme Thomson wrote, "The sweet, sad sigh of his slide guitar playing quickly became Harrison's signature sound—unmistakable . . . Slide suited him: it was unflashy, soulful and melodic, and seemed to capture the very essence of that 'weeping' sound."

Using a glass slide on his finger, he taught himself to produce a unique voice combining qualities of African American blues and classical Indian sitar. Tonally, it distinguished many of the songs on *All Things Must Pass.*

The danger in hiring so many splendid support players—Clapton, Whitlock, Frampton, Mason, Gary Wright, Billy Preston, Badfinger, Ringo, Gary Brooker, Jim Gordon, and Carl Radle, among others—was that he might just blend in and become a back-up player on his own album. Sometimes the players, trading licks, showed off, like a roomful of gunslingers proving who was fastest, and Harrison—by choice—faded into the background.

"One thing you'd learn about George very early was that if you talked to him like he was a Beatle, he would close up and walk away," said Joey Molland of Badfinger. "If you talked to him like he was a regular bloke, about your car break-ing down . . . or something, then he'd be all ears and get right into it with you."

Harrison was also in danger of being eclipsed by Phil Spector's Wall of Sound production. Harrison had chosen him because he was one of the best in the business, but his grandiose style did not always suit the intimacy of Harrison's songs. His dramatic flair, combined with Harrison's self-deprecation, made for an odd mix. "I went to . . . Friar Park, which he had just purchased, and he said, 'I have a few ditties for you to hear,'" Spector said. "It was endless! He literally had hundreds of songs, and each one was better than the rest." New songs and numerous songs the Beatles had rejected, including the title track. "He had all this emotion built up when it was released to me," Spector said. "I don't think he had played them to anybody, maybe Pattie."

"I'm twice the writer I was when we did *Revolver*," Harrison said at the time. This wasn't a statement of confidence. "Simply, I just know how to do it better now because I do it more often. I'm writing songs day and night—I can't stop. The reason I feel impelled to write now is that I believe you can say more in two or three minutes of a song than you can say in any way else in ten years. Add the music and there's more feeling. More truth." Songwriting wasn't a *craft* for him, he said; it was a means of self-expression and praise for God. "[The] songs are there, all around. All you have to do is reach out and capture one."

Bramlett believed Harrison "knew he had something special" with the music. "He wasn't covered with a blanket anymore . . . I didn't think he had much to develop—he was ready. How much development does a man need?"

"He was making a [huge] transition," Whitlock observed. "Can you imagine being him?" Stepping out as a solo artist (writing, singing, playing, producing), testing a new dynamic with a fresh coproducer, herding and caring for a group of musicians—while negotiating the Beatles' business affairs and their hurtful personal friction, renovating a massive property, producing other artists' albums, and trying to maintain a marriage and a spiritual life.

It was then that his mother's cancer returned. This was clearly too much stress for one man.

Some of the Apple Scruffs still lingered around Apple and Abbey Road, waiting for the Beatles. Carol Bedford had distanced herself from Harrison, but she mingled with the others. One night, outside Abbey Road, she would recall, "I heard [Harrison] playing at 4 a.m. He thought he was alone and no one could hear him so he was free of self-consciousness," she said. "It was the most beautiful guitar playing I have ever heard, a kind of bluesy Hawaiian sound."

Harrison's mother didn't know him.

It was early July. He had suspended recording *All Things Must Pass* to sit in his mother's hospital room, remembering how patiently she had doted on him and abided when, as a teenager practicing guitar, he bungled the same Carl Perkins or Roy Orbison riff hours on end. Even when he rejected Catholic practice, she didn't feel hurt or angry. She tried to understand. Now she stared at him uncomprehendingly from her hospital bed as the tumor took over. When his father, sister, and brothers left the room in the late afternoons, he'd sit quietly, reading to her passages from the Bhagavad Gita: "For the soul there is never birth or death. Nor, having once been, does it ever cease to be. It is unborn, eternal, ever-existing, undying, and primeval."

"One exhausted afternoon," a series of minor chords came into his head, he said, and he wrote a slow, finger-picking tune, "Deep Blue," by her bedside, "filled with the frustration and gloom of . . . hospitals, and the feeling of *disease*—as the word's true meaning is—that permeated the atmosphere."

Louise Harrison died on July 7, 1970, with her son chanting "Hare Krishna" in her ear.

He retreated for solace to Friar Park, asking his two brothers to move in with him. They could live in the outlying lodges on the grounds and work in the garden—the way they had all worked in their father's gardens as kids, growing runner beans, goldenrod, lupines, and night-scented stock.

Shaken by his mother's death, Harrison withdrew to meditate and pray in the private chapel with its latticed stained-glass windows. Always he carried a bag of japa beads, dipping his right hand into the bag, using the beads to count off prayers or the Sanskrit names of God. Carpenters hammering door frames asked him, "Did you hurt your hand?" Rather than try to explain, he would say, "Yeah, yeah, I had an accident."

He would lose himself among the "Perverted Proverbs" Sir Frank had carved into mantels in the house or into flat stones in the gardens (some of them inscribed in Latin): "Punctuality is the thief of time"; "People who live in glass houses should dress in the dark." Harrison cherished the humor as well as the gravity of the aphorisms.

In the late afternoons he would drop down into caves on the premises, light candles in the cool air, and sit among the skeletons, the oddly angled mirrors, the illuminated glass grapes, and the tiny wishing well. He would head up a path emerging into one of the lakes, giving him the illusion of walking on water.

Throughout his grieving, he was eager to record again but hesitant, fearful of breaking the serenity of his quiet mood. Little by little, he reassumed the responsibilities he had set for himself, first around the house. He helped engineers excavate rubbish-strewn lakes, digging hundreds of feet for water—"The more you get into something the more incredible it is," he said. He drew up elaborate to-do lists: "Leaded lights missing from window; Skylight on turret outside made bigger; Clear out and fix holes under tower; Remove all old wires."

He oversaw the transformation of the upstairs ballroom into his home recording studio, soundboards resting gently among Tiffany lamps, dark wooden paneling, and plush carpets. He tacked snapshots of his family and friends on the wall above the mixing console.

"Friar Park lifted his spirits [during this time]," Boyd later wrote, "[but] I felt it was George's house. . . . At Kinfauns I had felt that we had an equal partnership. At Friar Park I didn't. . . . Most of the time, even when he was in the house, I didn't know where he was. At meals, if he was there, too many other people were at the table for us to have any real conversation; and even though we shared a bed, he was often in his recording studio or meditating half the night." In particular, Boyd objected to the continuing presence of the Krishnas. "What finally got to me was that they didn't look after their children," she said. Twice, one of the women's toddlers, left alone to wander the grounds, fell into a fountain and nearly drowned. "You've *got* to look after your children," Boyd told them. "Krishna looks after them," they replied.

"Well, that was it," Boyd said. "I spoke to George about it, but he liked having them there. . . I felt more and more alienated."

It didn't help that she had not managed to bear children of her own. This pained the couple. Harrison told inquiring friends that the problem was his, though time would prove this not to be the case.

Finally, he reconvened his hired band and returned to Abbey Road. It was a joy to play music again, to hear his songs come to life, but recording introduced new problems. Spector was frequently drunk during the sessions, polishing off a couple of bottles of Courvoisier each day. He carried a pistol—for protection, he claimed—but Harrison didn't want it in the studio. The musicians, "looking," he said, "for 'unending pleasure,'" indulged in various substances. Starr couldn't remember later which tracks he had played on. Harrison was "very well behaved," said Ken Scott, a sound engineer. "There was too much riding on [the album]." "He was a pretty straight dude, all things considered," Bobby Whitlock would later write. On tour with Delaney and Bonnie, he had seen Harrison tempted each night to get "messed up on coke and booze." "[But] I never saw George do any blow at all on that tour," he said.

By 1970, cocaine had become rock and roll currency, as valued as cash in the music industry. It was rampant in LA, where the major record companies were headquartered. Delaney Bramlett was one of scores of artists who developed a destructive habit. "Initially it can be a creative catalyst," Joni Mitchell explained. "In the end it'll fry you, kill the heart. It kills the soul and gives you delusions of grandeur as it shuts down your emotional center."

It also had cachet. It was expensive and fashionable, a membership card into music's elite corridors.

Coke made its way into the *All Things Must Pass* sessions courtesy of Eric Clapton. It had become his drug of choice after the Delaney and Bonnie tour, deadening the anguish he felt at not possessing Pattie Boyd. Whenever Harrison stayed late at the studio, mixing songs at the end of a day when the other musicians had left, Clapton contacted Boyd and requested clandestine meetings with her. He suspected she was using him to make Harrison jealous, but their intimacy grew.

Along with some of the other session players—Whitlock, Gordon, and Radle (with Clapton, they would come to be known as Derek and the Dominoes)— Clapton recorded a song called "Layla," addressed directly to Boyd: "I'm begging, darling, please . . . / darling, won't you ease my worried mind." The name Layla came from a book by an ancient Persian poet—a story of unrequited love.

Clapton accused Boyd of destroying his heart. She was depressed by Harrison's withdrawals into music or meditation, and she felt overwhelmed by Clapton's pleas but touched by the song he had written. Her cuddles with him led to serious trysts.

One evening, Clapton blurted to Harrison, "I have to tell you, man, that I'm in love with your wife." "George was furious," Boyd said. "He turned to me and said, 'Well, are you going with him or coming with me?'"

Nevertheless, Harrison and Clapton resolved to shelve their conflict to play music together. The Abbey Road sessions continued. In the studio, Whitlock became aware of the bristling dynamic between them. "There were subliminal messages going back and forth between two good friends as a way of healing and setting each other free," he said. "Saying what they could not say any other way." Harrison went about his business like a man "who had a bigger kettle of fish to fry, rather than get down with what he had no control over anyway." Clapton did more cocaine.

Finally, with personal tensions, Spector's shenanigans, and peer pressure, Harrison occasionally joined his band in a drink or a snort. He would come home in the early morning, tapped out, carrying his guitar. One day, near dawn, he walked into the kitchen while Shyamasundar was scraping paint off the moldings. "I've been thinking about this," Harrison began abruptly, pacing as if angry, "and I don't believe Krishna in his human form is the highest manifestation of God. . . . Prabhupada's got it all wrong, Prabhupada just doesn't have a clue about it." Inexplicably, he kept needling Shyamasundar until Shyamasundar climbed off his ladder and pushed Harrison to the wall. He took a deep breath, stepped away, and started to leave the kitchen. Harrison grinned. "Just checking," he said.

On another morning, an Apple courier arrived from the office to deliver some cash. He walked in on Harrison and Boyd in one of the lodge houses. Harrison, startled, shouted, "Who the fuck are *you*?"' and nearly threw him down the outside stairs (Boyd had seen what she had taken to be a burglar on the grounds just days before). Harrison's nerves were fraying.

In the end, it was perhaps a blessing that Phil Spector deteriorated as thoroughly as he did during the album's recording, leaving Harrison to finish the production alone. Their working styles were never going to mesh. Spector would later say, "[Harrison] let me make all the basic tracks. He said, 'Go, go, go!'" Spector said. "In the overdubbing, he was in control of his parts. He wouldn't let anything go until it was right. 'My Sweet Lord' must have taken about twelve hours to overdub the guitar solos. He must have had that in triplicate, six-part harmony. . . . Perfectionist is not the word. Anyone can be a perfectionist. He was beyond that. He just had to have it so right. He would try and try and experiment upon experiment, to the point where I would leave the studio for several hours while he played different parts over and over with the engineer. Then I would come in and listen, and he would say, 'How does it sound? Are there too many parts? Too few parts?'"

Meanwhile, Clapton's cocaine use slipped out of control. He found a dealer who delivered to him in the Abbey Road tea room. Eventually the dealer insisted he buy a packet of heroin each time he purchased coke: pure pink Chinese, he said. "Pattie was not ready to leave George . . . [and] Eric decided . . . he was [going] to do heroin," Whitlock would write later. "I don't know why he chose to start doing smack at George's session. You would think that he would have done it at home with just us, or by himself."

Plainly, Clapton meant to rattle his friend.

"George asked me, 'What are you doing? What is your intention?'" Clapton recalled. "And I said, 'I want to make a journey through the dark, on my own, to find out what it's like in there. And then come out the other end.'"

And he intended to blackmail Boyd. He told her that if she didn't leave Harrison for him, he would become an addict. "Don't be so stupid," she said, unaware that he was already using.

In spite of the band's indulgences and the background drama, Harrison kept a tight focus, steered his group productively, and moved the sessions toward a successful close.

One night John Lennon stopped by the studio to say hello. Later, his public remarks revealed how much Harrison had shaken him, assembling an energetic band and steering it with expertise. "John was really negative" when the triple album appeared, Harrison remembered. "[He] said, 'He must be fucking mad, putting three records out. And look at that picture on the front, he looks like an asthmatic Leon Russell.'"

Attack was Lennon's mode whenever he perceived a threat. "When [John] heard the stuff we were doing he was completely blown away," Whitlock said. Whitlock recalled in his autobiography that John and Yoko showed up at the studio "dressed in army fatigues complete with helmets. . . . I remember how proud George was after John left the studio that night. He had a great big smile. John got his socks blown off by all of us, and George's new album was better than anything that John had ever done, and he knew that as well."

"I just felt that whatever happened, whether it was a flop or a success, I was gonna go on my own just to have a bit of peace of mind," Harrison said.

On August 15, 1970, a dismayed Ravi Shankar read that General Yahya Khan had postponed national elections in Pakistan, on the pretext of a flooding crisis in the East. In fact, Yahya was in the process of finalizing the legal framework he needed to consolidate his power. Pakistan, he said, would become a "Federal Islamic Republic." Despairing, recalling childhood images of British soldiers beating civilians in the streets, Shankar set his paper down, picked up his sitar, and played a plaintive Bengali folk tune.

Three months later, Cyclone Bhola turned East Pakistan into a seething swamp.

The recording of *All Things Must Pass* ended late at night on August 12, 1970. On that day, six time zones earlier, in Philadelphia, where Muhammad Ali then lived, Belinda, standing at her kitchen stove, making dinner, paused to answer the telephone. She was nine months pregnant with twins. Ali was sitting at the kitchen table eating a salad.

"Mrs. Ali, you got your wish," said a voice on the line. "Muhammad Ali got his license."

"What's the matter?" Ali asked, looking up, registering the shock on her face. "Take the phone."

"What's the matter?"

She whispered, "You got your license, baby."

"You lie!" said Ali. "Don't tell me that. You lie!"

She forced the receiver into his hands. Ali listened carefully as a man named Leroy Johnson, an attorney and the first Black person ever elected to the Georgia State Senate explained to him that Georgia had no state athletic commission. Cities, not the state, oversaw boxing rules. Lester Maddox, Georgia's governor and a strict segregationist, would naturally oppose an Ali fight in the South, but he didn't control the matter. Atlanta's mayor, a man who owed Leroy Johnson big time, had the power to sanction a match. The mayor, a white fellow named Sam Massell, had received ninety percent of Atlanta's Black vote thanks to Johnson. "Johnson cut himself a piece of [any future] promotion, and after that visited Massell to call in his chits," fight promoter Harold Conrad explained later. "Massell wasn't happy about it, but Johnson controlled a pile of Black votes, so the mayor went along with it. That's what it took . . . politics and money and three years of trying."

Now the time was right. Said one of Ali's lawyers, "The Vietnam War looked a lot worse . . . and Muhammad Ali looked a lot better." Sacrificing his career, maintaining his convictions, facing the threat of prison, exiled by his spiritual leader, he had become a martyr, an underdog, easier to support.

"This ain't no joke," he told Belinda. The phone shook in his hand. "My God, I got my license." At the table he began to cry.

Since his departure from boxing, the heavyweight division had been a mess. In 1968, the World Boxing Association sponsored an eight-man tournament to find a new champ after Ali had been stripped of his crown. Jimmy Ellis, small and quick, a Louisville native who had trained with Ali as a teenager and served as his sparring partner, won the championship by beating Jerry Quarry, an Irish-American from a family of California farmworkers. Angelo Dundee had agreed to be Ellis's trainer.

Joe Frazier, a compact scrambler who won a gold medal in the 1964 Olympics fighting as a heavyweight, did not participate in the WBA tournament, opting instead for a better deal competing for the New York World Heavyweight Championship. He won it, beating a nearly inexhaustible bruiser named Buster Mathis.

On February 16, 1970, Frazier knocked out Ellis in the fifth round of a fifteen-round match. At that point, his record was twenty-five wins, no losses. *Ring* magazine had continued to recognize Ali as the heavyweight champ throughout his ordeal, but now the editors conceded: since he might never fight again, Frazier had earned the honor.

Ali was gracious. "I can't blame Joe Frazier for accepting the title under the conditions he did," he said. "Joe's got four or five children to feed. He's worked in a meat-packing house all his life and deserves a break. He would have fought me if he had the chance . . . so I can't take nothing from him."

With the public warming to Ali, the sports world began picturing an Ali-Frazier bout even before Ali was licensed in Atlanta.

In the third week of August 1970, at the Medical College of Philadelphia, Belinda gave birth three months prematurely to Jamillah and Rasheda, twin daughters, each weighing under three pounds.

Shortly afterward, while the babies were still hospitalized, Ali moved into a Miami Beach hotel and began training again in the 5th Street Gym. A couple of the walls had been repainted, but it was the same rat trap it had been the day he met the Beatles there.

Following the Atlanta decision, promoters scheduled a bout between Ali and Jerry Quarry, to be held in the city on October 26. Frazier's handlers were forcing Ali to wait, to prove himself a worthy—and lucrative—opponent after the long layoff. He was twenty pounds overweight, but it "was all there," said Angelo Dundee after watching him work out. "Everything. He can still fake with the hip, the hand, and the shoulder."

Ali taped a five-year-old picture of himself to a mirror in the gym, a shot taken in his prime. "See how narrow and trim I was," he said wistfully. "Maybe I'll never look like that again."

Ferdie Pacheco joined Angelo Dundee and Bundini Brown in Ali's corner. "All the bricks are in place," Dundee said, satisfied, surveying his team. It was time to get to work.

Bundini said: "You can't become a soldier until you go to basic training" (a poor choice of words, given Ali's history). They would all have to up their game again.

"It's like a dead man rising," Ali said. "I tell you. There are young people who didn't get to see me six years ago." He said it was "like an old boxer of Sugar Ray Robinson's caliber being put into a time machine and suddenly being a contender again."

In the gym, he let his sparring partners trap him against the ropes and whale away on his kidneys, ribs, and head. He said he did this on purpose, to harden his body, to strengthen his stamina. Cus D'Amato, Floyd Patterson's trainer, who dropped in to watch the workouts, didn't buy it. "No fighter ever lets anybody hit him. It hurts. It rattles your brain. Clay simply couldn't stay away from those guys."

Pacheco observed the weakness in his legs. "Before . . . he'd been so fast, you couldn't catch him, so he'd never taken punches. . . . [but] when he lost his legs [not training in exile], he lost his first line of defense. That was when he discovered something that was both very good and very bad. Very bad in that it led to the physical damage he suffered later in his career. . . He discovered he could take a punch."

His hands had softened. "After the layoff, when Ali fought he was in pain," Pacheco said. "So what we did . . . was numb his hands. It was my idea. I was the doctor. . . . One of Ali's peculiarities is that he's scared of needles, so first I'd numb him with ethyl chloride. Then I'd put one cc of cortisone and Xylacene in each hand; two shots to each hand, in the webs between the three middle fingers. The shots didn't violate any rules that I know of, although we didn't brag about them."

One day, a reporter from a London newspaper, observing a workout, asked Ali why he let his sparring partner unload on him so fiercely (severely bruising a rib). Ali answered that astronauts always did ground tests before launching into space.

"Why don't you smile anymore?" the reporter asked.

"I don't play in training. This is serious business."

"No more poetry?"

"There is no time," he huffed, "to rhyme."

One day a courier arrived at the door of his Miami hotel room, bearing two gift packages. The boxes were neatly wrapped in white tissue, green and red ribbons: "To Cassius Clay from Georgia." Nestled in one: a rag doll wearing yellow shorts and tiny boxing gloves. A noose was wrapped around its neck. The other package held a small, decapitated Chihuahua puppy. A note said, "We know how to handle black draft-dodging dogs in Georgia. Stay out of Atlanta!" It was signed with a sketch of the Confederate flag.

As the fight date approached, Ali moved his operations to a cottage and its grounds near Atlanta, owned by Leroy Johnson. Though Johnson had convinced local leaders to host the fight in order to show the world that Atlanta—the city of Martin Luther King Jr.—was "too busy to hate," Ali received threatening notes at the cottage from the Ku Klux Klan and often heard gunfire in the woods.

"Cassius Clay . . . is gone forever. There's no way he can recapture the past or return to his prime," declared the *Chicago Tribune*. Ali promoted a different narrative. It became the defining story of his comeback years: "I'm not just fighting one man. I'm fighting a lot of men, showing them here is one man they couldn't conquer. Lose this one and it won't be just a loss to me. So many millions of faces throughout the world will be sad; they'll feel like they've been defeated. If I lose, for the rest of my life I won't be free. . . . I'm fighting for my freedom."

He knew that nothing exposed America's racial pathologies as viscerally as a Great White Hope battling a Black man.

Jerry Quarry was perfect for this drama. "My heritage was *The Grapes of Wrath*," Quarry used to say. At a press conference one day, before the Ali fight, he blurted, "If there are two black doctors handling the fight, I'm not going in. Screw it. They want equal rights and all that? Well, I want it, too."

His trainer, knowing how bad this sounded, tried to switch gears. He told the reporters, "You can say that when Jerry hits that big son of a bitch, he'll break his neck."

"And if you want to say 'big *Black* son of a bitch, you can say that too," Quarry said.

If Ali had risked nothing, if he had not returned to the ring, he would have retired undefeated, physically unharmed, a martyr of conscience in the history books.

But he needed the money. And he craved the attention.

He was guaranteed $200,000 for the fight, Quarry $150,000, and it was reported that 205 theaters in the United States and Canada would carry the bout live.

Ali had begun to believe his narrative, and outside Atlanta Municipal Auditorium on fight night, October 26, 1970, Jesse Jackson eloquently summarized the tale: "If he loses tonight, it will mean symbolically that the forces of blind patriotism are right, that dissent is wrong; that protest means you don't love the country. This fight is love-it-or-leave it versus love-it-and-change it. They tried to railroad him. They refused to accept his testimony about his religious convictions. They took away his right to practice his profession. They tried to break him in body and mind. Martin Luther King used to say, 'Truth crushed to the earth will rise again.' That's the Black ethos. And it's happening here in Georgia, of all places, and against a white man."

Hours before the fight, boxing historian Bert Sugar was standing in the lobby of Atlanta's Regency-Hyatt Hotel. "It was right before the crowd left for the arena," he said. "Ali was going up to his room in one of those glass elevators, ascending. And everybody in the throng below, his legion of followers who'd been waiting for his resurrection, looked up, cheering as he ascended. It was spine-tingling; it transcended anything I'd ever seen."

At the last minute, Governor Maddox called for a boycott of the fight. He said, "[I] would hope that Clay gets beat in the first round and he's flattened for a count of 30." He declared fight day to be a "day of mourning" in Georgia. When informed of this, Ali said he didn't know what "that word" meant. A sportswriter explained, "It means it will be a black day." "Oh yeah, there'll be a lot of my folks there," Ali answered.

Sugar described the arena—an old auditorium that opened in 1909—as "something out of *Gone with the Wind*." "The black community was there in force. It was probably the greatest collection of black power and black money ever assembled up until that time. Bill Cosby, Sidney Poitier, Jesse Jackson, Julian Bond, Ralph Abernathy, Andrew Young, Coretta Scott King, Whitney Young." Right in the heart of the old Confederacy. "People were arriving in hand-painted limousines dressed in colors and styles I'd never seen," Sugar said. Purple tuxedos, sequins, minks, frilled silk shirts unbuttoned to the navel. "They weren't boxing fans; they were idolators."

Julian Bond took his third-row seat with his wife, aware that this was "a coronation, the King regaining his throne." "That night," he said, "Atlanta came into its own as the black political capital of America." Two days earlier, at a cocktail party, Ali had warned Bond's wife, "Don't wear that [light blue] dress [if you sit in the third row], because I'm gonna spill blood all over you."

"Ali! Ali!" The crowd's chants echoed. He had become a genuine African American folk hero. "This probably is an event unparalleled in Negro history," the *Atlanta Constitution* said. In dormitories across the country, white college students gathered eagerly around radios to listen to the match.

For the first time in his career, Ali would be fighting a younger man. He glanced at himself in the mirror as he left his dressing room. He had shed most of his excess weight. He was beautiful.

Wali Muhammed, Herbert's brother, slid into his corner along with Angelo Dundee, Ferdie Pacheco, and Bundini Brown. Elijah Muhammad (no relation to Wali) had not officially lifted the Nation of Islam's ban against the boxer, but nothing more was ever said of it. With Ali's earning power at least temporarily restored, all was forgiven. (The Nation's quiet reinsertion into his life meant his on-again, off-again affair with Sonji Roi was over.)

Curtis Mayfield sang the national anthem.

"Ghost in the house! Ghost in the house!" Bundini yelled, referring to the spirit of Jack Johnson, the iconoclastic boxer whose defiance inspired Ali.

Ali dominated the first round, proving his jab was as fast as ever. He was bigger than before. He had more power. Quarry couldn't get near him. In the past, Ali would jab then dance away. Slower in the legs now, he'd jab then throw a huge right hand.

At the end of the round, he slumped on his stool, exhausted.

Quarry gained confidence in the second, scoring with a big hook to the body and Ali's still-sore rib. In round three, Ali came out flat-footed, and Quarry was finding his groove when Ali threw two left hooks and a right, opening a gaping cut over Quarry's left eye. Ali went after the wound twelve more times in the round until it bled from four different places. "I'd never seen a cut like that," said Tony Perez, the referee. "You could see the bone."

Because of the fuss Quarry had made about Black doctors, no medics were standing in his corner (officially, four doctors—two Black, two white—had been assigned to the fight, but they were nowhere to be seen). "I had to make a decision alone," Perez said. "Quarry wanted to keep going. He was screaming, 'No, no, Tony. Don't stop the fight!' But I had to stop it. His own trainer wanted me to. The eye was so bad."

In the ring afterward, Ali bragged to reporters, "I'm stronger and I hit harder than I did three and a half years ago." But later he admitted, "I knew better. Before exile, I could go six rounds at the fastest pace without feeling it. It took only three rounds to get Quarry, but . . . I was tired. My jab was off target. My uppercuts were off. I saw openings I couldn't cash in on. . . . I was shocked . . . I wondered what would have happened if he could have lasted ten rounds."

Ralph Abernathy and Coretta Scott King gave Ali a comeback trophy in the ring. "You are a living example of soul power," Abernathy said. "[You are] not only our champion, but a champion of justice and peace," said Coretta Scott King.

Quarry took fifteen stitches in the face, collected his check, and went home. A tough night's work, but not so bad, maybe, for a guy who'd grown up in a tent, picking fruit alongside his parents in fields owned by someone else and sprayed with tons of poison.

Late that night, at home in Philadelphia, Belinda, groggy, picked up the ringing telephone. "Ali won, you lose. The bomb goes off at midnight," a voice said. Then the caller hung up.

The Philadelphia Bomb Squad came and found no bomb at the house.

The following morning, in most of the nation's newspapers, Ali scored another victory, perhaps more important than the fight itself: articles referred to him by his chosen Muslim name, adding "Cassius Clay" only as an "aka."

Six weeks later, Ali (still unacquainted with his twins) fought again, in New York, determined to fast-track his shot at Joe Frazier's championship belt. A judge had forced New York to lift its restrictions on Ali, following the Atlanta decision. This time Ali's opponent was an Argentinian, Oscar Bonavena, nicknamed "Ringo" after his Beatle haircut. Bonavena had lost twice to Frazier, but both bouts had been fierce, and the decisions were close. Ali was not coasting. This would be a serious fight.

He had gotten little rest following the Quarry match. Ferdie Pacheco advised him to let "his body recuperate," but "Ali didn't know if he'd be fighting or in jail in four or five months, so he went after it."

The fight was scheduled for December 7, Pearl Harbor Day. Veterans' organizations protested Ali's appearance. Madison Square Garden received a heavy load of hate mail: "If you allow that coward nigger to make money on December 7, those brave boys who lie entombed in the USS *Arizona* will turn over in their graves. Now you made December 7, 1970 a day of infamy along with December 7, 1941."

"Why you no go in the army?" Bonavena taunted Ali in press conferences. "You chicken. Cluck. Cluck. Cluck."

In his hotel room, the day of the fight, Ali received an unusual visitor. His name was Judge Aaron, a Korean War veteran, stooped and hunched like a man twice his age, with a perpetual puzzled look on his face. A member of Ali's entourage brought him into the room: "Tell him who told you come," the man urged Aaron.

"I saw Martin Luther King a week before he died," Judge Aaron explained. "He told me I should see Muhammad Ali. He said you wouldn't let the world forget me."

"Give him the message," Ali's aide prompted him.

"I'm the message. I'm the living message." Slowly, Aaron unbuttoned the army jacket he wore. Cut into the flesh of his chest were the letters "KKK." He dropped his pants. Scars crossed his groin where his testicles should have been. He informed Ali that the Klan had castrated him one summer night in Alabama when he'd joined King's civil rights marches.

After a long, stunned quiet, Ali asked gently, "What do you want from me?"

"I don't know. I wanted to see you . . . I just didn't want to be left lying on the road . . ."

Ali rose and hugged him. "[F]or a moment the confusion [left Aaron] and I [saw] what he must have looked like in all his innocence before they wrecked him," Ali said later.

He declared he would publicly dedicate the Bonavena fight to "the unprotected people, to the victims."

Perhaps as a nod to angry veterans, Madison Square Garden did not play the national anthem that night as Ali stood praying in the ring.

And perhaps drawing strength from Judge Aaron, Ali somehow survived the grueling ordeal of fifteen rounds, the exhaustion of his arms and legs, the determination of a flailing but powerful opponent. "Ali absorbed more punishment against Bonavena than he had in any previous fight," Pacheco said. Late in the final round, as he was about to collapse, his mouth cut, his right eye bruised, Ali unloaded a left hook on Bonavena's chin and dropped him. Bonavena beat the count, but he was dazed. Ali floored him twice more, ending the bout. The Argentinian sprawled across the canvas, like Ringo posing with Ali in the 5th Street Gym all those years ago.

By returning to New York—the state that had first stripped him of the right to box—and emerging victorious in the ring, he had achieved the "gladsome termination of a holy crusade," said the *Boston Globe*.

The stage was set for Ali-Frazier.

Ali stood in the silence of a funeral home, in the harsh glare of two floor lamps, one on either end of the open coffin. He stared starkly into the casket.

"What was his name?" he asked the funeral director.

"He was Leslie Scott."

"Have a family?"

"Two children about grown."

"How about his wife? She take it pretty hard?"

"Very, very hard."

Gently, Ali touched the edge of the coffin. Dave Kindred, the Louisville sportswriter who had long covered Ali, had rarely seen him so somber. Kindred had traveled to Philadelphia to interview him. Ali told him about an article he had seen in the paper—two men arguing during a closed-circuit television broadcast of the Bonavena fight. One man pulled a knife, and an off-duty policemen killed him.

Ali wanted to see the corpse.

Now, standing over the casket, Ali asked, "What's he feel like? Is he hard?" He reached in and touched the dead man's body. He pushed against the thigh with his fingers, felt a hand, then a cheek. "Cold," he said.

He traced the coffin's edge. "Life is pitiful. One second, this man is alive. He's arguing that I'm a better fighter than Joe Frazier. The next second he's dead." He turned away. "I ain't worth dying for."

Cyclone Bhola smashed the coasts of East Pakistan during a Hindu full moon festival, raining death upon the land.

Ancient Hindus, noting the sun's apparent constancy, saw the sun as a symbol of immortality. The moon's many phases made it a natural representative of birth, death, and recurrence. On the days of full and new moons, many Hindus celebrated the circle of life, seeking waters in which to purify their bodies and minds as they contemplated the eternal.

This was why so many more people than usual—in the tens of thousands—had been thronging the shores when the worst winds hit, whipping up tidal surges of over thirty feet. It was why one UPI correspondent counted 350 floating bodies in the Bay of Bengal within hours of landfall, before he became exhausted.

In California, trying to concentrate on teaching at a music school he had founded, Ravi Shankar despaired for his relatives in East Pakistan. He received regular reports from family members describing their exodus to Calcutta, away from the storm damage and the worsening political situation.

Anguished, Shankar wrote a song beginning, "Oh Bhaugowan, Khoda tala." *Bhaugowan* and *Khoda* meant "God" to Hindus and Muslims, respectively.

Shankar sang: "Oh God, where are you? / To see us suffer like this, in this flood, / and this fight and this hunger. / Why should we suffer so, with all these calamities?"

"Maybe Nixon'll call [Frazier] if he wins," Ali said. "I don't think he'll call me." Ali worshipped the wrong God. Once more, he was promoting a fight as though it were something much greater than a sporting event.

On TV he had said, "The only people rooting for Joe Frazier are white people in suits, Alabama sheriffs, and members of the Ku Klux Klan. I'm fighting for the little man in the ghetto."

Watching at home, Frazier snapped, "What does *he* know about the ghetto?" Frazier had been born in South Carolina, one of a sharecropper's thirteen kids. Racial violence had forced him to move to Philadelphia where he'd worked in a slaughterhouse and taken boxing lessons at the police gym both to keep his weight down and to channel his anger in a more productive direction. At work, he would train by punching huge slabs of frozen meat.

He had thought he was friends with Ali. He'd given Ali money; gone to Muslim services at Ali's suggestion (just to be polite), and supported Ali's draft decision: "If Baptists weren't allowed to fight, I wouldn't fight either," he'd said.

But then Ali called him an Uncle Tom and turned him into a Black White Hope. "He isolated Joe from the Black community," recalled Dave Wolf, a boxing manager. "He constantly equated Joe with the white power structure, and said things like, 'Any Black person who's for Joe Frazier is a traitor.' He did it on purpose; he did it far beyond what was necessary to sell tickets. It was cruel, that's all."

"When he gets to ringside, Frazier will feel like a traitor. Fear is going to come over him, and he'll lose a little pride. . . . He don't have nothing. But me, I have a cause," Ali insisted.

Wolf understood that Ali uttered such things to give himself a psychological edge before the fight, but "there was a bullying, sadistic quality to what he did, like pulling the wings off a dying insect . . . the damage he did to Joe was never undone."

Frazier got so angry, he drove to Ali's house one night to demand an apology. Ali said it was all in fun, to promote their rivalry. Frazier said he didn't find it fun. Ali had no right to question his blackness or his manhood. When had Ali ever plowed a field? "Uncle Tom? Only one I've been Tommin' for is you," Frazier said. "Those sorry-ass Muslims leadin' you on me. It's gonna stop right here."

"Don't talk about my religion," Ali warned him. "I can't let you do that. Go home and cool down."

"Ain't never gonna be coolin' down now. Fuck your religion," Frazier said. "We're talking about me. Who I am . . . You can't take who I am. You turn on a friend for what? So you impress those Muslim fools, so you be the big man?"

"We're finished talking." Ali shut the door.

"I should be a postage stamp," Ali said. "That's the only way I'll ever get licked."

There was another way: by not training properly. His life was in an uproar. The city of Philadelphia was taking too much tax money out of Ali's purse now that he was earning large sums again. He and Belinda moved to Cherry Hill, New Jersey. The house had more room for the twins and Maryum. Not that Ali saw his wife and kids much: when he wasn't in Miami, training in the 5th Street Gym, he was running around with women. "All of a sudden, you know, you're trying to deceive a person, lie all the time . . . I could read him. I could read him real good. That's why it hurt me," Belinda said. "These women, they think women [at home] don't know? Women always know." She blamed the sudden money and the reignited fame. Ali and Frazier were on the cover of *Time* magazine, and the press compared their upcoming bout to Roman gladiatorial combat, claiming it was as momentous an occasion in US history as the moon landing—two great-grandsons of slaves earning $2.5 million each in a single night). Belinda also blamed Herbert Muhammad, who had plenty of girlfriends and encouraged Ali to get all he could. It's the way men were, Belinda figured: "[Ali] was weak . . . He had a father that went around with different women. Like father, like son. He didn't see the power in being strong."

The distractions—the move, the public spectacle, the women—made Ali reckless in the gym. Belinda realized that he wasn't taking Frazier seriously. "If the people around him would say, 'You're bad, man,' he'd get lazy," she said. "Wouldn't train. If he had it in his mind he could whip somebody, that's when he falls weak. I saw all these people telling him he was going to do this, going to do that, you're bad, man. I could see this. All day long. He wouldn't get up, wouldn't run. I said, 'Whoa, wait a minute' . . . [and he] was screwing around with every Tom, Dick, and Harry's woman. Bad." She told him flatly, he was going to lose the fight.

Frazier was training hard in his Philadelphia gym, turning up James Brown and Otis Redding on the wall speakers and giving the punching bags every kind of trouble.

"Muhammad Ali [has] become Lucky Lindy and the Brown Bomber, Bobby Kennedy and Joan Baez, all rolled up into one irrepressible folk hero hailed as our favorite defender of the truth and the resister of authority," Budd Schulberg wrote just days before the bout.

Ali was still facing prison. He was twenty-nine years old. For all he knew, the Frazier fight would be his last hurrah—which made it surprising that he prepared so recklessly. Or perhaps it explained his behavior as that of a man enjoying as much as he could before the world snatched it away from him.

He had always admired Sam Cooke's style, even when Sam's style might have gotten him killed in a grotty LA motel—flirting with the edge, courting dangerous thrills with insouciance. Ali was now carrying that attitude into the ring, taking severe beatings in practice before entering the biggest fight of his career against a determined opponent.

On the day before the fight, Belinda arrived in New York with the kids. Ali had booked fifteen rooms for his family and friends at the New Yorker Hotel ("I bet Joe Frazier doesn't have that many rooms," he bragged.) Belinda tried to find her husband. Finally, she got him on the phone—in a room with a woman. "Why you in there?" she screamed into the receiver. "This is what I'm talking about, Ali! This is *just* what I'm talking about! I'm gonna come up there and knock the hell out of you!"

She kicked at the door. Ali opened it, naked. The woman cowered in the shower. "I'm sorry, I'm sorry," she said. "This is just business. He gave me forty dollars. Please don't kill me."

When the woman had gone, Belinda told Ali, "I'm tired of these shenanigans, I really am." A forty-dollar hooker with a smack habit? *Seriously?* "I'm so embarrassed about this because she's ugly, and you're stupid. You've got a fight tomorrow night."

"I understand," Ali said. "I'm sorry."

Belinda said she'd root for Joe Frazier.

Each new Ali fight was bigger than the last, breaking viewership records. Madison Square Garden sold out almost immediately. This was the new Garden, the third in the city's history, erected in the mid-sixties where the magnificent Beaux Arts Pennsylvania Station once stood. Ringside seats sold at $150 apiece but were soon being scalped for $700 and more. Over three hundred million people in twenty-six countries would see the match on closed-circuit TV. Jerry Perenchio, a Hollywood talent agent in charge of promoting the fight, said, "It's potentially the greatest single grosser in the history of the world."

Parties the day before the bout convened entertainment royalty (e.g., Burt Lancaster, Frank Sinatra, Barbra Streisand, Miles Davis, Diana Ross, and Dustin Hoffman), political heavyweights (Ted Kennedy, Sargent Shriver, and John Lindsay), and writers (Norman Mailer, George Plimpton, Pete Hamill, and Bruce Jay Freidman).

Ali's narrative seemed to have influenced Alistair Cooke of London's *Guardian*. Cooke called Ali "pretty boy" and referred to Joe Frazier as "one of the gargoyles of Notre Dame."

The bout's early rounds were remarkable for their intensity and unexpectedness—neither fighter relied on his strengths. Ali did not dance; rather, he stood with Frazier toe-to-toe, taking big shots, trying to end the fight quickly. Frazier, usually a methodical body-puncher, adept at slowly wearying his opponents, went for Ali's head, also trying for a swift knockout. For him this was personal. Ali won the first two rounds on points, landing more punches more accurately. In the third round, Frazier began throwing hooks to the body, and Ali was visibly tired. He sagged against the ropes through several middle rounds, hoping Frazier would punch himself out, when he should have been trying to score points.

His clowning and his attempts at intimidation didn't work. "Don't you know I'm God?" he shouted.

"God, you're in the wrong place tonight," Frazier snapped back.

In round nine, Ali bounced eight straight jabs off Frazier's skull. Frazier's face swelled, misshapen, like a lump of worked-over dough. Doggedly, he responded with stinging uppercuts. Neither man fell.

Ali was vulnerable to a left hook winging-in over his right hand, whenever he dropped the right, preparing to throw an uppercut. In the eleventh round, Frazier saw the right hand dip. He timed his left exquisitely and caught Ali on the jaw. Ali shivered, backed up, dazed. He spent the rest of the round trying to gain control of his body again, to lose the numbness, but Frazier could not put him away.

"In round fifteen, Ali was tired, he was hurt, just trying to get through the last round," Ferdie Pacheco said. "And Frazier hit him flush on the jaw with the hardest left hook he'd ever thrown. Ali went down, and it looked like he was out cold. I didn't think he could possibly get up. And not only did he get up, he was up almost as fast as he went down. It was incredible. Not only could he take a punch. That night, he was the most courageous fighter I'd ever seen. He was going to get up if he was dead. If Frazier had killed him, he'd have gotten up."

Angelo Dundee was convinced Ali was unconscious as he fell and was jolted back awake when his ass hit the canvas.

"Ali made it," Bob Waters reported in *Newsday*. "His toes pointed in and sometimes the head didn't seem to want to go where the body was going. But when the [final] bell rang, Ali's face was even with Frazier's and both of Ali's feet were flat on the canvas. Frazier curled his lips at Ali. 'I told you I'd get you,' he said."

Frazier won by unanimous decision.

"I was devastated. It was awful," said TV sportscaster Bryant Gumbel. "I felt as though everything I stood for had been beaten down and trampled. We'd all seen those pictures of the people with flags and hard hats beating up kids with long hair who were protesting, and this was our chance to get even in the ring . . . it was a terrible, terrible night. I'll never forget it as long as I live. The feeling was like when Richard Nixon won [a] crushing reelection mandate a year later. That was devastating, but Ali losing was much more personal."

President Nixon crowed: "That draft-dodger asshole" got what he deserved.

"I suppose it will be taken in some quarters as a victory for hot dogs and apple pie, the Fourth of July and moonlight on the Wabash," Jim Murray wrote in the *Los Angeles Times*. "And it's safe to belong to the American Legion again, pack up your troubles in your old kit bag—but actually it was just a fist fight."

At a brief press conference, a stiff and swollen Frazier still demanded an apology from Ali. "What are guys going to say now?" he asked reporters. "You've been writing about the great Ali and what he was going to do to me. I can read, you know. Now let me go and get my face straightened out."

He spent nearly three weeks in the hospital, recovering from the damage Ali had inflicted on his body—before being invited to the White House by Richard Nixon to attend Sunday services.

Ali got his jaw X-rayed—it was not broken—and left the hospital after forty minutes. "It's all your fault," he told Belinda. "You said I was going to lose, that's why I lost." She didn't answer him.

Diana Ross had been far more consoling, kneeling beside him in his dressing room after the fight, caressing his swollen face and whispering to him.

The next day Ali told reporters, "You lose, you lose. I don't cry. I don't cry because I lose. The world will still go on. A plane can crash with forty-five people, Black and white. Is my losing as bad as forty-five people dying, and that's forgotten? Having presidents die and Martin Luther King die and that's forgotten. How many people in Vietnam are dying? . . . I've studied life. People have accidents, people die. My wife and my babies and my house is waiting. The sun is still shining."

With the loss in the championship bout behind him, he resumed his old rhetoric and became, once more, a warrior for justice. "Boxing introduced me to the real fight of freedom, justice and equality for twenty million Black people," he said. "I wouldn't mind going to jail because I'd be with my brothers. I'm ready to die for my people now."

The US Supreme Court didn't want to bother with his case—his conviction had been upheld twice now—but the fact that he dominated the sports pages again led Justice William Brennan to argue that "he'd become such an important and large public figure that the public wouldn't understand if the Supreme Court didn't review the case," Tom Krattenmaker, a law clerk for Justice John Harlan, explained.

Thurgood Marshall recused himself. He had been at the Justice Department in 1967 when Ali first refused the draft and the department prosecuted him.

Edwin Griswold, the US solicitor general, argued the government's case against Ali. He told the court, "The petitioner just doesn't want to fight a white man's war, and I can understand that. But that's not the same thing as being a pacifist."

On April 23, 1971, the court voted 5–3 to send Ali to prison. Justice Harlan, seventy-two years old, the court's senior member, in treatment for spinal cancer, was tasked with writing the majority opinion. Krattenmaker, his clerk, said, "My initial reaction was that I thought the decision was wrong." Krattenmaker was twenty-six. He knew plenty of sons of wealthy families who had played the political angles and bought military deferments. "I suppose it's fair to say—or accurate to say—that I . . . was one of those people who was most early opposed to the Vietnam War," he said. He had read *The Autobiography of Malcolm X*, and it convinced him the government's case was wrong: Malcolm made it clear that the Nation of Islam was a real religion and it opposed all wars not declared by Allah.

This was a hard sell in the courts, given the government's hostility to antiwar protesters and its view of the Nation as a terrorist organization. But Krattenmaker returned to Judge Lawrence Grauman's interrogation of Ali on the issue of conscientious objection: Grauman's conclusion—rejected by the Justice Department—that Ali was sincere.

The young clerk thought he saw some legal daylight here. He went to John Harlan. "So, yes, I sort of said, 'Mister Justice, I have an opinion on this. I think it should be coming out the other way, and here's why.'"

He convinced Harlan that the Nation of Islam would only allow Ali to fight in a theocratic war: Ali's convictions were sincere. This changed the court's vote from 5–3 to 4–4, still not enough to keep Ali out of jail. A tie vote affirmed the lower court's conviction. But no one on the court liked the look of a split decision in such a high-profile case. Even the bench's conservative justices recognized shifting public opinions and conceded that Ali's ongoing persecution had become a national embarrassment.

Krattenmaker had discovered that when the Justice Department dismissed Grauman's endorsement of Ali, they had failed to inform Ali's draft board of the judge's remarks. They had given the board the wrong impression of Grauman's opinion. Therefore, the Justice Department had offered "erroneous legal advice," upon which an "erroneous" judgment had been made.

Based on this technicality, the court wriggled out of the Ali mess without setting any precedents concerning the draft or conscientious objector status, without—in essence—making a ruling at all.

By an 8–0 vote, the court overturned Ali's conviction. He was free at last.

When he heard the news, he was back in Chicago, visiting the old neighborhood. It was shortly after nine in the morning. He had driven his Lincoln Mark III to a South Side store for some fresh-squeezed orange juice and had just walked out of the store when the owner ran after him. He'd heard the report on the radio. "I'm so happy for you," the man said.

Ali whooped and bought a round of orange juice for everyone in the place.

Later he thanked "Allah and the Honorable Elijah Muhammad." He said he would "try to live better . . . [and] try to do good." He said he felt like a "man been in chains all his life and suddenly the chains taken off": "he don't realize he's free until he get the circulation back in his arms and legs and starts to move his fingers." He said he couldn't be "mad" at those who'd prosecuted him, because "they did what they thought was right." "I . . . ask them to respect the rights to my beliefs. But if I'm going to ask that, then I got to respect the rights to their beliefs."

"It was biblical," *New York Times* reporter Sidney Schanberg said of the millions of desperate refugees slogging through marshes and monsoons from East Pakistan into northern India.

> There's a numbness. Either that or you feel like crying. There was a tremendous loss of life on those treks out. Their bodies have adjusted to . . .

germs in their water, but suddenly they're drinking different water with different germs. Suddenly they've got cholera. People were dying all around us. You'd see that someone had left a body on the side of the road, wrapped in pieces of bamboo, and there'd be a vulture trying to get inside to eat the body. You would come into a schoolyard, and a mother was losing her child. He was in her lap. He coughed and coughed and then he died.

Those who could not leave were selectively hunted down, killed at random, tortured, raped, or burned out of their villages. "Artillery, tanks, automatic weapons, mortars, aeroplanes, everything which is normally used against invading armed forces, were utilized [against civilians], and very large-scale killings took place," India's foreign minister, Swaran Singh, reported, adding that he was "deeply stirred by the carnage in East Bengal."

In the Oval Office, President Nixon said, "I hope to hell we're not [going to aid the refugees]." He didn't trust Congress. He and Kissinger assured each other they were right to do nothing. They told each other their support for Yahya was strategically sound. "He's a decent man, for him to do a difficult job trying to hold those two parts of the country . . . and keep them together," Nixon said.

Somehow, a copy of Ambassador Blood's "Selective Genocide" telegram reached Senator Edward Kennedy. Nixon was furious that the cable had leaked. Kennedy learned that 80 percent of West Pakistan's arms came from the United States, despite the arms embargo. He raised alarms all over Washington, but no one listened. He praised Pakistan's neighbor. "The government of India, as it first saw this tide of human misery begin to flow across its borders, could have cordoned off its land and refused entry. But to its everlasting credit, India chose the way of compassion," Kennedy said.

Nixon had remarked about India, "I don't know why the hell anybody would reproduce in that damn country but they do."

In Los Angeles Ravi Shankar said, "I [kept hearing] that many of my distant relatives, along with hundreds of thousands of other refugees, were fleeing to Calcutta. I felt very concerned. It was not political or religious feeling on my part; it was more linguistic. Being Bengali-speaking myself I felt sympathetic towards Bangladesh, but even more so for the refugees who had crossed the border into India and were suffering so much, especially the children."

"The idea . . . occurred to me of giving a concert to raise money to help these refugees—something on a bigger scale than normal. While I was thinking of this, George Harrison was in Los Angeles. He would come to my house in the mornings and spend time there, and he understood what I was going through. I asked him frankly, 'George, can you help me?' . . . He was really moved and said, 'Yes, something should be done.'"

"The war had been going on . . . and I had hardly even heard of it, so he fed me a lot of newspaper articles about it," Harrison recalled. "And so I got involved. The priority was to attract world attention to what was going on. It wasn't so much the money because you can feed somebody today and tomorrow they will still be hungry, but if they are getting massacred you've got to try and stop that first of all.

"I said, 'OK . . . We'll try and make it into a big show, and maybe we can make a million dollars instead of a few thousand.' So I got on the telephone trying to round people up. We pinpointed the days which were astrologically good, and we found Madison Square Garden was open on one of those days—1st August."

At this point, Harrison wielded massive clout in the music industry. *All Things Must Pass* had received overwhelmingly positive reviews. "Wagnerian, Brucknerian, the music of mountaintops and vast horizons . . . [an] extravaganza of piety and sacrifice and joy, whose sheer magnitude and ambition may dub it the *War and Peace* of rock and roll," Ben Gerson wrote in *Rolling Stone*. *Melody Maker* called it "the rock equivalent of the shock felt by prewar moviegoers when Garbo first opened her mouth in a talkie: 'Garbo talks!—Harrison is free!'"

Its most striking single, "My Sweet Lord," a tsunami of layered guitars, was "among the boldest steps in the history of popular music," one journalist remarked, but he said its overt religiosity might make it a "fatal career move." It was like Ali declaring himself a Muslim. Harrison worried about this too but decided to risk it: "Everybody is always trying to keep themselves covered, stay commercial. So I thought, 'Just do it.' Nobody else is, and I'm sick of all these young people just boogying around, wasting their lives, you know." He wanted to write the "Western equivalent of a mantra, which repeats over and over again the holy names," he said.

The refrain, several overdubs of Harrison accompanying himself singing harmony, meant to show that "'Hallelujah' and 'Hare Krishna' are quite the same thing." The song ended with an ancient Sanskrit prayer: *gurur brahma, gurur vishnu, gurur deva maheshwara, / gurur sakshat, parabrahma, tasmai shri gurave namah* ("I offer homage to my guru, who is as great as the creator Brahma, the maintainer Vishnu, the destroyer Shiva, and who is the very energy of God").

Bobby Whitlock recalled, "When we were doing 'My Sweet Lord' with all those names at the end, I said, 'What the hell are all these guys?' He said, 'They're all gods.' And I said, '*Way* too many gods, George!'"

Like the album, the single immediately topped international record charts. "Every time I put the radio on, it's 'Oh, My Lord,'" John Lennon complained. "I'm beginning to think there *must* be a God."

The album's other songs, a diverse offering of rock, country, gospel, and folk, of quiet acoustics and electric assaults, presented the full paradox of George Harrison—a very private man who wanted to share his thoughts with millions; a man eager to establish his own identity while acknowledging he would never escape his mythic past; a man eager to share his faith with others while freely admitting doubts; a man who had everything, expressing unfulfilled yearning; a man mourning lost friendships (in gentle contrast to the vitriolic attacks Lennon and McCartney would later launch against each other). *All Things Must Pass* was the contradictory testament of a spirit struggling daily in the material world. If the grandiose productions occasionally battled the tunes' intimacy, that tension—its honest raggedness (matching Harrison's voice and the quality of his lyrics)—made for compelling listening, and still lifts *All Things Must Pass* above any other solo effort by a former Beatle.

Harrison was "not the kind of person I would buy the records of," Lennon said, obviously jealous, after the album's sales surpassed three million. "I don't consider my talents fantastic compared with the fucking universe, but I consider George's less."

His view notwithstanding, the album's spectacular success, commercially and critically, put Harrison in a position to do just about anything he wanted.

What he wanted to do was help his friend, to relieve a humanitarian disaster that most of his audience hadn't heard about in a part of the world few of his fans realized existed. To say the least, this made his new manager Allen Klein and his record company nervous.

Nor was he certain he could, on short notice, talk any of his buddies into appearing with him, for no pay, in a benefit concert for a cause they didn't understand. It would be humiliating to have them turn him down. And by default, he would be the headliner—a role he had never sought, never relished, never wanted.

"He had to really steel himself and be very brave to do this," said Pattie Boyd.

"That was his sacrifice for Ravi," Chris O'Dell, the couple's personal assistant, observed.

He spent the second half of June and the first half of July calling musicians, sometimes spending twelve hours a day on the telephone. He knew he could count on Starr. McCartney turned him down, citing the Beatles' business differences. He didn't want to spread the impression that the Beatles were willing to reunite. Initially Lennon agreed but only if Ono could also perform. Harrison said no—he feared she would turn the show into a self-promoting art event, and that was not what this was about. Angrily, Lennon declined to participate (Ono was so upset with Harrison—and with Lennon, for not defending her vigorously enough—that she caught a jet out of the country). Harrison was stung by his mates' inability to abandon petty concerns for something larger than themselves.

Mick Jagger couldn't make it because of visa problems. Billy Preston agreed, impressed by the "charity" of it. Klaus Voorman and Carl Radle would play bass, Leon Russell piano. Badfinger volunteered to provide backing acoustic guitars. Claudia Lennear, a veteran session singer, lined up a large, diverse choir. Jim Horn and the Hollywood Horn Players happily came aboard. "Everybody wanted to help. Everybody wanted to be part of it," said drummer Jim Keltner. "You knew it was all going to come together because who's going to say no to George, you know?"

"I'll consider it, man," Dylan promised Harrison. Dylan had been in a self-imposed exile for almost five years now and seemed terrified at the prospect of performing again. In late July, Harrison moved into the Park Lane Hotel in New York, and booked rehearsal space in a room above Carnegie Hall. Dylan came to see him at the Park Lane and said he'd join some rehearsals to see if he "felt like" participating.

His ambivalence caused Harrison considerable anxiety but not nearly as much as Eric Clapton's unreliability. Initially Clapton agreed to fly from London to play. At this point, he kept himself in a daily opioid daze. He and Pattie Boyd had not seen each other in two years, but he continued to send her poems and entreaties through the mail. She responded, signing one of her letters, "Moons full of love." Harrison, aware of all this, let it pass. He hoped that by getting Clapton back onstage, even if he was propped up by drugs, his friends would begin to acknowledge his addiction and reach out to him.

"We had him booked on every flight out of London for about seven days," Harrison remembered. "'He's on this flight.' 'Okay.' So we'd go to the airport and he wasn't there."

Jonathan Taplin, the concert's production manager, said, "By the third day, George was getting a little anxious that he wasn't going to have a guitar player, and by the fourth day, word must have been getting out because all of a sudden a lot of guitar players started showing up in the lobby of the Park Lane. . . . George figured, 'I've got to get somebody,' so he hired Jesse Ed Davis, who had been in Taj Mahal's band."

When Clapton did finally reach New York, he holed up in a room at the Essex House with a female companion. He sent her out each day to buy heroin. He tried to attend a rehearsal but couldn't get through it.

"A lot of the last-minute logistics happened in the last two weeks . . . most of the musicians didn't gather until literally seven days before the concert," Taplin recalled.

"It was a miracle [that it came together]," Shankar said.

Rattled by all the details, the phone calls, the travel arrangements, the contract negotiations (nearly each musician was signed to a different record label), the equipment prep (for recording a live album and making a film), the rehearsals at which only a few players showed up at a time, the need to practice his own performance, and the rising air of Beatlemania in the streets outside the hotel, Harrison bordered on collapse.

He had learned he was being sued for plagiarism by Bright Tunes, the publisher of the Chiffons' 1962 hit record "He's So Fine." The publisher claimed "My Sweet Lord" was a direct copy of the song. Harrison, backed by Billy Preston, who said he was a witness, denied this, saying the song had its origins in a group sing-along on the Delaney and Bonnie tour and was influenced by the Edwin Hawkins Singers' "Oh Happy Day." Pattie Boyd also said, "I knew [George] had written it—I was there when he was working on it." But Bright went forward with a lawsuit. Klein said not to worry, he would handle it—and he suggested to Bright's president that Harrison buy the entire Bright catalog as a settlement. This sounded like a ploy to pad ABKCO's holdings. A long legal wrangle had begun.

Klein was driving Harrison crazy. Though he claimed ABKCO would not make a dime from the charity concert, Klein's demand that Harrison sign over more than £600,000 in management fees made Harrison wary. (In a demo for *All Things Must Pass*, on a song called "Beware of Darkness," Harrison had sung, "Beware of ABKCO.") Klein was using the pre-concert publicity to promote his business, falling just short of claiming credit for arranging the event. He had made a series of public gaffes. When Lord Harlech, the former British ambassador to the United States, and a close friend of Jackie Kennedy's, asked Klein why Harrison's concert was being staged in the United States instead of England, Klein erupted, "'Ferchrissakes, ya country hasn't been very nice to the Beatles, not very nice at all. . . . Why should anyone want to stay in England with

[your] tax situation?" His rudeness, never forgotten, would seriously damage Harrison later.

When Edward Kennedy's Senate office phoned asking for concert tickets, Klein refused. "Tell 'em we're all sold out. . . . What did Teddy Kennedy ever do for rock?"

Kennedy was preparing to tour the refugee camps on the border of India and East Pakistan.

But Klein's worst mistake, which Harrison would not discover until after the concert, was his failure to advise his client to choose in advance a specific charity organization to handle the money. This would prove to be a calamitous oversight.

Besides Klein, Harrison tried to keep watch on his father. He had invited his father, still grieving for his wife, to join him in New York—to reengage with the world. Rock and roll chaos was perhaps not the best venue for this, but to Harrison's surprise, the tumult appeared to amuse Harry. It gave him energy. He was enjoying himself—maybe too much, flirting with all the groupies in the hotel lobby hoping to bed a rock star, another reason for Harrison to worry.

Meanwhile, Boyd was out and about in Manhattan, seeking contacts for a return to modeling, and meeting Clapton, for all Harrison knew. He didn't see her much.

Shyamasundar showed up one afternoon. Harrison asked him to prepare *prasādam* to feed the band and crew. Everyone gathered on a hotel floor to share dal soup, saffron rice, chapati, and fried milk curd. As people ate, Dylan sat in a corner alone, morosely strumming "Like a Rolling Stone."

The New York days were muggy and humid, sweltering. This did not stop ticket-buyers from lining up outside the Garden overnight, around the block. They all wanted to see a Beatle onstage (though one young woman assured a reporter, "Like, I'm really into this East Pakistan thing"). "The level of energy outside [Madison Square Garden] . . . was *intense*," Jann Wenner said. "Block and half away, you know, and I could just feel the place buzzing."

The growing crowds in the streets unsettled Harrison, as did a joint press conference with Ravi Shankar on July 27. "When tickets for your concert went on sale . . . they sold out within minutes," Geraldo Rivera, then a local news correspondent, commented to Harrison. "It seems as if the same kind of mania that attached to [the Beatles] now attaches to you. How do you feel about that?"

Shankar gave his pal a sympathetic grin.

"I feel flattered, you know," Harrison said, looking dismayed. "I don't know why it should. It's a great honor."

"Mr. Harrison, with all the enormous problems in the world, how did you happen to choose this one to do something about?"

"Because I was asked by a friend if I'd help, you know, that's all."

In the Oval Office, Richard Nixon told Henry Kissinger, "I see now the Beatles are up raising money for [East Pakistan]." Obviously, he didn't know the group had disbanded. "You know, it's a funny thing the way we are in this goddamn country, is, we get involved in all these screwball causes."

"For whom are the Beatles raising money?" Kissinger asked. "For the refugees in India?"

"The goddamn Indians," Nixon said. But he wasn't worried: "Nobody . . . gives a shit . . . about India-Pakistan . . . you know, I think Biafra stirred people up more than Pakistan, because Pakistan, they're just a bunch of brown goddamn Muslims."

George Harrison, with a hit record on the charts, was in a hotel room prior to giving a concert as the mania swirled around him. The familiarity was disorienting. And this time he was alone—alone with the responsibility of bringing off a major performance, with finalizing arrangements, tempering tensions in his band, his crew, his friendships.

This is happiness?

Years later, a groupie who refused to be identified told a tabloid writer she had made it into Harrison's room (introduced to him, she said, by his naïve father, who had been harmlessly flirting with her in the Park Lane lobby). She claimed Harrison needed conversation more than intimacy. He seemed to her a painfully sad and lonely man, unhappy about the breakdown of his marriage, clinging to Krishna the way an addict craves a fix.

Countless such stories, impossible to corroborate, followed each of the Beatles everywhere they went, but this one rings true to the extent that it gives us a snapshot not of a sexually ravenous rock star but of a needy man under enormous pressure, grappling with depression.

The woman claimed she remained in touch, as a friend, with Harrison's father, for several years afterward. And less than a year later, Harrison would be back in New York, at the Park Lane Hotel, alone in the same suite overlooking Central Park South, writing a song on hotel stationery about the final collapse of his marriage: "Now the winter has come, / Eclipsing the sun / that has lighted my love for some time."

The night before the concert, Clapton was still in a bad way, unable to practice. Dylan stood onstage, gazing out at the auditorium's forty thousand empty seats, the microphones, the camera equipment. Finally he turned to Harrison and said, "Hey, man. This isn't my scene. I can't do this."

"By that time, I'd had so much on my plate, trying to get it all organized . . . I was so stressed," Harrison said. Exasperated, he told Dylan, "It's not my scene, either. I don't do this every day. In fact, this is the first time I've *ever* done anything on my own. You at least have been a solo artist."

Dylan still would not commit. Harrison agonized: he didn't have a proper lead guitarist; he had a potential gap in his show he didn't know how to fill.

He had insisted that a classical Indian music set begin the concert (really two concerts: an afternoon show and an evening performance). He did not want to create the impression that Bangladesh—or India, for that matter—was a squalid poverty pit, begging the enlightened West to save it. It was a proud, culturally rich, deeply spiritual part of the world, wounded now—bludgeoned—by rapacious politicians.

Though most of the young audience members did not appreciate what they were seeing, the occasion was remarkable even before a single note sounded. Ravi Shankar, a Hindu, took the stage beside Ali Akbar Khan, a Muslim, while a humble Englishman bowed to them, hands together in a prayerful gesture of respect. In that moment, an entire complex colonial history was evoked and rewritten, as a preface to staging a new historical vision—one of harmony, diverse peoples sharing space, creating music to relieve suffering.

It was a more potent moment than any art happening, street theater, or bed-in from the preceding decade. The audience members sensed its gravity even if they didn't comprehend it.

By referring to Bangladesh before it was Bangladesh, before it was an independent nation or recognized as such, and while the United States was supplying billions of dollars of arms to prevent the region from *becoming* independent Bangladesh, the international musicians, performing on American soil, made a powerful and dignified statement, akin to Malcom X's views of the world in the early 1960s.

Harrison, dressed simply in a light blue shirt and brown vest, received enormous waves of applause when he walked onstage, but he stilled the noise with the quietness of his voice and his muted demeanor. He thanked the audience for attending the benefit and then announced, "The first part of the concert is going to be an Indian music section. You're going to hear a sitar-sarod duet and, as you realize, the Indian music is a little more serious than our music, and I'd appreciate it if you could try to settle down and get into the Indian music section." He introduced Shankar, Khan, the great tabla player Alla Rakha, and Shankar's partner, Kamala Chakravarty, playing the tambura, the drone instrument.

Shankar acknowledged that the audience was "impatient" to hear its favorite stars, but he cautioned them that the Indian music required "a little concentrated listening. "We are trying to set the music to this special event, this historical program. . . . We are not trying to make any politic. We are artists, but through our music we would like you to feel the agony and also the pain and a lot of sad happenings in Bangladesh."

The Indian instruments had gone out of tune, and players adjusted their strings for about ten seconds, after which the audience burst into cheers. Grinning, Shankar said, "Thank you. If you appreciate the tuning so much, I hope you will enjoy the playing more."

It was essential, for him, to introduce the performance with a *dhun*, a light, ancient melody based on a Bengali folk tune. His mentor, Khan's father, Baba, was Bengali, so this was a regional homage on many levels. "Bangla Dhun" unfolded slowly, starting with a short, improvisatory *alap* on sitar and sarod followed by a mid-tempo *gat*, set by Alla Rakha's flying fingers. He beamed like a boy. Next to Ringo Starr, no drummer on a world stage had ever seemed so joyous.

The tune's melodic development, the *vistar*, gained speed as Shankar and Khan traded major themes. Then a sixteen-beat *tintal* cycle kicked in, a rapid call-and-response between the sitar and the sarod, the Hindu and the Muslim, expressing to each other, sitting side by side, their agony and anger, their harmony and shared understanding. The musicians rose, bowed to the audience and to one another; the most famous performance of Indian classical music in the West—still to this day—had come to an end.

Shankar was nearly moved to tears.

While a crew cleared the stage, a short film played, revealing the desperation of the refugee camps, fly-specked children starving in mud, skeletal bodies sprawled in wet ditches. The images, simple, straightforward, unadorned, needed no explanations.

Harrison reemerged onstage, arrayed now in a white suit with pink OM symbols stitched on its jacket lapels. He carried a white Stratocaster. Beneath his long, monk-like beard, he managed to convey a balance of gravitas and exuberance, befitting the occasion. He was quietly charismatic in a way he had never been before—and never quite would be again.

To the extent that he could, Harrison wanted to arrange the Western music sequence in a pattern as stately as a raga. Most of the songs he chose had an overwhelmingly spiritual thrust, leavened with nods to earthy rock and roll. He began with "Wah-Wah," an anthem celebrating his break from the Beatles and his desire to free himself from harmful things; "My Sweet Lord" came next (in the second show), a declaration of personal yearning for God, followed by "Awaiting on You All," a communal invitation invoking the Divine.

Billy Preston took the spotlight with a gospel tune, "That's the Way God Planned It," a plea for humility and calm after so much racial violence in America. Filled with the spirit, he danced across the stage midway through the song. He was followed by Ringo Starr (who received the biggest ovation of the night, not just a sign of affection for him but also of appreciation for his gesture of friendship to Harrison—a smidgen of the brotherly love the Beatles once represented). Starr sang "It Don't Come Easy," a blues homage written largely by Harrison, who gave Starr the composing credit. *Rolling Stone*'s reviewer of the concert wrote, "Seeing Ringo Starr drumming and singing on stage has a joy in it that is one of the happiest feelings on earth still."

Harrison's "Beware of Darkness" came next in the set, a warning to avoid Maya, the world of illusion. Claudia Lennear and her choir backed Harrison, and Leon Russell sang a verse. James Cushing, a music critic, later wrote of the performance, "We have essentially an African-American gospel group with a British lead singer trying to get us into Hindu religious mythology, and this long-haired Oklahoma boy, Leon, drawls a country-western take on the whole [thing] . . . [it's a] cultural salad bowl."

Russell was not the only Okie onstage. Guitarist Jesse Ed Davis, a Native American hailing from the former Indian Territory, stood as a witness to home-grown colonialism.

Harrison and Clapton (dosed with methadone) performed a stirring duet on "While My Guitar Gently Weeps," a personal give-and-take complementing the political call-and-response performed by Shankar and Khan. Poignantly, the two old friends smiled at each other as their guitars spoke what couldn't be expressed openly, given Clapton's continuing obsession with Boyd, the condition he'd gotten himself into, and the recognition that he had let his friend down by endangering the concert. "I made it really hard for myself," Clapton said later. "That guitar is not the right kind of guitar to play that song on. I should have [had] a solid Gibson or something, not a semi-acoustic, but [I was] . . . not really there."

For once, Harrison's strong, graceful playing far outshone his more virtuosic buddy.

Also "not really there" in the first show until the last possible moment was Bob Dylan. Harrison had taped a set list to the back of his guitar and had scribbled on the paper "Bob" followed by a huge question mark. Leon Russell played a hard-rocking R&B set, and this was followed by a lovely rendition of "Here Comes the Sun" featuring Harrison and Badfinger's Pete Ham on acoustic guitars.

Backstage, in a tiny men's room, Pete Bennett, an Apple employee, found Dylan leaning against cold tiles nervously strumming his guitar. He was due to go on. "Bob! What the hell . . . ?" he said.

"I like it in here. How's George doing?"

"Fine. Fine . . . You gotta get out there onstage, man."

"Maybe the people won't like me anymore, Pete."

"Bob, shit, Bob! Everybody's waiting to see you!"

"See me fuck it up, you mean."

"Do it for [George]," Bennett said.

He walked Dylan to the edge of the stage. Harrison was already squinting into the wings, to see if the show was about to come crashing to a halt. Relieved to glimpse a sleeve of Dylan's denim jacket in the reflection of a spotlight, he announced, before the singer could change his mind, "I'd like to bring out a friend of us all, Mr. Bob Dylan!"

Days before the show, Harrison had asked Dylan to play his early antiwar anthem, "Blowin' in the Wind." Dylan, always loathe to dwell in the past, had responded tartly by challenging Harrison to play "I Want to Hold Your Hand." (In 1966, hearing "Tomorrow Never Knows" for the first time, Dylan had teased Harrison, "Oh, I get it. You don't want to be cute anymore.")

But at the concert Dylan twice performed a set of his earliest tunes, including "Blowin' in the Wind," consciously reassuming—for this occasion only—the mantle of His Generation's Voice that he had worked so hard to erase.

Harrison accompanied him with gentle harmonies and delicate backing guitar. Perhaps in no previous setting had his melodic gifts been so apparent: "He could develop a simple little melodic idea that would be repeated in the course of a song, so that you would never be able to hear the song without hearing this hook," David Bromberg observed.

Onstage at Madison Square Garden, with Harrison's tasteful backing, aided by Leon Russell on bass and Starr on tambourine, Dylan had never sounded so urgent, so clear. "I really couldn't quite believe we were actually seeing what we were seeing. But we were, oh, yes, we were, and I'm not going to forget it, because it surely ain't going to happen again," wrote Don Heckman, reviewing the concert for the *Village Voice*.

When Dylan sang, "How many deaths will it take till he knows / that too many people have died?" he seemed to directly address Richard Nixon.

Harrison closed the show with a song he had written specifically for the occasion. Dispensing with lyricism, "Bangla Desh" opened with as blunt and straightforward a statement of purpose as any song of the era: "My friend came to me / with sadness in his eyes. / Told me that he wanted help / before his country dies. / Although I couldn't feel the pain, / I knew I had to try. / Now I'm asking all of you / to help us save some lives."

The honest, humane lyric "portrays the man behind the music," said Kofi Annan, the Ghanaian diplomat who would serve as secretary-general of the United Nations from 1997 to 2006.

"I have no quarrel with John Lennon's endless clattering around inside his psyche or Paul McCartney's search for sweetness and light, but at the moment I have to have stronger feelings about George Harrison's active efforts to do something about the misery in the world around him," said Don Heckman in the *Voice*. "How surprising that the most introspective of the Beatles should be the one who, in the long run, takes the most effective actions."

At the after-show party in Ungano's, a Manhattan nightclub, an exhilarated Dylan embraced Harrison, lifting him off the ground. "God!" he shouted. "If only we'd done *three* shows!" He would soon be touring again and writing his most politically engaged songs in years.

The next morning, Harrison wrote a song entitled "The Day the World Gets 'Round," a plea for political enlightenment. "It was a very emotional period for me," he would write later. The collaborative nature of the concert had filled him with optimism. "At the same time, I felt slightly enraged because, let's face it, the whole problem and how to solve it lies within the power of the governments and world leaders. They have resources, food, money, and wealth enough for twice our world's population, yet they choose to squander it on weapons and other objects that destroy. . . . It seems to me a poor state of affairs when 'pop stars' are required to set an example in order to solve this type of problem."

Two weeks after the concert, Ted Kennedy, chairman of the Senate Judiciary Committee on Refugees, flew to East Pakistan to tour the refugee camps. What he saw, he said, was an "outrage to every concept of international law," the direct consequence of "genocide." He said, "[The president's Asia policy] baffles me and after seeing the results in terms of human misery, I think it's an even greater disaster." On efforts to help the victims: "Obviously, the international response has been meager to date."

Nixon countered Kennedy's public rebuke by reminding the press of the senator's moral failings: Chappaquiddick still haunted Kennedy—the night, in July 1969, he'd drunkenly driven his car off a road, killing a young woman he'd just met at a party, Mary Jo Kopechne. He'd worked hard, since then, to shed his national disgrace, hoping for some measure of redemption. Nixon brushed him off angrily.

It was not as easy for Nixon to ignore the publication of the Pentagon Papers in the *New York Times* and the *Washington Post*, beginning in June 1971. The revelations further eroded public trust in government. Then the Democratically controlled US Senate voted to withdraw US forces from Vietnam. Nixon vetoed the bill, but it was a setback. It hardened his position on East Pakistan. He needed a foreign policy victory.

In November, Indira Gandhi visited Washington. Nixon and Kissinger tried to wheedle her into helping Yahya in East Pakistan, but she refused to accept this. Kissinger said she lectured Nixon "like a professor [talking to] a slightly backward student."

In early December, fed up with India's aid to the refugees and what he saw as interference in his affairs, Yahya declared war on India. Nixon told Kissinger, "[It] makes your heart sick" to see Yahya "done so by the Indians, and after we warned the bitch."

In support of West Pakistan, he sent the USS *Enterprise* to the Bay of Bengal, threatening a nuclear confrontation.

✿

Like Kennedy, George Harrison was, for Richard Nixon, an irritant to be waved away, though Nixon worried, a little, that Harrison might have surprising sway—the United States was preparing to lower its voting age to eighteen.

At first blush, it was easy to dismiss the Concert for Bangladesh as a feel-good party thrown by soft-headed, limo-driving rock stars to ease their consciences; easy to dismiss its fund-raising as just a drop in the bucket and its stance as problematical—one more East-West power imbalance, perpetuating the helplessness of poor people.

But the event had been a genuine collaboration between an Easterner and a Westerner. Neither would forget the cause and just move on. For Shankar it was personal. Harrison would spend years trying to manage the concert's legacy, through apparently endless tangles of contractual and financial difficulties, often at the expense of his career.

As he had said from the beginning, raising awareness had always been a more important goal than collecting money. "Overnight, the word 'Bangla Desh' . . . was all over the world because of the press coverage," Shankar wrote. "It created such a good wave of publicity for the newborn country"—a country now in danger of nuclear annihilation.

"It was a necessary morale booster for the Bengalis. . . . Thousands were dying every day . . . and it shone a light on some of the Pakistani Hitlers," Harrison would write in his autobiography.

To Nixon's consternation, the single "Bangla Desh" began to climb the charts (its B side was "Deep Blue," Harrison's song for his dying mother; the record was a moving combination of private and political mourning). Young Beatle fans who had never known where Asia was went door to door gathering funds for the refugees. Journalists who had never written "Bangladesh" began using the name regularly.

A Pakistani official warned diplomats in Pakistan's embassies around the world that an "Anti-Pakistan gramophone record entitled 'Bangla Desh,' which was sung by George Harrison, a member of the Beatles' Trio," was getting massive radio airplay. "It contains hostile propaganda against Pakistan," the official said, ordering embassies to do what they could to prevent it from being broadcast.

Meanwhile, music critics were writing that a side effect of the charity concert was nothing less than rock and roll's salvation. "What Woodstock was *said* to be, the Madison Square Garden Bangladesh concert was," Geoffrey Cannon wrote in the *Guardian*. "The concert will stand as the greatest act of magnanimity rock music has yet achieved."

Jann Wenner said, "The Concert for Bangladesh came along at a moment in which the rock and roll scene had been greatly dispirited. A number of things had happened that made you think, you know, maybe the light was going out. There were the prominent deaths of Jimi Hendrix and Janis Joplin, which suggested the drug scene was too heavy. Altamont had happened only eighteen months earlier, I think. Bob had not put out a record in a long time . . . and the Beatles had broken up; that was really depressing. . . . The leading voices of rock and roll were either stilled or quiet. . . . It was a moment of drift . . . and then to have something come along like this which had such a purpose and a spirit."

There were prominent nay-sayers. Greil Marcus wrote that the concert "seemed to be about one of three things": "1) God save us. 2) This is the way God planned it. 3) Chant the names of the Lord and you'll be free. All of the devout rockers on Harrison's stage seemed to be missing their own point. If this gibberish had any relation to reality . . . then the same god that allowed this wonderful concert to take place was also raining hot death on the other side of the globe."

But in the end, even Marcus conceded that Harrison's sincerity was touching: "[He] beats his fists against [the world's] wall of illusion as he sings." "His performance of 'Bangla Desh' gets through to you . . . [You] get some idea of why it was Harrison called all these people together in the first place."

Overwhelmingly, the response to the concert, and to Harrison in particular, matched the *Rolling Stone* review: "The Concert for Bangla Desh is rock reaching for its manhood. Under the leadership of George Harrison, a group of rock musicians recognized, in a deliberate, self-conscious, and professional way, that they have responsibilities, and went about dealing with them seriously. . . . Harrison emerges . . . as a man with a sense of his own worth, his own role in the place of things, and as a man prepared to face reality openly and with a judgment and maturity with few parallels among his peers. As much as the music . . . the spirit he creates through his own demeanor is inspirational."

In the five decades since the concert (as of this writing), continuing sales of the album (CDs and downloads) and concert film on DVD have earned millions of dollars and vastly benefited UNICEF, but in the months following the event, negative publicity surrounding Allen Klein tarnished Harrison's gesture.

Six months after the show, on February 28, 1972, *New York* magazine published a piece quoting Klein as claiming that "85 percent" of the money raised at the benefit had been "used for expenses." An amount of $1.14 of every album sale (at the list price of $12.98) was unaccounted for. Allegedly the money wound up in Klein's pocket. Since he had failed to advise Harrison to identify a receiving charity in advance, the governments of the United States and Britain considered the concert a for-profit affair, subject to heavy taxation.

In London, Harrison met with Patrick Jenkin, England's chief financial undersecretary. For two hours, he painstakingly described the suffering in Bangladesh and in the refugee camps bordering India. He begged the undersecretary not to shave cash from the charity's coffers. But Klein's rudeness to Lord Harlech was well known now inside the British bureaucracy. Icily, Jenkin informed Harrison, "Of course, we are genuinely sympathetic, Mr. Harrison, however . . . Have you ever heard the saying, 'Charity begins at home?'"

"Thanks for your time," Harrison said. "Perhaps you people would prefer it if I were to move out of England, like virtually every other major British pop star and take my money with me?"

"That, sir, would, of course, be entirely up to you."

Jenkin's office released a public statement praising Harrison for making his case so "very eloquently," adding that Jenkin had been "glad to talk with a man who has gone right to the top and has stayed there so long." Harrison responded publicly by describing "all the . . . bullshit" Jenkin had quoted him, "which is so much part of the game of politics. Until the [politicians] bec[o]me human," he said, "we must do our service to others without their help." He wrote a personal check to the British government for over £1 million to cover the concert's tax bill.

Meanwhile, Bhaskar Menon, head of Capitol EMI Music Worldwide, delayed immediate transfer of $400,000 in concert receipts to the people of Bangladesh because he insisted Capitol be compensated for releasing the live album. He blocked the album's release until the deal was settled. Harrison felt outraged, especially as he, through Apple, was financing the album's packaging and design. He had spent weeks arguing with Capitol about the cover. He wanted a stark photo of a starving Bengali child sitting before an empty bowl. The record company wanted a more benign image—an open guitar case filled with bottles of medicine. Harrison had to "jump on that and change it and shout at them," he wrote to his wife. "It's such a pain, all that messing around just because they didn't like the truth."

The album's delay allowed bootleg recordings of the concert to circulate widely, eating into money for the refugees.

On November 23, 1971 Harrison appeared on *The Dick Cavett Show*, ostensibly to talk about a film he had produced on the music of Ravi Shankar, but the conversation eventually turned to his struggle with the concert's ugly aftermath.

Cavett didn't know how to handle Harrison, who did not even attempt to be the chatty celebrity talk-show guest plugging his latest product. "I'm probably the biggest bore you've ever had on the show," Harrison said.

"You don't like to talk, then," Cavett responded nervously.

"If there's something to say, but there's really nothing to say."

When Harrison denounced American television as "rubbish," it became clear he was having Cavett on, but the host's nervousness returned when Harrison discussed the logistical nightmare of getting money to the Indian refugee camps. He said he'd chosen UNICEF as the receiving charity. "We were going to give [the proceeds] to the American Red Cross, who in turn could give it to the Indian Red Cross, but then we heard so many different stories about the Red Cross . . . and how these hurricanes hit someplace in America and they just take care of the whites, and all the Blacks are there and they're not taking care of them."

Plainly envisioning lawsuits, protests, and angry sponsors, a rattled Cavett croaked, "I hadn't heard that." He cut to commercial. When the show returned, he insisted that Harrison clarify his remark. It was just a rumor, yes? Surely he hadn't meant to single out the Red Cross for racial discrimination. Harrison sat silently. "Right, George?"

"Uh, yeah, right," Harrison muttered.

His passion for Bangladesh had now been stirred. Suddenly there was something to say, and he couldn't be stopped. He launched into a tirade against the record company's greed. "I'll release the damn album myself," he told an increasingly alarmed Cavett. Harrison called Bhaskar Menon a "bastard." He shook his fist at the camera and said, "Sue me, Bhaskar." Cavett jabbed a finger at Harrison, "Yeah, sue *him*, Bhaskar."

Days later, Menon relented but not until demanding a public apology from Harrison who, he said, was not in possession of all the facts. Part of the problem, Menon explained, was Allen Klein. Klein was using negotiations over the album to extort money from Capitol concerning old Beatles royalties.

If this weren't enough, contractually Harrison needed the other Beatles' permission to donate his share of the concert and album money to UNICEF. For weeks, Lennon and McCartney strung him along before agreeing.

Perhaps it was *those* exchanges, his buddies' refusal to help him with the concert, the memory of living in his bandmates' shadow, rarely receiving credit for his contributions to the Beatles that inclined him to keep the publishing rights to "Bangla Desh." All other proceeds from the concert, the movie, and album sales he gave away, but he retained the rights to the song. The decision, his weakness, and his stubborn *possessiveness* troubled him. Sadly one day, he said to one of Allen Klein's assistants, "I try so hard to be the person I'm not."

Nixon's nuclear threat was a "madman" bluff, and the Pakistani army was no match for Indira Gandhi's troops. Indian soldiers seized Dacca. On December 16, 1971, Gandhi forced Pakistan to unconditionally surrender its control of what would now be known as Bangladesh.

The young country's problems were just beginning, but it was a country now.

"I have been three times to Bangladesh," Ravi Shankar said years later. "I can't tell you the love and respect and the wonderful feeling they have for me. They really love me, and they really love George."

Perhaps to punish Harrison for staging the concert, or to frighten him from engaging in further activism, the Nixon administration detained Harrison at the airport in March 1973 when he flew to New York from Pakistan. He was told that, due to his old marijuana conviction in England, he could remain in the United States for only three months.

He cabled an angry telegram to "President Richard Nixon, White House, DC." He asked Nixon how he could, in good conscience, bomb the citizens of Cambodia while kicking a harmless man like him out of the country. He berated Nixon for his "repressive war-monger ways," and closed with the "Hare Krishna" chant.

By now, the public mind associated Nixon's face with the famous photograph by Nick Ut of the naked Vietnamese girl fleeing a napalm attack. It upset the president that rock music had become the soundtrack to repeated images of Asia's war rubble.

Occurring when it did, just after the twilight of the 1960s, the Concert for Bangladesh raised important questions about the uses of rock and roll. The concert's beauty lay in its marriage of politics and religion to spread generosity—placing spiritual consciousness at the center of social service. Generally, the public did not understand Harrison's Hinduism any more than it grasped the Islam of Muhammad Ali. But each man had displayed his faith in action, as a foundation for principles, as courage or charity.

For a while in the early 1970s, Harrison's gesture appeared to shake rockers from their complacency.

In the pages of *Melody Maker*, Lennon and McCartney engaged in a very public spat over politics and music. Their exchange was published in November 1971, the same month Harrison raised awareness of Bangladesh on *The Dick Cavett Show*.

In the pages of *Melody Maker*, McCartney said he didn't like most of Lennon's solo music because there was "too much political stuff." He preferred the softer *Imagine*. Lennon responded, in a long letter that was published in its entirety, "So you think 'Imagine' ain't political? It's [got] . . . sugar on it for conservatives like yourself!!"

A debate opened in the music press about rock and roll's social aspects. The discussion intensified after Lennon and Yoko Ono released their album *Some Time in New York City* in 1972, a collection of diatribes-set-to-backbeats about the women's movement, prison reform, "the Troubles" in Northern Ireland, and other topics torn from daily headlines.

Music or agit-prop?

Lennon and McCartney wouldn't have tangled so fiercely over the issue if Harrison hadn't shaken them up with the Concert for Bangladesh. Suddenly, their little brother was taken seriously as a musician, a humanitarian. Meanwhile, Lennon's musical efforts met stiff critical resistance. The same critics dismissed McCartney as trifling.

Bob Dylan faced a similar challenge. This was obvious in a *New York Times* article, "Won't You Listen to the Lambs, Bob Dylan?," published on November 28, 1971. It praised Harrison's concert, and noted that, at a recent Carnegie Hall performance, Joan Baez sang a song called "Won't You Listen to the Lambs, Bobby?" "They're dying," she sang. She suggested that Dylan had turned his back on social commitments, in life and in music. Her audience agreed. "Some critics have charged him with caring more about the steady growth of his investment portfolio than the problems of the world; of being a 'capitalistic pig,' to use the shrill rhetoric of the radical movement," said the article's author, Anthony Scaduto. "These accusations clearly have stung Dylan."

"What is this shit?" Greil Marcus had written of the singer's latest unengaged songs in 1970's *Self Portrait* album.

Meanwhile, Lennon's political music was causing him trouble. Beginning in the spring of 1971, and intensifying in February 1972 as Richard Nixon's reelection campaign ramped up, the US government initiated a concerted effort to silence Lennon, much as it had done with Muhammad Ali. In a memo to the White House, forwarded by Senator Strom Thurmond, the Senate Internal Security Subcommittee reported:

> Radical New Left leaders Rennie Davis, Jerry Rubin, Leslie Bacon, Stu Albert, Jay Craven, and others have recently gone to the New York City area. This group has been strong advocates of the program to "dump Nixon." They have devised a plan to hold rock concerts in various primary election states for the following purposes: to obtain access to college campuses; to stimulate 18-year-old registration; to press for legislation legalizing marihuana; to finance their activities; and to recruit persons to come to San Diego during the Republican National Convention in August 1972. . . .
>
> Davis and his cohorts intend to use John Lennon as a drawing card to promote the success of the rock festivals and rallies. [A State Department] source feels that this will pour tremendous amounts of money into the coffers of the New Left. . . .
>
> The source felt that if Lennon's visa is terminated it would be a strategy counter-measure.

After the success of the Concert for Bangladesh, staged by one Beatle, damaging Nixon's foreign policy, the prospect of more concerts organized by a second Beatle during the presidential campaign unnerved Nixon's team. The FBI seems to have been not much help. According to one FBI document, the International Society for Krishna Consciousness was backed by Lennon as well as Harrison ("It appears that these individuals are members of the Beatles singing group").

For the next four years—long past Nixon's reelection—Lennon's phone would be tapped and he would be tailed by FBI field agents and subjected to what the *New Yorker* called "wildly inefficient political persecution." "Inefficient" because the FBI spent considerable resources planting agents in concert audiences to document Lennon's subversive statements. They filed these statements in top secret memos, when in fact the words were readily available as printed song lyrics on the back covers of his albums.

Lennon's persecution felt part and parcel of the 1960s, a natural continuation of that decade's tumult. But it also felt *weary*, part of the miasma already apparent in 1970s American culture, as if the government, having failed to bag one famous, youthful dissident, had picked a substitute and wasn't even trying to justify its reasoning this time. Lennon too seemed to just mimic the motions. "Make love, not war," he sang, almost a sigh. "I know—you've heard it before."

As global crises escalated, the sports world seemed a poor reflection of its former self as well. In September 1972, television audiences watched in horror as commandos from the Palestinian Liberation Organization kidnapped and killed Israeli athletes at the Munich Olympic Games. Olympic leaders considered canceling or delaying the Games, prompting Bruce Jenner, US decathlete, to groan, "It's all a bunch of shit. Why do we have to cancel a day?" Nothing, he thought, should stand in the way of his chance at a medal.

It did not escape sportswriters that Jenner's selfishness stood in marked contrast to Ali's example of placing principle before career. Whatever had motivated the boxer, however confused or conflicted he may have been, he had publicly declared a moral stance, and he had not wavered in spite of the consequences. More and more observers remarked how rare this was, not just in sports but also in public life generally.

And, for the longest time, the Concert for Bangladesh remained one of a kind. In the 1980s, Bob Geldof would follow its example and raise money for famine relief, organizing the Live Aid Concert. After that, other large-scale charities would follow, none with the spontaneous innocence of the Harrison-Shankar collaboration.

In the 1970s, rock and roll drifted toward the Vegas-Elvis spectacle. Manufactured images, designed and poll-tested to manipulate emotions so people would purchase a particular product or vote a certain way, proliferated. The images grew more sophisticated. Their calculated use by politicians, artists, and advertisers, was frighteningly successful but tainted everything public. *Everyone* was Vegas Elvis, costumed and prancing. Few public figures escaped this trap.

In 1971 Muhammad Ali, on his comeback trail in the boxing ring, a survivor of persecution, and George Harrison, widely respected for his solo debut and his grand humanitarian gesture, were exempt from the disappointment enveloping most 1960s heroes. Ali and Harrison, rooted in their respective faiths, still seemed to embody their ideals. This was not because they shunned image-making—advertisers had created public personas for them, and they had profited. But what made them seem authentic was the way they had seized control of how they wanted to be perceived. On that score, they would both be sorely tested in the years ahead, but, for a time, Harrison expressed his preferred approach in a quote he attributed to Gandhi: "Create and preserve the image of your choice." That was a not such a simple practice. It violated the ethos of the decade into which he and Muhammad Ali were about to plunge.

PART FOUR

1974

CHAPTER 8

The Funeral of All Sorrows

George Harrison began 1974 by giving Richard Starkey a forty-three-page booklet by Swami Omkarananda entitled "Fourteen Scientific Reasons Why No One Dies." On the first page, he had circled the title and inscribed beneath it "Ringo," along with a drawing of a six-pointed star. Then he had written "to help us not feel too bad—as we continue dropping apart."

The two old friends were dropping apart because of the Beatle breakup and its bruising aftermath, and also because, during the Christmas season, Harrison had declared in front of Starkey, his wife Maureen, Pattie, and Chris O'Dell that he was in love with Maureen.

For months, Boyd had suspected an affair between Harrison and Maureen. To the end of their lives, he and Maureen both denied a physical relationship. Nevertheless, the intensity of their emotional bond was enough to rend the two marriages. Maureen was increasingly miserable. She said she had gone from being a "silly sixteen-year-old hairdresser dating the most popular drummer in Liverpool" to becoming a shell-shocked survivor of Beatlemania. But, for her, the mania at its worst was nothing compared to the effect of the band's breakup on her "Ritchie." She claimed he had always suffered from an "inferiority complex," but he had been "such a cheerful, peaceful man . . . [it was] wonderful to talk with him." Then the Beatles' troubles began. She remembered him stomping home from a recording session one day, upset with McCartney's dominance in the studio. He began to drink more and take more drugs. Even so, "he never let any drug get hold of him and when he thought it was, he'd stop immediately," Maureen confided to O'Dell. "I always admired that about him."

He wasn't a front man, and he wasn't a songwriter. He was still young, but he feared his best years were behind him. "He even tried to commit suicide once," Maureen said. "I shouldn't say he did it intentionally because it took place when he was drunk. . . . He tried to cut his throat with his razor in the bathroom. He really frightened me at first, but I knew he wasn't conscious of it."

Then cocaine "made him paranoid." "God's honest truth," Maureen said. "It changed his brain. I hate cocaine."

In 1972–73, when the Starkeys were frequent guests at Friar Park, "cocaine . . . crept into our repertoire," Pattie Boyd later wrote. In the rock world the drug was so accessible that no one could escape it. In Los Angeles, where Harrison and Starr flew for record industry meetings, someone, often a music executive, would press a packet on them wherever they went. "'Yes' people . . . were always hanging around George whenever he was in LA, the record producers, managers, sycophants, and general hangers-on who sat around swapping stories, drinking, smoking, reaching into their pockets to pull out some high-grade cocaine, and generally trying to outcompete one another for George's attention," O'Dell wrote.

Observed Peter Jenner, a veteran rock and roll manager, "I came to the conclusion that cocaine was introduced by the Mafia and the record companies so they could get their money back, by parting rock stars from their royalties. . . . It keeps everyone in wage slavery. It keeps the artist going out and working—the goose that lays the golden egg. If you've got to pay The Man, you do what you're told. It's always been a classic device in the music industry, keeping your people in debt." Sam Cooke knew that game. So did Allen Klein.

"George developed an interesting and extreme relationship with [coke]," Boyd said. "He was either using it every day or not at all for months at a stretch. Then he would be spiritual and clean and would meditate for hour after hour, with no chance of normality. During those periods he was totally withdrawn and I felt alone and isolated. Then, as if the pleasures of the flesh were too hard to resist, he would stop meditating, snort coke, have fun, flirting and partying. Although it was more companionable, there was no normality in that either."

"Normal" he had never known. Once past the bacchanalia of the Beatles' touring years, Harrison freely admitted that he wasn't always strong enough to resist the staggering array of temptations offered him. He knew better than to shave his head and remove himself to a Krishna temple, although that was also a temptation from time to time. As he expressed in "Pisces Fish," a song composed near the end of his life, "I'm . . . living proof of all life's contradictions: / One half's going where the other half's just been." (Lennon once quipped, "George is a frightened Catholic: God one day, coke the next. He gets so high he scares himself back to church.")

Maureen, fearing correctly that she was losing her husband to alcohol addiction, saw that, despite Harrison's extreme behavior, he was, in O'Dell's words, "never . . . much of a druggie . . . [just] an occasional imbiber."

Maureen came to Harrison as someone who was trying to break the cycle of despondency and indulgence gripping all the Beatles and their families following the acrimonious split. The band may have splintered when it came to music, but a cocoon still kept them together—distrusting outsiders, knowing that no one else could understand what they had experienced together. If Starr was unable to pay attention to Maureen, who else did it make sense for her to turn to for sympathy and understanding but another Beatle? If Boyd had gotten tired of Harrison's chanting, there was lonely Maureen, ready to listen to his struggle to balance his body's needs with his spiritual aspirations.

During such talks, "[George] would get so intense and so present—so intently focused—that it was almost unnerving . . . as if he could see inside [your] soul," O'Dell would write. It was another quality that drew Maureen to seek consolation from him. "It was scary to go into that deep internal place with him . . . and talk about the things that meant the most to me, thoughts and emotions that touched the very truth of who I was and what I believed in. . . . Then, all of a sudden, he'd switch into his fun, flirty side and everything would be light and we'd . . . be laughing and having a good time. With George the hard part was not knowing which side you were going to encounter."

By contrast, Maureen was always "authentically wholly herself," said O'Dell. "There wasn't an ounce of bullshit in [her]," which Harrison, surrounded by so many "yes" people, appreciated.

Physical or not, Harrison's bond with Maureen from late 1973 to early 1974 severely strained two Beatle marriages that had already been faltering. "[Maureen] and George go into a room and shut the door," Boyd complained to O'Dell one morning. "The other day I knocked on the door, and they told me to go away. They had locked the door! When they finally opened it, I asked Maureen when she was leaving, and she just looked at me and smiled. Oh!"

So, on New Year's Day 1974, Harrison gave his old buddy Ringo a book promising everlasting life. He scrawled in it, "I was in the greatest show on Earth," surrounding the sentence with musical notes. Beneath that, he wrote "death" and "rebirth." "Is there life after birth?" he wrote in the margin, "see p. 23." On page 23, he underlined, "for the more highly evolved man, death bursts the narrow circle within which material life has imprisoned a consciousness."

On another page Harrison wrote, "Neither are you the slayer nor are you slain (Bgvd Gita) . . . When the sun sets 'in the sky' do you say, it is dead, and all is over?"

During this same period, he had been writing a song titled "Simply Shady," about "what happens to naughty boys in the music business," he said dryly. In the song, he confessed that, by letting a certain lady in his door, he had caused a "minor war." He would most certainly reap what he had sown.

Harrison's closeness with Maureen followed a two-year period of financial and legal turbulence. He was under enormous pressure. After the spectacular successes of *All Things Must Pass* and the Concert for Bangladesh, he experienced what biographer Alan Clayson called "the George Harrison moment," a time of high public interest and expectations during which a new album or a tour might have cemented his status as the most powerful, most respected performer in rock and roll. Instead, his energies continued to be depleted by battles with Allen Klein, Capitol Records, the IRS, and the British government over the concert proceeds and his efforts on behalf of East Asian refugees. "It took up a few years of his life," Olivia Arias, his second wife, said. "It was a big undertaking for a young man."

The legal frustrations were "enough to make you go crazy and commit suicide," he admitted. Meanwhile, journalists only wanted to know what his next project would be or if the Beatles were going to get back together. "Is it a priority to go 'round the world being a rock and roll star?" he'd respond. "There's no time to lose, really, and there's gonna have to be a point where I've got to drag myself away and try and fulfill whatever I can." He said, "I wouldn't really care if no one ever heard of me again."

He finally freed himself of his contractual obligations to Allen Klein but not until Klein adopted "war mode," filing lawsuits and counter-lawsuits. In a power play meant to intimidate Harrison, Klein blocked an easy settlement of the "My Sweet Lord" plagiarism case. He purchased Bright Tunes for ABKCO. In essence, now Klein was the one suing Harrison (after Klein had already collected substantial royalties on the song).

If he thought this move would frighten his former client, he was mistaken. "Allen so completely misjudged the pulse of Harrison as to be talking about the man in the moon," said one of the lawyers involved in the negotiations. Harrison considered Klein's actions a personal betrayal. He fiercely maintained he was innocent of the plagiarism charge and the case dragged on for years. A judge finally found Harrison guilty of "subconscious plagiarism," but in the end, Harrison wound up owning the Bright catalog, settling the matter once and for all.

"When [I] got rid of Allen Klein . . . I was five years behind with my taxes and I needed someone to organise me out of all that mess," Harrison said. "I wanted someone to help me with my present and future, but unfortunately he would have to get involved with my past." Through an acquaintance in the Hare Krishna movement, he got in touch with an American lawyer and accountant, Denis O'Brien. "I was a fan of the Beatles but I didn't want to deal with one," O'Brien said. "The stories I heard of record people, I thought they had crawled out of the gutter. But George is an absolutely extraordinary individual. . . . [He] was very centered and I walked away from that first meeting thinking, 'This is the most powerful person I've ever met in my life.' I've met the chairman of Shell, of RTZ, of IBM, of Ford . . . all these people and I've never met anyone so together as George."

Unfortunately, O'Brien would exhibit his own shortcomings as a manager.

At about this time, Eric Clapton reentered the picture. With the help of Who guitarist Pete Townshend, Traffic keyboardist Steve Winwood, and Ronnie Wood of the Faces (later of the Rolling Stones), Clapton performed a concert on January 13, 1973, in London's Rainbow Theatre. Townshend hoped the concert would restart Clapton's interest in pursuing a career and help him kick his heroin habit.

Harrison and Boyd attended the show. "Eric didn't look well," Boyd said. He had borrowed a red 1957 Gibson guitar he'd given Harrison (it was the instrument Clapton had played when recording "While My Guitar Gently Weeps" with the Beatles). And he wore a white suit reminiscent of the outfit Harrison wore at the Concert for Bangladesh. He seemed to be *performing* George Harrison for Boyd's benefit.

The strange psychology underpinning the trio's relationships intensified over the next few months. Once more, Clapton entreated Boyd to leave her husband for him. In the meantime, Harrison had begun writing and recording songs with Ronnie Wood. Wood had "pinched" his wife Krissie from Clapton, he said. She was a model with a strong physical resemblance to Boyd. "Eric and I have always had this kind of sparring thing about girls we've known, and if you look at it sort of like a jigsaw puzzle you can see how our lives have fit together over the years," Wood said.

The old road ethos again—male bonding through partner-swapping.

Wood knew about Clapton's obsession with Boyd. He himself had flirted with her openly at Friar Park. In turn, Harrison got friendly with Krissie Wood.

"Perhaps he was hoping to provoke me," Boyd recalled, "hoping to make me put my foot down and reclaim him."

In the years since, Wood, Boyd, and Clapton have related conflicting stories, and Harrison never talked at all, so it is difficult to ascertain sequences and facts. At one point, Boyd flew to the Bahamas with Ronnie Wood, after which Wood bragged to the press, "It [the romance with Pattie] is definitely on." This prompted an angry response from Harrison: "Whatever Ronnie Wood has got to say about anything, certainly about us, it has nothing to do with Pattie or me. Got that? It has nothing to do with us."

He and Boyd began living separate lives. Delaney Bramlett remembered Boyd acting "very friendly" with him in LA. From there, she flew to Florida, where Clapton was recording an album. Harrison drove alone through Europe, chanting nearly fourteen hours without a break in the car.

When he planned to rent a villa with friends in the Algarve in southern Portugal, he asked Krissie Wood to come along. "Ronnie was happy for me to go. Everything was quite aboveboard and George was the kindest host you could expect," Krissie said. "At the villa George talked to me a lot about Indian religions. I don't think anybody taught me about spiritualism as much as George, and I'm still grateful to him for what he did. He was gentle, kind, and considerate, just what I needed at that moment."

All of this preceded, overlapped with, and perhaps precipitated whatever occurred between Harrison and Maureen Starkey. Additionally, the Krishna families living on his grounds, the careless parents who'd alienated Boyd and her friends, were straining nerves. "The washing machines were always full of diapers and kids' clothing," O'Dell would recall. "[And there was] the mess upstairs in the wing the Krishnas occupied—clothes strewn all over the place, candles leaving piles of wax, dishes piled up in the sink. The sickly sweet odor of saffron permeated everything, even our clothes and our skin . . . I could smell it in my hair. The little sayings on the blackboard, often taken directly from the *Bhagavad Gita* . . . began to piss us off. [Pattie and I] interpreted them as preachy little quotes intended to chide us for our profligate ways or undisguised attempts to convert us." Yet Harrison felt an obligation toward the families; he'd invited them to live there.

"I think owning that huge house and garden [finally] created confusion in him," Boyd said. "It was a constant reminder of how rich and famous he was . . . but in his heart he knew he was just a boy from Liverpool. . . . He had embraced spirituality with an obsessive intensity, yet he wanted to experience everything he had missed by becoming famous so young. He once told me that he felt something in life was evading him. But he wouldn't—perhaps couldn't—go out and be normal."

"He was angry a lot, and because of who he was it hurt people more," O'Dell recalled. To atone for his outbursts, he would disappear and chant until his jaw hurt. "Pattie and I used to joke that we didn't know if his hand was in the prayer bag or the coke bag."

On a pole at Friar Park, he liked to fly a flag featuring the OM symbol. As a joke, he also kept a pirate flag. Boyd was not laughing when one day she replaced the OM flag, hoisting the skull and bones instead.

One day Harrison told O'Dell, "You may think we're lucky because of all this," waving his hand at the large house and gardens. He left the unspoken *but* lingering in the air.

Playing music had always been a balm, but the music was difficult to get to then with so many responsibilities, troubles, and personal failings weighing on him. The plagiarism suit had made him skittish. "It made me so paranoid about writing," he said. "I thought, 'God, I don't even want to touch the guitar or the piano, in case I'm touching somebody's note.' Somebody might own that note, so you'd better watch out!" He didn't even listen to the radio much, and he felt out of touch. He liked "oldies," he said, though Bob Marley's reggae songs appealed to him as urgent and fresh. He tried to avoid journalists—they only wanted to ask about the Beatles. Irritably, he said, "I don't even think the Beatles were that good. . . . I wouldn't join a band with Paul McCartney. That's not personal; it's from a musician's point of view. The biggest break in my career was getting in the Beatles. The second-biggest break since then was getting out of them." (In March 1973, he *had* joined John and Ringo in an LA recording studio to cut a track called "I'm the Greatest" for Starr, hoping to boost his solo career. "It's the Muhammad Ali line," Lennon said of the song, which he had written. "I couldn't sing it but it was perfect for Ringo. He could say, 'I'm the greatest,' and people wouldn't get upset. Whereas if I said, 'I'm the greatest,' they'd all take it so seriously.")

Harrison had to travel great distances to find his muse again. On holiday in Portugal, he "work[ed] on a guitar he had brought along with him, sanding down and adjusting the neck till he was satisfied with how it felt when he played it," said Gary Wright, a keyboardist Harrison had befriended during the *All Things Must Pass* sessions. "I was impressed . . . with his versatility and the work he did with his hands." Harrison experimented with Dobros, mandolins, and ukuleles. "New instruments often sparked new songs," Wright recalled. "He might even change the tuning on the instrument in order to create unusual chords, which would inspire new vocal melodies. Many of his songs were written like this." In the evenings, after a day of playing, he cooked cauliflower and potatoes, rice and peas for his friends.

After dark, he'd read Yogananda aloud or quote Sri Yukteswar: "Remember that finding God will mean the funeral of all sorrows."

Finally, in mid-1973, armed with new songs, refreshed from meditating in peaceful surroundings, he decided to become proactive and address his problems head on. He purchased an ancient manor home on seventeen acres northwest of London, in the Hertfordshire countryside, and donated it to the International Society for Krishna Consciousness. He said he hoped it would be a "place where people could get a taste of the splendor of devotional service to the Supreme Lord." It was also a place where the Krishna families who had become such a problem at Friar Park could live. Prabhupada named the house Bhaktivedanta Manor and declared Harrison an "archangel." In time, devotee volunteers turned the manor into a productive working farm, growing potatoes and raising cows producing over forty thousand liters of organic milk a year.

Harrison gathered a small group of musicians in his studio at Friar Park, including Klaus Voorman, Ringo Starr, Gary Wright, Jim Keltner, and Nicky Hopkins, to record his new songs. Initially he asked Phil Spector to coproduce the sessions. "[But] Phil was never there," he said. "I literally used to have to go and break into the hotel to get him. I'd go along the roof at the Inn on the Park in London and climb in his window yelling, 'Come on! We're supposed to be making a record!' ... [Phil] used to have eighteen cherry brandies before he could get himself down to the studio." Harrison gave up on him. In any case, a quieter, less-ornate sound better suited his intimate new material.

"It was obvious to anyone who knew George that he was seriously stressed," John Barham, the orchestra arranger, would recall. "I think it was most likely the daunting task of attempting to match the extraordinary artistic and commercial success of *All Things Must Pass*. Added to that was the stress of litigation in connection with 'My Sweet Lord' and ... George and Pattie were having problems. ... I felt that George's stress was negatively affecting the working atmosphere in the studio." Barham noted, "I felt he was going through some kind of crisis. I think it may have been spiritual, but I cannot be sure. I felt an austere quality was entering his songs."

Nevertheless, Harrison came up with some of his most heartfelt work, backed by a strong voice and intricate slide guitar—his "country and eastern" sound, one critic said. The album's songs were rhythmically complex, often shifting time signatures abruptly, and graced with unusual chromatic intervals. *Living in the Material World* would become his third chart-topping album (shortly after the live recording *The Concert for Bangladesh* won a Grammy for Album of the Year). It included another number one single, "Give Me Love," a *bhajan*, a plaintive, childlike companion prayer to "My Sweet Lord."

The title track moved from chugging rock and roll (the material world) to a slow, meditative break featuring tabla and a drone (the spiritual sky), and a splashy Las Vegas finale indicated the showbiz-darkness clawing at Harrison's spirit. "The Lord Loves the One (That Loves the Lord)" was a tribute to Prabhupada, while "Be Here Now" was a call to meditation based on a book by Ram Dass.

On *All Things Must Pass*, Harrison, saddened, was gently forgiving of his old Beatle mates, particularly Paul McCartney, singing, "As the days stand up on end, / you've got me wondering how I lost your friendship, / but I see it in your eyes." He had been hardened by years of sniping and lawsuits: "Bring your lawyer, I'll bring mine, / Get together, we could have a bad time." Set to a swirling square dance reel, the song, "Sue Me, Sue You Blues," suggested that the Beatles' misery would never end in this crassly materialistic world: "You serve me and I'll serve you / Swing your partners, all get screwed."

As Simon Leng wrote, "While George Harrison was bursting with musical confidence, *Living in the Material World* found him in roughly the same place that John Lennon was when he wrote 'Help!'—shocked by the rush of overwhelming success and desperately wondering where it left him."

Even the album's cover art reflected Harrison's conflicts: on the front was a Kirlian photograph of his hand appearing to dematerialize while gripping a Hindu medallion; on the back, his palm cupped a pair of US quarters and a silver dollar. The inner sleeve of the LP featured a color portrait of Krishna and a photo of Harrison and friends arrayed in a possible parody of the Last Supper, with Harrison in priestly robes standing behind a table of food and wine; in the background a nurse is pushing a pram (the child he and Boyd had failed to conceive?) near an empty wheelchair (his dead mother?). Unapologetically, Harrison continued to be the world's most serious and eccentric rock and roll star.

The public response to the album was fully positive. The critical reaction was mixed. "Harrison has always struck me before as simply a writer of very classy pop songs; now he stands as something more than an entertainer," wrote Michael Watts in *Melody Maker*. "Now he's being honest." In *Rolling Stone*, Stephen Holding called the album "profoundly seductive," "an article of faith, miraculous in its radiance," and "the most concise, universally conceived work by a former Beatle."

Tony Tyler, in *NME*, differed. "[*Living in the Material World* is] breathtakingly unoriginal . . . turgid, repetitive and so damn holy I could scream," he wrote. "I have no doubt it'll sell like hot tracts and that George'll donate all the profits to starving Bengalis and make me feel like the cynical heel I undoubtedly am."

Harrison was indeed arranging to send most of his royalties to East Asian refugees. He had learned from his bitter concert experience. Coinciding with the album's release, he established the Material World Foundation, a charitable organization dedicated to humanitarian causes, artistic endeavors, and "alternative life views and philosophies." As an initial endowment, he donated his copyrights for nine of the eleven songs on *Living in the Material World*.

In the summer of 1973, he drove to Bhaktivedanta Manor to discuss his spiritual struggles with Prabhupada. He wore *tulsi* beads and carried a japa bag. He had tied his hair in a ponytail.

Fresh from establishing the Material World Foundation, he had earthly matters on his mind. In the presence of Shyamasundar and others, he warned Prabhupada that the International Society for Krishna Consciousness was rapidly becoming a huge worldwide organization in need of structural and financial management beyond the old man's trust in God. "You've really got to be prepared for the future, you know . . . In another five years—"

Prabhupada was briefly distracted and pressed *prasādam* on Harrison ("for your wife"), potatoes and cauliflower. Harrison continued, "It's like a snowball, the effect, you know. It's getting bigger all the time." Just like the Beatle Empire. "And in the next five years I'm sure it's going to double. . . . At that point there's going to be . . . it's going to need such fantastic management. It's going to be like high-level business management."

"Yes," Prabhupada said. "So that it may not deteriorate." He wasn't worried: Krishna would provide.

Prabhupada saw that Harrison was troubled. He asked, "Sometimes you are chanting Hare Krishna?"

Yes, Harrison was. "[But] I seem to keep going in cycles."

"Eh?"

"I . . . have periods when I just can't stop chanting, and then other periods where, you know, I turn into a demon again and then forget to. . ."

Prabhupada laughed. "You are not demon. You are demigod. Someway or other you have got attached to Krishna. That will help you . . . You are reading?"

"I'm reading the *Gita*."

"Yes. . . All answers are there."

Prabhupada read a passage, and Shyamasundar translated, "'Whatever action is performed by a great man, common men follow in his footsteps. And whatever standards he sets by exemplary acts, all the world pursues.'"

"So this is your duty now," Prabhupada informed Harrison. "By the grace of Krishna you are one of the great men. Although you are young man, but Krishna has placed you in such a high position that there are many young men who follows you. So that is the instruction."

"[But] when you commit yourself to something, in a way it's like putting your head on the chopping block," Harrison said. "Because people, you know, somebody can turn around and chop it off. . ."

"No, it is not chopping off."

"I find . . . the more commitment that you make, or that I make, even though it's such a little commitment, I mean, relatively speaking, it's such a little one, now I'm getting in the area where I find that people are . . . well, sometimes it provokes a bad reaction."

"[People are] envious, maybe," Shyamasundar said.

"I'm not sure how it . . . if it all balances out in the end . . ."

"If you reach one person . . ."

"But say you don't reach any people. . ."

"Yes, sometimes it happens," Prabhupada said.

The conversation continued for a while.

"People become sometimes angry. Otherwise we have nothing to make enemy. We are simply teaching, 'Love God.'"

Harrison pressed him further. "The build-up of the *mantra* is so subtle . . . there's that point where I just can't relate any more to anybody . . . to my friends, even to my wife. I mean to anybody. You know, it's. . ."

"But your wife is very favorable," said Prabhupada. "She is nice girl."

"Yes, she's an angel . . . But you see what happens is . . . the days, the periods when I'm so deeply into . . . chanting all the time, then when I finish . . . I come down . . . and I'm not smiling, and I'm not particularly happy. . . . There is more urgency involved. The realization that everybody is wasting their time and everybody is doing mundane things which are . . . you know, just having a little bit of mundane fun."

"But when you were chanting you wrote the song," Shyamasundar offered. "And it's proven by people's purchasing all those songs that they want to hear that."

"But the problem is this: where to find a balance? . . . I'm out on a limb and it's hard to pull all those people with you . . . there's a point where suddenly I'm not going to be . . ." He paused, as if it was too painful to contemplate his marriage. "I'm not going to know them anymore."

As he rose to leave for the drive back to Friar Park, which was under the banner of the skull and bones, Prabhupada asked him, "You are going alone, or is somebody going with you?"

"I go alone," Harrison said. "Well . . ." He laughed. He bowed to the old man, hands folded. "A little bit of you will be with me."

1974 began for Muhammad Ali with a defeat of Joe Frazier in their second bout at Madison Square Garden. The victory was not as joyous as it once might have been.

After their first fight in 1971, Frazier had rarely defended his heavyweight title. Sportswriters criticized him for playing it safe. But Ali had inflicted so much damage on his body that he wasn't the same fighter, and he knew it. He retained his heavyweight title with two wins in 1972 but then would lose the title to George Foreman in January 1973.

Meanwhile, after his loss to Frazier in '71, Ali fought thirteen times in twenty-seven months, despite Ferdie Pacheco's strong advice to quit. Quit now. Pacheco heard a slight slurring of Ali's speech after the first Frazier fight, a possible sign of brain damage from too many concussions. Ali brushed off his doctor. "There is no fucking cure to quick money," Pacheco lamented—the price of living in the material world.

Just like George Harrison, Ali had a powerful streak of self-determination bordering on self-denial, what Joyce Carol Oates, in her study of boxing, called the "fantastic subordination of the self in terms of a wished-for destiny." She wrote, "That which is 'public' is but the final stage in a protracted, arduous, grueling, and frequently despairing period of preparation . . . [the] systematic cultivation of pain in the interests of a project, a life-goal. . . . If this is masochism—and I doubt that it is, or that it is simply—it is also intelligence, cunning, strategy . . . the constant re-establishment of the parameters of one's being." To "invite what most sane creatures avoid—pain, humiliation, loss, chaos—is to experience the present moment as already, in a sense, past. *Here* and *now* are but part of the design of *there* and *then*."

To create oneself through periodic discipline, sacrificing pleasure, is to envision one's legacy—in a sense, to see oneself as dead. Clearly, death haunted

Harrison and Ali. It is not surprising that Harrison admired Frank Crisp for planting trees he would never see grow to maturity.

To create oneself is also to be here now, vividly alive in the instant.

Ali was driven to regain the championship he had worked for all his life, the honor that was stripped from him illegally, unethically. Redemption would be his legacy.

The process kept him constantly traveling, perpetually training, away from Belinda and his children, Maryum, the twins, and now a young son, Muhammad Jr. "They don't know me too well," he admitted. As much as he loved children, he still believed day-to-day child-rearing was women's work. He never learned to change a diaper. Belinda's parents, in Chicago, cared for the kids most of the time: the brief visits from their father were like vacations from ordinary life.

His forty-first pro boxing victory came on Valentine's Day 1973 against a tough journeyman named Joe Bugner. The fight was most notable for Ali's costuming: he wore into the ring a long, glittering robe given to him by Elvis Presley. On the back, rhinestones spelled out "People's Choice." "[Elvis] is one of the reasons I wanted to entertain people and be loved by the people and make the girls admire me so much," Ali said.

Years later, long after Presley's untimely death and about four years after his own last bout, Ali would remark, "People don't realize what they had till it's gone. Like President Kennedy—there was no one like him, The Beatles, and my man Elvis Presley. I was the Elvis of boxing."

By the time of the Bugner fight, Ali's road to redemption had become longer and harder. A month before, a diminished Joe Frazier had lost the heavyweight title to Foreman.

After winning a gold medal and proudly waving an American flag at the 1968 Olympics, Foreman had become, for a time, sparring partner of Sonny Liston, who continued fighting—and kept winning—after his 1965 loss to Ali. (Liston would win fourteen consecutive bouts between the summer of 1966 and the fall of 1969 during Ali's hiatus from boxing.) Foreman had grown up in Houston's rough Fifth Ward. He had been a petty thief, a young man whose finest achievement, prior to the Olympics, was eluding police by smearing himself in raw sewage, confusing police dogs, and hiding in the hot crawl spaces of abandoned houses. A television commercial for Lyndon Johnson's Job

Corps featuring Jim Brown turned his life around. He joined the Job Corps, and through contacts there he met a boxing coach who trained him and got him a spot on the Olympic team.

When he met Sonny Liston, about a year before Liston's death, the former champ had been reduced to "fighting in a Mexico bull ring" in front of "stoned college kids from El Paso," according to *Sports Illustrated*'s Richard Hoffer. (His first four bouts after his second loss to Ali were held in Sweden.) Liston had little to say, and Foreman didn't talk much either. "George, my grandmother always say, a man need two things," Liston told the young fighter one day—his one moment of mentorship. "A man need a haircut and shined shoes."

On that advice, Foreman turned pro and advanced quickly through the heavyweight ranks without a smidgen of boxing style, versatility, or strategic cunning. He simply had more power than anyone else. The press referred to him as Sonny Liston without the personality.

In the heavyweight championship bout on January 22, 1973, in Kingston, Jamaica, he demolished Frazier, knocking him down six times in four and half minutes. As a fight, it was disappointing; as an event, it was groundbreaking. Jamaica became the first of many former colonies to host a major boxing match. The fight's promoters chose the site over Madison Square Garden because the Jamaican government charged no taxes: good for tourism, national leaders reasoned. Certainly, most Jamaicans, earning an average monthly salary of roughly twenty-five dollars, couldn't afford to attend the spectacle. ("Come to fight. You will be safe," said the radio promos, implying that every other part of the country was highly insecure.)

As a component of Muhammad Ali's comeback, the result of the Frazier-Foreman bout was a formidable impediment. Now Ali would have to defeat Frazier in a rematch and then Foreman to regain the title.

Then disaster struck Ali—partially self-inflicted. He signed to fight a former marine named Ken Norton in the San Diego Sports Arena little over a month after beating Joe Bugner. It was too soon to return to the ring, and he didn't take his training seriously. He twisted an ankle, clowning around on a golf course. In the LeBaron Hotel, the night before the fight, he went to bed with two hookers. His weakness for prostitutes may have had something to do with his first sexual encounter as a teenager before the Golden Gloves tournament—an attempt to reclaim youthful vigor—and it certainly showed a love of danger consistent with the risks he took in the ring. It wasn't what he *should* have been courting.

"You got to get the hard-on and then you got to keep it. You want to be careful not to lose the hard-on, and cautious not to come," Bundini Brown advised him. He didn't mean women—he was referring to training.

But Ali could not get aroused for the bout with Ken Norton.

Afterward, Belinda, incensed about the hookers, disgusted with Ali's listless performance in the fight, said she "put three cops in the hospital," kicking her way past them to pummel her husband.

"We should have put *her* in the ring," Bundini said.

In the second round of the fight, Norton, lean and chiseled, convinced he would have "beaten Godzilla" that night, broke Ali's jaw. He had come prepared to brawl: he countered Ali's jabs with sharp jabs of his own, over Ali's lowered right hand. When Ali backed away from blows, Norton pursued him, still jabbing, then he went for the body, forcing Ali to cover his kidneys—when he did, Norton went for the head.

"[Ali] could move the [jaw]bone with his tongue and I felt the separation with my fingertips at the end of the second round," Pacheco said. "That's when winning took priority over proper medical care. It's sick. All of us—and I have to include myself in this—were consumed by the idea of winning that fight. . . . Norton was a guy Ali was supposed to beat hands down, and at that point in Ali's career he couldn't afford a loss. . . . Also, with Ali there was always politics involved . . . Everything had to do with Muslims and Vietnam and civil rights, and if Ali lost it was more than a fight. So you didn't just have a white guy say, 'Stop the fight' . . . When we told Ali his jaw was probably broken, he said, 'I don't want it stopped.' He's an incredibly gritty son of a bitch."

"Each round I was taking out the mouthpiece, and there was more and more blood on it," said Wali Muhammad, working the corner that night. "My bucket with the water and the ice in it became red . . . I had to shake the mouthpiece to get all the blood out of it into the water."

"The pain must have been awful," Pacheco said. "He couldn't fight his fight because he had to protect his jaw. And still, he fought the whole twelve rounds. God Almighty, was that guy tough. Sometimes people didn't realize it because of his soft, generous ways; but underneath all that beauty, there was an ugly Teamsters Union trucker at work."

Norton won a split decision. Ali left the ring in silence. "Muhammad Ali cannot talk!" Howard Cosell screamed to a national television audience. The voluble one had been muted. His jaw would soon be wired shut.

Now he would have to beat Norton in a rematch, Frazier in a rematch, *and* Foreman. "Losing to Norton was the end of the road, at least as far as I could see," Cosell said. "So many of Ali's fights had incredible symbolism, and here it was again. Ken Norton, a former Marine, in the ring against the draft-dodger in San Diego, a conservative naval town. Richard Nixon had just been re-elected with a huge mandate. Construction workers were marching through the streets supporting the war in Vietnam, which showed no sign of winding down. After that loss, it seemed as though Ali would never get his title back again."

The press was quick to write him off. "Ali's sun is setting fast," said Red Smith in the *New York Times*. Ali was a relic of the sixties, no longer relevant, Lee Winfrey wrote in the *Chicago Tribune*. It was no longer the Age of Aquarius; it was the Age of Nixon. "[Ali is] no different from Chubby Checker. People don't want to dance to his music anymore."

In boxing, it was about to become the Age of Don King. A Cleveland numbers runner, King had listened to the Ali-Frazier fight on a prison radio while serving time for homicide. He had killed a small-time gambler who had failed to pay a debt. Before going inside, King bought off several witnesses and one detective, getting his sentence reduced first to second-degree murder and then to manslaughter. He would be out in four years.

"I transcend earthly bounds," he said. "I never cease to amaze myself. I haven't yet found my limits. I am ready to accept the limits of what I do, but every time I feel that way, boom!—God touches me, and I do something even more stupendous."

The *Village Voice*'s Jack Newfield called King a "street Machiavelli, a ghetto Einstein." He "dressed like a pimp, [and] talked like an evangelical storefront preacher," offering rapid-fire pastiches of Shakespeare, Adam Smith, and Nietzsche.

When he got out of jail, he grew an Afro like a squat desert cactus and decided his next "stupendous" venture would be fight promotion. Through the Cleveland nightclubs, he knew a lot of singers, including Lloyd Price. He knew Price was friends with Muhammad Ali.

King lured Ali to Cleveland with a charity event: he promised to raise money in a boxing exhibition for a hospital in an all-Black neighborhood teetering on bankruptcy. (In the end, the hospital received $15,000 from Ali's appearance; King pocketed twice that much. The hospital closed.)

"Motherfucker" was King's favorite word. "A Black word. It's our heritage," he'd say. Ali didn't like hearing it, especially if women were present. But King knew how to cement his brotherhood with the boxer—"I resonate from slavery," he said—everywhere he went, he carried plenty of cash. Cash, like jewelry, cars, fine clothes and shoes, was an emblem of Black success, he said, not like the abstract trickery of white riches: credit cards, contracts, deeds, accounts. Ali thought of cash as something solid, something the white man couldn't take away from you with the flourish of his signature. The more King displayed his cash, the more Ali respected him—the more Ali *desired*. "Ali, he wanted it all," King saw. "You go [to] meet . . . two girls. Okay, you get one, I get one. No! Ali wanted 'em both. He had an insatiable appetite. You couldn't take that away from him."

It was something for King to work on.

He worked on other things too. The night of the Frazier-Foreman fight in Jamaica, King arrived as a guest of Joe Frazier. He left in a limo with George Foreman. "I came with the champion and I left with the champion," he explained matter-of-factly.

If Ali ever hoped to be champion again, he would need to regain his mental and physical discipline. These were eluding him more as he grew older. A tax dodge helped him. Advised to protect his money through investment, he bought a plot of land near Deer Lake, Pennsylvania, an hour northeast of Harrisburg. He began to clear the ground near Sculps Hill Road for a rustic training camp, felling many of the oak and ash trees himself, breaking one ax and ruining five more.

He had learned about the nicely forested area years earlier through one of his opponents, Ernie Terrell. Terrell had trained on a mink farm near Deer Lake owned by a furrier and boxing enthusiast named Bernie Pollack. Ali loved the wooded isolation, the rugged feel—like a setting in one of the westerns he had watched with Belinda. The place would later come to be known as Fighter's Heaven. It became Ali's retreat, his Friar Park.

Along with his team, he built eighteen bare-bones cabins—like slave dwellings—overlooking the Poconos. He filled them with wooden rockers, plywood tables, and coal stoves. Oil lamps provided the light. The dining hall was a large log structure. Lana Shabazz and Ali's aunt Coretta ran the kitchen, preparing Muslim staples, grains and vegetables, and bean pie, a custard pie made with navy beans in a whole wheat crust. The pie, a favorite of Ali's, was renowned in Nation bakeries, praised by the Messenger himself: "Allah (God) says that the little navy bean . . . would give us a life span of one hundred and forty years . . . [unlike] everything that the Christian table has set for us."

Years earlier, the Nation's bakers had begun using the bean as a replacement for the sweet potato, a remnant of the "slave diet."

At Fighter's Heaven, the cooks boldly posted the rules of their "KYTCHEN." Even Ali couldn't break them: "What goes in stews & soups is NOBODY's dam business"; "DON'T CRITICIZE the coffee you may be olde and weak yourself someday"; "this is my kitchen if you don't believe it START SOMETHING."

Down a gravel path from the dining hall Ali constructed a bunkhouse for his sparring partners, next to a small mosque. He hired a crew to deliver boulders and place them on the property. He asked his father to paint the names of famous fighters on the rocks. Joe Louis. Rocky Marciano. Sonny Liston.

The gym was spacious, with many windows and mirrors and pictures of Ali. In the mornings, at four thirty, he would rise from his rope bed (two hundred years old), sip water from a hand pump, ring an 800-pound church bell he had purchased at a local antique store, and go jogging down Drehersville Road. Sometimes he would be accompanied by local children who responded to the bell. In the evenings, he'd invite kids to join him in the gym to see magic tricks and watch old 16 millimeter fight films. Ralph Thornton, who cleaned the gym, later recalled the father of a twelve-year-old boy dying of leukemia. The man brought the child to see the boxer, his son's last wish, though "he'd been reluctant to do it because he didn't like Ali." Ali spent all of an afternoon with the boy, and later, after the boy died, the father returned "almost in tears," Thornton said. "He told me, 'Mister, I never liked Ali. I've hated him ever since I knew about him. I was always hoping someone would beat him, and beat him badly. But I'll never forget what he did for my son. He's a good man, and I'm sorry for the way I felt about him."

Thornton recalled, "At first the neighbors were very unhappy when we moved into Deer Lake. There were a lot of rumors. A lot of people said, 'Don't go up there and have anything to do with the Muslims. They'll kill you." One day Belinda went shopping in town, collecting furnishings for the cabins: refrigerators, tables, beds. One of the store owners called the police, complaining about a suspicious Black woman "making all these crazy orders."

When Ali paid to pave a prominent road, improving rural conditions, residents warmed to him. He developed a reputation as a big tipper in local cafés. His camp was open to visitors day and night. "People started coming around to meet the champ, and found out how friendly he was," Thornton said. "After a while, they realized we were good neighbors. They knew we weren't going to threaten them in any way, and they became good neighbors too."

Strangers appeared at the gate, begging for money. Ali always gave them cash. One day a man in a wheelchair whose legs had been amputated approached the camp wearing an LA Dodgers cap. He claimed to be baseball great Roy Campanella, fallen on hard times. Everyone, including Ali, knew he was lying, but Ali gave him a wad of dollars. *Why?* asked Angelo Dundee. "Ang, *we* got legs," Ali replied.

He was doling out salaries to an increasingly large retinue—many of whom just showed up randomly. Ali would tell them to find something to do around the cabins, and he put them on the payroll. "We loved Ali," said one. "We didn't even know how much we were going to get paid . . . I think all of us just wanted to be with [him] because he was who he was."

Within weeks, he trimmed down to 211 pounds. His jaw had healed. He felt fitter, happier. He even seemed to have reached a truce with Belinda. From an antiques dealer he had bought an old wooden surrey. He parked it among the boulders. At night, he and his wife sat on the buckboard scanning the stars for the Mother Ship while she recited to him words of wisdom from Elijah Muhammad.

Because he was who he was, he got his rematches in quick order. Ken Norton, feeling confident, agreed to meet him again at the Forum in Inglewood, California, on September 10, 1973. "There is no way you can eliminate the ravages of time. . . . They are all talking about Muhammad Ali like it's his life or death on the line," Ferdie Pacheco said before the bout. "Is he through or is he not? Is he still the fastest and most beautiful man in the world, or is he growing old and slow?"

This time Ali stayed focused. But Norton remained a tough opponent for him. "He was kind of awkward, which made him hard to hit," said Wali Muhammad. "[He] was afraid of guys with a big punch. . . . If you made Norton step back, he couldn't fight. But Ali always let him come forward. He made Norton look like a better fighter than he was."

For the first time in many outings, Ali danced. "You the boss with the hot sauce!" Bundini yelled from the corner. The fighters traded withering blows. They were evenly matched. In the fifth round, Ali slowed. Norton moved inside and landed several body punches. "I own you!" he shouted at a sagging Ali. In the sixth, Ali puffed Norton's right eye with a quick shot. They clobbered each other until the twelfth and final round. Whoever most impressed the judges during this last stand would win the fight. Ali rose to the challenge, punching furiously with a stubborn reserve of strength. Norton, a man caught in a windmill, was addled. Ali won by a split decision.

He did not brag about the victory or celebrate it much. Back at the camp, asked by a newsman what he was thinking, he muttered, "Age. People dying."

✧

Joe Frazier "had an unrealistic expectation of what would happen after he beat Ali," boxing manager Dave Wolf said. "He thought all of the Ali-related problems that existed in his mind, particularly in terms of acceptance by the Black community, would go away. And they didn't. Joe still wasn't perceived as the total champion, and he blamed that entirely on Ali."

Thoughts of Ali upset Frazier more than losing the title to George Foreman did. Only by beating Ali a second time, once and for all, could Frazier be satisfied. Less than five months after Ali defeated Ken Norton, Frazier gave him a rematch. The fight was scheduled for January 28, 1974 in Madison Square Garden.

Immediately, Ali announced that Joe Frazier was too ignorant and ugly to be the champ.

Both men had been damaged by years in the ring. Ali had avenged his loss to Norton, but it had taken everything he had. Frazier had looked like a rag doll against George Foreman. As before, when they came together, their styles were complementary. They gave each other just enough trouble. Neither man could find a way to be dominant.

Bundini was confident. "I taste Ali's sweat now, and it's got salt in it," he said. "The last time it was like water. But the salt means he's got his body juices working again."

This sounded strange, but it seemed to be true: Ali danced, avoiding the ropes, evading Frazier's hook, clenching when Frazier got too close (Tony Perez, the referee, allowed him to do so, to the bitter frustration of Frazier's corner). Ali would grab Frazier's neck and pull his head down. The ref let it go. "Joe would come in, punching, bobbing, weaving. He'd score one or two shots, and then just lay there in a clinch like he was resting," Perez said later, defending his calls. "All he had to do was bend at the knees. Get down so low Ali couldn't hold anymore . . . it seemed like he was content to be in a clinch."

Ali also had reasons to protest. In the second round, he had stunned Frazier with a straight right hand. At that instant, Perez thought he had heard the bell, ending the round. He stopped the action, but the round wasn't over. His error gave Frazier valuable recovery time.

As the fight neared its end, Frazier's right eye was swollen, and Ali's nose was bleeding. Frazier was landing heavy punches, but Ali moved stylishly, flicking his hands in Frazier's face, appearing to control the ebb and flow. Jonathan Eig wrote, "He fought with so much flair that it was difficult to take one's eyes off him." That, more than anything else, may be why the judges gave him the unanimous decision.

"I can't say nothing bad about him," Ali said afterward. "I actually thought Joe was finished. He isn't. He had me out on my feet twice."

"I want him again. One more time," Frazier said, angrier than ever.

Meanwhile, George Foreman "seemed to be auditioning for the ogre's role that was left vacant when the late Sonny Liston shriveled to mortal proportions before the iridescent talent of Muhammad Ali," said one sportswriter.

On March 26, Foreman took less than five minutes to dismantle Ken Norton in the ring, knocking him out in the second round, humiliating him even worse than he'd embarrassed Joe Frazier. "I want to hurt him so bad," Foreman had said before the fight, "[he] just won't be there anymore."

Iridescence seemed to stand little chance against such annihilating force.

By late April 1974, Eric Clapton had weaned himself from heroin. With Pete Townshend he was busy recording music for the film version of *Tommy*. One day he admitted "he was building up the courage" to make one last appeal to Pattie Boyd. He asked Townshend to go with him to Friar Park and "spend some time with George" while he maneuvered to get Pattie alone.

Harrison's intense interludes with Maureen Starkey had slacked off. Within the Beatle circle everyone remained friendly, if a little distant. "I would be civil to her," Boyd would recall much later. "But you know, I can forgive but I won't forget . . . I didn't know what she hoped to get out of this whole thing, except maybe she hoped that she would be with George, and he didn't want it, otherwise they would have stuck together."

More troubling to her then was her impatience with being "the little wife sitting at home." The night Pete Townshend arrived with Eric Clapton, he got the clear impression Boyd was more desperate "to escape the house . . . vast, rambling . . . than she was to leave George."

Clapton took her aside, down a long hall. "We were alone for what felt like hours," Boyd said.

"George was happy to talk with me about Indian mysticism and music," Townshend said, though they both knew exactly what was going on. "I fell in love with George that night. His sardonic, slow-speed Liverpudlian humor was charming, and his spiritual commitment was absolute." They sat together in Harrison's recording studio, Harrison explaining that he saw everything as an expression of God. There was no good or bad, really. The important thing was to develop an awareness of the Divine—"taste him on your tongue . . . hear him in the music." The Divine existed even in a line of coke. Whatever awakened your consciousness, like Krishna's flute calling—it couldn't be bad if it focused your attention on the eternal. A sitar. Elvis on the radio, singing "Heartbreak Hotel."

Our problem, Harrison believed, was to mistake our bag of bones and flesh as our final condition, when it's really only temporary. Once we discard our attachment to the temporary, we can still appreciate our daily experiences, still enjoy ourselves, but our activities won't affect us so much. Our troubles, while still upsetting, lose their edge.

As another man, in another part of his house, was trying to seduce his wife, Harrison was speaking of letting go.

"[Eric] was so passionate, desperate, and compelling that I felt swamped, lost, and confused," Boyd said. "But now I had to make a choice."

Years later, she would conclude, "[Eric's] behavior was wrong—[he] was morally wrong to entice me to leave George, because I was married to George and I really shouldn't have done that. But also, I was wrong as well to allow myself to be flattered."

Clapton recalled, "The very words were—I mean, when I announced I was in love with her, [George] said, 'Well fine,' you know, 'You go ahead.'" *There is no good or bad.* "[It] wasn't, I believe now, what he truly felt, but there was a certain . . . you know, he didn't want to appear to be, I guess, upset. The fact was he was very upset."

On July 3, Boyd told Harrison she was leaving him. "It was late at night and I went into the studio and told him we were leading a ludicrous and hateful life," she said. "When he came to bed, I could feel his sadness as he lay beside me. 'Don't go,' he said."

By 1974, "Muhammad Ali [had] gone through more periods and assumed more identities in his life than any person I've known," Jack Newfield wrote. "Manchild, con man, entertainer, poet, draft-dodger, rebel, evangelist, champion . . . along with Robert Kennedy and the Beatles . . . [he] captured the sixties to perfection. Ali, like Robert Kennedy and the Beatles, was full of passion and willing to challenge authority. In a rapidly changing world, he underwent profound personal change and influenced rather than simply reflected his times."

This read like an obituary. The United States was sinking into a valedictory mood. "We're not a global village, we're a global OUTPATIENT CLINIC," Lester Bangs wrote. The Vietnam War was finally stumbling to an inglorious end, the country's first military defeat (in spite of Richard Nixon's attempts to sell it as a shining moment of honor).

Nixon was in no position to talk about honor: the Watergate scandal, relentlessly exposed by that old *Sergeant Pepper* fan, Carl Bernstein, was beginning to unravel his presidency. According to opinion polls, a large majority of US citizens felt the government was "paralyzed, inept, and impotent." Inflation. The energy crisis. Missing POWs. The Symbionese Liberation Army. Wounded Knee. Traumatized vets bringing the war home to city streets. Court rulings radically changing the definitions of marriage, gender, birth, and death. "This kind of malaise atrophies the will of the people," *Time* magazine quoted Princeton historian Eric Goldman saying.

And in this moment of despondency, what of those symbols of the 1960s?

Ali's stock had risen as the war wound down, his opposition to it looking smarter than ever. Jim Brown said, "When Ali came back from exile, he became darling of America. . . . [but] I didn't feel the same way about him anymore, because the warrior I loved was gone. In a way, he became part of the establishment."

Yet Ali could still be a confounding figure to the mainstream—as when the Nation of Islam dispatched him to Libya to speak to President Muammar al-Qaddafi. After that, Ali flew to Uganda for a meeting with Idi Amin. The Nation's leaders had sent Ali to beg for a loan. The Nation was bleeding money and support. Elijah Muhammad, in failing health, had withdrawn from the public gaze while more aggressive, politically engaged Black groups seized the spotlight.

Amin challenged Ali to a fight, offering him $500,000 in cash. Ali didn't think so. Amin put a gun to his head: "Now what do you say, Muhammad Ali?" The dictator laughed and said he was joking. The tawdriness of the incident was a stark reminder that the world's problems, particularly in struggling, newly independent nations, had not been solved. The global revolution had not delivered on its promises. The change heralded by Bob Dylan and other troubadours had fizzled. Four days after Ali beat Joe Frazier in their second fight in the Garden, Dylan performed an underwhelming concert there, a show convincing some critics he was stuck in the past.

Around this time, in a *Rolling Stone* piece on John Lennon's latest work, a
jaded Nick Tosches said that "movement music" was passé. It was "completely
ludicrous" now to believe music had any sociopolitical importance. Lennon's
Walls and Bridges, was "just plain old fuckin' music" and the former Beatle
was part of the "great revolutionary consortium's going-out-of-business sale."
Lennon seemed to concede the point, retreating into nostalgia and in early 1975
releasing a collection of rock and roll oldies.

Harrison had fared better, earning enormous goodwill with the Concert for
Bangladesh—until Allen Klein's monkey business bruised the effort. Harrison's
failure to produce an immediate follow-up to the event, taking advantage of his
high visibility, slowed his career, as did the increasing somberness of his songs.

"Name me one sixties superstar who hasn't become a zombie," Lester Bangs
wrote, with the fury and melancholy of a spurned lover. "George Harrison belongs
in a day-care center for counterculture casualties. . . . His position seems to be
I'm pathetic, but I believe in Krishna, which apparently absolves him of any
position of leadership."

"What is this search for meaning, anyway?" Nick Tosches wrote. "Didn't
that go out in '68?"

The critics—many of whom had been the truest believers and now were
groaning like wounded victims—had gotten their fill of what James Mitchell
called the "spiritual-Aquarian overtones of a now by-gone era."

In the mid-1970s, the revolutionary enthusiasm of "the times they are
a-changin'" had been shoved aside by a nothing-to-lose, nothing-to-gain stance
given voice years later by Kurt Cobain: "Here we are now. Entertain us."

CHAPTER 9

The Show Goes On

On May 17, 1974, as Americans watched a live newsfeed of a house in Compton, California, explode, igniting the palm trees behind it as a swarm of cops and FBI agents closed in, a new line was crossed in the marriage of entertainment and information. This was news as show biz, pundits offering responses in real time, facts and information be damned. Patty Hearst was inside that house, reporters said: a poor young woman brainwashed by a religious race-cult, the Symbionese Liberation Army. (Never mind that Hearst wasn't really inside the house, and never mind that the SLA was not religious and did not advance a coherent racial agenda.)

The 1970s would offer further examples of extreme cultism—Jim Jones and the Reverend Sun Myung Moon, for example—smearing the authentic spiritual searches of the sixties and obscuring the pathologies of accepted extremism such as Christian fundamentalism and television evangelists. They all resembled Vegas Elvis or Gorgeous George.

The fact that, historically, the rise of mystery cults was almost always associated with fractured and dying cultures was a point rarely discussed, as the country rushed to embrace law and order again, to elect a fundamentalist Southern Baptist president and four years later a former movie actor whose greatest role turned out to be that of a conservative reformer.

Islam's long tradition of diversity, its acceptance of other religions, was forgotten as the Western press played up right-wing distortions of its teachings. Hinduism's influence on Western thought, through Jung and Schopenhauer, and in the United States through Emerson, Thoreau, and Whitman, was lost as the press emphasized its embrace by drug-crazed dropouts. Even the use of sex and drugs in religious practices was misunderstood by reporters looking for dramatic stories, trivializing ancient rituals the world over, the Romantic search for a higher sensibility pioneered by de Quincy, Novalis, Coleridge, and Baudelaire.

The sixties links to these traditions of seeking had distinguished the decade from other periods of American activism, such as the proletarian 1930s. But now exhaustion had set in and a backlash had begun. LSD, the sixties drug-catalyst, had dissolved the ego. Cocaine, the 1970s high, strengthened it. The culture, running on harsher fuel, was getting harder. Rougher. It was apparent in movies, songs, politics, and daily life.

✧

In the Vedas, *samsara*, the migration of souls, follows one of two paths. The atman, the eternal self, tucked like a kernel inside thick material layers, is freed at the death of the body to follow the ancestors, traveling to heaven and eventual rebirth in the world, or to follow the gods to the realm of the sun, never returning to the suffering of material life. In February 1974, when George Harrison flew to India for the first time in six years to meet Ravi Shankar, Shankar told him he hoped for another life to finish the plans he'd made in this one. Harrison replied he had no intention of coming back. He'd done enough. A better world awaited him: "The whole point to being here, really, is to figure a way to get out." His "ambition was to have no ambition." While in India, he very much wanted to see again, as a reminder of the bliss to come, *antyesti*, the final life-ritual by the banks of the Ganges. There, during the rituals, the fire god Agni consumed the physical body, releasing the soul.

In Calcutta, he wrapped a bag of 108 japa beads around his neck and nestled his hand in the bag, counting prayers. He wasn't about to die (as far as he knew) so it wasn't yet time to perform *savraprayascitta*—atonement for *everything*—but he sought forgiveness and healing.

His marriage was over. "I really do love Pattie. But . . . love alone isn't enough," he told his traveling companion, Gary Wright.

The Vedas proclaimed that, by walking in the footsteps of saints, one burned away karma. Wearing old sandals, Harrison stepped carefully through the streets, searching for sadhus in the bustling crowds of bikers and strolling families, warmed by the smell of incense lighted by holy men performing *pujas* and by chanting from nearby temples.

He was no longer looking for a living guru. Maharishi and Prabhupada—God had sent him these teachers when he had needed them and would send others when he was ready to learn from them.

Wright went with Harrison to meet Shankar's older brother, Uday, now in frail health. When Uday opened the door of his simple apartment building, "George immediately laid himself prostrate before [him] taking the dust from his feet," Wright later wrote. "I was emotionally overwhelmed by . . . [this] gesture of humbleness and respect. . . . Tears welled up in my eyes, and . . . I felt so grateful, so very special, to have witnessed this moment. This was the first time I had seen this side of George, which was almost childlike. Humility is a sign of greatness, and at this moment I clearly saw what that meant."

Uday offered them chai and sweets. He spent the afternoon telling them stories. Once he had danced across the world's most famous stages. Back in the days of youth and ambition.

One day, at dusk, Shankar, Harrison, and Wright arrived in Vrindavan. "Everyone, everywhere was chanting 'Hare Krishna' and various permutations on that," Harrison would later recall. Krishna was reported to have first appeared in the city five thousand years ago. Egrets, red-faced cranes, and gentle pheasants called from the shores of small lakes. Moorhens nested, cooing, in *parijata* trees. The swaying leaves shaded grazing goats.

The men circumnavigated Govardhan Hill, the hill that Krishna, as a child, lifted from the earth like a giant umbrella to shield his friends from rain.

They stayed at an ashram dating from the seventeenth century. For several days, they meditated, wrote music, discussed the art of devotion. The head of the ashram, a man named Shrivatsa Goswami, said, "There is an interesting dictum—if you read the Vedas a million times, that is equal to one recitation of *japa*. And if you do a million *japas*, that is equal to once making an offering of food with love to the Lord. And a million such offerings are equal to one musical offering. Then what is superior to a musical offering? Only another musical offering. Nothing is higher. That was one of the themes of discussion when George and Ravi came to visit."

In Vrindavan, through Shankar, Harrison met a Russian Indologist named Natalya Sazanova. She didn't recognize him. He asked her to teach him Hindi. "He had an absolute talent," she said. "George grasped the spoken language on the fly. He particularly learnt bhajans fast, and sang them." She heard him practicing sitar one day. "I was so impressed that I asked him, 'George, what do you do for a living?' He was terribly embarrassed. He said, 'Actually, I'm a professional musician.'" Shankar smiled. She remembered a lovely "moonlit night in a deserted spot on the banks of the Yamuna River . . . It was amazing: Ravi, George and an Indian flautist [played a concert together]. I hadn't heard anything like it before."

During this time, Prabhupada visited Vrindavan, staying in a place near the river, along with Gurudas, Yamuna, and several other devotees. "We were having a very strong, very nice kirtan in Srila Prabhupada's house," recalled H. G. Gunarnava Prabhu, a new disciple. "Gurudas came rushing in, [saying], 'George is in Vrindavan! Should I go bring him to you?' Prabhupada nodded. His eyes were like saucers. 'Yes, bring him straight away. I would very much like to see George.'"

Forty minutes later, Harrison and Shankar entered the room, Harrison wearing a tweed sport jacket and white yogi pants. He was chanting, his hand in the bag. "As soon as Srila Prabhupada saw him, he beamed," Prabhu said. "His smile was so wide and showed all his teeth. He welcomed George . . . like a father meeting his son. It was very warm."

Vrindavan "was my most fantastic experience," Harrison later wrote. "It's all so ancient, all these little streets and old temples."

Shankar had arranged for them to meet a locally revered ascetic, Sripad Maharaj. "We went down to where the river Yamuna used to flow, but now it's changed its course so it's a dry bed," Harrison recalled. "We went off with this man and I didn't know who he was . . . and the more we walked, the more I thought, 'God this guy is incredible'—everybody was coming up to him all the time and touching his feet. He looked like an old beggar; real matted long hair and he wore an old sack robe and had bare feet and all these Swamis with shaved heads and saffron robes were coming and bowing to him and touching his feet. . . . I was a stiff Westerner when we started off, but there was a moment when the atmosphere of the place got to me[,] melting all the bullshit away . . . It became a fantastic, blissful experience for me."

The man was the ascetic they had sought. He guided them through the city's temples. "Later, they gave us some rooms and we slept for just a few hours until [Sripad] came and got us at 4 a.m.," Harrison said. "We'd probably only slept for three hours but it was the deepest sleep I had ever had in my life and all through the sleep I could hear choirs singing. I still don't know to this day—I don't think it was temples I could hear—I think it was something else—all through the sleep I was hearing huge heavenly choirs."

Sripad took them to Sevakunj Garden, where Krishna, playing his flute, danced in ecstatic circles with the gopis. In some stories, he split himself into hundreds of avatars so each girl believed she alone was dancing with the god. Harrison was not the only modern musician to see these tales as examples of the itinerant troubadour's life. Shankar too had taken many lovers over many years in his travels round the world. "I felt I could be in love with different women in different places. It was like having a girl in every port—and sometimes it was more than one!" he admitted late in life. "It became very messy emotionally for everyone concerned, including me, as I suffered the reflected pains of all of them. Now I wonder how I could have loved [many] women at the same time in different cities." But he had encouraged them to think of him as a Krishna figure, spreading Eros and joy, without moral judgment, as the god had done in the garden.

Harrison remained in Krishna's park until sunset—at which time, it was said, even the birds and other animals left. Any creature lingering in the garden after dark went mad or died.

Sripad showed him a big brass bed by an altar in a nearby temple, honoring Krishna's resting place after a night of consorting with the Gopis. (Like a traveling rock star, Krishna never rose early in the day).

"That morning when we came back from the temple at about 5 a.m. it was still dark, and we sat in a room," Harrison said. "Sripad started singing a Bhajan to which we all sang the answering part, repeating it over and over. I got blissed out with my eyes shut, and didn't want it to stop. . . In the end . . . the sun was so high; it must have been 9 or 10 o'clock in the morning . . . and [Sripad] said to me, 'Why don't you make that into a song?'"

Months later, in his Friar Park studio, while recording music for his *Dark Horse* album, Harrison fused the bhajan with gospel, calypso, and country-and-western changes to create "It Is 'He' (Jai Sri Krishna)." He dedicated it to Sripad. It was one of the few upbeat songs on the otherwise melancholy album—and the only devotional song—and it featured Harrison's twelve-string acoustic guitar, the gut-stringed *gubgubbi*, and Moog synthesizer.

His trip to India had been filled with subtle signals, tugs on his soul, to place his music once more in service to Krishna and to spread the word as far as he could take it. *What is superior to a musical offering? Why don't you make that into a song?*

He had no urgent desire to travel the world as an entertainer. But Prabhupada had pointedly told him, "How long will you be George Harrison? While you're in this body, you should be as much as possible talking about Krishna consciousness." In Vrindavan, Prabhupada's commandment coincided with Harrison's rekindled wish, first imagined in 1967, to present true classical Indian music to the West—not just sitar, tabla, and sarod, but a full Indian orchestra, with santoors and sarangis, swaramandals and tanpuras, shais, damarus, and dholaks. Now that he'd established the Material World Foundation, he finally had the legal and financial means to stage such a spectacle in Europe, maybe even in the United States.

"[In Vrindavan, when] George . . . was telling me I should bring something like this over to [Western audiences], . . . I said, 'You must also take part in it,'" Shankar recalled. Not as mere entertainment but as a living example of Nada Brahma: sound as God; creative energy motivating the universe.

The cobbles glistened with raw sewage as men carried the corpse of an old woman wrapped in golden cloths on a bamboo handbarrow through streets choked with tuk-tuks and motorbikes, dogs and goats. An old man chanting in Hindi shuffled alongside the procession, throwing puffed rice on the body. Harrison, walking alone, curious, followed the group down to the Ganges, past gilded stone palaces and forts. At the river, the carriers set the body down, and each man took a turn bathing in the water. Rose petals floated on green-brown scum. Occasionally, downstream, the arm or a leg of a partially decomposed body would bob to the surface, limbs of a person whose family could not afford a cremation.

Hundreds of pyres steamed and hissed to clanging bells. Harrison felt the vibrations in his chest. Timber boats docked at the foot of worn stone steps on the banks, and crews began unpacking clumps of logs, carrying them to a wood-splitting area. There, men with axes prepared to feed the fire god, their swift chopping motions stirring ash in the air into pestilential swarms.

Standing beside the river Harrison would have seen family members prop their dead against the steps, trim their nails, bind their thumbs together, and anoint them, placing leaves from Tulasi trees into gaping, toothless mouths, sprinkling them with sacred water poured from smooth clay pots. He would have seen men spread ghee—clarified butter—on the bodies' stiff skin, chanting, "Rama nama satya hai," preparing for the "fire [that] burns out the 'seed' [of karma]." Using bamboo strands, the men would tighten the stacks of corkwood, camphor, sandalwood, and mango piled into pyres. Young sons would choose wrapping cloths—wedding dresses, white shrouds for widows, red for holy men. Harrison would have seen the Doms, the caste of Untouchables designated to do the burning, raise their torches to the bodies' heads and feet, stoke the fires with long wooden poles. He would have seen boys pour milk on finished pyres and other young men crack intact skulls nestled among smoking embers, so souls could fly away.

In the mud and ash by the lapping water, among lyre-shaped breastbones, Dom children scrabbled for rings, gold teeth, nose studs, coins. Cows stood among the flames, keeping warm.

Harrison gripped his wooden beads. He vowed that someday this river would cradle his material remains.

The man with the shaved head said "Pardon me," and he squeezed into a seat in the second row of the Senate Caucus Room beside the air force colonel. On the other side of the shorn man sat a small Japanese woman. The colonel, Elvin C. Bell, had recently completed his job as an advisor to President Richard Nixon during White House negotiations with the Soviet Union's general secretary, Leonid Brezhnev, concerning the Strategic Arms Limitation Agreement. Now the colonel was curious to hear testimony in the Senate Select Committee on Presidential Campaign Activities, otherwise known as the Watergate hearings.

The hearings had been convened, under the direction of Senator Sam Ervin from North Carolina, to investigate the break-in at the Democratic National Committee headquarters at the Watergate office complex on June 17, 1972, in Washington, D.C. Five men had been arrested for burglary and for the illegal wiretapping of DNC phones. One of the men, James W. McCord Jr., was discovered to be a salaried security coordinator for Nixon's reelection committee. Soon two other men, E. Howard Hunt Jr., a former White House aide, and G. Gordon Liddy, a finance counsel for the reelection committee, were also linked to the break-in. It took federal prosecutor Archibald Cox little time to uncover further evidence of widespread espionage sanctioned by the Nixon administration to persecute the president's political enemies. The hearings were arranged, during the course of which Senator Howard Baker, Republican from Tennessee, would famously intone, "What did the President know and when did he know it?," Nixon's tapes would be discovered, and former White House legal counsel John Dean would reveal that Nixon had been fully aware of multiple crimes and cover-ups. Dean pronounced a "cancer on the presidency."

On this warm June day in the Caucus Room, Colonel Bell had difficulty concentrating on Dean's testimony. He sat directly behind Dean's wife,

Maureen—quite aware of her "voluptuous and statuesque" figure, he said. He had to peer around her tightly wrapped blonde bun to view the witness.

Then the odd-looking man with the round, shaved head sat beside him along with his Japanese companion. It took the colonel a moment, but he recognized the pair as John Lennon and Yoko Ono. He remembered reading that Lennon had recently cut his hair to protest the war.

Lennon had his own reasons for attending the Watergate hearings, having learned that his name appeared on one of the president's enemy lists. He'd long been aware of FBI harassment. Some of the agents shadowing his movements even aspired to become entertainment critics, noting at one of his concerts that his latest material was "lacking Lennon's usual standards."

Like Colonel Bell, Lennon was eager to hear about the president's nefarious acts—curious as to how they might affect his immigration case.

"When a break was called during Dean's testimony, [Lennon] engaged me in a conversation that consisted of a running series of questions," the colonel said. "The subjects were . . . American politics, where I was born and lived, what I did for a living, did I play a musical instrument, am I a baritone or a bass when I sing, why did I come to Washington during the hot summer, did I believe in God, why does America insist on having a military, and would I join him and Yoko for lunch?"

After lunch, the colonel stood next to Lennon at the urinals. "Why is your country fighting in Vietnam?" Lennon wanted to know.

A couple of months earlier, in April 1973, Lennon and Ono had held a press conference to declare: "We announce the birth of a conceptual country, NUTOPIA. Citizenship of the country can be obtained by declaring your awareness of NUTOPIA. NUTOPIA has no land, no boundaries, no passports, only people. NUTOPIA has no laws other than cosmic. All people of NUTOPIA are ambassadors of the country. As two ambassadors of NUTOPIA, we ask for diplomatic immunity and recognition in the United Nations of our country and its people."

Three more years would pass before Lennon would be issued a green card and allowed to remain in the States.

George Foreman had assumed that once he had amassed a lot of money and reached the pinnacle of his profession, he would be happy. The American Dream. He had earned $70,000 in Jamaica for smashing Joe Frazier around the ring, and $700,000 in Venezuela for driving Ken Norton into the canvas. But now his life was a series of business contracts he barely understood, contested by various lawyers, managers, and corporate representatives. He felt like a piece of steak gnawed by a pack of dogs.

He bought a dog of his own, a beautiful German shepherd. Then a car hit the dog, killing it instantly. Foreman was inconsolable.

As the heavyweight champion of the world, he figured he could have any woman he wanted, anywhere, anytime, but to remain the champ, he believed he had to abstain from sex during year-round training.

He had gotten married, but now his wife, impatient with his long absences, his abstinence, and his general surliness, wanted a divorce. More lawyers. Endless contracts.

He was getting "meaner by the day," he said later—just like Sonny Liston—feeling a "terrible emptiness," almost a spiritual yearning. That's when Don King arrived at his Oakland training camp, in the Minerals and Gems Exhibition Hall on the Alameda County Fairgrounds. "George, I know these people been screwin' you," he said. "But I tell you this. I'm going to give you a chance to make $5 million. Don't lose this chance."

What's the hustle? Foreman wanted to know. King promised he could deliver Muhammad Ali and the greatest championship bout ever staged. Foreman didn't believe him.

In fact, King had met with Ali at Deer Lake to discuss the grand possibilities of such a match. "This [wouldn't be] just another fight," he had rapped. "Freedom. Justice. That's what you'll be gainin' for your people by gettin' back the title." He guaranteed Ali $5 million.

Ali agreed. Foreman agreed.

Now King had a problem. Where was he going to get $10 million?

Weathered, brain-damaged boxers wandered through the gates of Ali's camp, "the ring indigent, old and broken, like medieval supplicants from a ghostly past," wrote Mark Kram. Ali gave them all cash.

He was now intermittently in serious training for his fight with George Foreman. Don King had managed to cobble money together from a broadcast company called Video Techniques, from a wealthy British investor, and—according to an FBI memo—from a mob boss in Cleveland. The rest of the funding came from Mobutu Sese Seko, Zaire's despotic ruler. Over many years, Mobutu had robbed his own country for personal gain, becoming, in the words of international journalists, "a walking bank vault in a leopard-skin hat." He guaranteed $10 million up front, plus expenses, if the promoters would stage the match in Zaire.

King labeled it a "symbolic Black happening," two descendants of American slaves returning triumphantly to the homeland, finally free of colonial rule.

Angelo Dundee and Ferdie Pacheco were less concerned with symbolism than with George Foreman's "anywhere punch," so named by one of Foreman's sparring partners: "Anywhere [it lands] it breaks something inside you." "George is the first [fighter] I been with in the ring I know can kill you," the man said.

Few observers gave Ali a chance. Foreman had brutally crushed two opponents Ali could barely put away. "Ali's had it. He's at road's end," said Jerry Quarry.

"The time may have come to say goodbye to Muhammad Ali," Howard Cosell announced on ABC, "because, very honestly, I don't think he can beat George Foreman."

Foreman said Ali should retire: "He's been hit a lot."

Ali professed unconcern: "They figure he'll give me hell. But you can't give the devil hell, and I'm hell in the ring. . . . This man represents Christianity, the American flag. He's a bad image for the youth. He represents pork chops . . . God has set him up for me. God knows the world wants me to win. . . . Kings of countries worship me, women so happy to see me they cry when I touch them. *Me!* A little Negro boy from Louisville. I'm the Black Henry Kissinger!"

"Foreman's nothin'. I tell myself, I'm fightin' for my people's freedom . . . It takes faith to move mountains. Now I got the faith to move George Foreman. . . . The whole world gonna be shook up that night. I predict a miracle. We gonna rumble in the jungle."

He had toned down his racial rhetoric and rarely spoke of the war. He told Dave Kindred that, if he had it to do over again, "I wouldn't have said that thing about the Viet Cong. I would have handled the draft different. There wasn't any reason to make so many people mad."

A kinder, gentler Ali. A 1970s Ali. Between sparring rounds at the Deer Lake gym—against a gangly kid named Larry Holmes—Ali recited poems for visitors and newsmen, showered them with wisdom: "They say wise men go off and meditate on top of a mountain, and fast and think. I wrote something the other day: 'The world is a field, / And we are born to cultivate the field. / Once we learn to cultivate the field, / We can produce anything.'"

If someone mentioned Foreman's frightening strength, Ali regaled them: "The man who has no imagination / Stands on earth / He has no wings / He cannot fly."

For weeks he would work hard. Then his energy sagged. In the evenings, after a lackluster sparring match, he would slouch against the boulders—JACK JOHNSON, ARCHIE MOORE, ROCKY MARCIANO—as if searching for his place in this vast cemetery of giants.

Belinda goaded him. He was talking, not training, she said. She had a T-shirt made in the gift shop of a nearby amusement park: on the front, in block letters, "I LOVE HIM BECAUSE HE'S THE GREATEST"; on the back, "GEORGE FOREMAN." Ali raged at her. He called her a bitch. He said she embarrassed him. "I ain't taking it off until you start training seriously," she said.

Aside from his laziness, she was angry about the drifters in the camp, smuggling hookers and drugs into their rooms. She was mad at the champagne Ali sometimes sipped. She was mad at the girls he disappeared with in his cabin for half an hour. He'd fume at his wife and then give her flowers and apologize.

One day she told him she was going to Chicago with the kids to stay with her parents for a few days. Then she was coming back to clean up the camp: she would chase off the "hangerbangers, the niggers smoking reefer up there" . . . and all Ali's "damn girlfriends." "If you want the girlfriends, you go down to the hotel," she said, pointing to Route 61, where the Deer Lake Motel, smelling of insecticide, advertising "Discreet Lodging," offered rooms at hourly rates. It was reminiscent of the place where Sam Cooke had died. "You don't bring 'em up in the camp no more," Belinda said.

One of the girlfriends was a high school senior named Wanda Bolton, whom Ali had met after the second Ken Norton fight. Eventually Ali would take her as one of his Muslim wives. Belinda reluctantly agreed to this arrangement because in June 1974, while Ali was training for George Foreman, Bolton gave birth to his daughter, Khaliah.

Belinda knew *all* the girlfriends, including Areatha Swint, Barbara Mensah, and Patricia Harvell, with whom Ali had another daughter, Miya. "Ali failed as a man. He was a successful fighter, but he failed as a man," Belinda said flatly. For a while, after her ultimatum, he did as he was told. He sent the girlfriends away. He walked among the boulders patting his belly. "Gotta lose this," he'd say. "No women. No drinking. I got fresh air up here, fresh water, vegetables, you can breathe . . . gotta lose this."

At night, after sparring with Holmes, he'd watch summaries of the Watergate hearings on TV. "It's just a case of white people judging white people because white people were crooked to white people," he said. None of it was as important as the incredible number of Black children "killed daily by police throughout the country." Nixon's crimes didn't shock him: "To me the country's always been in lies and thieves, so it ain't no surprise to me this happened. My phone is tapped ... Elijah Muhammad's phone is tapped."

In interviews, he didn't precisely defend Nixon, but on one occasion he said, "We all do wrong so why are you going to get on a person because of they did this or they said that? Nobody perfect. The Judgment Day coming. God comes and judges all of us. On that day if your good outweighs your bad you can make it."

✸

The government of Zaire offered every hotel room in the country to Don King, if King could convince enough Americans and Europeans to travel to Africa to watch the Foreman-Ali fight, now scheduled for September 25. It was a hard sell: a $10,000 package (in today's currency), involving multiple inoculations for diseases and with lodging that was substandard in the eyes of most wealthy tourists. King bragged that he could deliver over seven thousand paying customers; in the end, he persuaded thirty-five.

As part of his stateside promotional blitz, he hired four Black young women and arranged for them to appear at various sports events around the country, wearing bikinis and boxing gloves, hawking brochures about Zaire. The women had been chosen after an open audition at the Century Plaza Hotel in Los Angeles. "They didn't have to tell us they wanted world peace and the end of hunger in America," said Bill Caplan, Foreman's PR manager and one of the judges. "All that mattered was looks!"

In late August, shortly after Richard Nixon resigned the presidency, Ali and Foreman traveled to Salt Lake City for a promotional exhibition also billed as a fund-raiser for Africa's drought-stricken regions. None of the money ever reached its destination. At the Salt Palace, Ali recited for reporters, "If you think the world was shook up when Nixon resigned, / Wait till I whip Foreman's behind!"

Bob Hope told jokes, and Ali and Foreman took turns sparring with listless partners. Between the boxing displays, King's beauties paraded across the ring wearing shiny ribbons touting "Foreman-Ali-Zaire." One of the girls, Veronica Porché, eighteen, just out of high school, grabbed the attention of Gene Kilroy, of Ali's entourage. She was tall, with waves of brown hair cascading over and around her light skin. The "most beautiful woman" Kilroy had ever seen, he said. He pointed her out to Ali. Ali looked her over, up and down, for several minutes. He agreed she was "breathtaking."

He told everyone that, win or lose, his fight with George Foreman would be his last. After that—Allah and Elijah Muhammad willing—he would become a minister for the Nation of Islam.

"He's in show business. It's hard to get out," Andy Warhol said of him a short time later. "I'm surprised fighters don't take drugs, because it's just like being a rock star. You get out there and you're entertaining 30,000 people. I mean, you're a different person."

But Ali's appeal traveled far beyond Warhol's imagination. "I attract people," Ali said matter-of-factly. "Pretty girls from all over the country charter planes to my fights because I say things that attract them: 'I'm beautiful! I'm too pretty to be a fighter!' . . . Then I attract the redneck white folks that don't like Black people: 'I'm the greatest!' . . . 'That nigger's too arrogant; he talks too much . . . Nigger needs a whoppin' . . . Then I attract the Black militants that don't like the whites: 'Yeah! Tell 'em, brother! Tell them honkies, brother!' . . . Then I got all the long-haired hippies, because I don't go to war. I ain't going to no Vietnam . . . Then I attract the Muslims, because of the name Muhammad Ali. Then the Israeli, who don't get along with the Muslims, might come to see me get whupped . . . So you add it all up, I got a helluva crowd."

Africans awaited him too, but in the days before he left for Zaire, he insulted those who would soon be his hosts. To journalists doubting his ability to beat George Foreman, he joked, "Mobutu's people gonna put you in a pot, cook you and eat you." Zaire's foreign minister phoned Deer Lake. "We're not cannibals," he said. "We're doing the fight to create trade and help our country, and Mr. Ali's remarks are damaging our image."

On the eve of travel, Ali seemed melancholy: "I'd never live anywhere but the United States. . . . But America's dying," he said. "You see a tragedy every day."

Sitting quietly in the camp kitchen one night he mused, "People die, and people bet and lose their houses on me when I fight and lose. It's a fact that people die of heart attacks every time I fight. It's not right. Too serious. No fun. Whole countries, sad. The women in Egypt cry. . . . I got to quit. One more fight . . . and I'll get out."

Covering Ali for *Sports Illustrated*, Mark Kram wrote, "He knew what the currency of earthly immortality was: get out in time on your own terms. . . . If the fall was too messy, the national psyche, so hooked on the bread-and-culture circus of film stars and athletes, would . . . recoil."

"It's a miracle I got through fightin' like I did," Ali said. "I'll retire with money, land, good health, and wise investments. No reason to hang around. All I can do is go downhill."

✺

"Might as well sit down," a gaunt, pale, and obviously fatigued George Harrison said, taking the stage at the Royal Albert Hall. He wore a yellow shirt with a red OM symbol on it. It was September 23, 1974. He was about to present Ravi Shankar's Music Festival from India, about which he had written in the program, "I hope this Music Festival may help a little, to nurture the wealth of the West. God only knows."

"I'm very nervous," he told the audience, "and we've all been rushed, and we're behind schedule. But, uh . . . we're really quite lucky to have anything, actually, if we all think about that. Without the blessing of you know who, the Lord"—he glanced up—"then where would we all be? So, it's my job to introduce Ravi Shankar and get out of here before I shake meself to death." He swallowed. "So let's hear it for the one and only blessing to the world in the form of Ravi Shankar."

Shankar appeared onstage. Harrison hugged him warmly and kissed the side of his head. Hands folded, Harrison bowed to the musicians, a full twenty-piece orchestra featuring flautist Hariprasad Chaurasia, Sultan Khan on sarangi, and the South Indian violinist L. Subramaniam. For weeks they had been rehearsing at Friar Park while Shankar improvised and composed the pieces they would perform. Harrison said, "It was amazing because [Ravi] would sit there and say to one person, 'This is where you play,' and the next one, 'And you do this,' and 'You do that,' and they're all going, 'What?' 'Okay, one, two, three . . . ' And you'd think, 'This is going to be a catastrophe'—and it would be the most amazing thing."

The program featured several classical styles, emphasizing instrumental and vocal call and response, moving to more contemporary percussion- and folk-based structures. It was a new sort of spectacle, a new experience, for European audiences; producing it fulfilled one of Harrison's longtime dreams.

The festival and the orchestra's short European tour in the following days were just part of a frenzied set of activities occupying Harrison in the weeks before his own massive US tour with Shankar, Indian musicians, and an assemblage of jazz, gospel, and rock players—another new sort of spectacle, and a bold risk for the first Beatle to tour the States since 1966.

When Pattie Boyd left him in July, he could have suspended all work, retreated into the vast rooms of his house, maybe to retile the walls, or he could have lost himself in his gardens, but instead he threw himself wholly into the several projects he had initiated as the year began.

Friends had told him that Boyd had flown to Buffalo, New York, to War Memorial Stadium, to join Eric Clapton on *his* US tour. "It was not an auspicious start," Clapton admitted. "I was almost blind from a severe bout of conjunctivitis caught from Yvonne Elliman, with whom I was . . . carrying on, and so drunk from nerves that I managed to crash into a huge potted plant on the stage."

Boyd, shocked by the indulgent realities of rockers on the road, flew back to England after the tour's first leg. "The minute she left, I was off having one-night stands and behaving outrageously with any woman who happened to come my way . . . while my drinking was steadily increasing," Clapton said. "It seemed like I was already trying to sabotage my relationship with Pattie, as if now that I had her, I didn't want her anymore."

When the tour was over, he retreated to Jamaica with Boyd for a "kind of honeymoon" and to record a new set of songs. Chris O'Dell joined them for a few days. One night she and Boyd "started talking about George and how much we both missed him," O'Dell said. "Pattie loved Eric but still cared deeply about George." O'Dell suggested they call him. Boyd was reluctant but admitted it would be nice to hear his voice. She dialed the number. Within minutes they were chatting "like old friends," but then Clapton walked into the room and demanded to know who was on the phone. "Why the fuck did you call him?" he said. O'Dell grabbed her purse and left the room.

Later, Harrison sent Boyd a note: "E + P God Bless Us All, love from G."

"George's note was like a forgiveness," she said. "It meant a lot to me. I didn't feel great about leaving him."

After she left, Harrison busied himself arranging the music festival and finishing the production of an album he had helped Shankar record a few months earlier, *Shankar Family and Friends*. It was a collection of raga- and tala-based songs as well as an extended ballet, "Dream, Nightmare, and Dawn." The ballet's theme was "Paradise Lost and Regained," inspired by the turmoil in Bangladesh. Part of it, "Dispute and Violence," would become a centerpiece of Harrison's US shows.

"I Am Missing You," a love song to Krishna, was "fantastic," Harrison thought. "It sounds to me like a hit record. You should write more of these," he urged Shankar.

"George, I've been trying *not* to write them for years!" Shankar replied.

Harrison was also, at this time, producing a record by a British duo, Bill Elliot and Bob Purvis, who called themselves Splinter. The Beatles' old roadie, Mal Evans, had discovered them playing in Newcastle pubs and brought them to Harrison's attention. He admired their harmonies and melodies, felt he could improve their songs with tighter arrangements, and even played with them, guitars and Dobro, to show them fresh musical possibilities. He offered them a recording contract—in May, he had signed with Jerry Moss and Herb Alpert of

A&M Records in Los Angeles to create his own record company—and he worked the duo hard, day and night, to produce a fine album, featuring some of his own best guitar work. "[He] bent over backwards to make us happy," Purvis said. As a result, Elliot believed, "his own album did suffer a bit." (As part of the deal with A&M, Harrison had promised a solo release; as he had always done, he put more effort into other people's music than his own.) "He was very hands-on, and it had to be perfect," Elliot said. "He would keep you there all night just to get one harmony right. . . . He was a good taskmaster and he taught me an awful lot about singing. If it was a difficult harmony he would sit and work it all out at the piano and give everybody their part."

When the boys arrived to record, he was often so shabby in his overalls, having planted trees all day, Purvis's wife once mistook him for the gardener.

He had a brief fling with a twenty-five-year-old model named Kathy Simmonds. It was a case of opposites attracting. He taught her to meditate, but she didn't warm to chanting. He tried to persuade her to quit eating meat, not to wear leather or furs. She tried to convince him to cut his hair and change his overall appearance. He missed Boyd more than ever.

"I went on a bit of a bender," he said. "I wasn't ready to join Alcoholics Anonymous or anything—I don't think I was that far gone—but I could put back a bottle of brandy occasionally, plus all the other naughty things that fly around. I just went on a binge."

Meanwhile, he was also attempting to write and record new songs. The blessings of the home studio were comfort and convenience; the drawback was a lack of outside pressure enforcing discipline or deadlines.

Joni Mitchell came to London to play two shows at the New Victoria Theatre, backed by Tom Scott and the LA Express, a jazz fusion band. Scott had played on *Shankar Family and Friends*; Harrison attended Mitchell's show one night and invited the band to Friar Park the following day. "We all got out there at about one in the afternoon, and George didn't get out of bed until around four, so we just hung out there for three and a half hours . . . until George appeared, all smiles with a Galois in his hand," said Robben Ford, the band's twenty-two-year old guitarist. His jazz-and-blues stylings greatly impressed Harrison. Ford too was impressed: "He was an amazing personality, one . . . of those people with so much energy coming off of him. He was big. You don't think of George Harrison that way, but to be around him, he was George Harrison, man!"

Harrison showed Ford his collection of vintage guitars and traded tour stories with him. "Eventually around midnight [the band] went up to the third or fourth floor where he had his studio," Ford said. "[There was] cocaine in boxes all around the room. We snorted coke and recorded two songs for the *Dark Horse* album—'Hari's On Tour (Express)'"—basically improvised on the spot—"and 'Simply Shady.' We recorded until the sun came up and then everybody went to bed, and I think we left the next day, but I'm really not sure."

Intermittently, Harrison gathered other musicians at his home to work on the album, pushing himself. His throat, always relatively weak, was problematic, and he began to lose his voice. He strained to be clear and to suppress his coughs on long-distance phone calls to the A&M offices in Los Angeles, where a team was preparing to launch his record company. A young woman named Olivia Trinidad Arias would always answer the phone and bring him up to speed on the company's progress. She was straightforward, matter-of-fact, and funny. They established an easy rapport. Harrison sent Chris O'Dell to Los Angeles to oversee arrangements. She was now working again as his personal assistant. "Would you . . . take a picture of Olivia?" he asked her. "I've been talking to her on the phone a lot. You know, we really have a connection. Sometimes we talk for hours. I just want to know if she's as beautiful as she sounds."

In October, Harrison flew to LA himself. No one at the record company had arranged a welcoming party for him. Arias ran out to meet him in the parking lot. "I thought *somebody* should," she said. "He drove onto the lot by himself in this little car, and I thought, 'Jeez, this is a big day in his life,' and I went outside and said, 'Welcome.' He said, 'What's going on?' He was very excited, but it was just me."

"My first impression of George was that he was smaller than life," she recalled. "Very humble, normal and thoughtful. He was very focused. He had such a strong sense of self. He didn't seem to be a frivolous person . . . from the first day I met him, he was working on music."

Arias was twenty-five-years old, with a dark complexion, long black hair, and a radiant smile. Like Harrison's parents, her folks were working-class. Her grandparents had emigrated to the United States from Mexico. Her father, Zeke, was a dry cleaner, her mother a seamstress. The family always grew corn in their front garden. Arias went to high school in Hawthorne, California, home of the Beach Boys (a point of interest to Harrison). A passion for multicultural art was another connection she shared with him. "I love Mexican cinema. I love *Macario* and *Maria Candelaria*. I love the films from the Epoca de Oro," she said. "Jorge Negrete is my hero. I grew up listening to Trio Calaveras and Trio Los Machos . . . George loved Mexican music [too]—He even had Jorge Negrete on his jukebox [at Friar Park]."

"It was our spiritual aspirations that provided [the strongest] bond between us," she said. "I was doing yoga and meditation and I had a great excitement about the spiritual path, as he did also."

Her sister, Linda, had become a follower of Prem Rawat, also known as Maharaj Ji, founder of the Divine Light Mission in California. He taught a form of meditation called the "Knowledge," not strictly related to Hinduism. It stressed the individual's ability to find peace and happiness within. Linda Arias lived in his ashram for a while and introduced Olivia to his teachings.

Harrison was not enamored of Rawat. Critics decried the guru's lavish Western lifestyle and accused him of greed and of falsifying ancient religious traditions. "He drives fast racing cars," Harrison once complained. "So do I, but I am an ex-pop star. He is a spiritual leader!" Nevertheless, he was pleased that Arias was serious about meditation, and he honored her respect for her guru.

"[George and I] had our differences," Arias said, "but [spirituality] was what kept us together."

As a child, she had twice seen the Beatles in concert—at the Hollywood Bowl in 1965 and at Dodger Stadium the following year. She once told a friend she dreamed she would marry George Harrison. In 1972, she went to work as a merchandising assistant and secretary at A&M. Then her boss assigned her to work with Harrison's fledgling label, in an office located in Charlie Chaplin's old movie studio.

Harrison had two years remaining on his contract at EMI, but the idea of being independent and poised to promote the work of other artists appealed to him. "If George liked you, he wanted to help you," said Jim Keltner.

Harrison called the label Dark Horse. The name struck him for several reasons. Keltner got it right away: "My dad worked at a race track all his life. [The] dark horse is the one not expected to win but who wins."

"George always considered himself to be a dark horse—under the radar," Arias said. Additionally, Hindu mythology revered Uchchaihshravas, a seven-headed horse who was always the best in battle, a protector and champion. Harrison had seen a depiction of the creature on a paint can in India and thought it would make a bold logo.

In the Rig Veda, the horse, a sacrificial animal, is often associated with the sun, the source of God's light: "The swift runner has come to the highest dwelling place."

Arias shared Harrison's excitement about the record label. He was clearly smitten with her. She reciprocated: "He had this way of looking at you that made you feel you were without limitations," she said. "It just went straight to your heart. Once you'd been with him, he had this way of making you want to bring out a truer version of yourself, unlocking something. It was profound and electrifying, and [thinking about it] can still bring prickles to the back of my neck."

She also saw that "he wasn't impressed by anything or anybody, even then, except Ravi Shankar. I think he'd maxed this planet out."

A&M had invested over $2 million in Harrison's vision, entering into a five-year agreement with him. From the first, trouble loomed. Moss and Alpert expected huge returns from their seed money. Harrison insisted, "I don't want Dark Horse to be a big label. I want to keep it reasonably small."

His work ethic was both a blessing and a curse. He had exhausted himself, damaged his throat, and shouldered too much at once, falling behind schedule. A&M wanted him to tour, and they wanted a new album right away. He didn't want to travel without Shankar and the Indian orchestra—for him, the whole point of touring was to offer the music he most loved to American audiences. "George wanted to give the impression of a band, with him as host, soloist, singer and guitarist," Tom Scott said.

Meanwhile, Harrison was preparing to release the label's first two albums, *Shankar Family and Friends* and Splinter's debut.

"He had [so much] on his plate," said David Acomba, a filmmaker hired to record the tour. "He had recently split up with Pattie, he met Olivia, The Beatles were trying to sign their separation papers, Allen Klein was trying to sue him. He had this incredible pressure. It was the first tour by a Beatle and he had to rehearse the band, bring over the Indian musicians, he had just started [the] Dark Horse record label and he had to attend to that, plus he was putting out an album to go with the tour. No wonder he didn't have a voice! His energy level was just drained every which way."

A smarter, more experienced manager would have seen the toll such stress was taking on his client and put the brakes on the frenzied activity. Rehearsing songs, trying to finish his album on the A&M soundstage, Harrison was forced to shout hoarsely over the band, worsening his badly strained throat. This did not bode well for performing forty-seven shows in forty-nine days in twenty-six cities, while overseeing and caring for an entourage of seventy-one people. Arias thought he should have canceled or postponed the tour, but too much money had been invested and George felt "tremendous responsibility" to his audiences and the promoters, she said. "His relatively new manager [Denis O'Brien] really didn't know the man. If he had, he would never have booked that type of tour."

The dates were set—a questionable decision, made, said Harrison's friend Eric Idle, from the combination of "George as an amateur saint and Denis as an amateur devil."

On October 4, 1974, the US embassy in Caracas, site of the George Foreman–Ken Norton fight, sent a cable to the US embassy in Kinshasa, warning the ambassadors there to steer clear of the upcoming championship bout between Foreman and Ali. The fighters and their promoters—especially Don King—were nothing but trouble: "[Ours was] a fairly bitter experience," Caracas wrote. "Neither [your] embassy nor USIS should be involuntarily dragged into the fight by [these] prevaricators.... [Our] first recommendation to [our] beleaguered friends in Kinshasa is that they make sure that there is a valid understanding between the Congolese collectors and the American fighters and their so-called managers on the tax issue."

Aside from the likelihood that funny money would create friction between the governments of the United States and Zaire, no one knew what Ali might say that could stir controversy. He was, after all, still the Louisville Lip.

On the Air Zaire flight to Kinshasa, Ali sat with reporters, telling them how "strange" it felt to "the American Negro" to see Black pilots flying a plane. It was a miracle! He was grateful to be invited into the cockpit with them, impressed with their skills and erudition.

The reporters didn't know it, or didn't remember, but nearly all of his oratory on the jet that day came from Malcom X. In one scene in the *Autobiography*, Malcolm had said, "I can't tell you the feeling it gave me. I had never seen a black man flying a jet. That instrument panel: no one could know what all those dials meant! . . . I had never been invited up into the cockpit. And there I was, with two Muslim seatmates."

On his way to Africa ("Lumumba Territory"), seeking to regain what he believed America had stolen from him, Ali repeatedly recalled his lost brother Malcolm.

CHAPTER 10

The Rumble in the Jungle

Ten years had passed since Ali had faced a monster, Sonny Liston, whose onslaught he could not possibly survive. Now here he was again, facing a similar situation. As the boxers arrived in Africa, as the fight date approached, the warnings grew darker. "George does not hit like other fighters. Even a punch on the arms leaves you feeling paralyzed," said Henry Clark, a heavyweight who had sparred with Foreman. "Ali is a friend of mine, and I'm afraid he's going to get hurt. George is the most punishing human being I've ever been in [the ring] with. . . . One round with [him] is like ten with another fighter."

Norman Mailer wrote, "[The] fight was a foregone conclusion that could not be altered. If Ali entered the ring with fear, there would be a scandalously quick end. If Ali came in bravely, well . . . it would be a more interesting fight . . . but it could not go on. Ali did not have the stamina to go fifteen rounds at top speed . . . it would be equal to avoiding a keyed-up lion in a cage for forty-five minutes."

"The flea goes in three, Muhammad Ali," Foreman bragged, mocking Ali's rhyming.

"Defeat was in the air," Mailer wrote. "Ali alone seemed to refuse to breathe [it]."

Breezily, Ali said, "[I've been] borrowin' my strength from the trees," referring to the oaks he'd felled at Deer Lake.

"I done something new for this fight," he said. "I done wrestled with an alligator . . . I done tussled with a whale, I done handcuffed lightning, throwed thunder in jail! That's bad! Only last week I murdered a rock, injured a stone, hospitalized a brick! I'm so mean I make medicine sick!"

More somberly he told reporters, "You are impressed with Foreman because he looks like a big Black man and he hits a bag so hard. He cuts off the ring. I am going to tell you that he cannot fight. I will demonstrate that the night of the fight. . . . You are going to get the shock of your life. . . . I let you in on a secret. Colored folks scare more white folks than they scare colored folks. I am not afraid of Foreman, and that you will discover."

In Zaire, Ali and his entourage were housed in a presidential compound at N'Sele, about forty miles from Kinshasa on the banks of the Congo River. The palace announced its presence with a large pagoda rising out of the forest, a gift from the Chinese government. Flat stucco buildings lined the acreage. Hyacinth clotted the water on which a three-tiered paddleboat, *President Mobutu*, floated next to a hospital ship.

The air was sticky—*stickiness* was the primary quality of the place's material reality. Putrescence of algae in the river, roasting cassavas, rotting meat, human sweat, and sun-dried fish assaulted the senses. The sunlight put palpable pressure on the skin. The displacement of long travel awakened Ali to the fact—experienced, he said, as a deep, dizzying feeling—that all individuals were immigrants on Earth. This feeling lent him strength: as a child of diaspora, he was convinced he would discover his essence in this land. He seemed to float on the smells of almonds, cloves, and cocoa, on the scents of vanilla and banana leaves, among the many layers of this heavily seared and striated continent: the layer of animals, people, plants, of water and mud; the layer of the ancestors, the living dead who thickened the air with the mulch and loam of their breath; the layer of the spirits, injecting their whispers, the jolt of good and bad humors, into people's lungs and hearts and veins. *N'golo:* the vital energy flaming all things, the *kuntu*, the primal substance of a cape or a cane or a hat.

Africa gave Ali a major advantage over Foreman. Don King's banter was absurdly hyperbolic: "Ali is Russian, Ali is Oriental, Ali is Arabic, Ali is Jewish, Ali is everything that one could conceive with the human mind. He appeals to all segments of our world . . . Ali motivates even the dead." Yet King was not entirely wrong in this ancient place with his passing reference to ghosts.

Zaire fed Ali, as if he were preternaturally attached to its past, its diversity, its mighty streams pulling the rest of the earth to its core. The contrast with his opponent couldn't have been greater—George Foreman, the tough street kid who had broken over two hundred windows in his lifetime because he liked to hear screaming and the sound of breaking glass; Foreman, who wanted to fly across the sea, talk to no one, knock Ali silly, collect his prize money, and go home.

Ali had been experimenting with ways to characterize Foreman in his pre-fight patter, his game of psychological fogging: Foreman was cursed by thousands of Africans sticking voodoo pins in Foreman dolls; he was a white, flag-waving Christian. Such talk hearkened back to the ugly, racist remarks Ali had made concerning Joe Frazier—but once Ali landed in Africa, the remarks seemed not only insulting to the place but also false.

Inadvertently, Foreman gave him the hook he wanted. Stepping off the plane in Kinshasa, wearing a floppy cotton hat and denim overalls, Foreman walked across the tarmac behind a large German shepherd on a leash, a wary dog named Daggo. Even young Zairians associated police dogs with the Belgians who had ruled the Congo until the early 1960s.

Foreman moved past the airport crowd as silently, as arrogantly, as the murderer who ran the country now.

Ali referred to Foreman as a Belgian. Without needing to strain the metaphor, he had won the nation's people. "I'm the greatest!" he shouted whenever he ran laps in the countryside, through open watermelon fields, by old dirt roads. George Foreman was an "oppressor of all Black nations!"

The crowds responded happily, "Ali, bomaye! Ali, bomaye!"

Ali, kill him.

"The horror! The horror!" Joseph Conrad's famous words from *Heart of Darkness*, describing Belgian rule of the Congo under King Leopold II, remained apt.

"They told you and me we came from the Congo. Isn't that what they told you? I mean, isn't that what they taught us in school?" Malcolm X had said to a rapt audience in the Audubon Ballroom on December 13, 1964. "They've been teaching me all my life I'm from the Congo. I love the Congo. That's my country. And that's my people that your airplanes are killing over there."

By "your" he meant "American."

Few Americans knew, or know even now, how deeply implicated in the horror of the Congo the United States has been. In 1895, four years before Conrad published *The Heart of Darkness*, crusading journalist Ida B. Wells knew of the terror in Africa and referred to it to illustrate the wretched conditions for people of color in US southern states. Memphis, where two of her colleagues had been lynched, was "a scene of shocking savagery which would have disgraced the Congo," she wrote.

In 1905 Mark Twain wrote a scathing indictment of Leopold's aggressions and, indirectly, those of his US supporters.

The United States was the first country to recognize Leopold's claim to be "King-Sovereign" of the International African Association, an allegedly philanthropic organization promoting free trade for European countries on the African continent and giving Christian missionaries unrestricted access to poor savages in need of conversion. In fact, the IAA was Leopold's cover for creating a military infrastructure to support "policing functions"—that is, to "suppress dissent." Under his rule, countless Congolese were enslaved, in deadly conditions seething with brutality and rampant disease, to serve Belgium's rapacious extraction of ivory and rubber from the forests.

Conrad barely fictionalized events in his novel. His descriptions came from what he saw and from on-the-ground reports, such as the following written by Black American missionary William Henry Sheppard: "We found a road had been made . . . and saw some . . . heavy iron wagon wheels lying by the roadside; also sun-bleached skeletons of native carriers here and there who by sickness, hunger, or fatigue, had laid themselves down to die, without fellow or friend."

US support of Leopold's murderous activities, mostly through the 1880s efforts of Henry Shelton Sanford, who had been US minister to Belgium from 1861 to 1869, had little to do with free trade or the spread of Christianity. Connecticut native Sanford held strong white supremacist views: he dreamed of shipping Black America's "descendants of slaves" to Africa to "regenerate their parent country," thus ridding the US of a troublesome population and providing a ready-made labor force to plunder the Congo's resources. (It bears noting that Sanford founded Sanford, Florida, the city where Trayvon Martin would be shot to death in 2012, sparking the Black Lives Matter movement.)

Forever scarred by the savagery he witnessed in the Congo, Sheppard returned to the United States and became the pastor of Louisville's Grace Presbyterian Church. He and his wife spearheaded civil rights activism in the city, helping to establish local chapters of the National Association of Colored Women, the NAACP, and the Urban League. His example inspired Cassius Clay Sr. as he matured in Louisville. Clay's son would spar in the church's rec center.

Ali, of course, heard Malcom X speak repeatedly, passionately about the Congo. Malcolm organized meetings with Congolese "liberation fighters," offering his full support. In the last weeks of his life, he railed against US aggression in Africa, linking it to domestic racism: "Old Lyndon is all tied up in South Vietnam and the Congo . . . but he's not minding his business in Mississippi, in Alabama."

When Patrice Lumumba stood up to the Belgians, ending their reign in his nation, Malcolm allowed himself a flicker of hope, even as he knew Lumumba's days were numbered. No Western country could tolerate the leader of an independence movement. He was too threatening. "The President [Dwight Eisenhower] . . . regarded Lumumba as . . . a mad dog," said Richard Bissell, CIA operations chief at the time, "and he wanted the problem dealt with." Eisenhower told CIA director Allen Dulles directly, "Lumumba should be eliminated."

Working with US-friendly factions in the Congolese government, and with Belgians still embedded in the army under the command of Joseph Désiré Mobutu (later called Mobutu Sese Seko), the CIA enabled the arrest and murder of Lumumba. His body was chopped up and dissolved in acid.

Since that time—1961—Mobutu, backed by billions of dollars in US military aid, had declared himself "the Guide, the Father of the Nation, the Helmsman, and the Messiah." He renamed the country Zaire, apparently because he liked the sound of it. When he discovered it was not an African word, but rather Old Portuguese, he insisted on it anyway. Said one American diplomat: "The first rule of dictatorship is reinforce your mistakes."

Every night on TV, Mobutu's head appeared in a cloud while Zaire's national anthem played. He continued King Leopold's rape of the land, enriching himself through his people's labor and killing his enemies. His reckless incompetence would destabilize the region, leading eventually to genocide in neighboring Rwanda.

Ryszard Kapuściński, one of Conrad's countrymen who lived in Africa in the 1970s, wrote that the mid-1970s were among the continent's darkest years:

> Civil wars, revolts, coups d'état, massacres, and hunger, such were some of the symptoms of the crisis. . . The epoch of the fifties and sixties, full of promise and hope, had come to an end. . . . Power struggles erupted within the new African states, [producing] tribal and ethnic conflicts, military might, corruption, murder. At the same time, the new states proved to be weak, incapable of performing their most basic functions. And all this was occurring during the Cold War, which the East and the West transplanted onto the terrain of Africa. . . Dependent countries were utterly ignored, their affairs and dramas treated as strictly subordinate to superpower interests.

In September 1974, seeking to grab a superpower's spotlight, Mobutu embraced Muhammad Ali. Ali's willingness to fight in Zaire, bringing massive publicity and prestige to the despot, appeared to clash with his religious principles. Distressingly, he seemed to mirror Louis Armstrong's tour of the Congo in 1960, shortly after the coup that toppled Lumumba.

Armstrong's travel had been sponsored by the US State Department. The trumpeter's presence in Africa as an American goodwill ambassador served as an entertaining diversion from America's atrocities in the region.

Now here was Ali—another American cover story, hiding the rot in Zaire?

"Watching Ali in Zaire was wonderful," said Ferdie Pacheco. "He'd go on walks into areas where I don't think they had electricity, let alone television sets, and everyone knew him. To see the looks on people's faces when they saw him, the love, the power he had over them. It was spine-tingling. And Ali was having a ball, talking about Black doctors, Black lawyers, Black heads of state, Black airline pilots. I'm not sure I ever saw him that excited."

"You could actually see and feel him drawing strength from the exuberant love of [the] people," said Kwame Ture, who had traveled with Ali to see the fight. "It was unbelievable. Wherever [he] went. I mean, even when he ran—no matter what time—it was as if the youth of the entire city ran with him. All around him, trailing behind, a joyous procession of ragged Black youth, eyes shining with pride."

N'golo. Gathering the forces.

Mobutu had erected billboards on roads across the country, obscuring filthy shanties: "A FIGHT BETWEEN TWO BLACKS IN A BLACK NATION ORGANIZED BY BLACKS AND SEEN BY THE WHOLE WORLD: THIS IS THE VICTORY OF MOBUTUISM" and "THE COUNTRY OF ZAIRE WHICH HAS BEEN BLED BECAUSE OF PILLAGE AND SYSTEMATIC EXPLOITATION MUST BECOME A FORTRESS AGAINST IMPERIALISM AND A SPEARHEAD FOR THE LIBERATION OF THE AFRICAN CONTINENT."

Publicity posters proclaimed, "FROM SLAVE SHIP TO CHAMPIONSHIP."

The slogan offended Zairians but affirmed their perceptions that Ali's quest concerned more than sport. He said he was fighting "for the little brothers sleeping on floors who got nothing to eat." He said, "I want to win for the wine-heads, dope addicts, prostitutes, people who got nothing, who don't know their own history. I can help these people by winning."

Foreman, whose entourage was ensconced in a military encampment near Kinshasa, grew more and more disconsolate. Lizards hung from the ceiling above his bathtub. His personal cook couldn't find the necessary ingredients to make him a decent cheeseburger. He loafed, bored, after training, reading *Superman* comics. Sportswriters referred to him, with undisguised racism, as sleepy and slow in the manner of a big cat drowsing on the veldt, catching the scent of prey.

Ali called him "The Mummy": "There ain't no mummy gonna catch me."

The satellite requirements and the demands of closed-circuit television markets meant the fight had to start at 3:00 a.m. in Zaire.

A reporter asked Foreman, "How do you feel about fighting at three o'clock in the morning?"

He replied, "When I was growing up in Houston, I had a lot of fights at three and four in the morning."

Ali meanwhile was remarkably disciplined in Zaire—until Don King, at Mobutu's expense (on the backs of the Zairian people) flew friends and guests over from the States, including the four young women he had hired to promote the bout. Veronica Porché almost declined the trip because she still had classes to take at the University of Southern California (she was pursuing a pre-med degree), but she had never traveled abroad and wanted the experience.

At first, when she arrived in N'Sele, at Ali's training camp, Ali ignored her, flirting instead with another, more outgoing woman. But Porché realized that he was self-consciously aware of her and a little shy. When the women boarded a bus for their hotel in Kinshasa, Ali rode with them, sitting next to Porché, asking serious and respectful questions about her family.

She was soon a regular guest at his camp. He managed to finagle time with her when Belinda was not around. She surprised herself, responding to his child-like charm. He was like a "country boy," she said. "He had these lectures he had written out on cards and they were really beautiful, on friendship, love. [One day] he was saying his lecture on love and . . . I fell in love with him. I felt there was sort of a palpable feeling."

She feared for him in the fight against Foreman. Everyone told her Ali had no prayer.

He told curious reporters she was his "babysitter."

He told her his marriage to Belinda was finished and that he wanted to marry *her*. One afternoon, he summoned a Zairian minister, a Christian, to perform a private ceremony at the N'Sele compound. "I can't say how legal it was," Porché said. "I know it's crazy, but we got married."

Ali promised her they would arrange a formal, public wedding once they returned to the States and he divorced Belinda.

Belinda left Zaire for several weeks, along with many reporters, when, nine days before the scheduled fight, one of Foreman's sparring partners, fearing for his life against the ropes, opened a cut over Foreman's right eye with an awkward thrust of his elbow. Doctors postponed the fight for six weeks to give the wound time to heal. Both fighters were distraught. Ali felt he had reached his physical peak. The delay deflated him. And Foreman had been eager to tear into some tough American meat.

Mobutu confiscated the fighters' passports, fearing that if they left the country they would never return. In effect, he placed them under house arrest. Wherever they went, child-soldiers waving Israeli Uzis trailed them (the soldiers were children—orphans—because most of the country's adults had died in massacres, droughts, or famines).

Mobutu used the extra time to order more buildings painted, to mow the weeds along the highways and plant colorful blossoms. He bulldozed hundreds of shanties.

Toward the end of October, reporters trickled back to Kinshasa, inoculated for yellow fever, smallpox, typhoid, tetanus, hepatitis, and cholera. The reporters carried plenty of cash for the *matabiches*, the bribes, they would be asked to pay at the airport, hotels, and restaurants.

Belinda returned and was not pleased with what she found.

Members of Ali's entourage saw her in the N'Sele compound hiding two black eyes beneath a large pair of sunglasses. She said Ali had hit her. Few of his aides believed her, but there was no doubt she had scratched Ali's face. In the next few days, he softened and became more solicitous of her, but he did not suspend his romance with Porché. In fact, he flaunted it. Conspicuously, Belinda wore a "Foreman" button.

✦

South African trumpeter Hugh Masekela and US record producer Stewart Levine arranged with Don King to present a three-day music festival, Zaire '74, in conjunction with the Rumble in the Jungle. When the fight was postponed, the festival went ahead, September 22–24.

"There had never been anything like it. . . . It was 1974, so there was hardly any consciousness [worldwide] of African music," Levine said. The concerts combined rhythm and blues and soul acts from the United States—James Brown, B. B. King, Bill Withers, and the Spinners—with cherished African performers, such as Masekela and Miriam Makeba.

Ali took Veronica Porché to the concerts. When Lloyd Price sang "Stagger Lee," he kissed her for the first time.

The joyous atmosphere was tinged with fear. Like children afraid of harsh punishment, the African musicians heaped praise upon Mobutu. Masekela and Levine worried correctly that Don King would cheat them out of their profits. "He was such a pig," said Levine.

The problem of engineering quality sound for the shows' unique mix of electric guitars, mikes, and traditional stringed instruments, hand drums, and wooden flutes was daunting. Multicultural musical extravaganzas were rare. On a massive scale, only the Concert for Bangladesh had offered a recent pioneering example. Sound wizard Gary Kellgren, with his precise knowledge of phasing, of balancing eight-track and sixteen-track boards, had made the Bangladesh shows a splendid success. Early in the planning stages for Zaire '74, Masekela sent word: get George Harrison's guy. Harrison is class. He knows how to do this stuff.

The fight's delay gave journalists, pundits, and observers additional time to articulate the impossibility of Ali's task. His chances of winning were as "remote as Zaire," Red Smith wrote in the *New York Times*.

The old boxer Archie Moore, serving as a training consultant for Foreman, said, "[George] not only has TNT in his mitts, but nuclearology as well. Even if [he] misses a punch, the whoosh . . . will lower the temperature in the air very considerably."

Again, it seemed that Ali alone believed otherwise. Leon Gast, an American documentary filmmaker on hand to record the music festival and the bout, said, "Ali was supremely confident. At least, that's how it seemed. It was as though the championship belonged to him, and getting it back in the ring was a formality to be dealt with at the appropriate time."

In the afternoons, Ali strode through Kinshasa "kiss[ing] babies with deliberation, slowly, savoring their skin, as if he could divine which infants would grow up healthy," Norman Mailer observed.

Ali sat quietly with his parents in the evenings, on drab orange sofas inside his compound, his plump, smiling mother failing to hide her concern for her son, his father grousing, "They's more good-looking womens in Louisville than's showing forth here."

One day, in the training gym, Ali shocked his African guests, clowning recklessly. He let his sparring partner pound him in the stomach then he fake-staggered and fell. He did it again. "The man been knocked down twice," he cried from the canvas. He popped up then wobbled and dropped two or three more times. "Well, the Lip has been shut. He's had his mouth shut for the last time. George Foreman is the greatest. Too strong," Ali whined. "Now, a defeated Ali leaves the ring. George Foreman is undisputed champion of the world."

Everyone knew he was kidding, but this was bad luck. One did not tempt the forces. Ali was taunting the dead, fiddling with powerful magic beyond his control.

In fact, he was *performing* magic, and it was magic of a different order than his Zairian admirers grasped. As always before a fight, he imagined every possible scenario, role-played each potential outcome. He envisioned a plausible future—then rejected it. He seized the future *he* wanted. He sent his spirit into everything, inhabiting each aspect of whatever time had in store. He was the canvas. He was the ropes. He was the crowd's energy. In his mind, he was Ali and his own opponent (*What's my name?*).

The real fight—the only fight—was the tussle with himself.

Days before the bout, in the belly of the beast, Muhammad Ali spoke incendiary words, words that would have gotten anyone else killed in Zaire, words whose wistfulness expressed the struggles of an era.

Speaking for Leon Gast's documentary (in a scene cut from the film), Ali said, "I'm fighting for God and my people. I'm not fighting for fame or money. I'm not fighting for me. I'm fighting for the Black people on welfare, the Black people who have no future. . . . I am a politician for Allah."

He paused to recall his brother Malcolm.

Then he said quietly, somberly, "I wish Lumumba was here to see me."

Warily, Gast's crew glanced around the room.

Lumumba, whom the current leader had murdered and chopped into pieces.

Did Ali mean it? Did he really know what he was talking about? It didn't matter. He had said it. The words were in the world now, a spreading force. And this was Ali.

Ali, bomaye.

✿

Viewers watching the fight on closed-circuit TV at 425 locations in the United States and Canada and on delayed home television broadcasts in 120 other countries could not get a proper sense of Kinshasa's Stadium of the 20th of May.

It was not only a vast cinder-block sports and entertainment complex built with slave labor, it was also a government processing center, a detention spot for immigrants, criminals, and enemies of the state, an interrogation facility, and a disposal unit for bodies. Underneath the stadium seats loomed a series of catacombs, dark spaces, some of which now served as the fighters' dressing rooms, in which people had been bludgeoned and shot to death. The design was such that quick exits were impossible should the police decide to stop you. The monolithic walls, the steel bars, mirroring Auschwitz and Kolyma, were reminders that the organized mass killings, the genocides that characterized the twentieth century, began with the African slave trade and its lingering colonial stench. Along with horrible humidity, blood was in the air.

At noon, the day before the fight, Angelo Dundee inspected the ring. It was a disaster. One corner had sunk into mud; Dundee had it bolstered with concrete slabs beneath the post. The padding was a foam rubber called Ensaflor, intended as cushion to protect the fighters from injury, but the high heat had nearly melted the stuff. The ring would be slow, an impediment to Ali's dancing. Dundee spread resin on the surface. Later, Foreman's camp would accuse him of having loosened the ropes to Ali's advantage, but Dundee pointed out, quite reasonably, that the ropes naturally went slack in the heat.

Just before 3:00 a.m., Don King appeared ringside wearing diamonds, gold pendants, and a light brown dashiki. Mobutu would not attend the fight in person, fearing assassination.

Ali's dressing room was like a "comfort station in a Moscow subway," Norman Mailer, who was there, would later write. "Big, with round pillars tiled in white . . . it also looked like an operating room."

"What's going on here?" Ali demanded when he entered. His trainers and his aides were glum. "Why is everybody so scared? What's the matter with you? . . . It's just another day in the dramatic life of Muhammad Ali. Just one more workout in the gym to me."

He shadowboxed around the sweating pillars, wearing only a jockstrap. "I'm afraid of horror films and thunderstorms." (He had watched the horror film *Baron Blood* on television just a few hours earlier.) "Jet planes shake me up. But there is no need to be afraid of anything you can control with your skill. That is why Allah is the only one who terrifies me. Allah is the only one of whom the meeting is independent of your will." Malcolm remained on his mind. He recalled "living with threats" after Malcolm's murder: far worse than facing George Foreman. "Real death threats. No, I have no fear of tonight."

Bundini had brought a special robe for Ali to wear into the ring: white, with the green, red, and black stripes of Zaire's flag running across it, and a map of the country stitched to the chest. Ali refused to wear it. It was too garish. Bundini sulked. Ali slapped him. He didn't need this nonsense right before the fight.

"It must be dark when you get knocked out," he mumbled to no one, considering once more a possible future—indulging it now, so it would not come to pass. "I never been knocked out ... down, but never *out*. That's *strange* ... being stopped. Yeah, that's a bad feeling waiting for night to choke up on you." Then he shook himself like a dreamer waking from a nightmare. He shouted to the room, "Let's get ready for the rumble in the jungle. Hey, Bundini, are we gonna dance?"

Bundini scowled. Everyone else was already grieving.

"Does anybody hear me?" Ali yelled. "Are we going to the dance?"

"We're going to dance and dance," said Gene Kilroy, trying to muster confidence. He sounded sorrowful.

"We're going to dance," Ali said. "Daaaance." He nudged Bundini. "Say, Bundini, we gonna dance?"

Bundini hung his head.

"Drew, why don't you speak to me? Bundini, ain't we going to dance?" Tenderly, then, "You know I can't dance without Bundini."

"You turned down my robe," Bundini murmured.

"Oh, man. I'm the Champ. You got to allow me to do something on my own. You got to give me the right to pick my robe or how will I ever be Champ again? ... Bundini, I am blue. I never seen a time like this when *you* don't cheer me up."

Mailer, watching this exchange, this elaborate seduction, saw Bundini smile reluctantly.

"Bundini, are we going to dance?"

"All night long."

"Yes, we're going to dance! We're going to dance and dance!"

Ali and Herbert Muhammad retreated to a toilet stall—the only private space—to offer praise to Allah. Then they headed for the ring through a maze of brick corridors.

Armed, white-helmeted soldiers lined the paths from the corridors onto the soccer field surrounded by stiff wooden seats, arranged in an oval, and then to the boxing ring, poorly sheltered beneath a corrugated tin roof supported by dubious girders. A tropical downpour might commence any minute, sweeping in off the sluggish Congo. Monsoon season was two weeks overdue. It was four o'clock in the morning, and the air felt woolen. The moon was bright.

The fight promoters had reserved two thousand premier seats next to the ring, selling for $250 apiece. Many were empty. The wire service reporters had grabbed their spots, along with celebrity guests—including Joe Frazier and Jim Brown—invited to offer commentary on various television and radio broadcasts. Frazier could barely contain his glee at the beating he knew Ali was going to get.

Among the sixty thousand seats around the soccer field—obscenely uncomfortable, far from the ring—*feticheurs* (witch doctors) waved chicken claws, beads, and feathers and chanted incantations, mostly in favor of Ali. Even with the moon and the first streaks of dawn, the night was so flatly dark that it was disorienting. People chattered nervously, welcoming voices so they knew they weren't alone, locked in an elastic emptiness.

An immense picture of Mobutu hung above their heads, eerily shadowed in the moonlight.

Ali's retinue followed him silently into the ring, subdued: a line of pallbearers.

Foreman made him wait—the privilege of the champion, raising expectations, creating anxiety through prolonged delay, forcing the challenger, this pretender to his crown, to endure awkward moments of doubt, exposed in the ring. In this case, the tactic misfired. Ali relished having the ring to himself, commanding the love of the crowd, channeling its throbbing excitement into his legs and arms, into his heart. He shuffled, he air-boxed. People roared. "Ali bomaye! Ali bomaye!" The black stripe on his white, gleaming shorts perfectly articulated the grace of his movements.

"Light came off him," Mailer swore. Ali was ready to reclaim what belonged to him. No one believed him (except his people, the faithful, the world's underdogs). No one had ever believed him. Now they would learn.

Back in the catacombs, just outside Foreman's dressing room, Archie Moore was "praying, and in great sincerity, that George wouldn't kill Ali." "I really felt that was a possibility," he said. So did the majority of the people who had gathered in the moonlight in the Stadium of the 20th of May.

Foreman entered the ring wearing the colors of the American flag. "That's some mean-lookin' man," Bundini whispered to Angelo Dundee. A band played the US national anthem, followed by the Zairean anthem. Referee Zack Clayton called the men to the center of the ring. He could barely spit out his instructions. Ali wouldn't shut up. "You have heard of me since you were young," he hissed at Foreman. "You've been following me since you were a little boy. Now you must meet me, your master!"

Foreman appeared genuinely startled. He didn't think he could be affected by Ali's nonsense. But now the moment was here. It was real.

"You been hearing about how bad I am since you were a little kid with mess in your pants! Tonight, I'm gonna whup you till you cry like a baby!"

Ali returned to his corner, bowed his head, and tucked his arms into his ribs in quiet prayer.

✪

A monsoon always announced itself with a stirring on the river, water evaporating and then reforming, cascading in rushing streams among the forested hills under warm trade winds from the sea. Even in years like this, when the rain was late, people felt its slow accumulation, for weeks sometimes—the awesome gathering of its forces. It was an everlasting storm, present even when it wasn't.

When it arrived, it was an all-encompassing waterfall, drowning human cries.

Some Western scientists claimed the Brahmaputra Valley in eastern India registered the planet's highest lightning flash rate during monsoon seasons, but Zairians doubted this. With an average of 158 lightning flashes per square kilometer each year, the Congo River valley was the most electric place on Earth. The hilly terrain, the uranium deposits in the bedrock, the methane pockets in the oil fields—they all combined to snatch the sky's power and bring it here. The tin roof above the small ring in the Stadium of the 20th of May waited to focus it.

✪

Ali's right hand had astonishing force. Foreman couldn't believe it: not just the strength of the punch but also the fact that he threw it. Against a skilled opponent, heavyweights rarely led with their right. The right hand was most fighters' haymaker, so they would save it, use it calculatingly, defending and jabbing with the left, preparing the right for the longer distance it needed to travel to reach an opponent's head with proper impact. Because of this distance, it was a dangerous punch to throw, especially early in a fight when an opponent was fresh and quick to seize advantage of openings. But damn if Ali didn't come out swinging his right. And connecting. Toe to toe. He wasn't dancing. On top of everything else, he was insulting Foreman, demonstrating lack of respect for the man. *I'm not afraid of you.*

Foreman was in a fight. This he didn't expect.

His corner was a brain trust of boxing: Archie Moore, Sugar Ray Robinson, Sandy Saddler. They had prepared him well in many ways, honed his speed, taught him sophisticated ring movement, briefed him on Ali's tics, tricks, and habits. A good young student, prepped by scholars, he couldn't fail.

But here, in the first thirty seconds of the fight, Ali, the old has-been, had flummoxed them all. He threw another right: the *thunk* of a machete cracking a melon.

Foreman's corner men yelled at him to do what he *had* to do, what he had learned so well to do: cut off the ring, herd Ali, trap him against the ropes, where, unable to move, he would be a punching bag. Swiftly, beautifully, with no effort, it seemed, Foreman charged like an enraged animal. He maneuvered Ali to the side of the ring. Or did he? Ali appeared to retreat willingly, into the most dangerous place he could stand. Why would he do that? It was "pugilistic suicide," Jonathan Eig would write.

"Oh Christ, it's a fix!" George Plimpton shouted ringside.

"I won't kid you. When he went to the ropes, I felt sick," said Angelo Dundee. "Everything we planned was built around not getting hit. Muhammad was going to move, stay on his toes, show George all kinds of angles. What can I say?"

Foreman unloaded long, whisking, imprecise punches on Ali's forearms and he went for the ribs. He knew he needed only one clean punch to end the fight. Ali covered expertly, and popped Foreman with another hard right.

Between the first and second rounds, Dundee screamed at Ali, "What you doing? Why don't you dance? You got to dance."

"Don't talk," Ali told him. "I know what I'm doing."

"Do it! Do it now!"

In the second round, he let himself be driven again to the ropes, with no room to move. He was like a man awaiting an execution. He withstood a barrage of blows, blocking many but not all. His kidneys were taking a pounding. Foreman's corner was ecstatic. They had Ali exactly where they wanted him. "A bird's nest was on the ground," Saddler said. Just waiting for the big cat to lap up the eggs.

"I . . . died two or three times [during the fight,]" said Lana Shabazz, Ali's cook. "I flat out died. I couldn't look. I just covered my face with my hands, and every now and then I'd ask, 'Is he still alive?' . . . I don't know what was wrong with that boy, standing by the ropes, taking all those punches."

But all those punches didn't seem to faze him, and Foreman's movements were so ponderously slow that Ali was able to send rights and left jabs past the man's big arms, raising welts on Foreman's face. Whenever Foreman achieved some accuracy, Ali would step around him and tie him up, wrapping his gloves around the back of Foreman's neck, wrestling him, pinning his arms to his sides and jabbing his ribs until the referee pulled them apart. Then Ali would retreat again.

The old man's experience was paying off. "I gave George what he thought he wanted," he said.

Archie Moore was the first to recognize Ali's strategy. "Oh, no, you beautiful thief! I know what you're up to!" he yelled across the ring.

"What Ali did that night was truly inspired," Ferdie Pacheco said. "The layoff had taken away his first set of gifts, so in Zaire he developed another. The man had the greatest chin in the history of the heavyweight division. He had as much courage as anyone who ever fought. He could think creatively and clearly with bombs flying all around him . . . Somehow, early in the fight, Ali figured out that the way to beat George Foreman was to let Foreman hit him. Now that's some game plan . . . tak[ing] punch after punch . . . But Ali took everything Foreman could offer."

The *feticheurs* knew: they had been called on so often to heal the wounds from terrible animal bites or to ease malaria's fevers.

The cure for pain is to experience pain. To experience pain is to learn that it is not a hostile force stalking our bodies from beyond. It is *us*. The pain is our muscles, our bones, our damaged tissues.

Like restless weather systems, hostile forces *do* circle the globe seeking to sweep us away. But if their primary power is pain, we may weaken them by *absorbing* their pain.

Once we have taken pain in, mulched it with our body's juices, it is ours to maneuver. To digest. We discover where and how to store it, embrace it, blunting its strength, maybe even—in the way of all old habits—to cherish it, ruefully. *This is mine. You can't frighten me, or take me down, using what is mine. You are* not *the controlling force.*

The *feticheurs* waved their yellow chicken claws in the fading moonlight, in the hot wooden seats above the ring: "Ali bomaye! Ali bomaye!"

☼

"I really didn't plan what happened that night. But when a fighter gets in the ring, he has to adjust according to the conditions he faces," Ali said.

> Against George, the ring was slow. Dancing all night, my legs would have got tired. And George was following me too close. . . . I used more energy staying away from him than he used chasing me. I was tireder than I should have been with fourteen rounds to go. . . So between rounds, I decided to do what I did in training when I got tired. It was something Archie Moore used to do. Archie . . . fought till he was as old as I am now, and he did it by conserving energy. He let younger men take their shots and blocked everything . . . and then, when they got tired, Archie would attack.

Foreman hurt him. "A couple of times, he shook me bad, especially with the right hand," Ali admitted. "But I blocked and dodged most of what he threw, and each round his punches got slower and hurt less when they landed. Then I started talking to him. 'Hit harder! Show me something, George. That don't hurt. I thought you were supposed to be bad.' And George was trapped. I was on the ropes, but he was trapped, because attacking was all he knew how to do."

In round six, Ali surprised Foreman by marching to the middle of the ring and snapping Foreman's head with three quick lefts before retiring again on the ropes. He leaned so far back—keeping his jaw clear of Foreman's fists—he could have been counting craters on the moon. The blows he *did* receive, to his ribs, to his gut, were partially absorbed by the slack ropes swaying with his torso and his thighs. He was passing the energy along, out of his body. Norman Mailer later wrote that he looked like a man swinging in the rigging of a ship.

Ali's corner screamed, "Careful! Careful! Careful!"

Ali stuck out his tongue.

The ringbolts yowled like cats. The ropes whipped back and forth.

Foreman was now waving his arms listlessly, like the mummy Ali said he was. Ali's joke was actually an insight into Foreman's boxing style—the key to beating it. Foreman moved relentlessly forward, hands extended, pawing at his opponent to knock away his opponent's arms. If you kept your arms up and wearied Foreman's arms, his style would cease to work.

"I got a feeling that George is not gonna make it," Joe Frazier told television viewers glumly.

Ali gyred and gyred on the ropes. Foreman flailed at him. Then Ali bruised him with another right. He looked over at Jim Brown, ringside, and gave him a playful wink: *Don't worry about me.*

"I really don't believe it," Brown said into his mike. "I thought he was hurt. I thought his body was hurt. He came back. He hit Foreman with everything. And he winked at *me*?"

"Is that all you got?" Ali taunted Foreman.

"Muhammad amazed me, I'll admit it," Foreman later said. "He outthought me, he outfought me. . . . I went out and hit [him] with the hardest shot to the body I ever delivered to any opponent. Anybody else in the world would have crumbled. Muhammad cringed. I could see it hurt. And then he looked at me. He had that look in his eyes, like he was saying I'm not gonna let you hurt me. And to be honest, that's the main thing I remember about the fight."

At the beginning of round eight, with Foreman completely out of gas, Ali shouted, "Now it's my turn!"

Foreman wobbled forward, throwing big, circular punches, missing each time. Ali waited against the ropes until the round's final twenty-one seconds. Then he stepped around his opponent, trading places, disorienting him, and hit him in the head with a left-right combo. Sweat flew from Foreman's forehead, glistening, rainbowed in the spotlights—a startled firefly swarm. He staggered. Ali spun into the center of the ring, landing a left, a right, and a second left. Foreman twirled off-balance, tilting toward the floor, holding out his arms, grasping at nothing. Ali circled him as he fell, ready to clock him one last time as the man went down, but he saw it wasn't necessary. "Oh, Lawdy!" Bundini shouted from the corner. "He on Queer Street!"

Muhammad Ali was redeemed.

Surrounded by arrogance—Foreman's arrogance, convinced that no one could resist his power; Mobutu's arrogance, convinced that for $10 million he could buy respect for his murderous regime; the press's arrogance, convinced that the Marvelous Mouth would be silenced in Africa—Ali adopted the stance of humility, curled against the ropes, humbling his opponent and his critics.

"Muhammad Ali has done it!" shouted the British broadcaster David Frost. "This is the most joyous scene ever seen in the history of boxing!"

Groggy on his stool in the corner, Foreman answered, "Yeah," when Saddler asked, "Feel all right?" "Well, don't worry," Saddler assured him, shaking his head. "It's history now."

"Yeah."

"You're all right. The rest will take care of itself."

Foreman asked where his dog was.

Ali was mobbed in the ring. He raised his arms. Though almost no one noticed, for a full ten seconds, propped up by others as they hugged and lifted him, he fainted on his feet.

✿

Afterward, in the dressing room, down in the dour catacombs, Norman Mailer watched Belinda slip through the door. "Husband and wife looked at each other silently as if a question of long standing was at last being resolved," he wrote later. "They kissed. . . . He gave her a smile as open as the sweetness of his feelings. There was something so tender in Ali's regard, so mocking, and so calm, that the look appeared to say, 'Honey, my ways got to be curious to you, and we both know I am crazy, but please believe me when I try to tell you that I am, my darling, by all scientific evidence a serious fellow.'"

The rain began as dawn broke fully, the green moon fled the sky, and Ali's entourage left the arena. Two buses followed a silver Citroën carrying the champ and his wife—"like a military column through a liberated territory," George Plimpton thought. Within minutes the catacombs were flooded, the dressing rooms swept away. Towels and Telex machines floated in gurgling, muddy currents. Ticket stubs, peanuts, and fruit peels glutted the underground mazes, stuffing the generators, which flickered and went out. The satellite systems beaming post-fight analyses to the world's corners shut down.

Plimpton recalled that a heavy rain had fallen after Ali's first victory over Sonny Liston.

Twice, on the way back to N'Sele, Ali's motorcade had to pull off the road and wait for the torrent to slacken so the drivers could see again. "Damn, do those trees look like they're moving to you?" Ferdie Pacheco mused aloud, squinting through the window at the downpour. He soon realized that hundreds of ghostly figures were emerging from the woods, men and women holding up their babies in the gale (protected by fraying palm fronds) so Ali could see them and bless them.

"When we left, Ali belonged to America," Pacheco said. "Now he belongs to the world."

The compound was deserted when they arrived. No press. Ali did not want to celebrate or gloat. He was quiet. The entourage dispersed. At one point, gazing at the river, sniffing the hyacinth in the air, he said, as if to himself, as if he'd been through a cleansing, "You'll never know how long I waited for this. You'll never know what this means to me."

I wish Lumumba was here to see me.

Sportswriter Pete Bonventre took a walk through the compound a little later in the morning. He found Ali "three hours after the greatest victory of his life . . . sitting on the stoop [of his cottage], showing a magic trick to a group of Black children. It was a rope trick, where the rope is cut in half and then it's suddenly back together again. And it was hard to tell who was having a better time, Ali or the children. All I could think was, I don't care what anyone says, there'll never be anyone like him again."

CHAPTER 11

Dark Horse

U S president Gerald Ford sent a telegram to Zairean president Mobutu Sese
Seko on October 31, 1974. "I would like to express my appreciation for the
warm hospitality extended by your great country to two outstanding American
fighters and to the many other Americans who went to Zaire for the heavyweight
championship fight. Through Zaire's support of this major sporting event, our
two peoples have learned more about each other and the basis of our friendship
has been strengthened. Warmest personal wishes."

Muhammad Ali always hated flying, and 1974 was a particularly bad year for the
American aviation industry. The Organization of Petroleum Exporting Countries
had decided to punish the United States for its support of Israel during the Yom
Kippur War and ordered an oil embargo. The move revealed how utterly dependent
the United States was on Arab oil. The resulting rise in fuel prices nearly crippled
the airlines, suffering already from Federal Aviation Administration fare restrictions, overcapacity, poor safety records, and adverse publicity from recent hijacks.

When the rest of the world's citizens imagined US aircraft, they envisioned
B-52s pounding Hanoi, but even those flights had failed, as America was now
beating a messy retreat from Southeast Asia.

Airline travel in 1974 was a grim experience, filled with foreboding, discomfort,
and the expectation of stale peanuts for lunch. Still, in early November, Ali flew
to Chicago to be feted for his victory over George Foreman. Mayor Richard J.
Daley declared November 1 Muhammad Ali Day.

While in town, Ali visited Elijah Muhammad. The Messenger was much diminished. Frail and quiet, his breathing more labored than ever, he had been telling his followers to condemn the "slavemaster" no more—we'll have no more talk about "blue-eyed devils," he declared. "[The slavemaster] said you could go free and we see that he is not angry with us." The fight had gone out of Elijah.

Ali affirmed that his faith was stronger than ever, though he admitted, "I feel real guilty, makin' so much money so easy. Fighting George Foreman was an easy $5 million. . . . From here on out . . . I don't want nothing but what it costs to train. I want my share to go to needy groups." He had long said that when he retired from the ring he wanted to become a full-time Nation of Islam minister. But now he confessed, "I don't want to be a leader. I don't live clean enough to be a spiritual leader."

On December 10, Ali flew again, this time to Washington, DC, to meet President Gerald Ford in the White House. It was a tough time for Ford. Three months had passed since he had pardoned Richard Nixon for his crimes; four months had gone by after having declared at his inauguration, "My fellow Americans, our long national nightmare is over." But the lingering depression had not abated, and Ford's pardon of his predecessor raised suspicions that the federal legal system was as rigged as a mob-fixed fight.

The nation's gloom was heightened by the humiliations of Vietnam and the Arab oil embargo. Ford, hapless, seemed incapable of solving these problems. On September 16, a week after pardoning Nixon, he signed a Vietnam War clemency act. It offered pardons and repatriation to draft resisters and military deserters in exchange for an oath of allegiance and two years of public service. It should have been a healing gesture, but it came too late—the public was years ahead of the government in its opposition to the war—and the offer seemed dubious in the swirl of cynicism clouding the Nixon arrangement. Few young men eligible for clemency trusted the deal enough to accept it.

The oil embargo uncovered the embarrassing fact that, with just 6 percent of the world's population, America consumed 30 percent of the world's oil, and it sparked not only an energy crisis but also a burst of inflation. Experts called it *stagflation*, a condition in which jobs and wages remained stuck as cost-of-living expenses ballooned (a circumstance some economists had thought impossible). When it became apparent that the financial damage would not be repaired any time soon, economists named the mess a full-scale recession. Recession would shape the remainder of the decade.

Ford's response to it, on October 8, was dismissed by the *Washington Post* as "one of the biggest government public relations blunders ever." He appeared before Congress announcing a campaign to "Whip Inflation Now." His strategy consisted of charging a surtax on large corporations and wealthy Americans, but its centerpiece lay in asking citizens to conduct a one-hour "trash inventory" of their houses; to throw away waste; to lower thermostats; to carpool; and to plant vegetable gardens. He asked citizens to organize voluntary task forces and send him lists of inflation-busting ideas. He ordered hundreds of thousands of red-and-white WIN buttons ("Whip Inflation Now") to be manufactured and distributed across the country.

The buttons immediately became objects of ridicule. People wore them upside down (NIM—"No Immediate Miracles"). Stagflation remained steady, and Congress showed no willingness to work with Ford. Both Democrats and Republicans considered him useless. The standoff between the executive and legislative branches increased Ford's impotency. When, in the name of greater transparency (and perhaps to atone for 1964's inadequate Warren Commission report), Ford convened a congressional team to investigate America's covert assassinations, the effort was merely cursory. J. Edgar Hoover's ghost still harnessed more power than the president. Ironically, Ford would be the victim of two botched assassination attempts in 1975—incidents giving journalist Rick Perlstein occasion to mock him further: "Was Gerald Ford ever really president? He couldn't even get himself shot straight."

With the nation's leadership so adrift, it was perhaps inevitable that the culture would snap. UFO sightings spiked, amid fears that no one was minding the nuclear arsenal. Community volunteerism dipped—it was the "Me Decade," Tom Wolfe declared—do it if it feels good. "Wife-swapping" parties were "in" among middle-class couples, bowls full of house keys and uppers laid out like favors on the coffee table.

In addition to sending the apocalyptic shrieks of *The Late Great Planet Earth* to the top of the best-seller lists, Americans made *The Exorcist*, a morality tale about satanic possession, the top-grossing film of the early 1970s. The special effects, of a young girl turning green, spewing vomit, and spinning her head in circles, may have struck many parents as an only slightly exaggerated portrait of the national mood. (In the movie, the girl's mother, a filmmaker documenting campus unrest, receives an invitation to the White House. Enter the Devil.)

It was at this point that Muhammad Ali emerged victorious against impossible forces from within the darkness of Africa. America fell in love with him as it never had before. Ford needed him. On Studs Terkel's radio show, Ali had said, "I think the masses root for me [now] because they're scuffling. . . . People are basically underdogs as a whole. And the things that I say [for] my people, and the freedom of all people, in the way I speak out . . . the places I go and the things I do and the odds being so much against me, they see themselves in there, they don't see me or they don't see color, they see themselves and they're fighting against untold odds. . . . They just pretend that's them."

George Plimpton pointed out, in a *Sports Illustrated* article naming Ali "Sportsman of the Year," that Ali's achievement suggested "all things are possible. . . the comeback from hard times and exile, the victory of an outspoken nature over a sullen disposition, the prevailing of intelligence over raw power, the success of physical grace, the ascendance of age over youth, and especially the confounding of the experts." "Moreover," he added, "the victory assuaged the guilt feelings of those who remembered the theft of Ali's career."

Ford welcomed a gracious Ali into the Oval Office. "We as a nation were pretty much torn apart," Ford reflected later.

> There were conflicts between families, in colleges, and on the streets. We'd gone through serious race problems. The Vietnam War had heightened differences. And of course, there was the heritage of Watergate. One of the major challenges my administration faced was how we could heal the country. Not that everybody had to agree, but at least we should lower our voices and listen to one another. . . . Having Muhammad Ali come to the Oval Office was part of our overall effort. I felt it was important to reach out and indicate individually as well as collectively that we could have honest differences without bitterness.

Ford sincerely believed Ali was a "man of principle." "I know there were some who thought he evaded his military responsibility, but I've never questioned anybody's dedication to whatever religion they believe in," he said. "I give people the maximum benefit of the doubt when they take a stand predicated on conscience . . . I never joined the critics who complained about what he did and didn't do during the Vietnam War. I accepted his decision."

The men talked sports—Ford was a fan of boxing and football—and the visit went "quite well," the president recalled. Ali no longer seemed angry. His sole aim appeared to be pleasing as many people as he could.

✿

Nixon had been banished, but he wouldn't go away. Healing the country was going to be harder than Ford thought.

On October 29, following surgery in California for phlebitis in his leg, Nixon suffered postoperative shock and fell into critical condition, delaying the Watergate trials. Eventually he evaded the trials altogether.

When he recovered, the press had a field day portraying him as a vampire who wouldn't die. Political cartoonists presented him with dark circles under his eyes and a perpetual five o'clock shadow. Rubber Nixon masks became a hit at Halloween parties.

Writer Garry Wills called Nixon "the least authentic man alive." He had stalked American politics for over two decades, conditioning the public to accept inauthenticity as the nation's norm. Obvious lying simply became the way leaders spoke—we were forced to acknowledge this. Image meant more than substance. Though Nixon began with a visceral hatred of television, vampiric in his televised debates with JFK, he learned to manipulate the medium, as Kennedy had, instructing every politician in his wake. By the early 1970s, the public had been well trained to see news and politics as dramatic acts in an ongoing spectacle. The Watergate hearings became a riveting television miniseries, featuring good guys and bad guys. At the center of it all: Nixon's dark, sweating face smeared with runny makeup. He looked like the Joker in *Batman* comic books. And in the 1970s, as he was assuming tragic immortality, more and more celebrities seemed to have adopted his appearance, including religious figures (such as Tammy Faye Bakker, whose facial mask gave members of the rock band Kiss a run for their money) and musical acts like Alice Cooper and David Bowie.

The inauthentic—the image, the spectacle—had spread so wide there seemed little choice but to embrace it. And what did the masks conceal? Blue-collar workers voting against their own interests—swayed by patriotic rhetoric, failing to mobilize their electoral power to demand equal distribution of wealth. The funneling of public money into lavish sports facilities, enriching athletic leagues and team owners, under the guise of community development. The rise of megachurches, as lavish as football stadiums. Tuxedoed preachers saying Jesus really didn't mean it about the rich and the eye of the needle.

Meanwhile, US industrial executives, convinced that the nation's post–World War II prosperity would never end, increased their profits by investing in foreign rather than domestic labor forces. In regulatory terms, they argued for the dissolution of national boundaries. Boundaries impeded corporate flexibility. In 1971, the United States experienced its first trade deficit since 1893. Leveraged-buyout firms buying and selling junk bonds guaranteed that the seventies would be the first decade since the thirties when most Americans had less money at the end of a ten-year period than when they began.

As for civil rights and the War on Poverty—Alex Haley's *Roots* became a hit television show, but rather than inciting a lasting national conversation about the legacy of slavery, it caused a genealogy craze among white families (many of whom were eager to prove they had no "tainted" blood). In response to the urban protests of the 1960s, investment banks created "mortgage-backed securities," allowing banks to escape geographic lending restrictions. This led to financial bundling, unethical mortgage practices, massive losses of low-income housing: the foundation for the economic crash of the early 2000s.

The "long national nightmare" (Nixon's dark face brooding over it all) wasn't a simple trauma resulting from events we couldn't control. The horror was deliberately, steadily fabricated.

Shea Stadium, site of Beatles concerts in the 1960s, had become, by the early 1970s, part of America's patriotic spectacle. Along with Dallas's Cotton Bowl, Shea hosted gala POW celebrations. The soldiers, released from Vietnamese prisons, some of them suffering severe culture shock, were lauded with lavish dinners, busty cheerleaders, Bob Hope jokes, and the US Merchant Marine Academy Band playing "This Land Is Your Land."

Music critic Rob Sheffield noted that Paul McCartney's single "Silly Love Songs" ("a strident defense of dippiness") joined such 1976 number one hits as "Disco Duck." "But 1970s pop trash was stranger than Paul realized," Sheffield wrote. "According to the charts, the People were into songs about streaking, kung fu fighting, doing the hustle, CB radio, muskrat love, cruising at the YMCA, sniffing pots of glue, and killing the entire city of Chicago."

It was not the country George Harrison had last toured in 1966.

"Compared to what I should be, I'm a heathen," Harrison said.

"I never met a more tortured person in my life," filmmaker David Acomba reflected. "Never. Between the material world and this other quest [for God]. This was the whole dichotomy of the tour, back and forth, back and forth."

After a performance at the Long Beach Arena on November 10, 1974, Harrison was dispirited and exhausted although the tour was just beginning and the show had been well-received that night.

He walked onto the dark, lonely stage after the crowd had dispersed and witnessed the mountains of "empty bottles of gin and bourbon and tequila and the brassieres and shoes and coats and trash" left behind, he said. "There was a bulldozer, a huge bulldozer, just moving this stack of garbage." He wondered what he had in common with his fans. "They are all spaced out. . . . You play a concert, and half of them don't even know who they are watching. . . . There was a lot of violence, just a lot of violence."

"He was frustrated, he was trying to reconstruct the entire nature of the rock and roll tour, he wanted to change things and move things forward," Acomba said.

"Had he pulled it off, George Harrison's tour of North America in late 1974 might still be talked about in hushed tones," Graeme Thomson writes in *George Harrison: Behind the Locked Door*. "It would have been widely recognized as a groundbreaking fusion of Western rock and Indian classical music. . . . On the heels of two number one records, either side of the Concert for Bangladesh, it would have sealed Harrison's status as one of the elite solo rock stars of the Seventies."

It was not to be.

Trouble was evident in the rehearsals, in the days before the tour, in Charlie Chaplin's old studio on the A&M lot. Harrison had arrived from England overworked, overtaxed. "It was the winter, cold, and his voice was just a mess," said Robben Ford. "I don't think he quite knew how to take care of himself in that way."

Unlike Muhammad Ali, who had spent the year honing his body to perfection and preparing mentally, Harrison had struggled to prepare himself spiritually. "It really is a test," he told a writer from *Melody Maker*. "I either finish the tour ecstatically happy, or I'll end up going back to my cave for another five years." He really did have a cave on his property. In fact, seventeen years would pass before he would tour again. At war with himself, he failed to train for the grueling months ahead. ("So far from home, / So far from OM," he would write once the tour was finished.)

"He was constantly hoarse and could barely sing most of the time," Ford said. "He had not been doing it, man, [this] was the only tour. He was obviously capable of it, but he wasn't ready."

Even with a shredded voice, he had earned enough goodwill from his Beatles past—and fans were so eager to see a Beatle—that he could have easily won over the crowds. But his struggle extended into battles with the concert promoters and audience expectations. Primarily he was touring to showcase Shankar and the Indian orchestra. He knew his name would be the heavy draw, but he had no desire to take center stage or enact Beatledom. He insisted the tour be billed "George Harrison and Ravi Shankar," with both men's photographs on the program cover, extensive biographies of every musician inside the brochure, and plenty of Krishna imagery. He even wanted the newspaper ads to read "Don't come if you don't like Indian music."

"I thought it would give people another kind of experience other than watching Led Zeppelin all their lives," he explained.

Bill Graham, the major concert promoter, nearly wept with frustration. His relationship with Harrison had begun with a series of mixed signals, and it then deteriorated. During the tour's planning phase, Harrison invited Graham to Friar Park and served a dinner of Indian dishes. "There's no silverware and Bill doesn't know what to do," recalled one of Graham's assistants. "George starts shoveling food into his mouth with his hand. So Bill thinks, 'Okay . . . ' Bill's left-handed, and so he starts shoveling food with his left hand. George looked horrified and explained that you eat with your right hand and wipe your ass with your left."

The other two men handling tour arrangements understood Harrison as little as Graham did. Harrison's financial manager, Denis O'Brien, was out of his depth in the rock world. Besides, he was busy trying to keep Allen Klein's process servers from crashing Harrison's backstage dressing rooms. (Klein was suing Harrison for money Klein said he had borrowed from ABKCO.) Jonny Podell, the hot young booking agent Graham had hired, spent most of his time skiing down a mountain of high-grade coke.

None of them had the standing with Harrison to move him from his stubborn, uncommercial positions. "At the rehearsal, during the first run-throughs, it took about two hours and eighteen songs before George would do a Beatles song," Shankar said. "I had to go to George to urge him to consider audience expectations and give people a couple of old songs. He [said that] people expect him to be exactly what he was ten years ago. He's matured so much in so many years. That's the problem . . . people like to hear the old nostalgia." Harrison just did not want to do it. Like Muhammad Ali ten years earlier, he insisted, "I don't have to be what you want me to be."

He was quite willing to "put his neck on the line," said Tom Scott. "By that I mean presenting a show with so much new material when people expect him to do a Beatles."

Finally, in deference to Shankar, Harrison agreed to slip a few of his well-known tunes into the sets, but he gave them radically new arrangements—not to augment them; rather, in the spirit of subversion.

After the warm response to the Concert for Bangladesh, Harrison naively believed listeners would welcome his experiments with world music, the postcolonial soundscape: Western rock melded with jazz, gospel, and Indian bhajans.

Two days after Muhammad Ali shook the world in Kinshasa, Harrison introduced his conception of Nada Brahma to an audience at the Pacific Coliseum in Vancouver, British Columbia. He had imagined something like the Haight's Mantra-Rock Dance in 1966, but it was a "fiasco, soundwise and everything," said Lakshmi Shankar, Ravi's sister-in-law, a vocalist with the orchestra.

The show began with a shrieking wail, like a World War II air-raid siren. The bombs were falling again on Liverpool. Then the LA Express launched into an intro.

Harrison took so little stage time that he seemed to be making a guest appearance at a Ravi Shankar festival. "George wanted so badly for people to hear what he had heard [in Indian music]," said Olivia Arias. "And honestly he was going to make sure you listened to it whether you liked it or not."

He didn't approach giving the audience what it thought it would hear until the fourth song. "George didn't want to do 'Something' at all," Billy Preston said. "I knew he was gonna have to do it, and he started rebelling against it by doing it a different way, rewriting the lyrics."

As if chastising the crowd—*This song doesn't mean as much to me as it does to you*—he coughed out, "If there's something in the way, we move it," and "Find yourself another lover—well, I did,'" changing the original sentiment.

The show's mixture of styles and instrumentation was exhilarating—for those who were open to it. But the pacing was off. In one segment, a musician would start to gain momentum and then step aside for another player exploring an entirely new direction. The audience never caught a head of steam.

"The way he started the show, the band would play a tune and George would kind of drift out into a guitar solo," Acomba said. "Bill [Graham] wanted it like, 'Okay, the band does a number, then the house goes dark, and all of a sudden you hear the opening strains to 'Here Comes the Sun.' *Please*, George, do it.' 'No, no,

I don't want to do that.' That was George, you know. He never wanted to be up front—he just wanted to play music. He didn't want to be the star."

To be fair, he had tried to warn everyone, at a pre-tour press conference at the Beverly Wilshire Hotel in Los Angeles, that he wasn't hitting the road as a guitar god.

In typical fashion, he was blunt with reporters. His playing was "not particularly" sharp at the moment, he said—lately, he'd been forced to waste time "turning into a lawyer or an accountant." It would be good to be a musician again. His greatest concern: "I've lost my voice." "I'd be panic-stricken," he said, "but I don't even have time to worry."

Hardly the words of a man preparing to take the world by storm.

He dashed the hopes of those expecting to see a Beatles celebration: "I realize the Beatles did fill a space in the '60s . . . [but] one of the problems in our lives is that we get attached to things."

He encouraged listeners to attend the concerts ready for new experiences: "I think the combinations of instruments that people may not have heard along with instruments they have heard is going to blow a lot of people's minds."

The reporters were not interested in musical innovation. They asked him if he planned a rebuttal to Eric Clapton's "Layla." He responded, "Rebuttal? That sounds nasty . . . I'd rather [Pattie] was with *him* than some dope."

If they wanted to know what was happening in his life, he said, "Get my [new] album. It's like 'Peyton Place.' I mean, it will tell you exactly what I've been doing."

He apologized for speaking so often about "the Lord." "[But] he is there," Harrison said. "I have experienced something in my life, and I know He's there." He admitted he didn't meditate regularly now, but he was always thinking about the Lord. It was an ongoing commitment. No one's life was saved in single strokes, by miracles.

Asked if it was hard to reconcile a spiritual path with the rock and roll life, he answered, "It is difficult, yeah. It's good practice . . . to be, as they say, in the world but not of the world. You can go to the Himalayas and miss it completely. Yet you can be stuck in the middle of New York and be very spiritual."

His crowning glory? "As a musician? I don't think I've got any yet. As an individual, just being able to sit here today and be relatively sane. That's my biggest accomplishment to date."

✿

A reviewer writing about the tour's first concert ended his piece:

> The press, arriving at the Coliseum . . . was surprised to find no waiting
> press conference . . . PR men announced there would be no interviews
> during the tour, no backstage access and . . . photographers had better
> be equipped with telephoto lenses. All this sounds as though Harrison
> wants to stay out of touch. . . . After the "My Sweet Lord" encore, his final
> words were "Good night and God bless you." He was an appealing figure
> on stage, obviously, even stupefyingly sincere, but it seemed he will need
> all the blessings that God can [muster] on the rest of the tour.

In the early 1970s, rock concerts were edging into dangerous territory, with
the prevalence of cheap heroin circulating around urban venues. Harrison was
shocked by the decadent atmosphere. Backstage at the Los Angeles Forum,
abandoning his no-interview rule, he told *Rolling Stone* writer Ben Fong-Torres,
"People have to *think* a little bit more. The audience has to sacrifice a little bit
of something. . . . They have to listen and look, and then they'll get it, they'll
get something good. They think it's going to be this or that, then that itself is
the barrier which stops them enjoying, and if you can just open your mind and
heart, there's such joy in the world to be had."

Fong-Torres, startled by Harrison's intensity, asked him, "But what about
those who scrounged up $9.50 wanting at least a taste of Beatle George?"

"I don't say I'm Beatle George."

"Well, one of the things you don't control is how the audience feels about you."

"I certainly am going to control my own concept of me. Gandhi says create
and preserve the image of your choice. The image of my choice is not Beatle
George. If they want to do that, they can go and see [Paul McCartney and] Wings
. . . fuck it, my life belongs to me. It actually doesn't. It belongs to *Him*. My life
belongs to the Lord Krishna . . . I'm the servant. . . . Never been so humble in all
my life, and I feel great."

"But you're in show business," Fong-Torres pressed him.

"So I am in show business. And this is my show, right? . . . You know, I didn't
force you or anybody at gunpoint to come to see me. And I don't care if nobody
comes to see me, nobody ever buys another record of me. I don't give a shit, it
doesn't matter to me . . . I'm gonna do what I feel within myself."

Harrison's refusal to offer media-ready sound bites, the way Ali did, profoundly affected the way he was received as he traveled across the United States in 1974. So did his cavalier treatment of Beatles tunes, hoarsely shouted over jazz riffs.

Ever the band player, he gave more and more stage time to Ravi Shankar, Alla Rakha, Harihar Rao, Billy Preston (playing the gospel riffs he'd performed at Sam Cooke's funeral), Tom Scott, and Robben Ford. But the nostalgic crowds wanted more of Beatle George.

Nostalgia was one of the most powerful driving sentiments behind the glam-rock tide Harrison was trying to buck, the make-up and high-heeled boots, the deliberately-styled inauthenticity of David Bowie, Elton John, the New York Dolls. Glam rock was progressive in advancing gender fluidity, but it was arguably regressive in embracing early-twentieth-century theatrical camp, such as ostentatious costuming and broad pastiches of musical styles. It mounted a backlash against the persona of "authenticity" adopted by many late '60s rockers, including Dylan and the Beatles.

On the road again in 1975, Dylan would paint his face.

Harrison didn't budge. He carried authenticity to painful extremes. "What you saw was who he was," said Andy Newmark, one of the tour's drummers. "He was very straightforward . . . open and honest with everyone. . . . No star bullshit going on." He was determined to dismantle the Beatle myth.

But that wasn't the worst of his sins. Finally, what audiences and rock journalists would not forgive him for was his betrayal of rock and roll (in their view). Onstage, he pointed to Ravi Shankar's sitar and said he would die for Indian music, not for Western rock.

To have one of the industry's biggest stars dismiss the industry was a serious economic threat—as the alarmed editors of *Rolling Stone* understood. With their guidance, Fong-Torres wrote the most scathing pan of the tour, of Harrison's music, of his talent in general: not a critique as much as a character assassination.

Headlined "Lumbering in the Material Word," the snarky piece began, "Holy Krishna! What kind of an opening night for George Harrison is this? Ravi Shankar asks for silence and no smoking during his music. Silence is very important, he says, because music is eternal, and out of silence comes the music. Something like that. But, instead, out of the audience comes this piercing death cry, followed by a rain of war whoops. After a few numbers, people start shouting, 'Get funky!' and 'Rock and roll!' . . . One reporter is guessing that the Sanskrit letter for Om, illuminated in shadowboxes at either end of the stage, is actually the Indian dollar sign."

Arguably, tolerance for Indian music in America had faded in 1967 when John Lennon said "We made a mistake" (talking about the Maharishi). After that, music producer Richard Bock said, "The record sales took an immediate nosedive. . . . Within six months from when you could sell a hundred thousand copies of Ravi, you could sell ten thousand. . . . The Beatles were that powerful an opinion-maker." On his own, Harrison could not restore enthusiasm for anything other than Beatles songs. Shankar faced physically hostile crowds. And despite future accolades, Harrison's career never fully recovered from the *Rolling Stone* attack.

The tour's harshest critics cited Harrison's proselytizing as one of his worst offenses. (It was a habit he had learned, in part, from Shankar's scolding of restless audiences). "In defense of his tour," one reviewer wrote, "George Harrison has argued that 'If you don't expect anything, life is one big bonus. But when you expect anything, then you can be let down.' So expect nothing—is that the moral of a shriveled career?"

The remark indicates how wide a gulf had opened between Harrison and his public. His statement was a paraphrase of the Bhagavad Gita, counseling against forming attachments in life. His refusal to peddle nostalgia as he believed Crosby, Stills, Nash, and Young, Eric Clapton, and Elton John were doing was not mere cussedness. It was a form of Krishna-consciousness, projecting an aspirational image.

If it was startling to see a self-avowed spiritual man surrounded by celebrity trappings (a sleek tour plane, catered meals, limos, and plenty of booze and coke), Harrison had made no secret in songs, in interviews, and in his stage patter that he was still struggling, a seeker, not a role model. In "My Sweet Lord," he did not claim to have seen God; he wanted to encounter the Lord, "but it takes so long"—the quest never ends.

Andy Newmark insisted, "[Harrison's] spiritual thing was real—he wanted to help people. . . . He was just trying to live his life and find some truth and reality. Within that, I don't think he had any conflict in his mind over whether getting high was against any kind of rule. . . . He was seeking peace of mind and something to balance all that hysteria and Beatles stuff."

But hundreds of people flocking to see him rejected his rejection of the past. Harrison's rejection discounted their happy memories, their younger selves. In their displeasure, they rebuffed his beliefs as well as the Indian music he treasured. They greeted his exhortations ("Chant Krishna! Christ! Krishna! Christ! Allah! Buddha!") with silence.

Pressured by Bill Graham, Harrison compromised and began to limit Shankar's stage time. This pained him terribly. Shankar's performances were the point of the tour. And in asking Shankar to trim his musical numbers, he was butchering the sacred structures of the pieces, something neither the audiences nor the promoters respected or understood.

That burst of exuberance from 1964, when Cassius Clay met the Beatles in the tragic wake of JFK's murder—Ali in Zaire had restored some of it, but Harrison was trying to take it away.

☼

"[It] was an extremely well-organized tour," Shankar recalled. "George had even arranged a Boeing 707 for us, complete with a big Aum painted on the outside, and the inside rearranged so that the first-class area was a floor with carpets and throw cushions, like a Maharajah's lounge. The entire plane was ours for the tour. Our musical instruments, cushioned in large protective boxes, were traveling by road along with the sound equipment. After a performance three trucks used to leave for the next city, while we would fly later on, so that when we landed and were whisked off from the plane directly to the hotel (by car), they were there to meet us. One of the trucks was even converted into a full kitchen run by Vasudevan [Shankar's cook], so that there was Indian food ready for us on arrival at the hotel!"

"The flights were the best times," Harrison said. "We got into the groove of escaping out of the hall, running to the airport and jumping on the plane. Then we'd take off and go to the next city and there would be a little after-show party on the plane, and we would arrive late at night so we would already be in town for the next gig. Jim Keltner, percussionist Emil Richards, and Tommy Scott were so into all the Indians—they would be hanging out with Alla Rakha on those plane rides, playing different rhythms. It was fantastic. And with the kitchen truck, it reached the stage where the Western musicians would be eating Indian food and the Indians would all be eating pizza."

"Trying to keep two bands with two crews from two different continents with two different cultures happy was a real organizational feat," Chris O'Dell would recall. "The grand total ended up being somewhere around 120 people schlepping from one city to another."

Once, on the plane, Willie Weeks, the bass player, mentioned that he loved lobster. One night he checked into his hotel room to discover that Harrison had arranged for dozens of lobsters to be packed in ice in his bathtub. "In spite of the hard time with the press, he still kept his sense of humor and his generosity," Weeks said. "It was the classiest tour I've ever been on, the best hotels, the best everything. He wanted to make everybody happy. It was beautiful."

When he registered at hotels, Harrison used the pseudonym "Jack Lumber" after Monty Python's "Lumberjack Song" (before the shows, the song played each night over the arenas' speakers). Olivia Arias traveled with him. "He seemed so happy when he was with Olivia," O'Dell remembered. "I was surprised to see how affectionate he was with [her], holding hands, heads touching as they talked, snuggling up next to her at every opportunity. I'd never seen George be very demonstrative with Pattie."

Shankar's orchestra stayed in less exclusive lodgings than did the rock and rollers. Many of the Indian musicians spoke no English; they were rural people, most of them traveling in the United States for the first time, willing to accept more modest surroundings. In each city, the crew would set up a hospitality suite in Harrison's hotel. They stocked it with Indian food. "I loved watching George wander into the hospitality suite and go straight to the portable kitchen to fill his plate with curries and chutneys," O'Dell said. "As he sat on the couch and ate quietly by himself, there was a prayerful presence about him. Food, meditation, solitude, silence—George held on to the spiritual realities that helped him get through the stress of being on the road."

Harrison dedicated the profits from three of the shows to the Material World Foundation, packaged as aid for Bangladesh. Proceeds from the sale of printed programs were funneled to various local charities wherever the tour was booked, including the Appalachian Regional Hospital and the San Francisco Free Clinic. The clinic had been established in 1967, the year Harrison made his frightening trip to the Haight. In 1974, it was about to lose its federal funding. The staff was preparing to close its medical facilities, which had treated ten thousand patients in a year. Harrison gave the doctors $66,000. Between the two San Francisco concerts, on November 6 and 7, he and Arias toured the Haight. "Nobody gaped [this time]," said the clinic's founder David E. Smith. "Nobody mobbed him or kissed his ass."

"He said he hoped to start a ripple with other musicians doing the same kind of things," Amie Hill, a clinic volunteer, recalled. "He said, 'Don't thank me. It's not me.'" Then for the doctors and nurses he sang "The Lord Loves the One," his tribute to Prabhupada.

Three nights later, at the LA Forum, unable to coax the crowd to chant with him, he croaked from the stage, "I don't know how it feels down there, but from up here you seem pretty dead."

When someone yelled "Bangladesh!" he responded, "Don't just *shout* Bangladesh. Give them something to help. You can chant, 'Krishna, Krishna, Krishna' and maybe you'll feel better. But if you just shout 'Bangladesh, Bangladesh, Bangladesh,' it's not going to help anybody."

The following afternoon, at the second LA show, he felt stronger. Bob Dylan had appeared backstage to offer moral support. "Good afternoon, just got out of bed," Harrison announced to the crowd. "Looks very nice out there. You all look very happy. God bless you. . . . We're all pretty knackered up here."

Midway through the first set, he introduced "Something" as one of his "comedy" numbers. Though he shouted the lyrics, his guitar soloing was impeccable and more tasteful than ever.

He mocked himself, hawking the printed programs: "Sell, sell, sell!"

He introduced the horn section: "You name it, they'll blow it."

Then he said, "At this pause in the show you're either going to be confused or joyous, because there's lots of Indian instruments . . . it's not like what you've heard before. We just need a little bit of your patience, 'cause there's lots of little microphones so it'll just take a moment." As the spotlight settled on Ravi Shankar, Harrison said, "I'd like to introduce somebody who came into my life and suddenly from that moment on my life became worthwhile."

The LA audience was slightly more polite during Shankar's set than the crowds had been in Vancouver and Seattle. "Your vibrations are very nice," Harrison said afterward. "I gotta say it helps."

He was lavish in his introductions of Billy Preston and the LA Express. He thanked the Lord for them.

"I'd just like to tell you that—you know, sometimes when you've not done this for so long, and I step up here and I see a lot of miserable faces, it just drains me energy," he said. "But seeing so many happy faces, it gives me strength. Thank you."

Closing the show, he sounded like a deeply injured man grateful for the smallest kind gestures. "God bless you," he said. "I mean, we all need a bit of love. The less people go around kicking the legs out from under each other. . . . Oh, but even when they do, it doesn't matter."

In many cities, the bands played two shows, afternoon and evening. The arenas were looming and drafty and sometimes featured "festival seating," meaning no seating at all, so promoters could cram more bodies into the hall. The schedule was brutal (almost every day a travel day), the environments harsh. On the plane and between shows, Harrison drank hot tea, vinegar, and honey. Some days his voice improved. Then it would crater again. "Yet he wasn't going through the motions—each night he turned in a committed vocal performance, with Preston gamely covering for him on the high notes," Thomson writes.

"We all read the reviews every morning, at breakfast, or on the plane," Andy Newmark said. "It was pulling him down. He would mention that he was really getting killed by the press. It was a difficult time for him, that tour. The press slammed him, he lost his voice, his wife had left him, and the shit was really hitting the fan."

"Some people used [his hoarseness] as an excuse to give him a hard time because of what he was trying to bring to the audiences," Willie Weeks believed. "It was a struggle. I remember feeling hurt for him." David Acomba said, "I remember him coming up to me one night and saying, 'I'm only going to get to heaven on Ravi's coattails, with this rock and roll life. . . . There were drugs around, the usual stuff. Spirituality helped him, but a lot of other self-medicating substances helped him too. Whatever gets you through the night. He was totally drained. He was a thin guy anyway, and when he lost his voice I don't know if he had the physical wherewithal to surmount that."

"We were all doing coke," Newmark said. "George would do that with us sometimes, but it's not like the fuel of the tour was substances—it was just normal. That's what everybody was doing in that period. He never seemed excessive to me, and it would alternate between a few days when he would partake and then a period when he meditated and had all the incense going."

Touring taught Newmark:

If you want to understand what part drugs play in the life of a rock musician . . . [imagine] you're on the road. Your life is in planes and hotels. There's no continuity, just moving from place to place, every day a different town. You're herded like cattle. There's nothing particularly human about it. And this substance becomes your friend. It goes with you wherever you go, this constant in an inconstant life. This friend gives you a familiar feeling wherever you go, and you begin to think it makes the reality of your life easier to cope with. It's there, in a vial, in your back pocket, your buddy. Ultimately, of course, you learn it's an unhealthy friend.

The historical record has stamped the tour "ill-fated." A glance at the reviews from city to city reveals that there were as many positive as negative responses, maybe a few more, an impressive balance given the boldness of the presentation. It was the December 19 appearance of Ben Fong-Torres's *Rolling Stone* piece that sealed the collective memory.

Early in the tour, the *Oregonian*'s John Wenderborn wrote, "It was a sheer delight to listen to the varied sounds from sitar, tabla, flute and other stringed instruments. Harrison brought [along] . . . Shankar's orchestra for a valid, viable marriage of musical cultures."

Jacoba Atlas, writing in *Melody Maker*, acknowledged the negative buzz in the music industry but said, "For me the George Harrison concert was a complete delight: incredibly good tight music, played by people who were not on ego trips and who were enjoying their time on stage. Harrison's voice was gone, but there was so much music to cover the rough spots that it really didn't matter. The band has got to be one of the finest assembled anywhere. . . . Harrison wore no glitter, pranced no prances, displayed no ego. If you wanted a superstar he was a disappointment. If you wanted good music, he was perfect."

Diehard Beatle fans continued to be distressed at the way he changed the lyrics to old favorites—slipping the phrase "I love God more" into his version of John Lennon's "In My Life." "God bless John, Paul, and Ringo, and all the ex-ex-ex-ex-exes," he offered by way of consolation. The fans who could overcome their preconceptions were swept away by the show. "You hear every different type of music there is in the world," one listener told *Rolling Stone.* "If you were gonna talk to God, that would be the way," said another. These comments were especially true of a long piece in the middle of the concert titled "Dispute and Violence," featuring jazz horns, gospel piano, classical Indian instruments, and Harrison's electric guitar: all the dissonance and harmony of 1974, as representative of its time as the sound-collage "Revolution #9" on the Beatles' *White Album.*

In Chicago, "George looked high as the band rocked out 'My Sweet Lord,'" a reviewer wrote. "The building almost rose several feet in the air from the combined happiness of singing audience and rocking musicians."

Even Ben Fong-Torres admitted the concerts were musically engaging, buoyed by the "appealing sincerity of George Harrison himself, blissed-out and beaming," despite Harrison "committing all manner of ghastly, anti-show business mistakes—over-introducing Ravi Shankar or Billy Preston, imploring the audience to 'have a little patience' for the Indian music."

For those disappointed in Harrison's refusal to project star quality (which he was capable of doing, as he did in the Concert for Bangladesh), the *New York Times* commented, "Mr. Harrison reverted to the role of the vocally silent, diffident lead guitarist, flashing quick smiles to his fellow players and playing his part in the larger whole. It was a role that suited him. He has had his hits and he has deserved them. But [what] suited him best was the role of the 'silent Beatle,' humbly taking second billing."

Most significantly, for Harrison, the *musicians* were happy. He considered this the hottest band he'd ever worked with. Happily, he said he was probably the worst player on stage. He had created the harmony he wanted between Western and Eastern musicians, among Blacks, whites, and Asians, among Christians, Hindus, and Muslims. "[It] was a dream come true for him," said flautist Hariprasad Chaurasia. "He treated everyone equally, irrespective of his or her race or nationality. . . . And, even while running around to get everything right and in place before the concert, George would also make sure that those who were backstage were getting tea and coffee."

Jim Horn said Harrison was the "sweetest person" he ever worked with: forthrightly, he accepted responsibility for the tour's ups and downs. "God is fair," he told the band. "He's not watching over everybody and saying, 'You did that, so give him a kick in the behind.' It's ourselves who get into a mess or get ourselves out."

Robben Ford remembered,

[One night] he invited me to his hotel room, just to kind of hang out a little bit. It was just the two of us, and I played him a song that I'd written, and he played "Be Here Now." It was when I was first impressed by his guitar playing. There was really a strong feel. When he played it had command in it, which was not something that I ever really necessarily noticed. It was like, 'Wow, this is a real guitar player here' . . . I was so into blues players and jazz, I wasn't aware of him as a guitar player. It gave me an even higher regard for him as a musician.

Ford also saw, quite clearly: "He wanted a life. And touring is not a life."

"Every show was hard for him," said L. Subramaniam.

He was trying sincerely to do something to benefit people. . . . [He] wasn't just looking to popularize Indian music but also [to offer] a path of spirituality. He was trying to make people aware of the music because he knew gradually they would get to the root. . . . But the press wasn't always sympathetic. . . . Anyone else under that kind of pressure would have said, 'Okay, I'm calling it off. We'll tell the press I have a sore throat, and I'll be on the next flight home.' But he took the risk of going on, of people again writing something negative about him, of putting in all that effort. Why did he do it? I always had the feeling someone very special was occupying that body.

President Ford's son Jack was in Salt Lake City, studying forestry at Utah State University in Logan. He attended one of the concerts, and afterward, he went backstage to meet Harrison. They hit it off. "I don't have any ideas about the first family," Harrison said. "The only impression I had of President Ford was that he was a person who was put in a job, which he didn't particularly want and maybe he didn't really need it at all." He could relate.

In Tulsa, Leon Russell joined Harrison onstage, and they received a thirty-minute ovation. Russell was a Tulsa native and had built an impressive recording studio in an old church downtown. Harrison visited him there and may even have jammed with him later at the Colony, a little club Russell owned.

Texas pleasantly surprised Harrison. He still associated it with JFK. "George was constantly worried about being shot," said David Acomba. "It was after Watergate, the Kennedys, Martin Luther King, and security wasn't great at these places. It could have happened at any time." In fact, Fort Worth supplied the most enthusiastic crowd Harrison had experienced. He plunked on a big cowboy hat and danced with Billy Preston. "I'm so happy that you should like it!" Harrison gushed at the end of the show.

"I played Fort Worth and Houston and it's amazing, the change, you know," he said later. "It just blows me out, the change in five years of the people's consciousness. It's incredible! It's like, say, four or five years ago in San Francisco or Los Angeles, it's like that now in Texas, the feeling of the people and what they liked. . . . I didn't have any of the old fears."

In Memphis, David Bowie met Harrison backstage. It was the future greeting the past. The Beatles had dabbled, briefly, in theatrical presentations—the suits and boots and shaggy hair, the *Sergeant Pepper* costumes—but Harrison had firmly rejected these. He had certainly never approached the heights of production Bowie excelled at. In 1974, Bowie, weary of his Ziggy Stardust mask, was touring behind *Diamond Dogs*, a "piece of theatre," according to one critic, "belong[ing] on Broadway." Harrison was a performer raised in the era of participatory democracy, communal happenings, and socially relevant art. Bowie practiced separation from the audience, power over it, raising walls of glittering artifice. "The idea of getting minds together smacks of the flower power period to me," Bowie had said. "The coming together of people I find obscene as a principle. It is not as natural a thing as some people would have us believe."

His was the prevailing view in the 1970s, as evidenced by the close connections he made with his audiences despite erecting barriers, and Harrison's frequent failures to excite group chanting.

"Ringo thinks [Bowie] is great, and John does too. But I don't have any concept of whether he's great or not," Harrison said. "I hope he wasn't offended by it, I pulled his hat off from over his eyes and said, 'Hi, man. How are you? Nice to meet you. Do you mind if I have a look at you to see what you are, because I've only ever seen those dopey pictures of you.' . . . I want to see who the person is."

Later Harrison would tell a reporter he had no patience with playing at being a rock star. "I'd rather be silly jumping up and down chanting Krishna than be silly jumping up and down with high-heeled mirrored boots on and eye make-up," he said. "There comes a time when you have to realize what life is all about."

Life was about death. And Ravi Shankar feared he was about to experience complete knowledge of it on the road. In spite of the Monterey Pop Festival, Woodstock, and the Concert for Bangladesh, he had been naïve in his expectations of young American audiences. He hadn't been prepared for the rudeness and indifference accorded the Indian sets, or the arena crowds shouting for Beatle George.

It proved too much for him. "I had [a] first alert from my heart while we were in Chicago," he said. "I was hospitalized in intensive care for five days. Luckily, it was not that serious, but I was cautioned to take care of my heart in the future."

He attributed the episode to the adverse effects on his muscles of the loud stage speakers, but doctors informed him that he had experienced a mild heart attack. He missed nine shows. Harrison, smiling, told the press, "Ravi's heart, with the Indian time signatures, happens to beat in seven and a half beats or something."

Shankar's scare was symptomatic of the toll the tour was taking on him and Harrison. The Indian musicians were not ingesting drugs all night (though Alla Rakha was fond of the Scotch on the plane and Shankar carried bags of hashish-laced candies from India). Nevertheless, Shankar was stunned at what the pressure, the atmosphere surfaced in him. He had commenced an affair with a secretary working for his booking agent. He resented the crowds' clamoring for rock and roll. "This tour has done a great deal to me," he wrote his partner Kamala. "For the first time I'm shocked to find (after many years!) all those depths of feelings I have. Such as anger, ego, jealousy—pettiness, being hurt."

The tour was so "ambitious," Olivia Arias observed. "Twenty years before its time. It capped four remarkable years in the public alliance between Ravi and George. And it . . . nearly destroyed them both."

Matters weren't helped by Harrison's manager, Denis O'Brien. One night O'Brien warned Shankar that he suspected him of taking financial advantage of Harrison. He had learned that, alone among the acts at the Concert for Bangladesh three years earlier, Shankar, always worried about money (and seeking respect for his music), had insisted on being paid for his performance—after talking Harrison and his peers into donating their services. O'Brien simply didn't trust him. Shankar's bitterness grew as the tour wound down. Afterward, he would not work again publicly with Harrison for many years, though their personal relationship remained strong. Shankar was determined to disengage from the world of rock and roll and return to his roots, as he had once advised his young friend to do.

There used to be an innocence to it all.

Even at the height of Beatlemania, Harrison felt a bond with his audience. He remembered Dallas in '64: he'd seen a kid screaming, bouncing up and down on a folding chair in the seventh row; next to him, his father was clearly sipping booze from a flask. Harrison glimpsed a cop moving toward them from the wings. He edged to the front of the stage and nodded a stern warning to them. They smiled at him. The man tucked his flask into his shirt.

Now a majority of the audiences seemed to use concerts as excuses to get loaded, no matter who was playing. And screw the cops.

He remembered the sweetness of the Apple Scruffs. Now there was a hard edge to fans' obsessions, their sexual come-ons—with the band and with one another. At the show in Providence, Rhode Island, Harrison witnessed from the stage two men assault a girl. Then they turned and pummeled each other. He shouted, "Krishna, Krishna, Krishna! Stop the fighting! We didn't come here for a fight. You can get one of them anywhere."

He remembered the joy and frustrations of trying to write his first songs. Now, every time he picked up a guitar, he expected a lawyer to tackle him, telling him he couldn't use those notes. It was humiliating. Between recording dates, he was forced to perform in courtrooms, to explain that he was a "jungle musician," composing by ear: you can build a song around the sound of a water pump outside your hotel room, he testified one day. He had grown so insecure that he once asked one of his lawyers whether he should take formal music lessons. The lawyer was startled. What a question from such a successful star! "Whatever you're doing, don't change it," he said.

Jack Ford attended a show in the Capital Centre in Largo, Maryland, in early December (accompanied by a large Secret Service retinue). He invited Harrison to the White House to meet his father. "Nixon had just left office, and . . . I was keen to go there. I wanted to see how many of the bad vibes were left," Harrison said. (In DC, the musicians lodged at the Watergate Hotel.)

Gerald Ford told Harrison that he had recently received a visit from Muhammad Ali. Harrison recounted the story of how the Beatles had met Ali in Miami, ten years ago now. Ali picked up Ringo, he said, and tucked him under his arm.

Harrison brought his father with him to the White House, along with Olivia Arias, Ravi Shankar, and Billy Preston. This is the Black and White House now, Harrison joked. Preston played "God Bless America" on a Steinway in the drawing room.

Ford knew what he knew about the Beatles from his son, but he had been thoroughly prepped by his staff. Prior to the visit, Ford's secretary had given him two questionnaires that Harrison had filled out for the *New Musical Express*, one in 1964 and one in 1974. The file was titled, "George Harrison: Then & Now." In 1964, asked to list his brothers and sisters, he had written, "Louise, Peter, Harry." Now he wrote, "Kumar [Shankar], Billy Preston." In 1964, he said he'd gotten his education at the Liverpool Institute. In 1974, he changed his answer to "on tour and [in] Hamburg."

"Most thrilling experience" in 1964: "First disc a hit within 48 hours of release." In 1974: "Seeing Krishna."

In the Oval Office, Ford tapped the buttons displayed on Harrison hound's-tooth jacket and asked what they were. Krishna, Babaji, and the OM symbol, Harrison explained. He gave the president an OM button. In return, Ford walked around the corner of his desk, opened a drawer, and pulled out a red and white WIN button. He handed it to Harrison, who pinned it to his lapel. (By now, the WIN campaign was a total bust, with only two volunteers in the White House promoting it to the press, and no budget to print reply cards to the thousands of citizens who had written the president, offering ideas for beating inflation.)

Harrison decided Ford was a decent man. This gave him hope for the future. "I couldn't believe the place felt as comfortable as it did, after Nixon," he said. (Eventually he met Henry Kissinger and gave him a copy of *The Autobiography of a Yogi*.) Harrison did not want to trouble the president with politics, but he felt relaxed enough in the White House to raise the issue of John Lennon's immigration status (a persecution as onerous as that of Muhammad Ali, he said). And he wore into the Oval Office a pair of handmade Tibetan boots—one of the first subtle protests in the West against China's brutal treatment of its neighbor.

An enthusiastic audience in Detroit brought Harrison back for a second encore and didn't want to let him go. In Philadelphia, a ten-minute version of "While My Guitar Gently Weeps"—Harrison and Robben Ford trading licks—prompted a long ovation. The music seemed to improve each night as everyone's energy flagged. "You either go crackers and commit suicide or you attach yourself more strongly to an inner strength," Harrison said.

On December 15, John Lennon attended the Long Island show at the Nassau Veterans Memorial Coliseum. "John smiled and tapped his foot the whole time, like a proud older sibling watching his kid brother score a touchdown," Chris O'Dell remembered.

"The band really cooked," Lennon said. "The show I saw was a good show. My personal opinion was that even though I know what George was trying to do, I don't think it worked with Ravi. . . . I think Ravi's great . . . [but] I want to see George do George."

Introducing "In My Life," Harrison said, "I'd like to do a song written by an old friend . . . You all allow him to come and stay here."

But afterward, backstage, depleted, exhausted, Harrison succumbed to frustration—the weeks of tension on the road, the years of condescension from his bandmates. He had given Lennon his all, he said, even after the breakup, playing on Lennon's records. But where was Lennon when Harrison needed him most, at the Concert for Bangladesh? Harrison got so heated he pulled the glasses from Lennon's face and hurled them to the floor. Lennon didn't move. "I saw George going through pain, and I know what pain is, so I let him do it," he said later.

Like brothers, they patched things up as soon as their anger fizzled. Lennon agreed to appear onstage with Harrison during the tour's closing show at Madison Square Garden. Meanwhile, "Allen Klein was chasing George all over New York," Lennon said. "George was even running down back elevators."

Through their lawyers, the Beatles had finally agreed on a terms-of-separation document legally ending the band. Lennon, Harrison, and McCartney were all in New York at the time of Harrison's final concerts. They agreed to meet at the Plaza Hotel to sign the papers. The lawyers had already secured Starr's signature in London.

McCartney recalled, "We all arrived for the big dissolution meeting at the Plaza. . . . There were green baize tables, like the Geneva Conference it was, with millions of documents laid out for us to sign. George [was coming] off tour. I had flown in especially from England . . . and John wouldn't show up. He wouldn't come across the park!"

"My astrologer said it wasn't the right time for me to sign it," Lennon said.

"George got on the phone, yelled, 'Take those fucking shades off and come over here, you!,'" McCartney said. "John still wouldn't come over. He had a balloon delivered with a sign saying, 'Listen to this balloon.' It was all quite far out."

"The planets weren't right and John wasn't coming," said a disgusted Linda McCartney. "Had we known there was some guy flipping cards on his bed to help him make his decision, we would have all gone over there. George blew his top but it didn't change anything. It's beyond words."

Lennon tried to smooth things over, sending word to Harrison that he was still willing to appear onstage in the Garden. Harrison wouldn't speak to him. Instead, he informed May Pang, Lennon's companion during a period of estrangement from Yoko Ono, "I started the tour without him and I'll finish it without him."

McCartney attended the first of the two Madison Square Garden shows, wearing a huge fake mustache, aviator sunglasses, and an Afro wig, a disguise guaranteed to call attention to him. He would learn a valuable lesson from the concert, and two years later he mounted a wildly successful US tour, generously playing several old Beatle songs. (Robbie McIntosh, one of the guitarists in McCartney's band, said, "I figured I would come up with some snappy new solos of my own to dress up Paul's old Beatles tunes. But as I listened to the records, I realized that George Harrison had come up with the absolutely *perfect* solo for each and every one of them, and that there was nothing I could have done to improve upon them. So I ended up just learning George's solos.")

At Harrison's final show, Jonny Podell, the booking agent, arrived at Madison Square Garden in a Rolls. He stumbled out of the car clutching a cosmetics bag. It bulged with coke. He stood backstage with Bill Graham, both men congratulating each other for the amazing success they had pulled off: in spite of the mixed reviews, the tour had earned a substantial profit. Graham wore a silver necklace proclaiming the word BAD. Podell's necklace said BADDER.

Onstage, Harrison announced, "For the last fifty gigs there have been those who've put us down. Some liked us, some didn't, some had too much ink in their pens. Well, for everyone, this is it. It all comes out in the wash." Launching into "My Sweet Lord," he said, "I'm here to tell you the Lord is in your heart."

The musicians, East and West, joined together, arm in arm, for the final bow.

"Afterwards, George gave gifts to everybody," Robben Ford recalled. "To me he handed a drawing of a guitar, and he said, 'This is your Christmas present, Robben. It's being custom-made by Gibson right now and it will be with you in a couple of months.' It was a beautiful big-bodied blonde Gibson with a single cutaway."

After showering, the band and crew repaired to the Hippopotamus, a chic Manhattan nightclub, to celebrate. Ringo was there with Maureen (though their marriage was on the rocks). Harrison chatted with her, relaxed and friendly. For the second time in as many days, Harrison and Lennon reconciled. They recalled old times, when, as the Beatles, they had hidden from their fans in a bathroom at the Plaza Hotel.

The next day, December 21, the men appeared together in public for the last time. They did a joint radio interview with New York's KHJ, both of them working very hard to be nice. Harrison lauded Lennon's "inventive" songs such as "Strawberry Fields Forever" and "Norwegian Wood." He chastised the press for its unfair treatment of Lennon during his immigration struggles.

In turn, Lennon praised Harrison's tour: "All the audiences have been digging his shows, [I know] 'cause I've got good spies, and the critics didn't like it because you changed it. If you'd done the same [old tunes] you would have been attacked for *not* changing it."

But huge differences remained between them, made worse by the endless legal battles, and no amount of playing-nice could hide the fact—as if it needed reinforcement—that the Beatles were done.

Discussing changes in the music scene, Harrison said, "Every picture I've ever seen of David Bowie or Elton John, they just look stupid to me."

Tersely, Lennon said, "I think they look great."

"Well, I think [they're] dopey."

The Beatles' formal partnership was dissolved in the London High Court on January 9, 1975. The decade over which they ruled, along with Muhammad Ali, had begun with dispute and violence, and it ended with a whimper.

In 1974, the differing public receptions given to George Harrison and Muhammad Ali—Ali's mostly joyous, Harrison's cruel—had much to do with the men's personalities, their performances, and their aims that year.

But on another plane, Ali's redemption in Zaire—or its perception in the press—suggested a final turning-away by a majority of Americans from the policies, public ethos, and military excesses that governed the 1960s.

Similarly, the perception that Harrison's US tour had been a disaster—a *mis*perception, objectively speaking—suggested that young people were turning away from any notion of popular music as authentic expression. Given that music had been the era's most powerful generational emollient, the rejection signaled massive disillusionment, more profound than was immediately apparent.

America had disgraced its principles in the 1960s. Our pop heroes affirmed this while our leaders lied to us. But, in the end, many of our heroes let us down, just like our leaders, pushing simplistic ideals, sloganeering statements weakened by the same excesses wrecking Vietnam.

What happened to trust when a corporate entity such as Columbia Records could boast, "The Revolutionaries are on CBS?"

What happened to trust when the old activists disavowed their pasts? "I've come to believe that all of our radical activity in the late 1960s might actually have prolonged the Vietnam War," Allen Ginsberg said.

John Lennon sang, "I found out . . . There ain't no guru who can see through your eyes."

"No one realized it at the time, but the Concert for Bangladesh marked the end of the age of innocence for rock music," said the *Toronto Star*. "It also ultimately led to the creation of today's corporate-influenced do-gooder. . . . Good things are still done in the name of rock, but they're more calculating, more cynical than what went down that hot August night [in 1971]."

Ralph Gleason, *Rolling Stone*'s cofounder, proclaimed, "When the pop star turned out not to be the revolutionary the politicos thought he was, they turned on him, cursed him and in the name of his failure pronounced rock dead."

Beneath the disillusionment, the economic scaffolding supporting sixties idealism was crumbling. Internationally, small, independent nations were struggling to survive. And then, late in 1974, George Harrison and Muhammad Ali, the Quiet One and the Marvelous Mouth, reappeared to remind us of their faiths, their visions for shaking up the world. They convinced or did not convince, unable to hide their flaws. But their flaws, no less than the sincerity of their yearning, were essential to what made fans turn to them in the first place: their willingness to mature publicly along with everyone else.

It was 1941 when Henry Luce, the publisher of *Time* and *Life* and *Sports Illustrated*, published his famous essay "The American Century," touting "America as the dynamic center of ever-widening spheres of enterprise, America as the training center of the skillful servants of mankind, America as the Good Samaritan, really believing again that it is more blessed to give than to receive." He insisted, "Out of these elements surely can be fashioned a vision of the 20th Century to which we can and will devote ourselves in joy and gladness and vigor and enthusiasm."

Instead, the American Century—the postwar period of prosperity and possibility—lasted about twenty-eight years, frittered away by hubristic leaders responding to Cold War imperatives, the breakup of colonial blocs, reckless uses of energy, and a changing global market.

For much of those twenty-eight years, Muhammad Ali and George Harrison, born one and two years, respectively, after Luce expressed his vision, enacted the "joy and gladness" Luce predicted, as well as the turbulence and tragedies he did not. In 1974, both men staged their climactic events inviting a worldwide reappraisal of the American Century. There was much to celebrate—the advancement of civil rights, the independence of young nations, artistic richness, spiritual reawakening; and much with which to be concerned—war, the persistence of racism and sexism, the destruction of natural resources, the worshipping of violence.

The year 1974 had painfully tested these men as well as Luce's vision. Everything that Ali and Harrison had done, everything their work had stood for in the 1960s, went baldly on the line. In assessing their efforts, audiences, critics, historians, artists, and politicians took the opportunity to reassess all that had come before, the meanings attached to it, and the worth of those meanings. The quality of the very culture giving those meanings substance lay bare.

Was it a worthy culture? Should it continue? If not, what changes needed to be made—in the areas of race and class, gender, sex and sexuality? International relations and the human weakness for war? Spirituality?

Audiences, critics, historians, artists, and politicians did not always agree on the answers, nor were their motivations and degrees of seriousness all the same. But as cultural representatives—living forms of shorthand for discussion—Ali and Harrison were central to the issues.

As myth-makers and media creations, as public men churning in the era's maelstrom, Ali and Harrison became synonymous with antiauthoritarianism, religious yearning, and war protests. They challenged yet reinforced gender stereotypes: Ali mocked fixed sexual beliefs by referring to himself in traditionally feminine terms ("I'm so pretty!"). Harrison did so by growing his hair long. Yet their confident personae were absolutely male—Ali exhibiting strength and aggression in the ring, Harrison seductive pressure, wielding his phallic guitar. In their private lives (exposed in the tabloid press) they could be appalling chauvinists.

They were imperfect messengers, but messengers they were.

In their rejections of Christianity, they challenged not only America's dominant religious dogmas but also the modes of behavior, the family structures, the particular brand of God-and-country patriotism keeping the culture together. In their acceptance of alternative beliefs and behaviors, they invited fear, curiosity, and ridicule in varying degrees. They put traditional philosophies to the test.

Ali was a powerful symbol of courage, of individual resolve against massive odds. Harrison, as a member of the Beatles, was a warm reminder of the collective's strength; as a solo artist, he became an example of determined will, struggling to be recognized.

Both men transcended their fields, their work linked to regions of the world ravaged by colonialism and its deadly aftermath.

In 1974 a president resigned, and an ignominious war juddered to an end. It followed a year in which abortion was legalized and preceded a year in which the digital revolution arrived with the founding of Microsoft. Virtual worlds were about to be fought over as fiercely as terra firma. Europe's old colonial powers, having lost their grip on empire, melded as an economic unit. In the United States, New Deal liberalism, appearing to reach fulfillment with LBJ's initiatives, gasped for breath.

A blockbuster mentality seized entertainment, publishing, journalism, and business, consolidating power and money in the hands of a few, diminishing diversity—a particularly frightening evolution in the areas of news and information.

The marches for civil rights and for women's rights paved the paths for identity and social justice movements, a growing ethic of personal liberation, of grievance politics.

Ali and Harrison and their pasts were judged, in the fall of 1974, in the contexts of each of these developments. The Vietnam War still dominated US headlines, and Ali's name was forever fixed to it, but their meanings had changed and were changing still. Though only three years had lapsed since the George Harrison moment with the triumph of the Concert for Bangladesh, a cultural chasm had opened wide in the realm of popular entertainment.

Together, the Rumble in the Jungle and the Dark Horse Tour became coda to one distinctive period in Western culture and prelude to another, very different vision of what the West could—would—turn out to be.

"People who were never really keen on me just really hate my guts now. It has become complete opposites, completely black and white," Harrison said.

"When I got off the plane [from America], and back home [after the tour], I went into the garden and I was so relieved. That was the nearest I got to a nervous breakdown. I couldn't even go into the house. I was a bit wound up . . . getting dragged into [a] hole . . . then when I came in, I looked in the mirror and decided: 'Oh, I'm not that bad after all.' Ego. That [false] reflection."

Afterword

The Final Round

The death of Elijah Muhammad on February 25, 1975—heart failure at the age of seventy-seven—freed Muhammad Ali, though publicly he still expressed fealty to his mentor. When Ali heard the news, he flew from Deer Lake to the funeral in Chicago. Muhammad's son Wallace, once Malcom X's friend and admirer, was the new leader of the Nation of Islam. Almost immediately, he disavowed many of his father's old teachings. The Nation would turn toward a form of orthodox Islam. Dress codes would be relaxed. Smoking and dancing were allowed at certain public functions. White people would be invited into the fold.

Eventually Wallace Muhammad announced an end to the Nation of Islam. The organization would henceforth be called the World Community of al-Islam in the West. (Louis Farrakhan broke from Wallace and continued to lead a group called the NOI.)

One day, weeks prior to Elijah's death, back from Zaire, Ali had told Dave Kindred, in a whisper, "They always got somebody watching."

"Who's they?" Kindred asked.

"I would have gotten out of this a long time ago. But you saw what they did to Malcolm. I ain't gonna end up like Malcolm."

"You afraid?"

"I can't leave the Muslims. They'd shoot me, too."

But now Elijah was gone, and Wallace was busy atoning for the father's sins. Ali, still wary, wanted to know what he should think about all this. He asked the Messenger's son Herbert, his fight manager. Everyone in Ali's circle resented

Herbert: he had cheated the boxer for years. "I knew [Herbert] would tell me just what's happening, how I should feel, what I should say, what I should do," Ali said.

Herbert told him to embrace Wallace's reforms.

To a private gathering of mourners in Chicago, Ali said, "If every Muslim was killed tomorrow, and I was the onliest one left, I would go out somewhere and set me up a little mosque and continue . . . I make my pledge here today . . . that I will be faithful and loyal and honorable to the Honorable Wallace Muhammad."

He said he no longer believed in the Mother Ship or the divinity of W. D. Farad, but his faith in God was stronger than ever. "Elijah taught us to be independent, to clean ourselves up, to be proud and healthy. He stressed the bad things the white man did to us so we could get free and strong. Now, his son Wallace is showing us there are good and bad regardless of color, that the devil is in the mind and heart, not the skin. We Muslims hate injustice and evil, but we don't have time to hate people. White people wouldn't be here if God didn't mean them to be."

He was champ again. History had affirmed his stance on the war. Released from a fearful sect, he was preaching reconciliation of the races, tempering his politics. People loved him. "Ali has entered folklore," Wilfrid Sheed wrote.

But he felt restless. He had achieved his professional goals—what more could he do? He was freed from the threats of the Nation, but its absence left him puzzled about the nature of his faith. He lacked the structure he was accustomed to. He had damaged his marriage, for which he was genuinely sorry, but he couldn't stem his desires (and he was bothered by Ferdie Pacheco's suggestion that he had suffered brain injury: perhaps his impulse control was compromised).

The one constant in his life now was his worldwide celebrity. "Ali does not . . . sit around thinking of how he can [stay] famous. It is a blind biologic groping for the limelight, awesome in its accuracy," Sheed said. Ali's celebrity depended on dancing in the ring, which could only injure him further.

The problem with entering folklore, Sheed warned, was that there was "no place to go but down."

After his 1974 tour, George Harrison also softened his rhetoric. He spoke little of chanting, of Krishna, of reincarnation in the material world. This was partly the result of exhaustion, recognition that his proselytizing wasn't welcome, partly the result of ill health and a plunge back into the LA rock scene.

Five months after the tour ended, he was at the A&M sound studio in Los Angeles, cutting an album to fulfill his contract with Capitol/EMI, so he could become independent and pursue his vision of Dark Horse Records.

"I think he wasn't up for it, really," said Klaus Voorman. "It was a terrible time because there was a lot of cocaine going around, and that's when I got out of the picture . . . I didn't like his frame of mind."

Harrison's activities depressed and sickened him: over the course of the next two years, his muscles weakened and his skin grew sallow. He developed a severe case of hepatitis. Olivia Arias accompanied him back to Friar Park, reduced his diet of drugs and drink, fed him healthy food, and found him an acupuncturist. Not only did his health improve, so did his mood.

Arias reminded him of the benefits of meditation: "When you strive for something higher in the next world, you have a much easier time in this one."

In 1976 Harrison told rock journalist Lisa Robinson it had always been "difficult" for him to avoid the seediness of the music business. He had been raised in it: "I really relate to these people. I love them, and they're my friends, and from time to time I've really gotten into that—being crazy and boogying . . . parties and whatever all that involves," he said. "I go from being completely spiritual and straight. Then, after awhile, I've gone back in with the rockers again. But I've got a good sort of tilt mechanism in me. And when that hasn't worked, I've had hepatitis."

Harrison met Prabhupada at Bhaktivedanta Manor one last time on July 26, 1976. The visit followed a two-year period during which Prabhupada wondered whether he could trust Harrison. Though Harrison had bought the manor and its grounds for ISKCON, he retained ownership. Without saying so, Harrison seemed to worry about the organization's direction once Prabhupada was gone. Future events would justify his concern.

In any case, Prabhupada, true to his nature and faith, finally severed his attachment to the concept of ownership. "I know that George will not ask us to vacate," he told his devotees. "He is not that type of man."

When Harrison arrived at the manor, he saw that Prabhupada had grown very frail. The old man lay in bed, his hand scrabbling in a bead bag.

"How do you feel?" Harrison asked gently.

"I have old man's disease, cough and cold, so coughing. But still, work is going on, and I shall complete eighty years this month. September, eighty-one. So now, due to age, it is becoming [a] little difficult."

"Yes."

"Anyway, by the grace of Krishna, how are you?"

"Quite good."

"Chanting is going on?"

"Yes."

"That is our life and soul . . . We are inviting everyone, 'Come here. Such a nice house given by George. You live here comfortably, eat nicely, and chant Hare Krishna.'" Chuckling, he added, "We don't want any factory work."

"No."

"Still, people do not come. They'll prefer to go to the factory, whole day work in the hell." He and Harrison laughed together.

"I suppose someday the whole world will just be chanting in the country," Harrison said.

"That is not possible . . . I am very much pleased that you take so much trouble to come here," Prabhupada said.

"It's my pleasure."

The old man pressed *prasādam* on him: cauliflower and samosas. Harrison said he could eat very little because he had been sick. "I had something. I went yellow. I had jaundice . . . I was working as well, so I, you know, I think I was pretty tired."

Harrison returned to the subject of Prabhupada's health. "Are you ever going to stop traveling?"

"If that is Krishna's desire." Prabhupada said his fondest wish was to be conscious of the Lord as he drew his last breath. "If at the time of death one can remember Krishna, then his whole life is successful. Immediately he goes to Krishna."

"When my mother died, I had to send my sister and father out of the room because they were getting emotional, and I just chanted Hare Krishna," Harrison said.

"She chanted?"

"I did."

"Oh, very nice. So she could hear?"

"I don't know, I don't know. She was in, like, a coma or something. It was the only thing I could think of."

"If she has heard Hare Krishna, she will get the benefit."

Prabhupada asked one of the disciples to pull a book from a shelf and read a prayer to Krishna. Then he told Harrison, "If you chant this verse according to the Sanskrit tune, your admirers will take it very nicely."

Harrison laughed and said his "admirers" rarely responded to him now even when he sang in English.

As he rose to leave, Harrison urged Prabhupada to rest. Prabhupada wished him "long life."

Despite his frailty, the old man continued to travel in the next year and a half, to the United States, back to England, then to India.

In the States, self-proclaimed deprogrammers were declaring ISKCON a cult, a bogus religion. They accused its leaders of brainwashing vulnerable young people. Prabhupada considered it a personal victory when the New York high court ruled that the Hare Krishna movement was a "bona fide religion with roots in India that go back thousands of years."

His health problems persisted—"*pitta* and *vāhyu*, bile and air," he said. When the devotees fussed over him, he shooed them away: "I have nothing to do with this body."

As for the future of the movement, he said, "Don't be anxious . . . even if I go, where is the harm? I have given my ideas and direction in my books. Just you have to see it. I think I have done my part. Is it not? Do you think so or not?"

In November 1977, as he lay on a thin mattress in a hot room in Vrindavan, he asked the disciples who'd gathered around him to please forgive him, for he was the most fallen man on Earth.

"Is there anything you want?" someone asked him.

"I have no desire."

Back at Bhaktivedanta Manor, Shyamasundar told Harrison that the guru was gravely ill in India. At least he had managed to return to Krishna's birthplace.

"Will he live?" Harrison asked.

"It doesn't really look too promising."

Harrison spent the rest of the afternoon driving alone through the back roads of Oxfordshire, chanting.

Just before he died, Prabhupada removed a gold ring from his finger and placed it in a weeping disciple's palm. "Please, give this to George Harrison," he said. "He was a good friend to us all. He loves Krishna sincerely and I love him. He was my archangel."

The American public was not in a forgiving mood. Voters punished Gerald Ford for his lenience with Richard Nixon. Although he won 48 percent of the popular vote in the November 1976 presidential election, the electoral vote was decisive against him.

In January 1977, at a gala held before the inauguration of Ford's successor, Jimmy Carter, Muhammad Ali met John Lennon again. Lennon had finally been cleared of the immigration charges against him. "Yoko and John were so enamored of Ali," said Joel Sacher, a New Jersey entrepreneur and friend of the fighter. "They were more excited about seeing him than [they were about seeing the president]."

The two old sixties warriors, wearing tuxes, shook hands warmly. *You ain't as dumb as you look*. Carter was already warning the nation that its resources were not inexhaustible, that energy needed to be conserved. (Four years later he would not be reelected, in part for this unwelcome message.)

The media asked whether anything in the 1960s had been what it seemed.

Ali moved slowly. Fighting had damaged him. "The object of the game of boxing is hit and don't be hit. . . . You wanna show people how strong you are, show 'em how strong you are by *not* taking those shots. But you know, [Ali] didn't do that," Larry Holmes lamented. "Hit me! Show me something! And they did." And this had taken a toll. "You can't [take shots like Ali did] and think you're gonna come out of it whole."

But less than a year after his Rope-a-Dope victory over Foreman, Ali was back in the ring against Joe Frazier. He'd had three fights, all wins, in between. Ferdie Pacheco refused to be his doctor anymore. Ali continued fighting against his advice. "It's time for me to face another test," Ali said. "Things have been going too good lately. Allah must make me pay for all this fame and power. . . . Allah's always testing you. He don't let you get great for nothing."

Frazier said, simply, "This is the end of him or me."

In essence, it would be the end of them both—the "closest thing to death" Ali had ever experienced, he later said. Afterward, though both fighters continued to box, they were broken men. They had permanently damaged each other's bodies.

The fight occurred in the Philippines—the "Thrilla in Manila," Ali named it—next door to Vietnam. Mark Kram called the Philippines "America's first Vietnam." In 1900, President William McKinley had sent US troops there to wrest the archipelago from Spain. America's colonial venture spawned the "first genocide in modern history before Hitler," Gore Vidal wrote (discounting the fate of North American natives).

The match took place on October 1, 1975, just six months after Operation Frequent Wind, America's final evacuation from Vietnam. In late March, fixed-wing aircraft began airlifting American civilians and at-risk Vietnamese to safety. Then, as the North Vietnamese People's Army approached Saigon, panic erupted at the US embassy. The world witnessed a series of horrifying television images: Vietnamese citizens climbing on the embassy rooftop, desperately grabbing at US helicopters, losing their final chance to escape as the choppers rose into smoke; US sailors on aircraft carriers in the South China Sea, shoving choppers overboard to make room on the flight decks for the next set of pilots to land. It was a humiliating end to a wasteful war.

Vietnam had finally freed itself from invading forces, as had the Philippines.

In 1966 Ferdinand Marcos had sent his military thugs to Manila's airport to rough up the Beatles because he believed they had not paid him proper respect. Now, like Mobutu before him, Marcos hoped to gain favorable publicity for his deadly regime by hosting the world's most famous man.

Ali arrived in Manila surrounded by a new entourage. Belinda remained at home in Chicago, while Veronica Porché, "sometimes known as 'Ali's other wife,'" according to sportswriter Pete Bonventre, toured Manila with the champ.

"You have a beautiful wife," Marcos remarked to Ali, nodding at Porché.

"Your wife is quite beautiful, too," Ali replied.

This was the final indignity, Belinda said later, confronting Ali. She yelled, "You tell that bitch, if I see her I'm gonna break her back." She gave up on him. She and Ali would divorce, and he soon married Porché—officially.

"When we got married, he was an innocent guy, but he changed during the course of our marriage," Belinda said. "Some of it, I guess, wasn't his fault. So much was happening around Ali that he couldn't always see himself. The world was spinning by so fast; he didn't have time to stop and think. And he was influenced by certain people in the religion who he looked up to for guidance, and they led him wrong. Some of them were married and fooling around themselves. And instead of trying to be like him, they tried to make him like they were, and they were successful. It could happen to anyone. I don't think he would have been the way he was with other women if he'd been surrounded by the right people."

Even Wallace Muhammad—Ali's new leader—disappeared into rooms, Ali said in a whisper, winking.

An eighteen-year-old Louisville woman named Lonnie Williams, whom Ali had known since she was little, also accompanied the entourage to Manila. In 1986, she would become his fourth wife after his divorce from Veronica Porché.

Belinda wasn't the only one unhappy with Ali's companions. In the days before the Frazier fight, Ali's father paced the training gym, calling his son a nut. Elijah Muhammad had left over $5 million to Herbert and Wallace, yet Ali had once bought the Messenger a house in Phoenix. He had paid his hospital expenses. "The old man took him to the cleaners, and [the Muslims are] still not done," Cash muttered.

Meanwhile, Don King skimmed his share.

"I used to go to bed at night crying because of the way people were ripping off Ali," Howard Bingham said. "All someone had to do was walk in the door and say, 'As-salaam-alaikum.' That was the easiest way to plug him."

In Manila, Joe Frazier was the one shouting "Rip-off!" Ali's racist taunting of him was worse than ever. "First two fights, he tried to make me a white man," Frazier said. "Then he tried to make me a nigger."

"All night long, this is what you'll see," Ali told reporters, pulling a small black rubber ape from his pocket. He pummeled the toy. "Come on, gorilla. We're in Manila. Come on, gorilla. This is a thrilla."

"Ugly! Ugly! Ugly! [Frazier] not only looks bad! You can smell him in another country!" Ali would yell. "If he's champ again, other nations will laugh at us."

Impoverished Filipinos lapped it up. They had never seen such a show. Keenly studying Ali's appeal, Marcos said, "If he was Filipino, I'd have to kill him. So popular." Then he added, "That's a joke . . . of course."

"No nation can contain me!" Ali proclaimed. He reached even larger audiences now. Home Box Office, a brand new cable television station, began shipping its equipment to the Philippines, preparing to open a fresh broadcasting era. It became the first cable network to air a live sports event nationally using satellite technology.

Near the Araneta Coliseum, the site of the fight, morning sunlight strafed the stone walls of an old Spanish fort, revealing bullet holes and shadowy shell fragments left from the Second World War. The walls were like murals documenting the twentieth century's violent history. Nearby, the South China Sea quivered with a ship's wake in the day's rising heat. The air, especially inside the arena, would soon be unendurable. Pungent. Malarial. Rotten. Vendors, working out of jeepneys (old American army jeeps converted into food carts) sold pork and rice and sweet and sour chicken outside the arena and jacked up their prices on iced San Miguel beer.

Many in the crowd of twenty-eight thousand were used to watching cocks fight, rather than Black men.

Ferdinand and Imelda Marcos took their lavish chairs, seated like the monarchs they had replaced when Filipinos declared their independence.

Ali won the early rounds, nearly knocking Frazier out. Then Frazier rallied, "wedg[ing] himself under Ali's chest and . . . banging like a man trying to get out of a locked trunk," Jonathan Eig wrote.

"Lawd have mercy!' Bundini screamed from Ali's corner as the men murdered each other. Cigar smoke settled like fog in the ring. The stench of sweat was overpowering. Frazier's face absorbed sharp flurries, blows like staple-guns; he moved obsessively forward, a man numbed by rage. He twisted his punches into Ali's torso as if trying to scrape out his liver. Ali would sag, then shake back to life—where did the energy come from? Allah was surely stretching him to the limit. He smashed Frazier's eyes until, in round thirteen, both were about to close. Frazier could no longer see Ali's right fist when it came whistling round his head. A vicious hook sent Frazier's mouthpiece flying across the ring, glistening like the Mother Ship glimpsed from a misty distance.

In the fourteenth round, every one of Ali's punches—jabs, hooks—connected, bloodying Frazier's face. Frazier's head bounced like a tire on loose shock absorbers. He trudged ahead. Ali rolled his eyes heavenward, as if to implore his punishing God, *How is this creature still standing?*

At the end of the round, Ali, so exhausted he was falling asleep, told his corner to cut his gloves off. He couldn't go on. In Frazier's corner, a similar conversation was taking place. Eddie Futch, Frazier's trainer, had seen eight men die in the ring. He wasn't about to watch the ninth go down. Frazier couldn't see. He was going to stumble straight into death. "Joe, it's over," Futch said.

Unwillingly, Frazier quit mere seconds before Ali did. Ali rose from his stool, raised his arm, the survivor more than the winner. Then he collapsed, in a heavy faint, onto the canvas.

He would be pissing blood for weeks. He told Mark Kram, "I was thinking at the end, why am I doing this? What am I doing in here against this beast of a man? It's so painful. I must be crazy. I always bring out the best in the men I fight, but Joe Frazier, I'll tell the world right now, brings out the best in me. I'm gonna tell you, that's one helluva man, and God bless him."

Joe Frazier, his eyes just slits, was unable to see visitors to his room. "Who is it? Who is it? Turn the lights on!" he'd say. The lights *were* on. "Man, I hit him with punches that'd bring down the walls of a city," he told Kram. "Lawdy, Lawdy, he's a great champion."

Before journalists left the island and the Philippines vanished once more from the world's mental map, Ferdinand Marcos spoke an uncomfortable truth: "No matter what one says, Ali symbolizes success in [this] part of the world which sees white men as colonial. . . The old voices against colonialism are all over Asia again because of the Vietnam debacle, and Ali symbolizes a continuing protest against this racism and dominance because of color and birth. And while this may not be fascinating to the Western world, it is to Asians a highly charged matter."

In February 1978 Ali flew to Bangladesh on a "pilgrimage." He intended to spread joy and recognition to the young nation still struggling with its legacy of genocide and famine: "[I want to] help more people in the world know about Bangladesh. To draw attention to some of the positive things about [it]; so [many] negative things have been said."

The government—which had honored George Harrison as one who "stood next to us in our war of liberation"—made Ali an honorary citizen. Humbly, he said, "Thank you so much. Now if they kick me out of America, I have another home."

The twilight of Ali's boxing career sent his dependents scrambling for money, shelter, and support. Howard Cosell was not hurting. He held a secure position as a sportscaster for ABC, and he had achieved immense popularity as a color commentator each week on *Monday Night Football*. Still, the thrills of his professional life diminished along with Ali. As one of Ali's few public supporters during the trials of the 1960s, Cosell had become more than just a sportscaster. His voice had assumed political force. He relished being *relevant*. Sports? He could take the games or leave them.

There had never been a story like Ali. Cosell was convinced there never would be again.

Briefly, in 1975, Cosell made another bid to be relevant: he convinced ABC to give him a live weekly variety television show, modeled after Ed Sullivan's old revue. He wanted to book the kinds of guests that would have all of America talking the next day. "Get me the Beatles!" were his first instructions to his young staff. If he could reunite the Beatles, live, on national television, he would blow Ed Sullivan's ghost out of the ether. (Sullivan had died in October 1974.)

As fellow New Yorkers, Cosell and John Lennon had become acquainted at a few social affairs. Cosell met with Lennon one day at Manhattan's 21 Club. Lennon arrived wearing a black velvet jacket adorned with a diamond-studded "Elvis" pin.

"John, I want you guys on my show," Cosell informed him.

"What do you mean, 'you guys?'"

"You, George, Paul, Ringo."

Lennon hesitated. "I don't know, I don't know. After what's gone down, I don't know."

"Let's be realistic," Cosell said. "This is bigger than both of us. . . . Think of it, John. Imagine restaging the most electrifying moment in American television."

Lennon finally said no. It would never happen. Not even an offer of millions of dollars, a stadium arena, closed-circuit television, an album and movie deal could bring the Beatles together again. They weren't the same players. The past was past.

In the end, Cosell booked a now largely forgotten group, the Bay City Rollers, and attempted to convince his audience they were "the next Beatles." His variety show was canceled shortly afterward.

December 8, 1980, gave Cosell another shot at national relevance. That Monday night, along with Frank Gifford and Don Meredith, he was calling a football game between the Miami Dolphins and the New England Patriots. Meanwhile, in Manhattan, an accident and a coincidence were about to give Cosell the news scoop of his life. Alan Weiss, a news producer for WABC-TV in New York, was riding his motorcycle through Midtown when he collided with a taxi, injuring his leg. He was taken to the emergency room at Roosevelt Hospital on West Fifty-Ninth. An anxious clamor consumed the ER. Weiss saw police officers rush breathlessly through the halls. He overheard the name "John Lennon."

The Beatles' "All My Loving" was playing on the hospital radio.

Weiss was soon on the telephone to WABC. The station contacted Roone Arledge, head of national programming at ABC. The football game was about to go into overtime when Arledge called the broadcast booth. "Howard, I know you can handle this," he said to Cosell. "The country doesn't even know. They just shot John Lennon."

Minutes later, with a trembling voice, Cosell announced to the nation, "ABC News has confirmed that John Lennon, a member of the famed Beatles, maybe the best-known member, was shot twice in the back outside of his apartment building on the West Side of New York tonight. Rushed to Roosevelt Hospital. Dead on arrival. An unspeakable tragedy."

After a stuttering pause, he pronounced sports irrelevant at a time like this. He quoted John Keats: "My heart aches, and a drowsy numbness pains my sense."

Within days, Pete Hamill wrote:

> If you were there for the sixties, the ritual [processing the knowledge of a man with a gun having killed a public figure] was part of your life. You went through it for John F. Kennedy and for Martin Luther King, for Malcolm X and for Robert Kennedy. . . . We knew there would be days of cliché-ridden expressions of shock from the politicians; tearful shots of mourning crowds; obscene invasions of the privacy of The Widow; calls for gun control; apocalyptic declarations about the sickness of America; and then, finally, the orgy over, everybody would go on with their lives.
>
> Except . . . this time there was a difference. *Somebody murdered John Lennon.* Not a politician. Not a man whose abstract ideas could send people to wars, or bring them home; not someone who could marshal millions of human beings in the name of justice; not some actor on the stage of history. This time, someone had crawled out of a dark place, lifted a gun, and killed an artist. This was something new.

Yet as Susan J. Douglas, a communications analyst, pointed out, the Beatles, in spite of their "great spirit," had always intersected with the "subterranean recesses of hatred and paranoia" in the United States. She called Lennon a victim of America's "pathologies": the pathology of sexism, evident in the country's labeling of Beatlemania as female hysteria; the pathology of homophobia that evinced countless derisive comments about the Beatles' long hair; the pathology of religious fanaticism evident in the burning of Beatles albums under the sign of a lighted cross; the pathology of intolerance for dissidents in the FBI's persecution of Lennon for exercising free speech; and finally the pathology of gun violence.

As long as the four ex-Beatles walked the earth, there was always a chance they might come together again, rekindling the utopian ideals of the 1960s. But in Douglas's reading, American pathologies proved too strong, too immovable. Five gunshots rejected the 1960s once and for all. John Lennon was dead, and so were the Beatles.

Harrison's old mate had settled in New York because he could be himself there, he said. While he was still alive, fans gathered outside Lennon's apartment at the Dakota on West Seventy-Second Street, hoping for autographs, but they were generally quiet and respectful. The chaos of the past was gone, and Lennon could walk the city freely—something he had never known as an adult. He was forty years old. In many ways, he felt he was experiencing life—outside the Beatle bubble—for the first time.

On the morning of his death, he and Yoko Ono had posed for *Rolling Stone* photographer Annie Leibovitz: Ono fully clothed on a bed, Lennon, nude, clinging to her body, fetus-like, kissing her face. "You've captured our relationship exactly," he informed Leibovitz.

Later that day, he told an interviewer from San Francisco's RKO radio, "Maybe in the '60s we were naïve and like children and later everyone went back to their rooms and said, 'We didn't get a wonderful world of flowers and peace. . . The world is a nasty horrible place because it didn't give us everything we cried for.' Right? Crying for it wasn't enough."

Outside the apartment building, in the late afternoon, he autographed an album cover for an apparently shy young man named Mark David Chapman.

Lennon spent his last evening doing what he had always loved: playing, arranging, and recording music.

At 10:50 p.m., he and Ono returned to the Dakota. As he stepped out of his limo, he briefly noticed the young man who had asked for his autograph earlier. Lennon walked past him toward the building's entrance. "Mr. Lennon?" Chapman said. Before Lennon could fully turn, Chapman fired five shots from a .38 revolver into his back and chest.

Symptoms of Chapman's mental illness had included hearing phantom voices and identifying so strongly with Lennon that he signed the singer's name on his worksheets. Psychologically, for Chapman, the murder was also a suicide. He had loved the Beatles; he had believed in peace and love; he had worked with children as a YMCA camp counselor; he had once shaken Gerald Ford's hand when Ford was on the road campaigning; he had become disillusioned and had, in fact, shattered mentally when crying in the '60s didn't work.

Cosell's sources had pronounced Lennon dead on arrival at Roosevelt Hospital, but at least one of the ER doctors disputed this. He said Lennon was still alive when the paramedics rolled him in on a gurney. For several minutes the doctor massaged his heart.

The obscene, sadly unsurprising details were these: tabloid photographers gathered outside the emergency room, hoping to catch a money shot of the bullet holes in John Lennon's body. A female news anchor burst into the ER with cameras and lights and microphones and screamed that her First Amendment rights were being violated by doctors who refused to let her film the resuscitation attempts. An orderly stepped outside to address a few fans lighting candles on the sidewalk. "You want me to tell you what happened, man?" he said. "Where's twenty dollars? Come on. Why should I be doing anything for you for nothing?"

A curious detail was this: four blocks from the hospital, at West Fifty-Fifth Street, was New York's Hare Krishna temple. Two devotees, Bakula and Surottama, had welcomed into the world that morning a baby daughter, Shringara. By mid-afternoon Shringara had developed a cough. To be on the safe side, the couple asked another devotee, a young woman named Keshiha, to drive them to Roosevelt's emergency room. A nurse began to examine their baby but then she was called out of the room to attend Lennon. In the years since that night, the facts have blurred: one story says Ono spotted Surottama and said hopefully to her dying husband, "John, the Hare Krishnas are here." Another story says the last sounds Lennon ever heard were the lilting, whispered syllables of the Hare Krishna chant.

George Harrison was awakened at 5:00 a.m., at Friar Park, by Olivia Arias, now Olivia Harrison, who had heard the news of Lennon's murder from Harrison's sister Louise. Louise had phoned from the United States. It took the full morning for the news to sink in.

Derek Taylor, the Beatles' old PR manager, called to say, "George, maybe you should make some sort of statement [to the press], just to get the bastards off your back."

"I can't now. Later, maybe," Harrison replied.

A crowd began to gather and sing outside the gates of his house. Harrison stood alone at a window watching a ring of bobbies link arms to keep people back. He admitted later that, from that moment on, traveling anywhere in public, he'd always wonder "which person might have a gun."

Weeks later, he told an interviewer, "[John and I] saw beyond each other's physical bodies. If you can't feel the spirit of some friend who's been that close, then what chance have you got to feel the spirit of Christ or Buddha or whatever else you may be interested in? . . . I believe what it says in the scriptures and the *Bhagavad-gita*: 'Never was there a time when you did not exist, and there will never be a time when you cease to exist.' The only thing that changes is our bodily condition. . . . I feel him around here."

On the day he had heard the awful news, Harrison, in his home studio, turned to a few of his friends. Quietly, he said, "I just wanted to be in a band. Here we are twenty years later, and some whack job has just shot my mate. I just wanted to play guitar in a band."

He withdrew from public view. He preferred staying home pruning magnolia trees or planting jasmine bushes. In India, nature was considered God's "universal form," and Harrison approached his garden as though he were its servant. He themed certain sections of the property, devoting areas to Japanese or Hawaiian plant species, but his greatest pleasure came in nourishing flowers he saw blooming spontaneously and in cultivating contrasting colors in thickets appearing to grow wild. Sometimes he would garden by moonlight to see his lawns from a different perspective.

One night in the spring of 1978, Harrison had awakened to blue and gold light glowing intensely in his room. From out of the glow his father appeared. Later, Harrison would describe the experience as a vision more than a dream. His father gazed at him lovingly and then said good-bye. The following day, Harry Harrison died of emphysema at the home his son had bought for him.

The grief was mitigated, somewhat, by the birth of Harrison's son three months later, on August 1, in the Princess Christian's Nursery in Windsor. He and Olivia named their boy Dhani, after a pair of notes in the Indian musical scale: *Sa-Ri-Ga-Ma-Pa-DHA-NI-Sa.*

For the longest time, Dhani knew little about his father's life as a musician. "I was pretty sure he was just a gardener," Dhani said.

My friends would . . . end up back at my house . . . and it would be like around twilight on a Saturday night, and we'd find my dad somewhere in the garden. Sooner or later it would turn into . . . five teenagers sitting there, listening to him lay things down in a very Obi-Wan kind of way. He had that kind of gravity to him. You know, you didn't mess with him. He was tough but he was also like a father to everyone that I knew. It came with his life experience . . . years and years of just the weirdest life that anyone could imagine, and with that came great wisdom. He would sit there and before long it would be like some sort of Jedi Master class. . . He wouldn't talk about stuff that other parents would talk about. He would talk about miracles and yogis and levitation and flying and astral projection. That, to him, was not in any way weird. But, of course, the *Star Wars* generation, for us that was just great. That was just brilliant. So all my friends would love coming over and hanging out, listening to the crazy old wizard in the garden.

On September 2, 1978, when Dhani was one month old, Harrison married Olivia Arias at Friar Park, in front of her parents and a handful of local friends. Mariachi music played on the jukebox.

Four months earlier, Pattie Boyd had married Eric Clapton (despite her well-founded fears that his alcoholism would undermine their marriage). The couple held a reception in Clapton's backyard garden. Harrison and Boyd remained on good terms—he referred to himself as the husband-in-law. Paul McCartney, Ringo Starr, and Harrison joined Elton John, David Bowie, and Clapton in a drunken jam—the first time the three ex-Beatles had performed together since 1969. (They had recently turned down a $100 million offer to reunite for a single concert. "It's trying to put responsibility for making the world a wonderful world again onto the Beatles," Harrison had said. "I think that's unfair.")

George Harrison and Muhammad Ali met one last time in 1988, at New York's Waldorf Astoria Hotel on the night the Beatles were inducted into the Rock and Roll Hall of Fame. Ali sat stiff and mostly silent, enjoying the public outing, a rare occasion for him because of his physical infirmities by then. Harrison and Ringo Starr represented the Beatles. McCartney refused to attend the ceremony, citing ongoing business disputes with his former mates.

Starr was mildly drunk, unable to give a fully coherent speech. This left Harrison to mark the occasion properly. At the podium, accepting the honor, he said, "I don't need to say much because I'm the Quiet Beatle." Graciously, he said he loved McCartney and was sorry he wasn't there. "We all know why John isn't here." He gave a nod to Ali (after being prompted by Ringo: "Don't forget Muhammad Ali"): "We won't forget Muhammad Ali. He picked us up in Miami Beach one day."

Harrison noted how strange it was to speak for the group: "All that's left, I'm afraid."

☼

Why did millions of Americans, and many more people around the world (three and a half billion, according to some estimates) weep when Muhammad Ali, dressed in white, his face stiff, his hands fluttering with Parkinson's, walked out of the shadows in Atlanta on July 19, 1996? It was the opening ceremonies of the Olympic Games, and the venue was the Centennial Olympic Stadium, built for the occasion. Children ran through the stands, waving paper-mâché doves. Echoes of Martin Luther King Jr.'s "I Have a Dream" speech, piped through the stadium speakers, rang in the air.

Ali gripped the Olympic torch. He struggled to keep his arm steady so he wouldn't burn himself. With this spark, cherished the world over, he would light the sacred flame and declare the Games open.

People wept not because fifteen years had passed since his last sad fight against Trevor Berbick in the Bahamas—a fight no one had wanted him to fight, a fight so poorly organized that his trainer was forced, at the last minute, to airlift Ali's left-behind gloves from Miami. The ring bell had to be shanghaied from a fat cow grazing in a weedy field. Almost nobody had seen that fight.

His late career had been "an exercise in torpor not to be believed," said Howard Cosell. Watching him was like witnessing a man being murdered in slow motion.

Herbert Muhammad's unreliable doctors had misdiagnosed Ali as suffering from pesticide poisoning, then from a hyperthyroid condition, for which the doctors prescribed medications that left him severely dehydrated. The treatment's effects nearly killed him in the ring in his pathetic loss to Larry Holmes in 1980, which was actually Ali's first defense of the heavyweight crown he had regained two years earlier against Leon Spinks. Afterward, he had been tested again, this time by more competent professionals. They claimed he was suffering from Parkinsonism, a diagnosis later refined to Parkinson's disease, almost certainly the result of repeated blows to the head. Most Americans didn't know these details. They just knew that, in his increasingly rare public appearances, he barely moved and spoke slowly, unclearly. The Marvelous Mouth had become the Quiet One.

Since retiring, he'd had two more children, Hana and Laila, with Veronica Porché. Porché, unwilling to serve as his nurse, divorced him after talking him into nullifying their prenuptial agreement. Ali married Lonnie Williams and adopted a ninth child, Asaad, with her. He sold Fighter's Heaven and moved to Berrien Springs, Michigan, with Lonnie and Asaad.

All his kids got along. Jamillah said she never minded sharing her father with a passel of stepsisters and brothers: "We had to share him, anyway. We had to share him with the world."

Ali had buried his father in 1990, after Cash had collapsed in a Louisville parking lot, dead of a heart attack. He had buried his mother four years later, after she'd suffered a stroke. Odessa lingered for weeks in a hospital. He sat by her bed each day, whispering, "I love you, Bird. Are you in pain, Bird?"

He had buried Bundini Brown in 1987, after Bundini, intent on drinking himself to death, idle now that the champ was out of business, had fallen, incurring serious head injuries. Sitting next to Bundini in the hospital, Ali held his old friend's hand. "Man, just think, you're gonna be up there in heaven with Jesus and Shorty, Joe Louis, Jack Johnson, and all the great ones, and someday me, too," Ali said. "And you're gonna be walking up there on streets of gold and diamonds and rubies, like the Bible says." Bundini tried to talk, but Ali told him to lie still. He dabbed his face with a towel. "My turn to wipe *your* sweat off," he said gently.

Most Americans didn't know what was happening with Ali because most no longer considered him relevant—and because Ali had removed himself from the public gaze. After watching a tape of himself on the *Today* show in 1990 he said, "That man looks like he's dying. . . . If I was a fan, I'd be shocked." Lonnie tried to tell him he gave hope and inspiration to others suffering disabilities, but he wouldn't hear of it. He withdrew.

Unable to control his hands, he still tried to perform magic tricks for children, friends, reporters. Then, mumbling, he'd explain the tricks, insisting that his Muslim principles meant he couldn't deceive people. He said God had struck him with disease as a lesson for the world. We all age and die, even the greatest.

Then the Olympic Committee called. In 1960, the Olympics had been the site of his first world triumph. Now here was another shot at redemption.

Millions of people wept when they saw Ali in Atlanta because his condition *did* shock them. But then, as the crowd chanted, "Ali! Ali!" and he held the flame aloft with his right hand while his left arm shivered, shock gave way to a variety of emotions, primary among them nostalgia and admiration for his courage. Even most cynics, convinced this was a form of commercial packaging—yet another rehabilitation of Muhammad Ali for financial gain—admitted he was brave to reveal his weakness to the world, and to demonstrate his indomitability in spite of illness.

There was one dissenter. "I wish he'd fallen into [the flame]," Joe Frazier said, as bitter as ever. "If I had a chance, I'd have pushed him in."

"My God! That white shimmering figure! The hand trembling. Ali, again!" George Plimpton wrote, expressing majority opinion: Ali conquering his infirmities to unify the world. "It was just wonderful."

"Until that instant . . . Ali's legacy had not been fully considered," Richard Hoffer reflected. "Here he was, at the age of fifty-four, long past his prime, and he, now that we thought about it, still hadn't been defined. . . . No sooner had that [Olympic] cauldron caught fire than America, probably the world, realized what he'd come to mean to us. . . . We suddenly understood that the turbulence he'd imposed on us, and the punishment he'd accepted on our behalf, had been altogether necessary, good for us, actually." As tragic as his frailty was, "it was not humiliating. In his physical humility, he seemed prouder than ever."

George Harrison also experienced further moments of redemption. His creativity—especially his ability to help other people glimmer in the spotlight—turned to films. Working with members of the Monty Python comedy troupe, he established HandMade Films. The company wound up producing some of the finest independent British cinema of the 1980s.

In 1988 he scored the last number-one single enjoyed by any ex-Beatle. His hit cover of "Got My Mind Set on You" came from his album *Cloud Nine*. The album's songs were tasteful, layered with gentle guitar, seemingly effortless and therefore charming. Harrison was having *fun*. In the title track, he urged listeners to take his love, his hopes, his jokes . . . and if he wore thin, well, that was okay. He would accept that. The album was so popular that the US press referred to it as Harrison's comeback (he insisted he had never gone anywhere).

In the late 1980s, he enjoyed another round of critical acclaim, teaming with Bob Dylan, Roy Orbison, Tom Petty, and Jeff Lynne to record as the Traveling Wilburys. The songs were carefree, light, tributes to and parodies of every rock and roll riff these old pros could muster. Harrison played with a fluid ease only years of experience could impart.

Then Eric Clapton, divorced from Pattie Boyd, coaxed him into public performance, just as Harrison had urged Dylan back to the stage in 1971. Clapton suggested they do a short tour of Japan together: "Come on, George, you don't get out there in the trenches like the rest of us—you need to get out there and play." Harrison would have the support of Clapton's backing band, and Clapton to shore him up. "He was really scared to death," Clapton said. "He changed his mind about five different times."

Though Harrison worried about his voice, haunted by the '74 tour, the shows went well. Audiences were enthusiastic. This time around, he agreed to perform a generous portion of Beatles songs and not to mess with the lyrics. Keyboardist Chuck Leavell said, "He seemed very comfortable in his skin playing them," prompting speculation about 1974. *What if?* "It was very obvious that he liked being part of a band."

"Something," his love song for Boyd, was the crowd favorite each night. Onstage, during the tune, trading solos, he and Clapton smiled sadly at each other.

As the band traveled through Japan on bullet trains, Hare Krishna disciples appeared at various stations to honor Harrison. They handed food through the windows. "It was very touching," said Tessa Niles, a backing singer on the tour. "He didn't vocalize any of his [spirituality]. He didn't discuss it. He would light incense wherever he was. I think it was ritualistic, it wasn't about the smell. You just knew that this was something that he carried in him. He was *kind*, and I think I was thrown by that. We were employees [of his] at the end of the day, but he was so much fun to be with, and very empathetic."

Olivia and thirteen-year-old Dhani joined the entourage near the end of the tour. At the final night's concert, Harrison invited Dhani onstage with him to play "While My Guitar Gently Weeps" and "Roll Over Beethoven."

The experience had been so pleasant and successful, the band urged Harrison to tour Europe and the States again. "We were begging George," said Chuck Leavell. "'People would eat this up. We would work with you in a heartbeat.' He would just kind of smile and laugh and nod, but at the end of the day that wasn't what he wanted to do. We were terribly disappointed."

"[He] wasn't seeking a career," Tom Petty said. "He didn't really have a manager or an agent. I don't think he valued rock stardom at all."

Olivia felt he was still suffering post-traumatic stress disorder. "If you had 2 million people screaming at you, I think it would take a long time to stop hearing that in your head," she said. "George was not suited to it." During the 1974 tour, she said, "George talked a lot about his nervous system, that he just didn't want to hear loud noise anymore."

Also distressing to him was ISKCON's drift toward corruption following Prabhupada's death—a development he had feared. He had tried to warn Prabhupada about it. "I am always a bit skeptical about organizations and since the Swami died it does seem to be chaotic, with all kinds of guys thinking they're the gurus," he said. "To me, it's not important to be a guru, it's more important just to be, to learn humility."

Mukunda Goswami admitted that after Prabhupada's death, "[Many of the Swami's] leading disciples experienced personal and spiritual difficulties which, in many cases, increased in tandem with their power. . . . The movement suffered from the corrupt and errant leadership of some of Prabhupada's foremost disciples, a few of whom [got] involved in criminal activities. The children of Prabhupada's disciples suffered at the hands of unqualified, abusive teachers in the schools [and] numerous disillusioned devotees abandoned the movement."

Eager not to be bothered, not even by the Krishnas, Harrison bought properties in Hawaii and Australia, the edges of the world. "George was always on a quest to get as far away as he could," Olivia said.

"George would [tell me], 'Look, we're not these bodies, let's not get hung up on that,'" Tom Petty said. "[He] would say, 'I just want to prepare myself so I go the right way, and go to the right place.' I'm sure [he] got that worked out."

Since the 1960s, the Maharishi had been dogged by credible reports of womanizing. Meditation had become an obscenely lucrative business, often falsely advertised as providing benefits it could not deliver. Nevertheless, Harrison had always felt badly about the Beatles' abrupt departure from the Maharishi's ashram in Rishikesh.

In September 1991, he sought a conciliatory meeting with the Maharishi, whom he had not seen since 1968. He flew to the Netherlands where the Maharishi was staying. He bore a single rose for his old teacher.

The time for judgments was past.

"How have you been?" the Maharishi asked him.

"Some good things, some bad things," Harrison answered quietly. "You must know about John being assassinated."

"I was very sorry to hear about it."

After a pause, Harrison said, "I came to apologize."

"For what?"

"You know for what."

He asked if the Maharishi could forgive the Beatles' behavior. "We were so young."

The Maharishi smiled and said he remembered hearing that when the Beatles first appeared on *The Ed Sullivan Show* in 1964, there was no crime in the United States for that one hour. Everyone was glued to a television set. "When I heard this, I knew the Beatles were angels on earth. It doesn't matter what John said or did, I could never be upset with angels," he said.

Harrison wept.

"I don't need . . . money [now] and neither do the Beatles," Muhammad Ali told the *New York Daily News* on January 15, 1977, around the time he met John Lennon at Jimmy Carter's inaugural ball. Still, he had hatched a plan, along with his pal Joel Sacher, the New Jersey entrepreneur, to raise $200 million to establish an agency for "feeding and clothing the poor people of the world . . . and to help people develop a quality of the heart." The only cultural event with the power to jump-start such a grand effort was a reunion concert by the Beatles.

"If there was anybody in the world who could have pulled this off and reunited the Beatles, it was Muhammad Ali," Sacher said.

At the ball, Ali discussed his idea with Lennon. Lennon listened seriously. He didn't dismiss the thought. He invited Ali to visit his apartment at the Dakota. We'll talk it over, he said.

According to Sacher, many behind-the-scenes meetings took place over the next few months between representatives of the four musicians and the boxer. The Beatles' business affairs remained tangled because of Allen Klein. Nothing could happen quickly.

Ono was so enamored of Ali that she bought, one day, a stylized portrait of him by the painter Jean-Michel Basquiat. She displayed the painting on the wall of the Lennons' apartment in the Dakota. Titled *Cabra*, or "Goat" ("Greatest of All Time"), the canvas depicted a glowing bull's head shimmering against a deep crimson background. Ali had entered the realm of animal-spirits, deity-icons, *milagritos*, myth.

"More and more he is like a soul walking," said sports reporter Frank Deford.

By the time a lingering scrap of Beatlemania swept into Harrison's house intending to kill him, he had already decided that, apart from giving his son a father, he didn't have much reason to be here.

In July 1997, while gardening, he had wiped some sweat from the back of his neck and discovered a lump. In early August, surgeons removed several enlarged lymph nodes. They were malignant. Harrison returned to his garden, meditated, chanted, and played the ukulele.

A few days later, he received a visit from his old friend Shyamasundar. Shyamasundar called him "Dad" and joked that his own memory was shot: "I can't even remember how to tie my friggin dhoti."

Now, trying to sound casual, he asked, "What's all this about some cancer thing? I saw something in a newspaper."

Harrison pulled back his shirt collar to reveal the surgical scar. "You know, they told me at the clinic . . . they could cut it out, and I thought, Why bother? I don't really care about sticking around. . . . I mean—I didn't even want to tell anyone, just let it go. I had it removed, but really there's nothing, I mean, I've done it all, I've had it all."

He felt he had come full circle in recent years, returning to India, recording again with Ravi Shankar. He had bought Shankar a house in Encinitas, California, and looked after his old friend's health. He considered buying a house of his own in Southern California because he enjoyed meditating at the Self-Realization Fellowship, but he was put off one day, in 1992, while house-hunting with real estate agent Jeff Paiste. "He couldn't believe all the trash people throw out of their cars," Paiste said. "We were on the highway and saw a couch on the curb, then a chair, and then some busted up furniture. George looked really disgusted and said, 'You should drive the homeless around and pick this stuff up, furnish an apartment for them.'"

In the early '90s, Harrison collaborated with Paul McCartney and Ringo Starr to complete *The Beatles Anthology*, a lengthy film documentary presenting the band's saga from their point of view, accompanied by remastered recordings and rescued demos and outtakes. Relations had warmed. Watching old films, Harrison commented, "You know, Paul *was* a cute-looking guy, really, wasn't he?" But tension was never far from the surface. One day, McCartney overheard Harrison mixing a track in Friar Park. "Ah, that sounds nice, George. When the fuck did you learn to do all this?" he said. Harrison replied, "Remember me? I was second on the right."

He had written and recorded several new songs. Eventually he would put them out. No hurry.

In India, traveling with Shyamasundar and Mukunda, he'd done *kirtan* in a temple in Vrindavan, quietly chanted on his beads while the odor of incense mingled with wet forest smells wafting through windows after warm rain showers. At one point, he said, "To think that Prabhupada is right here." With his bead bag he wiped a tear. "Starting to get a little misty. . ."

He had drifted down sacred rivers, watching cattle graze on the muddy banks as the evening stars appeared, the sky full of swift satellites. Red-assed monkeys scampered through bamboo thickets, fields of blue flowers, trees with low-hanging limbs. In Vrindavan, trees were thought to be souls experiencing one last material incarnation before entering the spiritual sky.

In Madras, he and Shankar recorded a collection of traditional mantras. Shankar's hope was to create a meditative atmosphere for the listener, sounds of healing for souls made ill by the Western world. "This is our effort to achieve some semblance of balance," Harrison said. "There is something in this music that goes beyond any language. This stuff is so ancient that everything stems from it."

When they had completed the recording months later at Friar Park, calling it *Chants of India*, Harrison told Shankar, "Thank you for this music."

Then, on December 31, 1999, Harrison and his wife, in their upstairs bedroom, were awakened at around 3:30 a.m. by the sound of breaking glass. Harrison got up. From the top of the stairs, he saw a dark figure roaming the house. Later he would learn this was Michael Abram, a thirty-four-year-old heroin addict and paranoid schizophrenic who believed the Beatles were "witches." He was convinced that Harrison's chanting was "the language of Satan spoken backwards . . . [and that] such sorcerers should not be allowed to live." For days, Abram had been drinking in pubs in Henley-on-Thames, wearing a Walkman to submerge the voices in his head.

Abram had smashed a pair of tall French windows with a small statue from the garden. From another statue he had plucked a long steel lance. "You get down here!" he yelled at Harrison.

Olivia's mother was staying in the house. Dhani was sleeping in one of the lodges. Harrison feared what Abram might do if he didn't stop him. Chanting "Hare Krishna, Hare Krishna," he moved quickly downstairs and tackled the intruder. Abram had a six-inch knife. Repeatedly, he stabbed Harrison in the chest. "I can't believe after everything that's happened to me I'm being murdered in my own home," he later recalled thinking.

Olivia ran from the bedroom, picked up a fire poker and bashed Abram's head. He turned and seized her throat. Harrison, bleeding, jumped him. Abram stabbed him again. Olivia crawled across the room, grabbed a table lamp, and smashed Abram's face. Two police officers arrived, alerted by an alarm. They subdued the man. Dhani, awakened by the noise, ran to his father. Harrison was struggling to breathe, slipping in and out of consciousness. "Oh, Dhani," he croaked.

Paramedics arrived at 4:00 a.m. and worked on him for twenty minutes, stabilizing his blood pressure, attaching him to a saline drip. He had a punctured lung; one of the stab wounds had come within half an inch of rupturing a major blood vessel. He and Olivia were driven to the Royal Berkshire Hospital in Reading. Days later, Harrison joked that Abram "definitely wasn't auditioning for the Traveling Wilburys." His lung was permanently damaged. Air leaked from it, weakening his voice.

"Aren't you glad you married a Mexican girl?" Tom Petty faxed him.

His friends believed the attack, coming so soon after cancer surgery, took years off his life. "The trauma that George had, the break-in, nobody will know what that did," one said. "It was a dreadful, dreadful time. He never quite recovered."

In spite of the shock, "he was very positive," said Ken Scott, one of the Beatles' old sound engineers. "He had seen and completely understood his own mortality, and he was very comfortable with that."

Monty Python's Michael Palin, now a close friend, said, "He had become so serene. . . . There was precious little anger or blame. He'd changed."

He went into his garden and planted four hundred maple trees.

No one was really surprised when doctors at the Mayo Clinic found cancer in his lungs in March 2001. Soon a malignancy had spread to his brain.

He flew to Benares and bathed in the Ganges.

At Friar Park, "he was editing all this stuff he had done with the intention that Dhani and Olivia would put it all out," Emil Richards said. "He knew he was going, but he was working on music right to the end."

The songs released posthumously on an album he titled *Brainwashed* were a pop music version of the Bhagavad Gita, the journey of the self through a treacherous world toward spiritual salvation.

The last song he recorded, "Horse to the Water," featured anecdotes about foolish human behavior, built around the old bromide, "You can take a horse to the water but you can't make him drink." The song's prevailing sentiment was "You can expose people to wisdom but you can't make them wise." Harrison, the dark horse, did not exempt himself. On one level, the song was a frank admission that, in spite of knowing better, he had repeatedly done things harmful to his health.

His voice cracked, yet it remained poignant and clear. He copyrighted the song under the name "R. I. P. Music Ltd."

Klaus Voorman visited him at Friar Park before Olivia took him for cancer treatments at various medical clinics around the world. Harrison drove Voorman around the garden in a small golf cart. He was too weak to walk. "I listened . . . to his passionate speeches about the Canadian goldenrod, indigenous rhododendron bushes or the little bamboo forest that transported the visitor into a Japanese Zen garden. . . . It was like a botanical tour. He knew every centimeter of his estate," Voorman said. "After a while we came to a place where different types of grass grew that I had never seen before. George stopped the cart and looked at the softly swaying grass for a long time. After a while he turned to me. 'You know, it took many, many years until I understood that this grass has a special meaning to me. Somehow I feel connected to it. So when I'm not here anymore, then you just have to imagine me as a swaying sea of grass and I'll be close to you.'"

From Switzerland to New York, Olivia engaged specialists in differing treatments, including forms of fractionated stereotactic radiosurgery, a procedure focusing radiation beams directly on the tumors. The press hounded the couple wherever they went, despite major news stories requiring urgent attention: the 9/11 attacks, the drumbeat for another Gulf War.

"You'll be fine, Olivia, you'll be fine," Harrison assured his wife.

"Fine is okay, but it is not really good enough, is it?" she said.

One day, one of Harrison's doctors, Gil Lederman of the Staten Island University Hospital forced the desperately ill man to listen to his son play guitar and urged him to sign the instrument. "I don't even know if I know how to spell my name any more," Harrison whispered. Ledermen guided his hand: "Come on, you can do this."

In New York, Harrison said goodbye to his sister Louise, to Ringo Starr, and Paul McCartney. "He was *very* ill," Starr said. "My daughter had a brain tumor [at the time]. And I said, 'Well, you know, I've got to go, I've got to go to Boston [where she is], and he was . . . it's the last words I heard him say, actually . . . he said, 'Do you want me to come with you?' So you know, that's the incredible side of George."

With McCartney he laughed and cried. He held his friend's hand, gently rubbing the skin with his thumb. They joked about the time he'd lost his virginity in Hamburg with the other Beatles listening. "It was good. It was like we were dreaming," McCartney said. "He was my little baby brother . . . because I'd known him so long. . . . It's funny, even at the height of our friendship—as guys—you would never hold hands. It just wasn't a Liverpool thing. But it was lovely."

Harrison entered palliative care in Los Angeles at the UCLA Medical Center. To avoid press madness, he and his family secluded themselves on Heather Road at an undisclosed Beverly Hills house owned by Paul McCartney.

In 1966, Harrison had told an interviewer his goal in life was to "do as well as I can do, whatever I attempt, and someday to die with a peaceful mind."

He positioned pictures of Krishna and Rama in the room so he could see them from his bed. Olivia and Dhani surrounded him. Ravi Shankar played sitar quietly in a corner. Shyamasundar and Mukunda chanted. George Harrison passed away just before 1:30 p.m. on November 29, 2001. He was fifty-eight years old. Reportedly, his last words were, "Love one another."

"He was a giant, a great great soul," Bob Dylan said. "He inspired love and had the strength of a hundred men. He was like the sun, the flowers and the moon."

Muhammad Ali's final years involved a slower, more painful decline, but he never lost his humor, his delight in entertaining. He applied lessons learned in boxing to his daily circumstances: "It's what you can do after you're tired that counts in the ring," he said.

With visiting friends, he would pretend to fall asleep in the middle of conversations, prompting sad, whispered comments about his condition. Then he would jump up, startling everyone. He'd laugh: *Gotcha!*

He loved telling jokes: "What did Abraham Lincoln say after a four-day drunk? 'I freed the who?'"

He hid behind doors wearing fright masks, leaped out at his children, and lumbered after them as they ran through the house screaming and laughing. He ate all their vitamins at the breakfast table so they wouldn't have to. He showed them magic tricks and then said, "This is all deception. I'm doing this to teach you a lesson, and it is this: do not believe your eyes. There are people who will tell you lies and try to trick you, but you must always be on your guard."

He watched old films of his fights and smiled wistfully. "Wasn't I something?" he'd say.

He looked at old photographs of friends and colleagues—always lingering on one in particular. "That was Malcolm," he would say, "a great, great man."

Ali constantly made tapes of household conversations for his children. "These tapes are something I'm making because I am history conscious," he said. "We only come through this world once and we're only young once. We're only babies once, teenagers once, old men and old women, and then we die. But I knew it would be so beautiful . . . that one day you [my children] would be intelligent enough to appreciate that your daddy made all these tapes so you could hear them someday."

He made peace with his rivals. "George Foreman!" he barked into the phone one day, in one of the many conversations he recorded.

"Praise God, man! It's a miracle," Foreman said. He had retired from boxing (although he would make a middle-aged comeback, regaining the heavyweight crown in 1991). He had become a born-again Christian.

"How you doin', George?"

"I'm doin' just fine, man. I'm just thinking about you every day. . . . Can you please call me a little bit more?" Foreman said. Who could have predicted that, of all the fighters of his era—given his once-snarly demeanor—Foreman would turn out to be the sweetest? "You and I are closer than you think. . . . We're going to be old men and old friends together. You should call me up at least once every month, man."

Even Joe Frazier came around. Though at the time of his death in 2011 he still didn't like Ali, he had made amends. In 2002 the aging antagonists had attended the NBA All-Star Game in Philadelphia. Standing courtside while "America the Beautiful" played on the loudspeakers, Frazier gave Ali support, propping a steadying hand under his left arm. "We sat down and made up," Frazier told reporters. "Life's too short. He said his apology and I accepted it. Let's bury the hatchet, please."

Like Harrison, Ali became more and more serene. Once Hana took her father to visit her mother in Los Angeles. Nearly a decade had passed since Porché had divorced Ali, and she had remarried. At the door to her house, she hugged him, and then her eyes welled with tears. She rushed to a bedroom. "Why is she crying?" Ali asked.

Hana followed her mother. "Dad wants to know why you're crying," she said. "He might think you feel sorry for him or something."

"No, it's not that," Porché said.

"Then what is it?"

"When I looked in his eyes, I saw God."

He had always maintained his faith, but he admitted he had never practiced his religion with proper discipline until his illness humbled and frightened him. His beliefs continued to evolve. "The man who views the world the same at fifty as he did at twenty has wasted thirty years of his life," he said.

Most often now he studied books by Hazrat Inayat Khan, the great teacher of Sufi, often described as the mystical branch of Islam. "[My father] is more spiritual . . . than he's religious," Hana said. Khan stressed internalizing one's God-awareness, accepting all religions, all the names of the Lord, seeing past the world's illusory veils to celebrate the eternal. These beliefs brought Ali into harmony with George Harrison's views. Ali no longer prayed five times a day, Hana said: the ritual was hard on his body. But he followed the Koran's dictum to practice "submission, faith, and doing the beautiful."

In 2005 he received the Presidential Medal of Freedom from George W. Bush. In 2009 he attended Barack Obama's inauguration. His memory was starting to slip. One day he asked Hana, "Don't we have a Black president?"

"Yeah, Obama, remember? You were at his inauguration."

"Yeah, that's right. Tell Lonnie to get him on the phone and see if there's anything I can do to help with public relations."

In 2016, when presidential candidate Donald Trump called for a ban on Muslim immigration to the United States, Ali released a statement: "Speaking as someone who has never been accused of political correctness, I believe that our political leaders should use their position to bring understanding about the religion of Islam."

Ali spent less time in Michigan and most of each year in Paradise Valley, Arizona, near Scottsdale, where Lonnie's sister helped care for him. "Everything now is about protecting him and making sure he is healthy," Lonnie said.

In late May, 2016, at the age of seventy-four, he was hospitalized in Phoenix for a respiratory infection. Treatments did not help. On June 3, at the Scottsdale Osborn Medical Center, his family gathered round him. "Can he hear us?" Jamillah asked.

"Yes. His spirit can hear us," Hana answered.

One of the machines connected to his body began to chime like a bell between rounds. "That's your eight-count, Daddy! Now get your ass up!" Rasheda said. Everyone laughed. The doctors disconnected him from the ventilator. An imam named Zaid Shakir bent and whispered the call to prayer in his ear: "There is no God but Allah, and Muhammad is his messenger."

At 9:10 p.m., Muhammad Ali breathed his last, dead of septic shock.

"You're free now, Daddy," Hana said, stroking his hand. "You don't have to fight anymore."

He was buried in Louisville, his hearse passing enormous crowds chanting, "Ali, bomaye!"

Sometime after the press frenzy faded, Olivia and Dhani Harrison flew to Allahabad, India, to the intersection of Hinduism's three most sacred rivers, the Yamuna, the Saraswati, and the Ganges. There they scattered Harrison's ashes. Mohandas Gandhi's ashes had been released here in 1948. Every twelve years the Kumbh Mela, the world's largest religious festival, which Harrison had attended in 1966, opened where the rivers met. Allahabad was known as the Garden of God; the Yamuna's deep green currents spilled into the light blue ripples of the Ganges, flowing in two directions; while the mythical river, the Saraswati, mentioned in the Rig Veda, was said to erupt from underground, another realm entirely. Rare birds, the whistling teal and the lesser whistling duck, migrated here each year from China, Tibet, and Siberia, restlessly searching for a peaceful place in the world.

The idea of a Beatles reunion, brought about by Muhammad Ali, was still a tantalizing possibility as late as December 1980, when Mark David Chapman shot John Lennon outside the Dakota.

"Ali was devastated," Joel Sacher said. "Not the fact that we couldn't get the Beatles back together, but that another person could take [someone's life], such a talented individual. It had a profound effect on Ali. . . . Why? Why end a life like that?"

Just days before Lennon died, his lawyers filed an interesting legal document in a New York court. It was designed to block an unauthorized Beatle-themed Broadway show. In connection with the suit, Lennon had testified that he and his three former partners planned to perform again soon.

The night of the Jimmy Carter ball, Lennon felt tremendous delight seeing Ali. "It brought back such memories for [the two of] them," Sacher said. Ali was the only other person on the planet who understood what it was like to achieve the level of fame the Beatles had experienced. Lennon "couldn't stop talking about having met [Ali] in '64 and all that had transpired in the world since then. It was a moment in time you could never [re-create]."

But the fighter wouldn't stop trying. Said a beaming Ali, days after the gala—in what turned out to be a valediction—"It would be a personal joy to see [the Beatles] together again. The man who helps unite the Beatles makes a better contribution to human happiness than an astronomer who discovers a new star."

Notes

Prologue: "You Don't Ever Want to Die"

1   *It was an astonishing sight*: Pattie Boyd, *Wonderful Tonight: George Harrison, Eric Clapton, and Me* (New York: Three Rivers Press, 2007), 88.

2   *bears and monkeys*: Pattie Boyd, "Foreword: My Journey to Rishikesh with George," in Paul Saltzman, *The Beatles in India* (San Rafael, Calif.: Insight Editions, 2018), 6.

2   *"Kumbh" and "Mela"*: Nityananda Misra, *Kumbha: The Traditionally Modern Mela* (London: Bloomsbury Academic, 2019), 1–2.

2   *I remember sitting with Ravi*: Saltzman, *Beatles in India*, 7.

2   Bhang ti thandai: Oliver Crasske, *Indian Sun: The Life and Music of Ravi Shankar* (New York: Hachette Books, 2020), 317.

4   *I love the feel [here]*: Adam Kilgore, "How a Small, Mostly White Town in Pennsylvania Became Home for Muhammad Ali," *Orange County Register*, June 9, 2016, ocregister.com/2016/06/09/how-a-small-mostly-white-town-in -pennsylvania-became-home-for-muhammad-ali.

4   *Muhammad, are you afraid of dying?* Dave Kindred, *Sound and Fury: Two Power-ful Lives, One Fateful Friendship* (New York: Free Press, 2006), 193–94.

4   *I want to say something right now*: Samuel Osborne, "Muhammad Ali Death: The Boxer's Response When Asked What He wanted to Do When He Retired," *Independent*, June 4, 2017, independent.co.uk/news/people/Muhammad-ali-death -quotes-boxer-dead-aged-74-watch-answer-when-asked-about-retirement. I have quoted Ali speaking here, in 1977, but this was a practiced spiel he'd delivered for years.

5   *dishonor and dysfunction*: Richard Hoffer, *Bouts of Mania: Ali, Frazier, Foreman, and an America on the Ropes* (Philadelphia: Da Capo Press, 2014), 1.

5   *perfect Seventies symbol*: Charlie Haas, "Goodbye to the '70s," *New West*, January 29, 1979, 29.

6   *How can people consider Ali a historic figure from the 1960s?* Mark Kram quoted in Kindred, *Sound and Fury*, 317.

8   *As Ali noted*: see Hoffer, *Bouts of Mania*, 141–43.

One: The Quiet One and the Mouth

13   *It is not an overstatement*: quoted in Andreas Killen, *1973 Nervous Breakdown: Watergate, Warhol, and the Birth of Post-Sixties America* (New York: Bloomsbury, 2006), 13.

14   *You know your boss*: Liston cited in Bob Mee, *Ali and Liston: The Boy Who Would Be King and the Ugly Bear* (New York: Skyhorse Publishing, 2011), 57.

15   *Those boys really went at it*: Jonathan Eig, *Ali: A Life* (Boston: Mariner Books, 2017), 22.

15   *looked no better or worse*: Thomas Hauser, *Muhammad Ali: His Life and Times* (New York: Touchstone, 1991), 19.

15   *At twelve years old*: quoted in Eig, *Ali*, 23.

16   *baddest dude*: Eig, 36.

16   *This guy is such jerk*: quoted in David Maraniss, *Rome 1960: The Summer Olympics That Stirred the World* (New York: Simon and Schuster, 2008), 285.

16   *Television, money, and drugs*: Maraniss, xi–xii.

16   *increasing tension*: Maraniss, 347.

17   *Uncle Sam's unofficial goodwill ambassador*: Maraniss, 77.

17   *I know how far I can go back*: quoted in Eig, *Ali*, 37.

17   *He slept with it*: Wilma Rudolph quoted in Dave Zirin, "The Hidden History of Muhammad Ali," *Jacobin*, June 4, 2016, www.jacobinmag.com/2016/06/the-hidden-history-of-muhammad-ali.

17   *With the intolerance in your country*: Maraniss, 77.

17   *We got qualified men*: quoted in Mee, *Ali and Liston*, 41.

17   *To make America the greatest is my goal*: quoted in Zirin.

17   *They were very scruffy characters*: Bryan Wawzenek, "55 Years Ago the Beatles Make Their TV Debut," October 17, 2017, *Ultimate Classic Rock*, ultimateclassicrock.com/beatles-television-debut.

18   *We'd walk down Lilly Lane*: Iris Caldwell quoted in "Iris Caldwell," It's Only Love: Beatlegirls Website, sentstarr.tripod.com/beatgirls/caldwell.html.

18   *every single time*: Wawzenek, "55 Years Ago."

18   *We don't all speak like [the] BBC* and all other details of the Queen's Royal Variety Performance: Andrew Grant Jackson, "The Beatles Play for the Queen," *Slate*, November 4, 2013, slate.com/culture/2013/11/the-beatles-royal-variety-performance-when-john-lennon-told-the-queen-of-england-to-rattle-yourjewelry.html.

19   *One reason for [their] popularity*: Steve Greenberg, "How the Beatles Went Viral: Blunders, Technology and Luck Broke the Fab Four in America," *Billboard*, February 7, 2014, billboard.com/articles/news/5894018/how-the-beatles-went-viral-in-america-1964.

19   *popularity of transistor radio*: See Roger Handy, Maureen Erbe, Henry Blackham, and Aileen Antonier, *Made in Japan: Transistor Radios of the 1950s and 1960s* (San Francisco: Chronicle Books, 1993).

19 *juvenile and maddeningly repetitive*: Greenberg, "How the Beatles Went Viral."

20 *Who the hell are the Beatles?* Greenberg.

20 *On the plane over*: John Lennon, *Lennon Remembers*, ed. Jann S. Wenner (1971; repr., New York: Verso, 2000: 108–9.

20 *always knew exactly where he was going*: "Iris Caldwell."

20 *America's got everything so why should they want us?*: quoted in Geoffrey Giuliano, *Dark Horse: The Private Life of George Harrison* (New York: Dutton, 1990), 44. See also Philip Norman *Shout! The Beatles in their Generation* (New York: Simon & Schuster, 1981): 245. Norman attributes the line to Paul McCartney. Though the quote has been attributed to more than one Beatle, in a variety of sources, it seems most reliably to be Harrison's comment.

20 *We needed a fling*: Lester Bangs quoted in Greenberg, "How the Beatles Went Viral."

20 *an early indicator*: Simon Leng, *While My Guitar Gently Weeps: The Music of George Harrison* (Milwaukee: Hal Leonard, 2006), 12.

21 *"Don't Bother Me" felt like the spookiest song*: Greil Marcus, *The History of Rock 'n' Roll in Ten Songs* (New Haven: Yale University Press, 2014), 173.

21 *because he never thought he was any good*: Dhani Harrison quoted in Jayson Greene, "Notes You Never Hear: The Metaphysical Loneliness of George Harrison," October 13, 2014, Pitchfork, pitchfork.com/features/overtones/9522-notes -you-never-hear-the-metaphysical-loneliness-of-george-harrison.

21 *Whatever media you put [me] in*: Lennon, *Lennon Remembers*, 21.

21 *My father once said to me*: quoted in Greene, "Notes You Never Hear."

21 *naughty chords*: George Harrison quoted in Tony Frye, "The Harrison Sound: Naughty Chords," *Extra Texture*, accessed May 17, 2023, https://web.archive.org /web/20050315045109/www.freewebs.com/extratexture/thesignaturesound.htm.

21 *He looked very hard*: Greene, "Notes You Never Hear."

21 *It is just one voice*: Greene.

21 *to lift the spirits*: "How the Beatles Went Viral."

22 *The Beatles are coming* and *Get these Beatle wigs*: Greenberg, "How the Beatles Went Viral."

22 *If they ever submitted*: quoted in Greenberg.

22 *"Great," said Ringo*: Greenberg.

22 *Mr. Harrison, who is known as the quiet Beatle*: "Beatles Prepare for Their Debut," New York Times, February 9, 1964.

22 *Yesterday and today*: quoted in Greenberg, "How the Beatles Went Viral."

23 *there wasn't a single hubcap*: quoted in Greenberg.

23 *publicist's dream* and other Condon quotes: Hauser, *Muhammad Ali*, 44.

23 *Muhammad was never as talkative*: quoted in Hauser, 40.

23 *Man, how about shooting me*, quoted in Hauser, 40–41.

24 *It may not seem like much*: quoted in Hauser, 56.

24 *I'm a beatnik*: quoted in Hauser, 103.

24 *Cassius Clay is Hercules*: quoted in Hauser, 101.

24   *Maybe if we make enough personal appearances*: quoted in Hauser, 109.

25   *If the world was all sports*: quoted in Hauser, 111.

25   *Sonny Liston rather take off his sport coat* and other quotes from the Jack Paar Show: "Liberace and Cassius Clay on *The Jack Paar Show*," November 29, 1963, dailymotion.com/video/x8ukzq.

25   *You didn't have to push*: Hauser, *Muhammad Ali*, 36.

25   *Niño con boca grande*: Mee, *Ali and Liston*, 74.

26   *The hardest part of the training is the loneliness*: Mee, 57.

26   *trip around the world*: Eig, *Ali*, 40–41.

26   *Winning the World Light heavy Weight*: Eig, 82.

27   *Tell the boys to come over*: "Oh Yeah: Hanging with the Beatles in Miami in 1964," *Tampa Bay Times*, January 30, 2014, www.tampabay.com/features/humaninterest /oh-yeah-hanging-with-the-beatles-in-miami-in-1964.

27   *Are these motherfuckers*: Sonny Liston quoted in Hauser, *Muhammad Ali*, 63.

27   *loudmouth who's going to lose*: John Lennon quoted in Andy Greene, "Flashback: The Day Muhammad Ali Met the Beatles," *Rolling Stone*, June 4, 2016, rollingstone .com/culture/culture-news/flashback-the-day-muhammad-ali-met-the-beatles -153381.

27   *It was all just part of being a Beatle*: Beatles, *The Beatles Anthology* (San Francisco: Chronicle *Books*, 2000), 123.

27   *He claimed that he tricked the Beatles*: Robert Lipsyte, "Winner by Decision," *Smithsonian*, February 2004, smithsonianmag.com/arts-culture/winner-by-a -decision-106452969.

28   *capo di tutti capi*: Ferdie Pacheco, *Tales from the 5th Street Gym: Ali, the Dundees, and Miami's Golden Age of Boxing* (Gainesville: University Press of Florida, 2010), 49.

28   *I'm on my way to hell*: Willie Pastrano quoted in Pat Putnam, "The Death of a Fabled Fight Factory: The 5th Street Gym," December 6, 2004, *The Sweet Science* (International Brotherhood of Prizefighters), tss.ib.tv/boxing/articles-of-2004 /1419-the-death-of-a-fabled-fight-factory-the-5th-st-gym.

28   *Fifty cents, bub*: Pacheco, *Tales from the 5th Street Gym*, 55–56.

28   *I was unworthy* and all other quotes from Robert Lipsyte: cited in JP Finlay, "The Day the 60s Began—The Unbelievable Story of Muhammad Ali First Meeting the Beatles," NBC Sports, June 13, 2016, www.nbcsports.com/washington/other -sports/day-60s-began-unbelievable-story-muhammad-ali-first-meeting-beatles.

29   *Lennon said, 'I'm Ringo'* and subsequent Beatle quotes in this paragraph: Finlay, "The Day the 60s Began."

29   *Gateway to the British Empire*: George E. Curry, "Slavery Was Music to the Beatles' Hometown," *Black Voice News*, December 11, 2008, blackvoicenews .com/2008/12/11/slavery-was-music-to-the-beatles-hometown.

29   *The first known slave ship*: Curry.

29–30   *There was an honesty that we had*: Olivia Harrison, *George Harrison: Living in the Material World* (New York: Abrams, 2011), 15.

30   *just* gone: Bob Spitz, *The Beatles: The Biography* (New York: Little, Brown, 2005), 23.

30   *Britain declared war on Germany*: see Spencer Leigh, *The Beatles in Liverpool* (Chicago: Chicago Review Press, 2012), 14.

30   *Cold?* Quoted in Leigh, 21.

31   *Lord willing*: quoted in Giuliano, *Dark Horse*, 4.

31   *terrified that I was going to die next*: Graeme Thomson, *George Harrison: Behind the Locked Door* (London: Omnibus Press, 2013), 29.

31   *[Priests smelling of tobacco]used to come round*: Beatles, *The Beatles Anthology*, 26.

31   *Christ dragging his cross*: Beatles, *The Beatles Anthology*, 26.

31   *the darkness [really] began*: George Harrison, *I Me Mine* (San Francisco: Chronicle Books, 2002), 21.

32   *I had already made my mind up*: Harrison, 24–25.

32   *I had a really sore throat*: Beatles, *The Beatles Anthology*, 27.

32   *cheapo horrible little guitar*: Beatles, *The Beatles Anthology*, 27.

32   *Time wasted is existence*: "Picton Clock Tower," Wikiwand, https://www.wikiwand .com/en/Picton_Clock_Towers. See also Richard Pollard, *Lancashire: Liverpool and the Southwest* (New Haven: Yale University Press, 2006), 497.

32   *Would you pack in work*: Beatles, *The Beatles Anthology*, 44.

33   *was known to be a dodgy place*: Beatles, *The Beatles Anthology*, 45.

33   *I wanted to get out*: John Lennon quoted in Pete Hamill, "The Death and Life of John Lennon," *New York Magazine*, December 20, 1980, nymag.com/news /features/45252.

33   *naughtiest city in the world*: Thomson, *George Harrison*, 38.

33   *The Allies had relentlessly bombed Hamburg's shipyards*: See Alan J. Levine, *The Strategic Bombing of Germany, 1940–1945* (Santa Barbara, Calif.: Prager, 1992), 149.

33   *We were put in this pigsty*: Beatles, *The Beatles Anthology*, 46.

33   *All these gangsters would come in*: Beatles, *The Beatles Anthology*, 49.

34   *over nothing*: Beatles, *The Beatles Anthology*, 53.

34   *We all got our [sexual] education*: Beatles, *The Beatles Anthology*, 53.

34   *I certainly didn't have a stripper*: Beatles, *The Beatles Anthology*, 54.

34   *crappy suitcase*: Beatles, *The Beatles Anthology*, 55.

35   *Deliveries and Female Disorders*: Eig, *Ali*, 7.

35   *the darkest spot*: Eig, 3.

35   *He could beat on anything*: Eig, 11.

36   *Once he asked her*: see Eig, 16.

36   *Black lawyers would try to screw him*: Tim Shanahan, *Running with the Champ* (New York: Simon and Schuster, 2016), 170.

36   *They'll kill each other*: Eig, *Ali*, 29.

36   *I knew the kid was scared*: Eig, 30.

36   *you saw the two component parts*: Hauser, *Muhammad Ali*, 122.

37   *He used to ask me to throw rocks at him*: Hauser, 17.

37   *He was like a live chick*: Eig, *Ali*, 54.

38   *We're [getting] the fuck out of here*: Finlay, "The Day the 60s Began."

38   *But [then] some state troopers* and all other Lipsyte quotes: Finlay.

38   *Hello there, Beatles*: Eig, *Ali*, 135.

38   *Who were those faggots?*: Joey DeVille, "When Muhammad Ali Met the Beatles," May 15, 2010, joeydeville.com/2010/05/15.

39   *called McCartney the prettiest*: Eddie Deezen, "When the Beatles Met Muhammad Ali," *Today I Found Out*, February 11, 2014, www.todayifoundout.com/index .php/2014/02/beatles-met-muhammad-ali.

39   *Squirm, you worms!*: Deezen.

39   *The bigger you get*: John Lennon cited in Muhammad Ali, *The Greatest: My Own Story*

39   *You're not as dumb as you look*: Deezen, "When the Beatles Met Muhammad Ali."

39   *I am a man of destiny*: Muhammad Ali quoted in Randy Roberts, "Remembering Muhammad Ali," *Politico*, December 31, 2016, politico.com/magazine/story/2016 /12/obituary-muhammad-ali-greatest-boxng-214584.

39   *I don't know what it was*: Muhammad Ali quoted in William Nack, "Young Cassius Clay," *Sports Illustrated*, January 13, 1992, si.com/boxing/2015/09/23 /muhammad-ali-childhood-cassius-clay-louisville-si-vault.

39   *If you can't stand the world you live in*: quoted in Randy Roberts and Johnny Smith, *Blood Brothers: The Fatal Friendship between Muhammad Ali and Malcolm X* (New York: Basic Books, 2016), 19.

Two: Elijah and Malcolm

41   *He's the fifth Beatle*: Jonathan Eig, *Ali: A Life* (New York: Mariner Books, 2017), 134.

41   *Clay is a freak*: Hauser, *Muhammad Ali*, 67.

41   *Sonny Liston was a mean fucker*: Hauser, 58.

42   *A boxing match is like a cowboy movie*: Mee, *Ali and Liston*, 92.

42   *got[ten] out of hand*: Remnick, *King of the World: Muhammad Ali and the Rise of an American Hero* (New York: Random House, 1998), 147.

42   *[This will be] the most popular fight*: quoted in Mee, *Ali and Liston*, 16.

43   *manipulat[ing] odds*: quoted in Mee, 55.

43   *Saint v. Sinner*: quoted in Mee, 91.

43   *If the public will give me a chance*: quoted in Mee, 115.

43   *The leopard cannot change*: quoted in Mee, 121.

43   *muscular mass of menace*: quoted in Mee, 122.

43   *I want to reach my people*: quoted in Mee, 129.

44   *I watched Sonny*: quoted in Mee, 129.

44   *Some day they'll write a blues song*: quoted in Mee, 96.

44   *[Liston] is a man unafraid*: quoted in Mee, 115.

44   *insufferable . . . bullying*: Mee, 132.

44   *Colored people*: quoted in Remnick, *King of the World*, 23.

45   *He's got one of them bulldog kind of minds*: quoted in Remnick, 142.

45   *The big thing for me*: quoted in Remnick, 141.

45   *Come on out of there!*: Remnick, 142.

45   *fished off a street corner*: Roberts and Smith, *Blood Brothers*, 15.

45   *Why are we called Negroes?* Eig, *Ali*, 49.

46   *brainwashed*: Eig., 50.

46   *They musta fed him something*: Kindred, *Sound and Fury*, 43.

46   *My brother*: Eig, *Ali*, 86.

46   *I liked that cartoon*: Michael Tisserand, "The Cartoonist and the Champ," Comics Journal April 24, 2018, www.tcj.com/the-cartoonist-and-the-champ.

46   *fishing for the dead*: Roberts and Smith, *Blood Brothers*, 13.

46   *Why are we called Negroes?* Remnick, *King of the World*, 128.

47   *Anybody can sit*: Remnick, 129.

47   *How could a black man talk about the government?* Roberts and Smith, *Blood Brothers*, 65.

47   *Poke give me a headache*: Myron Cope, *Double Yoi!* (New York: Sports Publishing, 2016), 62.

47   *No, I'm not, not now*: Remnick, *King of the World*, 135.

48   *other side of the Cotton Curtain*: Remnick, 92.

48   *life might be better*: Elijah Poole quoted in Louis A. DeCaro, *Malcolm and the Cross: The Nation of Islam, Malcolm X, and Christianity* (New York: NYU Press, 2000), 28.

48   *Allah has proved to be very much of a human being*: November 9, 1943, Federal Bureau of Investigation file, "Allah Temple of Islam, et al, SELECTIVE SERVICE," vault.fbi.gov/Wallace%20Fard%20Muhammad/Wallace%20Fard%20Muhammad%20Part%201%20of%207.

48   *I asked Him*: Elijah Muhammad, *Message to the Blackman in America* (Chicago: Muhammad's Temple Number 2, 1965), 17.

48   *Negroes were Moslems*: vault.fbi.gov/Wallace%20Fard%20Muhammad/Wallace%20Fard%20Muhammad%20Part%201%20of%207.

49   *many [fanatical] beliefs*: "Chicago file #100–12899," vault.fbi.gov/Wallace%20Fard%20Muhammad/Wallace%20Fard%20Muhammad%20Part%201%20of%207.

50   *made like the universe*: Louis Farrakhan, "'The Wheel'—That Great Mother Plane: Allah's (God's) Calling Card," *Final Call*, December 11, 2013, finalcall.com/artman/publish/minister_louis_farrakhan_9/article_101093.shtml.

50   *cut off the head*: Kevin Baker, "Lost-Found Nation," Historynet, historynet.com/lost-found-nation.

50   *a racket*: Baker.

50   *Don't worry*: Baker.

51   *give life to the dead*: Muhammad, *Message to the Blackman in America*, 306.

51   *hypocrites*: Baker, "Lost-Found Nation."

51   *All members . . . were told not to register*: "Chicago file #100–12899," vault.fbi.gov
        /Wallace%20Fard%20Muhammad/Wallace%20Fard%20Muhammad%20Part
        %201%200f%207.

51   *patient . . . diagnosed*: Michael Lieb, *Children of Ezekiel: Aliens, UFOs, the Crisis
        of Race, and the Advent of End Time* (Durham: Duke University Press, 1998), 135.

52   *peculiar authority*: James Baldwin, *The Fire Next Time* (New York: Dial Press,
        1963), 78.

52   *Why, you have to be almost totally illiterate*: quoted in Jack Olsen, *Black Is Best:
        The Riddle of Cassius Clay* (New York: Dell, 1967), 148.

52   *And I looked*: Ezekiel 1:4, quoted in Lieb, *Children of Ezekiel*, 2.

52   *Without the failings*: quoted in Eig, *Ali*, 49.

52   *Detroit Red; Satan*: "Becoming Malcolm X: Incarceration and Conversion,
        1946–51," *Malcolm X: A Search for Truth*, Schomburg Center for Research in
        Black Culture, New York Public Library Online Exhibition Archive, web-static
        .nypl.org/exhibitions/malcolmx/becoming.html.

53   *subversive*: Manning Marable and Garrett Felber, eds., *The Portable Malcolm X
        Reader* (New York: Penguin Books, 2013), 75.

53   *In Bandung*: Malcolm X, transcription of King Solomon Baptist Church speech,
        November 10, 1963, The Autobiography of Malcolm X: Speeches and Interviews,
        ccnmtl.columbia.edu/projects/mmt/mxp/speeches/mxt26.html.

54   *You're not in Alabama*: Marable and Felber, *The Portable Malcolm X Reader*, 81.

54   *No one man*: Marable and Felber, 82.

55   *assist Castro*: Marable and Felber, 167.

55   *strongest link*: quoted in Peniel E. Joseph, *The Sword and the Shield: The Revo-
        lutionary Lives of Malcolm X and Martin Luther King, Jr.* (New York: Basic
        Books, 2020), 97.

55   *I am interested in him as a human being*: quoted in Joseph, 291.

55   *Malcolm X and [Clay]*: quoted in Roberts and Smith, *Blood Brothers*, ix.

55   *He's a fag*: quoted in Roberts and Smith, 151.

55   *swore by all that's holy*: quoted in Roberts and Smith, 162.

55   *I'm not mad*: quoted in Roberts and Smith, 164.

55   *I feel free*: quoted in Roberts and Smith, 107.

56   *I believe it's human nature*: quoted in Roberts and Smith, 106.

56   *[When] Cassius Clay declares*: quoted in Roberts and Smith, 105.

56   *violently anti-white*: Roberts and Smith, 159.

56   *determine . . . motives*: Roberts and Smith, 156.

56   *Our children were crazy about him; loved [Clay] like a younger brother*: quoted
        in Roberts and Smith, 157.

57   *tricky; diplomat*: Manning Marable and Garrett Felber, *The Portable Malcolm
        X Reader*, 291.

57   *done with him*: Eig, *Ali*, 132.

57   *nice, sweet kid*: quoted in Roberts and Smith, *Blood Brothers*, 163.

57   *In Cleveland*: quoted in Roberts and Smith, 164.

57   *Clay, through his association with Malcolm X*: quoted in Roberts and Smith, 172.

57   *My religion is more important*: quoted in Roberts and Smith.

58   *The hell I can't*: quoted in Roberts and Smith, 172–73.

58   *Revolution is bloody*: quoted in Marable and Felber, *The Portable Malcolm X Reader*, 263.

58   *I've just spent four hours with God*: quoted in Roberts and Smith, *Blood Brothers*, 128.

58   *Whenever sheep*: Joseph, *Sword and the Shield*, 151.

59   *circus; Toms*: Roberts and Smith, *Blood Brothers*, 132–133.

59   *he would not have been shocked*: Joseph, *Sword and the Shield*, 164.

59   *While King was having a dream*: quoted in Joseph, 164.

59   *I'm David*: quoted in Roberts and Smith, *Blood Brothers*, 108.

59   *I believed he was divine*: quoted in Roberts and Smith, 69.

60   *Be careful about mentioning Kennedy*: quoted in Marable and Felber, *The Portable Malcolm X Reader*, 274.

60   *That devil is dead*: quoted in Roberts and Smith, *Blood Brothers*, 143.

60   *The death of President Kennedy*: quoted in Marable and Felber, *The Portable Malcolm X Reader*, 279.

60   *chickens coming home to roost*: quoted in Marable and Felber, 275.

60   *the rise of the dark world*: quoted in Joseph, *Sword and the Shield*, 168.

60   *We with the world*: Marable and Felber, *The Portable Malcolm X*, 276.

61   *trying to crawl back to the plantation*: quoted in Roberts and Smith, *Blood Brothers*, 137.

61   *racial trouble*: Marable and Felber, *The Portable Malcolm X Reader*, 137.

61   *We are proud of [our] struggle*: Patrice Lumumba cited in Leo Zeilig, *Lumumba: Africa's Lost Leader* (London: Haus Publishing, 2008), 97.

61   *Lumumba [is] the greatest man*: "Malcolm X on Lumumba," www.hartford-hwp .com/archives/45a/459.html.

62   *I've been hearing about* (and following conversation): quoted in Roberts and Smith, *Blood Brothers*, 141–42.

62   *If you knew what the Minister did*: quoted in Roberts and Smith, 148.

63   *Hey, sucker* and all quotes in this paragraph: quoted in Roberts and Smith, 179, 180.

63   *This fight is the truth*: quoted in Eig, *Ali*, 138–39.

63   *To be a Muslim is to know no fear*: Roberts and Smith, *Blood Brothers*, 181.

64   *The final take*: Details about the closed-circuit broadcast of the 1964 Clay-Liston fight are drawn from Michael Ezra, *Muhammad Ali: The Making of an Icon* (Philadelphia: Temple University Press, 2009), 80–89.

65   *Dedicated to Peace*: Mee, *Ali and Liston*, 188.

65   *would [always] walk past a good girl*: quoted in Pamela Saldana, "Roulette with the Mob, Part I: Sam Cooke," *All Things Thriller*, allthingsthriller.com/2019/05 /15/playing-roulette-with-the-mob-part-i-sam-cooke.

65   *OOOO*: Olsen, *Black Is Best*, 150.

66   *Watch out* and other details concerning the water bottle: Remnick, *King of the World*, 187–88.

66   *somber and menacing*: Steve Ellis commentary, in Muhammad Ali, "Muhammad Ali vs. Sonny Liston (II) 1965-05-25," youtube.com/watch?v=S872eqTMtso (hereafter "1964 fight video").

67   *It's even money*: Eig, *Ali*, 144.

67   *This bout is under the auspices*: 1964 fight video.

67   *In fact, the VFW had nothing to do with the fight*: Mee, *Ali and Liston*, 166.

67   *He hit hard*: Hauser, *Muhammad Ali*, 74.

67   *He was the most perfect physical specimen*: quoted in Remnick, *King of the World*, 118.

67   *Liston hadn't trained properly*: Remnick, 177.

67   *The punches you miss*: quoted in Remnick, 194.

68   *I remember I came to my corner*: quoted in Remnick, 191.

68   *It was obvious*: quoted in Remnick, 193.

68   *Liston's eyes tip you*: quoted in Remnick, 190.

68   *The old champ*: quoted in Roberts and Smith, *Blood Brothers*, 188.

68   *Cassius went after Liston*: quoted in Hauser, *Muhammad Ali*, 75.

69   *I saw the blood*: Remnick, *King of the World*, 193.

69   *Liston is in desperate trouble!*: 1964 fight video.

69   *Come on, you bum*: Remnick, *King of the World*, 193.

69   *Sensation*: 1964 fight video.

69   *That left hand*: 1964 fight video.

69   *Liston had aged*: quoted in Mee, *Ali and Liston*, 195.

69   *He's got something in his eyes!*: 1964 fight video.

69   *trainers [were] dirty*: 1964 fight video.

69   *Cut 'em off!*; *This is the big one*: quoted in Remnick, *King of the World*, 195–96.

69   *He was ready to quit*: Hauser, *Muhammad Ali*, 76.

70   *This white man*; *looking to do a number*: Hauser, 77.

70   *Run!*: Remnick, *King of the World*, 196.

70   *Clay isn't putting up much of a defense*: 1964 fight video.

70   *Take a stiff tree branch*: quoted in Remnick, *King of the World*, 197.

70   *I was just trying to keep alive*: quoted in Remnick.

70   *[Clay] is playing around!*: 1964 fight video.

70   *Cassius can't see*: quoted in Hauser, *Muhammad Ali*, 77.

70   *Liston has got a scowl*; *the most . . . sensational*: 1964 fight video.

71   *It's all Clay*: 1964 fight video.

71   *That's it*: Remnick, *King of the World*, 199.

71   *an instant middle-aged man*: quoted in Remnick, 202.

71   *That wasn't the guy*: Hauser, *Muhammad Ali*, 79.

71   *Something has happened*: 1964 fight video.

71   *Police are lining*: 1964 fight video.

71   *I folded my arms*: quoted in Roberts and Smith, *Blood Brothers*, 193.

71   *It was all bullshit*: quoted in Remnick, *King of the World*, 201.

71   *I'm the greatest thing that ever lived!* and other post-fight dialogue: 1964 fight video.

72   *I tried to throw a left hook*: Remnick, *King of the World*, 202.

72   *Don't [people] know*: Mee, *Ali and Liston*, 191.

72   *Sonny's better off dead*: Remnick, *King of the World*, 202.

72   *one hundred percent*: Remnick, 211.

72   *Well . . . don't you think it's time*: Eig, *Ali*, 152.

73   *Sam Cooke had three beautiful young ladies*: Olsen, *Black Is Best*, 150–51.

73   *I'm through talking*: Eig, *Ali*, 153.

73   *I feel sorry*: Remnick, *King of the World*, 205.

73   *Card-carrying?* Eig, *Ali*, 153.

73   *Black Muslims is a press word* and continuing Clay quotes: Hauser, *Muhammad Ali*, 82–83.

74   *Most of the writers*: quoted in Hauser, *Muhammad Ali*, 83.

74   *The fight racket*: quoted in Remnick, *King of the World*, 209–10.

74   *conduct detrimental*: quoted in Remnick, 210.

74   *poor example*: Eig, *Ali*, 162.

74   *His parents were dismayed*: see Olsen, *Black Is Best*, 133–34; Eig, *Ali*, 109; Hauser, *Muhammad Ali*, 65.

74   *sport and play*: Eig, *Ali*, 156.

74   *nursing . . . like a baby*: Eig, 157.

74   *Jonathan Eig has determined*; *Comedian Dick Gregory*: Eig, 164–65.

75   *solidly in Malcolm's corner*: Eig., 157.

75   *I'm the champion of the whole world*: quoted in Eig, 158.

75   *It was "obvious"*: quoted in Roberts and Smith, *Blood Brothers*, 215.

75   *Malcolm X has cost him*: quoted in Roberts and Smith, 215.

75   *twenty-four hours before the match*: Mee, *Ali and Liston*, 203.

75   *I saw the Liston-Clay fight*: quoted in Robert Ecksal, "Sonny Liston's Lonely Hearts Club Band," Boxing.com, December 31, 2016, boxing.com/sonny-listons -lonely-hearts-club-band-htm.

76   *There is no doubt in my mind*: quoted in Mee, *Ali and Liston*, 194.

76   *I said I was the greatest*: quoted in Mee, 212.

76   *I don't like that name*: quoted in Eig, *Ali*, 161.

76   *I just want to do what's right*: quoted in Roberts and Smith, *Blood Brothers*, 216.

76   *This Clay name*: Eig, *Ali*, 158.

76   *That's a political move!*: Roberts and Smith, *Blood Brothers*, 218.

76   *He did it*: Eig, *Ali*, 159.

76   *I am stunned*: Joseph, *Sword and the Shield*, 175.

76   *They promised him a wife*: Remnick, *King of the World*, 214.

77   *Rudy considered this blasphemy*: Roberts and Smith, *Blood Brothers*, 217–18.

77   *stop seeing Malcolm starting today*: Roberts and Smith, 217.

77   *I don't want to talk about him*: Remnick, *King of the World*, 214.

77　　　*swift low-voiced chat*: Roberts and Smith, *Blood Brothers*, 237.

77　　　*We are brothers*: quoted in Roberts and Smith, 237.

77–78　*I am religious*: quoted in Roberts and Smith, 230.

78　　　*Nobody leaves the Muslims without trouble*: quoted in Roberts and Smith, 219.

78　　　*source of inspiration*: Roberts and Smith, 241.

78　　　*Who's the king?* quoted in Roberts and Smith, 245.

78　　　*I'm like Columbus*: quoted in Hauser, *Muhammad Ali*, 80.

78　　　*I'll remember that trip*: quoted in Hauser, 80.

78　　　*getting killed*: quoted in Hauser, 255.

79　　　*A brotherhood!*: quoted in Hauser, 247.

79　　　*colonial power*: quoted in Manning Marable, *Malcolm X: A Life of Reinvention* (New York: Viking, 2011), 317.

79　　　Omowale: Marable, 314.

79　　　*The next moment froze* and further details of Malcolm-Ali meeting: Roberts and Smith, *Blood Brothers*, 251–52.

80　　　*Because a billion of our people*: quoted in Remnick, *King of the World*, 216.

80　　　*I've lost a lot*: quoted in Roberts and Smith, 252.

Three: Ravi and Prabhupada

81　　　*full of bullet holes* and *crazy guys*: Harrison, *I Me Mine*, 41.

81　　　*I loved it*: Beatles, *The Beatles Anthology*, 147.

81　　　August 21, in Seattle: Felicks Banel, "Remembering the Beatles' Seattle Invasion in the Summer of '64," KUOW, KUOW.org/stories/remembering-beatles-seattle-invasion-summer-64.

81　　　*Till death*: quoted in Greg Lange and Alan J. Stein, "Beatles Play at the Seattle Center Coliseum on August 21, 1964," *HistoryLink: The Free Encyclopedia of Washington State History*, March 17, 2003, www.historylink.org/File/5435.

82　　　*There had been riots*: Harrison, *I Me Mine*, 39.

82　　　*I wake up*: Robert Wilonsky, "Officer Down," *Dallas Observer*, November 26, 1998, www.dallasobserver.com/content/printView/6401409.

82　　　*more scared here*: Donna Canada and Thomas C. March, "Dallas Press Conference—Datebook Magazine Story," June 19, 2012, *Meet the Beatles for Real*, www.meetthebeatlesforreal.com/2012/06/this-is-one-of-those-girls-who-let.html.

83　　　*Pigman met us*: Harrison, *I Me Mine*, 41.

83　　　Pigman heart attack: "Crash of a Lockheed L-188c Electra in Ardmore: 83 Killed," Bureau of Aircraft Accidents Archives, baac-acto.com/crash/crash-lockheed-1-188c-electra-ardmore-83-killed; UPI, "Pilot Involved in Fatal Crash Had Ailment," *Times-News* (Henderson, NC), May 14, 1966.

83　　　*It smells but it sells*: Fred Goodman, *Allen Klein: The Man Who Bailed Out the Beatles, Made the Stones, and Transformed Rock and Roll* (New York: Eamon Dolan/Houghton Mifflin Harcourt, 2016), 15.

83　　　*The artists never had any money*: quoted in Goodman, 19.

84　　　*You exist in this kind of vacuum*: Beatles, *The Beatles Anthology*, 147.

84 *We used to play clubs*: quoted in Martin Nethercutt, "How George Harrison—Who Had Strong Irish Connections—Was Far from the Quiet Beatle," *Irish Independent*, February 26, 2018, McCartney.com/?p=10896.

84 *okay as far as he was concerned*: Thomson, *George Harrison*, 88.

84 *The music was dead*: Lennon, *Lennon Remembers*, 20.

85 *Dylan had misinterpreted*: Lennon, 20.

85 *Because we were famous*: Lennon, 103–4.

85 *All these poor unfortunate people*: Beatles, *The Beatles Anthology*, 143.

85 *They gave their money*: quoted in Eoghan Lyng, "45 Years of George Harrison's Song, 'Crackerbox Palace,'" *Far Out*, January 24, 2022, faroutmagazine.co.uk/45-years-of-george-harrisons-song-crackerbox-palace.

85 *The Beatles and Elvis*: Boyd, *Wonderful Tonight*, 71.

86 *Modern, secular spectator sports*: Mike Marqusee, *Redemption Song: Muhammad Ali and the Spirit of the Sixties* (London: Verso, 1999), 271–72.

88 *fairy world*: Boyd, *Wonderful Tonight*, 18.

88 *I didn't resent his presence*: Boyd, 63.

88 *slave contract*: quoted in Eli Attie, "Did the Beatles Get Screwed?," *Slate*, March 4, 2013, https://slate.com/culture/2013/03/the-beatles-start-northern-songs-was-it-really-a-slave-contract.html.

88 *As an 18- or 19-year-old*: quoted in "Jan. 10: Only the Northern Songs, Part I," *They May be Parted*, https://theymaybeparted.com/2020/02/28/jan-10-only-the-northern-songs-pt-1, from *Billboard*, June 19, 1999, 77.

89 *Why don't you just leave us alone?* Thomson, *George Harrison*, 83.

89 *You see what you're doing* and *I haven't done anything*: Roberts and Smith, *Blood Brothers*, 290.

89 *I have no compassion*: quoted in Marable, *Malcolm X*, 419.

89 *Just tell [Malcolm]* and *I'm probably a dead man*: Roberts and Smith, *Blood Brothers*, 265.

89 *Any man who will go to bed*: Roberts and Smith, 264–65.

89 *that no good long-legged Malcolm*: Roberts and Smith, 230.

89 *Malcolm will soon die*: Roberts and Smith, 264.

89 *Malcolm should have been killed*: Roberts and Smith, 268.

89 *worthy of death*: Roberts and Smith, 281.

90 *Malcolm X and anybody else*: quoted in Douglas Perry, "17 Things You Didn't Know about Muhammad Ali: Book Reveals Brazen Infidelities, Malcolm X Attacks," *Oregonian*, September 29, 2019, oregonianlive.com/trending/2017/09/17_things_you_didn't_know_about.html.

90 *He'd be talking with you*: quoted in Roberts and Smith, *Blood Brothers*, 275.

90 Ameer: Roberts and Smith, 283.

90 *support fully*: "Malcolm X," Biography, Martin Luther King, Jr. Research and Education Institute, Stanford, California, kinginstitute.stanford.edu/encyclopedia/malcolm-x.

90 *You can't legislate goodwill*: quoted in Joseph, *Sword and the Shield*, 4.

90   *Well, Malcolm*: Joseph, 7.

90   *At the time, FBI reports*: ibid., 174.

91   *era in which we witnessed*: Marable, *Malcolm X*, 418.

91   *chickens coming home to roost*: Marable, 386.

91   *When you put a fire*: Marable, 413.

91   *I believe in one God*: quoted in Marable, 427.

91   *As long as you call it*: quoted in Charles Lewis Nier III, "Guilty as Charged:
        Malcolm X and His Vision of Racial Justice for African Americans through
        Utilization of the United Nations International Human Rights Provisions and
        Institutions," *Penn State International Law Review*:16, no. 1 (1997): 161.

91–92   *manifestations of racial bigotry*: quoted in Nier, 158.

92   *the United Nations shall promote*, Nier, 163.

92   *Negro problem*: quoted in Nier, 164n96.

92   *deliberately inflicting*: Nier, 175.

92   *Outline for Petition*: Nier, 179.

92   *covert action*: Nier, 183.

92   *Wa-Alaikum-Salaam*: Roberts and Smith, *Blood Brothers*, 294.

93   *Wake up, brother*: Roberts and Smith, 292.

93   *I don't feel right about this meeting*: quoted in Roberts and Smith, 294.

93   *They had the mentality*: quoted in Marable, *Malcolm X*, 430.

93   *Brothers and sisters* and next two Malcolm quotes in this paragraph: Roberts
        and Smith, *Blood Brothers*, 294.

93   *Hold it!*: Marable, *Malcolm X*, 486.

93   *I was there that day*: Ilyasah Shabazz, *Growing Up X* (Waterville, Maine: Thorn-
        dike Press, 2002), 24.

93   *Noise and screaming*: quoted in Shabazz, 30–31.

93   *Are they going to kill everyone?* Marable, *Malcolm X*, 439.

93   *They're killing my husband!*: Roberts and Smith, *Blood Brothers*, 245.

94   *Thomas Hagan*: Roberts and Smith, 261.

94   *Butler and Johnson*: Roberts and Smith, 305.

94   *convergence of interests*: Marable, *Malcolm X*, 424.

94   *Socialist Weekly of the African Revolution*: Nier, "Guilty as Charged," 161.

94   *There ain't no goddam hope*: quoted in Roberts and Smith, *Blood Brothers*, 295.

95   fire in Ali's apartment: Roberts and Smith, 297.

95   *somebody started it on purpose*: Roberts and Smith, 298.

95   *I'm with God* and following quotes: Roberts and Smith, 298.

95   *Malcolm was a hypocrite*: quoted in Marable, *Malcolm X*, 457–58.

95   *Amen!*: Roberts and Smith, *Blood Brothers*, 299.

95   Ossie Davis eulogy: Ossie Davis, "Eulogy for Malcolm X," American Radio
        Works, americanradioworks.public radio.org/features/blackspeech/odavis.html.

96   *No white man*: Roberts and Smith, *Blood Brothers*, 301.

96   *Turning my back on Malcolm*: quoted in Adam Lusher, "Muhammad Ali's One
        Regret: Turning His Back on Malcolm X," *Independent*, June 5, 2016, www

.independent.co.uk/news/world/muhammad-ali-dead-dies-one-regret-malcolm
-x-a7066446.html.

96   *I wish I'd been able* and following quotes in this paragraph: quoted in Lusher.

96   *[My father] informed me*: Sam Pollard interview with Herbert Muhammad, June 4, 1989, Eyes on the Prize II Interviews, Washington University Digital Gateway Texts, digital.wustl.edu/e/eii/eiiweb/muh5427.0439.116marc_record _interviewee_process.html.

97   *I don't want you around the ring*: Roberts and Smith, *Blood Brothers*, 234–35.

97   *I delivered her picture*: Pollard interview.

97   *I wasn't impressed*: quoted in Hauser, *Muhammad Ali*, 114.

98   *I didn't know if he was serious*: Hauser, 115.

98   *Man, you don't marry*: quoted in Roberts and Smith, *Blood Brothers*, 272.

98   *Legally you still ain't married*: quoted in Hauser, *Muhammad Ali*, 116.

98   *She agreed to do everything*: Roberts and Smith, *Blood Brothers*, 273.

98   *I told him*: quoted in Hauser, *Muhammad Ali*, 130.

98   *wanted to control his entire life*: quoted in Roberts and Smith, *Blood Brothers*, 273.

99   *Woman, you're too wise*: Roberts and Smith, 273.

99   *tarnished the victory*: Roberts and Smith, 274.

99   *chance meeting*: Beatles, *The Beatles Anthology,* 171.

100   *lubricating routines*: Marci McDonald, "Swami Vishnu-Devananda Is Not Like You and Me," *Maclean's*, December 1, 1974, archive.macleans.com/article/1974 /12/1/swami-vishnu-devananda-is-not-like-you-and-me.

100   *[Vishnu Devananda] told me years later*: Harrison, *I Me Mine*, 47.

100   *whole Beatle thing*: Beatles, *The Beatles Anthology*, 171.

100   *The Beatles were [already] doomed*: I Me Mine, 39.

100   *See what you've done*: Thomson, *George Harrison*, 111.

101   *When I first consciously heard*: Beatles, *The Beatles Anthology*, 196.

101   *It does seem like he already had some Indian background*: Olivia Harrison, *George Harrison*, 244.

102   *I'm sure [Riley] thought*: Beatles, *The Beatles Anthology*, 177.

102   *going about ten miles an hour*: Beatles, *The Beatles Anthology*, 178.

102   *It was if we suddenly*: quoted in Mikal Gilmore, "Beatles Acid Test: How LSD Opened the Door to 'Revolver,'" *Rolling Stone*, August 25, 2016, www.rollingstone .com/music/music-news/beatles-acid-test-how-lsd-opened-the-door-to-revolver -251417.

102   *suddenly . . . the most incredible feeling*: Beatles, *The Beatles Anthology*, 177.

102   *There was a God*: quoted in Gilmore, "Beatles Acid Test."

102   *everything in the physical world*: Beatles, *The Beatles Anthology*, 179.

102   *I had this lingering thought*: quoted in Olivia Harrison, *George Harrison*, 190.

102   *[Muhammad Ali] once asked [me]*: quoted in Hauser, *Muhammad Ali*, 51.

103   *Since [Malcolm's] assassination*: quoted in Hauser, 110–11.

103   *There was a whole new atmosphere*: quoted in Hauser, 122–23.

103   *Cassius is about the cleanest thing*: quoted in Eig, *Ali*, 173.

103	*Why can't women*: quoted in Eig, 182.
104	*My wife and I*: quoted in Eig, 174.
104	*There ain't but one way* and other quotes from Ali-Liston press conference: Mee, *Ali and Liston*, 215.
104	*That damned fool*: quoted in Eig, *Ali*, 178.
104	*Blood is like champagne*: quoted in Gilbert Rogin, "Still Hurt and Lost," *Sports Illustrated*, November 16, 1964, https://vault.si.com/vault/1964/11/16/sonny-liston -profile-muhammad-ali-first-fight.
104	*almost tragic expression*: Rogin.
105	*I believe that sometime*: quoted in Hauser, *Muhammad Ali*, 124.
105	*I'm so beautiful*: quoted in Eig, *Ali*, 171.
105	*I slapped her*: quoted in Hauser, *Muhammad Ali*, 129.
105	*Don't worry*: quoted in Hauser, 184.
105	*I didn't like the way*: quoted in Hauser, 125–26.
106	*Maine is the land of the bear*: quoted in Mee, *Ali and Liston*, 242.
106	*I can't wait for this fight*: quoted in Mee, 244.
106	*They act like the Beatles are in town*: quoted in Mee, 247.
106	Zulu: Hauser, *Muhammad Ali*, 126.
106	Lewiston, Maine: Mee, *Ali and Liston*, 234.
106	Shelby, Montana: Jeff Welsch, "Once Red-Faced, Shelby Now Embraces 'The Fight That Won't Stay Dead,' and the Massive Stadium Built for It," April 18, 2020, *406 MT Sports*, 406mtsports.com/406sports/once-red-faced-shelby-now -embraces-the-fight-that-wont-stay-dead-and-the-massive/article_7888ddfe38 -87d5-56ad-99f6-a29089a5356e.html.
106	*We'd run at sunup*: quoted in Earl Gustkey, "Muhammad Ali: A Fix or a Fist?," *Los Angeles Times*, August 5, 2015, www.latimes.com/sports/la-sp-ali-earl-gustkey -19900525-story.html.
106	*The Negro has the fear put in him*: quoted in Paul Gallender, "'Phantom Punch'—Mystery Solved," Boxing.com, May 25, 2014, https://web.archive.org /web/20140530040516/boxing.com/phantom_punch_mystery_solved.html .
106	*They're coming to get* him, *not me*: quoted in Gallender, "Phantom Punch."
106–7	*He just didn't seem like Sonny*: quoted in Eig, *Ali*, 188.
107	*At the same moment Clay and Liston*: quoted in Mee, *Ali and Liston*, 249.
107	*All those police*: quoted in Mee, 251.
107	*poison gas bombs*: Roberts and Smith, *Blood Brothers*, 303.
107	*ugly*: quoted in Hauser, *Muhammad Ali*, 125.
107	*dawn's early light*: Mee, *Ali*, 257.
107	Robert Goulet; *Clay hit the wrong guy*: Allen Barrra, "Muhammad Ali's 'Phantom Punch on Sonny Liston Explored in New Book," *Chicago Tribune*, December 3, 2015.
107	*Are you sure*: Mee, *Ali*, 257.
107	*They come out of Chicago*: quoted in Mee, 252.
107	*We're in the front row*: quoted in Mee, 256.

108 *Did you notice the way Liston was sweating?* ChiTownView, "Muhammad Ali / Sonny Liston Controversial Second Fight," youtube.com/watch?v=DjNimg3DGuo.

108 *"The Phantom Punch"*: Gallender, "Phantom Punch."

108 *throwing Corn Flakes*: quoted in Eig, *Ali*, 191.

108 *Get up and fight, sucker!*: quoted in Roberts and Smith, *Blood Brothers*, 303.

108 *Liston still has reflexes*: ChiTownView, "Muhammad Ali / Sonny Liston Controversial Second Fight."

108 *It's over!*: Hauser, *Muhammad Ali*, 127.

109 *Fix!*: Eig, *Ali*, 191.

109 *Fake!*: Roberts and Smith, *Blood Brothers*, 303.

109 *He laid down* and dialogue with Rudy Clay unless otherwise noted: Eig, *Ali*, 190–91.

109 *Did I hit him?* Gallender, "Phantom Punch."

109 *ugly as a Maine lobster*: William Nack, "O Unlucky Man: Fortune Never Smiled on Sonny Liston," *Sports Illustrated*, August 22, 2014, www.si.com/boxing/2014/08/22/o-unlucky-man-sonny-liston-william-nack-si-60.

109 *left hook or a right cross*: 1964 fight video.

109 *You could have got up!*: Mee, *Ali*, 259.

109 *Tell her*: quoted in Mee, 259. See also Nack, "O Lucky Man."

109 *It was a perfect shot*: quoted in Mee, *Ali*, 259.

109 *I have a feeling*: quoted in "Muhammad Ali vs. Sonny Liston (2nd Meeting)," *BoxRec*, https://boxrec.com/media/index.php?title=Muhammad_Ali_vs._Sonny_Liston_(2nd_meeting)&oldid=609639.

109 *We learned*: quoted in "Muhammad Ali vs. Sonny Liston (2nd Meeting)."

109 *I was groggy*: Mee, *Ali*, 260.

109 *it was the way the fight had to go*: quoted in Gustkey, "Muhammad Ali."

109 *I was down but not hurt*: quoted in Hauser, *Muhammad Ali*, 128.

109 *I think Sonny gave that second fight away*: quoted in Eig, *Ali*, 191–92.

109–10 *He is inarticulate*: quoted in Nack, "O Lucky Man."

110 *You have never seen the real Muhammad Ali*: 1964 fight video.

110 *that lousy bum Clay*: quoted in Mee, *Ali and Liston*, 261.

110 *Come upstairs* and quotes in next two paragraphs.: Hauser, *Muhammad Ali*, 128–29.

110 *How [can] I stand by*: quoted in Eig, *Ali*, 196.

111 *You traded heaven for hell*: quoted in Hauser, *Muhammad Ali*, 129.

111 *They've stolen my man's mind*: quoted in Eig, *Ali*, 196.

111 *I just about went crazy*: quoted in Hauser, *Muhammad Ali*, 129.

111 *He went through hell*: quoted in Eig, *Ali*, 196.

111 *I know what it's like to be loved*: quoted in Hauser, *Muhammad Ali*, 131–32.

111 *I know what it's like to be dead*: quoted in Gilmore, "Beatles Acid Test."

111 *an all-out war zone*: Tracy Daugherty, *The Last Love Song: A Biography of Joan Didion* (New York: St. Martin's Press, 2015), 187.

112   *John and I had decided*: Beatles, *The Beatles Anthology*, 190.

112   *I'd take anything*: Beatles, *The Beatles Anthology*, 190.

112   *never get back home*: Gilmore, "Beatles Acid Test."

112   *We were all slightly cruel*: Beatles, *The Beatles Anthology*, 190.

113   *There were girls at the gates*: Dean Nelson, "Beatles Introduced to Ravi Shankar's Music at LSD Party, Byrds Singer Recalls," *Telegraph*, April 19, 2010, https://www
        .telegraph.co.uk/culture/music/the-beatles/7603772/Beatles-introduced-to-Ravi
        -Shankars-music-at-LSD-party-Byrds-singer-reveals.html.

113   *I had a concept*: Beatles, *The Beatles Anthology*, 190.

113   *I told him that there was nothing*: quoted in Gilmore, "Beatles Acid Test."

113   *For Christ's sake*: quoted in Gilmore.

113   *[Lennon] looked at me*: quoted in Gilmore.

114   *morbid and bizarre*: Gilmore.

114   *What do you think about God?*: Nelson, "Beatles Introduced to Ravi Shankar's Music at LSD Party."

114   *an orange and blue ass pit*: Colin Fleming, "Why the Beatles' Shea Stadium Show Was Even Greater Than You Knew," *Rolling Stone*, August 14, 2015, www
        .rollingstone.com/music/music-news/why-the-beatles-shea-stadium-show-was
        -even-greater-than-you-knew-227621.

114   *started zooming round the stadium*: Beatles, *The Beatles Anthology*, 188.

114–15 Details of Shea Stadium performance, unless otherwise noted: Spitz, *The Beatles*, 577–78.

115   *he who has taken shelter*: "A. C. Bhaktivedanta Swami Prabhupada," Wikipedia, https://en.wikipedia.org/wiki/A._C._Bhaktivedanta_Swami_Prabhupada.

116   *They fought, and so many died*: Satsvarūpa Dāsa Goswami, *Prabhupada, Your Ever Well-Wisher* (1983; repr., Watford, UK: Bhaktivedanta Book Trust, 2003), 12.

116   *But those difficulties*: Goswami, 17.

116   *Do not fear*: Goswami, 30.

116   *My dear Lord Krishna*: Goswami, 31–32.

117   *he looked like the genie*: Goswami, 59.

117–18 *I am an old man*: Goswami, 71.

118   *"Matchless Gifts"*: Goswami, 51.

118   *In the next twelve years*: Goswami, 1.

118   *little carvings and incense* and *"crummy-quality" sitar*: Beatles, *The Beatles Anthology*, 196.

118   *He knew that he would have ended up*: quoted in Ajoy Bose, *Across the Universe: The Beatles in India* (India Viking, 2022), 30.

118–19 *Working with [you]*: Bose, 25.

119   *grating fuzz-box and abrupt chord changes*: Ian Macdonald, *Revolution in the Head: The Beatles' Records and the Sixties* (1994; repr., Chicago: Chicago Review Press, 2007, 178.

119   *first classical Indian song*: Macdonald, 168–69.

119   *This was, after all*: Geoff Emerick, *Here, There, and Everywhere: My Life Recording the Music of the Beatles* (New York: Avery, 2007), 126.

120   *It features an E major drone*: Emerick, 163–64.

120   *We were at the point*: Beatles, *The Beatles Anthology*, 146.

120   *[the] sound was bad*: Bose, *Across the Universe*, 43.

121   *cram everything in*: quoted in Bose, *Across the Universe*, 43.

121   *Do not cling*: quoted in Bose, 43.

121   *ego-death*: Bose, 43.

121   *sound like the Dalai Lama*: Emerick, *Here, There, and Everywhere*, 8.

122   *lay down all thoughts*: Beatles, *The Beatles Anthology*, 210.

122   *The Indian drone*: Macdonald, *Revolution in the Head*, 192.

122   *Mr. Harrison*: Shiv Dayal Batish, "My Episode with the Beatles and George Harrison," *RagaNet*, raganet.com/Issues/3/beatles.html.

122   *came forward with folded hands*: Batish.

122   *awe and wonder*: Batish.

122   *unreal life*: Boyd, *Wonderful Tonight*, 89.

123   *It was so terrifying*: Boyd, 92.

123   *founder of Britain's Indian empire*: Boyd, 77.

123   *jolly and friendly*: Boyd, 65.

123   *We'd be in the same room*: Boyd, 81.

124   *guess who's coming?* Bose, *Across the Universe*, 52.

124   *Something clicked*: Ravi Shankar, *Raga Mala* (New York: Welcome Rain Publishers, 1999), 189–90.

124   *was very friendly*: Shankar, 189–90.

124   *Sound is God*: Bose, *Across the Universe*, 67.

124   *Ravi was my link*: Shankar, *Raga Mala*, 190.

124   *From the moment we met*: Shankar, 189–90.

124–25 *My goodness*: quoted in Bose, *Across the Universe*, 67.

125   *I told him*: Shankar, *Raga Mala*, 190.

125   *Ravi came to my house*: ibid.

125   *proper use of the pick*: Harrison, *I Me Mine*, 56.

126   *I felt strongly*: Shankar, *Raga Mala*, 190.

126   *Where do you think*: quoted in Ezra, *Muhammad Ali*, 64.

126   *An altercation with his father*: Leigh Montville: *Sting Like a Bee: Muhammad Ali vs. the United States of America, 1966–1971* (New York: Doubleday, 2017), 71.

126   *Come on, black man*:quoted in Montville, 30.

127   *An FBI memo*: Ezra, *Muhammad Ali*, 130.

127   *Spooktown*: Montville, *Sting Like a Bee*, 19.

127   *For two years*: quoted in Montville, 20.

127   *How many roads*: Montville, 20.

128   *I'd just like to let him know*: Montville, 21–22.

128   *Black Benedict Arnold*: Montville, 31.

128   *Not since A. Hitler*: quoted in Montville, 31.

128   *You got nothing against those Viet Cong*: quoted in Montville, 25.

128   *I am a member*: quoted in Montville, 23.

128   *makes as much sense*: quoted in Montville, 31.

128   *Those Vietcongs*: quoted in Ezra, *Muhammad Ali*, 99.

129   *First of all* and all other details of the Illinois Athletic Commission meeting: Montville, *Sting Like a Bee*, 36–37.

129   *[America's] a lousy country*: quoted in Gilmore, "Beatles Acid Test."

129   *Christianity will go*: quoted in Gilmore.

130   *We were the generation*: Beatles, *The Beatles Anthology*, 201.

130   *Epstein [has] always tried to waffle on at us*: quoted in Alan Clayson, *George Harrison* (London: Sanctuary Publishing, 2001), 196.

130   *You won't live*: Beatles, *The Beatles Anthology*, 216.

130   *We think about [the war] every day*: Beatles press conference, Japan, June 30, 1966, Beatles Interviews Database, beatlesinterviews.org/db1966.0630.beatles .html.

130   *hot/Catholic*: Beatles, *The Beatles Anthology*, 217.

131   *[Before long] we were woken up*: Beatles, *The Beatles Anthology*, 219.

131   *This is what happens*: Steve Turner, *Beatles '66: The Revolutionary Year* (New York: HarperLuxe, 2016), 381–82.

131   *Mania was going on*: Beatles, *The Beatles Anthology*, 220.

131   *freak show* and *Who fucking needs this?*: Spitz, *The Beatles*, 625.

131   *We're going to have a couple of weeks*: quoted in Jordan Runtagh, "Remembering Beatles' Final Concert," *Rolling Stone*, August 29, 2016, www.rollingstone.com /music/music-features/remembering-beatles-final-concert-247497.

132   *I'm pleased*: quoted in Montville, *Sting Like a Bee*, 41.

132   *robbing* and *You want to make a bum*: quoted Montville, 41.

132   *This whole thing has been disturbing*: quoted in Montville, 44.

132   *in deference to the many families*: Ezra, *Muhammad Ali*, 107.

132   *Outbursts over [Ali's] draft status*: quoted in Ezra, 109–110.

133   *They want to stop me*: quoted in Ezra, 111.

133   *The American press keeps me*: quoted in Montville, *Sting Like a Bee*, 55.

133   *Don't laugh*: quoted in Montville, 58.

133   *Boxing is nothing*: quoted in Ezra, 111.

134   *JOHN LENNON SAYS*: Spitz *The Beatles*, 627–28.

134   *What I said stands*: quoted in Spitz, 629.

134   *We have been Beatles*: quoted in Spitz, 631.

134   *Why can't we bring all this out*: Beatles, *The Beatles Anthology*, 223.

134   *What [Lennon] meant*: quoted in Spitz, *The Beatles*, 629.

134   *I didn't want to talk*: Beatles, *The Beatles Anthology*, 225.

134   *Look, you do realize*: quoted in Spitz, *The Beatles*, 632.

134   *I didn't mean to cause all this*: quoted in Spitz, 632.

134   *another little piece of hate*: Gilmore, "Beatles Acid Test."

134   *If I'd have said* and other details of the press conference: Spitz, *The Beatles*, 632–63.

135   *So this is where* and *Send John out*: Spitz, *The Beatles*, 634.

135   *We're known as a terror organization*: Jordan Runtagh, "When John Lennon's More Popular than Jesus Controversy Turned Ugly," *Rolling Stone*, July 29,

2016, rollingstone.com/feature/when-john-lennons-more-popular-than-jesus
-controversy-turned-ugly-106430.
135 *I will never forget*: quoted in Spitz, 634.
136 *My heart stopped*: quoted in Spitz, 635.
136 *mud hut*: quoted in Spitz, 637.
136 *Bring the GIs home now*: Montville, *Sting Like a Bee*, 102.
136 *War is wrong*: Beatles press conference, New York City, August 22, 1966, Beatles Interview Database, www.beatlesinterviews.org/db1966.0822.beatles.html.
137 *It's true*: quoted in Montville, *Sting Like a Bee*, 83–84.
137 *I'll die right now*: quoted in Montville, *Sting Like a Bee*, 85.
137 *I do not believe that*: quoted in Montville, 103.
137 *I . . . hope very much*: quoted in Montville, 106.
137 *It was clear from the start*: quoted in Spitz, *The Beatles*, 636.
138 *We've had four years*: quoted in Riley Fitzgerald, "Unearthed Interview Reveals the Beatles' Thoughts on Old Songs prior to Sgt. Pepper's," *Cosmic*, www.cosmicmagazine.com.au/news/unearthed-interview-reveals-beatles-thoughts-on-old-songs-prior-to-sgt-peppers-lonely-hearts-club-band.
138 *I haven't learned to play the sitar*: Beatles press conference, New York City.
138 *I've noticed that George Harrison*: quoted in Spitz, *The Beatles*, 676.
138 *Can I please* and other details of the Candlestick Park concert unless otherwise noted: Runtagh, "Remembering Beatles' Final Concert."
139 *puppet show*: Spitz, *The Beatles*, 640.
140 *Right—that's it*: quoted in Spitz, *The Beatles*, 640.

Four: Within You

143 *may have been the most momentous spiritual retreat*: Philip Goldberg, *American Veda* (New York: Three Rivers Press, 2010), 7.
143 *It just wasn't you*: Michael Lindsay-Hogg, dir., *Let it Be*, film (1970; United Artists, 1981).
143 *Jai Guru Deva, Om*: John Lennon, "Across the Universe," genius.com/The-Beatles-Across-the-Universe-lyrics.
144 *constellation of forces*: Goldberg, *American Veda*, 8.
145 *Despite more than fifty years*: quoted in Goldberg, 70.
145 *a handsome monk*: quoted in Goldberg, 74.
145 *Sisters and Brothers of America*: quoted in Goldberg, 73–74.
145 *The struggle to become . . . divine*: quoted in Goldberg, 74.
145 *the paragon of all monastic systems*: quoted in Goldberg, 79.
145 *God-consciousness, or the realization of God*: quoted in Goldberg, 113.
146 *spiritual India*: Goldberg, 118.
146 *I do not believe that sitar*: quoted in Bose, *Across the Universe*, 64.
146 *It was quite amazing*: quoted in Bose, 65.
146 *My heart melted*: quoted in Bose, 80.

147 *Ravi and his brother gave me a lot of books*: quoted in Doug Yurchey, "George Harrison and God," *World-Mysteries Blog,* January 26, 2013, https://blog.world-mysteries.com/guest_authors/doug-yurchey/george-harrison-and-god.

147 *Ravi used to say*: quoted in Bose, *Across the Universe,* 66.

147 *But I am a Hindu*: Bose, 66.

147 *My hips were killing me*: quoted in Bose, 75.

147 *hero of popland*: Bose, 75.

148 *I'm not pretending*: quoted in Bose, 76.

148 *All the great philosophers*: quoted in Bose, 77.

148 *I believe much more in the religions of India*: quoted in Greene, Here Comes the Sun, 68.

148 *bandwagon gimmick*: quoted in Bose, 70.

148 *Making love*: Bose, 78.

148 *To suddenly find yourself*: quoted in Bose, 80.

149 *They were polite*: quoted in Muzafffar Raina, "A Week with Ravi and George—Boatman Recalls Days Spent by the Musicians on Dal Shikara, *Telegraph India,* December 14, 2012, telegraphindia.com/india/a-week-with-ravi-george-boatman-recalls-days-spent-by-the-musicians-on-dal-shakira/cid/352904.

149 *The world is one family*: S. Shah and V. Ramanourthy, *Soulful Corporations* (New York: Springer, 2014), 449.

149 *Krishna . . . is always shown*: Paramahansa Yogananda, *Autobiography of a Yogi* (New York: Philosophical Library, 1946), 133.

149 *Let's develop alter egos*: quoted in Bose, *Across the Universe,* 106.

150 *Classes*: Mukunda Goswami, *Miracle on Second Avenue: Hare Krishna Arrives in New York, San Francisco, and London, 1966–1969* (Badger, Calif.: Torchlight Publishing, 2011), 6.

150 *There are eighty-four species*: quoted in M. Goswami, 17–18.

150 *Krishna's name*: quoted in M. Goswami, 50.

150 *Whenever a new musician*: quoted in Satsvarūpa Dāsa Goswami, *Prabhupada,* 93.

151 *STAY HIGH*: M. . Goswami, *Miracle on Second Avenue,* 88.

151 *But have you,* and subsequent conversation with Millbank members: M. Goswami, 87.

151 *"Slum Goddess of the Lower East Side"*: M. Goswami, 98.

151 *If God is so kind* and *You are daily killing*: quoted in M. Goswami, *Miracle on Second Avenue,* 71.

151 *If we want peace*: quoted in M. Goswami, 73.

152 *To systematically propagate*: S. D. Goswami, *Prabhupada,* 66–67.

152 *The main thing*: quoted in S. D. Goswami, 84–86.

152 *Hey, Buddha!*: S. D. Goswami, 91.

152 *Swami's Flock Chants in Park*: M. Goswami, *Miracle on Second Avenue,* 107.

153 *How can we change America?*: quoted in M. Goswami, 116–17.

153 *Thousands of people*: quoted in M. Goswami, 119.

153 George Harrison in an old issue of the *Oracle*: M. Goswami, 120.
154 *We were quite an assorted lot*: quoted in S. D. Goswami, *Prabhupada*, 107.
154 *The houses looked like match boxes*: quoted in M. Goswami, *Miracle on Second Avenue*, 148.
154 *Swami says even Ravi Shankar*: quoted in M. Goswami, 114.
155 *Hey, you're one of the Krishnas, right?*: quoted in M. Goswami, 153.
155 *You can speak something*: S. D. Goswami, *Prabhupada*, 116.
155 *I'd like you to sing aloud* and Ginsberg's subsequent remarks: M. Goswami, *Miracle on Second Avenue*, 154–55.
155 *This chant . . . will lead us to the spiritual world*: quoted in M. Goswami, 155.
155 *People didn't know*: quoted in S. D. Goswami, *Prabhupada*, 116.
156 *The ballroom appeared*: quoted in S. D. Goswami, 117.
156 *Om Vishnupāda*: S. D. Goswami, 116–17.
156 *Because I never lose my head*: quoted in Montville, *Sting Like a Bee*, 96.
156 *Look! There's another one*: quoted in Montville, 105.
156 *impressed by [Ali's] statements* and other Grauman comments: Montville, 117.
157 *Neither the fact*: Montville, 118–19.
157 *What's my name?*: Montville, 127.
157 *It was a kind of lynching; while thousands of our finest*: quoted in Hauser, *Muhammad Ali*, 165–66.
157 *Look at what was happening then*: quoted in Hauser, 157.
157 *If I put [Terrell] away*: Montville, *Sting Like a Bee*, 129.
158 *If what you say is true*: quoted in Montville, 131.
158 *I don't care what Muhammad told you* and following conversation: quoted in Montville, 133–34.
158 *I never thought of myself as great*: Hauser, *Muhammad Ali*, 171.
158 *We [Black people] weren't brought here*: quoted in Eig, *Ali*, 230.
159 King-Ali conversation and subsequent press conference comments: Montville, *Sting Like a Bee*, 137.
159 *Rather than have the American Dream slain*: quoted in Montville, 141.
159 *an instrument in the hands of subversives*: quoted in Eig, *Ali*, 249.
159 *Why should they ask me*: quoted in Ezra, *Muhammad Ali*, 125.
160 *Tell little children*: Kindred, *Sound and Fury*, 109.
160 *Tell all the fans*: quoted in Montville, *Sting Like a Bee*, 144.
160 *ten thousand men a month*: Kindred, *Sound and Fury*, 110.
160 *22.4 per cent*: Montville, *Sting Like a Bee*, 158.
160 *Gee Gee*: Kindred, *Sound and Fury*, 110.
160 *"We Love Ali"*: Hauser, *Muhammad Ali*, 161.
160–61 *You all look very dejected; Viet Cong don't scare me*: quoted in Montville, *Sting Like a Bee*, 153.
161 *It would lighten our trip*: Eig, *Ali*, 240.
161 *I kind of feel sorry*: quoted in Montville, *Sting Like a Bee*, 152.
161 *See that black man over there?* quoted in Montville, 153.

161   *You are about to be inducted*: quoted in Hauser, *Muhammad Ali*, 169.

161   *Cassius Marcellus Clay* and subsequent dialogue: Kindred, *Sound and Fury*, 111.

161–62 *Ladies and gentlemen*: PBS *Eyes on the Prize* transcript, "Ain't Gonna Shuffle No More (1964–1968)," http://www.shoppbs.org/wgbh/amex/eyesontheprize/about/pt_205.html.

162   *I strongly object*: Kindred, *Sound and Fury*, 112.

162   *unanimously decided to suspend*: quoted in Kindred, 113.

162   *Backed at home; My country, right or wrong*: quoted in Montville, *Sting Like a Bee*, 157.

162   *Mama, I'm all right*: quoted in Eig, *Ali*, 241.

162–63 Povich, Cannon, Collins quotes: Montville, *Sting Like a Bee*, 160.

163   *Your attorneys* and subsequent dialogue, Montville, 161.

163   Lyndon Johnson offer: Eig, *Ali*, 245.

163   *[Ali] has something*: quoted in Eig, 249.

163   Ali sketching an airplane crashing into a mountain: Kindred, *Sound and Fury*, 121.

163–64 Guyana, Egypt, Ghana, Pakistan, and Britain: Ezra, *Muhammad Ali*, 128.

164   *What bothers me is*: Ezra, 128.

164   *left-wing writers, alcoholics*; and *injustice on a historical scale*: Kindred, *Sound and Fury*, 113.

164   *Without so much as a hearing*: quoted in Kindred, 114.

164   *We need a national voice*: quoted in Kindred, 114.

164–65 Plimpton-Cosell conversation: Kindred, 114–15.

165   *flower-waving crowds*: Spitz, *The Beatles*, 702.

166   *Princess of Islam* and following two quotes: Montville, *Sting Like a Bee*, 175.

166   *Do you know who I am?*: Eig, *Ali*, 243.

166   *You're proud of this name?* Montville, *Sting Like a Bee*, 174.

166   *I certainly am*: quoted in Montville, 174.

166   *Clay? Is that like dirt and mud?*: quoted in Kindred, *Sound and Fury*, 121.

166   *If I had to be a man*: Montville, *Sting Like a Bee*, 174.

166   *You gonna butt the line?* Eig, *Ali*, 243.

166   *I wasn't interested . . . I wanted to mold him*, quoted in Eig, 245.

167   *I think [I] was a challenge*: quoted in Hauser, *Muhammad Ali*, 184.

167   *[S]he don't say nothing*: Hauser, 184.

167   *I liked it that way*: quoted in Hauser, 184.

167   *married a man with no job*: Eig, *Ali*, 245.

167–68 turbulent summer of 1967: Montville, *Sting Like a Bee*, 179–80.

168   Black Power conference: Montville, 181.

168   *The Beatles are here*: Boyd, *Wonderful Tonight*, 104.

168   *I went there expecting*: Beatles, *The Beatles Anthology*, 259.

168   *Everybody looked stoned*: Boyd, *Wonderful Tonight*, 104.

168   *It certainly showed me*: Beatles, *The Beatles Anthology*, 259.

168   *a better, more honest*: quoted in Spitz, *The Beatles*, 698.

168   *Paul needs an audience*: quoted in Spitz, 698.

169   *I thought Paul should have been quiet*: quoted in Spitz, 699.

169   *the plane went into a stall*: Beatles, *The Beatles Anthology*: 259.

169   *People who'd never thought about the war*: quoted in Eig, *Ali*, 250.

169   *What kind of America*: quoted in Eig, 250.

169   *You better get out of town*: Eig, 252.

170   *I'm a whore-runner*: quoted in Eig, 253.

170   *I was happy*: quoted in Eig, 253.

170   *The government had taken away*: Hauser, *Muhammad Ali*, 185.

170   *part German marching band*: Spitz, *The Beatles*, 676.

170   *To help us get into the character*: quoted in *The Beatles Anthology*, 248.

170   *At that time, EMI*: Beatles, *The Beatles Anthology*, 252.

170   *No, I won't be in it*: quoted in Robert Ecksel, "Sonny Liston's Lonely Hearts Club Band," *Boxing.com*, December 31, 2016, www.boxing.com/sonny_listons_lonely _hearts_club_band.html.

171   *They were going to melt old Sonny down*: Ecksel.

171   *I'd just got back from India*: Beatles, *The Beatles Anthology*, 242.

172   *nobody was really expecting . . . much of*: Emerick, *Here, There, and Everywhere*, 179.

172   classical music of Northern India: Peter Lavezzoli, *The Dawn of Indian Music in the West: Bhairavi* (New York: Continuum Books, 2006), 18–39.

172   *In the Vedas of the Hindus*: quoted in Lavezzoli, 17.

172   *raga . . . color*: Lavezzoli, 19.

172–73 *Technically . . . a raga lies*: Lavezzoli, 19.

173   *[My sitar training] really did help me*: Harrison, *I, Me, Mine*, 58.

173   "Oriental" folk themes: I have drawn from David R. Reck, "Beatles Orientalis: Influences from Asia in a Popular Song Tradition," *Asian Music* 16, no. 1 (1985): 86–89.

174   *prostitute's quarters*: Amit Chaudhuri, "Indian Classical Music, the Beatles and the Blues," *Guardian*, September 21, 2012, www.guardian.co.uk/music/2012/sep /21/indian-classical-music-darbar-festival.

174   *[George] really wanted to learn*: quoted in Lavezzoli, *The Dawn of Indian Music in the West*, 171.

174   *It became like a fashion*: quoted in Lavezzoli, 171.

174   *To me it is the only really great music*: quoted in "'Love You To' History," Beatles Music History, www.beatlesebooks.com/love-you-to.

174   *The session came out of the blue*: quoted in "'Love You To' History."

175   *"Love You To" remains the most accomplished*: Lavezzoli, *The Dawn of Indian Music in the West*, 175.

175   *boredom*: Emerick, *Here, There, and Everywhere*, 125.

175   *One cannot emphasize enough*: Reck, "Beatles Orientalis," 108.

175   *George barely even noticed*: Emerick, *Here, There, and Everywhere*, 180.

176   *Klaus had a harmonium*: quoted in "'Within You Without You' History," Beatles Music History, http://www.beatlesebooks.com/within-you-without-you.

176   *dreary*: Reck, "Beatles Orientalis," 108.

176   *They [had] jobs*: quoted in "'Within You Without You' History."

176   *carpet on the floor*: "'Within You Without You' History."

176   *It was very calm*: Emerick, *Here, There, and Everywhere*, 179–80.

176   *Indian music is written*: quoted in "'Within You Without You' History."

177   *The results were nothing short*: Emerick, *Here, There, and Everywhere*, 186.

177   *Thankfully he had the help* and two following Emerick quotes: "'Within You Without You' History."

177   *Finally, with the lights*: quoted in "'Within You Without You' History."

177   *Well, after all that long Indian stuff*: quoted in "'Within You Without You' History."

177   *I think he just wanted to relieve*: quoted in "'Within You Without You' History."

177   *He is clear on that song*: quoted in "'Within You Without You' History."

177–78   *a hallucinatory cabaret*: Reck, "Beatles Orientalis," 108.

178   *A few days ago two friends*: quoted in Reck, 113–14.

178   *Without going out of your door*: quoted in Reck, 114.

178   *South Indian temple hymns*: see Lavezzoli, *The Dawn of Indian Music in the West*, 183.

Five: Sour Milk Sea

179   *With "Sgt. Pepper's Lonely Hearts Club Band"*: Nick Scalera, "When Carl Bernstein Reviewed 'Sgt. Pepper," Boundary Stones: WETA's Washington DC History Blog, June 5, 2017, https://blogs.weta.org/boundarystones/2017/06/05/when-carl-bernstein-reviewed-sgt-pepper.

179   *The war in Viet Nam*: Richard M. Nixon, "Asia after Viet Nam," *Foreign Affairs*, October 1, 1967, https://www.foreignaffairs.com/articles/asia/1967–10–01/asia-after-viet-nam.

180   *The power structure*: quoted in Hauser, *Muhammad Ali*, 187.

180   *Putting the lectures together*: quoted in Hauser, 185.

181   *I was as close to him*: quoted in Montville, *Sting Like a Bee*, 187.

181   *No intelligent white man*: Hauser, *Muhammad Ali*, 188.

181   *Go home*: Montville, *Sting Like a Bee*, 186.

181   *No, brother*: Montville, 148–49.

181   *I ain't doing this* and *Yes, you are*: Montville, *Sting Like a Bee*, 186.

181   *Ladies and gentlemen*: quoted in Montville, 186.

181–82   *Whatever the punishment*: quoted in Hauser, *Muhammad Ali*, 187.

182   *Damn the money*: quoted in Hauser, 189.

182   *The speeches were important*: quoted in Hauser, 190.

182   *If you want to see a man at his best*: quoted in Hauser, 201.

182   Details and quotes from Alabama episode: Montville, *Sting Like a Bee*, 188.

183   FBI memorandum: Hauser, *Muhammad Ali*, 191.

183 *the last man on earth* and *aggressively oratorical*: Jill Hudson, "Muhammad Ali's 1968 'Esquire' Cover Is One of the Greatest of All Time," *The Undefeated*, May 31, 2017, https://theundefeated.com/features/muhammad-ali-1968-esquire-cover.

183 *Hey, George!*: quoted in Eig, *Ali*, 256.

184 *The world knows*: quoted in Hauser, *Muhammad Ali*, 193.

184 *We'd practiced*: quoted in Hauser, 183.

184 *My conscience won't let me*: quoted in Alexxa Gotthardt, "The Photograph That Made a Martyr out of Muhammad Ali," *Artsy*, November 7, 2018, https://www.artsy/article/artsy-editorial-photograph-made-martyr-muhammad-ali.

184 *cooperative news sources*: Taylor Branch, *At Canaan's Edge: America in the King Years, 1965–1968* (New York: Simon & Schuster, 2006), 735.

185 *Make sure you play*: Branch., 770.

185 *Martin Luther king dedicated his life*: quoted in Eig, *Ali*, 257–58.

185 *In this difficult day*: quoted in Eig, 257.

185 *Dr. King was my great Black Brother*: quoted in Eig, 257.

186 *the systematic exclusion*: Hauser, *Muhammad Ali*, 192.

186 *resulted in no prejudice*: Hauser, 192–93.

186 *I'm being tested*: quoted in Hauser, 193.

186 *Allah made men*: quoted in Eig, *Ali*, 262.

186 *If I go to jail*: quoted in Montville, *Sting Like a Bee*, 199.

187 *George is a few inches*: quoted in Gary Tillery, *Working Class Mystic: A Spiritual Biography of George Harrison* (Wheaton, Ill.: Theosophical Publishing House, 2011), 151.

187 *The mystery* inside *George*: quoted in Mikal Gilmore, "The Mystery Inside George Harrison," *Stories Done: Writings on the 1960s and Its Discontents* (New York: Free Press, 2008), 107.

187 *The way George is going*: quoted in Bose, *Across the Universe*, 193.

187 *I believe in reincarnation*: quoted in Dana Spiardi, "The Queen's Speech: The Beatles Are Turning Awfully Funny, Aren't They?," *Hip Quotient*, November 25, 2013, hipquotient.com/the-queens-speeech-the-beatles-are-turning-awfully-funny-arent-they.

187 *Once you take the vows*: quoted in Bose, *Across the Universe*, 121.

187 *[The Swami] never trained me*: quoted in Bose, 125.

188 *WHO WANTS INSTANT*: Bose, 129.

188 *The truth of Indian philosophy*: quoted in Bose, 129.

188 *[In] India in the 1950s*: Bose, 132.

188 *dance in a hurry*: Bose, 135.

188 *Americans are always interested in pills*: Bose, 135.

188 *richest girl in the world*; *life-destructive plant*: Bose, 140.

189 *fake gurus*: quoted in Bose, 19.

189 *I suppose we were so absorbed*: Boyd, *Wonderful Tonight*, 108.

189 *I had no misconceptions*: quoted in Bose, *Across the Universe*, 152.

189 *an apple on sale*: Lennon, *Lennon Remembers*, 37–38.

190   Details of Indian countryside drawn from Greene, *Here Comes the Sun*, 90.

190   *The group stopped for lunch*; *Accha*: Bose, *Across the Universe*, 189.

190   ashram description: Bose, 177.

190   *meditate with dysentery*: Bose, 183.

190–91   *The Beatles and hippies*: quoted in Bose, 11.

191   *stupid*: Bose, 13.

191   *Is it a new song, George?*: Greene, *Here Comes the Sun*, 91.

191   *Music is the highest form of education*: Greene, 60.

191   *Because of the conscious mind expansion*: quoted in Greene, 95.

191   *sparsely furnished*: Boyd, *Wonderful Tonight*, 114–15.

191   *John and George*: Boyd, 119.

191   *I had a strange experience*: quoted in Bose, *Across the Universe*, 211.

191–92   *The goal is really to plug*: Greene, *Here Comes the Sun*, 95–96.

192   *a decent guy*: quoted in Greene, 92.

192   *You can have everything in life*: quoted in, 93.

192   *It took you back to childhood*: quoted in Bose, *Across the Universe*, 211.

192   *We're not here to talk music* and *Calm down*: quoted in Greene, *Here Comes the Sun*, 95.

192   *I believe that I*: quoted in Greene, 95.

192   *there are bods [people] up here*: quoted in Bose, *Across the Universe*, 192.

193   *Kalladadi Samuda*: Harrison, *I Me Mine*, 142.

193   *suggestion of death*: MacDonald, *Revolution in the Head*, 323.

193   *what made the music of the Beatles*: quoted in Paul Saltzman, *The Beatles in India* (San Rafael, CA: Insight Editions, 2018), 100.

193   *My belief*; and *Until 1966*: quoted in Saltzman, 100.

194   *George didn't really want to learn*: quoted in Jon Solomon, "Donovan on Teaching the Beatles the Fingerstyle that Became the White Album," *Westword*, September 20, 2011, westword.com/music/Donovan-on-teaching-the-beatles-the-fingerstyle-that-became-the-white-album-8326737.

194   *under the tropical stars*: "Hurdy Gurdy Man," Donovan Unofficial, https://web.archive.org/web/20150314202338/http://donovan-unofficial.com/music/songs/hurdy_gurdy_man.html.

194   *This will do me*: Greene, *Here Comes the Sun*, 96.

194–95   McCartney feeling constricted: Bose, *Across the Universe*, 248.

195   *He's not a modern man*: quoted in Bose, 167.

195   *Look up at the sky* and *I got so excited* Bose, 254.

195   *Wild Orgies*; *Beatle Wife*: Bose, 198.

195   *He was a wicked man*: quoted in Bose, 262.

195   *[George and I] stayed up all night*: Lennon, *Lennon Remembers*, 27.

196   *Being a Beatle*: quoted in Bose, *Across the Universe*, 254.

196   *All Maharishi ever gave me*: quoted in Greene, *Here Comes the Sun*, 97.

196   *total bullshit*: Beatles, *The Beatles Anthology*, 285.

196   *As usual*: quoted in Bose, *Across the Universe*, 264.

196   *Wait; Talk to me*: Bose, 266.

196   *a lot of flakes*: Beatles, *The Beatles Anthology*, 285.

197   *We made a mistake*: Bose, *Across the Universe*, 278.

197   *cunt*: Bose, 266.

197   *I don't want to hear about it* and following conversation: Bose, 269.

197   *Western Communism*: Bose, 281.

197   *chaos waiting for him in England*: Boyd quoted in Bose, 269.

197   *great scribes; Year of the Guru*: Greene, *Here Comes the Sun*, 98.

197   *exchange for . . . teenyboppers*: quoted in Bose, *Across the Universe*, 159.

198   Details of Harrison's twenty-fifth birthday: Bose, 213–14.

Six: And in the End

199   mlecchas: S. D. Goswami, *Prabhupada*, 161.

199   *I am very much eager*: quoted in M. Goswami, *Miracle on Second Avenue*, 282–83.

199   *No matter*: quoted in M. Goswami., 292–93.

200   *First they ignore you*: quoted in M. Goswami, 294.

200   *It is understood*: Prabhupada to Shyamasundar, December 21, 1968: "George Harrison (Letters)," Vaniquotes, vaniquotes.org/wiki/George_Harrison_(Letters).

200   *So far [as] Mr. George Harrison is concerned*: Prabhupada to Mukunda, September 15, 1968, "George Harrison (Letters)."

201   *So. I hear Ginsberg's a friend* and following exchange: quoted in M. Goswami, *Miracle on Second Avenue*, 337–38.

201–2 *Hell's Angels*: quoted in Thomson, *George Harrison*, 141–42.

202   *These three [guys]*: quoted in Thomson.

202   *[And] I think George did it very well*: Beatles, *The Beatles Anthology*, 312.

202   *Just doing my job* and other details of Harrison-Shyamasundar meeting: Greene, *Here Comes the Sun*, 102–3.

203   *Stop showing your titties; all them niggers; baaaad, the man was immaculate*: quoted in Montville, *Sting Like a Bee*, 200.

203   *Yeah, I'd go back*: quoted in Kindred, *Sound and Fury*, 132.

203   *WE TELL THE WORLD*: Kindred, 133.

203   *I want the world to know*: Montville, *Sting Like a Bee*, 207–8.

204   *LET THIS BE A LESSON*: Montville, 209.

204   *It was terrifying*: quoted in Eig, *Ali*, 266.

204   *I made a fool of myself*: quoted in Kindred, *Sound and Fury*, 134.

204   *Boxing is temporary*: Montville, *Sting Like a Bee*, 209.

204   *Do you know these people* and subsequent conversation: Greene, *Here Comes the Sun*, 103–5.

205   *Yes, I remember your name*: quoted in M. Goswami, *Miracle on Second Avenue*, 339–40.

205–6 *closet Krishna; I always felt at home*: Mukunda Goswami, "George Harrison Interview: Hare Krishna Mantra—There's Nothing Higher (1982)," Krishna

.org, https://krishna.org/george-harrison-interview-hare-krishna-mantra -theres-nothing-higher-1982.

206   *Mr. George Harrison is sometimes coming*: Prabhupada to Shyamasundar, May 6, 1969, "George Harrison (Letters)."

206   *tackling very consistently*: Prabhupada to Shyamasundar, May 26, 1969, "George Harrison (Letters)."

206   *I am glad that your friendship*: Prabhupada to Shyamasundar, June 29, 1969, "George Harrison (Letters)."

206   *These monied men*: Prabhupada to Shyamasundar, September 19, 1969, "George Harrison (Letters)."

206   *It will cost nineteen thousand dollars*: quoted in Greene, *Here Comes the Sun*, 158.

206   *Swami, we must be very careful* and next four paragraphs: quoted in Greene, 158–60.

207   *You've got to record the mantra* and following three paragraphs: M. Goswami, *Miracle on Second Avenue*, 341.

207   *Repeat Until Death*: Olivia Harrison, *George Harrison*, 240.

208   *the biggest thing in London*: Prabhupada to Shyamasundar, June 11, 1969, "George Harrison (Letters)."

208   *everyone in the world*: Goodman, *Allen Klein*, x.

208   *George came back from Rishikesh*: quoted in Thomson, *George Harrison*, 153.

208   *We're in the happy position*: quoted in Goodman, *Allen Klein*, 155.

208   *psychedelic sugar daddy*: Goodman, 155.

208   *We're just going to do*: quoted in Spitz, *The Beatles*, 727–28.

208   *We want to set up a system*: quoted in Goodman, *Allen Klein*, 155.

208   *Scotch, VSOP brandy, vodka*: Boyd, *Wonderful Tonight*, 132–33.

209   *The [world's] longest cocktail party*: Richard DiLello, *The Longest Cocktail Party: An Insider's Diary of the Beatles, Their Million-Dollar Apple Empire and Its Wild Rise and Fall* (Edinburgh: Canongate, 2000).

209   *George Harrison was really*: Emerick, *Here, There, and Everywhere*, 319.

209   *I sensed that he was*: quoted in Thomson, *George Harrison*, 154.

209   *I'd open my guitar case*: quoted in Thomson, 146.

210   *I felt more at home in India*: Harrison, *I Me Mine*, 57.

210   *Tension Album*: Mikal Gilmore, "Why the Beatles Broke Up," *Rolling Stone*, September 3, 2009, https: //www.rollingstone.com/music/music-features/why -the-beatles-broke-up-113403.

210   *Paul said, "Come and see the show"*: Gilmore, "Why the Beatles Broke Up."

210–11   *As David R. Reck wrote*: Reck, "Beatles Orientalis," 104.

211   *The way I see it*: quoted in Olivia Harrison, *George Harrison*, 232.

211   *what the Beatles and their pals did to us*: quoted in Kenneth Womack, "In 1969, the Fifth Beatle Was Heroin: John Lennon's Addiction Took Its Toll on the Band," *Salon*, February 15, 2019, https://www.salon.com/2019/02/15/in-1969-the -fifth-beatle-was-heroin-john-lennons-addiction-took-its-toll-on-the-band.

211   *This was a fairly big shocker*: quoted in Womack.

211 *John started talking*: quoted in "The Beatles and Drugs," in *The Beatles Bible*, beatlesbible.com/features/drugs/8.

212 *The other Beatles*: Womack.

212 *Fuck me*: Gilmore, "Why the Beatles Broke Up."

212 *You sit through sixty sessions*: Lennon, *Lennon Remembers*, 45.

212 *lightness [going] out of his soul*: Boyd, *Wonderful Tonight*, 122.

213 *George could be very easy*: quoted in Thomson, *George Harrison*, 169.

213 *I don't think I knew half*: Boyd, *Wonderful Tonight*, 124–25.

213 *impure . . . At least you try . . . It's crazy*: Carol Bedford, *Waiting for the Beatles: An Apple Scruff's Story* (Poole and Dorset, England: Blandford Press, 1984), 162.

214 *I was one of his nightmares*: Bedford, 140.

214 *trying to set me up*: Eric Clapton, *Clapton: The Autobiography* (New York: Broadway Books, 2007), 106–7.

214 *And I enjoyed the attention he paid me*: Boyd, *Wonderful Tonight*, 141.

214 *work out*: Thomson, *George Harrison*, 167.

214 *I was shocked*: Boyd, *Wonderful Tonight*, 123.

214 *was always surrounded by young maidens*: quoted in Boyd, 122.

215 *I hated everything about my ego*: quoted in Thomson, *George Harrison*, 168–69.

215 *Bob was an odd person*: quoted in Thomson, 159.

215 *He was totally free*: quoted in Thomson, 160.

215 *Beatles' winter of discontent*: Thomson, 160.

215 *asked me if I would stay behind* and *I remember listening*: quoted in Thomson, 161.

216 *Our songs*: quoted in Thomson, 164.

216 *Look, I'll play whatever*: quoted in Spitz, *The Beatles*, 808.

216 *Something had just blown up* and *Violence is as American as cherry pie*: quoted in Montville, *Sting Like a Bee*, 248.

216 *make the Viet Cong*: quoted in Malcolm McLaughlin, *The Long, Hot Summer of 1967: Urban Rebellion in America* (New York: Palgrave MacMillan, 1974), 122.

216 *[So] we're sitting there*: quoted in Montville, *Sting Like a Bee*, 248.

217 *Jack Johnson is the original me*: quoted in Montville, 239.

217 *You've had us in your lock*: Montville, 239–40.

217 *Was you scared?* Montville, 240.

217 *Ali was brilliant*: Adam Langer, "Muhammad Ali in a Broadway Musical? It Happened," *New York Times*, November 28, 2019, www.nytimes.com/2019/11/28/theater/muhammad-ali-broadway-buck-white.html.

217 *Why can't I just ad lib*: quoted in Montville, *Sting Like a Bee*, 245.

218 *I'd never do a love scene*: quoted in Montville, 247.

218 *I thought growing up*: quoted in Eig, *Ali*, 272.

218 *a sex addict*: Eig, 272.

218 *He would tell me 'I'm just weak, man'*: Eig, 273.

218 *That would leave the 150 women*: Montville, *Sting Like a Bee*, 246.

218 *gangster mosque*: Eig, *Ali*, 272.

219   *Clive Barnes*: quoted in Hauser, *Muhammad Ali*, 197.

219   *I think the FBI shut it down*: quoted in Montville, *Sting Like a Bee*, 251.

219   *Writing is as good as fighting*: Montville, 252.

220   *We haven't got half the money*: quoted in Goodman, *Allen Klein*, 157.

220   McCartney tormenting Epstein: see Peter McCabe and Robert D. Schonfeld, *Apple to the Core: The Unmaking of the Beatles* (New York: Pocket Books, 1972), 26.

220   *I got 'em!*: Peter Doggett, *You Never Give Me Your Money: The Beatles after the Breakup* (New York: HarperCollins, 2009), 67.

220   *all the charm*: Doggett, 65.

220   *fast-talking*: Doggett, *You Never Give Me Your Money*, 65.

220   *Because we were all from Liverpool*: quoted in Doggett, 69.

220   Lennon responding to Klein's stories: McCabe and Schonfeld, *Apple to the Core*, 125.

220   *sentimental old Jewish mommy; I believe him*: quoted in McCabe and Schonfeld, 130.

221   *fucked around by everybody*: Spitz, *The Beatles*, 821.

221   *I'm . . . trying to help you; You're not annoying me*: quoted in Doggett, *You Never Give Me Your Money*, 59.

222   *I don't see why any of you* and subsequent studio conversation: Doggett, 59–60.

222   *We used to do it*: quoted in Greil Marcus, *The History of Rock 'n' Roll in Ten Songs* (New Haven: Yale University Press, 2014), 134.

222   *I'm a tidy man; conspiracy to pervert*: Greene, *Here Comes the Sun*, 42.

222   *Ten pounds, two shillings*: Greene.

222   *psychological problems*: Thomson, *George Harrison*, 205.

223   *skin was covered* and following quotes: Boyd, *Wonderful Tonight*, 136.

223   *Do you plan to meet* and following dialogue: M. Goswami, *Miracle on Second Avenue*, 365.

223   *nice young boy*: quoted in S. D. Goswami, *Prabhupada*, 164.

223   *Prabhupada just looked*: quoted in S. D. Goswami, 163.

223–24   *What kind of philosophy are you following* and subsequent conversation, except where otherwise noted: Greene, *Here Comes the Sun*, 151–52.

224   *We've done meditation*: quoted in Greene, 177.

224   *Could you live like that?* quoted in Greene, 154.

225   *just a hair short of lunatic; Must be one of yours*: Greene, 148.

225   *Hare Krishna record*: Prabhupada to Shyamasundar, September 19, 1969, "George Harrison (Letters)."

225   *Klein and Eastman lurched*: Derek Taylor, *As Time Goes By* (London: Faber and Faber 2004), 142.

225   *They're not four little boys*: quoted in Doggett, *You Never Give Me Your Money*, 86.

226   *Everything got too big*: Taylor, *As Time Goes By*, 204.

226   *I looked to the Beatles*: Taylor, 218–19.

226   *I guess you could say*: quoted in Goodman, *Allen Klein*, 190.

226   *I think I'll be leaving the band now* and following dialogue: Doggett, *You Never Give Me Your Money*, 61. See also Doug Sulphy and Ray Schweighardt, *Get Back: The Beatles' Let It Be Disaster* (London: Helter Skelter Publishing, 1997), 130.

227   *I'd like to say thanks*: Spitz, *The Beatles*, 817.

227   *The event is so momentous*: Martin Scorsese, dir., *George Harrison: Living in the Material World*, film (Grove Pictures, 2011).

227   *It's always cold*: quoted In M. Goswami, *Miracle on Second Avenue*, 389.

227   *The British Empire is finished*: M. Goswami, 408–9.

Seven: "My Friend Came to Me"

231   *Bingos*: Gary J. Bass, *The Blood Telegram: Nixon, Kissinger, and a Forgotten Genocide* (New York: Alfred A. Knopf, 2013), 21.

232   *The state language of Pakistan*: Anirban Mahapatra, "When Bangladesh Went to War over Language," *True Stories* (Ozy), May 3, 2018, https://web.archive.org /web/20220518023650/https://www.ozy.com/true-and-stories/when-bangladesh -went-to-war-over-language/85912.

232   *There were still bodies*: quoted in Bass, *The Blood Telegram*, 23–24.

233   *gross neglect*: Reuters, "East Pakistani Leaders Assail Yahya on Cyclone Relief," November 23, 1970.

233   Joi Bangla!: Bass, *The Blood Telegram*, 28.

233   *It is the duty*: quoted in Bass, 29.

233   *I've seen the beginning of the break-up*: quoted in Bass, 28.

233   *I feel that anything*: quoted in Bass, 3.

233   *I don't like the Indians*: quoted in Bass, 5.

233   *Pakistan is a country* and *Nixon found the Pakistanis*: quoted in Bass, 3.

233   *There is a psychosis*: quoted in Bass, 6.

234   *basket case*: Bass, 18.

234   *obsequiousness*: quoted in Bass, 6.

234   *At least two mass graves*: quoted in Bass, xii.

234   *deafening silence*: Bass, xii.

234   *promptly, publicly, and prominently deplore*: quoted in Pankaj Mishra, "Unholy Alliances," *New Yorker*, September 16, 2013, https://www.newyorker.com /magazine/2013/09/23/unholy-alliances-3.

234   *The Indians need* and *They're such bastards*: quoted in Mishra.

234   *Kill three million*: quoted in Ershad Ahmed, "Bangladesh: Remembering Genocide and Celebrating Victory Day," *Global Voices*, https://globalvoices.org/2006/12 /18/bangladesh-remembering-genocide-and-celebrating-victory-day.

234   *We are . . . operating*: quoted in Bass, *The Blood Telegram* xix.

234   *It looks . . . as if Yahya* and following dialogue: quoted in Bass, 57.

234   *Selective Genocide*: quoted in Bass, 58.

235   *mass murder*: Bass, 67.

235   *Horror stories . . . Pray for us*: Bass, 79–80.

235   *U.S. policy related to*: quoted in Bass, 77–78.

235   *conjur[ing] peace; There is no problem*: quoted in Peter Doggett, *You Never Give Me Your Money: The Beatles after the Breakup* (New York: HarperCollins, 2009), 91.

236   *We all have to sacrifice a little* and *The fact that we're all here*: "George Harrison Interview: Howard Smith, WABC-FM, New York, May 1, 1970, Beatles Interviews Database, *Beatles Ultimate Experience*, https://www.beatlesinterviews.org/db1970 .04gh.beatles.html.

236   *our civilization is being questioned*: quoted in Bruce J. Schulman, *The Seventies: The Great Shift in American Culture, Society and Politics* (Cambridge: Da Capo Press, 2001), 1.

237   *There isn't going to be any revolution*: quoted in Schulman, 14.

237   *You take drugs*: quoted in Schulman, 16.

238   *All I want to do is look at the trees*: quoted in Boyd, *Wonderful Tonight*, 146.

238   *The house was going to be knocked down*: Harrison, *I Me Mine*, 67.

238   *Shadows we are*: Greene, *Here Comes the Sun*, 165.

238   *a bit like Lewis Carroll or Walt Disney*: Greene, 165.

239   *My God! What's he done?* quoted in Olivia Harrison, *George Harrison*, 268.

239   *There were . . . blue firs*: quoted in Olivia Harrison, 270.

239   *[Sir Frank's] attention to detail*: quoted in Thomson, *George Harrison*, 191.

239–40 *Those first few weeks*: Boyd, *Wonderful Tonight*, 151.

240   *I was hoping*: quoted in Greene, *Here Comes the Sun*, 166.

240   *The idea was that*: Boyd, *Wonderful Tonight*, 160.

240   *lost souls*: Boyd, 160.

240   *They may have been spiritual*: Boyd, 161.

240   *[And] George was a slightly soft touch*: quoted in Thomson, *George Harrison*, 195.

240   *They were just a bunch of moochers*: quoted in Thomson, 196.

240   *I began to feel*: Boyd, *Wonderful Tonight*, 161.

240   *John Lennon said it was so dark*: Boyd, 151.

241   *He was always laid back*: quoted in Thomson, *George Harrison*, 202.

241   *The sessions felt very comfortable*: Bobby Whitlock, *Bobby Whitlock: A Rock 'n' Roll Autobiography* (Jefferson, N.C.: McFarland, 2011), 76–77.

241   tonsillectomy: Clayson, *George Harrison*, 272.

242   *I really feel that your voice has got to be heard*: quoted in Leng, *While My Guitar Gently Weeps*, 77–78.

242   *George was really a great guitar player*: Whitlock, *Bobby Whitlock*, 74.

242   *He always bowed to Eric*: Scorsese, *George Harrison*.

242   *I've always liked the way George plays*: "Watch Bob Dylan's Emotional Cover of the Beatles' 'Something,' in Tribute to George Harrison," *Far Out Magazine*, https://web.archive.org/web/20200524174917/https://faroutmagazine.co.uk/bob -dylan-george-harrison-beatles-cover-something-2002.

242   *The sweet sad sigh*: Thomson, 186.

242   *One thing you'd learn about George*: quoted in Greene, *Here Comes the Sun*, 183–84.

243   *I went to . . . Friar Park*: quoted in Olivia Harrison, *George Harrison*, 282.

243   *I'm twice the writer*: George Harrison Stories, http://harrisonstories.tumblr.com.

243   *he knew he had something special*: quoted In Leng, *While My Guitar Gently Weeps*, 76.

243   *He was making a [huge] transition*: quoted in Thomson, *George Harrison*, 203.

243   *playing at 4 a.m.*: Bedford, *Waiting for the Beatles*, 158.

244   *For the soul*: Cited in Giuliano, *Dark Horse*, 129–30.

244   *One exhausted afternoon*: quoted in Clayson, *George Harrison*, 319.

244   *work in their father's gardens*: Harrison, *I Me Mine*, 70.

244   *Did you hurt your hand?* Greene, *Here Comes the Sun*, 173.

244   *Perverted Proverbs*: Giuliano, *Dark Horse*, 118.

245   *The more you get into something*: Harrison, *I Me Mine*, 72.

245   *Friar Park lifted his spirits*: Boyd, 157–58.

245   *What finally got to me* and next paragraph: Boyd, 161.

245   *Looking for "unending pleasure"*: Greene, *Here Comes the Sun*, 172.

245   *very well behaved*: Thomson, *George Harrison*, 206.

245   *There was too much riding*: Thomson.

245   *He was a pretty straight dude*: Whitlock, *Bobby Whitlock*, 113.

245   *I never saw George do any blow*: Whitlock, 56.

246   *Initially it can be a catalyst*: quoted in Cliopatria, "Kirk Bane: Review of Barney Hoskins's *Hotel California*," History News Network, September 7, 2008, https://historynewsnetwork.org/blog/54220.

246   *I have to tell you, man*: Boyd, *Wonderful Tonight*, 155.

246   *There were subliminal messages*: Whitlock, *Bobby Whitlock*, 77.

246–47 *I've been thinking about this*: quoted in Greene, *Here Comes the Sun*, 168–69.

247   *Who the fuck are you?* Bryan Rooney, excerpts from "Working for the Beatles at Apple," in *Backstage with Bryan Rooney: From Liverpool to Ringo to Donna Summer*, http://www.frugalfun.com/backstage.html.

247   *[Harrison] let me make all the basic tracks*: Scorsese, *George Harrison*.

247   *Pattie was not ready to leave George*: Whitlock, *Bobby Whitlock*, 77–78.

247   *George asked me*: quoted in Michael Schumacher, *The Life and Music of Eric Clapton* (New York: Citadel Press, 2003), 162.

247   *Don't be so stupid*: Boyd, *Wonderful Tonight*, 156.

248   *John was really negative*: quoted in Giuliano, *Dark Horse*, 130–31.

248   *When [John] heard*: quoted in Thomson, *George Harrison*, 208.

248   *I remember how proud George was*: Whitlock, *Bobby Whitlock*, 77.

248   *I just felt that whatever happened*: quoted in Giuliano, *Dark Horse*, 131.

248   *Federal Islamic Republic*: Mishra, "Unholy Alliances."

249   *Mrs. Ali, you got your wish* and subsequent dialogue: Montville, *Sting Like a Bee*, 266–67.

249   *Johnson cut himself a piece*: quoted in Hauser, *Muhammad Ali*, 208–9.

249   *The Vietnam War looked a lot worse*: quoted in Montville, *Sting Like a Bee*, 254.

249   *This ain't no joke*: quoted in Montville, 267.

250   *I can't blame Joe Frazier*: quoted in Hauser, *Muhammad Ali*, 208.
250   *was all there*: quoted in Eig, *Ali*, 289.
250   *See how narrow and trim I was*: quoted in Eig, 291.
250   *All the bricks* and *You can't become a soldier*: quoted in Montville, *Sting Like a Bee*, 271.
251   *It's like a dead man*: quoted in Montville, 273.
251   *No fighter ever lets anybody hit him*: quoted in Eig, *Ali*, 290.
251   *Before . . . he'd been so fast*: quoted in Hauser, *Muhammad Ali*, 213–14.
251   *After the layoff*: quoted in Hauser, 213.
251   *Why don't you smile* and following dialogue: quoted in Montville, *Sting Like a Bee*, 274.
251   *To Cassius Clay from Georgia*: Ali, *The Greatest*, 304.
252   *too busy to hate*: Eig, *Ali*, 289.
252   *Cassius Clay . . . is gone forever*: quoted in Ali, *The Greatest*, 312.
252   *I'm not just fighting one man*: quoted in Hauser, *Muhammad Ali*, 210.
252   *My heritage was*: quoted in Montville, *Sting Like a Bee*, 272.
252   *If there are . . . Black doctors* and subsequent dialogue: quoted in Montville, 275.
252–53 *If he loses tonight*: quoted in Eig, *Ali*, 294.
253   *It was right before the crowd left*: quoted in Hauser, *Muhammad Ali*, 210.
253   *[I] would hope Clay gets beat; day of mourning*: quoted in Montville, *Sting Like a Bee*, 274–75.
253   *something out of* Gone with the Wind; *black community was there in full force*: quoted in Hauser, *Muhammad Ali*, 210.
253   *a coronation; Don't wear that [light blue] dress*: quoted in Hauser, 211.
253   *This probably is an event unparalleled*: quoted in Montville, *Sting Like a Bee*, 276.
254   *Ghost in the house!*: Ali, *The Greatest*, 326.
254   *I'd never seen a cut like that; I had to make a decision*: quoted in Hauser, *Muhammad Ali*, 212.
254   *I'm stronger*: quoted in Montville, *Sting Like a Bee*, 277.
254   *I knew better*: quoted in Ali, *The Greatest*, 326.
254   *You are a living example; a champion of justice and peace*: quoted in Montville, *Sting Like a Bee*, 277.
255   *Ali won, you lose*: quoted in Montville, 278.
255   *Cassius Clay . . . aka*: Montville, 278.
255   *Ali didn't know if he'd be fighting*: quoted in Hauser, *Muhammad Ali*, 216.
255   *If you allow that coward*: Ali, *The Greatest*, 337.
255   *Why you no go in the army?* quoted in Montville, *Sting Like a Bee*, 280.
255–56 Judge Aaron details and dialogue: Ali, *The Greatest*, 340–45.
256   *Ali absorbed more punishment*: quoted in Hauser, *Muhammad Ali*, 216.
256   *gladsome termination of a holy crusade*: quoted in Montville, *Sting Like a Bee*, 281.
256   *What was his name?* and subsequent details and dialogue: Kindred, *Sound and Fury*, 139.

257   UPI correspondent: United Press International, "'Thousands killed' in East
        Pakistan," UPI Archives, November 14, 1970, https://www.upi.com/Archives
        /1970/11/14/thousands-killed-in-East-Pakistan/8141510514511.

257   *Oh Bhaugowan*: Shankar, *Raga Mala*, 218.

258   *Maybe Nixon'll call [Frazier]* : quoted in Montville, *Sting Like a Bee*, 285.

258   *The only people rooting for Joe Frazier*: quoted in Hauser, *Muhammad Ali*, 219.

258   *What does he know*: Hauser, *Muhammad Ali*, 219.

258   *If Baptists weren't allowed*: quoted in Hauser, 217.

258   *He isolated Joe*: quoted in Hauser, 219.

258   *When he gets to ringside*: quoted in Hauser, 221.

258   *there was a bullying, sadistic quality*: quoted in Hauser, 220.

258   *Uncle Tom?* and dialogue the follows: quoted in Eig, *Ali*, 304–5.

259   *I should be a postage stamp*: quoted in Hauser, *Muhammad Ali*, 223.

259   *All of a sudden, you know*: quoted in Montville, *Sting Like a Bee*, 289.

259   *[Ali] was weak*: quoted in Montville, 288–89.

259   *If the people around him*: quoted in Montville, 289.

260   *Muhammad Ali [has] become Lucky Lindy*: quoted Eig, *Ali*, 309.

260   *I bet Joe Frazier doesn't have that many*: quoted in Montville, *Sting Like a
        Bee*, 292.

260   *Why you in there?* and next two paragraphs: quoted in Eig, *Ali*, 314.

260   *I understand . . . I'm sorry*: quoted in Montville, *Sting Like a Bee*, 295.

261   *It's potentially the greatest single grosser*: quoted in Eig, *Ali*, 308.

261   *pretty boy* and *gargoyles*: Montville, *Sting Like a Bee*, 297.

261   *Don't you know I'm God?* Eig, *Ali*, 317.

261   *In round fifteen*: quoted in Hauser, *Muhammad Ali*, 228.

262   *Ali made it*: quoted in Montville, *Sting Like a Bee*, 299.

262   *I was devastated*: quoted in Hauser, *Muhammad Ali*, 224–25.

262   *That draft-dodger asshole*: Larry Platt, "Muhammad Ali's Philadelphia Story,"
        Philadelphia Citizen, June 6, 2016, philadelphiacitizen.org/muhammad-alis
        -philadelphia-story.

262   *I suppose it will be taken in some quarters*: quoted in Montville, *Sting Like a
        Bee*, 300.

262   *What are you guys going to say now?* quoted in Montville, 300.

262   *It's all your fault*: quoted in Montville, 300.

262   *You lose, you lose*: quoted in Montville, 300–301.

263   *Boxing introduced me*: quoted in Montville, 307.

263   US Supreme Court details and quotes, unless otherwise noted: Bill Littlefield,
        "The SCOTUS Clerk Who Helped Muhammad Ali Avoid Prison," *Only a Game*,
        September 8, 2017, https://www.wbur.org/onlyagame/2017/09/08/muhammad
        -ali-supreme-court-vietnam-war.

263   *The petitioner just doesn't want to fight*: quoted in Montville, *Sting Like a Bee*, 310.

264   *I'm so happy for you; try to live better*: quoted in Montville, 318–19.

264   *It was biblical*: quoted in Bass, *The Blood Telegram*, 119.

265   *Artillery, tanks, automatic weapons*: quoted in Bass, 120.

265   *I hope to hell we're not*: quoted in Bass, 141.

265   *He's a decent man*: quoted in Bass, 149.

265   *The government of India*: quoted in Bass, 190.

265   *I don't know why the hell*: quoted in Bass, 154.

265   *I [kept hearing] that many of my distant relatives*: Shankar, *Raga Mala*, 217–18.

265–66 *The idea . . . occurred to me*: quoted in Shankar, 219.

266   *The war had been going on* and next paragraph: Shankar, 219–20.

266   *Wagnerian, Brucknerian*: quoted in Greene, *Here Comes the Sun*, 182.

266   *Garbo talks!*: quoted in Greene, 181.

266   *among the boldest steps*: quoted in Greene, 182.

266   *Everybody is always trying*: quoted in Greene, 182.

266   *"Hallelujah" and "Hare Krishna"*: quoted in Greene, 181.

266   *gurur brahma, gurur vishnu*: Greene, 182.

266   *When we were doing*: quoted in Thomson, *George Harrison*, 190.

267   *Every time I put the radio on*: quoted in Greene, *Here Comes the Sun*, 183.

267   *not the kind of person*: quoted in Doggett, *You Never Give Me Your Money*, 148.

267   *He had to really steel himself*: quoted in Thomson, *George Harrison*, 213.

267   *That was his sacrifice*: quoted in Thomsen, 226.

268   *charity* (Billy Preston): *The Concert for Bangladesh*, DVD (1972; Apple Films, 2005).

268   *Everybody wanted to help*: *The Concert for Bangladesh*, DVD .

268   *I'll consider it, man*: quoted in Giuliano, *Dark Horse*, 134.

268   *Moons full of love*: Boyd, *Wonderful Tonight*, 172.

268   *We had him booked*: *The Concert for Bangladesh*, DVD.

268   *By the third day*: *The Concert for Bangladesh*, DVD.

269   *A lot of the last-minute logistics*: *The Concert for Bangladesh*, DVD.

269   *It was a miracle*: *The Concert for Bangladesh*, DVD.

269   *I knew [George] had written it*: Boyd, *Wonderful Tonight*, 80.

269   *Beware of ABKCO*: George Harrison, "Beware of Darkness" demo, *The Making of All Things Must Pass* (Cellar Dweller Records, 2010).

269–70 *Ferchrissakes*: quoted in McCabe and Schonfeld, *Apple to the Core*, 16.

270   *Tell 'em we're all sold out*: quoted in McCabe and Schonfeld, 3.

270   Shyamasundar: Greene, *Here Comes the Sun*, 189.

270   *I'm really into this East Pakistan thing* and *The level of energy*: *The Concert for Bangladesh*, DVD.

270   *When tickets for your concert went on sale* and following: *The Concert for Bangladesh*, DVD.

271   *I see now the Beatles; For whom are the Beatles*: quoted in Bass, *The Blood Telegram*, 213.

271   *Nobody . . . gives a shit*: quoted in Bass, 210.

271   groupie who refused to be identified: Giuliano, *Dark Horse*, 138–39.

272   *Now the winter has come*: Harrison, *I Me Mine*, 244.

272   *Hey, man. This isn't my scene*: *The Concert for Bangladesh*, DVD.

272   *By that time*: quoted in Thomson, *George Harrison*, 213.

273   *The first part of the concert* and next two paragraphs: *The Concert for Bangladesh*, DVD.

273   tune's melodic development: See Lavezzoli, *The Dawn of Indian Music in the West*, 191.

274   *Seeing Ringo Starr drumming*: quoted in Nicholas Schaffner, *The Beatles Forever* (New York: McGraw-Hill, 1978), 148.

274   *We have essentially*: quoted in Harvey Kubernik, "With a Little Help from his Friends: George Harrison and the Concert for Bangla Desh," *Rock's Back Pages*, July 2011, https://teachrock.org/article/with-a-little-help-from-his-friends-george -harrison-and-the-concert-for-bangla-desh.

275   *I made it really hard for myself*: *The Concert for Bangladesh*, DVD.

275   *Bob! What the hell* and subsequent dialogue: Giuliano, *Dark Horse*, 135.

275   *I'd like to bring out a friend of us all*: *The Concert for Bangladesh*, DVD.

275   *Oh, I get it*: quoted in Steve Turner, *Beatles '66: The Revolutionary Year* (New York: HarperCollins, 2016), 269.

276   *He could develop a simple little melodic idea*: quoted in Leng, *While My Guitar Gently Weeps*, 107.

276   *I really couldn't quite believe*: Don Heckman, "George Harrison, Bob Dylan, Eric Clapton: The Concert for Bangladesh," *Village Voice*, August 5, 1971, https:// www.villagevoice.com/2010/12/23/george-harrison-bob-dylan-eric-clapton-the -concert-for-bangladesh.

276   *My friend came to me*: Harrison, *I Me Mine*, 229.

276   *portrays the man behind the music*: *The Concert for Bangladesh*, DVD.

276   *I have no quarrel*: Heckman, "George Harrison, Bob Dylan, Eric Clapton."

276   *God! If only we'd done three shows*: Rolling Stone editors, *Harrison* (New York: Simon & Schuster, 2002), 146.

276–77 *It was a very emotional period for me*: Harrison, *I Me Mine*, 226.

277   *outrage to every concept of international law*: quoted in Sydney H. Schanberg, "Kennedy, in India, Terms Pakistani Drive Genocide," *New York Times*, August 17, 1971, www.newyorktimes.com/1971/08/17/archives/kennedy-in-india-terms -pakistani-drive-genocide.html.

277   *like a professor; [It] makes your heart sick*: Mishra, "Unholy Alliances."

278   *Overnight, the word*: Shankar, *Raga Mala*, 220.

278   *It was a necessary morale booster*: Harrison, *I Me Mine*, 60.

278   *Anti-Pakistan gramophone record*: Bass, *The Blood Telegram*, 213.

278   *What Woodstock was* said *to be*: Geoffrey Cannon, "The Concert for Bangla Desh Album Review—Archive, 1972," *Guardian*, January 4, 1972, https://www .theguardian.com/music/2022/jan/04/concert-for-bangladesh-album-reviewed -george-harrison-1972.

279   *The Concert for Bangladesh came along*: *The Concert for Bangladesh*, DVD.

279   Greil Marcus on the concert: Greil Marcus, *Bob Dylan by Greil Marcus: Writings 1968–2106* (New York: Public Affairs, 2016), 37, 39.

279 *The Concert for Bangla Desh is rock reaching*: Jon Landau, "Concert for Ban-gladesh," *Rolling Stone*, February 3, 1972, https://www.rollingstone.com/music /music-album-reviews/concert-for-bangladesh-248989.

280 *85 percent*: *New York Magazine*, February 28, 1972, 47–48.

280 *Of course, we are genuinely sympathetic* and following dialogue: quoted in Giuliano, *Dark Horse*, 136.

280 *very eloquently* and *bullshit*: quoted in Clayson, *George Harrison*, 316.

280 *jump on that*: quoted in Thomson, *George Harrison*, 232.

281 *I'm probably the biggest bore* and other dialogue from Cavett Show: transcript, "The Dick Cavett Show, November 23, 1971," Beatle Links: The Beatles Internet Resource Guide," http: www.beatlelinks.net/forums/showthread.php?t=17254. See also Greene, *Here Comes the Sun*, 193.

282 *I try so hard to be the person I'm not*: quoted in Goodman, *Allen Klein*, 221.

282 *I have been three times to Bangladesh*: quoted in Thomson, *George Harrison*, 235.

282 *repressive war-monger ways*: quoted in Steve Marinucci, "George Harrison Sent Nixon an Angry Telegram after 1973 Immigration Troubles," *Billboard*, April 5, 2019, https://www.billboard.com/articles/columns/rock/8528598/jonathan -something-number-one-dad-video-pays-irreverent-tribute-to-god.

283 Lennon and McCartney public spat: *Melody Maker*, November 20, 1971, and December 7, 1971, Beatles Interview Database, www.beatlesinterviews.org/db1971 .11jp.beatles.html.

283 *Won't You Listen to the Lambs*: Anthony Scaduto, "Won't You Listen to the Lambs, Bob Dylan?," *New York Times*, November 28, 1971, https://www.nytimes .com/1971/11/28/archives/-wont-you-listen-to-the-lambs-bob-dylan-wont-you -listen-to-the.html.

283 *What is this shit?* quoted in Mikal Gilmore, "Bob Dylan's Lost Years," *Rolling Stone*, September 12, 2013, www.rollingstone.com/music/musicnews/bob-dylans -lost-years-66632.

284 *Radical New Left leaders*: quoted in Jon Weiner, *Gimme Some Truth: The John Lennon FBI Files* (Berkeley: University of California Press, 1999), 4.

284 Lennon's alleged affiliation with ISKCON: Weiner, 78.

285 *Make love, not war*: John Lennon, "Mind Games," genius.com/john-lennon -mind-games-lyrics.

285 *It's all a bunch of shit*: quoted in Kindred, *Sound and Fury*, 183.

286 *Create and preserve the image of your choice*: quoted in Greene, *Here Comes the Sun*, 215.

Eight: The Funeral of All Sorrows

289 *Fourteen Scientific Reasons*: "George Harrison's Personal, Hand-Annotated Booklet on Spiritual Regeneration Given to Ringo Starr—With Notes on the Beatles—'I was in the greatest show on Earth,'" Nate D. Sanders Auctions, March 2012 auction, https://natedsanders.com/george_harrison_s_personal_hand _annotated_booklet-lot572.aspx.

289   *silly sixteen-year-old*: Maurice Devereux, "Interview with Maureen Cox, 1988,"
        Le Chroniqueur, July 1988, in *The Daily Beatle*, wogew.blogspot.com/2015/01
        /interview-with-maureen-ocox-1988.html.

289   *he never let any drug*: quoted in Chris O'Dell with Katherine Ketchum, *Miss
        O'Dell: My Hard Days and Long Nights with the Beatles, the Stones, Bob Dylan,
        Eric Clapton, and the Women They Loved* (New York: Touchstone, 2009), 312.

290   *[H]e even tried to commit suicide*: Devereux, "Interview with Maureen Cox,
        1988."

290   *made him paranoid*: quoted in O'Dell, *Miss O'Dell*, 312.

290   *cocaine . . . crept into our repertoire*: Boyd, *Wonderful Tonight*, 66.

290   *"Yes" people*: O'Dell, *Miss O'Dell*, 186.

290   *I came to the conclusion*: quoted in Paul Du Noyer, "Cocaine: The Devil's Dan-
        druff," Q, October 1986, pauldunoyer.com/ cocaine-the-devils-dandruff.

290   *George developed*: Boyd, *Wonderful Tonight*, 166–67.

291   *George is a frightened Catholic*: quoted in Thomson, *George Harrison*, 12.

291   *never . . . much of a druggie*: O'Dell, *Miss O'Dell*, 188.

291   *[George] would get so intense*: O'Dell, 186–87.

291   *authentically wholly herself*: O'Dell, 250.

291   *[Maureen] and George go into a room*: quoted in O'Dell, 262.

291   *I was in the greatest show on Earth*: "George Harrison's Personal, Hand-Annotated
        Booklet."

292   *what happens to naughty boys*: Harrison, *I Me Mine*, 282.

292   *minor war*: Harrison, 286.

292   *George Harrison moment*: Clayson, *George Harrison*, 318.

292   *It took up a few years of his life*: quoted in Thomson, *George Harrison*, 238.

292   *enough to make you go crazy*: Jay Spangler, "George Harrison Interview: Craw-
        daddy Magazine, February 1977," Beatles Interviews Database, https://www
        .beatlesinterviews.org/db1977.0200.beatles.html.

292   *I wouldn't really care*: quoted in Clayson, *George Harrison*, 318.

292   *war mode*: Goodman, *Allen Klein*, 237.

292   *Allen so completely misjudged*: quoted in Goodman, 240.

293   *subconscious plagiarism*: Elliot J. Huntley, *Mystical One: George Harrison After
        the Break-Up of the Beatles* (Toronto: Guernica, 2006), 133.

293   *When [I] got rid of Allen Klein*: quoted in Keith Badman, *The Beatles: The Dream
        Is Over: Off the Record 2* (London: Omnibus Press, 2002), 101.

293   *I was a fan of the Beatles*: quoted in Badman, 101.

293   *Eric didn't look well*: quoted in Johnny Black, "Desperation Blues: The Show
        That Brought Eric Clapton Back from the Brink," *Classic Rock*, January 12, 2023,
        https://loudersound.com/features/fly-on-the-wall-28-erci-clapton-s-all-star
        -comeback-concert.

293   *pinched; Eric and I have always had*: "What Ronnie Wood Says about Pattie,"
        Harihead, November 12, 2007, https://harihead.livejournal.com/2049.html.

294   *perhaps he was hoping to provoke me*: Boyd, *Wonderful Tonight*, 179.

294   *It . . . is definitely on; Whatever Ronnie has got to say*: "British Press Report, Monday November 26, 1973," posted by YouGotTheSilver69, *Rocks Off—The Charlie Watts Message Board*, July 2, 2008, https://rocksoff.org/cgi-bin/messageboard /YaBB.pl?num=1214583846/68.

294   *very friendly*: Marc Shapiro, *Behind Sad Eyes: The Life of George Harrison* (New York: St. Martin's Press, 2002), 122.

294   *Ronnie was happy for me to go*: "What Ronnie Wood Says about Pattie."

294   *The washing machines*: O'Dell, *Miss O'Dell*, 153–54.

294   *I think owning that huge house*: Boyd, *Wonderful Tonight*, 167.

295   *He was angry a lot*: quoted in Thomson, *George Harrison*, 237.

295   *Pattie and I used to joke*: O'Dell, *Miss O'Dell*, 188.

295   *You may think we're lucky*: quoted in O'Dell, 254.

295   *It made me so paranoid*: quoted in Giuliano, *Dark Horse*, 157.

295   *oldies*: Clayson, *George Harrison*, 325.

295   *I don't even think the Beatles were that good*: quoted in Shapiro, *Behind Sad Eyes*, 125.

295   *It's the Muhammad Ali line*: quoted in Badman, *The Beatles: The Dream Is Over*, 117.

295   *work[ed] on a guitar*: Gary Wright, *Dream Weaver: Music, Meditation, and My Friendship with George Harrison* (New York: Jeremy P. Tarcher/Penguin, 2014), 102.

295   *New instruments*: Wright, 105–6.

296   *Remember that finding God*: quoted in Wright, 110.

296   *place where people could get a taste*: quoted in Giuliano, *Dark Horse*, 106.

296   *archangel*: Clayson, *George Harrison*, 268.

296   *Phil was never there*: quoted in Thomson, *George Harrison*, 240.

296   *It was obvious*: quoted in Thomson, 242.

296   I felt he was going through: quoted in Leng, *While My Guitar Gently Weeps*, 137.

296–97 *country and eastern*: Clayson, *George Harrison*, 323.

297   *As the days stand up on end*: Harrison, *I Me Mine*, 187.

297   *You serve me*: Harrison, 236.

297   *While George Harrison was bursting with musical confidence*: Leng, *While My Guitar Gently Weeps*, 138.

297   *Harrison has always struck me*: Michael Watts, "The New Harrison Album," *Melody Maker*, June 9, 1973, 3.

297   *profoundly seductive*: quoted in Greene, *Here Comes the Sun*, 195.

298   *so damn holy*: Tony Tyler, "Holy Roller: Harrison," *NME*, June 9, 1973, 33.

298–300 Harrison-Prabhupada conversation: "Conversation with George Harrison, July 22, 1973," Śrīla Prabhupāda Archive, https://prabhupada.io/spoken/730722r2.lon.

300   *There is no fucking cure*: quoted in Eig, *Ali*, 330.

300   *fantastic subordination*: Joyce Carol Oates, *On Boxing* (New York: Ecco Press, 1987, 1995), 26.

301   *They don't know me too well*: quoted in Eig, *Ali*, 336.

301   *People's Choice; [Elvis] is one of the reasons*: Trina Young, "When Muhammad Ali Called Elvis Presley 'The Greatest,'" Elvis Presley Biography, https://elvisbiography .net/2019/01/15/when-muhammad-ali-called-elvis-presley-the-greatest.

301   *People don't realize*: quoted in Young.

302   *stoned college kids*: Hoffer, *Bouts of Mania*, 26.

302   *George, my grandmother*: quoted in Hoffer, 27.

302   *Sonny Liston without the personality*: Eig, *Ali*, 342.

302   *Come to fight*: Hoffer, *Bouts of Mania*, 95.

303   *You got to get the hard-on*: quoted in Eig, *Ali*, 344.

303   *put three cops in the hospital; should have out her in the ring*: Eig, 348.

303   *beaten Godzilla*: Eig, 345.

303   *could move the [jaw]bone*: quoted in Hauser, *Muhammad Ali*, 252.

303   *[E]ach round I was taking*: quoted in Hauser, 252.

303   *The pain must have been awful*: quoted in Hauser, 252.

303   *Muhammad Ali cannot talk!*: Hoffer, *Bouts of Mania*, 109.

304   *Losing to Norton was the end*: quoted in Hauser, *Muhammad Ali*, 253.

304   *Ali's sun is setting*: quoted in Hoffer, *Bouts of Mania*, 111.

304   *No different from Chubby Checker*: quoted in Eig, *Ali*, 341.

304   *I transcend earthly bounds*: quoted in Eig, 337.

304   *street Machiavelli*: quoted in Eig, 337–38.

305   *Motherfucker*: quoted in Eig, 339.

305   *I resonate*: quoted in Eig, 341.

305   *Ali, he wanted it all*: quoted in Eig, 340.

305   *I came with the champion*: quoted in Eig, *Ali*, 343.

305–6   bean pie and *Allah (God) says*: Rossi Anastopoulo, "The Radical Pie That Fueled a Nation," *Taste*, November 13, 2018, https:// www.tastecokking.com/the-radical -pie-that-fueled-a-nation.

306   *KYTCHEN*: Eig, *Ali*, 352–53.

306   *he'd been reluctant to do it*: quoted in Hauser, *Muhammad Ali*, 248.

306   *At first the neighbors; making all these crazy orders*; and Thornton in next paragraph: quoted in Hauser, 247.

307   *Ang, we got legs*: quoted in Eig, *Ali*, 355.

307   *We loved Ali*: quoted in Eig, 354.

307   *There is no way you can eliminate*: quoted in Hoffer, *Bouts of Mania*, 120.

307   *He was kind of awkward*: quoted in Hauser, *Muhammad Ali*, 254.

307   *You the boss*: Eig, *Ali*, 355.

307   *I own you!*: Eig, 356.

308   *Age. People dying*: Hoffer, *Bouts of Mania*, 130.

308   *had an unrealistic expectation*: quoted in Hauser, *Muhammad Ali*, 254.

308   *too ignorant and ugly*: Eig, *Ali*, 357.

308   *I taste Ali's sweat now*: Eig, *Ali*, 357.

308   *Joe would come in*: quoted in Hauser, *Muhammad Ali*, 256.

309   *He fought with so much flair*: Eig, *Ali*, 360.

309   *I can't say nothing bad*: quoted in Hoffer, *Bouts of Mania*, 131.

309   *I want him again*: Hauser, *Muhammad Ali*, 258.

309   *seemed to be auditioning*: quoted in Hoffer, *Bouts of Mania*, 136.

309   *I want to hurt him so bad*: quoted in Hoffer, 136.

309   *he was building up the courage*: Pete Townshend, *Who I Am* (New York: Harper-Collins, 2012), 285.

309   *I would be civil to her*: quoted in Martin Nethercutt, "Pattie Boyd Admits George Harrison Was the Love of Her Life," *McCartney Times*, January 22, 2018, www.mccartney.com/?p=10636.

309   *the little wife*: Shapiro, *Behind Sad Eyes*, 120.

309   *to escape the house*: Townshend, *Who I Am*, 286.

309   *We were alone*: Boyd, *Wonderful Tonight*, 183.

309   *George was happy*: Townshend, *Who I Am*, 286.

310   *taste him on your tongue*: *George Harrison Stories*, http://harrisonstories.tumblr.com.

310   *[Eric] was so passionate*: Boyd, *Wonderful Tonight*, 183.

310   *[Eric's] behavior*: quoted in Nethercutt, "Pattie Boyd Admits George Harrison Was the Love of Her Life."

310   *The very words were*: quoted in *George Harrison Stories*, http://harrisonstories.tumblr.com.

310   *It was late at night*: Boyd, *Wonderful Tonight*, 184.

310   *Muhammad Ali [had] gone through*: quoted in Hauser, *Muhammad Ali*, 259.

311   *We're not a global village*: quoted in Killen, *1973 Nervous Breakdown*, 11.

311   *paralyzed, inept, and impotent*: Hoffer, *Bouts of Mania*, 133.

311   *This kind of malaise*: quoted in Hoffer, 133.

311   *darling of America*: quoted in Eig, *Ali*, 365.

311   *Now what do you say*: Eig, 364.

312   *movement music*: quoted in James A. Mitchell, *The Walrus and the Elephants: John Lennon's Years of Revolution* (New York: Seven Stories Press, 2013), 189.

312   *Name me one sixties superstar*: Lester Bangs, "Dandelions in Thin Air," *Cream*, June 1975, 40.

312   *What is this search for meaning*: quoted in Mitchell, *The Walrus and the Elephants*, 198.

312   *spiritual-Aquarian overtones*: Mitchell, 197.

312   *Here we are now*: Kurt Cobain, "Smells like Teen Spirit."

Nine: The Show Goes On

314   *The whole point to being here*: quoted in Tillery, *Working Class Mystic*, 112.

314   *ambition was to have no ambition*: Oliver Craske, *Indian Sun: The Life and Music of Ravi Shankar* (New York: Hachette Books, 2020), 510.

314   *I really do love Pattie*: quoted in Shapiro, *Behind Sad Eyes*, 121.

315   *George immediately laid himself*: Wright, *Dream Weaver*, 125–26.

315   *Everyone, everywhere*: Harrison, *I Me Mine*, 296.

315 *There is an interesting dictum*: quoted in Greene, *Here Comes the Sun*, 210.

315 *He had an absolute talent*: quoted in Ajay Kamalakaran, "Tuitions in Vrindavan: When a Russian Indologist Taught George Harrison Hindi," *Open*, September 20, 2019, https://openthemagazine.com/feature/tuitions-vrindavan-russian -indologist-taught-george-harrison-hindi.

316 *We were having a very strong, very nice kirtan*: ISKCON Vrindavan, "George Harrison Visiting Prabhupadha House (Vrindavan)," youtube.com/watch?v= xyfJ-60IVsw.

316 *As soon as Srila Prabhupada saw him*: ISKCON Vrindavan.

316 *my most fantastic experience* and next two paragraphs Harrison, *I Me Mine*, 296–97.

317 *I felt I could be in love*: Shankar, *Raga Mala*, 265–66.

317 *That morning*: Harrison, *I Me Mine*, 296–97.

317–18 *How long will you be George Harrison?*: ISKCON Vrindavan, "George Harrison Visiting Prabhupadha House (Vrindavan)."

318 *[In Vrindavan, when] George . . . was telling me*: Shapiro *Behind Sad Eyes*, 126.

318 *the fire [that] burns out the seed [of Karma]*: Harrison, *I Me Mine*, 180.

318–19 Cremation details: Boyd, *Wonderful Tonight*, 88.

319 *Pardon me* and all other details and quotes from Watergate hearing: Elvin C. Bell, "A Chance Meeting with Watergate's John Dean, John Lennon and Yoko Ono," *Fresno Bee*, September 14, 2018.

320 *lacking Lennon's usual standards*: Adam Cohen, "While Nixon Campaigned, the F.B.I. Watched John Lennon," *New York Times*, September 21, 2006, https:// www.nytimes.com/2006/09/21/opinion/21thu4.html.

320 We announce the birth of a conceptual country: Mitchell, *The Walrus and the Elephants*, 200–201.

321 *George, I know these people*: quoted in Eig, 362.

321 *This [wouldn't be] just another fight*: quoted in Eig, 362.

321 *the ring indigent*: Mark Kram, *Ghosts of Manila: The Fateful Blood Feud between Muhammad Ali and Joe Frazier* (New York: Harper Perennial, 2002), 195.

322 *a walking bank vault*: Eig, *Ali*, 366.

322 *symbolic black happening*: Eig, 367.

322 *anywhere punch*: quoted in Hoffer, *Bouts of Mania*, 146.

322 *Ali's had it*: quoted in Eig, *Ali*, 375.

322 *The time may have come*: quoted in Eig, 375.

322 *He's been hit a lot*: quoted in Eig, 371.

322 *They figure he'll give me hell*: quoted in Kindred, *Sound and Fury*, 197.

322 *Foreman's nothin'*: quoted in Kindred, 195.

322 *I wouldn't have said that thing*: quoted in Eig, *Ali*, 374.

322 *They say wise men*: quoted in Victor Bockris, *Muhammad Ali in Fighter's Heaven* (London: Arrow Books, 1998), 35.

322 *The man who has no imagination*: quoted in Bockris, 36.

323 *I LOVE HIM*: Eig, *Ali*, 375–76.

323   *hangerbangers*: quoted in Eig, 377.

323   *Ali failed as a man*: quoted in Eig, 416.

323   *Gotta lose this*: quoted in Bockris, *Muhammad Ali in Fighter's Heaven*, 29.

323   *It's just a case of white people*: quoted in Bockris, 82.

324   *We all do wrong*: AP Archive, "Muhammad Ali Said Too Many People Are Condemning President Nixon for the Watergate Scandals," https://www.youtube .com/watch?v=-ZydvpxfPP8.

324   *They didn't have to tell us*: quoted in Eig, *Ali*, 372.

324   *If you think the world was shook up*: quoted in Eig, 378.

324   *most beautiful woman* and *breathtaking*: Eig, 379.

325   *It's hard to get out*: quoted in Bockris, *Muhammad Ali in Fighter's Heaven*, 127.

325   *I attract people*: quoted in Bockris, 40–41.

325   *Mobutu's people* and response: quoted in Hoffer, *Bouts of Mania*, 146.

325   *I'd never live anywhere*: quoted in Bockris, *Muhammad Ali in Fighter's Heaven*, 81.

325   *People die*: quoted in Kindred, *Sound and Fury*, 197–98.

325   *He knew what the currency of earthly immortality was*: Kram, *Ghosts of Manila*, 196.

325   *It's a miracle*: quoted in Kindred, *Sound and Fury*, 198.

326   *Might as well sit down* and next paragraph: *Music Festival from India: Live at the Royal Albert Hall (1974)* (Umlaut Corporation, 2010), DVD.

326   *I hope this Music Festival*: Ravi Shankar and George Harrison, *Collaborations* (Dark Horse Records, 2010), booklet.

326   *It was amazing*: quoted in Thomson, *George Harrison*, 266.

326–27 *It was not an auspicious start*: Clapton, *Clapton*, 158.

327   *The minute she left*: Clapton, 161.

327   *kind of honeymoon*: Clapton, 161.

327   *started talking about George*: O'Dell, *Miss O'Dell*, 297–98.

327   *E + P*: Liz Thomas, "The 'Love' Note That Showed George Harrison Had Finally Forgiven Patti Boyd after She Left Him for Eric Clapton," *Daily Mail Online*, March 28, 2011, https://www.dailymail.co.uk/tvshowbiz/article-1370462 /Love-note-shows-George-Harrison-forgave-Patti-Boyd-left-Eric-Clapton .html.

327   *fantastic . . . It sounds to me like hit record*: Craske, *Indian Sun*, 403.

328   *bent over backwards*: quoted in Leng, *While My Guitar Gently Weeps*, 144.

328   *his own album did suffer*; *He was very hands on*: quoted in Thomson, *George Harrison*, 263.

328   Kathy Simmonds: see "George's Girlfriend Kathy," Meet the Beatles for Real, March 24, 2020, http://www.meetthebeatlesforreal.com/2020/03/georges -girlfriend-kathy.html.

328   *I went on a bit of a bender*: quoted in Thomson, *George Harrison*, 264.

328   *We all got out there*: "The Robben Ford Interview," *Tone Quest Report*, November 2009, https://www.tonequest.com/robben-ford-interview.

328   *He was an amazing personality*: "The Robben Ford Interview."

328–29 *Eventually around midnight*: "Robben Ford Interview," *Tone Quest Report*, November 2009, https://www.tonequest.com/robben-ford-interview.

329   *Would you . . . take a picture*: O'Dell, *Miss O'Dell*, 305.

329   *I thought somebody should*: quoted in David Browne, "George Harrison's Dark Horse Label Rides Again," *Rolling Stone*, March 8, 2020, https://www.rollingstone.com/pro/features/george-harrison-dark-horse-label-olivia-harrison-dhani-harrison-interview-961427.

329   *My first impression of George*: quoted in Doggett, *You Never Give Me Your Money*, 217.

329   *I love Mexican cinema*: "Interesting/Cool George Harrison Stories?," Steve Hoffman Music Forums, https://forums.stevehoffman.tv/threads/interesting-cool-george-harrison-stories.329645.

330   *it was our spiritual aspirations*: quoted in Robert Sandall, "George Harrison—Jolly George, the Unsung Story," *Sunday Times*, October 12, 2003.

330   *He drives fast racing cars*: quoted in Joe Creighton, "1983 I Was in the Black Sorrows," https://www.joecreighton.com/259/1983_I_was_in_The_Black_Sorrows/1983-I-was-in-The-Black-Sorrows.html.

330   *[George and I] had our differences*: Sandall, "George Harrison."

330   *If George liked you* and next paragraph: Browne, "George Harrison's Dark Horse Label Rides Again."

330   *George always considered himself*: quoted in Browne.

330   *The swift runner*: "Hymn to the Horse," in *Rig Veda*, translated by Wendy Doniger (London: Penguin, 2005), 1.163, 13.

330–31 *He had this way of looking at you*: quoted in Caroline Frost, "George Harrison 'Had This Way of Looking at You,' Remembers His Wife Olivia, on Release of 'Apple Years' Music," *Huffington Post*, September 24, 2014, http://www.huffingtonpost.co.uk/2014/09/24/george-harrison-the-apple-years-albums-olivia-harrison.

331   *he wasn't impressed*: quoted in Sandall, "George Harrison."

331   *I don't want Dark Horse to be a big label*: quoted in Browne, "George Harrison's Dark Horse Label Rides Again."

331   *George wanted to give the impression*: quoted in Thomson, *George Harrison*, 268.

331   *He had [so much] on his plate*: quoted in Thomson, 273.

331–32 *[George felt] tremendous responsibility*: quoted in Craske, *Indian Sun*, 409.

332   *George as an amateur saint*: quoted in Clayson, *George Harrison*, 334.

332   *[Ours was] a fairly bitter experience*: "The Department of State Reports on the George Foreman-Muhammad Ali Fight ('The Rumble in the Jungle'), Part I," *Text Message*, https://text-message.blogs.archives.gov/2016/09/13/the-department-of-state-reports-on-the-george-foreman-muhammad-ali-fight.

332   *strange [to] the American Negro*: Hoffer, *Bouts of Mania*, 147.

332   *I can't tell you*: Malcolm X with Alex Haley, *The Autobiography of Malcom X* (1964; repr., New York: Ballantine Books, 2015), 331.

332   *Lumumba Territory*: Lewis A. Erenberg, "Rumble in the Jungle: Muhammad Ali vs. George Foreman in the Age of Global Spectacle," *Journal of Sport History* 39, no. 1 (Spring 2012): 92.

Ten: The Rumble in the Jungle

333   *George does not hit*: quoted in Norman Mailer, *The Fight* (New York: Bantam Books, 1976), 42.

333   *One round with [him]*: quoted in Mailer, 79–80.

333   *[The] fight was a foregone conclusion*: Mailer, 79.

333   *The flea goes in three*: quoted in Mailer, 82.

333   *Defeat was in the air*: Mailer, 77.

333   *borrowin' my strength from the trees*: quoted in Kram, *Ghosts of Manila*, 157.

333   *I done something new for this fight*: quoted in Eig, *Ali*, 378.

334   *You are impressed with Foreman*: quoted in Mailer, *The Fight*, 55.

334   *Ali is Russian*: quoted in Mailer, 90.

335   *I'm the greatest!*: Eig, *Ali*, 383.

335   *Ali, bomaye!*: Eig, *Ali*, 384.

335   *They told you and me we came from the Congo*: quoted in Ira Dworkin, *Congo Love Song: African American Culture and the Crisis of the Colonial State* (Chapel Hill: University of North Carolina Press, 2017), 2.

335   *a scene of shocking savagery*: Dworkin, 5.

336   *King-Sovereign*: Dworkin, 7

336   *policing functions*: Dworkin, 9.

336   *We found a road*: quoted in Dworkin, 70.

336   *descendants of slaves*: Dworkin, 8.

336   *liberation fighters*: Dworkin, 281.

336   *Old Lyndon*: quoted in Dworkin, 280.

337   *The President . . . regarded Lumumba*: quoted in Adam Hochschild, *King Leopold's Ghost: A Story of Greed, Terror, and Heroism in Colonial Africa* (Boston: Mariner Books, 1998), 302.

337   *the Guide, the Father*: Hochschild, 303.

337   *The first rule of dictatorship*: quoted in Mailer, *The Fight*, 88.

337   *Civil wars, revolts, coups*: Ryszard Kapuscinski, *The Shadow of the Sun* (New York: Vintage, 2001), 128–29.

338   *Watching Ali in Zaire*: quoted in Hauser, *Muhammad Ali*, 265–66.

338   *You could actually see and feel him*: quoted in Eig, *Ali*, 385.

338   *A FIGHT BETWEEN TWO BLACKS*: Kindred, *Sound and Fury*, 199.

338   *FROM SLAVE SHIP TO CHAMPIONSHIP*: David Mosley poster, http://www.webgalleria.com/ali-forman-rumble-jungle-poster.

338   *for the little brothers*: quoted in Bockris, *Muhammad Ali in Fighter's Heaven*, 16.

339   *There ain't no mummy*: quoted in Hauser, *Muhammad Ali*, 266.

339   *How do you feel; When I was growing up*: quoted in Hauser, 267.

339   *country boy*: quoted in Eig, *Ali*, 387.

339   *babysitter*: Eig, *Ali*, 387.

339   *I can't say how legal*: quoted in Eig, 387.

340   matabiches (bribes): Eig, 389.

340–41 Quotes and details from Zaire '74: Zachary Lipez, "Zaire '74 Was Woodstock for African Artists," *Vice*, August 14, 2017, https://www.vice.com/en_us/article/j5584g/zaire-74-was-woodstock-for-african-artists.

341   *remote as Zaire*: quoted in Eig, *Ali*, 390.

341   *[George] not only has TNT*: quoted in Hoffer, *Bouts of Mania*, 151.

341   *Ali was supremely confident*: quoted in Hauser, *Muhammad Ali*, 268.

341   *kiss[ing] babies*: Mailer, *The Fight*, 109.

342   *They's more good-looking womens*: quoted in Mailer, 121.

342   *The man been knocked down twice*: quoted in Mailer, 58–59.

342   *I'm fighting for God and my people* and *I wish Lumumba*: quoted in Mike Marqusee, *Redemption Song: Muhammad Ali and the Spirit of the Sixties* (London: Verso, 1999), 271–72.

343   *Stadium of the 20th of May*: see Mailer, *The Fight*, 111–12.

343   *comfort station*: Mailer, 133.

343   *What's going on here?* and next paragraph: quoted in Mailer, 133–34.

344   *It must be dark*: quoted in Mailer, 136–37.

344   Ali-Bundini exchange: Mailer, 137–38.

345   *Light came off him*: Mailer, 142.

345   *praying, and in great sincerity*: quoted in Mailer, 143.

345   *That's some mean-lookin' man*: Hoffer, *Bouts of Mania*, 162.

346   *You have heard of me*: quoted in Mailer, 144.

346   *You been hearing about how bad I am*: quoted in Eig, *Ali*, 395.

346   *A monsoon always announced itself*: see Ella Davies, "At One Lake in Venezuela, Lightning Flashes 28 Times a Minute," BBC, August 10, 2015, www.bbc.com/earth/story/20150810-the-most-electric-place-on-earth.

347   *pugilistic suicide*: Eig, *Ali*, 395.

347   *Oh, Christ!*: quoted in Eig, 398.

347   *I won't kid you*: quoted in Hauser, *Muhammad Ali*, 276.

347   *What you doing? Don't talk*: Hoffer, *Bouts of Mania*, 163.

347   *Do it!*: Kindred, *Sound and Fury*, 201.

347   *A bird's nest was on the ground*: quoted in Hoffer, *Bouts of Mania*, 163.

347   *I . . . died two or three times*: quoted in Hauser, *Muhammad Ali*, 276.

348   *I gave George what he thought he wanted*: quoted in Hauser, 277.

348   *Oh, no, you beautiful thief!*: Hoffer, *Bouts of Mania*, 164.

348   *What Ali did*: quoted in Hauser, *Muhammad Ali*, 274.

348   *Ali, bomaye!*: Dave Anderson, "A Comeback Chant: 'Ali, Bomaye,'" *New York Times*, October 31, 1974, https://www.newyorktimes.com/2016/06/11/sports/a-comeback-chant-ali-bomaye.html.

349   *I really didn't plan* and following quotes: Hauser, *Muhammad Ali*, 276–77.

349   *a man swinging in the rigging of a ship*: Mailer, 159.

349   *Careful!*: Mailer, 160.

349   *I got a feeling*: quoted in Eig, *Ali*, 398.

350   *I really don't believe it*: quoted in Mailer, 161.

350   *Is that all you got?* Eig, *Ali*, 398.

350   *Muhammad amazed me*: quoted in Hauser, *Muhammad Ali*, 277.

350   *Now it's my turn!*: Eig, *Ali*, 397.

350   *Oh, Lawdy!*: quoted in Hoffer, *Bouts of Mania*, 165.

350   *Muhammad Ali has done it!*: quoted in Mailer, 171.

350   *Yeah* and Saddler quotations: Mailer, 170.

351   *Husband and wife looked at each other*: Mailer, 173.

351   *like . . . a military column*: quoted in Eig, *Ali*, 400.

351   *Damn, do those tree look like they're moving?* quoted in Kindred, *Sound and Fury*, 202.

351   *When we left*: quoted in Kindred, 202.

352   *You'll never know*: quoted in Kindred, 202–3.

352   *three hours after the greatest victory of his life*: quoted in Hauser, *Muhammad Ali*, 279.

Eleven: Dark Horse

353   *I would like to express my appreciation*: "Department of State Reports on the George Foreman-Muhammad Ali Fight ('The Rumble in the Jungle')," *Text Message*, https://text-message.blogs.archives.gov/2016/09/13/the-department-of-state-reports-on-the-george-foreman-muhammad-ali-fight-the-rumble-in-the-jungle-1974-part-i.

354   *slavemaster*: Eig, *Ali*, 403.

354   *I feel real guilty; I don't want to be a leader*: quoted in Eig, *Ali*, 404.

354   *My fellow Americans*: "Gerald R. Ford Remarks When Taking the Oath of Office as President," Gerald R. Ford Presidential Library and Museum, http://www.fordlibrarymuseum.gov/library/speeches/740001.asp.

355   *one of the biggest government public relations blunders*: Martin Crutsinger, "Ford's WIN Buttons Remembered," *Washington Post*, December 28, 2006, https://www.washingtonpost.com/wp-dyn/content/article/2006/12/28/AR2006122801002.html.

355   *No Immediate Miracles*: Crutsinger.

355   *Was Gerald Ford ever really president?*: Rick Perlstein, "The Seventies Show," *Nation*, December 8, 2010, 26.

355   *Me Decade*: Killen, *1973 Nervous Breakdown*, 9.

356   *I think the masses root for me*: quoted in "Muhammad Ali Discusses His Book, 'The Greatest: My Own Story,'" Studs Terkel Radio Archive, November 26, 1975, https://studsterkel.wfmt.com/programs/muhammad-ali-discusses-his-book-greatest-my-own-story.

356   *all things are possible*: George Plimpton, "Return of the Big Boxer," *Sports Illustrated*, December 23, 1974, https://www.si.com/vault/1974/12/23/628163/muhammad-ali-sportsman-1974.

356   *We as a nation* and all other Ford quotes: Thomas Hauser, "When Muhammad Ali and Gerald Ford Met," International Brotherhood of Prizefighters, July 19, 2019,

https://tss.ib.tv/boxing/featured-boxing-articles-boxing-news-videos-rankings
-and-results/59013-when-muhammad-ali-and-gerald-ford-met.

357   *least authentic man alive*: quoted in Killen, *1973 Nervous Breakdown*, 65.

358   *1970s pop trash*: Rob Sheffield, *Dreaming the Beatles: The Love Story of One Band and the Whole World* (New York: Dey Street, 2017), 276–77.

358   *Compared to what I should be*: quoted in Tillery, *Working Class Mystic*, 116.

358   *I never met*: quoted in Thomson, *George Harrison*, 285.

359   *empty bottles of gin*: quoted in Badman, *The Dream Is Over*, 146.

359   *He was frustrated*: quoted in Thomson, *George Harrison*, 277.

359   *Had he pulled it off*: Thomson, 259.

359   *It was the winter*: quoted in Thomson, 273.

359   *It really is a test*: quoted in Thomson, 259.

359   *So far from home*: Harrison, *I Me Mine*, 276, 278.

359   *He was constantly hoarse*: quoted in Thomson, *George Harrison*, 273.

360   *Don't come*: Thomson, 270.

360   *I thought it would give people*: quoted in Thomson, 270.

360   *There's no silverware*: quoted Thomson, 261.

360   *At the rehearsal*: quoted in Badman, *The Dream Is Over*, 136.

360   *put his neck on the line*: quoted in Ben Fong-Torres, "Lumbering in the Material World," *Rolling Stone*, December 19, 1974, reprinted in Beatles.ru, https://www .beatles.ru/books/paper.asp?id=1121.

361   *fiasco*: quoted in Craske, *Indian Sun*, 409.

361   *George wanted so badly*: quoted in Craske, 410.

361   *George didn't want to do "Something"*: quoted in Thomson, *George Harrison*, 274.

361   *If there's something in the way*: Thomson, 274.

361   *The way he started the show*: quoted in Thomson, 258.

362   All quotes from press conference: "Press Conference, October 23, 1974, Los Angeles," *George Harrison on George Harrison: Interviews and Encounters*, edited by Ashley Kahn (Chicago: Chicago Review Press, 2020), 184–90.

363   *The press, arriving at the Coliseum*: quoted in Badman, *The Dream Is Over*, 145.

363   *People have to* think *a little bit more* and other quotes from *Rolling Stone* piece: Fong-Torres, "Lumbering in the Material World."

364   *What you saw*: quoted in Thomson, *George Harrison*, 279.

364   *Holy Krishna!*: Fong-Torres, "Lumbering in the Material World."

365   *We made a mistake*; *The record sales*: quoted in Craske, *Indian Sun*, 365.

365   *In defense of his tour*: Jim Miller, *Rolling Stone*, "Dark Horse," February 13, 1975, https://rollingstone.com/music/music-album-reviews/dark-horse-206130.

365   *[Harrison's] spiritual thing was real*: quoted in Thomson, *George Harrison*, 282.

365   *Chant Krishna!*: Greene, *Here Comes the Sun*, 213.

366   *[It] was an extremely well organized tour*: Shankar, *Raga Mala*, 225.

366   *The flights were the best times*: quoted in Shankar, 226.

366   *Trying to keep two bands*: O'Dell, *Miss O'Dell*, 306.

367   *In spite of the hard time*: quoted in Greene, *Here Comes the Sun*, 217.

367   *He seemed so happy*: O'Dell, *Miss O'Dell*, 307.

367   *I loved watching George*: O'Dell.

367   *Nobody gaped* and other quotes from Free Clinic episode: Ben Fong-Torres, "Harrison Had Love-Haight Relationship with S.F.: Former Beatle Bolstered Free Clinic, but Found Hippies 'Hideous,'" *San Francisco Chronicle*, December 2, 2001, reprinted in Dr. Dave, http://www.drdave.org/Rock-n-Roll/GorgeHarrison -SFGate.htm.

368   *I don't know how it feels; Don't just* shout: Thomson, *George Harrison*, 276.

368   *Good afternoon* and all other concert quotes: personal transcript from bootleg recording of the afternoon performance at the LA Forum, November 12, 1974.

369   *Yet he wasn't going through the motions*: Thomson, *George Harrison*, 274.

369   *We all read the reviews*: quoted in Thomson., 280.

369   *Some people used [his hoarseness]*: quoted in Greene, *Here Comes the Sun*, 216–17.

369   *I remember him coming up to me*: quoted in Thomson, *George Harrison*, 281.

369   *We were all doing coke*: quoted in Thomson, 281–82.

369–70 *If you want to understand*: quoted in Greene, *Here Comes the Sun*, 228.

370   *ill-fated*: Nick DeRiso, "40 Years Ago George Harrison Begins Ill-Fated 1974 North American Tour," Ultimate Classic Rock, November 2, 2014, http:// ultimateclassicrock.com/george-harrsion-1974-tour.

370   *It was a sheer delight*: quoted in Leng, *While My Guitar Gently Weeps*, 160.

370   *For me the George Harrison concert*: quoted in Leng, 161.

370   *I love God more; God bless John*: Rob Sheffield, *Dreaming the Beatles: The Love Story of One Band and the Whole World* (New York: Dey Street, 2017), 265.

370   *You hear every different type of music*: Fong-Torres, "Lumbering in the Material World."

370   *George looked high*: quoted in Leng, *While My Guitar Gently Weeps*, 163.

371   *appealing sincerity*: Fong-Torres, "Lumbering in the Material World."

371   *Mr. Harrison reverted*: quoted in Leng, *While My Guitar Gently Weeps*, 165.

371   *[It] was a dream come true*: quoted in Anuradha Varanasi, "George Wanted to Be Reborn in India," *Week*, February 25, 2018, https://www.theweek.in/theweek /cover/2018/02/17/the-beatles-pandit-hariprasad-chaurasia.html.

371   *sweetest person*: "Tulsa Counterculture of the 70s: George Harrison in Tulsa, November 21, 1974," *Tulsa TV Memories*, http://tulsatvmemories.com/harrison .html.

371   *God is fair*: quoted in Greene, *Here Comes the Sun*, 218.

371   *[One night] he invited me to his hotel room*: quoted in Dan Furre, "Robben Ford, the One and Only," *Vintage Guitar*, https://vintageguitar.com/3401/robben-ford.

371   *He wanted a life*: quoted in Thomson, *George Harrison*, 226.

372   *Every show was hard*: quoted in Thomson, 218.

372   *I don't have any ideas*: quoted in Badman, *The Dream Is Over*, 147.

372   thirty-minute ovation in Tulsa: "Tulsa Counterculture of the 70s."

372   *George was constantly worried*: quoted in Thomson, *George Harrison*, 281.

372   *I'm so happy that you should like it*: Leng, *While My Guitar Gently Weeps*, 171.

372 *I played Ft. Worth and Houston*: quoted in Badman, *The Dream Is Over*, 147–48.

373 *belong[ing] on Broadway*: Philip Auslander, *Performing Glam Rock: Gender and Theatricality in Popular Music* (Ann Arbor: University of Michigan Press, 2006), 12.

373 *The idea of getting minds together*: quoted in Auslander, 131–32.

373 *Ringo thinks [Bowie] is great*: quoted in Badman, *The Dream Is Over*, 140.

373 *I'd rather be silly*: quoted in Thomson, *George Harrison*, 286.

373 *I had [a] first alert from my heart*: Shankar, *Raga Mala*, 227.

373 *Ravi's heart*: quoted in Craske, *Indian Sun*, 411.

374 *This tour has done a great deal to me*: Craske, 410.

374 *Twenty years before its time*: quoted in Craske, 411.

375 *Krishna, Krishna, Krishna!*: Leng, *While My Guitar Gently Weeps*, 270.

375 *jungle musician*: quoted in "Interesting/Cool George Harrison Stories?"

375 *Nixon had just left office*: quoted in Shankar, *Raga Mala*, 227.

375 *George Harrison: Then & Now*: Evan Phifer, "An Ex-Beatle at the White House," White House Historical Association, https://whitehousehistory.org/an-ex-beatle-at-the-white-house.

376 *I couldn't believe the place felt as comfortable as it did*: quoted in Shankar, *Raga Mala*, 227.

376 *You either go crackers*: quoted in Greene, *Here Comes the Sun*, 216.

376 *John smiled*: O'Dell, *Miss O'Dell*, 311.

376 *The band really cooked*: quoted in Badman, *The Dream Is Over*, 151.

376 *I'd like to do a song*: Personal transcript of bootleg recording of the November 15, 1974 show in Long Island.

377 *I saw George going through pain*: quoted in Clayson, *George Harrison*, 341.

377 *Allen Klein was chasing George*: quoted in Badman, *The Dream Is Over*, 151.

377 *We all arrived for the big dissolution meeting*: quoted in Badman, 152.

377 *My astrologer*: quoted in Badman, 151.

377 *George got on the phone; The planets weren't right*: quoted in Badman, 152.

377 *I started the tour*: quoted in Thomson, *George Harrison*, 283.

377–78 *I figured I would come up with some snappy new solos*: "Interesting/Cool George Harrison Stories?"

378 *For the last fifty gigs*: Thomson, *George Harrison*, 283.

378 *Afterwards, George gave gifts*: quoted in Thomson, 283–84.

378–79 joint radio interview: Nebo Sha Music, "John Lennon and George Harrison Last Interview Talking Beatles Songs in 1974," YouTube, youtube.com/watch?v=kv2Bj_BEXPQ.

379 *The Revolutionaries are on CBS?*: Doggett, *There's a Riot Going On*, 347.

379 *I've come to believe*: quoted in Doggett, 515.

379 *I found out*: lyrics to "I Found Out."

379 *No one realized it at the time*: quoted in Uch Onyebadi, *Music as a Platform for Political Communication* (London: IGI Global, 2017), 166.

380 *When the pop star*: quoted in Doggett, *There's a Riot Going On*, 397.

380 *The American Century*: quoted in Rick Perlstein, "That Seventies Show," *Nation*, November 8, 2010, 28.

382 *People who were never really keen on me*: quoted in Thomson, *George Harrison*, 296–97.

382 *When I got off the plane*: Harrison *I Me Mine*, 69.

Afterword: The Final Round

383 *They always got somebody watching* and subsequent conversation: Kindred, *Sound and Fury*, 204.

384 *I knew [Herbert] would tell me*: Eig, *Ali*, 406.

384 *If every Muslim was killed*: ibid., 406–7.

384 *Elijah taught us*: Robert Lipsyte, "King of All Kings," *New York Times*, June 29, 1975, nytimes.com/1975/06/29/archives/king-of-all-kings-lonely-man-of-wisdom-champion-of-the-world.html.

384 *Ali has entered folklore*: quoted in Eig, *Ali*, 409.

384 *Ali does not . . . sit around* and *no place to go*: quoted in Hauser, *Muhammad Ali*, 304.

385 *I think he wasn't up for it*: quoted in Leng, *While My Guitar Gently Weeps*, 179.

385 *When you strive for something higher*: quoted in Greene, *Here Comes the Sun*, 221.

385 *I really relate to those people*: quoted in Lisa Robinson, *There Goes Gravity: A Life in Rock and Roll* (New York: Riverhead Books, 2014), 149.

385 *Prabhupada wondering whether he could trust Harrison*: Prabhupada to Hamsaduta, October 15, 1974, "George Harrison (Letters)."

385 *I know that George will not ask us*: Prabhupada to Madhavananda, October 1, 1974, "George Harrison (Letters)."

385–87 *How do you feel?* and subsequent conversation: Prabhupada Vani, "Conversation with George Harrison, July 26, 1976," https://prabhupada.io/spoken/760726r1.lon.

387 *bona fide religion*: S. D. Goswami, *Prabhupada, Your Ever Well-Wisher*, 323.

387 pitta *and* vāhyu, *bile and air*: quoted in S. D. Goswami, 321.

387 *I have nothing to do*: quoted in S. D. Goswami, 341.

387 *Don't be anxious*: S. D. Goswami, 327.

387 *Prabhupada asks disciples to forgive him*: S. D. Goswami, 350.

387 *Is there anything you want? I have no desire*: S. D. Goswami, 352.

387 *Will he live?*: Giuliano, *Dark Horse*, 107.

387 *Please, give this to George Harrison*: quoted in Giuliano, 108.

388 *Yoko and John were so enamored of Ali*: Steve Politi, "The Forgotten Story of How Muhammad Ali and a Jersey Guy Tried to Reunite the Beatles," NJ Advance Media, January 16, 2019, https://www.nj.com/sports/2016/06/the_forgotten_story_of_how_muhammad_ali_and_a_jers.html.

388 *The object of the game of boxing*: quoted in Eig, *Ali*, 413.

388 *It's time for me to face another test*: quoted in Eig, 424.

388 *This is the end of him or me*: quoted in Eig, 426.

388 *closest thing to death*: quoted in Hauser, *Muhammad Ali*, 324.

388   *Thrilla in Manila*: Eig, *Ali*, 425.

388   *America's first Vietnam*: Kram, *Ghosts of Manila*, 165.

388–89 *first genocide in modern history*: quoted in Kram, 165.

389   *You have a beautiful wife*: Hoffer, *Bouts of Mania*, 184.

389   *You tell that bitch*: quoted in Hauser, *Muhammad Ali*, 319.

389   *When we got married*: quoted in Hauser, 307–8.

389   *Wallace disappeared*: Kram, *Ghosts of Manila*, 168.

390   *The old man took him to the cleaners*: quoted in Kram, 168.

390   *I used to go to bed at night crying*: quoted in Hauser, *Muhammad Ali*, 371–72.

390   *First two fights*: quoted in Hauser, 325.

390   *All night long*: quoted in Hauser, 313.

390   *Ugly!*: quoted in Kram, *Ghosts of Manila*, 169.

390   *If he was Filipino*: quoted in Hoffer, *Bouts of Mania*, 183.

390   *No nation can contain me*: quoted in Hoffer, 195.

391   *wedg[ing] himself under Ali's chest*: Eig, *Ali*, 428.

391   *Lawd have mercy!*: Eig, 429.

391   *Joe, it's over*: Hoffer, *Bouts of Mania*, 203.

391   *I was thinking at the end*: quoted in Hoffer, 203.

392   *Who is it?* quoted in Hauser, *Muhammad Ali*, 325.

392   *No matter what one says*: Hoffer, *Bouts of Mania*, 182.–

392   *[I want to] help more people in the world*: quoted in Naeem Mohaiemen, "Muhammad Ali, We *Still* Love You: Unsteady Dreams of a Muslim International," June 2016, https://www.researchgate.net/publication/305653220_Muhammad_Ali _we_still_love_you_uneasy_dreams_of_the_Muslim_International.

392   *stood next to us*: Dean Nelson, "Bangla Desh to Honour Bob Dylan and George Harrison," *The Telegraph*, October 19, 2012, https: //telegraph.co.uk/news /worldnews/asia/Bangladesh/9620324/bangla-desh=to-honour-bob-dylan-and -george-harrison.html.

392   *Thank you so much*: quoted in Mohaiemen, "Muhammad Ali, We *Still* Love You."

393   *Get me the Beatles!* and Cosell dialogue with Lennon: Kindred, *Sound and Fury*, 219.

393   *the next Beatles*: Kindred, 219.

393–94 *Howard, I know you can handle this*: Kindred, 245–46.

394   *ABC News has confirmed; my heart aches*: quoted in Kindred, 245–46.

394   *If you were there for the sixties*: Pete Hamill, "The Death and Life of John Lennon," *New York*, December 20, 1980, https://nymag.com/news/features/45252.

394   *great spirit; subterranean recesses*: Susan J. Douglas, "We Shot John Lennon," *In These Times*, February 6, 2014, https://inthesetimes.com/article/16142/we_shot _john_lennon.

395   *You've captured our relationship exactly; Maybe in the '60s we were naïve*: quoted in Jackie Nash, "John Lennon's Death: A Timeline of Events," *Biography*, June 16, 2020, https://www.biography.com/news/john-lennon-death-timeline.

395   *Mr. Lennon?* Hamill, "The Death and Life of John Lennon."

396   *You want me to tell you what happened*: quoted in Hamill.

396   *John, the Hare Krishnas are here*: "How John Lennon Heard the Ahamantra Just Before He Left His Body," ISKCON Desire Tree, February 26, 2018, https:// iskcondesiretree.com/profiles/blogs/how-john-lennon-heard-the-mahamantra -just-before-he-left-his-body.

396   *George, maybe you should make some sort of statement; I can't now*: quoted in Giuliano, *Dark Horse*, 167.

396   *which person might have a gun*: quoted in Greene, *Here Comes the Sun*, 233.

397   *[John and I] saw beyond*: quoted in Greene, *Here Comes the Sun*, 232–33.

397   *I just wanted to be in a band*: quoted in Thomson, *George Harrison*, 314.

397   *blue and gold light*: Giuliano, *Dark Horse*, 162.

397   *the Indian musical scale*: Greene, *Here Comes the Sun*, 228.

397   *I was pretty sure he was just a gardener*: "George Harrison: The Beatle Who Hated Fame," *The Week*, September 30, 2011, https://theweek.com/articles/481422 /george-harrison-the-beatle-who-hated-fame.

397–98 *My friends would . . . end up*: quoted in Dan Brooks, "'It Had Such an Impact on Everything': Dhani Harrison Talks Star Wars," StarWars.com, November 30, 2017, https://www.starwars.com/news/it-had-such-an-impact-on-everything -dhani-harrison-talks-star-wars.

398   *It's trying to put responsibility*: quoted in Greene, *Here Comes the Sun*, 231.

398   *I don't need to say much* and following quotes: Rock & Roll Hall of Fame, "Beatles Accept Rock and Roll Hall of Fame Inductions 1988," YouTube, https://www .youtube.com/watch?v=NO-HK_csGwk.

399   *an exercise in torpor*: quoted in Eig, *Ali*, 448.

400   *We had to share him anyway*: quoted in Eig, 506.

400   *I love you, Bird*: Eig, 521.

400   *Man, just think*: quoted in Eig, 512.

400   *My turn to wipe*: quoted in Eig, *Ali*, 512.

400   *That man looks like he's dying*: quoted in Eig, 519.

401   *I wish he'd fallen*: quoted in Hoffer, *Bouts of Mania*, 234.

401   *My God!*: quoted in Kindred, *Sound and Fury*, 309.

401   *Until that instant*: Hoffer, *Bouts of Mania*, 208–9.

401   *Come on, George*: quoted in Thomson, *George Harrison*, 357.

402   *He was really scared to death*: Thomson, *George Harrison*, 358.

402   *He seemed very comfortable*: quoted in Thomson, 360.

402   *It was very touching*: quoted in Thomson, 361.

402   *We were begging George*: quoted in Thomson, 363.

402   *[He] wasn't seeking a career*: quoted in "George Harrison: The Beatle Who Hated Fame."

402   *If you had 2 million people*: quoted in "George Harrison: The Beatle Who Hated Fame."

403   *I am always a bit skeptical*: quoted in "George Harrison Knew ISKCON Gurus Were/Are Bogus," HareKrsna,org, November 17, 2015, https://harekrsna.org /george-harrison-knew-iskcon-gurus-wereare-bogus.

403 *[Many of the Swami's] leading disciples*: Mukunda Goswami, *Miracle on Second Avenue*, 424.

403 *George was always on a quest*: quoted in Thomson, *George Harrison*, 330.

403 *George would [tell me]*: quoted in "George Harrison: The Beatle Who Hated Fame."

403–4 Exchange with Maharishi: "Beatles Are Angels on Earth, Said Maharishi," Bienfaits de la Méditation, https://www.bienfaits-meditation.com/en/the_beatles _and_tm/the-beatles/beatles-are-angels-on-earth.

404 *I don't need . . . money now* and subsequent quotes: Politi, "The Forgotten Story of How Muhammad Ali and a Jersey Guy Tried to Reunite the Beatles."

404 *More and more he is like a soul walking*: quoted in Eig, *Ali*, 527.

405 *Dad*: Greene, *Here Comes the Sun*, 245.

405 *I can't even remember*: quoted in Greene, 246.

405 *What's all this about some cancer*: quoted in Greene, 262.

405 *You know, they told me at the clinic*: quoted in Greene, 262.

405 *He couldn't believe all the trash*: quoted in Bart Mendoza, "The Beatles in San Diego," 2004, Jon Moore Presents: San Diego Concert Archive, www .sandiegoconcertarchive.com/beatlesinsandiego.html.

405 *You know, Paul was a cute-looking guy*: quoted in Thomson, *George Harrison*, 375.

405 *Ah, that sounds nice, George; Remember me?* quoted in Thomson, 378.

406 *To think that Prabhupada is right here*: quoted in Greene, *Here Comes the Sun*, 253.

406 *This is our effort*: quoted in Bradley Bamberger, "Shankar Illuminates 'Chants of India,' Collaboration with Harrison Draws on Ancient Texts," *Billboard*, May 8, 1997.

406 *Thank you for this music*: Greene, *Here Comes the Sun*, 259.

406 *witches*: Thomson, *George Harrison*, 387.

406 *the language of Satan*: quoted in Greene, *Here Comes the Sun*, 265.

406 *You get down here!*: Greene. 265.

406 *Hare Krishna; I can't believe after everything*: Thomson, *George Harrison*, 387.

407 *Oh, Dhani*: Scorsese, *George Harrison*.

407 *definitely wasn't auditioning*: quoted in Greene, *Here Comes the Sun*, 266.

407 *Aren't you glad you married a Mexican girl?*: Thomson, *George Harrison*, 388.

407 *The trauma that George had*: quoted in Thomson, 384.

407 *He was very positive*: quoted in Thomson, 391.

407 *He had become so serene*: quoted in Greene, *Here Comes the Sun*, 266.

407 *he was editing*: quoted in Thomson, *George Harrison*, 392.

408 *I listened*: quoted in "Interesting/Cool George Harrison Stories?"

408 *You'll be fine, Olivia*: quoted in Minnie Wright, "George Harrison: The Beatle Star's Heartbreaking Words to His Wife Before He Died," *Express*, November 29, 2019, https://express.co.uk/entertainment/music/1210402/george-harrison -the-beatle-death-wife-died-paul-mccartney-anniversary.

408   *I don't even know if I know how to spell my own name:* quoted in Thomson, *George Harrison*, 393.

408   *He was* very *ill:* Scorsese, *George Harrison.*

408–9   *It was good:* quoted in "Last Hours, Moments, and Words of George Harrison," https://beatlesdaily.com/2018/11/30/last-hours-and-moments-of-george-harrsion.

409   *do as well as I can do:* quoted in Greene, *Here Comes the Sun,* 271.

409   *Love one another:* "Last Hours, moments, and Words of George Harrison."

409   *He was a giant:* quoted in Jason Fine, editor, *Harrison* (New York: Simon and Schuster, 2002), 221.

409   *It's what you can do:* quoted in Hana Ali, *At Home with Muhammad Ali: A Memoir of Love, Loss, and Forgiveness* (New York: Amistad, 2019), 42.

409   *What did Abraham Lincoln say:* Hana Ali, 65.

409   *This is all deception:* quoted in Hana Ali, 184.

409   *Wasn't I something?* Hana Ali, 388.

410   *That was Malcolm:* Remnick, *King of the World,* 303.

410   *These tapes:* quoted in Hana Ali, *At Home with Muhammad Ali,* 413.

410   *George Foreman!* and subsequent conversation: Hana Ali, 240, 248.

410   *We sat down and made up:* quoted in Jack Cashill, *Sucker Punch: The Hard Left Hook That Dazed Ali and Killed King's Dream* (Nashville: Nelson Current, 2006), 248.

410   *Why is she crying?* and subsequent exchange: Hana Ali, *At Home with Muhammad Ali,* 386–87.

411   *The man who views the world:* quoted in Hana Ali, *At Home with Muhammad Ali,* 374.

411   *[My father] is more spiritual:* quoted in Masood Farivar, "Was Muhammad Ali a Sufi?," VOA News, June 8, 2016, https://www.voanews.com/a/some-sufi-adherents -claim-spiritual-kinship-muhammad-ali/3367977.html.

411   *submission, faith, and doing the beautiful:* William C. Chittick, *Sufism: A Short Introduction* (Oxford: One World, 2005), 4.

411   *Don't we have a Black president? . . . Tell Lonnie:* Hana Ali, *At Home with Muhammad Ali,* 39.

411   *Speaking as someone:* quoted in Eig, *Ali,* 531.

411   *Everything now is about protecting him:* quoted in Eig, 532.

411   *Can he hear us?* and subsequent exchange: Hana Ali, *At Home with Muhammad Ali,* 419–20.

411   *There is no God but Allah:* Eig, *Ali,* 534.

412   *You're free now, Daddy:* Hana Ali, *At Home with Muhammad Ali,* 421.

412   *Ali, bomaye:* Eig, *Ali,* 536.

412–13 *Ali was devastated* and subsequent quotes: Politi, "The Forgotten Story of How Muhammad Ali and a Jersey Guy Tried to Reunite the Beatles."

Index